DATE DUE

~~MR 11 '89~~			

DEMCO 38-296

The Letters of
MATTHEW
ARNOLD

Matthew Arnold at Field Foot, about 500 yards from Fox How, September 10, 1856, at 1:00 P.M. (Photograph courtesy The Masters and Fellows of Balliol College)

The Letters of
MATTHEW ARNOLD

Edited by
Cecil Y. Lang

VOLUME 1
1829–1859

THE UNIVERSITY PRESS OF VIRGINIA

Charlottesville and London

VICTORIAN LITERATURE AND CULTURE SERIES
Karen Chase, Jerome J. McGann, *and* Herbert Tucker, *General Editors*

THE UNIVERSITY PRESS OF VIRGINIA
Copyright © 1996 by the Rector and Visitors
of the University of Virginia

First Published 1996

Library of Congress Cataloging-in-Publication Data

Arnold, Matthew, 1822–1888.
   [Correspondence]
   The letters of Matthew Arnold / edited by Cecil Y. Lang.
       p.   cm. — (Victorian literature and culture series)
   Includes index.
   Contents: v. 1. 1829–1859.
   ISBN 0-8139-1651-8 (v. 1. : cloth : alk. paper)
     1. Arnold, Matthew, 1822–1888—Correspondence   2. Poets.
English—19th century—Correspondence.   3. Critics—Great
Britain—Correspondence.   I. Lang, Cecil Y.   II. Title.
III. Series.
   PR4023.A44   1996
   821'.8—dc20
   [B]   95-50448
                                                                         CIP

∞ The paper used in this publication meets the minimum requirements
of the American National Standard for Information Sciences–Permanence of Paper for Printed Library Materials, ANSI Z39.48-1984.

Printed in the United States of America

To Violette
and
In Memoriam
Amanda Stewart Bryan Kane

Contents

Acknowledgments   ix

Introduction`   xiii

Editorial Principles   lxi

Short Titles and Abbreviations   lxii

Chronology   lxvii

Illustrations follow page lxx

The Letters (1829–1859)   1

Appendixes   523

Index   531

Acknowledgments

This edition of letters was made possible by the cooperation and support of Matthew Arnold's grandson, the late Arnold Whitridge (1891–1989), and it remains pain and grief to me that he did not live to see it completed. *His* son, Frederick Whitridge, extending the cooperation and support and friendship begun by his father far beyond the imperatives of duty, has transfused them all with new meaning and renewed vitality. In these volumes their name probably occurs more often than that of any other except the writer of the letters.

The edition was made feasible by a five-year grant from the National Endowment for the Humanities, without which it could not have been undertaken. I acknowledge the support with heartfelt gratitude.

Five close friends imprint every page of the work—Beverly Kirsch, Paul Barolsky, Jerome McGann, Marjorie Wynne, and Kathleen Tillotson. Three works also impress every page of this edition, which in a well-ordered world would have preceded them all, and to these works mine is heavily indebted: R. H. Super's edition of *The Complete Prose Works of Matthew Arnold*, Kenneth Allott's and Miriam Allott's editions of *The Poems of Matthew Arnold*, and Park Honan's biography, *Matthew Arnold: A Life*. All three are acknowledged over and over again in these volumes, and each reference rests on a silent gratitude at once personal, admiring, and profound.

Librarians—warders, in Swinburne's happy phrase, of the "sevenfold shield of memory"—are the unsung heroes and heroines of civilization as we would like to know it, and they have all, everywhere, given evidence repeatedly of devotion to an ideal of work and learning that the writer of the letters collected here would have admired as much as the writer of this sentence appreciates it. A librarian in Paris once telephoned me in Charlottesville about a comma in an Arnold letter, one in Ottawa telephoned to give me an address that I needed, one in Leeds to say that an item I was looking for was indeed there, one in New York to call my attention to some special information, one in San Marino (California) to answer a question, one in New Haven to reassure me that my patience (!) was paying off. One in Oxford pulled himself away from the Oxford-Cambridge boat race, then in a dead heat, to let me know that I was pursuing a dead end. Lord Coleridge, not a librarian but a man with all the good qualities of one, telephoned to make sure an invitation to visit his library had not gone astray. The curator of the Spoelberch de Louvenjoul collection (then) in Chantilly deposited the album of Arnold's letters to Sainte-Beuve in the library of the chateau, where it was wonderfully taken for granted by all the *gardiens* that I was a connection of Jack Lang, the minister of culture. The Acting Director General of the Educational Advising Center, in Moscow (Felicity, thy name is Glasnost!), Ekaterina U. Genieva, moving mountains that neither the post office nor the American State Department, working through the Embassy, had budged, sent me a Fax and caused Faxes to be sent me from the State Museum of L. N. Tolstoi in Moscow and the Pushkin House in St Petersburg.

I owe a massive, long-standing, and continuing debt to the staff of the Library of the University of Virginia, especially to Kendon L. Stubbs, Associate Librarian (himself an Arnoldian figure in all the essentials), Michael Plunkett, Curator of Manuscripts, James Campbell, North Europe Bibliographer, Linda Lester, Director of Reference Services, and her admirable staff, including Bryson Clevenger, Martin Davis, Susan Marcell, Karen Marshall, Francis Mooney, Mohammad Yusuf. Some others have taken a personal interest in this work and made Arnold's cause and my cause their cause. Penelope Bulloch, Librarian of Balliol College, Oxford University; Vincent Giroud, Curator of Modern Books and Manuscripts, Beinecke Library, Yale University; Christopher Sheppard, Librarian of Special Collections, Leeds University; and John Bell, Archivist, National Archives, Ottawa, have all repeatedly gone far beyond the call of professional duty.

Two notable groups of letters would have remained unknown to me without the intervention of (as it seems to me) providence. Christopher Stray, Department of Sociology and Anthropology, University College of Swansea, called my attention to Arnold's letters to Henry John Roby, Secretary of the Taunton Commission (belonging to Roby's grandson, John King, who gave me permission to publish them) and sent me photocopies of them as well of Roby's *Reminiscences of My Life and Work* ("For My Own Family Only") from the unique copy in the library of St John's College, Cambridge. John Bell wrote to A. K. Davis, Jr, drawing his attention to the Arnold letters in the (then) Public Archives of Canada, at a time when Davis was already beyond the reach of mortal communication, and Wilma MacDonald then telephoned and wrote to me about them. Margaret L. Evans, Laurier House, Ottawa, sent me lists of Arnold books, bookplates, and inscriptions there.

Among those whose learning and generosity have supported me specifically as well as generally are Raul Balìn, Peter Beal, William Bell, Georgiana Blakiston, T. A. J. Burnett, Manfred Dietrich, Pauline Dower, Shiela Sokolov Grant Duff, Katherine Duff, Charlotte Fisher, Alastair and Jenny Fowler, Eeyan Hartley, Patrick Jackson, Roger Lonsdale, Jennifer Macrory, A. C. W. Mitford-Slade, Vanda Morton, Richard and Leonée Ormond, Tim Procter,

John Spedding, Virginia Surtees, Alan Tadiello, Peter Thwaites, Raleigh Trevelyan, Clive Wainwright, H. B. Walrond, C. D. Watkinson, Martin Williams, Timothy Wilson, Robert Woof. Also, Mildred Abraham, Edmund Berkeley, Jr, Staige Blackford, Sidney Burris, John Clubbe, Morton N. Cohen, Philip K. Cohen, Betty A. Coley, Ann C. Colley, Lowell W. Coolidge, Sidney Coulling, A. Dwight Culler, Kenneth Curry, David DeLaura, Robert T. Denommé, Leo M. Dolenski, Donald H. Dyal, William E. Fredeman, Donald Gallup, William Godshalk, Jennifer Hamilton, Martin J. Havran, the late Walter Houghton, Ann Hyde, Philip Kelley, Karen Lang, Mark Samuels Lasner, Larry Mazzeno, Patrick McCarthy, Mark Morford, John Powell, Mark Reed, Elizabeth Richardson, Harold Ridley, David Riede, Clyde Ryals, Nicholas Scheetz, Bernard Schilling, Alexander Sedgewick, H. L. Seneviratne, Sue Surgeson, Vincent Tollers, John Unsworth, Aram Vartanian, John O. Waller. Also, Lucien Carrive, Annie Chassagne, Jean Favier, G. Laflaquière, and (what a pleasure to conclude with these two names!) Georges Lubin and Christiane Sand.

"Grâce à l'exorbitance de mes années," as Chateaubriand wrote at the conclusion of *Mémoires d'Outre-Tombe*, "mon monument est achevé." Mine has been a privileged life, a thesaurus of experiences, of sensations and ideas. Who else, on a train from Waterloo Station to Devonshire to see Coleridges, has been picked up and engaged in conversation by a Dickens? Who else identifies as the very pleasure principle the satisfaction of editing Swinburne's letters, Tennyson's, Arnold's, and, with it, of meeting and knowing personally Swinburnes and Trevelyans, Capheaton and Wallington, Rossettis and Cheyne Walk, Speddings and Tennysons, Mirehouse and Farringford and Aldworth, Coleridges and Ottery St Mary, Wordsworths and Arnolds, Rugby School and Oxford, Grasmere and Fox How? "Thou hast forgotten, O summer swallow, But the world shall end when I forget."

Cecil Y. Lang
Charlottesville, 1995

Introduction

Matthew Arnold (1822–1888) has never returned from oblivion because, somehow, he has never been there. Even becalmed in the doldrums for half a century after his death, he remained visible because of one poem, "Dover Beach," honored wherever English literature is honored, and because of one segment of society, the academy. To scholars he has always seemed something like an idealized "one of us." Not because of exceptional learning—he *was* learned, but English poets have generally been well educated and in any case he was not more learned than, say, Milton or Gray or Swinburne. Not because of his academic positions—he had none, except for a few months spent filling in at Rugby School and his appointments as Professor of Poetry at Oxford. Certainly not because of his father's influence and example or the Old Boy network or his own impeccable credentials—he mended his fences and kept them in good repair, but they were the kind of fences that make not only good neighbors but also good survivors. Or, as another poet put it, "Always it is by bridges that we live." Yet unquestionably in England this son and grandson of Oxford University "belonged" all his life, in some real sense, to the very academy that he never belonged to professionally, the academy that in the United States adopted him, as foster son, with the passion and veneration reserved today for literary theorists, as, in the world at large, for rock stars and professional athletes. (Arnold, thou shouldst be living at this hour!)

As poet, critic, *moraliste*, Arnold stood foursquare for what the academy, middle-class and closet poets or delitescent belletrists to a man, always aspired to be—repository, watchdog, evangelist, keeper of the flame of liberal education, apotheosis of its aspirations, representative of "culture" raised to the highest power of excellence with an intellectual horniness equaled among English poets only by Shelley's. But no professional academic, then or now, could match his prose style, the unfaltering urbanity so deliberately nurtured (that "smile of heartbroken forbearance as of a teacher in an idiot school"), his breadth of vision, his range of interests, his fierce commitment to civilization and revulsion from anarchy, his perfect ease in mingling, at home and abroad, with cardinals, archbishops and bishops and deans, theologians, royals, politicians and statesmen, including half a dozen prime ministers, American presidents, diplomats, educators (including schoolmasters), grubby schoolchildren, poets, painters, playwrights, actors, novelists, journalists, editors and publishers, generals and admirals, aristocrats (blue-blooded or green-backed), judges and barristers and solicitors, surgeons and doctors, society ladies, Jews, Catholics, Quakers, Evangelicals, and of course Anglicans (high, low, middle). His voracious appetite for meeting and talking with everybody in the known world, from the highest levels to mere *fonctionnaires*, was perhaps most nearly satisfied in Europe in 1859, when the Newcastle Commission dispatched him to investigate and report on the educational systems of France, Holland, Switzerland, and Italy (as later to Austria and Prussia). His diary for that period, printed here for the first time, supplementing his frequent and lengthy letters, shows, what the government and then the world learned, that this young man, not yet forty years old, was the perfect ambassador, the right man at the right time for the right job.

In literary history Arnold is unquestionably a major figure, and his reputation is secure. The reasons are not self-evident, for hardly anyone, perhaps no one, would maintain that he is, unassailably, a major *poet*; no one would rank him with Blake, Wordsworth, Coleridge, Byron, Shelley, Keats, with Tennyson, Browning, Yeats. As a literary critic, though he is not in fashion at the moment, he is situated conspicuously in the mainstream of Dryden, Johnson, Coleridge, Sainte-Beuve, Taine, Renan, Eliot. And as much as any of them he was an important student of society—cultural milieu, church (theology, polity), state (education, domestic politics, international relations). His book *God and the Bible*, which no one reads, has been called his best work; *Essays in Criticism*, which everyone reads, has been discredited and yet remains influential—"a real event in one's mental life," said George Russell, who will figure so largely in this Introduction. Even if he were not famed for his poetry and essays, however, Arnold would still have a place in history: "My poems represent, on the whole," he wrote in a famous letter in 1869, "the main movement of mind of the last quarter of a century, and thus they will probably have their day as people become conscious to themselves of what that movement of mind is, and interested in the literary productions which reflect it." *Mutandis mutandis*, the claim could fairly describe this edition of Arnold's letters—a body of letters that may well be the finest portrait of an age and of a person, representing the main movements of mind and of events of nearly half a century and at the same time revealing the actual intimate life of the participant-observer, in any collection of English letters in the nineteenth century, possibly in existence. With an almost Stendhalian detachment and an almost epic sweep, concerned not merely with England but also with France, Italy, Austria, Prussia, and of course Ireland, as well as the Vatican, Spain, Russia, Turkey, Australia, New Zealand, India, Canada, and the United States, it takes on something approaching a fictional dimension and shape—an anti-epic, perhaps, without a conclusion and without an epic hero.

Two extraliterary indictments of Arnold continue to be brought against him. This Introduction is not their natural tribunal, for, whatever their place in a total view of him, they are relevant to these volumes only by implication. They can be mentioned briefly.

One of them, to be taken seriously only because of the distinction of its author, a gifted poet-critic who ought to have known better, can be dismissed out of hand—W. H. Auden's poem "Matthew Arnold," of which the best that can be said is that it is ungenerous and facile: "I am my father's forum and he shall be heard, / Nothing shall contradict his holy final word." The opposite would be equally close to the "truth." Dr Arnold was no Darth Vader. He died when his son was not yet twenty-two. Matthew Arnold loved and admired him and (like most of those who came in contact with him) revered his memory. This hardly seems discreditable. But the son was not a clone, not even a disciple, he had no desire to walk in the paternal footsteps, and, even after the self-conscious flippancies of a reactive young manhood, he said, wrote, and thought much that would have horrified his father as it troubled his mother and his sisters and brothers. In no sense did he "thrust his gift in prison till it died" because of his father. It died a slow death "in prison" because of his "hampered" existence, the grinding demands of inspecting provincial schools.

Arnold is also charged (to adapt his own lines on Wordsworth) with having averted his eyes "from half of human fate." This criticism, "staled by frequence, shrunk by usage into commonest commonplace," is neither facile nor ignorant, and, though it reduces Arnold to a stereotype, faulting him, essentially, for not being Yeats or Nietzsche, it is probably valid, but it is not the "central issue" of these letters. It may well be the central issue in any comprehensive view of Matthew Arnold, however, and I will advert to it later.

Background

He has had to wait a long time for a complete edition of his letters, and the explanation of the delay is easily available.

It is the story of one man, Arthur Kyle Davis, Jr (1897–1972), a member of the Department of English at the University of Virginia from 1923 till his death. Before beginning his instructorship, Davis spent four years as a Rhodes Scholar at Balliol College, Oxford, and there, like so many before and since, he was possessed by "that sweet city with her dreaming spires" and there too began his lifelong association (to use too neutral a word) with the Balliol man who had sent forth those lines to enchant the world. From that day forward Davis had *two* ruling passions (*two* aims, *two* businesses, *two* desires)—the

Commonwealth of Virginia and Matthew Arnold. In the fullness of time he began to assemble records (including photoduplicates, microfilms, typed or handwritten transcriptions) of all known Arnold letters, published or unpublished, institutionally or privately owned, excerpted or merely listed in sales catalogues or auction records, and in 1968 he issued *Matthew Arnold's Letters: A Descriptive Checklist*, published for the Bibliographical Society of the University of Virginia, the deliberate preliminary, he said, of a "well-annotated complete edition of the letters." Some of this information, with much more, including a "History of the Publication of Arnold's Letters to Date," is set forth in Davis's Introduction—in such detail and with such authority that to recapitulate it here would be supererogatory.

Davis's "Statistical Report" in the same Introduction is of course out of date. It always has been. The "checklist of the known letters of Matthew Arnold," he wrote, "has reached a total of approximately 2658 letters," of which, he goes on, "about 1600 . . . are now on deposit in the Manuscript Division of the University of Virginia Library (Alderman Library) in some form of photographic or facsimile copy, with varying restrictions." The larger figure is misleading. The *Checklist* is like an alluring landscape proud in its display of myriad articles of value and objects of beauty but littered with *disjecta membra*, mined with booby traps, haunted by the undead. It records not only those letters for which a text or partial text has been found but also letters *presumed* to have been written. On the other hand, the "1600 [letters] . . . in some form of photographic or facsimile copy" are another matter, a matter beyond praise, and it is no exaggeration to say that as much as any other single archive they reanimated scholarly work on Matthew Arnold. From 1968 (or earlier) to the present day, consulted and studied by students from everywhere in the English-speaking world, they have constantly nourished it. At the same time, paradoxically, Davis, who had made such study feasible, made progress improbable. He presided over this well-defined turf for nearly half a century, by which time his presidency, virtually unchallenged, was effectively unchallengeable. He was deposed only by mutability. The present editor joined the Department of English at the University of Virginia in 1967. Soon afterwards Davis invited and then urged him to become the editor of the Matthew Arnold letters. But he had promises to keep.

At this point the editor turns gratefully to the inaugural issue of the *Arnold Newsletter*, and the narrative of its first editor, Nadean Bishop. "In mid-October 1972," she wrote there, "I invited 60 people to an MLA seminar ostentatiously entitled 'The Sesquicentennial Celebration of the Birth of Matthew Arnold.' The stated purpose was both to discuss the future of Arnold scholarship and to pay tribute to Arthur Kyle Davis, Jr . . . . and his Advisory Board: Kenneth Allott, Louis Bonnerot, Dwight Culler, Fraser Neiman, Robert Super, Lionel Trilling, and Arnold Whitridge. I discovered that the Advisory Board had never met, but these eminent scholars responded to the invitation with warmth and grace, though ultimately only Neiman and Culler were able to attend.

"Shortly after the invitations were extended, word came of the death of A. K. Davis in a letter from Kenneth Allott: 'I should imagine that some time would be spent at your MLA meeting on the question of editing Matthew Arnold's letters, I mean since the reported death of A. K. Davis. It will obviously be necessary to find an editor for the project and to get the thing going properly.' Requests for recommendations were widely distributed."

In due course I was approached and invited to express interest in undertaking the editorship, and I accepted. The rest is history, but it is a history somewhat murkier than has been allowed in previous accounts.

Previous Editions

Russell's *Letters of Matthew Arnold*

The first (and only) "collected" edition of Arnold's letters was edited in two volumes by George William Erskine Russell (1853–1919) in 1895, *Letters of Matthew Arnold, 1848–1888*. Russell was the younger son of Lord Charles Russell, last and least of the six sons of the sixth duke of Bedford, and a nephew of Lord John Russell, the great Whig statesman (of whom he penned a sketch in *Collections and Recollections*). He was a lively, learned, witty, charming, privileged, High Church man-about-town, younger than Arnold's first two sons and not three years older than the charming, unreliable Dick (Richard Penrose), the only son surviving after 1872. The attraction seems to have been something very like wish-fulfilment in both directions. Temperament contended with genes. The Arnolds, who had known Russell "from a boy" at Harrow, where both families lived for a period, must have come to view him as the incarnation of what Dick ought to have been; Russell, for his part, seems to have found in Arnold a more congenial father-figure than the lieutenant-colonel of the Royal Horse Guards, Member for Bedfordshire, and then (1848–75) serjeant-at-arms (disciplinary officer) to the House of Commons. "Though I had admired and liked him in a reverent sort of way, when I was a Harrow boy and he was a man, I found him even more fascinating when I met him on the more even terms of social life in London," he wrote in *One Look Back* (1911), an autobiographical memoir: "He was indeed the most delightful of companions; a man of the world entirely free from worldliness, and a man of letters without the faintest trace of pedantry. He walked through the world enjoying it and loving it; and yet all the time one felt that his 'eyes were on the higher loadstars' of the intellect and the spirit. In those days I used to say that, if one could fashion oneself, I should wish to be like Matthew Arnold; and the lapse of years has not altered my desire."

Russell, the author of several books, including much elegant anecdotage in the *Manchester Guardian* and elsewhere, wrote, with a rare grace, a prose that had gone to school to Arnold's and that even a carping critic could not accuse of either tedium ("I do not know the sensation of dulness," he once said) or inelegance. Only four letters (or fragments) to him from Arnold are known, including a sentence from one written "on the last day" of Arnold's life. His personal papers (intolerable in the massive Bedford Estate archives, for Russell, as the putative author of an irreverent obituary of the tenth duke, was persona non grata) have not proved traceable. History, in consequence, is not only murkier than it need have been but it is also disrupted by serious lacunae.

For many of Arnold's letters survive only in these two volumes. Russell was more or less "commissioned" to edit a substantial selection of Arnold's letters. The task was "undertaken," as he wrote, "in obedience to the wish of Mrs Matthew Arnold and of her sisters-in-law, Mrs Forster and Miss Arnold"—Jane and Frances ("K" and "Fan"), the oldest sister and the youngest. "The two volumes," Davis wrote in the *Checklist*, "contain the text or partial text of 533 letters of Arnold. . . . Its weaknesses are apparent, and are largely explained by the date of publication and the fact that many of the people addressed or referred to were still alive; excisions by the Arnold family, omissions or suppressions by Russell, inadequate annotation, absence of an index, in general a late-Victorian caution as to inclusions and exclusions, understandable perhaps but in some cases regrettable." The list of weaknesses can be extended. Russell's silly, annoying, inefficient practice of heading letters "To the same" (instead of "To his mother," etc.) was an invitation to trouble that Trouble accepted at least a dozen times in the first volume, the infection spreading like a virus not only to letters following but also, necessarily, to the *Checklist* when Davis had no manuscript authority to controvert Russell's (1 : 90–91, 104–11, 125–28, 131–45, 146–48). Russell created a *tertium quid* out of two (or three?) letters at least once (1 : 53–54). He simply omitted some words or phrases that he could not read—and also included some. (In 2 : 430 he rose to sublimity with "a keg of whiskey" instead of "a key of Fridley.") He called attention to some omissions but finessed many, many more. He misdated many letters. And, most devastating of all, he left no paper trail of his transcriptions or files or correspondence, personal or otherwise.

In such circumstances, no one would expect sisters with scissors and a widow wielding a blue pencil to be less than zealous, but some opportunity exists now for any reader willing to take the trouble to compare a Russell text with one here and observe the nature and extent of disfigurement. On balance, the present editor would conjecture that Arnold's letters, so far as we know them, weathered familial surveillance and censorship in better health than, in almost identical situations, those of Tennyson (whose widow and son were pyromaniacs) or perhaps Swinburne (whose sisters and cousin were merely arsonists). "As far as we know them" is a crucial qualification. We know something about the limits of our knowledge, little about the extent of our ignorance. Among the family letters Russell saw only what they chose to show him. This could properly be called "family policy." Undoubtedly he never read many of the letters written to Frances Lucy Arnold, and certainly he did not know those to Clough or Sainte-Beuve or those in the Public Record Office (which in any event he would have disdained). To the family archive he seems himself to have added, among others, the twenty-two letters to Ernest Fontanès, a genuine series and an excellent one, as well as those to Arnold's friends Wyndham Slade, John Morley, and Francis Palgrave. The letters to Fontanès are probably fairly reproduced, whereas those to members of the Arnold family have often been dismembered almost beyond recognition.

To speak of "*Russell's* two volumes" is not altogether just, for they were not wholly his. It was "my happy task," he wrote in an excellent little book on Arnold in 1904, "to collect, and in some sense to edit, the two volumes of his Letters which were published in 1895. Yet in reality my functions were little more than those of the collector and the annotator. Most of the Letters had been severely edited before they came into my hands, and the process was repeated when they were in proof." The result, he says, "was a curious obscuration of some of Arnold's most characteristic traits—such, for example, as his overflowing gaiety, and his love of what our fathers called Raillery. And in even more important respects than these, an erroneous impression was created by the suppression of what was thought to be too personal for publication." William S. Peterson, in a fine article, "G.W.E. Russell and the Editing of Matthew Arnold's Letters" (*Victorian Newsletter*, 1970), quotes a letter from Russell to Mrs Humphry Ward in 1918:

> Mrs. A. wished me to edit them; and I wished to make them as much of a biography & a portrait as might be. But hardly anyone except Mrs. A. & Miss A. supplied me with any material; Mrs. A. deleted every admiring reference to herself, & Miss A. every trace of humour. This was done deliberately—she said, "Everyone knew my brother's lighter side; but few his serious & domestic side."

I felt that if only his serious side were presented in the book, the world wd. never know in the least what he was like. So I was constrained to insert the very few *playful* letters which reached me, although I fully realized that they were, in quality, inferior to the serious ones.

Blue pencil triumphed over blue blood, but two comments must be subjoined here. In the first place, Russell, most urbane of sophisticates, was disingenuous, though what he says was worth saying even if not quite true. In the second, what with the publication in 1932 of the Clough letters and now of many totally uncensored family letters, his complaint, though justified, is no longer of crucial importance. That Russell was disingenuous we know in this way. "A comparison of the letters addressed to Mr. John Morley and Mr. Wyndham Slade with those addressed to older members of the Arnold family," he wrote, "will suggest to a careful reader the nature and extent of the excisions to which the bulk of the correspondence was subjected." The statement is arresting—unhelpful and so nearly meaningless that it has to be recognized as a coded warning.

The manuscripts of the Morley letters and the Slade letters have disappeared. To Morley thirteen are on record—one holograph (a first, formal letter), two fragments of one sentence each, and the ten letters printed in Russell's volumes. Morley, who survived Arnold by thirty-five years, ordered his personal archive with such scrupulous attention that one has to assume them to have been destroyed. If this is so, authentication of the texts is forever unlikely. To Slade fourteen are known—thirteen in Russell, one in Tinker and Lowry, *The Poetry of Matthew Arnold: A Commentary*, pp. 169–70. Of Russell's thirteen texts ten were written in the 1850s and of these ten all but the first were censored. These thirteen Slade letters, however, are revenants, for the holographs, which have not been found, were seen by Kenneth Allott, the "careful reader" par excellence, who transcribed into his own copy of Russell's volumes all the objectionable passages. Thus, with the integral texts and therefore a reliable control we can say now that Russell, as he surely foresaw, has got his own back.

In Arnold's letters, neither here nor elsewhere, will the prurient achieve gratification. This is of course a matter for regret, but what *is* here is the relaxed but self-consciously discreet language of a Benedict and a bachelor who had been randy college boys together (male bonding in a miasma of testosterone), who still shared digs from time to time, and who now, barely in their thirties, clinging to "Raillery" and auld lang syne, selves in search of a self, were perceptibly and a little awkwardly moving into the world of adult conformity—knocking at preferment's door, earning wages, borrowing money, spawning children, accommodating in-laws, dining out, coping with overwork and overweight, with costive organs and hypertensive arterial systems, with ailing or recalcitrant children, chafing at the neglect of an unappreciative public, envying the success of others, and sadly, necessarily, accepting the universe—in brief exemplifying in every way the inexorable biological law that ontogeny recapitulates phylogeny.

Lowry's *Letters to Arthur Hugh Clough*

In the history of Arnold's letters the most notable event after the appearance of Russell's two volumes was of course the publication by the Clarendon Press in 1932 of *The Letters of Matthew Arnold to Arthur Hugh Clough*, edited with an introductory study by Howard Foster Lowry (1901–1967). Their appearance, as Robert H. Super has observed, "was comparable to the publication in 1848 of Keats's letters. . . . Both are the frank, enthusiastic outpourings to intelligent and sympathetic friends of young poets as they gradually mature in their thinking about their own work and the nature of the poetic art" (Allott-Super, p. 563).

Lowry, the son of Presbyterian missionaries and legally (almost) as well as spiritually a Victorian, attended as a matter of course The College of Wooster, in Wooster, Ohio, a Presbyterian institution long identified with the same "moral earnestness" that characterized Rugby College in the days of Dr Arnold. From Wooster he went to Yale University for graduate study, where, like so many others in that place and at that time (and later), he majored in Anglophilia and sniffed High Anglicanism (without, however, inhaling). But he preferred New Presbyters to Old Priests, and from Yale he went back to Wooster and then, inevitably, to Princeton University as professor of English, and from Princeton back to Ohio to become president of his old college.

When I myself was in graduate school, just before and after the Second World War, the Clough letters had been exalted to the status of Holy Writ, an aura that suffuses them even now. It was "the 'onlie begetter' of modern Arnold scholarship," as Kenneth Allott (repeating his own earlier praise) wrote in the Preface to his edition of *The Poems of Matthew Arnold* published by Longman in 1965, adding that "the phrase is not too strong." Indeed, it is not too strong. The importance of the letters is beyond cavil. Lowry, who in many ways seems himself a sort of latter-day Arnold, wrote a useful, learned, graceful Introduction, he performed deeds of valor in dating the letters, he resuscitated Clough, whose reputation at that time seemed sucked away permanently into a literary black hole, drawing extensively upon unpublished Clough papers, and he reanimated or even reinvented Arnold's reputation. All of these tasks, unpropped by the scholarship that today we take for granted, were incomparably more difficult in those bad days than we can realize now, some six decades later, without a deliberate act of will. Lowry was thirty-two years old when he brought it off!

Something more must be said, however. A. K. Davis, Jr, observing, in the Introduction to the *Checklist*, that reviewers of the volume were as one about its importance, names about a dozen, who, he says, "were prompt . . . to commend strongly Lowry's scrupulous editing." The importance of the letters is indeed "beyond cavil," but the quality of the editing demands stricture. The editor's youth was like a fault plane underlying his scholarship, conceptually, practically.

Trifles that the law does not concern itself with are the life-support systems of scholarly collections of letters. No detail is too niggling, no nuance too nice, no mite of pointing or mote of orthography or midge of grammar too puny for the dainty appetence of what Carlyle called the "Able Editor," who "pores over a little inexactitude in phrases, and pecks at it like a domestic fowl," as Mrs Mountstuart said of a professor in Meredith's novel *The Egoist*. For example, a sounding (strictly of manuscript evidence) through the year 1865 shows that Arnold gradually moved from an early characteristic preference in certain verbs for the suffix *ize* (surprize, authorize, sympathize, criticize, civilize, recognize, etc.) to an absolute preference, by 1860, for *ise*. In his early letters Arnold usually wrote "it's" for the possessive (eight times in the long journal-letter in August 1839 to his brother Edward). Similarly, and more to the point here, in his complimentary closes ("very truly yours") before 1863 or thereabouts Arnold generally wrote the possessive pronoun with an apostrophe and often did so after that date, even so late as 1887. In every one of the thirty-six letters to Clough closing with "your's" the apostrophe was omitted in Lowry's transcription.

Few literary works are innocent of misprints. In a copy of his book now in the Library of The College of Wooster, Lowry made many corrections of misprints or adjustments of editorial practice, mostly alterations of punctuation such as the conversion of double quotation marks (") to single but including the emendation of "longness" in "Yours with apologies for longness" (Lowry, p. 73; below p. 90) to "longueurs." A misprint, however, is different from a misreading, all misreadings are not created equal, and disingenuousness is not an error but a fault. He did not correct "Bhunlis Alp" to "Blümlis" (Lowry, p. 110; below p. 156) or the weird "Hanli Loui" (in Auvergne "the mountain country of the Hanli Loui, about Puy") in the last of his letters to Clough, May 6, 1861 (Lowry p. 156), to "Haute Loire." R. H. Super, the editor of Arnold's *Prose Works*, has silently corrected half a dozen misreadings in the dozen Clough letters selected for The Oxford Authors *Matthew Arnold*, edited with Miriam Allott, mentioned above. Of these corrections—all of course adopted and acknowledged below—I draw attention to two because they are not only misreadings of Arnold's hand (sometimes difficult though seldom impenetrable) but also faults of technique in Lowry's editing (which never draws attention to doubtful readings). Arnold did not write nonsense, and he did *not* write (Lowry, p. 97; below p. 129) "So much for this inspired 'cheeper' as they are saying on the moon." What he wrote was "on the moors." Similarly, he did *not* write (Lowry, p. 133; below p. 133) "and beyond Moore's etc.—constantly." This too has no meaning. What Arnold wrote was "and Byron's Moore's etc.—constantly," meaning that though Wordsworth's manner was often bad his diction was scarcely ever bad, whereas Byron's and Moore's diction was constantly bad. This has a great deal of meaning and is good criticism besides.

There are other similar instances. Lowry (p. 94) misunderstood the sentence "Who had the clearest insight into the way in which business proceeded in the schools?" (below p. 126) because he did not know the special meaning of the word *schools*—"the periodical examinations for the degree of B.A." (*OED*).

He missed the remarkable significance of the poem by Henry Robert Skeffington, "The Etruscan Tombs at Perugia and Chiusi" (Lowry, p. 102; below p. 132) that so excited Arnold (who quoted fourteen lines of it to Clough) and then slumbered like the Kraken in his subconscious depths for two and a half years before it rose at the Grande Chartreuse.

He very nearly enveloped Arnold in a Pauline epiphany or transformed him into a Presbyterian or perhaps a Quaker, making him appear to have written the contrary of what he meant in a crucial passage of a poignant letter: "for I find that with me a clear almost palpable intuition (damn the logical senses of the word) is necessary before I get into prayer" (Lowry, p. 110; below p. 110). In sober fact, Arnold wrote "before I get into praxis"! And what was a merely interesting passage (though a subversive misrepresentation!) becomes now an intimate and profound revelation, relevant to, say, the opening stanzas of "Resignation," to "The Scholar-Gipsy," "Thyrsis," and so much else, poetry and prose.

Lowry did not find it improbable, in another letter, written from Derby (Lowry, p. 118; below p. 233), that elementary schools and inspections "in the Pittener" should *start* at the end of the year, "shortly after December 19, 1851" (as he dated the letter), nor implausible that a bridegroom of about four months would spend the Christmas holiday away from a bride well into her first pregnancy, nor incredible that he could not possibly gloss the word *Pittener*, a region unknown to guidebooks and gazetteers that exists only in his transcription. It is in fact a misreading of "Potteries"—a "district in N. Staffordshire, including Hanley and Stoke upon Trent, the chief seat of the

English pottery industry" (*OED*), the Five Towns of Arnold Bennett, now a federated borough.

"The manuscripts of all the letters but two are now in the possession of the Sterling Memorial Library at Yale," Lowry wrote (p. vii). Which two? and does it matter? No answer to either question is offered by the editor nor, as far as the present writer is aware, has either question even been posed before. The answer to the first question, available to anyone willing to mate the holographs with the printed texts, is Number 15 (May 24, 1848) and Number 22 (September 29, 1848); the answer to the second is Yes. It matters because the issues are moral, ethical, practical.

Obviously, compelling reasons required the withholding of some of the information; equally compelling reasons should have required some (minimal) explanation. An owner has a right to stipulate whatever conditions of privacy he pleases for whatever reasons; an editor, along with his obligation to honor that right, has equally an obligation to call attention to it. Yet why did the two letters have to remain unidentified? This too matters. A plain, forthright statement (e.g., "Letters 15 and 22 are privately owned") would have enabled the admiring reviewers to point out that these two letters, and in the entire volume only these two, have ellipses. These ellipses could of course be Arnold's, *but there is only one other ellipsis, verifiable by manuscript, in the entire range of Arnold's letters in these several volumes!* The contexts of the two omissions are similar in one respect ("at the door stands a postillion and pair," "I ordered a char yesterday morning to remount the Simplon"), but far more arresting is the fact that the second letter contains the notorious passage that gave rise to the Marguerite cottage industry—"Tomorrow I repass the Gemmi and get to Thun: linger one day at the Hotel Bellevue for the sake of the blue eyes of one of its inmates"—the first evidence outside the poetry that Marguerite could be flesh and blood. Lowry takes no notice of it, though a year or so later he was sleuthing in hotel and castle registers in Thun (Tinker and Lowry, pp. 154–55). In his own copy of his book, mentioned above, Lowry scribbled in the bottom margin on p. 90, with a guideline leading to the letter number, 22 (the "blue eyes" letter)—"See Ms. at Wooster particularly possidetes." One is driven to the conclusion, unpleasant but hardly avoidable, that Lowry himself owned them and sold them at some point to a collector knowledgeable about Arnold and Arnold scholars.

Lost Letters

Much could be written about the letters *not* in these volumes. Some letters have disappeared, and some, for whatever reason, have proved untraceable. The Davis *Checklist*, for instance, records a series of eleven letters to Henry Dunn, secretary of the British and Foreign School Society (see below

p. 206), of which only three have surfaced. The other eight belonged at one time to Lowry and then to Frederick L. Mulhauser, the editor of Clough's letters and poems, but no trace of them remains either in the Mulhauser archive in the Honnold Library, Claremont, California, or, as his son assures me, elsewhere in family papers. Presumably, they were bought from Mulhauser by a collector knowledgeable about Arnold and Arnold scholars. In December 1987 William Doyle Galleries in New York offered a series of six letters (33 pages) written to Charles Butler, Arnold's American friend and host, which were acquired ultimately by Roger Brooks. The letters to Ernest Fontanès and the mysterious will-o'-the-wisp (now you see them, now you don't) letters to Wyndham Slade have already been mentioned. Arnold's closest friends were, with the exception of John Duke Coleridge and Arthur Stanley, exactly those present at his wedding, in June 1851—Clough, Slade, John Blackett, and Theodore ("Todo") Walrond—and to this quartet of "best men," and only these, not to his best-loved brother Tom, for example, nor to Coleridge nor to Stanley, would he have written the kind of unbuttoned, spontaneous letter that we so prize today. And not even to Clough did he say, as he said to Slade in November 1854 (Russell omitted it), "The plague of babies is for the present stayed. The matter to which you refer is one of considerable mystery: It looks easy, indeed, as you say: but these things are not precisely as they seem." With Blackett and Walrond he would probably have been similarly relaxed. To the former a single letter is known; to Walrond, not one. The loss is crippling.

Deletions in Russell's Edition

What has been deliberately censored? It is an interesting question, but to some extent the question is more interesting than the answer, for many of the deletions are wholly trivial, domestic chitchat, often an afterthought in a postscript. But the answer begs the question, for triviality and insignificance are the very essence, the sine qua non, of family letters. To every English person, not merely those in Wordsworth-land, the daffodil (which Arnold spells correctly half the time) seems a national icon. To every mother the diarrhœa—mentioned only less frequently than daffodils—of her son, daughter-in-law (who suffered from London to Paris and then from Paris to Nancy), and grandchildren is fraught with interest. Arnold well knows that his mother *wants* to hear "While I was dressing yesterday morning the nursery maid came down to me with this charming message; 'Please, Sir, Miss Nelly and Master Dick has got the croup, and the baby is very ill with diarrhœa.' " She *wants* to hear about their bad teeth and visits to the American dentist, about the French doctor in Paris and the old family doctor at home (so much a part of daily life that he does not merit a first name), domestic details, especially of the nursery (Mrs Tuffin and Mrs Goose and the Goosery were not invented), about the fevers and chills, biliousness and face-ache, cod liver oil, lumbago, gallstones, corns, about the "new dessert service . . . which took my fancy extremely" (he bought it without consulting his wife), whether to give a wedding present to Stanley ("he gave us none," said his wife), and, most certainly, about the adorable children decked out in their velvet finery for a *bal costumé*, about their childish prattle ("I love to hear of the sayings and doing of my midget," Arnold wrote later of his own infant granddaughter), as well as about the birds, cats, dogs, ponies, cows, pigs, and a score of sheep belonging to the butcher. And, truth to tell, so do we. For, though nothing sinister or indiscreet lurks in a large majority of the deletions nor, considered item by item, even anything specially interesting, the cumulative effect is considerable. These are the details that humanize the poet-critic-theologian-educator-political observer.

Occasionally, a deletion avoids repetition, as when Arnold tells both his mother and sister of meeting Byron's mistress, Teresa Guiccioli, now Mme Boissy, in Paris. Sometimes a bar or a mere initial letter stands for a proper name, e.g., Gladstone or Palgrave, both of whom were alive when the letters were first published, an editorial principle of which the observance was, to say the least, whimsical. The briefest deletion was of a two-letter abbreviation in a letter to his sister in March 1848, where Arnold, writing from Lansdowne House, refers to "my great Fh. table" (below, p. 97).

Many family letters, as we have seen, were undoubtedly withheld from Russell and perhaps destroyed. Of all the family letters printed in his two volumes of which we have the holographs (about 230), only 17 escaped without any deletion indicated. Some of the survivors have crossed-out or occasionally heavily obliterated passages, most of which are at least partially decipherable (omissions or cancellations italicized). *"Lady Wightman talks of going into lodgings at Kensington Palace, but nothing is as yet settled, except that she cannot stay in Eaton Place,"* Arnold wrote to his mother on the death of his father-in-law on December 24, 1863. This sentence and the four following are so heavily inked over that, even with an infrared lamp, the words cannot be recovered with certainty. *I keep as distant as I can about affairs,"* he goes on, *"and not being an executor I am not driven to mix myself much up with them. The Judge's will was made three years before my marriage. Lady Wightman will surely not have more than I told you. The girls will have, in the end about £[illegible: 100] a year."* The Byzantine procedures, the stone walls, mazes, and blind alleys of the Probate Registry at Somerset House can be circumvented, however, for the plain evidence of the financial accounts in the diaries, scrupulously recorded year after year, quarter by quarter, is that in 1851 Wightman ("The

Judge") settled on his daughter £100 a year and moreover that this was continued without change in the remaining years of Lady Wightman, who died in April 1871.

It seems to have been the blue pencil of Frances Arnold, the youngest sister and the most provincial and insular of all the children, that bore down most frequently, most inconsequently, and most inconsistently. She was not concerned with indiscretions, for probably none came her way. In a letter to her in June 1876, in which the first five sentences were omitted in the printed version, the second half of the postscript is blotted out: *"I saw Mrs Walrond the other day; looks older than Walrond & [?] severe; but nice."* There are deletions within deletions: in another letter to her in October 1886, of which about a page and a half is marked for omission, she heavily inked over, *"I am glad that Ld Salisbury has given Trinity to Butler; I am not particularly fond of him, but Flu is, and I think he will be a good Master."* (Russell's edition of the letters is dedicated to Henry Montagu Butler, headmaster of Harrow during Russell's years there.) And almost certainly it was Fan who did *not* delete Arnold's slur, "a sort of pseudo-Shelley called Swinburne," from a letter written to his mother in June 1863, before the younger poet's days of fame and ill-fame. In that year and in those circumstances and in a private letter the remark was not reprehensible. But to let it stand in a work published many years before Swinburne's death and in which so many inconsequential deletions had been made was inexcusable, especially if, as seems probable, it was a moral judgment for which Russell must share the blame with the family. (Swinburne, who did not take this sort of thing lying down, read it, was not amused, and called Arnold "a sort of pseudo-Wordsworth" and a great deal more—and worse! He must have missed the reference in July 1869, in which Arnold refrained from sending his mother a critical article in *Temple Bar* because "the passages quoted from Swinburne are really too strong to send into a decent family-circle.") And neither sister nor editor thought the reference to an old friend (Palgrave, diminished in print to a transparent initial) offensive— "P____'s verses always seem to me to want any real reason for existing." (If Palgrave had read this, his letter to Grant Duff in 1890—in the final volume—might have been less sweetly reasonable.)

Other instances are more typical. In Russell's second volume (pp. 83–85), for example, in the letter dated "Hampden, Tuesday, December 12, 1871" (which should be "Sunday, [December 10, 1871]") two passages are omitted. The first one, indicated by the three dots of an ellipsis, tells us in half-a-dozen lines that Arnold's host's house is unbearably cold (*"I see my breath and can hardly hold my pen"*) and that he is glad *"Flu is not with me, for I think she really could not bear it."* Fair enough—for his host, Grant Duff, a close friend, lived a good decade after the publication of the letter. The second omission, unindicated, is more savory, dealing not with a domestic inconvenience but with a national crisis so timely that it could be today's headlines. The prince of Wales's chances of recovery from a life-threatening bout of typhoid fever suddenly seem more promising. "His illness and the feeling it excites very much strengthens the crown," Arnold wrote (going on, in the deletion) "*and adds to the dissatisfaction raised by Sir Charles Dilke's proceedings. However, he has a line to take which if he sticks to it and is not frightened out of it before he has well entered it,*" Arnold continues, presciently, "*will sooner or later make him an important personage, with the turn men's minds are now taking.*" This has nothing to do with the notorious divorce case that so titillated the whole country some years later, it refers to the expense of maintaining the royal household and the queen's not paying income tax—with Arnold not quite betraying his own sympathies. Dilke, on friendly terms with Arnold, also outlived him.

Russell's next letter (pp. 85–86), dated "December 23, 1871" (instead of [December 24 or 25]), a birthday-Christmas thank-you, deletes without indication more than half of what Arnold wrote, printing all that shows him as a learned and discriminating student of the Bible in English, Greek, Latin, German, and Hebrew, omitting all that shows him as son, husband, father, brother, neighbor, huntsman ("*I am nearly decided to buy a breech-loader . . . you bore people if you keep them waiting with a muzzle-loader*") and, with tongue in cheek, as financial adviser to William Forster, his affluent brother-in-law.

The damage done to Arnold's pathetic letter to his mother (February 18, 1872) on the devastatingly sudden death of his son Budge, age eighteen, four years after the deaths of Basil and Tommy, is surely the most neurotically self-protective of all—seven separate silent deletions plus a passage heavily inked over: "I do not know that I shall write much, but I must tell you what pleasure it gave us to have your letter and Fan's this morning. I think Flu will write to you tomorrow. When I wrote last Sunday there was not even a trace of illness to be seen in Budge," Arnold went on,

> though I hear now he had been knocked up by running a mile very fast the day before: but he was entirely himself all Saturday evening ["*evening*" omitted] and Sunday, and indeed particularly gay *because he was so pleased at having the Toogoods here to whom he felt we owed a debt of hospitality; and again and again he said to me how awfully Mr Toogood seemed to like being here.* When I came home on Monday evening just in time to dress for dinner at the Leafs before coming to the theatricals here, Flu told me that Budge had gone to bed with a bad cold and toothache. I saw him three times that evening and found him very sick

and miserable; I concluded he had a bilious attack such as I used often to have when a boy, and that he had a cold with it. So it went on, head-ache taking the place of face [Russell: "tooth"] ache, and I cannot say I was the least uneasy *when Flu remained in his room without coming to bed on Wednesday night, because I knew he was sick from time to time and understood that she did not like him to be sick and miserable in solitude.* But when Victorine called to us on Friday morning, and I found him light-headed, wandering about the room, pressing his head with his hands, throwing himself on the bed again and again getting up, I was very uneasy; he knew me, however, and said—"Ah, Papa!" but I went off at once for Dr Tonge, the doctor who lives nearest. *He had not attended him, or heard of the case from Mr Hewlett—but when he saw him he said the light-headedness was "of no importance"—that it came from his feverish cold and the want of nourishment owing to his sickness, and that the thing was to get him to take nourishment as he would then go to sleep. And he asked me to go home with him for a dose of chloral. I went, but* when I came back *I found Flu had got him to take some spoonfulls of beef tea and* he seemed dropping into a heavy doze; *so we did not torment him with the chloral, which I am glad of as it would have been the worst possible thing for him.* I had to go very early to London, and he seemed in the same heavy doze when I left him. The rest you have heard; when I saw him again at 2 P.M., all the doctors were there besides Hutton, who had come down with me; and it was clear there was no hope. He never showed the least spark of consciousness, till his breathing ceased with a sort of deep sigh. How fond you were of him, and how I like to recall this! He looks beautiful, and my main feeling about him is, I am glad to say, what I have put into one of my poems, the "Fragment of a Dejaneira." *Flu sleeps well, as she did after Tommy's death, also: this is the great help for her, but she looks a ghost.* William Forster has just come.

Walter has just written a very feeling and kind letter.

The passage "as she did after Tommy's death . . . kind letter," crowded into the side- and top-margins of pages 1–3 of the holograph, is followed by several short lines heavily inked over that cannot be certainly recovered but may read: "*I think you lay too great stress on his* [?]*drink* [*drink* underlined] *leading to* [two words impenetrable, followed by] [?]*and* [?]*scorn; when* [p. 2] *one is aware of any fault indulged in, any bad habit given way to, one does not mention the fault or habit to those one respects; it is* [p. 3] *a necessary part of the* [?]*case.* Love to my dear Fan and to Rowland."

And so on. For the drawing of attention to omissions from the family letters is not, like certain diseases, self-limiting, since the process has no natural end other than the necessary termination imposed by the supply of letters and the atrophy resulting from the proliferation of inconsequentialities.

Family Letters

The Forsters

The family letters are the valve pumping the lifeblood of this entire work, and among them all, if we had a linguistic calorimeter to measure the emotive value of words, Arnold's letters to his sister "K" would score highest (those to his wife are disqualified, as will be seen). Not until his older daughter married and moved to New York did he again allow himself the warmth of language or the emotional outreaching that he reserved for Jane, the first-born, his elder by a year and a half. She was an admirable lady, and undoubtedly the most sympathetic of the children. Like all the Arnolds, she walked in duty, but all that was best in her mother (intelligence and principled self-lessness) and in her father (intellect, learning, humor) met and combined their strengths within her, and it would be a chilly heart indeed that could not understand Arnold's attachment. His known letters to her range in date from March 1848 to May 1887, but no letter at all has come forth during a dozen years of these several decades (e.g., 1869–73, 1876–78). Of those that remain all but four are holographs, and of these four only two are in Russell's edition. She censored not by penciling, nor yet by scissoring, but by withholding and (apparently) destroying. The missing letters to her may be the most desolating loss of all in the canon of family letters.

She felt in herself "the right of seniority of mind" (in Jane Austen's phrase) as well as of age, and it colored their very special relationship. She had been his superior in childhood, and in his maturity she was manifestly the only one, including his mother, that he regarded as his intellectual equal. The first six children were all born at Laleham, where their father (with John Buckland) kept a school before moving on to Rugby in 1828, but it was Jane, always Jane, whom he always associated nostalgically with their days there. "Jane is the only one I connect with Laleham, and her I do at every point," he wrote to his mother in January 1848. "On Sunday afternoon I went to Laleham, which you have never seen," he wrote to Fan, his youngest sister, in August next year. "It changes less than any place I ever go to. I should like to go there with your sister Jane." With a Tennysonian tenderness and in a Tennysonian idiom, he breathes the language of flowers: "It is beginning to grow dusk—but it has been a sweet day, with sun & a playing wind and a softly broken sky. The crocusses which have long starred the lawn in front of the windows, growing like daisies out of the turf, have nearly vanished—but the lilacs that border the court are thrusting their leaves out to make amends," he wrote to Jane at the end of March 1848, falling, uncharacteristically, into measured phrases and subtly prefiguring the meter, diction, and personation of "Come into the garden, Maud' " and then modulates into cryptic and possibly reproachful verse:

> " 'The clouds of sickness cast no stain upon
>   'Her vallies & blue hills:
> 'The doubt that assails all things never won
> 'This faithful impulse of unfaithful wills'—

—It gets more & more grey and indistinct, and the musical clock behind me is quickening its pace in preparation for its half hour peal."

And then in the other half of the letter he addresses himself to the intellectual side of Jane—England's deficiency and inferiority to "the Continent" in ideas and general culture, Lamartine, and a flourish of astronomy. Exactly a year later, abasing himself and calling over a vast, he says "I am fragments, while you are a whole," and in the altogether remarkable (and devastatingly mutilated) letter written on the subject of her engagement in [?May 1850] he breathes the spirit of the Psalter (without its cadences): "You my darling have been a refreshing thought to me in my dryest periods." But—"The heart knoweth its own bitterness and a stranger intermeddleth not thereof"— about four-fifths of page 3 (and therefore of p. 4) has been cut off. In October 1854, three years married, he said to her, not to his wife or mother or best friend: "There is no one and never will be any one who enters into what I have done as you have entered into it, dearest K,—and to whom I so want to communicate what I do." Jane Forster, for her part, perceptively (and perhaps a little uncomfortably) wrote to her brother Tom in May 1855: "I believe he never sees me without going back to the old times when we were 'the three older ones,' " and in August 1856, sending a belated birthday letter (also hitherto unpublished), Arnold tells her that she is "one of those oftenest in my mind and who first occur to me in connexion with what interests me deeply." Again the thought of her invokes his lyrical-pastoral-metrical mode—the thyme-scented air, "rabbits stirring in the fern," the "murmur of the Teme in the forest valley beneath—and far away in the beautiful sunlight the soft ranges of the Welsh hills fading away one behind the other in the distance." And then the nostalgia becomes explicit: "I was quite alone and as I rested on the stiles I thought of you because what it all brought to my mind was the story of Emma and her Nurse which we used to read when we were children." The "description of the pleasant hills" took "powerful hold" upon him indeed, and the first sentence of that description begins:

"The pleasantest time Jane [the Nurse] spent was in walking out with her little mistress [Emma]." And, as the excerpt below (p. 341n) reveals, Arnold's recall was total as well as vivid and revealing. It seems certain that her marriage created a great emptiness in the penetralia of his psyche: for she was to him, as he put it, falling easily into Wordsworthian intimations, "what no one else ever was, what no one else ever will exactly be again" (below p. 206).

William Edward Forster (1818–1886: *DNB*), her husband, was an affluent Quaker woollen manufacturer from Bradford, nephew of Sir Fowell Buxton (see below p. 164n), of whom he seems the very clone, and decidedly liberal in politics. The only child of a strong antislavery father and mother, he "left" the Society of Friends and on August 15, 1850, married Jane Martha Arnold at Rydal Church. Apparently, nephritis had rendered her infertile (see below pp. 190n. 4, 337n. 6, 341 n. 1), and, childless, they later adopted the four orphaned children of her brother William and bestowed on them the love they were so full of—requited in full measure by the children. He of course figures in these letters, and as M.P. (from 1861), under-secretary for the Colonies, privy councillor and vice-president of the Council, and in 1880 chief secretary for Ireland appointed by Gladstone (to whom he remained loyal, dying before the cards were on the table about Home Rule), he figured in the life of the nation. Largely self-educated, he attended neither public school nor university, and yet his Elementary Education Bill of 1870 has made his name survive. Of his and Arnold's relationship wars and rumors of wars have always been bruited, an oral tradition persists of muted tensions, unacknowledged and perhaps unrecognized—the urgencies of jealousy? professional resentment? temperamental incompatibility certainly. ("Diffidence," as Henry Adams remarked, "was not one of Forster's weaknesses.") And this man, who married the most important person in Arnold's life, was in most ways Arnold's very antithesis—no family circle to cosset him, no Old Boy network (his friends were made, not begotten), no Homer or Goethe, no Béranger or Rachel or Obermann or George Sand, no French spellings of ordinary English words, no Church of England to discard and then draw as a sort of joker or wild card. The wonder is not that tension existed but that it did not snap.

The Other Family Letters

Yet, though much was taken, much abides. The dutiful son wrote to his mother pretty faithfully once a week, gradually beginning at some point in the 1850s and continuing until her death in 1873, and manifestly taking pains to make his letters, all emanations from the heart, interesting and informative. He succeeded. Of them nearly four hundred survive, ranging over a period of four decades—literally, 1832–1873, though seriously from 1848— and the total number *written* must have been double or triple that figure. By any reckoning this is an extraordinary showing, and probably unique. The obvious comparisons are the letters of Chesterfield to his son and to his godson and, more to the point, those written to her daughter by Madame de Sévigné, who instructed the echoing ages in the art and whose example, wholly benign, must have flowed into Arnold's reversal of the pattern. His reference in a late essay to her "sheer elementary soundness of nature" and "her perfect lucidity" sounds self-reflexive.

Next, ranked by the number of letters surviving, are the youngest and oldest sisters, the two whose assistance was acknowledged by George Russell, Fan, with ninety letters, K (Jane Forster), with eighty-two. Fan, the younger, remaining at Fox How after her mother's death, functioned as the anchor of the family, and Arnold wrote to her then: "I shall try to keep up with you too my old habit of writing a weekly letter to her." K, the most appealing of them all, obviously remained the most cherished. After these two sisters ranks his favorite brother Tom, with sixty-eight. At this point a sharp falling off occurs: Susy, with thirteen (or thirteen and a half, sharing one with William), followed by Walter, the youngest child, who outlived Arnold and of whom so little is known, with three; William, who died in 1859 (the least appealing, combining his mother's rigidity and his father's self-righteousness, without their redemptive graces) with one (or one and a half), Edward (not quite the ninny he seems in these letters but certainly a house plant) with one, and Mary, who married three times and was perhaps the most interesting (and troublesome) of them all, with none. Richard Penrose Arnold, the only surviving son, is represented by six letters, Lucy Arnold Whitridge, the older daughter, by fifty-seven, and Eleanor, the younger, who married twice, by only ten.

In this tally must of course be included the seventy-odd letters to Frances Lucy Arnold, wife and then widow, whose resolute cooperation in Russell's two-volume compilation made it possible and whose self-righteous vigilance made it insipid. They were husband and wife for thirtyseven years, during many of which, especially early on, Arnold was at home only on weekends, and over long stretches of time, especially when abroad, he tended to write to her daily. No estimate about the total number written can even be attempted, but for nearly two dozen of those thirtyseven years no letter is known; of the tiny fraction surviving all but five are printed in Russell's edition, and among them all only eight holographs are known—the only letters to her in existence with a both a greeting ("My darling Flu," "My darling," "My dear darling," "My own darling," and, best of all, in 1879, "My extreme darling") *and* a close ("Your own always," "Your own always tenderly attached," "Your own tenderly and greatly attached," and, from abroad in 1858 and 1859, "I am again and again and always your fondly and tenderly attached and devoted *Cangrande*," which was not printed, and "Your own, always, *Cangrande*," which was muted in print to "Ever yours, M. A."

The effect of their destruction is of course incalculable—as it always is in such circumstances. The burning of Swinburne's letters to his college friend John Nichol (the equivalent of Arnold's to Clough) impoverished literary history. The burning of those of the tenderest of English poets to his fiancée, Tennyson's to Emily Sellwood, probably deprived the world of the only letters that could have rivaled Keats's in amatory expressiveness. Of the loss of Arnold's to his fiancée and then wife, especially those in the early 1850s, when he was sleepless in the Midlands, we can only speculate helplessly, though we can be confident that what remains has been denatured. To his widow, in her fierce determination to emmarble the Dead Poet, the slightest endearment seemed an indiscretion, gossip an abomination, the trivia of personal relations almost unclean. The younger sister's weapon of choice, as we have seen, was a blue pencil; the widow's—one gropes for an acceptable conceit!—was a shredder.

The Diaries

The most important sources of information about Arnold are of course his works (poetry and prose) and his letters, especially, as we have seen, the letters to Clough and to his family. But another quarry, long known to scholarship, is indispensable, almost equally valuable, and far more intimidating than his published works or his letters—the so-called diaries, sometimes referred to as "pocket diaries," a more accurate name, or "Note-books," a misleading name. The works and letters can be pored over or dipped into with pleasure; the diaries, invaluable but unreadable, cannot. Each of them, year after year, is an aide-mémoire, an "account-book," as Gladstone described his own diaries, "of the all-precious gift of time." They can be *used*. They *must* be consulted, for they are a mother lode of information—dates, places, itineraries, books and articles read or to be read, often with brief extracts or quotations, letters written or to be written, rendezvous, social and professional, scheduled or to be scheduled or canceled, records of sums borrowed or debts paid, a strict accounting of monthly bills and income, of presentation copies of books, patent medicines, domestic wages, and much, much else. The diaries for thirty-six years, 1852 to 1888, all in the Yale University Library (and all described in *The Tinker Library*, compiled by Robert F. Metzdorf) were transcribed by William Bell Guthrie as "A Dissertation Presented to the Graduate Faculty of the University of Virginia in Candidacy for the Degree of Doctor of Philosophy 1957" under the direction of A. K. Davis, Jr.: *Matthew Arnold's Diaries, The Unpublished Items: A Transcription and Commentary* (omitting only "the text of the literary entries" harvested in *The Note-Books of Matthew Arnold*, edited by Lowry, Karl Young, and Waldo Hilary Dunn, in 1952)—512 pages in one volume of commentary and apparatus followed by 1,781 pages in three volumes of transcription, the whole now available from University Microfilms International. By no means a menial or mechanical bean-counting grind, it could have been accomplished only by a compleat Arnoldian, and, in the finest sense of a wretched, pretentious phrase, it was a startling "contribution to knowledge" that cannot easily be overpraised.

There is more. Also at Yale are the diaries for the three years 1845–47, not transcribed by Guthrie and, except in one respect, to which I will return, not manifestly worth the effort; the "Reading-Lists" from them were published by Kenneth Allott in *Victorian Studies* in March 1959. For the next three years, 1848–50, the diaries have not been found. For 1851, the year of Arnold's marriage, a microfilm copy (also in the Yale Library) of the diary is transcribed here for the first time, interspersed among the letters below in separate chronological entries. Yet another diary is also transcribed and published for the first time in this edition of the letters, one maintained by Arnold in 1859 from March 15 till August 26, when he was abroad for the Newcastle Commission for the works known as *The Popular Education of France*, and including French Switzerland and Holland, and *A French Eton*.

In this connection it is necessary now to mention *The Oxford Diaries of Arthur Hugh Clough*, edited by Anthony Kenny, for the period January 1838, when Clough, four years older than Arnold, was nineteen, to August 1848. I quote now from Kenny's discerning Biographical Introduction, pp. lxi-lxii:

> In describing his sins and emotional crises, Clough adopts some disguises, so that the meaning would not be obvious, say, to a Balliol scout. . . .
> One of the most transparent of Clough's symbols is the one which he uses in connection with what he calls "the wretched habit" which he contracted when he was at Rugby and brought with him to Oxford. On 6 April [1838], in the second diary, he notes, "I was as nearly as possible committing my worst sin this Morning. I was not *quite* roused from sleep, but fully conscious." Two weeks later he notes on one day, "my wickedness and weakness have gone their full length" and on 3 May, "I have gone my full length—precisely in the same way as twice before." At the end of the diary he lists four times, including these three, on which "I have committed my worst sin."
> In later diaries on particular days he marks a large star, sometimes

encircled and sometimes hedged about with lines. From the prose which sometimes accompanies these stars we can see that they are meant to mark the commission of sin; and from the description of the context it seems certain that what is meant is solitary masturbation ("* after not getting up," "* almost wilful though asleep," "* after too much exercise and perhaps too much wine"). I have reproduced the stars in the text, because it is clear that the guilt and tension engendered played an important part in the depression which beset Clough at the time. At one point he went so far as to discuss the matter with his father, and to consult a Liverpool surgeon about it: he clearly was tempted to regard his self-abuse as something almost pathological.

Arnold's diaries for the years 1845–47 are marked like Clough's, though with crosses rather than stars, and perhaps for the same reason—the coercions of the postpubertal, premarital libido. The diaries for 1845–46 have for each month two printed numbered pages (with facing blank unnumbered pages), listing, column by column, on the left-hand pages (1) "the day of the month," (2) "the corresponding day of the week," (3) "Sundays, Royal Birth-days, Holidays, Terms [university and law], &c.," (4, 5) "the Sun's rising and setting," (6) "the Moon's rising or setting." The right-hand numbered pages list the day of the month, "the time of high water just above London New Bridge," "the equation of time," the moon's changes, and other such information. On the facing blank right-hand pages Arnold drew up by hand his own column of days of the month, with Sundays indicated ("S") to the right of the appropriate date (5, 12, 19, 25 for January 1845) and, after that, brief notations of a change of geographical location (January 20, "Left Fox How," 21, "Came to Oxford") or (January 24, 26) "chapel morning" or "o"(zero) on January 27–31. The next column records day by day the number of hours spent reading—zero on January 1 and 9, 1 or 2 thereafter, except for 3 on the twenty-ninth, and no entries on the twentieth and twenty-first. The last column lists "Skating" on January 2, with "do" (ditto) on the third and fourth, "Thaw" on the fifth, tenth, and twenty-second, and "Frost" on the ninth, twentieth and twenty-ninth. The left-hand blank pages list his disbursements in pounds, shillings, pence. And so on throughout the three years. The diary for 1847 is slightly different in physical format but not in ways relevant to this description.

To the left of certain dates on the blank pages throughout the three years are crosses, which demonstrably have nothing to do with chapel (attendance or avoidance), tardiness at prayers (or presence or absence), or inclement or fair weather (barometric pressure was less insistent than biological), and are not explained or commented on in any way at any point. A tally for the first quarter of 1845 shows that in January a cross was marked beside the dates 3, 5, 9, 11, 12, 24, 26, and 30; in February beside 2, 8, 9, 10, 13, 15, 19, and 24; in March, 9, 23, 25, and 30. And so on, once more, throughout the three years. For evidential completeness a tabulation of all the dates marked with a cross during the three years will be found in Appendix A. No diaries are known for 1848–50, as we have seen, and no crosses are in the 1851 diary.

Collections of Arnold Letters

Arnold papers girdle the globe—from England to New Zealand and Australia, to the United States and Canada, coast to coast, to Russia, Germany, Norway, the Netherlands, France, and Italy. As a writer, Matthew Arnold was never wildly popular like Byron or Tennyson or Dickens or Kipling, but he had a well-known, well-connected, and extremely influential father, whose moral force spread exponentially throughout the English-speaking world. Two of Arnold's brothers were, each in a small way, apostles of English culture and education in the farthest reaches of Empire—one went to India, married, and remained there for several years; another went to Australia and New Zealand, married, and remained there for several years. (His only son went to Australia, married, and remained there briefly.) His sisters married well, one to a high government official. His two daughters also married well—the older, wed to an American, established a vigorous family of American descendants. All Arnolds, mother, father, children, and children's children, were keepers of travel journals and ordinary diaries, and, in those days that are no more, they were one and all compulsive letter-writers and, for the most part, letter-savers.

Of Arnold papers the three largest collections are in the Library of Balliol College, Oxford; the Brotherton Collection, University of Leeds; and at Yale University. The forming of these collections is an interesting story in its own right.

Balliol, Arnold's old college, remained all his life one of the focal points of his intellectual and social existence, as it still is of his posthumous life. In the Balliol College Library the "Matthew Arnold Collections" number well over three hundred letters in Arnold's autograph, as well as poems and essays, early and late, in Latin and English, notebooks, journals, drawings, and books from Arnold's library, among them *De Imitatione Christi, Isaiah of Jerusalem*, and Claude Fauriel's *Histoire de la poésie provençale*, with notes in his hand. In 1973 Matthew Arnold's American grandson, Arnold Whitridge, son of the older daughter, Lucy, presented 313 autograph letters, as well as one by his wife and a marvelous letter by his sister "K" (Mrs William Forster). In 1983 the late Mary Moorman, the distinguished biographer of Wordsworth and great-great granddaughter of Thomas Arnold, gave a collection that included three autograph letters of Matthew Arnold as well as Arnoldiana. From time to time a few other letters have been bought or donated, among the latter a series of 7 letters to T. S. Baynes presented by Peter Spalding.

The William Delafield Arnold Collection was given in 1964 by Kyril Bonfiguoli, of Sanders of Oxford Ltd, a Balliol man. A collection (including forty-five autograph letters) that had formerly belonged to another Arnold grandson, Roger Wodehouse (son of Arnold's younger daughter, Nelly, later Viscountess Sandhurst, by her first husband) was bought in 1971. In 1982 Balliol acquired a vast collection of autograph materials (essays, notebooks, diaries, correspondence—upwards of two thousand letters, to and from family members and others) of Matthew Arnold's charming, unworldly younger brother, Thomas Arnold, from Tom's grandson, Francis Arnold, and his daughter Mrs Jane Davies. It should be pointed out also that *The Oxford Diaries of Arthur Hugh Clough*, edited by Anthony Kenny, was based on the Clough journals, "seven notebooks, which between them cover events from March 1835 to August 1848," in the Balliol College Library.

The Brotherton Collection in the Library of the University of Leeds has over two dozen autograph letters by Arnold (including sixteen to Robert Browning). Among library collections it is supreme in Arnold family "background" materials thanks to the generosity of Mary Moorman and through her good offices to that of two other family connections, Arnold Whitridge and Brigadier Penrose. The supremacy of the Brotherton Collection is concentrated especially in early background materials, much of it drawn upon by A. P. Stanley for his *Life and Correspondence of Thomas Arnold, D.D.*—twelve journals or notebooks of Arnold's father and mother concerning travel, Rugby School, and family matters, over a hundred and fifty letters from Dr Arnold to various correspondents, and over a hundred letters from his wife, chiefly to her sisters. As will be seen below, many of these, extraordinarily interesting in themselves, also and necessarily tell us much about Matthew Arnold, his brothers and sisters, and some of the closest friends of the early period.

The Arnold collection in the Beinecke Library, Yale University, is a tribute to the learning, discrimination, taste, determination, and alertness of one man, Chauncey Brewster Tinker, professor of English at Yale and, from 1930, Keeper of Rare Books in the Yale University Library. His collections (of which the Arnold materials are a small part) are admirably described in *The Tinker Library: A Bibliographical Catalogue of the Books and Manuscripts Collected by Chauncey Brewster Tinker*, compiled by Robert F. Metzdorf (Yale University Library, 1959).

The Arnold collection at Yale is wide-ranging—284 autograph letters

(44 of them from *The Tinker Library*), among them the incomparable (and celebrated) letters to Arthur Hugh Clough as well as several other series (Knowles, Ward, Smith), several family letters, and many, many others. The collection also includes manuscripts of poems and of a lovely twenty-eight-page prose essay, "George Sand," described by Marjorie G. Wynne in *The Arnoldian* (Fall 1975), as well as presentation copies and books from Arnold's own library, some catalogued by Metzdorf, others acquired later (e.g., *Logique de Kant*, annotated, *Critique de la raison pure*, Sainte-Beuve's *Tableau historique et critique de la poésie française et du théâtre français au XVIe siècle*). And, in addition to all this, the Yale collections also comprise the famous "Yale Manuscript," edited (1989) by S. O. A. Ullman, as well as *all* the diaries known to exist, a considerable number—those for 1845–47 and, as described in Metzdorf's catalogue, those from 1852 to 1888, a microfilm copy of the 1851 diary, the diary of the Newcastle Commission continental months in 1859, and Frances Lucy Arnold's 1867 diary. These diaries, a spectacular sweep of the board, are the underpinning of all modern biographical study of Matthew Arnold.

The Arnold material in the National Archives of Canada, the National Library, and in Laurier House, Ottawa, is choice—and, in a special sense, *rarefied*. All of it came from Canada's most famous political figure, William Lyon Mackenzie King, who served as prime minister, in three different terms, longer than any other first minister in the entire British Empire. An ardent admirer of Matthew Arnold, he knew and visited Arnold's niece, Mrs Humphry Ward, first in 1899, and through her came to know Arnold's American grandaughter, Eleanor Whitridge (later Greenough, then Thwaites), from whom over the course of a couple of decades or so he acquired his Arnold collection—twenty-nine autograph letters, of which two dozen are to members of the family, including one of the eight holograph letters to Frances Lucy Arnold—unlisted in the Davis *Checklist* and, heretofore unknown to scholarship, first printed in the present edition. The collection includes, moreover, four letters to other correspondents as well as four from the father, Dr Arnold—comprising the first two letters printed below, to his wife dated December 31, 1825, mentioning the three-year-old son ("I am sorry dear Matt is not more recovered") and to his Aunt, Susan Delafield, November 25, 1829, the *perfect* letter for this edition, mentioning all the six children; to G. J. Fox, January 19, 1832 (excerpted below); and finally, another perfect letter for this edition, a letter to Matthew Arnold, age nine, written March 1, 1832, from Rugby, where he was headmaster, to Laleham, where he got his start professionally with his brother-in-law, John Buckland, to whose school he had sent his son.

"Choice—and, in a special sense, *rarefied?*" Rarefied, because Mackenzie King's collection included a number of books from the Arnold family now in the National Library of Canada and in Laurier House. The books so far identified are Dr Arnold's three-volume edition of Thucydides' *History of the Peloponnesian War*, with ninety-two pages of notes as well as numerous annotations, his *History of Rome* (3 vols, no annotations), his copy of Carlyle's *The French Revolution* (3 vols, very few annotations), and Gilbert Burnet's *History of the Reformation in England* (no annotations), all in the National Library; in Laurier House, Matthew Arnold's copy of the Tom Moore seventeen-volume edition of the works of Byron; *The Poetical Works of S. T. Coleridge* (vols 2, 3, Pickering, 1836; inscribed: "Fifth Form / Matthew Arnold / From the Master of Rugby School. Examination, Decr. 1837"); Nicolas Perrot d'Ablancourt, *Lucien* (vols 1, 2, Amsterdam, 1709); James Reynolds, *Biographical Notices of Persian Poets* (London, Oriental Translation Fund of Great Britain and Ireland, 1846); *The Strayed Reveller and Other Poems* (London, Fellowes, 1849); and *The Poetical Works of Percy Bysshe Shelley* (vols 1–4, Moxon, 1839), all with Arnold's bookplate; also in Laurier House are these titles, with inscriptions: Coleridge's *Poetical Works*, as noted above; H. W. Beechey, *The Literary Works of Sir Joshua Reynolds* (inscribed to him in March 1869 by John Duke Coleridge); *A View of the Scripture Revelations Concerning a Future* (London, Fellowes, 1837), inscribed: "M. Arnold/from his Mother"); *Selected Poems of Matthew Arnold* (Macmillan, 1878, inscribed: "To Dick. / M. A. / Novber. 10th, 1878"); *Poetical Works of Matthew Arnold* (London, Macmillan, 1908, inscribed: "To / Mackenzie King, / from Matthew Arnold's/granddaughter; Eleanor/December 17th, 1915"); and *Selected Poems of Matthew Arnold* (London, Macmillan, 1910, inscribed: "To an old friend / from / Eleanor Whitridge / Greenough").

The British Library has about a hundred and forty letters, including the sixty-five in the Macmillan Archive, and several to Gladstone, Swinburne, Lady de Rothschild, one to his brother Tom (and one to Anthony Panizzi, Librarian of the British Museum, recommending Tom for a reader's "ticket of admission"). In addition, it contains a fine album of twenty-six letters addressed *to* Arnold by various notables.

The National Library of Scotland has about a hundred and thirty letters, of which the charming series (just over a hundred) to the "Prince of Publishers," George Smith, is the centerpiece, but it has also a notelet to Thackeray, an excellent letter to Arnold's brother Tom, several letters to the earl of Rosebery, a series of ten to John Aitchison, a couple to Mrs George Smith, and an assortment of others.

The Bodleian Library, it may be taken for granted, has a substantial "body" (not a "collection") of over five dozen Arnold letters and also a "collection" of about a hundred and twenty letters written by his father, mostly to his old friend, a fellow-judge, John Taylor Coleridge, himself father of

Arnold's close friend John Duke Coleridge (described in *The Arnoldian*, Autumn 1973, by Mary Clapinson). In addition the main body of the Clough Papers is here, among them Thomas Arnold's letters to Clough and J. C. Shairp.

Another library must be mentioned in this context—the Alexander Turnbull Library, Wellington, New Zealand, center for all study of Arnold's younger, favorite brother, Thomas Arnold. Two excellent books edited by James Bertram are indispensable, *New Zealand Letters of Thomas Arnold the Younger with Further Letters from Van Diemen's Land and Letters of Arthur Hugh Clough 1847–1851* (1966) and *Letters of Thomas Arnold the Younger 1850–1900* (1980). The latter volume (p. viii) lists the various collections containing letters by him and some family letters as well as a checklist (pp. 259–70) of the four hundred and thirty "known letters of Thomas Arnold the Younger."

The Public Record Office, London, also owns over five dozen letters, submerged or even buried in the official Council Office reports of most of the years during which Arnold was an inspector of schools, a job that sapped his *physical* energies but otherwise did not encroach on his intellectual self. They give us a sense of his professional life at once vivid and inert (resonant of the Circumlocution Office!), and, formulaic though they are, writing them must have trained him in precision and economy of prose style.

The University of Virginia Library has about two hundred letters and also a fifty-one page manuscript *Special Report on . . . Elementary Education in Germany.* The Pierpont Morgan Library has an excellent group of seventy-three Matthew Arnold letters (enriched by the bequest of the late Gordon N. Ray), including a specially fine letter to Tom Arnold, and in addition—a great rarity—a letter *from* Sainte-Beuve *to* Arnold. The collection also has the corrected proofsheets for *Isaiah of Jerusalem* as printed in the *Nineteenth Century* in April and May 1883.

In such a tabulation as this one expects certain libraries in the United States to stand up and be counted, even though their Arnold holdings are not spectacular. Harvard University, the possessor of a spectacular Tennyson collection, owns fifty-four Arnold letters, many of them addressed to standard Harvard names—Charles Eliot Norton (12), James Russell Lowell (6), whom Arnold knew as minister to England, Emerson (3), of course, whom he lectured on (the manuscript is in the Houghton Library) and whose family he visited in Concord, Henry James (3), a friend and admirer, and Francis James Child—as well as a good many others, including Thomas Bailey Aldrich and William Dean Howells.

Texas A&M University has fifty letters, the New York Public Library thirty-three (with the fine series to Andrew Carnegie, a smaller one to Richard Watson Gilder, and an excellent letter to Mary Penrose Arnold), the Berg Collection, down the hall, has eleven (and the Pforzheimer Collection one),

Bryn Mawr College thirty-two, the Huntington Library twenty-seven (as well as seven from Dr Arnold to Sir Francis Beaufort, two by Mary Penrose Arnold, and one by Frances Lucy Arnold), and the University of Rochester, with fewer than a half-dozen Matthew Arnold letters, has something unique and interesting, a collection of two dozen or so from various Arnolds—the parents, two from William Delafield Arnold (rarities), several from Frances Arnold—nearly all addressed to the Reverend or Mrs James Hearn (he was Dr Arnold's curate at Laleham in the 1820s) or their son Jamie, who lived at Fox How with them in the 1840s, tutored by Jane and then by Mary, and then died tragically still a young man.

The family collection of Matthew Arnold's great-grandson Frederick Whitridge, whose name occurs so often in these volumes, was formed by his father, the late Arnold Whitridge, and included the Arnold papers of *his* two sisters, Eleanor Whitridge Thwaites and Joan Whitridge Forsyth, both of whom predeceased him. It was enormous. Indeed, at its largest its size must have been hallucinatory, for it comprised virtually *all* that is now at Ottawa as well as much that is now at Yale (e.g., the notebooks, books, letters), much that is now at Balliol College and in the Brotherton Collection, and, obviously, some of the books that appear from time to time in dealers' catalogues. Arnold Whitridge presented to Balliol College 313 letters by Matthew Arnold, 304 of them addressed to Mary Penrose Arnold, and in addition made substantial gifts to the Brotherton Collection. Remaining in his collection on his death in 1989, were nearly two hundred Arnold letters, of which about a third were addressed to Jane Arnold Forster (with two to her husband, William E. Forster), another third to his great-grandmother, Mary Penrose Arnold, many to his mother, Lucy Arnold Whitridge, a few (rarities all) to his great-aunt Susy Cropper, and many to his great-aunt Fan, presiding over Fox How for many years after her mother's death, and half-a-dozen to the Arnold children. He also had the collection of letters addressed *to* Arnold published as *An Arnold Family Album* in *The Arnoldian* 15, no. 3 (Special Issue 1989–90). At one time the six honeymoon letters written by Frances Lucy Arnold (now lost to sight but printed in this volume from photocopies) as well as the 1851 notebook (also printed in this volume) were in his possession.

Matthew Arnold's extended family of course includes the four orphaned children of his brother William Delafield Arnold who, adopted by the Forsters, changed their name to Arnold-Forster. The library of Trinity College, Dublin, has the correspondence of two of them, Hugh Oakeley Arnold-Forster and Frances Egerton Arnold-Forster, a total of well over a thousand letters, all indexed in the National Register of Archives, Quality House, Quality Court, Chancery Lane (and on Chadwyck-Healey microfiche). The collection includes one Matthew Arnold letter (to his sister, Mrs

Forster) and a few from all his siblings but Tom and Walter as well as one from Frances Lucy Arnold.

Among other private owners, the Rothschild Archive has nearly a hundred letters addressed by Arnold to his close friend Lady de Rothschild (who outlived him by twenty-two years). Ten others to her and her daughter Constance Flower (later, Lady Battersea) are in the W. Hugh Peal Collection in the Library of the University of Kentucky. Arnold's friendship with John Duke Coleridge began earlier and lasted longer than any other on record (there are more letters to him than to Clough), and in the wonderful and vast Coleridge archive at Ottery St Mary the relationship is documented in five dozen letters, dated from 1843 to Arnold's death (and, counting the letters to the widow, well beyond it). Nearly three dozen letters to Mountstuart Grant Duff, from 1862 to 1887, formerly in the possession of Shiela Sokolov Grant Duff, are now in the British Library Oriental and India House Collections.

The only private collection of Arnold letters known to the editor not included in this edition belongs to Roger L. Brooks, professor of English at Baylor University and director of the Armstrong Browning Library, Waco, Texas, a collector as knowledgeable about Arnold and Arnold scholars as any man. A. K. Davis, Jr, describing him as among "the most assiduous searchers for Arnold letters in recent years," wrote a subacid paragraph about him in the Introduction to his *Checklist* (p. xxxviii).

Brooks has provided photocopies of several Arnold letters in the Armstrong Browning Library for inclusion in this edition, and, though he several times expressed his willingness to send copies of those in his private collection, they have not been forthcoming. I inquired about the possibility of remunerating him for the *use* (not the purchase) of his "twenty five unpublished letters" and he replied (I quote from his handwritten letter, April 13, 1989, before me): "Now arriving at a fair price is difficult, but considering the depreciation of the value of the collection, I would think $10,000 would be fair and reasonable." "And when I heard this thing," as Ezra says, "I rent my garment and my mantle, and plucked off the hair of my head and of my beard, and sat down astonied." I replied (I quote from a copy of my letter, April 29, before me): "Before I can go any further, I will have to have a listing of the letters, dates, addressees, and number of pages." No reply has been received.

The Letters Discussed

We have seen, in a general sense, what is *not* in these letters, what is partially in them, what *is* in them, and where they come from, and we may now properly inquire what they are like.

Tennyson once said, famously, that he "would as soon kill a pig as write a letter." Wordsworth told DeQuincey that he found painful the very "act of holding a pen." Swinburne, who certainly had pleasure in writing letters in his youth, described "the mere physical act of writing" as "a positive and often a painful effort." Arnold, on the contrary, loved it. He belonged to another school, the school of the marquise de Sévigné, Cowper, Gray, Fitz-Gerald, James. His letters are not emotional spillways. Indeed, apart from Keats's, no such series of letters exists, and even Byron's, for all their impromptu air, are artful to the last degree. Spontaneity, most treasured (and most overrated) of epistolary virtues, originates either in hormones, in substance abuse (Keats's hemlock or "draught of vintage"), in the creative imagination when language becomes amative release (Wordsworth's "overflow of powerful feelings" begins with arousal: "an emotion kindred to that which was before . . . is gradually produced"), or possibly in religious exaltation. In the first instance, it is the exclusive property of the young, and Arnold, like Byron and Swinburne, comes close to it solely in his hot youth (the only season ever experienced by Keats, who wrote all his surviving letters when he was twenty to twenty-five years old). The equivalent period for Arnold would be 1843 to 1848. In his letters after, say, 1850, spontaneity diminished, necessarily, and it was a dimming of glory, superseded by something he had learned from Goethe by way of the "Everlasting Yea" in Carlyle's *Sartor Resartus*: "The Fraction of Life can be increased in value not so much by increasing your Numerator as by lessening your Denominator." Or, more elegantly but still depressingly, as Empedocles rephrased it to Pausanias: "Make us, not fly to dreams, but moderate desire." Or, in contemporary slang, "Cut your losses."

> What Poets feel not, when they make,
> A pleasure in creating,
> The world in *its* turn will not take
> Pleasure in contemplating,

he once wrote (see below p. 250), and it is obvious from the best of these letters (and they are numerous), early and late, from childhood to grandfatherhood, that Arnold took pleasure in creating them.

What, then, do the letters *give* us, what do they amount to? Arnold discusses poetry and his own poems freely, most familiarly and memorably of course in the well-known letters to Clough but also in letters to his mother and his sister Jane. "My poems are fragments . . . I am fragments," he wrote to Jane, profoundly, in 1849 (below p. 143). Unlike Wordsworth, Shelley, and Byron, he could not "give his whole life to it," as he points out in one of his finest letters, his own apologia pro vita sua (below p. 402), and, unlike the latter two, could not be (or declined to be) Attis, driven by his "demon"

to an "actual tearing" of himself "to pieces." Less familiar but equally revealing is his stubborn fixation on *Merope*, which, straining the loyalties of his
friends and stretching those of his family, makes Arnold sound for all the
world like Wordsworth's Betty Foy sending on, on his well-girt saddle, "Him
whom she loves, her Idiot Boy." Arnold was equally obtuse about his very
late poem "Westminster Abbey," but he writes movingly about "Thyrsis,"
and on reading "Clough's letters and journals which his wife has just printed
for his private friends" said that it brought Clough "vividly" back to him.
"The loose screw there was in his whole organization, is, however," he went
on (December 4, 1865), "much more evident to me in reading this book
than it was in consorting with him in life . . . Poor, poor Clough. I have long
had a design, in some part already fulfilled, of making some memorial in verse
of what I saw of him and felt, and feel, about him."

This edition of the correspondence opens in 1825, when Arnold was
just barely three years old and living at Laleham, with the anxious concern of
his father, a provincial schoolmaster, that "dear Matt is not more recovered"
and his "hopes soon to be with him again"; it closes sixty-two years later,
with Matthew Arnold (unable to attend the funerals of a sister-in-law and a
brother-in-law on the same day) concerned for his daughter's health (she had
a cold) and looking forward to her arrival from New York with his only
grandchild, the "Midget," as the doting grandfather called her, said to be
"more fascinating than ever." In the first letter we have from his hand, July
1832, not yet ten years old, he writes "I have fished a good deal since you
went away," and in one of the very last, not a week before his death, he
wrote, "I was at Wilton last week, and found myself fishing in a greatcoat
amid snowstorms." In between, the provincial schoolmaster becomes, at
Rugby School, England's most famous headmaster (and probably the most
famous headmaster who ever lived!) and dies at the age of forty-seven; "dear
Matt" becomes a poet, a government school inspector, England's most famous living critic, and dies at the age of sixty-six.

The headmaster (himself exemplifying so much of the "movement of
mind" of his own generation) had five sons and four daughters. Of the sons
two lost the faith of their fathers, one kept misplacing it, one conformed
outwardly, and the fifth (the youngest), enigma and rebel though he was, is
said to have died a "faithful Churchman"; the daughters stood steadfast. Like
many of us, the Arnold children observed the first five of the Ten Com-
mandments as selectively as they pleased and the second five (as far as we
know) scrupulously. Certainly, they honored their father and mother all the
days of their lives. One and all highly intelligent, they were educated to move
among the best and brightest, required to be orderly, led by example to love
nature, to identify flora and fauna, to be fond of pets, to cherish old servants,

learning, religion, and tradition, brought up to be literary, and trained to be responsible, civic-minded *citizens*. Some of them were compulsive diarists, but only for chronometrical or mnemonic reasons and sometimes for self-improvement, but never with self-indulgent or confessional or egotistical motives.

They cleaved one to another, were always in touch with each other, were all anchored to their Lake Country home where the younger ones were born and where they all grew up. Something about family—the idea, the fact, the individuals—inspired the Arnold soul to transports of reverence. They had no dynastic aspirations, certainly, but—only Walter resisted the nuclear cohesion—they seem bound each to each by something like natural piety. They all had a large capacity for love (one is tempted to say "capacitance") that infuses these letters.

"Happy families are all alike," Tolstoi wrote in the famous first sentence of *Anna Karenina*. It would not be amiss to claim that the trajectory of the growth of the poet-critic's mind could be traced from Lélia to Anna Karenina, both rebels with a cause, both tragic, for the Russian novel, unlike George Sand's, does not conclude with the death of the heroine. Arnold's late essay on Tolstoi (whom he had met in the early sixties) and whom he certainly influenced) is flavored with autobiography when, near the wonderfully moving end of the novel (which he read in French), he renders Levine's meditation on the phrase of the old peasant, "living by the rule of God, of the truth":

> Then he reflected that he had been born of parents professing this rule, as their parents again had possessed it before them, that he had sucked it in with his mother's milk; that some sense of it, some strength and nourishment from it, had been ever with him, although he knew it not; that if he had tried to do the duties of his station it was by help of the secret support ministered by this rule; that if in his moments of despairing restlessness and agony, when he was driven to think of suicide, he had yet not committed suicide, it was because this rule had silently enabled him to do his duty in some degree, and had given him some hold upon life and happiness in consequence.

Anyone who peruses these letters thoughtfully will register the impression of Arnold's repeated use of the phrase "dear old" for the expression of affection for persons, pets, places (Rugby, Fox How, the Athenæum Club, Balliol College, the Avon) and, at least once, a *thing* (his watch fob!). Its numbing repetition (well over two hundred times) comes to seem a sort of verbal tic and therefore meaningless, but study will reveal it in another aspect. For it is quintessential Arnold—Tennyson's bone-and-nerve nostalgia, Swinburne's "Old thoughts, old thanks, old aspirations," joined to the names of all his brothers and sisters (habitually to Edward and Tom), to Clough and Shairp from school and university, to old men (Wordsworth, his neighbor, Banks, the gardener, and several others), to Budge and Dick and Nelly, but, most interestingly and tellingly, *never* to Rowland, his nanny, or to his mother, the two who seem to inhabit a sphere of white radiance that renders a qualifier redundant. Jane (K) lags in "dear old" only because of her special epithet, "dearest." "Precious" and "darling" are for Nelly and Lucy.

Poetry loves the past, its creator. Tennyson, all his life, nurtured a strong attachment to Lincolnshire, where his formative years had been so troubled. Swinburne adored the Northumberland and the Isle of Wight of a happy childhood. Matthew Arnold treasured Laleham, where he was born ("I blend more and more with the place," he wrote when he was twenty-five), and, though they toed the line in professing love for Rugby School, they all, like their father, drew it at Warwickshire. (Later on, he could stomach Harrow for a few years because London was so accessible and, as a resident, he could afford to put the boys in school there, but, he said, "it is ugly country like the neighbourhood of Rugby where I lived so long").

"Men should desire to have a home, which they do not wish to quit any more, suited to their habits of life and likely to be suited to them until their death," wrote Ruskin. The focal point of the Arnolds' lives—father, mother, children, children's children—was Westmorland, with its hills and lakes. Probably no note in these letters sounds more recurrently than a very Tennysonian "passion of the past" blended with a very Arnoldian passion of the place—that place was their revered Fox How, the house that Dr Arnold built (with some help and advice from Wordsworth) in 1832–34. Tutored in this reverence by Wordsworth, their friend and neighbor, they certainly were, but he merely educed what was latent in themselves. For they loved stones (not sermons in stones), grass, trees (cedar, stone pine, elm and beech, balsam poplar, ilex, peach, apple, pear, cherry, may, kalmia, myrtle, chestnut, bay, cupressus, plane, thuja, fir, magnolia, and juniper); like George Sand ("closely and truly intimate with rural nature"), they were *connoisseurs* of plants and flowers (purple helleborine, stinking iris, pennywort, ringwort, butterwort, cowslips, wild parsnip, sheep's parsley, bee, bird's nest, and butterfly orchis, as well as Lady's-slipper, aconite, anemone hepatica and white anemone, white violet, osmunda, pitcher plant, shrubby Cinque-foil, and even pokeweed—in the United States Arnold traveled with Asa Gray's *American Botany*); and they loved also four-footed and winged creatures, birds of course—stuffed, shot, eaten, or rescued from cats, but especially on the wing (robins, sparrows, wrens, blackbirds, thrushes—song and missel—cuckoos, stockdoves, nightingales—"almost maddeningly beautiful," "you do not know what you lose by being out of hearing of nightingales," he wrote to his sister in the last year of his life), but unexpectedly not of clouds, to which Arnold seems indifferent (a good sky is a cloudless sky, except for trout fishing). He was a faithful meteorologist. As to "dear Matt," his mother wrote in August 1867, "the delights he feels in the pure air & bright water—and in the old hills—& I am sure in the old recollections connected with the place are so great there it is a great joy to me to see them." Again, "the longer I live," he wrote to her ten months later, "the more I feel the charm of mountains and clear water." This feeling became part of his emotional baggage in France, Belgium, Italy (where the muddy streams and dry watercourses made him yearn for the "innumerable clear rivers of Scotland"), and of course Switzerland and the Tyrol.

Like so many other poets—Cowper, Crabbe, Hardy, William Carlos Williams—Arnold had a strong, enduring sense of place. Not Rugby but Oxford was notoriously the "sweet city," and the closest he came to wavering in his attachment was in 1873, in Italy. Paris, which he had found so nourishing and so thrilling on so many occasions, now "positively revolted" him, but Florence, he wrote to his brother, is "the loveliest city by far I have ever seen. Oxford is what comes nearest to it, but Oxford has no such perfect centre as the Duomo, standing in the midst of the city grouped around it, as a hen gathers her chickens under her wing." This was an aesthetic judgment, however, not infidelity to an ideal, for Oxford remained, always, *the* city, the city built "To music, therefore never built at all / And therefore built for ever," the "bourg" of which he took the rustic murmur "For the great wave that echoes round the world." Arnold—who had been several times to France (with a foot across the border in Spain) and Switzerland, had honeymooned in what is now northern Italy, had toured Scotland, Wales, and most of England, including the Isle of Wight and the Isle of Man—saw Cambridge for the first time in his life in February 1853, when he was thirty-two years old, finding it "strange to be in a place of colleges that is not Oxford." From his room in The Bull in Trumpington Street he was unable to identify "a long collegiate-looking building opposite" as Corpus Christi College, he found the "statue" of Newton not "the marble index of a mind for ever Voyaging through strange seas of Thought, alone" but "hardly as effective as I had expected," and, unlike Pater, who could discern "the mysticism of the middle age" even in the Mona Lisa, he considered King's College Chapel, not proud in its bearing, not eloquent of its old splendors, but somehow not quite measuring up, because the "Middle Ages and all their poetry and impressiveness are in Oxford and not here"! Only at Oxford did he feel himself "Matriculated to Eternity."

But Fox How was a *base*, the home his father had created ("Look: This was his house," as Ruskin put it in *Lectures on Architecture and Painting*, speaking exactly of such centers of stability); Oxford was a *way station*, home of the "masters of the mind" and cradle of a restless intellect. Each was a source where memory was refreshed and strength renewed. What Arnold needed was something that George Meredith had already found ("I am every morning on the top of Box Hill—as its flower, its bird, its prophet," he wrote of his new home. "I drop down the moon on one side, the sun on t'other. I breathe fine air. I shout ha ha to the gates of this world") or that William Morris would find at Kelmscott Manor:

> But kind and dear
> Is the old house here,
> And my heart is warm
> Midst winter's harm.

Arnold too needed to be able to say, "This is my house."

He was finally able to pronounce this benison in June 1873, when he moved into Pains Hill Cottage, Cobham, Surrey, the home of his last decade and a half, with which he is associated as much as Hardy with Max Gate or Shaw with Ayot St Lawrence. There, when he settled in, he was fifty years old, his wife forty-eight, his son, Dick, was nearly eighteen, Lucy, the older daughter, fourteen, and Nelly twelve. There, with London so near and yet so amiably distanced, Arnold came into his own: "A lovely morning, with the sun rising opposite my window and filling the grass and trees with light, and through the trees the blue line of the Surrey hills," he wrote, soon after moving in, in a birthday letter to his brother Tom. "How beautiful things are, and in spite of clouds within and without, may we go on feeling this to the end and die when we can no longer feel it. . . . I want you to see this place," he goes on in a Tennysonian (or Hardyan) mode, "the soil is so beautiful and so favourable to trees, and we stand so well placed, that the fibres of attachment which generally take two or three years to push out of one and take hold of a place have begun to push out here after a few months." And there, though "it is not yet what I hope to make it," he became something of a country squire, Tolstoi's Levine, and, as these letters disclose so vividly and refreshingly, spent the next fifteen years realizing its possibilities—and his own.

Important work lay ahead—*Literature and Dogma, God and the Bible, Last Essays, Mixed Essays, Irish Essays, Discourses in America, Essays in Criticism*. In the poetic vein only half a dozen poems were possible, and of these the last four were elegies, "Westminster Abbey" (on the death of A. P. Stanley) and the three marvelous animal poems, so bittersweet, so moving, "Geist's Grave," "Poor Matthias," and "Kaiser Dead," two dogs and a canary.

English poets, from Skelton to Eliot, glory in their animal poems, and among them Arnold's hold their own with the very best. Strikingly original and wholly charming, they are not pressed into the service of allegory or symbolism or a sense of the mystery of life or mutability or ethical insight or spiritual repair. They are not even agnostic, like Hardy's poem "Shelley's Skylark," they are *Arnoldian* and, bizarre as it is to describe these short, slight, humorous poems in the words used to describe a long, famous, tragic novel, they are perfectly defined in what Arnold wrote of *Anna Karenina*: "A piece of life it is. The author has not invented and combined it, he has seen it. . . . The author saw it all happening—saw it and therefore relates it. . . . This is the result which, by his extraordinary fineness of perception, and by his sincere fidelity to it, the author achieves; he works in us a sense of the absolute reality of his personages and their doings." In no sense bleak, they are rather a tender, affectionate acceptance of last things.

Other sides of Arnold we see in glimpses, not in broadsides. He was the most humorous of men, with a gift for satire not always kept in hand and a self-deprecating irony, both more characteristic of his essays than of his letters. "A Colonel Baird, a cousin of Mrs Arnold's, has forwarded to the India Board a memorandum on the unsavoury subject of *Earth-closets* in which he is an adept," he wrote to Grant Duff, in a letter that Russell shied away from. "You will have seen, with the pleasure and amusement of a true friend, all the earth closets lately emptied on my head for my Culture and Anarchy Essays." (Swinburne, whose very muse in certain moods was Cloaca, would have sympathized: "As to the Asinaeum," he wrote, "it is my wash (or rather p——) pot; over the Saturday have I cast out my shoe." The young Tennyson went him one better and, for the amusement of his friends, acted out "a man on a close stool.")

"Why, Uncle Matthew, oh why, will you not be always wholly serious?" asks his niece, deliciously, in Max's caricature. Arnold had caught the tone at an early age. Even in his little "autobiography" at the age of perhaps twelve he recorded an older boy's pun on "bough" and "bow"; at thirteen he wriggled out of writing *two* letters by addressing one to Willy and Susy together (neither of them could read, but "each of you would think it a shame if I did not write to you in particular"); and in August 1837, at the age of fourteen, in his journal-letter to his brother, he showed a degree of sophistication: "I went with Mamma to a great draper's warehouse," he wrote from Paris, "& assisted her with my exquisite taste in forming a selection of Pelerines Lace Cambric, Silks &c: a tasteful assortment of which it would have been impossible to have procured without my assistance."

Being a poet, he of course loved gossip. Tennyson, who said it was his "abhorrence," adored it, Swinburne, with none at hand, would invent it as part of his imaginative life, Browning dined out on it, Meredith elevated it into an art form, it was Byron's bread-and-butter, Pope's stock-in-trade, Milton's ultimate weapon, Oscar Wilde's arterial system.

"Scandal," wrote Wilde, "is gossip made tedious by morality." Arnold did not find it tedious when Sainte-Beuve regaled him with the latest Parisian titillations, especially the "letters he had had from G. Sand and Alf. de Musset at the time of their love affair, and then again at the time of their rupture," but then it was not trammeled by morality. "At Grillions' breakfast last week," Arnold wrote to his daughter shortly before his death, "Chamberlain came on for a ballot and was blackballed; it shows how high party feeling runs. At the Athenæum Canon MacColl who is thought to be a creature of Gladstone's received 59 blackballs!"

Gossip shades into satire, which came so easily to Arnold, as any reader of his essays knows. Ordinarily discretion personified, he was as susceptible as the rest of us to great wealth—repelled by vulgar display, admiring of quality, quiet good taste, elegance—and, even on his two American visits, he never failed to mention the wealth of his various hosts. Mentmore, the home of the Mayer de Rothschilds, "surpasses belief—it is like a Venetian palace doubled in size, and all Europe has been ransacked to fill it with appropriate furniture," he wrote, without irony, in 1863. "This place of Lord Lytton's stands well on a hill in the pretty part of Hertfordshire," he wrote to his mother after a visit to Knebworth, one of the "great fortified posts" of the Barbarians, in May 1869; "but like Lord Lytton himself the place is a strange mixture of what is really romantic and interesting with what is tawdry and gimcracky; and one is constantly coming upon stucco for stone, rubbish from Wardour street instead of real old curiosities, and bits in the taste of a second-rate Vauxhall stuck down in a beautiful recess of garden. The house loses no doubt by my seeing it so soon after Hatfield, which is a first-rate to a second-rate, compared with this at its best; but this might be a much more impressive place than it is, if it had been simply treated. Lord Lytton is kindness itself, but theatrical in his reception of us and in his determination to treat the Prince as a royal personage." Even Cardinal Newman was not (wholly) exempt. At a reception for him in May 1880, Arnold was well aware of the combination of theatricality and royalty, writing that "Newman was in costume, not full Cardinal's costume, but a sort of vest with gold about it and the red cap; he was in state at one end of the room . . . and people filed before him as before the Queen, dropping on their knees when they were presented and kissing his hand." Here he modulates into a different key. "It was the faithful who knelt in general, but then it was in general only the faithful who were presented. That old mountebank Lord Houghton dropped on his knees, however, and mumbled the Cardinal's hand like a piece of cake."

He can sound like Jane Austen's Mrs Bennet. Of his wife's niece he wrote to his mother in December 1870: "Edith Wood is just engaged to a Mr Wingfield, a nephew of the late Lord Dynevor's, with a fortune of nearly £30,000 a year. He is in the 60th rifles, very young and very steady, does not even dance. . . . You may imagine what an excitement this makes in Caroline's family, and how Flu listens to all the particulars." And then he becomes Mr Bennet: "She is a singular girl, but has many steady qualities, and I hope and think will not lose her head, as her Mamma would certainly have done in like case."

And he can even throw away a line—Lady Bracknell would not have disdained it—of elegant Arnoldian balance, equal parts of malice and sympathy. Of Charles John Vaughan, the former headmaster of Harrow incriminated in scandal but so much an Establishment figure that he had been merely shunted off to Doncaster as vicar and now redeemed as master of the Temple, Arnold wrote to his mother in December 1869: "I met the Vaughans and they both seem radiant with happiness in being at the Temple." The remainder of the sentence, inked over, reads: "she said they saw no one at Doncaster but the poor people and the middle class tradespeople and she felt Vaughan had done all he could in that position and needed change."

He could direct his gift against himself. As a lecturer, especially in the United States, he was (to put the matter forthrightly) guilty of every sin, so dreadful that he had to take elocution lessons, and he was not prepared for American newspaper reporting—"the rowdy newspapers here, with their daily specimens of figment, joke, caricature and ill-natured comment"—but his account of it and of the American scene in general on his two visits are as interesting as anything in these volumes. Arnold kept his balance. "A Detroit paper compared me, as I stooped now and then to look at my manuscript on a music stool, to 'an elderly bird pecking at grapes on a trellis.'" "'He has harsh features,' said another, 'supercilious manners, a single eye-glass, hair parted down the middle, and ill-fitting clothes.'" As far as it goes, this view (except for the "single eye-glass") seems a more or less accurate description of Tissot's caricature in *Vanity Fair* in 1871, to the "badness and absurdity" of which Arnold calls attention, adroitly attributing the judgment to Browning. (Two months later he spoke of his portrait in the *Illustrated Review* as "rather like an old sheep," and ten years before he sent a photograph to his brother Tom, "which is not good: but with my huge mouth and want of eyebrows, I never shall take well.")

Was there no rift within the lute? Was Arnold's life really so seamless as this Introduction seems to allow? Was he all *that* imperturbable? He lost his father when he was not yet twenty-two years old, his mother when he was fifty, two sons in 1868 and a third less than three years later. For several decades he worked unbelievably hard at a school-inspecting job for which he had no liking and no vocation, during much of the time away from home and family five days a week, so poor that he was constantly borrowing money from his mother, friends, publishers. Do these several thousand letters arranged in chronological order over a period of six decades reveal no fatal flaw, no defect of character, no imperfection of personality, no psychic weakness, no secret sin?

The answer is that indeed these letters hint at no kind of general dissatisfaction or nonspecific unhappiness, no variety of indiscretion or impropriety. Stalkers of *Angst* must seek another hunting ground. Arnold may have worn the scars of a "deep psychic wound," as I (and others before me) have suggested, but the concrete evidence is not here. Brother Tom's religious tergiversations undoubtedly disturbed them all, but they knew he was far more troubled than they were, and, though his New Zealand wife was antipodean culturally and socially as well as geographically, the varnish of acceptance shows at most only hairline cracks. His sister's third wedding stung Arnold (even Arnold!) into mentioning the "amusing but not pleasant accounts of what is said in Leicstershire about Mary's absurd marriage," and the dozen or so references to her husband (who died shortly before Arnold himself) are invariably to *Mr* Hayes. Edward Arnold, a school inspector wedded to Devonshire, was a problem because of ill health and because he was a widower in his last eighteen years. (David Hopkinson, himself a school inspector, has written admirably about him in *Edward Penrose Arnold: A Victorian Family Portrait*.). His sister Fan wrote to Mrs James Hearn, an old family friend, in August 1881 (MS, University of Rochester): "The beloved brother with whom I used to stay in Devonshire, became a confirmed invalid in 1877—from heart complaint. He was obliged to give up his Inspectorship and come to live with me. And I had the happiness of being able to nurse him and care for him during the last ten months of his life. He died in the spring of 1878."

Of Walter Arnold more needs to be said. He was the youngest and most obscure of them all, something of a maverick, and about him precious little has been printed. He is frequently mentioned in these volumes and virtually everything said is new, but the more one learns, the more enigmatic he seems.

His life is a domestic novel. He entered Rugby School in August 1846, where for whatever reason (including unruliness) he did not thrive, and shipped off as a "boy sailor" in (about) September 1847, when he was twelve years old. A letter from his mother to her sister Jane Penrose, October 17, 1847, in the Brotherton Collection, says that she can think with "repose of my Walter—so great a safety does there seem in his being so early placed under the salutary discipline of distinct duty." Exactly four months later Jane, writing to the "New Zealander," her brother Tom, reports: "We had three delightful letters yesterday from Walter. . . . He seems to be very happy on the S. Vincent and thoroughly interested in his work, the study of navigation, &c."

Matthew Arnold, nearly thirteen years older, seems to have been a sort of substitute father and to have paid the usual price. In July 1853 he wrote mysteriously to his mother (in the coded language of letters that will be saved): "It is affecting what you say about Walter, but perhaps he can hardly feel too much and too bitterly. It will be good for him in the long run." And in October he wrote to K: "All doing very well at Derby. I think of having Walter there, and putting him to a tutor." In the event, the sailor home from the sea was admitted as a student in Arts in University College, University of Durham, October 20, 1855. "His academic record," according to a letter from C. D. Watkinson, deputy librarian, "was to say the least undistinguished, even for the time, as he passed in the 8th class in the first year examination in Arts in Michaelmas Term 1857, the 6th class in second year Arts in 1858 and was awarded a Bachelor of Arts degree with 7th class honours, conferred upon him on 28 June 1859."

Walter was far more nearly a Robinson Crusoe than an Enoch Arden, however, and of him Arnold wrote presciently in March 1861: "Still, what he gets now is comparatively of little importance: if at 50 he is the rich man of the family, that is sufficient. And the rich man of the family he may easily be." He became an insurance underwriter, found favor in the sight of Lloyd's, and prospered mightily. He joined the Reform Club (of which Forster, his brother-in-law, was a member). Twice in 1866 Arnold mentions his marrying—"He will marry one of the Smithson sisters of his Richmond companion" (April 4, omitted by Russell); "Is he going to marry into the Gillman family?" (August 4). In the event, he married Sarah Anne Blissett, on November 18, 1871, as the marriage license in the General Register Office reveals. And he acquired a boat ("He went out for his first cruise in his new Yacht last Friday," Fan wrote to Tom in April, 1874, "but though he likes his boat very much he was hardly able to judge of his sailing power as there was hardly any wind"—Balliol MS), and, in due course, perhaps, an insurance brokerage firm of his own.

His relations with Arnold (whom he found "so much more formidable than Jane" even so late as October 1867) were gingerly, but the letters show him finally reintegrated into the family, and according to Florence Arnold-Forster's *Irish Journal* he was often at Eccleston Square for tea or dinner. The only reference in Arnold's letters to Sarah Blissett Arnold (if indeed it is that) occurs in January 1887 (the passage is heavily inked over): "Love to Walter and his two companions. I hope [?]Sarah's cold is better." He died on September 27, 1893, at Dingle Bank, Merseyside, the home of his sister Susy, where Matthew Arnold himself had died, and, as the brother of one famous Arnold and the son of another, earned a brief obituary in *The Times* (October 5) that, mentioning no surviving family, neither widow nor children, said: "He had a strong character, of which the elements—originality, solidity of judgment, deep affections—constantly recalled his father; he was a faithful Churchman, with a living and eager interest in the Church's work; and the heroic gentleness and patience with which he bore the suffering and weakness of his last years will not soon be forgotten by those who knew him." (A photograph of him is in Hopkinson's monograph.)

Arnold's wife has been written about with great sympathy and sensitivity in two articles by Patrick J. McCarthy, "Mrs. Matthew Arnold: Some Considerations and Some Letters," *Harvard Library Bulletin* (1969) and "Mrs. Matthew Arnold," *Texas Studies in Literature and Language* (1971). Her ties to her family were quite as strong as Arnold's to his, her relations with his family, as his with hers, seem unblemished. Arnold was of course totally loyal (as he was to all his family), though a suggestion of her assertiveness comes through now and then. Blanche Smith, Clough's fiancée, calling on her in April 1853, reported that she "was nice, but a little Belgravian"—to which Clough (recognizing marriage and male bonding as incompatible) replied, "You are quite right about Mrs M. Arnold." And (a most puzzling passage) Arnold wrote to his mother two years later (below p. 313): "Flu told you the abominable news about herself, I think. She is very properly sorry and ashamed."

On the other hand, the letters can rise to high comedy, for on Good Friday 1867 she made Arnold eat crow and apply to Gladstone ("respect is the very last feeling he excites in me") for the librarianship of the House of Commons; "I do not thoroughly fancy the place," he wrote to his mother; "however, Flu would like it, and that is a great thing." She was skilled in creative nagging. In 1870, when he failed to succeed Ralph Lingen as secretary to the Council Office, she felt aggrieved. "You see Fraser, who was sent to report on the American scene is made a bishop," he wrote to his mother; "to Fanny Lucy it seems as if every one who had done what I have was promoted, and I alone passed over." Arnold justifiably had a sense of injured merit, in this instance as in others, but, as he wrote to his mother, "There is no good in letting one's mind run on these things, and I had rather she neither dwelt on them nor suggested them to me."

Their life together appears to have been unruffled. "A charming woman; she has all my graces and none of my airs," Arnold is reported to have said of her. Cadmus and Harmonia ("placid and dumb"!) they were not; "happier than the cleverest, smartest, rarest" they were. And this perception is implicit in every syllable of the obituary of Frances Lucy Arnold signed "Bystander" (probably, George Russell) in *The Pilot*, July 6, 1901:

> It is difficult to state in words that would not seem exaggerated the perfect union of mind and heart which subsisted from first to last between Matthew Arnold and his wife. Theirs were indeed the "mutual society, help, and comfort" which the Prayer Book sets forth so prominently among the objects of marriage. There was, to borrow a phrase of Mr. Arnold's from another connexion, "'a radical good intelligence" between him and his wife, "based on a natural affinity," which no difference of mere opinion could disturb. The husband's political and social traditions were Liberal, as Liberalism was understood at Rugby in the 'forties; the wife was the stiffest of Tories, with Jacobite sympathies peeping through her Toryism. The husband's bias in theology we know from his books; the wife was a zealous and consistent High Churchwoman of the Tractarian school . . . . Like all people of her school she was an indefatigable churchgoer; and the friends, who, during her last illness, used to read the daily service in her room, found that the act of reading was little more than a formal exercise, for the patient always seemed to know the Psalms and Lessons of the day by heart.

Conclusion

In fine, these letters, like all such collected editions, show us an author remarkably like the one we have always known—different not in kind but in degree.

At the beginning of this Introduction it was said that Arnold is often charged with having averted his eyes "from half of human fate" and that this could well be the "central issue" in any comprehensive view of him. To it one has to return a commonplace, worth registering here because it is quintessentially what these letters are: for whatever reason, Arnold thought (or came to think) not in Wagnerian extremes—Ortrud-Elsa, Venus-Elizabeth, Gutrune-Brunhilde—but in existential dilemmas—Iseult of Ireland and Iseult of Brittany, Empedocles and Callicles, "primal law" and "self-selected good," two views of life, two modes of existence. *If* he shrank back from some "aboriginal abyss of real Being" (Emerson) and *if* the evidence is in these letters, it resides in an abstraction and in a vacuum—in a subtle alteration in tone and in what has been censored out of the maimed, mutilated, wrenching letter written to his sister Jane ("K") on receiving the news of her engagement to William Forster, of which only remnants (remarkable remnants) remain. To the present editor it seems probable (as many have thought) that Arnold suffered a grievous psychic wound and that he healed himself, willed himself into wholeness.

These statements push Arnold studies back to the condition of, say, seventy-five years ago. But more can be said. No one doubts that Arnold's poetry is intensely subjective, that his ringing rejection of "the dialogue of the mind with itself" is interesting precisely because it is only one small step removed from his own poetic practice, which is a dialogue of the mind explaining why he rejects the dialogue of the mind with itself. "Tristram and Iseult" and *Empedocles on Etna* come to mind. Of the former the Allotts write: "That the whole story developed a shadowy autobiographical significance for Arnold (with Marguerite and Frances Lucy Wightman as 'the two Iseults who did sway / Each her hour of Tristram's day') can hardly be doubted."

In the opinion of the editor (as of others before him) the only thing dubious about "Marguerite" is her *existence*. The cottage industry that has grown up about her concerns itself with her identity as a real person, almost as a Real Presence, but she is rather, I think, a member of that spectral band that includes in their various ways Laura, Beatrice, Shakespeare's Dark Lady, Shelley's Emily, Carlyle's Blumine, Tennyson's Rosa Baring, Poe's Helen, Rossetti's Blessed Damozel, Swinburne's Mary Gordon, and Meredith's "young love sleeping in the shade" (as well as Dickens's Mrs Harris and Oscar Wilde's Bunbury!): "This sort of adoration of the real / Is but a heightening of the 'beau ideal' "—the embodiment of an "old fancy" or the enfleshing of a *rite de passage*. He might have said (with the epigraph from Augustine heading Shelley's "Alastor") *Nondum amabam, et amare amabam, quærebam quid amarem, amans amare*—"I loved not yet, yet I loved to love, I sought what I might love, in love with loving." Insofar as she is any one existing person she seems an *emblem* of George Sand, the creator of *Indiana, Jacques, Consuelo, Mauprat*, and "days of *Valentine*, days of *Lélia*, days never to return . . . yet how ineffaceable is their impression!" We have to remember Tristram's question to Iseult of Ireland, "Madcap, what jest was this to meet me here?," when we read that in her English-speaking Couvent des Anglaises in Paris George Sand's nicknames were "*Madcap et Mischievous*" (*Histoire de ma vie*, 3.12—Pléiade, ed. Georges Lubin, 2:908), and, though Arnold's eyes could not have seen this before the mid-fifties, his ears might well have *heard* it when he called on her in Nohant in August 1846, among "her few questions and remarks, upon England and things and persons English—upon Oxford and Cambridge, Byron, Bulwer." "The hour of agony and revolt passed away for George Sand," Arnold wrote, "as it passed away for Goethe, as it passes away for their readers likewise. It passes away and does not return. Yet those who, amid the agitations more or less stormy, of their youth, betook themselves to the early works of George Sand, may in late life cease to read them, indeed, but they can no more forget them than they can forget *Werther.*"

Arnold loved to live—the world within and the world without chiming together, the life of the mind (society was a gymnasium) at one with the life of the body (the outdoors was a seminary). "When we last heard from Chester Square," his mother wrote in February 1860, "poor dear little Tom was ill again—& one of the servants completely laid up—but dear Matt still was in good spirits. Is it not wonderful how cheerily he gets through his work—& how hopefully & happily he looks at things." And he learned to live with a boring, demanding, underpaid, unrewarding occupation largely because—questing intellectual, husband and father, school inspector, clubbable man-about-town and cosmopolite-about-Europe and America, hunter, fisherman, skater, voracious reader—he lived to learn. "Certainly I feel no older, and that is one great benefit of going on reading and thinking, one's sense of a freshness and newness in things remains," he wrote to his mother in June 1866, on the fifteenth anniversary of his wedding.

To be an Arnold was to be an educator. "The idea of a general, liberal training is, to carry us to a knowledge of ourselves and the world," he wrote in *Schools and Universities on the Continent.* "We are called to this knowledge by special aptitudes which are born within us; the grand thing in teaching is to have faith that some aptitudes of this kind everyone has." To be an educator was to be a missionary, and the Arnolds in a missionary mode always sound so like the Holy Family networking that reminiscences of *Paradise Regained* crowd the mind. (The man who, as someone said, "liquefied the Apostles' Creed into a 'Stream of Tendency' and compared the doctrine of the Trinity to a story of 'Three Lord Shaftesburys' " could not reasonably object to the analogy.) Of his article on Joubert, Arnold wrote to his mother: "You say just what I like when you speak of 'handing on the lamp of life' for him. That is just what I wish to do, and it is by doing that that one does good."

> These growing thoughts my mother soon perceiving
> By words at times cast forth, only rejoiced.
> And said to me apart, "High are thy thoughts
> O Son, but nourish them and let them soar
> To what height sacred virtue and true worth
> Can raise them.

A few months earlier, he had written: "It is very animating to think that one at last has a chance of *getting at* the English public. Such a public as it is, and such a work as one wants to do with it!"

Holy Families are all alike. To be a missionary was to persuade, and the note sounds persistently. He has learned a "precious truth"—that "every-thing turns upon one's exercising the power of *persuasion, of charm*; that with-out this all fury, energy, reasoning power, acquirement, are thrown away and only render their owner more miserable. Even in one's ridicule one must preserve a sweetness and good-humour." "In the long run one makes ene-mies by having one's brilliancy and ability praised; one can only get oneself really accepted by men by making oneself forgotten in the people and doc-trines one recommends." Of *A French Eton*: "In this part I am really labour-ing hard to *persuade*, and have kept myself from all which might wound, provoke, or frighten." He "held it more humane,

> more heavenly, first
> By winning words to conquer willing hearts,
> And make persuasion do the work of fear;
> At least to try, and teach the erring soul
> Not wilfully misdoing, but unaware
> Misled; the stubborn only to subdue.
> (*Paradise Regained*, 1.228−32, 221−27)

For, Arnold went on, "to school oneself to this forbearance is an excellent discipline, if one does it for right objects."

Arnold sounds the "note" persistently, though it is not certain that he hears it consistently or that he entirely frees himself of the power not our-selves that makes for self-righteousness. Our best and brightest, impatient of his "evaporation effect" (elusiveness of meaning) or of his equivocal rather than "univocal" discourse, seem to reduce his core of belief to "Manners makyth man." "I do not know my future; is the future predictable for anyone today?" wrote Chateaubriand (Arnold scribbled it in his diary, below, in April 1851). "Our time is not a time of revolution but of social transforma-tion. These transformations take place gradually, and the generations caught up in one of these periods of metamorphosis disappear, forgotten and piti-able. If Europe—it could well be the case—is used up, that is another matter. Creating nothing, it will wither away impotently in an maelstrom of passions, morals, and doctrines."

Periods of social transformation are all alike. We ourselves, in the midst of one, can no longer take it for granted that cultivation of "the best that has been known and thought in the world" is the ultimate good or even a very high priority. *What* world, we ask? the Western world? the Third World? World without end? The old order changeth. If you are not part of the so-lution, we hear, you are part of the problem. Mediation has been displaced by immediation, moderation by polarization, antithesis by tautology. The antonyms of *Culture and Anarchy* have yielded to the synonyms of multiculture and anarchy, Philistinism has become a virtue, anti-intellectualism a badge of honor, Zeitgeist been trivialized to "What's hot and what's not."

In such a context Arnold may be considered, in Chateaubriand's terms, *obscure et misérable*, forgotten and pitiable. He was never accused of pomposity or insincerity, however, and he stood for right things in the right way (Leslie Stephen: "I often wished . . . that I too had a little more sweetness and light that I might be able to say such nasty things of my enemies"), for principles (liberal humanism, endearingly undefined) retaining still, more than a century later, their vitality and fecundity, their radiant freshness, their ability to speak to us. In no sense "a beautiful and ineffectual angel beating in the void his luminous wings in vain," he was a partially effectual messenger bearing a message about the art of the possible and the possibility of art, in the broadest sense, to the whole of Western society; and, though dismissed and patronized by his very progeny, he has not been deposed or superseded. His message remains as urgent now as it was a century ago: "We have met the enemy and he is us," as it has been put, immortally.

Editorial Principles

In all letters the date, return address, salutation, and closing have been normalized, with most abbreviations spelled out; square brackets indicate that an *essential* part of the date is an editorial addition. The names of addressees, occasionally written by Arnold at the foot of the letter, are placed at the head.

Letterheads (and seals) are centered; handwritten return addresses are printed flush right.

Angle brackets, in letterheads or in letters, indicate cancellations.

In the texts of letters printed from manuscript ampersands have been preserved, superior letters lowered, abbreviations retained or, occasionally, expanded in square brackets. A period is used when the last letter is not the last letter of the word. Numbers, punctuation, and capitalization follow the source.

Printed texts follow the source, except that the hyphen is omitted in *tomorrow, today, tonight,* in conformity with Arnold's invariable practice.

In general, previous publication has not been recorded, except that all letters or parts of letters included in Russell's *The Letters of Matthew Arnold 1848–1888* are indicated by an asterisk after the name of the addressee in the heading.

Reviews of Arnold's works and books and articles referred to by him have been identified whenever possible.

All contemporaries referred to, even unto wives and children, have been identified whenever possible—to the verge of scrupulosity. Perfection here, perhaps happily, is unrealizable, but no halfway house seems defensible.

Cartoons (usually caricatures) of persons formally identified in these letters as they appeared weekly in *Vanity Fair* magazine from Jan. 30, 1869, to Jan. 14, 1914—2,358 in all, typically with a biographical sketch, leading off with Disraeli and then Gladstone—have been noted, usually with this formula: (*VF*, 1/30/69). The excellent book *In "Vanity Fair"* by Roy T. Matthews and Peter Mellini is definitive—occasionally supplemented in the annotations by quotations from the cartoons or biographical sketches in the collection of the editor.

Arnold, regarded by many as England's foremost French writer, wrote a French that, though very good indeed, was less than perfect—inferior to Swinburne's, superior to Tennyson's, superior to the editor's, inferior to the editor's wife's—and his occasional breaches of idiom are noted throughout.

Short Titles and Abbreviations

Album	*An Arnold Family Album*, ed. Cecil Y. Lang, *The Arnoldian* 15, no. 3 (Special Issue 1989–90)
Allibone	Samuel Austin Allibone, *A Critical Dictionary of English Literature and British and American Authors*, and J. F. Kirk, *Supplement*, 5 vols (Philadelphia: J. B. Lippincott, 1897)
Allott	*The Poems of Matthew Arnold*, ed. Kenneth Allott; 2d edn ed. Miriam Allott (London and New York: Longman, 1979)
Allott-Super	*Matthew Arnold* (The Oxford Authors), ed. Miriam Allott and Robert H. Super (Oxford and New York: Oxford University Press, 1986)
Annual Register	*The Annual Register; A Review of Public Events at Home and Abroad* (London: Rivingtons, 1758—)
Arnold-Forster	*Florence Arnold-Forster's Irish Journal*, ed. T. W. Moody and Richard Hawkins with Margaret Moody (Oxford: Clarendon Press, 1988)
Baldwin	A. B. Baldwin, *The Penroses of Fledborough Parsonage* (Hull: A. Brown & Sons, 1933)
Bertram	*New Zealand Letters of Thomas Arnold the Younger*, ed. James Bertram (University of Auckland, 1966)
Boase	Frederic Boase, *Modern English Biography*, 6 vols (London: Cass, 1965)
Bonnerot	Louis Bonnerot, *Matthew Arnold Poète* (Paris: Librairie Marcel Didier, 1947)
Cohen	Lucy Cohen, *Lady de Rothschild and Her Daughters 1821–1931* (London: John Murray, 1935)
Coleridge	Ernest Hartley Coleridge, *Life and Correspondence of John Duke Lord Coleridge Lord Chief Justice of England*, 2 vols (London: William Heinemann, 1906).
Connell	W. F. Connell, *The Educational Thought and Influence of Matthew Arnold* (London: Routledge and Kegan Paul, 1950)
Coulling	Sidney Coulling, *Matthew Arnold and His Critics* (Athens: Ohio University Press, 1974)

County	*Walford's County Families of the United Kingdom* (London: Robert Hardwicke, 1871, Chatto and Windus, 1904)
Crockford	*Crockford's Clerical Directory*, 15th edn (London: Horace Cox, 1883)
Dawson	*Matthew Arnold The Poetry* The Critical Heritage, ed. Carl Dawson (London and Boston: Routledge and Kegan Paul, 1973)
DNB	*The Compact Edition of The Dictionary of National Biography*, 2 vols (Oxford University Press, 1975; *A Supplement*, ed. R. W. Burchfield, 1987)
Foster	Joseph Foster, *Alumni Oxonienses*, 2 vols (Oxford: Parker, 1887)
Guthrie	William Bell Guthrie, *Matthew Arnold's Diaries, The Unpublished Items: A Transcription and Commentary*, A Dissertation Presented to the Graduate Faculty of the University of Virginia for the Degree of Doctor of Philosophy 1957. 4 vols (University Microfilms International).
Harding	Joan N. Harding, *From Fox How to Fairy Hill* (Cowbridge and Bridgend: D. Brown and Sons, 1896)
Harrow	*Harrow School Register*, 1st edn ed. R. Courtenay Welch, 1894, 2d edn ed. M. G. Dauglish, 1901 (London: Longmans Green and Co., 1901)
Hillairet	Jacques Hillairet, *Dictionnaire historique des rues de Paris*, 2 vols (Paris: Editions de Minuit, 1963)
Honan	Park Honan, *Matthew Arnold: A Life* (London: Weidenfield; New York, McGraw Hill, 1981)
Hopkinson	David Hopkinson, *Edward Penrose Arnold: A Victorian Family Portrait* (Penzance: Alison Hodge, 1981)
Jowett	Evelyn Abbott and Lewis Campbell, *The Life and Letters of Benjamin Jowett*, 2 vols (London: Murray, 1897)
Kelly	*Kelly's Handbook to the Titled, Landed & Official Classes for 1896* (London: Kelly, 1896)
Kenny	Anthony Kenny, *The Oxford Diaries of Arthur Hugh Clough* (Oxford: Clarendon Press, 1990)

Landed	*Burke's Landed Gentry* (London: Burke's Peerage Limited, 1939)
Lowry	Howard Foster Lowry, ed., *The Letters of Matthew Arnold to Arthur Hugh Clough* (London: Oxford University Press, 1932)
Lyonnet	Henry Lyonnet, *Dictionnaire des comédiens français* (Geneva: Slatkine Reprints, 1969)
Martineau	*Harriet Martineau's Directory of the Lake District 1855. An Alphabetical Index Compiled by R. Grigg* (Beewood Coldell, 1989)
McCalmont	*McCalmont's Parliamentary Poll Book British Election Results 1832–1918*, eighth edn by J. Vincent and M. Stenton (Brighton: Harvester Press, 1971)
Mulhauser	*The Correspondence of Arthur Hugh Clough*, 2 vols ed. Frederick L. Mulhauser (Oxford: Clarendon Press, 1957)
OCAL	James D. Hart, *The Oxford Companion to American Literature* (London: Oxford University Press, 1941)
OCFL	Paul Harvey and H. E. Heseltine, *Oxford Companion to French Literature* (Oxford: Clarendon Press, 1959, 1961)
OED	*The Oxford English Dictionary*
POLD	*Post Office London Directory* (London: Kelly)
Reid	T. Wemyss Reid, *Life of the Rt. Hon. W. E. Forster* 3d edn (London: Chapman and Hall, 1888; rptd Bath: Adams and Dart, 1970)
Rugby	*Rugby School Register*, 2 vols, rev. A. T. Mitchell (Rugby: Printed for Subscribers, 1901, 1902)
Russell	George W. E. Russell, ed., *Letters of Matthew Arnold 1848–1888*, 2 vols in one (London: Macmillan, 1895)
Senior	Nassau William Senior, *Conversations with M. Thiers, M. Guizot, and Other Distinguished Persons during the Second Empire* (London: Hurst and Blackett, 1878)
Spoelberch	Vicomte Spoelberch de Louvenjoul, *George Sand étude bibliographique sur ses œuvres*, 1914, rptd New York: Burt Franklin, 1971)

Stanley	Arthur Penrhyn Stanley, *The Life and Correspondence of Thomas Arnold, D.D* (London: B. Fellowes, 1844)
Super	R. H. Super, ed., *The Complete Prose Works of Matthew Arnold*, 11 vols (Ann Arbor: University of Michigan Press, 1960–77)
Swinburne	Algernon Charles Swinburne, *The Swinburne Letters*, ed. Cecil Y. Lang, 6 vols (New Haven: Yale University Press, 1959–62)
Tennyson	*The Letters of Alfred Lord Tennyson*, ed. Cecil Y. Lang and Edgar F. Shannon, Jr, 3 vols (Oxford: Clarendon Press, 1981–1990)
Tinker and Lowry	C. B. Tinker and H. F. Lowry, *The Poetry of Matthew Arnold: A Commentary* (London: Geoffrey Cumberlege, Oxford University Press, 1940, 1950)
Tuckwell	William Tuckwell, *Reminiscences of Oxford* (London: Smith, Elder, 1907)
Upper Ten Thousand	*Kelly's Handbook to the Upper Ten Thousand for 1878* (London: Kelly, 1878)
Venn	John Venn and J. A. Venn, *Alumni Cantabrigienses*, 6 vols (Cambridge: Cambridge University Press, 1922–54)
VF	*Vanity Fair: A Weekly Show of Political, Social, and Literary Wares*, 1869–1914
Ward	Mrs. Humphry Ward, *A Writer's Recollections*, 2 vols (New York and London: Harper & Brothers, 1918)
Wellesley	Walter E. Houghton and others, *The Wellesley Index to Victorian Periodicals 1824–1900*, 5 vols (Toronto: University of Toronto Press, 1966–89)
Whitaker	*Whitaker's Naval and Military Directory and Indian Army List* (London: J. Whitaker & Sons, 1900)
Whitridge	Arnold Whitridge, *Dr Arnold of Rugby* (London: Constable, 1928)
Woodward	Frances J. Woodward, *The Doctor's Disciples* (London, New York, Toronto: Geoffrey Cumberlege, Oxford University Press, 1954)

WWW	*Who Was Who* (London: A. & C. Black; New York, Macmillan)
Wymer	Norman Wymer, *Dr Arnold of Rugby* (London: Robert Hale, 1953; rptd Greenwood Press, 1970)

Chronology

1822   (Dec. 24) Matthew Arnold born at Laleham-on-Thames, oldest son and second of the nine surviving children of the Rev. Thomas Arnold and Mary Penrose Arnold.

1828   Rev. Thomas Arnold appointed headmaster of Rugby School.

1834   Fox How, in the Lake Country, built and occupied by the Arnolds as a holiday home and later as permanent home of the family.

1836   Matthew Arnold and his brother Tom enter Winchester College.

1837   Arnold enters Rugby School in September.

1841   Dr Thomas Arnold appointed Regius Professor of Modern History at Oxford, and Matthew Arnold enters Balliol College on an open scholarship.

1842   (June 12) Dr Thomas Arnold dies of a heart attack at Rugby.

1844   (Nov.) Matthew Arnold takes the degree of B.A., Oxford.

1845   (Feb.-Apr.) Substitutes as assistant master at Rugby. (Mar.) Elected fellow of Oriel College, Oxford.

1846   (Apr.) Appointed private secretary to the Marquis of Lansdowne, Lord President of the Council.

1849   (Feb. 26) Publishes *The Strayed Reveller, and Other Poems.*

1851   (Apr. 15) Appointed inspector of schools by Lord Lansdowne. (June 10) Marries Frances Lucy Wightman. (Sept.-Oct.) Honeymoon, France, Switzerland, Italy. (Oct.) Takes up duties as school inspector.

1852   (Oct.) Publishes *Empedocles on Etna, and Other Poems.*
Thomas Arnold born July 6 (d. Nov. 23, 1868).
Inspectorial Districts: "'The midland district in which these schools are situated is a new district, formed in 1851'—for British Wesleyan and other Non-Conformist Schools, included the English counties of Lincoln, Notts, Derby, Stafford, Salop, Hereford, Worcester, Warwick, Leicester, Rutland, Northamptonshire, Gloucester, and Monmouth together with all of North Wales except Flintshire and Derbyshire [*for* Denbighshire], and all of South Wales" (Connell, p. 229n).

1853   (Nov.) *Poems. A New Edition.*
Trevenen William ("Budge") Arnold born Oct. 15 (died Feb. 16, 1872).

Inspectorial Districts: "Gloucester, Hereford, Worcester, Monmouthshire, and South Wales withdrawn. Middlesex, Hertford, Bedford, Essex, Huntington, Cambridge, Suffolk, Norfolk added" (Connell).

1854   (Dec.) *Poems, Second Series.*
Inspectorial Districts: "4 counties in North Wales and 7 North Midland and Eastern counties withdrawn. Kent, Sussex, Bucks, Oxford, and Worcester added. Many of the schools of his district were in London" (Connell).

1855   Richard Penrose Arnold born Nov. 14 (d. 1908).
Inspectorial Districts: "The title of the district became 'Midland Metropolitan and S. Eastern Division of England' " (Connell).

1856   Inspectorial Districts: "Arnold referred to the extent to which his district had changed by speaking of South Staffordshire as 'the nucleus of my original district but which forms nearly the remotest portion of my present district, the centre of which is London' " (Connell).

1857   (May 5) Elected Professor of Poetry, Oxford.
Inspectorial Districts: "The district originally 'extended from Milford Haven to the Humber' now consists of Middlesex, Kent, Essex, Hertford, Buckingham, Oxford, and Berks" (Connell).

1858   Lucy Charlotte Arnold born Dec. 15 (d. 1934). Married Frederick W. Whitridge of New York in 1884. Their three children married and there are many, many Arnold descendants of several generations and names in the United States as well as in England.

1859   (Mar.-Aug.) In France, Holland, Belgium, Switzerland as assistant commissioner to Newcastle Commission.
(Aug.) *England and the Italian Question.*

1861   (Jan.) *On Translating Homer.*
(May) *The Popular Education of France.*
Eleanor Mary Caroline Arnold born Feb. 11, 1861. She married (1) Armine Wodehouse (3d son of the earl of Kimberley) in 1889 (d. 1901) and (2) William Mansfield, Baron (later, Viscount) Sandhurst, in 1909.

1864   (June) *A French Eton.*

1865   (Feb.) *Essays in Criticism.*
Basil Francis Arnold born Aug. 19, 1866 (d. 1868).
(Apr.-Nov.) In France, Italy, Germany, Austria, Switzerland as

> assistant commissioner to Taunton Commission (Schools
> Enquiry Commission).

1867 (June) *On the Study of Celtic Literature.*

(July) *New Poems.*

(Mar.) Left Chester Square, the Arnold home for ten years, and
moved to Harrow, their home for five years.

Inspectorial Districts: "District restricted to Middlesex, Herts,
Essex, Suffolk, and Norfolk" (Connell).

1869 (Jan.) *Culture and Anarchy.*

Inspectorial Districts: "Lost the counties of Suffolk and Norfolk,
and gained Bucks" (Connell).

1870 (May) *Saint Paul and Protestantism.*

1871 (Feb.) *Friendship's Garland.*

Inspectorial Districts: "Reduced to the Metropolitan district only
of Westminster with Hendon and Barnet and Edmonton
districts of Middlesex, also designated one of the eight new
Senior Inspectors with general responsibility for Essex,
Middlesex, and London districts north of the Thames"
(Connell).

1873 (Feb.) *Literature and Dogma.*

(June) Moves to Pains Hill Cottage, Cobham, Surrey, his
permanent home.

1875 (Nov.) *God and the Bible.*

Inspectorial Districts: "Lost the districts of Hendon and Barnet"
(Connell).

1877 (Mar.) *Last Essays on Church and Religion.*

1878 (June) *Selected Poems of Matthew Arnold.*

1879 (Jan.) *Mixed Essays.*

(Sept.) *Poems of Wordsworth.*

Inspectorial Districts: "Lost Edmonton" (Connell).

1881 (June) *Poetry of Byron.*

1882 (Mar.) *Irish Essays.*

1883 (Oct.) First American tour.

Inspectorial Districts: "Retained Westminster and was made
Senior Inspector for the whole Metropolitan District consisting of the District of the London School Board, Middlesex
(extra-metropolitan), and Essex" (Connell).

1884 Inspectorial Districts: "Title changed to Chief Inspector, lost part
of Essex. England and Wales in this year divided into 10
chief Inspectorates" (Connell).

1885 (June) *Discourses in America.*

1886   (May-Aug.) Second American visit.

(Nov.-Dec.) In Germany for Royal Commission on Education.

1887   (Feb.-Mar.) In France, Switzerland, Germany for Royal Commission on Education.

(Apr. 30) Retires as Inspector of Schools

1888   (Apr. 15) Matthew Arnold dies of a heart attack at Liverpool.

(Nov.) *Essays in Criticism (Second Series)*.

Views of Fox How

the bright stood indifferent; the king dismissed the Ministers. Still in different style: he sent for better Thiers — a home. His cry issued Tom before. Still Graph memorable the crowd. Continues of attacks a different Posto with slight flourishes. opened the Bois front the Count of Paris or opposite — was taken by his on their to the Chambers in the heights bribe in — the Vote — 2/3 straight — a report replied to the People. The royal family the fate, Orleans Etc. England, a Republic and You with me live thy 2:

Remus + the wolf, the two children fighting like mad, (a)
the limp-uddered she-wolf affectionately snarling at the
little. Demons struggling on her back. Above it a great
picture, the Jewish Exiles, which would do for Consuelo and
Albert resting in one of their wanderings worn out upon a
wild stony heath sloping to the Baltic — she leaning
over her two children who sleep in their torn rags at her
feet. Behind me a most musical clock, marking now
24 Minutes past 1, P.M. On my left two great windows
looking out on the court in front of the house, through one
of which slightly opened comes in by pushes the soft
damp breath with a tone of spring-life in it which the
close of an English February sometimes brings — so different from
a November mildness. The green lawn which occupies nearly
half the court is studded over with crocuses of all colours—
growing out of the grass, for there are no flower beds, delightful
for the large still-faced whiterobed babies whom their nurses

Letter to Tom Arnold, Lansdowne House, February 28, 1848

Letter to Jane Forster ("K"), Lansdowne House, Tuesday, March 28, 1848

My darling Flu — No letter from you, which is a grievous disappointment, but there is nothing of which I am surer than that it is not my darling's own fault. But all through yesterday I had been looking forward to hearing today — and I went out to breakfast this morning comforting myself with the thought that when I came back I should see your dear handwriting. I think it must be that you are still at Teddington — and that your letters posted there did not reach London in time for the mail train. I start tonight for Bordeaux and I am afraid it is too much to expect a letter from you there from me but I have told the people here to forward your letter to me there, as soon as it comes. — After I wrote to you on Sunday I wrote a long letter to my mother — I never thank you for sending me that most interesting letter of Fan's: then I

Letter to Frances Lucy Arnold (p. 1), Paris, Tuesday, May 10, 1859, 3:00 p.m., signed "Cangrande"

school agency: then at 11 to
breakfast with the Seniors – Miss Minnie makes
herself very pleasant: they had the P[rince]
who commanded the Sardinian Army
in the Novara Campaign and the talk was
all about battles: the P[rince] gives the Sardinian
Army a bad name but to look at him,
you would say their defeats must have been
more owing to the general than the men.
It appears certain that Francis Joseph, who is
the most obstinate young fool on earth, keeps
Hess at Vienna because he is jealous of him
& has quarrelled with him: and Giulay is a
mere general d'antichambre. If this is so, as
is most likely, the Austrians will be well
beaten and well they will deserve it. But
it is said here that the French do not
at present expect to do more than drive them
back upon Verona: Verona, Mantua, &c are
very hard to take. Duvergier d'Hauranne, who
was a deputy & minister under Louis Philippe,
was also at Senior's, & another old most
Ex-deputy, Languinais. After breakfast I went
to the bank for money, went in and talked
to the girls at the shop at the corner about
the children, and came back here to have my
great disappointment about the letter: then

*Letter to Frances Lucy Arnold (p. 4), Paris, Tuesday, May 10, 1859, 3:00 P.M., signed
"Cangrande"*

The Letters of
MATTHEW ARNOLD
VOLUME I
1829–1859

Thomas Arnold to Susan Delafield[1]

Rugby

My dearest Aunt   November 25, 1829

I do not know when I have written a Letter addressed to yourself, and as I am now in School with the Boys writing Exercises, and have thus a little Time on my Hands to spare, I think I cannot do better than write to you, although we sent a Letter to Laleham so recently.—You must not therefore be alarmed, or think that any Thing is the Matter, when my Epistle makes its' Appearance; for the Children's Coughs are still so slight that we cannot tell whether it is the hooping Cough or no, and both Mary and I continue very well.—I think it may interest you to hear my Report of all the Fry in Order.—K you have seen very lately, and therefore you will know her better than any of them:—her Love for Laleham is unabated:—it was only this Morning when Matt was drawing a Church after his Fashion with a high Steeple, and I told him that I thought Churches with Towers were prettier, that K cried out that she thought so too, because Laleham Church had a Tower.—She gets on with her Latin Grammar, and knows the New Testament remarkably well;—and she is at once the merriest and one of the most obedient & tender hearted of all the Fry;—this Morning when she saw the Snow she wanted immediately to go out and play in it, and she was delighted when I brought them in a great Snowball to eat and to throw into the Fire.—Crab is also getting on with his Grammar, and I think with all his Work.—He is less active than K or Prawn, but I do not think that one of them has a stronger Understanding, nor more self Command: and I have dearly loved to see the Struggles which he has had with himself, and how much he has got the better of the Faults that are most natural to him.—They have made Lists of all their Possessions, and these I call over sometimes, to see if all their Things are safe;—and when any Thing is missing I take some other Thing away as a Pledge, and do not give it back till the lost Article is found.—And on the other Hand, I promised to give each Child a Shilling, if all their Things proved safe. I called over on Sunday, & one of poor Matt's Things being missing, he had no Shilling and I took a Pledge: but when I called over Tom's Things, & something was missing there, Matt sprung down from his Dinner to look for it, & had the Pleasure of finding it for Tom to save his Shilling.—Afterwards his own lost Article was found, & I gave him his Shilling;—but after a moment he gave it back to me saying, "Papa, there was another of my Things missing, which has not been yet found, so I ought not to have the Shilling."—You will believe that I was not sorry when Miss

Rutland produced it almost immediately afterwards, and Crab could have his Shilling.—Prawn is as fond of the geographical Cards as I [use]d to be, and will stay for Hours trying to find out the Places.[2]—He seems now quite well and strong,—and so good a Boy both to Miss Rutland and to us that it is delightful to see him. He is very curious in whatever he reads to be able to understand every Thing thoroughly.—Small Wild Cat is still as [paper torn: 1 or 2 wds missing: ? much a cor]morant and as improved in Temper and Conduct a[paper torn: ? s when] I saw you in the Holydays.—Didu is fonder than [paper torn: ? ever of] his Mamma and me; but he too is become [paper torn: ? less calm] in the Nursery than he was, and with us [paper torn: ? more so]. He is very quick with his Letters and his [paper torn: ? learning] Things by Heart;—but I do not want any of [paper torn: ? them pushed] forward, and I have yet begged that the Hours of their Lessons may be diminished to two Hours and a half a Day—for I think that mine with you in former Times used not to exceed an Hour, and I am afraid of their little Brains being over exerted.—As to dear little Widu, he shows some Violence, but he has been whipt, and he does not seem to like the Operation, for he is quiet in an Instant whenever he sees me look angry at him.—He is very fond of me, and delights to be in my Hole, that is, my little dressing Room. And thus I have given you a long Letter all about Fry,—but you are so affectionate to Fry's Papa that I think you will like to hear about them. I wish you were given to write Letters,—but you never were fond of it, and it is now too late to begin.—With our dearest Love to Susy and the Bucklands,[3] believe me my dearest Aunt　　　Ever your most dutiful & affectionate Nephew,

T. Arnold.

MS. National Archives of Canada.

1. Thomas Arnold (1795–1842: *DNB*), the famous headmaster of Rugby School and father of Matthew Arnold, was the son of William Arnold (1745–1801) and Martha Delafield (1750-Apr. 1829) and the nephew of Susan Delafield (d. 1834), to whom this letter is addressed. The best sources of information about them all are Whitridge, Wymer, and Honan.

Thomas Arnold married Mary Penrose (1791–1873) on Aug. 11, 1820. They had eleven children, of whom nine survived; the six born before this letter, a sort of Bestiary, are named in it (the seventh was born exactly nine months later). The children, referred to collectively as the "Fry" (later "Dogs"), all had nicknames (see below p. 18 and Honan, pp. 427–28):

> Jane Martha (1821–99), "K"
> Matthew (1822–88), "Crab"
> Thomas (1823–1900), "Prawn"
> Mary (1825–88), "Small Wild Cat" (later "Bacco")
> Edward Penrose (1826–78), "Didu"
> William Delafield (1828–59), "Widu"

For the record, the three children not yet born were:
> Susanna Elizabeth Lydia (1830–1911), "Babbat Apbook"
> Frances Bunsen Trevenen Whately (1833–1923), "Bonze"
> Walter Thomas (1835–93), "Quid" or "Corus"

In Dec. 1827, Thomas Arnold had been "appointed Headmaster of Rugby at a salary of £113 6s 8d a year, plus £2 a head extra for every boy living within ten miles of the town, and a 'handsome house and spacious apartments for the reception of 50 pupils' " (Wymer, p. 86). He took up his duties as headmaster in Aug. 1828.

2. Miss Rutland, the governess, taught the children by the same method that Susan Delafield had taught their father—"how to identify the counties of England with the aid of geography cards" (Wymer, p. 16).

3. His sister Susanna Arnold, afflicted with paralysis since 1811, died in 1832 (Wymer, pp. 44–45, 133). Another sister, Frances Arnold (1790–1863), married the Rev. John Buckland (1785–1859) in 1816, and with him Thomas Arnold joined forces in establishing a school at Laleham, Middlesex, a village on the Thames near Staines.

Mary Penrose Arnold and Thomas Arnold
to Matthew Arnold

Rugby
My dearest Matt   Wednesday, August 24, [1831]

You will not I hope forget that you were to write to us on Friday, the day you will receive this. It is the day of your own choice, and after what we have said to you I shall be sorry and disappointed, if you do not manage to send us longer letters than you did. If you can tell us that you get on well you will make us very happy, but if not, still we had rather you wrote plainly and openly to us, for you are our own dear child, and we like to know all about you. You may think with pleasure that you pleased us while you were at home with us, and you may also be very sure that you please us now, every time you overcome idleness or try not to be selfish or tell the truth from your heart when you are tempted to do otherwise.

Rugby looks very different now from when you were at home, for our three hundred Boys are nearly all arrived, and the whole place is as busy as it can well be. Mr Price has 40 Boys, and I have just been over his house, and his bedrooms you may tell your Aunt Buckland look quite comfortable now, they are so improved by the beds being altered as she advised. There are now eighty Boys at Mr Price's and Mr Ansteys, so that I see a great many making all haste to school when I get up in a morning, for you know my bed room looks out on the school field.

We have a new Master come to help M: Pons in teaching French and German and Italian, but he cannot speak English himself, and he must learn it as fast as he can.[1]

I am afraid you will not think of dear little Susanna's birth-day tomorrow, when she reaches the great age of one year. Will you tell your Aunt Susanna with my love that I did not bring with me the little book she was kind enough to give me for Edward—Tom or you had been reading it, and I did not put it away, but she will perhaps send it by Elizabeth,[2] by whom I shall be so glad to hear of you all at Laleham—I have often thought of that nice kiss, I had of you in your comfortable little bed—and I should like another hug at this minute, but I must wait patiently till Christmas, when we shall see more of one another than we could in all that [torn]iling about, pleasant as it was. How many new places we have seen together dear Matt: and how good of your dearest Papa to go over so much of his old Tours again to give us pleasure. This has been a whole school day and I have hardly seen him all the day, but now I see the Boys going home, and I hope he will soon be here. He always likes to add a line to his own dear Matt if he can. With my love to all, believe me ever my dear child your   Most affectionate Mother & friend

Mary Arnold

Do you remember any of the three things I told you?

My dearest Crab,

I must write you a few Lines, though Dinner is very pressing, and I very hungry. I have had a nice Bathe to Day at my old Place, and Mamma & I walked in the Garden, where our one Water Melon is really I think getting ripe.—We had not nearly so pleasant a Journey down to Rugby as we had up to S. Albans: for besides that you, dear Crabby, were not with us, Mamma was inside, & Tom and I could only find Room on the outside behind, for all the Front was full of Foundationers going down to Rugby with their Mammas & Friends inside.—But then, Crabby, we had four Horses all the Way in to Rugby from Daventry:—was not that grand? I am   your own affectionate Father,

T. Arnold.

MS. Brotherton Collection.

1. Bonamy Price (1807–88: *DNB*) had been at Laleham for two months under Arnold (see his letter in Stanley, pp. 47–49) and in 1830, after Worcester College, moved to Rugby as mathematics and then classical master under Arnold and remained there till 1850. J. C. Shairp described the Prices as "a sort of king and queen of Rugby" (William Knight, *Principal Shairp and His Friends*, p. 101). He seems to have spent the next eighteen years justifying his last name by making money in business in London and from 1868 to 1883 served as Drummond Professor of Political Economy at Oxford. His lifelong relationship with the Arnolds amply vindicated his first name, and, with Stanley and the

servants, he seems to have been the only "outsider" present at the funeral and burial of Dr Arnold, at which Thomas Trevenen Penrose "administered the Communion" (Stanley, 1:312).

The Rev. Charles Alleyne Anstey (c.1797–1881), B. A. Trinity College, Oxford, 1820, an assistant master at Rugby 1819–64, was also chaplain (until Oct. 1831, when Arnold took over) and "the first official house master" (Wymer, pp. 106, 114; Rugby).

Louis Pons was French master from 1830 to 1837. He was housemaster at 33, Bilton Road, Price and Anstey at Barbey Road (Rugby).

2. Her sister-in-law, Elizabeth Cartwright Penrose (1780–1837: *DNB*), wife of the Rev. John Penrose (1778–1859: *DNB*), rector of Langton and vicar of Bracebridge; as "Mrs Markham" she was the author of two popular text-books for children, *Mrs Markham's History of England* (1823) and *Mrs Markham's History of France* (1828). See Baldwin, *passim.*

Thomas Arnold to Matthew Arnold

Rugby
My dearest Matt   September 20, 1831

I thank you very much for your long Letter which we received this Morning.—To be sure there was a long Gap between the Beginning and the End of it, but still it was a very nice Letter.—I am sorry, my own Crabby, that you are in Trouble about your Greek Grammar:—it puts me very much in Mind of my own Trouble when I was first put into Phaedrus.—You cannot think how many Impositions I got, and how many hard Knocks;—but still the End was that I learnt Phaedrus, and so will the End be, that you will learn your Greek Grammar.—You know, Crabby, that nothing is to be done without Trouble,—but I would have you cheer up your old Heart, and set your Neck to the Collar, and pull very hard, and then the Coach will at last get up the Hill.—I like your telling us all about your Condition, and your Malé [= unsatisfactory] and your Pessimè—it is an ugly Word, that same Pessimè;—and I hope you will not have it often,—but work away, Crabby, and do your best, and be my own true Boy, and I shall love you always very dearly, and you will soon find that Pessimè and you have nothing to say to one another.—My own Boy will think and remember that he must expect Trials in this Life,—and whether the Trial be a hard Bit of Greek Grammar to you at your present Age, or the Love of Money or of Power at an older Age, still God loves us when we fight against our Temptations manfully and beg of him to help us.—And you who wrote so nicely about Pilgrim Love will understand that we are all Pilgrims, and must expect to meet with Enemies on our Way, and must fight with them as with great & bloody Giants.[1]—Your dearest Mamma will write to you soon: but we wished a Letter to go to you immediately: and to pat you on the Back, and say to you,

"Never mind, Crabby," "To it again, Crabby:" and get through your Work well.—God bless you, my dearest Boy, we all join in kindest Love to you, and believe me to be ever your most loving Father,

T. Arnold.

MS. Frederick Whitridge.

1. The letter is addressed to "Mr Matt Arnold, Revd J. Buckland's, Laleham, *Staines.*" A year earlier Arnold had written his own version of Bunyan—"Pimgrim's Progress in 4 vol., 8th Edition, Vol 1st" by "Matthew Arnold, LATE Fellow of CHRIST-CHURCH COLLEGE, OXFORD" (quoted in Honan, pp. 18–19). See *Album*, pp. 53–66.

Thomas Arnold and Mary Penrose Arnold to Matthew Arnold

Rugby
My dear Crabby,   October 18, 1831

I am afraid indeed that you are become a Tory, as you call it, since you have got Malè twice in one week. You do not say what it was for, but I am very sorry for it, be it what it will, for it makes me sadly afraid that my Boy Matt is an idle Boy, and thinks that God sent him into the world to play & eat & drink instead of to work.—I do not like writing to my Crabby when I am obliged to find fault with him,—but I must write to him, and I like his Letters very much, when he tells us what he has been doing, and what the Boys are doing in School.—We have got a Holyday here on Thursday, for Lawrence Sheriff's Day:[1] and there is going to be a great Dinner at the Eagle in Honour of the Day, when we expect several Gentlemen in from the Neighbourhood—and I am to be in the Chair.—Leach is here on his Way to Oxford, and dined with us yesterday, and Entwisle dines with us to Day.[2]—Dear little K is so much better that it would do your Heart Good to see her;—and dear Bacco is better, I think, though she still looks rather dismal. As for little Nemi, she is the funniest and dearest little Thing you ever saw—she gets about very cleverly, and can all but walk alone,—Widda chooses now always to sit and wait for me to come up from locking up: he sits on the Table in the Hall, and watches me come up from the Hall.—We have got a very nice Book lately, called Landscape Illustrations of Sir W. Scott's Novels, that is, Pictures of all the Places mentioned in his Novels, and you cannot think how many of them you saw in the Summer in our nice Tour.[3]—I have not written to Mr Wordsworth yet about our House at Rydal for the winter, though we still mean to go there, if it please God;—but, my

Boy, so many Things happen in two Months which we cannot at all foresee, that I do not like making Schemes long beforehand, except as far as talking about them amongst ourselves is concerned.—God bless you, my dearest Crabby, and believe me to be always your very loving *Pappy*, as you used to call me,—

T. Arnold.

Give my kind Love to Uncle, Aunts, and Cousins.—

My own dear Matt, Will you remember to send a letter to us next Sunday if you are well able, but else on the Sunday after—and be an honest Boy, & tell us how you get on, and how you like Virgil. Though I do not write more now, I think of you & love you very dearly & mean to begin a letter to send, when I get yours. Give our love to your dear Aunts & tell Aunt Susanna how we rejoice in hearing of her Drives. When will my Boy get his work so well done that he can go with her.   Your most affectionate Mother

Mary Arnold

MS. Brotherton Collection.

1. "Rubgy was founded not by a bishop as was Winchester, but by a grocer of the yeoman class, one Lawrence Sheriffe . . . . Anxious that his name should be perpetuated locally in some practical fashion, Sheriffe decided to establish a 'Free Grammar School' to serve the children of Rugby and neighbouring villages: and in July 1567 he made a will providing for same" (Wymer, pp. 98–99).

2. Possibly Henry Leach (1794–1864), an old Rugbeian and then, in 1813, at Oriel College, Oxford, of which Thomas Arnold became a fellow in 1815 (*Landed*; Rugby). John Entwisle (1784–1837), of Foxholes, Lancs, and Kilworth House, Rugby, was from 1832 M.P. for Rochdale (*Landed*).

3. "Nice" (except for Matthew Arnold's "smart attack of nettle-rash" in Edinburgh—see Feb. 25, 1865) and also fateful, for it changed their lives. The tour (see Wymer, pp. 146–50), took them through the Lake Country, where they called first on Southey and then on the Wordsworths—a visit that led directly to a Christmas visit and then, with all deliberate speed, after more visits and the shrewd, knowledgeable advice of Wordsworth, to the purchase of twenty acres and the building of the house at Fox How.

The Arnolds at Rydal Water, December–January, 1832

K has a small and very nice room to herself, and Crab another to himself, while Prawn & Didu sleep together in another. . . . I only wish Buckland . . . would put himself into the Mail and come down to us. . . . Will you urge him to do this, and at the same time thank him very much for his *letter* about Matt—He seems to me greatly improved in everything.

(Extract, Thomas Arnold to Susan Arnold, Dec. 20, 1831: Brotherton Collection)

We are actually here and going up Nabb's Scar presently, if the morning holds clear: the said Nabb's Scar being the mountain at whose foot our house stands; but you must not suppose that we are at Rydal Hall; it is only a house by the road-side, just at the corner of the lane that leads up to Wordsworth's house, with the road on one side of the garden, and the Rotha on the other, which goes brawling away under our windows with its perpetual music. The higher mountains that bound our view are all snow-capped, but it is all snug and warm and green in the valley,—nowhere on earth have I ever seen a spot of more perfect and enjoyable beauty, with not a single object out of tune with it, look which way I will. In another cottage, about twenty yards from us, Capt. Hamilton, the author of Cyril Thornton, has taken up his abode for the winter; close above us are the Wordsworth's; and we are in our own house a party of fifteen souls, so that we are in no danger of being dull. And I think it would be hard to say which of us all enjoys our quarters the most. We arrived here on Monday, and hope to stay here about a month from the present time. (Extract, Thomas Arnold to Rev. G. Cornish, Dec. 23, 1831: Stanley p. 192)

Crab certainly does construe Virgil very well, and seems to understand it very well, when made to think about it. His grammar is Pain & Grief to him, as I suppose it always must be to every Boy, (Extract, Thomas Arnold to Frances Arnold Buckland, Jan. 3, 1832: Brotherton Collection)

We have been here for five Weeks, enjoying it most exceedingly, and on Monday we must turn our Faces southward.—But we are going in the first Instance to my old Home, Laleham, near Staines, and shall not be at Rugby till the 3rd of February. (Extract, Thomas Arnold to G. J. Fox, Jan. 19, 1832: National Archives of Canada)

I could still rave about Rydal—it was a period of five weeks of almost awful happiness, absolutely without a cloud; and we all enjoyed it I think equally— mother, father, and fry. Our intercourse with the Wordsworths was one of the brightest spots of all, nothing could exceed their friendliness—and my almost daily walks with him were things not to be forgotten. Once, and once only, we had a good fight about the Reform bill during a walk up Greenhead Ghyll to see "the unfinished sheepfold" recorded in "Michael." But I am sure that our political disagreement did not at all interfere with our enjoyment of each other's society; for I think that in the great principle of things we agreed very entirely—and only differed as to the τα καθ' εκαστα. We are thinking of buying or renting a place at Grasmere or Rydal, to spend our holidays at constantly; for not only are the Wordsworths and the scenery a very great attraction, but as I had the chapel at Rydal all the time of our last visit, I got acquainted with the poorer people besides, and you cannot tell what a home-like feeling all of us entertain towards the valley of the Rotha. (Extract, Thomas Arnold to J. T. Coleridge, Apr. 5, 1832: Stanley, pp. 195–96)

Mary Penrose Arnold to Matthew Arnold

Rugby
My dearest Matt   February 29, 1832
    I am afraid your Papa will again today be too much ocupied to write to you—but our letter must go that we may get another from you as soon as possible. Whenever I hear of your dining in on a Friday, I will directly [?]assure you the pleasure of a letter with news of all at home. You have therefore only to write & tell me you have given this proof of a [?]necessary diligence, & our letter shall be written & sent without loss of time.—If you heard from your Aunts of my tumble from the pony, you will like to have the particulars from me.—You must know then that on Thursday last, when the sun shone and all [?]seemed bright & pleasant I went out with your father Mr Lee & Mr Grenfell,[1] and I enjoyed my ride, & felt that every step the pony made was doing me good, when, behold, on our way back in the Barby Lane the pony struck his foot as I suppose against something, & instead of recovering himself directly as I think & feel sure he would have done if my large saddle had not been so far forward—he fell completely—& Mr Lee who was nearest drew me off as well as he could, but not till I had received a violent blow on my throat, which is still black & blue as if I had been in the wars. I cannot blame my pretty pony, which you know to be so sure-footed—and when the weather is fine I believe I must mount him again—for the sun & air do me so much good, & walking so much harm that I know not how to give up my rides.[2]
    I shall not perhaps be able to add more, for morning visitors are just arrived—but I must add that Miss Robertson is as kind as possible to the Children & they all like her. Miss Rutland does not go for some weeks to the Thursbys.[3]   Ever your most affectionate Mother
Mary Arnold

MS. Balliol College.

1. James Prince Lee (1804–69: *DNB*) and Algernon Grenfell (c. 1804–45) were assistant masters at Rugby brought in by Arnold. Lee resigned in 1838 to become headmaster of King Edward's School, Birmingham, ten years later was consecrated first bishop of Manchester. Matthew Arnold substituted for Grenfell in 1845. "Matt Arnold," Clough wrote, "is probably going to act as Master at Rugby in the place of Grenfell, who is ill, indeed I am afraid very ill indeed, a relapse after a water-cure which [is] rather a dangerous matter" (Mulhauser, 1 : 145; Foster).

2. She was pregnant with Frances Trevenen, who "was born May 13, 1832, and died in infancy" (Honan, p. 428).

3. Ellen Robertson was the new governess, replacing Miss Rutland. The Thursbys were probably the Rev. William Thursby (1795–1884) and his wife, the former Eleanor Mary Hargreaves (d. 1884), who had inherited Ormerod House, Burnley, Lancs. Their son, the Rev. William Ford Thursby (1830–93), entered Rugby School in 1845 (*Landed*; Rugby; Crockford).

Thomas Arnold to Matthew Arnold

My dearest Crabby   [March 1, 1832]

I am writing to you in School, while the sixth Form are busy with their Translations.—You are a very dear Crabby and I think of you much oftener than I am able to write to you, for I have had a great deal to do lately of one Kind or another, and you know my Coat Pocket has a great many Letters generally which require to be answered.—I have given K and Prawn a sort of Paper on which I shall mark down how they do their Latin Lessons to me daily,—giving them 20 if they do very well,—10, if they do tolerably, and 0 if they do very ill indeed.—And I wish your old fat Sides were to be seen in the Class with them. You remember the Accident that happened to little Howard Lake about two Years ago, when he shot himself with a Pistol at Play,—He is just now dead, after having been in great Pain for some Time past, but whether it had any Thing to do with his former Accident or not, we do not know.[1]—Mrs Walker also is dead, the Mother of some of our Foundation Boys.—She was out shopping in Rugby on Wednesday last, and she died yesterday Morning.[2] So you see, dearest, that "Death is near and sure," as your old Hymn says, oftener than we are apt to think of.—Thank God we are all very well ourselves, but ought we not to be very thankful that dearest Mamma was no worse for her sad Accident on the Pony, and do you not think that I must have been sadly frightened when I saw her fall on the Ground?—I heard from Mr Wordsworth two or three Days ago, and he begged to be remembered to each of our Fry.—so you must not lose his Remembrance because you are away from us.—He says that there is a Gentleman talking of taking our House at Rydal for a twelvemonth, so that I fear we shall be obliged to look out for another House in the Summer—but the

Summer is a long Way off, and all Things are very uncertain with all of us.— Good bye, my dearest Crabb, and you may be certain of one Thing, that I love you very dearly, and am always   Your own affectionate Father,

T. Arnold.

MS. *National Archives of Canada*

1. Probably, a son of Capt. Charles Lake (father of William Charles Lake, later dean of Durham: see below p. 52), who had settled in Rugby about 1825, "having determined to live there for the education of his sons," of whom two enrolled that year and a third in 1827—none listed as "Howard" (Katherine Lake, *Memorials of William Charles Lake*, pp. v, 5; Rugby).

2. Thomas Walker, of Newbold-Revel, a hamlet nearby, had four sons admitted to Rugby in Jan. 1830.

The Arnolds at Winandermere, Summer, 1832

The Parents

Much has happened since April, but nothing to me of so much interest as the death of my dear sister Susannah, after twenty-one years of suffering. We were called up hastily to Laleham in June, hardly expecting then to find her alive; but she rallied again, and we went down with all our family to the Lakes for the holidays, intending to return to Laleham for a short time before the end of the vacation. But the accounts became worse, and we went up to her, leaving the children at the Lakes, towards the end of July. We spent more than a fortnight at Laleham, and returned to Rugby on the 18th of August, expecting, or at least not despairing of seeing her again in the winter. On the 23rd we heard from Mrs. Buckland, to say that all was over; she had died on the night of the 21st, so suddenly that the Bucklands could not be called from the next house in time. . . .

You may have heard, perhaps, that great as is the loss of this dear sister, I was threatened with one still heavier in May last [1832]. My wife was seized with a most virulent sore throat, which brought on a premature confinement, and for some time my distress was greater than it has been since her dangerous illness in 1821. But she was mercifully recovered, not however without the loss of our little baby, a beautiful little girl, who just lived for seven days, and then drooped away and died of no other disorder than her premature birth. We had nothing but illness in our house during the whole spring; wife, children, servants, all were laid up one after the other, and for some time I never got up in the morning without hearing of some new case, either amongst my own family or amongst the boys. Then came the cholera at Newbold; and I thought that, beat as we were by such a succession of illnesses, we were in no condition to encounter this new trouble; and therefore, with the advice of our medical men, I hastily dispersed the school. We went down bodily to the Lakes, and took possession of Brathay Hall, a large house and large domain, just on the head of Winandermere. It was like Tinian to Anson's crew,[1] never was there such a renewal of strength and spirits as our children experienced from their six weeks' sojourn in this Paradise. And for their mamma and papa, the month that we spent there was not less delightful. Our intimacy with the Wordsworths was cemented, and scenery and society together made the time a period of enjoyment, which it seemed almost wholesome for us not to have longer continued, μη νοστοιο λα-θωμεθα. (Thomas Arnold to John Taylor Coleridge, Sept. 17, 1832: Stanley, p. 201)

The Children

I

My own dear Mamma.   Saturday, July 28, [1832]

How is poor Aunt Susanna Mary Fletcher[2] went to-day and she told me to tell you that she thought the view from the rock very fine. On my birthday Miss Robertson says we may have tea on the knoll and have a half-holiday. We found some wild Cherries to-day but Miss Robertson said we might not eat them because they were not ripe. Yesterday Mary and I got some rushes and made two little brooms. Last night Mary Fletcher took me with her to visit Mr Allan Harden and staid there till I was quite sleepy. Matt is just come up from the Lake. I am my dearest Mamma your very affectionate daughter

Jane Martha Arnold

II

My dear Papa and Mamma   Saturday, July 28

How is Aunt Susanna.

I have fished a good deal since you went away but I have only caught a full sized Perch and a few minnows. Miss Robertson has been so kind as To give Tom and me a line and she has bought a dozen hooks and gives us one when ever ours are broken. presently we three eldest are going to gather fruit in the garden as only gooseberries and cherries came up for dinner and we only had two cherries and no gooseberries. Miss Robertson says I have been very good we saw Mr Twining[3] just now he came into the boat when I was fishing I fish a good deal and catch a very little Thank Dear Papa for his letter.   Your affectionate Son

Matthew Arnold

III

My dear Mamma and Papa

I hope you are quite well, We are thinking of going to Rydal this evening, to get some reeds for Jane to make pens of. I have got a new fishing line
which dear Miss Robertson gave me. We are going to have a half holiday,
and tea on the knoll if we are good children on Jane's birthday. the lake [*paper
torn* has] gone down very much indeed: it looks very heavy as if we should
have rain. it is exceedingly hot and everything looks parched and drooping.
I am your affectionate son

Prawn Creatura so small.

IV

Brathay Hall

My dear papa and mamma

it is a very nice day for us to bathe Miss Wordsworth is here give my
love to fan and tom[4] Miss Wordsworth has invited us to come and and have
dinner at Rydal on Friday. it is Jane's birthday and we are going to have tea
out of doors to day. there was some rain last night it is Just dinner time Good
by my dear mamma and papa i am Your   affectionate child

Mary
arnold

V

My dear Papa and mamma

it is Jane's birt[h]day Miss Wordsworth told us that she would take some
of us in her carriage on friday.   I am your affectionate son

Edward P. Arnold

The Governess

Ellen Robertson to Mary Penrose Arnold

Brathay
My dear Mrs Arnold   August 1st, [1832]

As the children's letters will go To day I will add a few lines to let you
know that all is going on well. The dear little ones, Susy & Willy particularly,
are looking extremely clear & well. Mrs & Miss Dora Wordsworth rode over
this morning to see the children and desired their kindest love—they were
happy in hearing a better account of Miss Arnold than they expected. They
have asked us all to dinner on Friday and I have accepted the invitation, for I
thought you would have done the same. Miss Harden has been here to day
& asked after you particularly. The elder Twining has just been here and went

down to the lake to see the little ones. I cannot tell you the pleasure it gives me to send you a good account of dear little Matt who has been a *very* good boy since last I wrote. The others have been equally deserving of praise. As it is Jeanie's birthday and the weather is very fine we intend drinking tea out of doors provided it is quite dry. Your letters reached us this morning and it gave us great pleasure to find so much better an account of Miss Arnold than we had dared hope for. We have collected those books which Dr Arnold sent for & I hope he will find them right. I directed John[5] to send them off directly. I am afraid of being too late for the post and must therefore leave off as Eddy has his letter to complete.

With kind regards to Dr Arnold and all at Laleham I remain   very sincerely your's

Ellen Robertson

I will be very careful about the windows.

MS. Brotherton Collection.

The Neighbors

William and Mary Wordsworth
to Thomas and Mary Penrose Arnold[6]

Rydal Mount
My dear Sir   ⟨Wednesd⟩ Tuesday, 19th [*for* 18], Septbr [1832]

Yesterday Mr Greenwood of Grasmere called with a Letter he had just received from Mr Simpson the owner of Fox How empowering Mr G. to sign for him an agreement either with yourself or any Freind you may appoint for the sale of that Estate, for £800.—possession to be given and the money paid next Candlemas, up to which time the Rent to be paid to him. The title deeds he adds are all complete with the exception of his admittance at the Court, which can be done at the time the business is settled. I need not say that it will give me pleasure to facilitate the purchase as far as is in my power.

Most sincerely do we all condole with you on the loss of your excellent Sister—Knowing however at the same time that neither your own mind nor that of Mrs Arnold will be wanting both in general consolations and especial ones rising out of the long suffering of your lamented Relative.

My own Sister is still in a very languishing state. About a month ago she made a wonderful start towards recovery, but by change of weather most likely, she was soon thrown back, and is now full as weak as when you left her.—Mr Tatham who succeeded you as Minister in Rydal Chapel, has, you will be glad to hear, just been presented by Lord & Lady Grenville to a valuable Rectory in Cornwall.—Mr Hamilton has been some weeks in Scotland—Lady Farquhar & Mrs and Miss Hook are still with Mrs Luff—and the neighbourhood of Rydal has been overrun with the numerous family of Winyards. We have had Mr Pickersgill with us who has done all that was needful on the spot and in my presence, towards completing a Portrait of me, for St John's Coll. The Likeness is said to be admirable, and every one is pleased w[it]h [it]. It will be engraved, if as we presume the College has no objection. Since your departure I have carefully read your Letters printed in the Sheffield paper. With a great portion of their Contents I can clearly agree, but there are points seeming to me material, on which you are for pushing change farther than I am prepared to go—I hope it will not be disagreeable to you and Mrs Arnold if I fill the remainder of this Sheet with a Sonnet called forth by the Pickersgill Picture.—

> Go, faithful Portrait! and where long has knelt
> Margaret, the saintly Foundress, take thy Place;
> And if Time spare the Colors for the grace
> Which to the work surpassing skill hath dealt,
> Thou, on thy rock reclined, tho' Kingdoms melt
> Before the breath of Change, unchanged wilt seem,
> Green hills in sight, & listening to the Stream,
> To think—& feel as once the Poet felt.
> Whateer thy fate, those features have not grown
> Unrecognized thro' many a ⟨falling⟩ starting tear
> More prompt, more glad to fall, than drops of dew
> By Morning shed around a flower half-blown;
> Tears of delight that testified how true
> To Life thou art, &, in thy truth, how dear!

with Kind remembrances to you rs[*mutilated*: elf] & Mrs Arnol[d], and love to The Children, in which all unite   faithfully yours,

                                                    Wm Wordsworth

My dear Mrs A.

    I have broken the seal of this letter to say, at the request of Miss Harden, who is one among a crowd of spectators—looking at the wonderful Portrait, that she has recd your letter—& she also mentions a *borrowed* vessel for warming a Carriage which she finds in the house & does not know how to find the Owner? God bless you all—ever sincerely & affly yrs. M. W.

MS. Frederick Whitridge.

1. The landing at Tinian in the Mariana Islands in the South Pacific in Aug. 1742, described in Richard Walker, *Anson's Voyage round the World in the Years 1740–44*, bk. 3, chs. 2–3: "there was great plenty of very good water . . . there were an incredible number of cattle, hogs, and poultry running wild on the Island . . . ; the woods produced sweet and sour oranges, limes, lemons and coco-nuts . . . . the prospect of the country . . . had . . . the air of a magnificent plantation, where large lawns and stately woods had been laid out together with great skill, and where the whole had been so artfully combined, and so judiciously adapted to the slopes of the hills, and the inequalities of the ground, as to produce a most striking effect, and to do honour to the invention of the contriver . . . . this delightful Island . . . where alone all our wants could be most amply relieved, our sick recovered, and our enfeebled crew once more refreshed, and enabled to put to sea."

Walker was echoing the description of the palace of Alcinous in *Odyssey* 7.112–32, and Dr Arnold, rising to the occasion as Odysseus safeguarding his crew, adapts *Odyssey* 9.102, "lest anyone should eat of the lotus and forget his homeward way"—the germ of Tennyson's poem "The Lotos-Eaters."

2. Mary Fletcher (1802–80), daughter of Archibald and Eliza Fletcher (see below p. 142), who married Sir John Richardson (1787–1865: *DNB*), the Arctic explorer, as his third wife in 1847. Robert Allan Harden (1803–75) and (below) Jane Sophia Harden (1807–76), son and a daughter of John Harden (1772–1847), formerly of Brathay Hall. See Daphne Foskett, *John Harden of Brathay Hall 1772–1847* (Abbot Hall Art Gallery, Kendal, 1974).

3. Mr Twining: Among several possibilities, one is irresistible—William Aldred Twining (1813–48: *DNB*; son of Richard Twining 2d, 1772–1857, *DNB*, the tea-merchant), who entered Rugby in 1825, Balliol College in 1832, and who married Mary Arnold in 1847 (see below pp. 72, 95). Stephen H. Twining, *The House of Twining 1706–1856*, is exclusively (as the titlepage reads) "A Short History of the Firm of R. Twining and Co. Ltd Tea and Coffee Merchants 216 Strand W. C. 2."

4. "Fan" and "tom" are Frances and Thomas Buckland, and Miss Wordsworth is Dorothy ("Dora") Wordsworth (1804–47: *DNB*), daughter of the poet, who married Edward Quillinan in 1841.

5. John, being a servant, remains a monomym. He is mentioned several times below. Jeanie and Eddy are of course Jane Martha Arnold ("K") and Edward Penrose Arnold.

6. Far more interesting than Wordsworth's census of the Rydal community is the history of the text of this letter: "Half a dozen lines or so were printed in *Letters of the Wordsworth Family* (1907), edited by William Knight, sometimes referred to as Chaos and Old Knight, Professor of Moral Philosophy at St Andrews and founder of the Wordsworth Society (of which Arnold was president in 1883). He was the first and last Wordsworth editor to see the original manuscript [before its appearance in *Album*, pp. 5–7], and it seems likely that he saw it through Matthew Arnold's good offices. This is substantially the first printing of the letter [in book form]. All the persons mentioned in it are identified in one place or another in Alan G. Hill's . . . revision of Ernest de

Selincourt's *The Letters of William and Dorothy Wordsworth, The Late Years*. Hill prints Wordsworth's letter to Greenwood carrying on from this one and also supplies details from letters to Wordsworth from Thomas and Mary Arnold in the Wordsworth Library, Grasmere . . . .

"The portrait of Wordsworth was commissioned by St John's College, Cambridge; Wordsworth himself chose Henry William Pickersgill as the artist. The sonnet, 'To the Author's Portrait,' No. XXIV in Miscellaneous Sonnets (*Poetical Works*, ed. De Selincourt and Helen Darbishire, 3:50−51) was first published, somewhat revised and damaged in revision, in *Yarrow Revisited and Other Poems* (1835). The damage, indeed, may have been partly attributable to Dr Arnold [who said 'Once, and once only, we had a good fight about the Reform Bill'], for it is precisely in the reference to the Reform Bill (which became law in June, 1832), in lines 6−7, that the worst damage occurs" (*Album*, pp. 63−64).

For an interesting detail on Mrs Winyard see below pp. 63−64.

To Thomas Trevenen Penrose[1]

My dear Uncle Trevenen   Sunday, December 15, 1833

I can quite well remember when I used to construe Herodotus to you, but I never do it now to anyone. When first I went to Mr Hill's,[2] I used to construe only Homer and Xenophon, but I have lately been put into Aeschylus and am construing the Persae, where the Chorus and the Messenger from Xerxes are calling out οτοτοτοi together. We are going to Laleham together on Thursday.

We now do not play at Cricket, or Football, but we have hoops. And I spear with Mr Hill or play battledore and shuttlecock in the afternoon. I can drive my hoop quite round the school-field when we go there on whole school-days. I like drawing armed men as well as ever, but I wish very much to draw cavaliers, but I do not know how to draw their Spanish cap and feather, therefore as Mr Hill is going to Oxford with us he says he will get a trooper which he had at college and show it me. I have got a wooden sword. We shall go to tutor at half past seven tomorrow. I am   your affectionate nephew

Matt Arnold

MS. Formerly held by Mrs Harry Forsyth.

1. See below pp. 67−68.

2. Herbert Hill (1750−1828), an old Christ Church man and rector of Streatham, Surrey, 1810−28, was the brother of Robert Southey's mother. His second son, Herbert Hill (1810−92), a New College man who married Southey's daughter Bertha in 1839, had been "summoned to Rugby" (Honan, pp. 21-22) in order to "keep Matthew and Tom stuffed full of Latin and Greek." (Twenty-four years later Arnold stuffed *him*—see below pp. 371−72.)

Autobiographies of Jane Martha and Matthew Arnold

[? late 1835]

The History of Janes Life

I was born August 1st 1821 I am told but I cannot remember it, that when I was a baby I was very ill indeed, and that poor Mamma was so anxious about me that when I recovred she fell ill and was very near dying—We lived at Laleham a small village on the Thames, 16 miles from London. We had a very nice large garden and we had a digging place in it—And we had a dog called Spot, because he was white with black spots all over him, he was a very good dog and when we were tired of digging we used to make him scratch out the earth for us—Papa took pupils I forget how many but they were very kind to us. And they used to put Matt and Tom and me into a little carriage we had upon wheels, and harness Spot to it and make him drag us around the garden.

There were some Jackdaws up in a tree in the garden which we were very fond of looking at, but my pleasure was partly taken away, because there was a cow in a field close by which used to bellow, and make a great noise, and I was rather frightened at it—As far as I can remember I never liked playing with dolls, my greatest amusement was digging. I am not sure whether I was fond of drawing then but I am now.—Uncle Buckland lived almost close to us at least at the other end of the village and kept a school, and dear Aunt Susanna and Aunt Delafield who is however my great Aunt lived next door to them. I used to be very fond of playing with my Cousin B's. In the summer of 1828 Miss Rutland came to live with us, an arrangement which neither Matt Tom or myself liked at first, but she was so kind that we soon got reconciled to it—In the August of that same year Papa was made head master of Rugby school and we went to live at Rugby. I was very sorry to leave dear Laleham I loved it so much.—

Six of us were born then Jane (that is) myself, Matt, Tom, Mary, Edward and Willy who was a baby—.Papa gave us all new names when we were quite babies and we have kept them ever since. I was K. and now I am called K. much oftener than Jane. Matt is Crab—, Tom, Prawn, Mary Bacco: Edward Didu, Willy, Widu, Susy Apbook, Fan Bonze, and Walter Quid— When we had been some time here Matt Tom and I went with Papa and Mamma to Malvern and Worcester. And on the hollidays, the same party with the additions of Mary and Miss Rutland went into Scotland as far as Inverary. In December 1831 we first went to the Lakes, to Rydal. The summer after that to Braythay. Then to Fox-Ghyll. Then to Allan-Bank. Then the rest went again to Allan-Bank, but I stayed at Laleham.

Then Papa built a house called Fox how, and now we go there every hollidays.

Tradition says that I was born at Laleham in 1822 on the 24th of December. I think my memory must be very good, for I remember such quantities of things wch occurred there. I have not however any string of facts in my head, but only abstruse ones. One of the first things I remember is my asking one of Papa's pupils who were very kind to us, one morning a⟨f⟩t⟨er⟩ breakfast to get me a bough, and he greatly vexed me by making a bow. We used also to be in the parlour after breakfast, putting together our dissected maps. I also remember when one of the pupils gave a book of beasts to Papa, and the going out to see a particular pig killed, & seeing a great hole dug till they came to water, and being carried about the garden by Spot, and being obstinate, and going up to London about my crooked legs, & wearing irons[1], & seeing Aunt Lydia copy the house from the Lawn. Also cutting the thistles with Willy Buckland & Jane & Tom, in the garden.

MS. Brotherton Collection.

1. To straighten a leg curved (probably) by rickets (Honan, 11–12, 431–32).

To Martha Buckland

My dear Martha   [Rugby, May 15, 1836]

You cannot say that I have not fulfilled my promise in writing a letter in verse even as it is,[1] but I would have even finished the sheet, if I had had time. But judge for yourself. I was under the impression that yesterday was the 8th of May instead of the 14th & I did not know that if I sent my letter to morrow it wld not reach you. I really could hardly squeeze out the 5 first lines of my epistle which I wrote last night, for I was barking continually was as dull and heavy with a cough as possible, (perhaps you will say I must have been remarkably so, to manage to be more than ordinary) and had a tumbler of *Senna & Jalop* [for *Jalap*][2] in contemplation for this morning which consummation actually took place. I put it to you therefore whether the poet's pen could run, "auspice Musa,"[3] in such a state of, what shall I call it? of *Nervousness*. I have to [*omission*: ?say to] night that I am better. No bad disposition to go on but I could not write more verse than I did, for I have got the before-mentioned Scripture History,[4] an essay for Papa, (a new regulation for Sunday invented for the benefit of the 3 elder ones) and my chapter to look over again. Give my love to Charly, and tell him I congratulate him on being able to express himself so aptly by hieroglyphics, as well as drawing animal life so exactly [*paper torn*: in] a letter to Matty, which he showed me.

Also to Fanny and Tommy, and Uncle & Aunt. Also to Mr & Mrs Spraggs.[5] Every one sends their best love to the so poetically described

"Maid of the merry blue eye,"[6]

by you know whom, & as I have filled my sheet with nonsense, which was my special object, for your edification you know believe me my dear Martha   Your affectionate Cousin,

M. Arnold.

MS. Yale University.

1. Printed in Allott, p. 617 ("The verses are the earliest known to survive in A.'s hand").
2. Senna and Jalap, purgatives.
3. "Under direction of the Muse" (Horace, *Epistles* 1.3.13).
4. Mentioned in the closing lines of his poem: "Now though my Muse has not as yet broken down / Yet Mr. Hill will greet me with a frown / Unless I have my Scripture Hist'ry ready. / Yet still, in answering me I hope you will be steady."
5. Charly, Matty, Fanny, and Tommy are her sister and brothers. The Spraggs have not been identified.
6. "Presumably alluding to an earlier poem by A." (Allott p. 617).

To William Delafield and Susanna Arnold

East Cowes[1]

My dear Willy and Susy   July 10, 1836

As I see Edward has been writing to Mary, I thought that it was but fair for me to write to you, and as I supposed each of you would think it a shame if I did not write to you in particular, I took a middle course & am writing to both of you together. As you will not be able, I suppose, to read this you must ask Mary to read it to you. When we had left Rugby we saw in a field near Dunchurch, several crows sitting on the backs of the sheep, wch would have made Master laugh very much, especially if she had seen them walking down again off their backs, as we did. At Towcester we saw Mr Browne the Examiner,[2] who lives near Buckingham. About 6 miles from Towcester we came to a great big Park called Stowe wch belongs to the Duke of Buckingham. There were a great many very nice Deer here wch you would both have liked to see. This Park is a Part of a Forest called Whittlebury. There are not many Forests now left in England, but this is one of them. Near Amersham there is a very Pretty Place wch belongs to Mr Drake.[3] When we got to Laleham we had our Dinner, and after Dinner went down to the old Thames. The next morning we bathed in it, and Then went on to a place called Bagshot. We passed through Windsor Park, about wch I dare say Willy has got a poem in his book of Poetry, beginning with, "Thy forests [*sic*], Windsor, and thy green retreats," wch Mr Pope wrote when he was only 13 years old.[4] There is a waterfall too in this stage, wch is made by a stream coming down from Virginia Water where the King sometimes goes. Then we went to Farnham where there are more hops than anywhere else in England. Then to Winchester where there is a beautiful Cathedral. We saw Dr & Mrs Moberly[5] here where we are going to school. Dr Moberly's House is not near such a nice one as the School House at Rugby. Then we got some Buns and went on to Eagle Hurst, and bathed in the sea the Next morning. I see that Edward is going to tell Mary about all that we did after Eagle Hurst so I shall not say any more about it. I hope Willy has had Plenty of Cricket, and Master Plenty of bathing. Give my love to dear Aunt Ward & all my cousins, to Miss Robertson, Rowland & Mrs Osborn and the servants,[6] & believe me dear Willy & Susy   your affectionate brother.

M. Arnold.

MS. Brotherton Collection.

1. On a "holiday visit to the Isle of Wight" (Allott, p. 621, with Arnold's poem "Lines written on the Seashore at Eaglehurst July 12, 1836"). Eaglehurst, near Southampton, was the country seat of the 7th earl of Cavan (d. 1837), whose second wife was Lydia (m. 1814), Dr Arnold's sister (see below p. 80n). "Slatwood," East Cowes, was the birthplace of Dr Arnold, who wrote to a sister on July 18: "I certainly was agreeably surprised rather than disappointed by all the scenery. I admired the interior of the island, which people affect to sneer at, but which I think is very superior to most of the scenery of common countries. As for the Sandrock Hotel, it was most beautiful, and Bonchurch is the most beautiful thing I ever saw on the sea coast on this side of Genoa. Slatwoods was deeply interesting; I thought of what Fox How might be to my children forty years hence, and of the growth of the trees in that interval; but Fox How cannot be to them what Slatwoods is to me,—the only home of my childhood,—while with them Laleham and Rugby will divide their affections. I also had a great interest in going over the College at Winchester, but I certainly did not desire to change houses with Moberly; no, nor situation, although I envy him the downs and the clear streams, and the southern instead of the midland county, and the associations of Alfred's capital with the tombs of Kings and Prelates, as compared with Rugby and its thirteen horse and cattle fairs" (Stanley, pp. 281–82). For Matthew Arnold on Slatwoods and Rugby see below the letter to his mother Oct. 16, 1861.

2. Edward Harold Browne (1811–91: *DNB*), of Eton and Emmanuel College, Cambridge (M.A. 1836), later bishop of Ely and then of Winchester. "In the summer of 1836 he was selected to examine the upper forms at Rugby; and went thither to Dr. Arnold's house to carry out his engagement . . . . It was said that immediately upon his arrival at the school he was shown up into the Headmaster's Library, where his brother examiner, Mr. [Thomas Legh] Claughton [1808–92: *DNB*, later bishop of Rochester and then of St Albans], was already established. He and Claughton had never met; and the latter looking up from his book, beheld a tall stripling somewhat bashfully entering the

room; he at once jumped to the conclusion that this was a sixth form boy, quietly ordered him to sit at the table, and handed him an examination paper. In vain did Harold Browne protest, the inexorable Oxonian would not be induced to loosen his grasp until Dr. Arnold had been sent for to vouch for the truth of his declaration that he was not a victim but a brother examiner" (G. W. Kitchin, *Edward Harold Browne . . . A Memoir*, pp. 38–39).

　　3. Thomas Tyrwhitt-Drake (1783–1852), of Shardeloes, Amersham, Bucks, M.P. 1805–32, and sheriff 1836 (Boase; *Landed*).

　　4. Alexander Pope's "Windsor Forest."

　　5. George Moberly (1803–85: *DNB*), headmaster of Winchester College (where Dr Arnold had enrolled in 1807 and which Matthew and Tom would enter in September), 1835–66, bishop of Salisbury, 1869. See Stanley, pp. 79, 126–27.

　　6. "Aunt Ward" was Dr Arnold's sister Martha ("Patty"), married in 1803 to John Ward, who succeeded her father, William Arnold (1745–1801), as customs officer at East Cowes, I.W. After John Ward's death she moved, about 1835 or 1836, to or near Rugby (Wymer, p. 178).

　　Mary Rowland (nurse, companion, friend), the very type of the faithful retainer, whose name occurs often in these letters, was with the Arnolds about half a century; she is last mentioned on Nov. 6, 1882. (Her first name is revealed—only?—in Reid, 2:302.) Mrs Osborn remains unidentified.

Mary Penrose Arnold and Thomas Arnold
to Thomas Arnold [son]

Fox How
Sunday, April 9, [1837]

We have recd our dear Matts letter today & are very thankful for the better account. . . . [Dr Arnold resumes here] Tell us whether dearest Matt is likely to have the full use of his fingers again—It is so cold! Snow by day & frosts by night coming upon us [in margin], now that Easter is over.—If this Weather lasts, it is likely to be a long Time before we shall have any Bathing.—I shall be very anxious to hear your Report of dear Crab.—Ever, my own Boy,　your most loving Father,

T. Arnold

MS. Brotherton Collection (extract).

To Edward Penrose Arnold

August 11–21, 1837 [1]

Journal &c

August 11th Dover. We left the school:House at Rugby at about 8 o'clock on Wednesday morning, August 9th: we set off for Daintry in

Northamptonshire our first stage with Horses and Postboy decorated with dark blue rosettes, the Whig:Radical colours at the election for North Warwickshire, wch was going on at the time, and caused a great ferment at the various inns in that Part of the County. The course of the stages, Daventry, Towcester, Stony Stratford, Brickhill, Dunstable, St Albans, Barnet & London afforded no new variety of any kind, except perhaps leaving the great road through Islington & the city, and turning off by the road to the West End, and thereby to Tavistock Square, where we dined at Mr Hulls,[2] and met the Bucklands, whose eldest son accompanies us on our route. We slept at Campbell's Family Hotel, the Bedford Arms in Southampton Row. The Beds looked comfortable, but Experience taught J Buckland and myself that seeing was not feeling. Suffice it, however without entering into particulars, to say that there were venomous little animals within them. On this day we had a comfortable breakfast previous to starting, and a dinner in Tavistock Square, & fruit & biscuits at intervals during the day atoned very fairly for Luncheon; as for tea I do not reckon it after a late dinner seeing that it is a mere amusement. If we fare as well every day, it will be well. However I must not anticipate. The next morning we rose at a comfortable Hour & having dressed went to Tavistock Square to breakfast. After breakfast leaving K and Mamma at home, and sending Tom to the Adelaide Gallery, I went with Papa and Mr Hull to the Temple and called on Prior: He was not at Home when I called and after waiting for him about 3 Quarters of an hour during which time I made notes from the Expresses of the Times which I found there of the latest Elections. Meanwhile Papa had been to Baldwin & Cradocks Paternoster Row about the first volumes of his R[oman] H[istory] and called for me in his way back. We then called a coach and drove to the French Passport office Poland Street, Oxford Street, where we discovered that getting the Passport would detain us an hour. Upon this we left Papa and Buckland at the office, and Mr Hull & myself walked homewards, and I got an Eye-Glass at Harris's the Optician's in Gt Russell Street. On returning to Tavistock Square we had an early dinner and after that went to the Bedford Arms Hotel to pack the Luggage. However when on arriving here we found Papa and Buckland, they did not know where the carriage had been [put] up: at last we got it from Woburn Mews and started for Dartford, a 17 mile stage. By the way we called at Mr Ware's the Oculist No 23 Bridge Street Blackfriars about my Eyes, and he told me not to wear a glass, and said plenty more which I need not repeat. After this we went on through Camberwell over Blackheath & Shooter's Hill, through Deptford & Bexley to Dartford a very beautiful Stage to Dartford: after changing here we went on to Rochester 15 miles: the views of the Thames with its vessels, sail, and steamer, of Tilbury Fort and Gravesend, through Part of which we passed were most beautiful, for I had never seen anything in that line before. Rochester Stroud and Chatham with the Medway which separates the two former towns & the Castle and Cathedral, we opened upon splendidly from the top of a hill a mile above the Town. Both this stage & the former were very long and hilly. The next stage 10 miles to Sittingbourne I was alone outside, and every Place I came to I longed to see the inn: Chatham Hill is one of the largest I ever saw on a turnpike road except perhaps the one out of Otley in Yorkshire: in fact all the stage was hilly: we slept at the George at Sittingbourne, and had tea, wch I needed at 8 o'clock, for I had eat nothing save gooseberries since 1 o'clock. The Inns at which we stopt, were the Bull, at Dartford, the Crown at Rochester, the George at Sittingbourne. At 10 o'clock I went to Bed. August 11th Friday Morning: Got up at 4 in the Morning!!! Horresco referens![3] I drank some milk & water which was the only thing procurable and got up behind the carriage with Jane half asleep. It was a 16 mile stage and the sun not rising for an hour & the dew being copious, I was frizzled in a style no Tonseur [*for* tonsor] could have surpassed. I believe I might have been more alive to the beauties, but not only my sleeping Propensities but a fine fog also hindered anybody's seeing anything. However just before we got to Canterbury the fog cleared up, and we had a beautiful view of Canterbury. When we got here we were to have breakfasted there [? then], but no one knowing about the Packets, we came on here 16 miles, passing Bishopsbourne, Hooker's Place, where we breakfasted, & I have written journal since. ——

Boulogne, Salon, Hotel des Bains
Saturday August 12th

After breakfast yesterday we saw Mr Eyre riding round our Hotel,[4] looking for us, and after some conversation we walked down to his house No 10 Marine Parade, and found Mrs Eyre: we sat there about an hour & lunched: there had been thoughts of bathing but there was not time, and on this being discovered, Mrs Eyre walked down towards the Hotel with us and we stopped at a Chymist's, and got some Diachylon Plaister for my foot. After that having returned to the Hotel, we waited there arranging luggage &c during wch waiting I saw Lord Holland and his carriage,[5] till the Packet was ready to sail: we then walked down to the Pier & got aboard the Water-Witch, a tolerably large Packet, and as comfortable as a steam Packet can be. The Packet went on almost directly after we got on board: the Harbour was as smooth as a Mill Pond, but as soon as we got out we began the delightful (to those that like it) motion of ascent and descent which sent admonitory twinges through & through me

"A vague Presentiment of Ill, a feeling worse than fear"[6]

What all this terminated in, all the minutiae of sea sickness, it is by no means necessary to state: at last I lay on deck in a cloak and went to sleep: I woke just at Boulogne and Napoleon's Pillar & the bare coast & Boulogne harbour with the Quantities of white bathing machines & People thronging the Piers was worth waking to see—on landing the variety of dresses & the appearance of every thing was almost confusing: we went to the Hotel des Bains & Papa returned to the Customhouse with the Commissioner: after this we dined moderately and went to bed: The bedroom furniture was like that of a very elegant private House in England would be. The Hotel was I think the largest I ever saw and the Salon where we dined was beautiful. Next morning we breakfasted in the Salon and came on with four horses: the Postillions in blue short tailed jackets with a broad red border covered with metal buttons, and with a large metal Plate resembling an oblong medal on the right arm: add to this the Jack:Boots immense Spurs & long thick thonged Whips, and you have the outside of a French Postillion. Samer, two Postes from Boulogne was our first stage: and being the first stage from the coast was very interesting: the roads were broad & firm bottomed: but not at all particular about hills: they seemed to have no idea of going round or cutting through, but to go on a straight forward Principle of up one side & down the other. The Poste aux Chevaux at Samer is a miserable Place: The Hotel La téte de Boeuf is a very good one apparently: Samer is not on a river: the next stage is Cormont only one Poste: here the country is chalk & hilly as a natural consequence of it's being chalk: we walked up one & the view being extensive & on a very large scale was very interesting: from hence to Montreuil was a Poste and a half: the country was well wooded, and in one Place the road running through some wood with no Hedges or Fences on either side was very picturesque and foreign in it's appearance. There are not Hedges along the road side as in England but in many Places Avenues of trees: which though rather stunted give the Country a Parklike look which is very picturesque: where there are hedges they have a curious way of knitting them together by passing flexible boughs along through them, & along them, wch keeps them upright & firm together. Montreuil is a fortified town with a drawbridge: we were stopped here for a minute while our Passport was visèd: I saw a Lamp Post such as men were in the habit of getting hanged upon in the French Revolution. Altogether I was much interested it being the first fortified place we saw. Montreuil is on the Canche, and has a moat, and a deep trench round it. Changing here we went on to Nampon a village on the Authie: we passed through a very pretty village of the name of Wailly where I saw some hemp growing & a little beyond Bernay afterwards some flax: there are two Nampons each with a church: the river divides them & the Poste aux Chevaux is at the second: this stage was a Poste and three quarters: at the inn we got down from the carriage, and while the Horses were changing walked onwards up the hill getting flowers: we remounted the carriage at the top and drove on up and down through the village of Vèron to Bernay where we dined at the Hotel de la Poste: we drank the vin ordinaire de Bourgogne which is drunk as the beer is in England in ⟨glasses⟩ tumblers, and I think very refreshing: There was here some conversation with the Marèchal about the Linch Pins one of which had been out for the two last stages, so that in fact we had stopped at Wailly at a Marèchal's, but as he was not a[t] home we went on: This stage was only one Poste: From hence we went on a stage of only one Poste along the large forest of Cressy, to Nuvions, and St Valery with it's shipping was seen though not by me far out on our right: Nuvions to Abbeville was one Poste and a half: rather on the Abbeville side we saw a large manufactory & close beyond it we met a young Priest in a long black Robe very like an English Lady's riding habit: The view of Abbeville from a hill above was very fine, the cathedral church partakes considerably of the character of the other French cathedrals I have seen draw-ings of such as the Notre Dame in Paris. After getting to the Hotel here and ordering tea and coffee in a salon inspecting bedrooms &c we walked out in the town which is completely French both in the Appearance & height of the Houses. It is a fortified town, and the Fortifications seem very like those of Montreuil sur Mer; (so called because there is no sea near it) This town is on the Somme: we went on to the Cathedral Church which we went into, and it's being dusk and many People kneeling at their devotions up the aisle, and the solemn stillness of every thing around, together with the indistinctly seen altar at the upper end had a very imposing effect: we returned and had tea and since then I have been writing this at the Hotel de l'Europe in the large manufacturing town of Abbeville. I must go to bed: but first I must mention how much I was struck in going over the little churchyard at Bernay at the inscriptions on the Wooden Crucifixes which are the Monuments here: The Form is thus

"Ici repose"—then follows the name & age &c, and it thus concludes
"Priez Dieu pour le repose de son Ame," or "Requiescat in Pace, Amen."

The Simplicity of this is very beautiful.

Between Montreuil and Nampont we drove with one Postboy who sat on the wheelers & drove the Leaders before him with a long whip. It is so late now that I must go to bed hoping to sleep sound, & not to be hot.——

Evroux Monday Night August 14th. Here we are at Evroux in conse-quence of a change of Plans: not going direct from Rouen to Paris as we had originally intended, but coming through Evreux Chartres, & to Orleans & the Loire, in order to see the country of vineyards; and thus to have only one instead of two days at Paris. At Abbeville we breakfasted on Sunday morning,

& afterwards read the service. We then left Abbeville along the banks of the Somme for a short way then turning up through some very hilly country through the following route to Rouen

Postes	
Abbeville to Huppy	1 & ½
Huppy to Blang⟨y⟩ is	1 & ½
Blangy to Foucarmont	1 & ¼
Foucarmont to Neufchatel	2
Neuchatel to La Boissiere	1 & ½
La Boissiere to Vehr Galant	1 & ½
Vehr Galant to Rouen	2

The first stage was hilly, & in walking up one hill I gathered some Hemp. In this part of France there are rows of Fruit trees, Apples & Pears growing along the borders of the Huge fields of corn which line the roads in every direction. These trees have continued till now and the Pears being many of them ripe, they present a very tempting appearance. Tuesday morning, Hotel de la [*for* du Grand] Cerf, Evreux. My journal is in arrears & I must fill up the space between Abbeville & Evreux very briefly. Huppy the first stage was a single house on the left side of the road.—Rambouillet Tuesday night Hotel du Lion D'Or, August 15th. Journals do not flourish: anything but in fact: arrears, or at best brief snatches of time after and before meals—

"Like angel visits few & far between,"[7]

seem to be the order of the Day. Never the less I must give a skeleton of the Events wch have intervened between the Present & the Past: i.e. the last time I wrote my journal properly, at Abbeville. To proceed—At Huppy I walked on while they changed Chevaux I walked on with Mamma & got some huge bearded corn & some detestably unripe apples. We then reascended the carriage and after some amusing incidents relative to the inclination of the Horses' Heads homewards, as the Pauvre Garçon did not understand driving, and walking down a very steep and long hill we reached Blangis. The Church is very insignificant both in architecture and ornaments, but we went into it and looked over it, and as it was nearly dark when we were in Abbeville Cathedral, it is to the gewgaw ornament & worthless Pictures of the Church of Blangis that I owe my first ideas of the inside of the Roman Catholic Churches in France. Blangis lies in a valley between two very steep Ridges of Hills & in walking up one on the Foucarmont side I got some Hellebore. We made at Foucarmont a kind of a shambling scrambling Lunch of cold boiled Eggs and Vin ordinaire de Bourgogne: between this and Rouen I do not know that there was anything remarkable, except that we

travelled without a Linch Pin, wch has now occurred so often as to be quite
an every day affair. We had a splendid glimpse of the Seine lighted up with
the moon from the hill above Rouen, & the whole city seen very dimly &
indistinctly through the waning light was very fine. We first drove to the
Hotel de Rouen on the Quay: but that being full, we went on up the great
street of the town to the Hotel de France an old inn. Directly after we got
there J. Buckland & myself went to the Public Promenade which runs along
the Quay: It being Sunday Evening the French Holiday it was thronged with
People sitting or sauntering. On returning we found tea coffee & Eggs &
went to bed [?]there My bed very large & tolerably soft. Next morning after
breakfasting at 8 we hired a Landau to see the town in. First we went to the
Church of St Ouen: the nave of which is in the beauty of it's architecture
one of the first in Europe: though for myself I prefer that of Winchester
Cathedral. We saw the Mass & the Priests, & after walking all over the church
we returned to the Landau, and drove to the Cathedral. This is very inferior
in many respects to St Ouen & was injured by a fire in 1822. After going over
it we went up the tower from the top of which we had a very good view of
the town all around us: on descending we found Mamma in the carriage and
went to the Palais de Justice which is a curious old Place but not very remarkable. We saw one of the Courts, wch did not seem very orderly. Thence
through the Place de la Pucelle the statue of the Maid of Orleans to the Bank
where Papa had business, and we learnt about the Passport. Then returning
to the Hotel de France we had a little shopping, dined and started for Porte
St Ouen a Poste & a half from Rouen. I must break off here & go to
bed———.

Hotel de Bristol: Place Vendaume, Paris, Wednesday August 16th—
    We are at Paris—a capital in size only inferior to London, and that but
slightly: in fashion elegance public buildings &c inferior to none—superior
almost to any in Europe. But instead of Rhapsodizing I must finish up my
arrears of Journal as quickly as possible. A little way beyond Porte St Ouen
the Road ascends a very considerable eminence, and in walking up the view
of Rouen in the distance, & the gigantic Seine with it's Poplar Islands winding beneath us, the high and broken chalk cliffs along the road, & the
glimpses of the river in front through the woodlands was quite superb. From
hence to Louviers the road ran through the forest of Pont de Larchy: but hill
& dust & heat combined to make the stage anything but agreeable. At a small
town about half way we took our Leave of the Seine, wch we crossed, but
here we have him again. At Louviers a town of 8000 inhabitants we were
detained 3/4 of an hour before the Postillions arrived. The church here
though nothing remarkable has some fine old arches about it: Hence to Ev-

roux 2 Postes & 3 quarters the longest we have had yet, we drove along the Eure amongst some fine trees for the first part of the way, and then from a fine hill we had a good view of Evroux, a Cathedral Town of about 9000 Inhabitants. It is on the Isson [*for* Iton]. We went over the Cathedral which is nothing particular i.e. after St Ouen & Rouen Cathedral: but a Part of the building which is called the Lantern is very beautiful here: the bishop's Palace joins the Cathedral. We had tea at the Hotel du grand Cerf & two of our Party had warm baths, wch Luxury I shall enjoy to night. Next morning we breakfasted and departed, towards Chartres. The first stage was Thomer a Poste & a half from Evroux: in coming up the hill out of Evroux, we saw the College, which was old & venerable in appearance, but had no pretensions to beauty of architecture. Hence to Nonancourt where Henry King of Navarre slept the night before the battle of Ivry: the field of Ivry is very near this place: Between this & Dreux, we passed a beautiful village down in the Hollow on the left, & Mr Waddington's Chateau.[8] From La Payarge to Chartres 2 Postes we had a little rain: & sprung a covey of Partridges from some corn, which were very strong on the wing, it being now near the first of September. From a high hill about 4 miles from Chartres we had a beautiful view of the Cathedral: we saw several vineyards: one hill in particular was covered with them: wch was very beautiful: we had to go a terrible distance on the Pavè before reaching Chartres wch jolted the Carriage considerably: we passed the public Promenade & arrived at the Hotel du Grand Monarque: wch is also the Poste aux Chevaux. It was the Festival of the Assumption & while Dinner was preparing we walked to see the Cathedral: the Entrances to which have most beautiful carved stone work. But beautiful as this was the carving along the Quire inside, & the Statuary over the altar seemed to me more beautiful still: the Cathedral was filled with People: who at first looked very attentive, each with their books in their Hands: but on a close inspection, I do not think they seemed at all more so than an English Congregation. We then returned from the Cathedral & dined & then set off for Maintenon. The road was very good hard bottomed, & well directed: and whereas from Evroux to Chartres the country had been the dullest we had yet seen to my taste, this stage was diversified with hill and wood: it seems to me to show the taste of the French, that in a long aqueduct for a canal to Maintenon the banks wch were steep and high, seemed more like a low well wooded Range of even hills than a bricked aqueduct for a canal, of all unromantic things to look like a wooded range of hills. At Maintenon we changed & went on to Epernon a stage of one Poste wch we did after being under half an hour about it. Hence to Rambouillet the Lion D'Or Hotel was a Poste & demi, roads shocking bad: but a beautiful drive through the Park of the Chateau of Rambouillet where King Charles the 10th of France retired after his expul-

sion. Here we drank tea & coffee & slept in a room where there was just
about room enough for 2 beds. We did not breakfast here but went on 1
Poste & 3 Quarters to the village of [?]Coignieres through a very wooded &
Parklike appearance: Hence two Postes to Versailles where we had a dejeuner
à la fourchette at the Hotel d'Europe after which we walked under a broiling
sun to see the Gardens and Orangery which were filled with large Ponds
adorned with marble vases & statuary. The building in extent is absolutely
enormous, but has no pretensions to handsome architecture & is of modern
appearance having been entirely built by Louis Quatorze of whom in the
entrance Court there is a handsome Equestrian Statue: also there are fine
statues of Turenne & other great Frenchmen on foot: as also in the town
there is one of Hoche. I had a racking headache owing to the dreadful Power
of the sun on one's head just after dinner & on leaving Versailles which we
did on our return from the Palace the jolting of the carriage on the Pavè
increased it yet more. On reaching the Palace at St Cloud we got out of the
Carriage and enquired of the Soldier on Guard if we could see the House or
terrace but Louis Philippe being there we could not: However from the
height on which we stood & where the House is built we had a beautiful
view of Paris & all the buildings with a beautifully clear ⟨defined⟩ outline
defined on the sky, owing to the absence of smoke: the church of St Gene-
viève, the Hopital des Invalids, the Church of Notre Dame &c were clearly
seen, with the Seine winding close below us. We then returned to Sèvre, a
place famous for it's china manufactory, which was 1 Poste from Versailles,
where we changed. We then proceeded crossing the Seine 1 Poste & a Quarter to Paris: I must confess that I went soundly to sleep till we were stopt at
the Barrière close to Paris to have the Passport vise'd by the Police, and so
missed seeing the Champ de Mars & the Champ d'Elyseè: but in driving
along the Seine I had a beautiful view of the Chamber of Deputies & in fact
of most of Paris. We entered by the Rue Rivoli, and through the Place de la
Concorde where Louis Sieze was guillotined, and where Cleopatra's Needle
wch was brought from Ægypt, is erected: thence to the Place Vendome
where Napoleon's Pillar was put up and where is our Hotel, the Hotel de
Bristol: where as the Newspapers would say, "we have a splendid suite of
Apartments." I write this late on Thursday Evening: and we got here
Wednesday Afternoon. When we arrived I went to my bedroom & lay down
to get rid of my headache wch was very bad. Then I came down & wrote
journal & read Galignani's Messenger while the rest all went to the Gardens
of the Tuilleries. On their return we drank tea: and I having had a warm bath
retired early: i.e. about ½ past nine. This morning I rose quite well, and after
breakfast, the day being so hot that though shutters were closed windows and
doors open & and Room darkened, we were nearly broiled alive. After

breakfast we sat reading the Papers writing &c till nearly eleven, when I went with Mamma to a great draper's warehouse, & assisted her with my exquisite taste in forming a selection of Pelerines Lace Cambric Silks &c: a tasteful assortment of which it would have been impossible to have procured without my assistance. On returning we went in a carriage to the Louvre & saw the immense Picture Gallery with Paintings by Rembrandt Reubens, Poussin, Claude, Teniers Vandyke & others: thence to the Statues which I did not like so well though I much admired the Ægyptian Porphyry Vases. I must go to bed now for I am hot tired sleepy, and what not? Thursday Night Hotel de Bristol August 17th Paris 1837.

Hotel d'Europe Abbeville Sunday Morning August 20th 1837.—
Though I have to make up still some arrears, yet I shall be enabled to finish it off briefly, there not having been anything worth seeing or mentioning since Paris, save the Cathedrals of Beauvais and Amiens. However to resume where I left off I must mention that of the statues at the Louvre two colossal ones of Melpomene & Jupiter pleased me most, and a figure of the Sphinx; After this we drove to the Jardin de Roi, the Zoological Gardens of Paris, from whence in fact the Gardens of that name in London were copied.

Hotel des Bains, Boulogne sur Mer, Monday, August 21st 1837.
Here we are where we began, but in the meanwhile have seen more than a single week has ever before exhibited to us. And now—what a pleasant Prospect! At 12 o'clock Lurching Vessel; Lee side of the Boat: breakfast rendered useless: a subsequent dinner necessary. But I must finish up to Boulogne where we now are, nor shall I attempt to describe our English Part of the Journey that yet remains, nor our Passage, and the concomitant Sickness about to be. After the Jardin de Roi where I saw a Giraffe, wch was the only beast there I had not seen before alive, Papa went to the bank, and then we drove home and dined: after wch we had some shopping & came home to Tea about 9 o'clock: when Papa and Jane & myself it being very hot, drank Tea enough to be drowned in. Next morning I walked to the Palais Royale with Jane & J. Buckland, and there also we shopped: The shops, Jewellers in Particular, were beautiful. We then lunched, and went off for St Denis 1 Poste. After this, about half way between it & Beaumont sur Oise we had a beautiful view of Paris in the distance behind us: we arrived at Beauvais about 7 or 8 o'clock and dined at the Hotel de France. Next morning we went over the cathedral, the Quire of which is the most beautiful in France, & set off about ten A. M. We went out of our road to see Amiens and it's Cathedral, the nave of which is said to be as beautiful as the Quire of Beauvais, but here again as in the case of St Ouen I prefer that of Winton [*sic*]. We dined here

& arrived again at Abbeville about 10 at night, where we had slept that same evening week, on our first setting out in France: with feelings how different did we revisit it! Then everything seemed to surprise, as new and interesting: now the novelty of the thing being worn off, though still every thing interested and amused, there was not that interest in every little thing that there had been. At the Hotel d'Europe we drank tea, slept and breakfasted, and then came on here by the same road that I have mentioned at the beginning of my journal. Here it must end, & no 10 days' tour ever gave more gratification. To you my dear Didu I take the Liberty of inscribing it, trusting that if ever you make the same tour, you will find it useful to your travelling Propensities in mentioning towns, routes &c, and to your no less Natural Piggish Propensities, in it's being in some small measure a "journale Gastronomique."   Believe me your's & affectionately

M Arnold

Hotel des Bains: Boulogne sur Mer

MS. Balliol College.

1. Facing p. 1, in Arnold's hand: "M Arnold/Bought at Dover July [*for* August] 11th 1837, and respectfully inscribed, to D. D. D. F. P. wch is being interpreted—/E. P. Arnold."

2. William Winstanley Hull (1794–1873: *DNB*), liturgical writer and hymnologist, at Brasenose College from 1811 (fellow, 1816–20), and an intimate, then and later, of Whately, John Taylor Coleridge, and Thomas Arnold. "One of my father's oldest and dearest friends . . . a barrister with little practice . . . whose five children were about contemporary with the eldest five of us" (*Passages in a Wandering Life*, p. 26). "He was three times married, in 1820, 1850, and 1861, and left a family by each wife" (*DNB*). See below p. 147 n. 2.

3. "I shudder in referring to it" (*Aeneid* 2.204—a tag).

4. Perhaps Charles Wasteneys Eyre (1802–62), of Rampton, Notts, rector of Hooton Roberts, Yorks, who entered Rugby School in 1813 and was at Brasenose 1820–23. His wife was the former Lucy Dorothea Foulis (*Landed*, 1871; Rugby). Arnold called on Mrs Eyre in London in 1851 (below p. 199).

5. Henry Richard Vassall Fox (1773–1840: *DNB*), 3d Baron Holland, prominent Whig politician (and nephew of Charles James Fox).

6. Untraced.

7. Thomas Campbell, "The Pleasures of Hope," pt. 2 (near end).

8. Thomas Waddington, of Rouen, father of W. H. Waddington (see below p. 423n).

Mary Penrose Arnold to Jane Penrose

September 2, 1838

You have not I think heard about our great fright about Matt, when he went out on the Lake—so I will tell you. In the first place, all of us except Matt & Mary who did not wish to be of the party, went on the Monday to a

Pic Nic at Elterwater with the Miss Hardens—We went to Dungeon Ghyll, both dined & had tea, in a little cottage close to the Lake which belonged to the Hardens & came home rather late at night over Loughrigg, having had some adventures during the day—As we came home we found the wind very high, which made us much more frightened on remembering it afterward. We found Mary at home, who said that she believed Matt was gone to dine with Mr Balston[1] in Ambleside—Matt was not home at prayers, but that had happened before, so I only told Carly that I should wait for him, & she would too—We sat very comfortably till about ½ past 10, when Carly began to get rather fidgetty about him, but I thought nothing of it still supposing he had left Mr B. to go & drink tea with Mr Wrightson, who would be likely to keep him. However I was uneasy too when he was not come home by eleven, so we sent John to Ambleside to know whether he was there—& while he was away Carly & I, too anxious & unhappy to stay in the house put on the boys Mackintoshes & paraded up & down the Birch Copse & sometimes going further in hopes of seeing something of him—in vain— neither he appeared, nor John, so we thought that the latter must have heard some bad news at Ambleside which he did not like to tell us—At 1 oclock we called up Tom—& then we all thought any [thing] better than staying there, so we three put on cloaks & bonnets & set off for Water Head, think- ing it possible he might have gone on the lake—before we got very far we met John who told us that he had not been heard of at Ambleside that no one knew what was become of him, but that he & Mr Balston's brother & Mr Freeman, had set off together somewhere, about 3 oclock, & were either on the Lake or on the Mountains, neither very consoling to us at that time of night—so we sent Tom & John to Water Head to see whether the boat was come in & heard that it was not—we sat waiting till 4 & then went to bed—desiring to be called at 6. After an hour & a half of sleep we got up, found that he was not returned, & that Mr Balston, had come over in great alarm to say that he & Tom would take a boat & go out on the Lake in search of them wch they did immediately—while Carly & I directly after breakfast, went to Waterhead & from there to Lowwood, mounting every high point near the road, to try to discover the sail. At length after a fruitless search we returned to make diligent enquiries of all the boatmen at Waterhead whether they had seen the boat go out? What sort of night it had been, whether the Black Dwarf could upset? &c—they could tell us nothing but that it had been blowing *fresh* & were evidently much surprised themselves! Well to make a long story short, we were too unhappy to stay long any where, so went to Ambleside to enquire of Mr Freeman's party, whether they knew any thing about them; found they did not & were much alarmed; that Mr Warden at the Post, who seeing our frightened looks & learning what was the matter, offered kindly to take his sail boat & go after them, he went immediately & we returned to the Lake to wait as we best might—A little after 12, he returned in triumph, having found them! I believe I never thought any one so beautiful as I did him then—we thanked him again & again till he must have wondered when we meant to have done, but it was a relief to say any thing, instead of doing as we had, all the night & morning, each forming all sorts of horrible ideas, & trying to persuade the other they could not possibly happen, firmly believing oneself all the time that they had—John & Mr B. returned soon after in the rowboat, bringing Matt whom they had exchanged for Tom—he said they had becalmed at their end though it had been rough at ours—that they had been on the Lake till 5 in the Morning, when they were so knocked up as to be obliged to put in a sleep at the Ferry—The Black Dwarf with the others did not return till past 3. Thus the matter ended having cost us the most wretched day & night we had ever spent.

MS. Brotherton Collection.

1. Probably William Balston, of Springfield, Maidstone, the father of Henry Balston (and six other sons, Oxonians all), who entered Rugby under Arnold in 1828, went on to Oriel and Magdalen, was ordained, and died of consumption in 1840 (Rugby). There are several letters to the son and one to the father in Stanley. Wrightson, Freeman, and Warden, below, have not been identified. Nor has Carly, but see below p. 158.

Mary Penrose Arnold to Jane Penrose and C. Lydia Penrose

Rugby
[December 8, 1838]

Matt: is not at home, having been invited to the dig at Sir Gray Skip-withs[1]—& the promise of a double barrelled gun for his entertainment so filled him with joy that I believe he has thought of little else since the invitation came—This shooting mania I cannot like—but we have given him to understand that it must be indulged sparingly, & his father does not think it right to debar him from an amusement he so delights in. A gun is bought accordingly which is to go to Fox How, & live there—only with these conditions that it shall be considered the gardener's gun, & that there is to be no hedge popping or slaughter of little birds. I was interrupted by his return from Newbold Hall—& hearing his history of his day of enjoyment—Now he is gone to bed.

MS. Brotherton Collection.

1. Sir Gray Skipwith (1771–1852; 8th bt), of Newbold Hall, nearby, had been a trustee of Rugby School since 1804.

To Jane Penrose and C. Lydia Penrose

Fox Howe
My dearest Aunts   Sunday, February three 1839
This Period of the year puts me naturally in Mind of our delightful visit to you about this time last year: and reminds me to thank you for your great kindness then to me and Tom. We shall not now however have so long an interval between our departure from Fox Howe and the Beginning of our Rugby Labours as last year: for we shall spend but 3 days Thursday Friday and Saturday at Rugby before the Halfyear begins. Mamma & Papa go on to London. Mamma to consult Dr Dunsford: [1] the experiment may *amuse* her: but I do not think that she has the least chance of deriving any real Benefit from him or his System, and I am sure she herself does but half believe in it. But I really think being in London will amuse her & do her good: and Papa will feel the change less in going from London to Rugby and his work than he would as a change from the everlasting Quiet of this Place. There has been a long frost here & rather severe: but mixed with snow: so that there has been no Skating to speak of here. I have no more Room left but Fan & Susy desire their love. Believe me   ever your affectionate

M. Arnold.

MS. Brotherton Collection

1. H. Dunsford, physician at 28 Somerset Street, Manchester Square (*POLD*, 1840).

Mary Arnold to C. Lydia Penrose

Rugby
My dear Aunt Lydia   December 7, 1839
Here we are at the end of the Half year and to day, the Class Papers are coming out, so you may suppose how anxious the Boys are, and my own Brothers not the least so. This evening there is to be a grand Supper, to which Matt, Tom, Edward, Willy, and little Walter were invited. But only Matt and Tom are going, for Edward and Willy are going up to Aunt Wards to drink tea, and Papa and Mamma think Walter too young to go. . . . I must tell you the Class Paper is just come out and Matt and Tom have a first in Classics, and Tom is first in Modern Languages, is not this good news Edward has a second class in Divinity and History.

MS. Brotherton Collection.

To Susanna Brooke Penrose, Jane Penrose, and Lydia Penrose

[Rugby]

My dear Aunts   Sunday Afternoon, August 30, [1840]

Mamma tells me she thinks you will be interested in hearing what Tom and I have been doing: so I will tell you as fully as my Papa will allow me. On the last Tuesday of the half year Tom went to Birmingham and from thence through Bristol to Tenby, to stay with the Whatelys':[1] while I started with John Penrose to go to fish in Derbyshire.[2] We found Frank at Ashbourne, & fisht all three together. I had never seen Dovedale before, so I was very glad to have the opportunity of fishing all through it. We then went on to Bakewell and after a day and a half there I left John to go to Hull & start for Norway: while I went to Manchester, and so on to Fox: Howe. After being a fortnight there I got a Letter from Lake telling me to meet him at Chester: so I went thither through Liverpool: and did not arrive till 12 o'clock. There I found Lake and a Pupil of his, an Irishman of the Name of Carden,[3] whom I thought a very pleasant Person. We then went for a fortnight touring about Wales: and were fortunate in having very fine weather the whole Time. At Bangor we found a Letter from Tom, who said that as there were no Coaches through S. Wales, he should go to Ireland with the Whatelys': and cross from Dublin to Holyhead and thence join us by Coach. He did not arrive till nearly the end of the Time: so we all went back to Beddgelert together, where we took lodgings & staid for a fortnight, with constant Rain the whole Time. Wales being only a bad second Edition of the Lakes I got heartily tired of it: and was not sorry to change our quarters to a Place called Abergele which is on the sea. Here we staid for another fortnight, and then went by see [*sic*] to Liverpool & on to Rugby, where we arrived the day before the Rest of the Party. If you have heard this before, dear Aunts, I cannot help ⟨this⟩ it's being stupid: but Mamma tells me you certainly Have not. Believe me   ever your most affectionate Nephew—

M. Arnold.—

MS. Brotherton Collection.

1. Richard Whately (1787–63: *DNB*), archbishop of Dublin 1831–63), formed a lasting friendship with Thomas Arnold at Oriel College, tutored Nassau William Senior (see below p. 194 n. 14), married the former Elizabeth Pope (d. 1860) in 1821, fathered a family that, as these letters reveal, was and remained close to the Arnold family. For Whately's influence on Arnold's thought see William Blackburn, "Matthew Arnold and the Oriel Noetics," *Philological Quarterly* 25 (1946):70–78.

2. John Penrose (1815–88), Rugby, Balliol, and a fellow of Lincoln College, 1837–43; he was an assistant master at Rugby 1839–46 and then became master of Exmouth School. He died in Norway June 20, 1888. See *The Right Honourable Hugh Oakeley Arnold-*

Forster: A Memoir by His Wife, pp. 22–23. His brother Francis Cranmer Penrose (1817–1903: *DNB*), of Winchester and Magdalene College, Cambridge, archaeologist, astronomer, antiquary, and architect, was possibly the most distinguished of a notable family—except perhaps for his daughter, Dame Emily Penrose (1858–1942: *DNB*), principal of Bedford College, Royal Holloway, and then Somerville, her alma mater.

3. Lionel Carden, from Barname, co. Tipperary, who entered University College in Dec. 1837 (Foster). Arnold recalls this Welsh stay nearly a quarter of a century later (see below his letter July 22, 1864).

Edward Walford to the Editor of *The Times*

I am the only survivor of a batch of five freshmen who were matriculated at Balliol on November 28, 1840; and I well remember how, when we waited in the Vice-Chancellor's ante-room for admission,[1] Arnold professed to us his great aversion to sundry statements in the Thirty-nine Articles, which at that time we were all forced to subscribe, especially that article which expresses an approval of the Athanasian Creed, and that which denounces and renounces the Pope of Rome. In his early days, when we dined at the same scholars' table, I shall never forget how, in opposition to the Tractarianism of the day, he used to say that the strict imposition of creeds had done more to break up than to unite churches, and nations, and families, and how even then, in our small and highly privileged circle, he was the apostle of religious toleration in every direction. His cheerfulness, geniality, and universal charity combined to make him as general a favourite at Balliol as he became afterwards in the wider world of society in London. Lord Coleridge, Mr F. Palgrave, Bishop Temple, and myself are now, alas! almost the only survivors of that pleasant scholars' table to which Arnold added "sweetness and light."   Your obedient servant,

E. Walford, formerly Scholar of Balliol College.

Hyde-park-mansions, N. W., April 17.

Text: The Times, Apr. 20, 1888, p. 13 (excerpt).

1. See below p. 45.

Tour in France, July 1841
Dr Thomas Arnold and Two Sons (Matthew and Thomas)

June 25, 1841: I purpose leaving this place for the Continent with my two eldest sons on Monday next [June 28]. (Stanley, p. 397).

June 26, 1841: If you could see the beauty of this scene, you would think me mad to leave it, and I almost think myself so too. The boys are eager to be off, and I feel myself that the work of Rugby is far more welcome when I come to it as a home after foreign travelling, than when I go to it from Fox How, from one home to another, and from what is naturally the more dear to the less dear (Stanley, p. 395).

C. *July 1, 1841:* I was at the same inn at Fontainebleau when Tom and I were with papa twenty-four years nearly ago. We did not go over the Palace then, but arrived late in the evening, and started early next morning—a wet morning, I remember it was.   (Russell, 1 : 306, Arnold to his sister Fan, May 14, 1865)

July 5, 1841 (MS, Brotherton Collection, p. 3a): Sails of the Barges gliding along the Band of Wood & Vines on our Left; the Plain of yellow Corn on the R. bounded by it's Band of Wood & Vines, and this perfect Road, a complete Terrace giving a full View of every Thing. You must certainly come hither one of these Days dearest with Bacco & Didu, for a short two Days outing from Fox How. At this Point, near La Frilliere, the Cliff on the opposite Bank with it's Face burrowed into at different Heights by these strange rock dwellings looks exactly like the Lycian Rock Tombs drawn in Fellowes' Book. The Chimneys of these old Houses rise out of the Ground on the Top of the Cliff. Arrived at La Frilliere, 6.28. Left at 6.33. And now the Hill on our R. is come close to us, and we are gazing as at Pangbourn between the Cliff & the River.—Tours is in sight.—And here are these rock Houses just above us—the Windows look so odd set in the Cliff, with the Vines above [MS p. 4] & below them, and all Sorts of old Entrances for Closets, Cellars, &c, at all irregular Heights.

Tours, July 5. We have been here, dearest, since 7.22, so expeditiously did we perform the last Stage, along the same magnificent Road, and under that strange Cliff, the very oldest Thing that ever I saw, yet very beautiful, so picturesquely did the Gardens & Vineyards & the natural Copsewood blend with the Rock & the old Windows.—This lasted for five or six Miles, and we had seen much of the same Sort of Thing at a Distance on the other Bank of the Loire.—At last we came upon a Quay just in Front of Tours, and then crossed the Loire by a Bridge of 16 Arches, one of the finest in Europe, the Continuation of which is the Rue Royale, moving directly through the City,—a broad & perfectly straight [MS, p. 4a] Street, built of very good Stone Houses, & with exceedingly good Shops below. Our Hotel, du Faisan, is in this Street, and my Room opens on a Balcony where Tom has been walking up & down in this glorious Night singing to himself, while the Calm of the cloudless Sky is strangely contrasted with the thronging of the busy World below, the Street swarming with People, & the Shops being still partly open, at past 10 o'Clock.—After having been settled here, we walked out to see the Cathedral, where I expected little & found much: a very rich west Front, a very fine Nave, & a great Deal of very rich painted Glass, two or three Windows being of that old Glass of which there were such beautiful specimens at Bourges. On our Way Home I called at a Shop where Galignani was to be had, and [MS, p. 5] there I learnt some later News of the Elections than I had before heard; but I will not enlarge on this Subject now.—I must call in the Boys from the Balcony & go to Bed, though we need not be up very early tomorrow, our Linen detaining us till 10 o'Clock. Good Night, my dearest Mamma, & Dogs all,—

Tours, July 6th. We are waiting quietly in my room—but we did not sit long, for Matt & I went out to get Straw Hats, & I got also a small View of Tours, but I tried in Vain to get one which represented the old Rock Houses, with their Windows & Chimneys, [drawing of two rock houses, in cliff side, with trees above and below]

July 7, 1841. Between Angoulême and Bordeaux. Left Barbiceaux 10.35, very rich and beautiful. It is not properly southern for there are neither olives nor figs; nor is it northern, for the vines and maize are luxuriant. It is properly France, with its wide landscapes, no mountains, but slopes and hills; its luminous air, its spread of cultivation, with the vines and maize and walnuts, mixed with the ripe corn, as brilliant in colouring as it is rich in associations. I never saw a brighter or a fresher landscape. Green hedges line the road; the hay, just cut, is fragrant; every thing is really splendid for man's physical well being;—it is Kent six degrees nearer the sun. (Stanley, pp. 482–83).

July 11, 1841, St Jean de Luz (Stanley, p. 483).

July 12, 1841, Bayonne: Letter, Thomas Arnold (son) to his sister Frances
(MS. Brotherton Collection).

	Bayonne
My dearest Fan	*July 12, 1841*

I told you that I would write to you if possible from our Journey, and accordingly I will send you a few Lines from this Place.—Our great impediment, strange to say, has been the Weather.—Every day since we landed at Calais it has been more or less cold & rainy, and though I expected it to mend as we got farther south, yet we have been to the very Frontier of Spain & still it has been as bad as ever.—Yesterday we slept at S. Jean de Luz:—a little

Place on the very Shore of the Bay of Biscay, and the Sea came roaring in with a driving south wester & drizzling Rain in a Manner very unlike the Summer Sea in Latitude 43 and a half.—All the Pyrenees were veiled, & when I looked out this Morning betweem four & five it was just the same, so I went to Bed again, & we did [not] set out till between seven & eight, so that it was then too late, besides that the Weather was still rainy, to go on to St Sebastian & return the same Day.—We went on however to the Bidassoa, and leaving the Carriage on the French Side we walked over and went as far as Irun, the first town in Spain. The Weather had now cleared, and the Mountains round us were visible. They were very like our own Westmorland Mountains, for which I loved them all the better,—but more thickly wooded with Pollard Oaks, which cover all their lower Parts.—The Road changed the very instant we were out of France from one of perfect Goodness to a very bad one, and the Street of Irun was intolerable. The Style of the Houses & Shops resembled the dirtiest Places which I have ever seen in central Italy; but every Body seemed civil, and a Man whom we met on a Hill outside of Irun when he found that we were English paid us many Compliments.—After our Return to S. Jean de Luz, we had a famous Bathe, for the Sea was got quite clear & blue again, and then while Matt prowled on the Shore, Tom & I walked up the Nivelle to see the scene of Lord Wellington's Victory in November, 1813. The Walk was very beautiful through a great Deal of Wood & Heath, the Heaths being in Flower very luxuriantly, & the Views of Mountain & Sea were very fine.—Then we set off for Bayonne, where we now are; and we propose to start tomorrow for Pau, & thence if the Weather continues so unfavourable, to return Home at once by Toulouse.—We came here by Orleans, Tours, Poitiers, Angouleme, and Bordeaux:—but what most surprized & delighted me was the Country of the Landes; between the Garonne & this Place. It is an enormous Bed of the Bagshot Heath Sand, but the Country is more like the new Forest than the mere Heath Country,—being a continued Forest of Oak & Pine, with Glades of Heath in the middle of it as about Eaglehurst.—Every Thing was so green & beautiful that I thought it one of the most delightful Countries I had ever seen in France. It ended with a Cork Tree Forest,—the Trees of which are exceedingly picturesque, and have an Underwood of Arbutus which is very striking.—I was very much pleased also with Bordeaux, which is one of the most complete Contrasts in every Thing to Marseilles, a finer Town, and with a Neighbourhood rich and ornamented beyond any Thing I have seen in France, but it is not a Greek Colony, nor is the Garonne the Mediterranean.—We shall get Home in Time I trust to have nearly a Fortnight at Fox How, which will be very delightful;—for it's Beauty is certainly not to be surpassed by any Thing that we are likely to see here.—Give my

best love to all your Party and believe me to be, my dearest Fan,   Your
most affectionate Brother and Friend,

T. Arnold.

Pau, July 13th. We have arrived here this Afternoon, and depend on the
Weather for future Movements.

July 14, 1841, Near Agen: For some time past the road has been a terrace
above the lower bank of the Garonne, which is flowing in great breadth and
majesty below us.

From these heights in clear weather you can see the Pyrenees, but now
the clouds hang darkly over them. (Stanley, p. 483).

July 14, Auch (Stanley, p. 483).

July 15, 1841 (MS. Brotherton Collection, p. 37a): the Lot & the Dor-
dogne, the View is almost boundless, but the Country is furrowed with many
Valleys, so that there is a great Variety of Surface, and the View embraces
Heights & Vallies, Slopes & Combes, Villages & scattered Houses, Corn,
Maize, Vines, Fruit Trees & Woods, absolutely in Extent & Numbers
infinite.

Arrived at Cancon, 6.43. The Road latterly has followed the narrow &
winding Top of the highest Ridge of all the Country, so that the Views have
been enormous—we have had again the Erica arborescens, & another Plant
that I never saw before, with curiously notched, or drilled Berries, quite
black when ripe, something like the Seed of the Nasturtium. They are acrid
& noxious, as the Postilion said, & as my Taste partly confirmed. Left Cancon, or rather were some way out of it, 6.58. Established at Castillonez, in
one of the queerest Places that ever I was in in my Life, 8.40. This last Stage
has [MS p. 38] been very beautiful:—a gradual Descent from our high Point
at Cancon toward the Valley of the Dropt, the Name of the little River below
this Town:—the same wide Views continuing, over a Country no less rich
& varied.—But the Town itself is a Curiosity;—the Road does not pass
through it, but by it, and few Travellers I should think ever enter it, fewer
still sleep at it.—The Pavement is worse than that of Irun, and the Place,
surrounded with it's heavy Arcades with a rude Gothic Arch, looks as primitive as possible. The Inn is a very odd place, undergoing Repairs, my Hostess
said,—and not without Need.

—Nevertheless our Bed Room Windows look out of a most delicious
View, and the Salle in which I am seated is large and papered [MS. p. 38a]
with one of those nice painted Papers that I so like.—What the Food will be
Time will show;—mine this day has been of the scantiest: an Egg and a Slice

of Toast for Breakfast at 6 A.M. and a very small Chicken's Wing & Piece of
Bread about 2.—Crab is well nigh famished, because he can eat nothing
early in the Morning, and could get nothing to eat since.—But being over
the Garonne & over the Lot seems like coming northwards again, and I anticipate with no small Delight a Period of more than a Fortnight at Fox
How.—And now good Night, my dearest Wife.—

July 16th, 1841: Left Castillonès, 6.25, the strangest Place that ever was
seen, but the Town after all was fair, the people very civil, & the Charge
moderate. [MS. p. 39] The Supper was curious.—Figs & pickled Cucumbers
were set on the Table before hand, just as Pickles would be in England. .Then
came the Potage, full of Bread & of Herbs, the manifold Produce of Garden
or Ditch, but of Mint guiltless.—Then came a Quarter of Goose hashed,—
a fricassed Poulet, and a Fricandeau of Veal,—so full of Garlick that I swallowed and retained it with extreme Difficulty.—Thirdly came a natural
roasted Poulet with Sallad, & French Beans, after which was the Dessert of
Cheese, Pears, little Cakes & Almonds. But ere the Dessert came, the Figs
were taken away: being regarded more as ὄψον [relish] than as ἐπι-
φόρημα [dessert]:—of which Practice Tom being unsuspicious, had nearly
lost his Fig, & was obliged to call the Dish back again. The Beds were [MS.
p. 39a] clean as usual, though I saw so many Rat Holes about in the Room
that I expected some gambolling; but the Rats were peaceful & so was I.—
There was a little Terrace Garden before the Salle Windows, out of which
our Hostess gave me a Nosegay this Morning.—The Country is still very
pretty, much varied & well clothed; but the Cold is remarkable, & the Rain
seems to have fallen [?]madly.—Left Bergerac, where we stopped for Breakfast for the Sake of Crab's Enteron, at 9.45.—We have now crossed the Dordogne, and are ascending one of it's Feeders, along a very nice Green Valley,
to get out upon the great Plains of Perigord, said to be the driest County in
France, & the only one therefore I suppose, which rejoices in these perpetual
Rains. [MS. p. 40] I cannot tell what this Limestone is which we find everywhere. I suppose it is tertiary, but in their external character the Oolite &
Calcaire grossier so resemble each other that one cannot tell which it is.—
Here it lies just below the Surface, covered often with ferruginous Sand.—
We have wound up a long Hill to get to the Top of the Plateau which divides
the Feeders of the Dordogne from those of the Isle. It is very pretty, for here
again the Chesnuts grow gracefully, and there is Plenty of Copse and Heath
besides.—Arrived at S. Mametz, 11.30. Left it at 11.40. Again this Country
which Vaysse abuses is in my Eyes extremely pretty; It is exactly the Hampshire Country about Otterbourne & Stoneham, with the Addition of the
Chesnuts besides. Arrived at Rossignol at 1.0. Left it at 1.11. The Country
has been quite beautiful. Our Map [MS breaks off for fifteen pages]

July 18, 1841, Bourges (Stanley, p. 483).

July 20, 1841, Paris (Stanley, p. 484).

July 23, 1841, Boulogne (Stanley, p. 484).

July 23–4, 1841 (MS. Brotherton Collection, pp. 55a–59): Arrived at Dover, and settled in the Ship, at 5.25.—Thank God, my dearest Wife, for his great Goodness!—It was a miserable Time, and I was at once very sick & very cold; but here we are in our beloved Country, & the Distance between Fox How & us seems now to be reduced to comparatively nothing.—God grant that we may meet happily on Sunday Morning!

July 24, 1841. Left Euston Square Station by my Watch at 10.8. . Journal has been lagging, dearest, but it does not much signify, and here I hope is our last Day of Absence, and instead of a Week at Fox How we shall have if it please God more than two.

—We dined yesterday at the Ship, & after Dinner we went to call on the Eyres.—Mr Eyre had been very unwell, but was, as Emma said, better: he still however looked very ill.—We started by the Mail at 9½, and were at the Victoria Hotel by six: there we dressed & I went to Hull's to Breakfast, and was received with their usual Kindness, but I left Matt & Tom to breakfast at the Hotel.—And now our Places are taken to Lancaster, and we are whirling along through Middlesex like Lightning.—Arrived at Watford, 10.49. Left it 10.51. Arrived at Tring, 11.20,—Left it, 11.27. And here we are leaving the Chalk, and descending into the central Plain of England,—how different, to be sure, from the Centre of France.—It is so green & so neat, & so quiet, and yet so full of Life & Power.—arrived at Wolverton, 12.5. . Arrived at Blisworth, 12.41. Left it 12.45. We have not yet been 24 hours from Boulogne, and here we are in the Heart of England, 130 Miles from Dover. Arrived at Wisdon, 1.2. Left it, 1.6. And arrived at dear old Rugby, 1.38. It does seem very odd not to be getting out; and I do not think that I ever passed it before without having something to do with it;—but now all my Attractions are at Fox How, and I have no Wish to linger any where on the Road. . But the Weather seems more heartily clearing since we have come out of the Kilsby Tunnel, than I have known it to do since we left Fox How. And this Warwickshire Country looks exceedingly beautiful under the bright Sky—so green & so flourishing.—Left Rugby, 1.44.—Arrived at Coventry, 2.7. Left it 2.10. And arrived close to Birmingham, and in Sight of all the little Houses in the Gardens, 2.50.—

Left Birmingham after a Feed not to be enough commended at 3.27.—Now as we do not enter that pleasant Refreshment Room when we go back to Rugby, I will just describe it for my Nigger's Sake.—You enter a large

Room & find three or four Tables covered with all Sorts of good Things, and with Plates set of very handsome China, and civil Servants come & take your Hat, & one asks if you will eat Beef, and another if you will eat Veal; and they carve for you most expeditiously & liberally, & goodly Dishes of Potatoes & of Peas are on the Table:—and when you are getting on with your Food, a civil Servant asks if he shall get you some more, and to this I say "no," but Pigger & Nigger would say "Yes."—and then they ask if you have Gravy enough,—and then if you will have some Cheese. . and Beef & Peas & Potatoes & Cheese & excellent Ale are all had for 2s., with as much Civility & Attention & Niceness as any Dinner can possibly be served. . —And now we are in the green Valley of the Ray, & they are beginning to mow; but I see here no Floods, whereas on Thursday in France we found all the Streams flooded & the Corn in one Place was standing in Water.—Arrive at Wolverhampton, 3.59. Left it, 4.2.—Arrived at Stafford, 4.30. Left it, 4.33. Arrived at Whitmore, 5.7. Left it 5.11. Arrived at Crave 5.22. Left it 5.37.—Arrived at Hartford, 6.3. Left it 6.6.—Arrived at Warrington, in the next County to you, my Darling, 6.31. Left it, 7.10. Arrived at Parkside, 7.3. Left it, 7.10. Arrived at Preston, and across the Ribble, 8.6. Left Preston 8.18. We have passed the Garstany Station, & are speeding on like mad; but we are behind our Time.—Passed Galgate, & within three Miles of Lancaster: and now coming close upon it, and opening on the Sight of it, 9.0

Milnthorpe, WESTMORLAND. July 24th.
Here we are, dearest, thank God, in our own County, and we shall I hope be with you to Breakfast tomorrow.—We dined here last Monday three Weeks, when we had just left you;—how infinitely happier is our being here now than then! I have kept our last Milnthorpe Bill ever since in my Pocket to comfort me when I was abroad.—and I resolved to keep it till we came back again; and now, thank God, here we are. We are expecting Preston, & then we shall not be unready to go to Bed, as [we] were up all last Night in the Mail.—So this will be the first English Bed that we shall sleep in, although we are now more than 300 Miles from the Place where we landed.—Good Night, dearest.—

July 25th: Left Milnthorpe, .44. It is much too late, dearest; but after having been a Night in the Mail I could not wake myself, & they did not call me till 5½. The P[wd illeg.] was again excellent, & the Bill no less so: and we are starting in finer Weather than we had with one Exception any Day abroad.—The fresh cut Grass fills the Air with Fragrance, and the Clouds which hang heavily & full of Rain in the Hills when we get there, seems now like light Mist ready to disperse on our near Approach.
The Beauty of these Walls by Levens, with their Stonecrops & their

Mosses,—and here we are over the Kent.—We are going up the great Hill, after having got on splendidly all the Way.—Again I am struck with the incomparable Beauty of the Flowers & Banks;—the tall lilac Campanula, the Valerian, the Meadow Sweet, the Geraniums, the Fox Gloves, all are delicious.

Windermere opens! The Mountains veiled in Haze towards his Head, but bright Gleams lighting them up below the Ferry.—Descending to Bowness, and arrived at Ullock's, 8.8. Marvellous. Such going is not often to be had, so safe & so speedy!.—Left Bowness, 8.20. & going famously, Robinson driving.—The Mountains are cleaving as we advance, & the Sun comes out brightly.—Here is Raynigg. 8.24. And here we go up the Bowness Hill to the Terrace [end of MS].

Texts: MSS Brotherton Collection; Stanley, pp. 482–84; Russell, 1: 306.

Thomas Arnold to William Empson[1]

Rugby
October 15, 1841
Our eldest son is gone up to Oxford this day, to commence his residence at Balliol. It is the first separation of our family, for, from our peculiar circumstances, all our nine children have hitherto lived at home together, with very short exceptions, but now it will be so no more.

Text: Stanley, p. 405 (extract).

1. William Empson (1791–1852: *DNB*) was a schoolfellow of Arnold's at Winchester and a frequent contributor to the *Edinburgh Review* (which he edited 1847–52) for which Arnold had written two articles (Stanley, p. 486).

Thomas Arnold to Frances Buckland

Rugby
My dearest Fan   December 7, 1841
I wished to tell you about our visit to Oxford,[1] yet really it is hard just now to be able to do any Thing beside my necessary Work.—But I must just tell you briefly how much I was interested and delighted at what I may call my second Entrance at Oxford, after an absence of just two & twenty years, since I came up to Hampton preparatory to our settling at Laleham.—We started at 5. A. M. precisely, Mary & I in the Carriage, and we reached Oxford about 11½. We drove to Laura's[2] & there found Stanley & Matt, & others soon after assembled to welcome us.—I went to Hawkins[3] & walked

with him to the Vice Chancellor's, to be admitted, and then we set out for the Theatre, it having been understood that the Lecture was to be there, as the Room at the Clarendon was not likely to hold the Numbers.—Here I waited at least half an hour for the Vice Chancellor, he having mistaken the Time,& it was very vexatious, for I knew that young Men are not fond of waiting, and I was in a great Fright lest my Lecture coming when their Patience was nearly exhausted might seem unreasonably long.—However there was no Remedy, & we should have waited longer had we not sent to St John's to fetch the Vice Chancellor out.—When he came, I marched into the Theatre with him & the Proctors, Hawkins, &c, and took my Station at the End of the Doctors' Seats, in the Place of one of the Curators of the Theatre. I was obliged to lecture with my Cap on, to my great Annoyance, such being the Etiquette.—I found that I could manage my Voice well enough, but I was in a Fidget as to the Length of the Lecture, & at last I began to skip vigorously, resolving that they should rather complain of it's being too short than too long. However they were very quiet to the End, & then came the speaking to different People, at which I worked hard, but could not speak to half of those whom I knew, nor indeed so much as see them. The Rugby men amongst the Undergraduates were all capping me as I past, and I spoke to every One whom I could mark, but their Number was so great, & we had no Time to lose.—However Mary & I walked up to Balliol to see Matt's Rooms, & to call on Jenkyns, who had the Gout & so could not come out to the Lecture.—We were in the Carriage with K about 4 or little after, & arrived at Home just at eleven.—Every Body was very kind, & certainly it satisfied me that in returning to Oxford I was going to no Place full of Enemies,—It delighted me to hear the high Character which our Rugby Men bear, Stanley especially,—who is more considered, I am told, than any Man of his Age in Oxford,[4]—I saw Buckland & Mrs Buckland,—and Bridges.—We are going if we can to get a House to which we may take up all the Children,—& the Pony will go with us too.—If Lydia is with you, will you tell her with my Love, how vexed I am to find that she never received my Sermons, which I fully thought Fellowes had forwarded to her.—I will take care that she does get it, as also a Copy of my inaugural Lecture, which is printing, & which I can send to both you & her by Post.— Love to all.—   Ever your most affectionate Brother & Friend,

T. Arnold.

MS. Brotherton Collection.

1. This letter, describing Dr Arnold's inaugural lecture as Regius Professor of Modern History at Oxford (see Stanley, ch. 10) and showing the "strong soul" in an uncharacteristic (unique?) "Fidget," invites comparison with the inaugural lecture fifteen years later of the Professor of Poetry, "On the Modern Element in Literature" (about

which we know little)—both spoke in the Sheldonian Theatre, both had to cope with a vice-chancellor, both were concerned with Europe, not just England, for both modernity began in the 14th c., both their schemes included a lecture on Dante, and, most important, both, in the most intimate way, cherished the occasion as the realization of a dream.

2. Laura Ward Greenhill, his niece, daughter of John and Martha Arnold Ward (see above p. 22 n. 6). In 1840 she married William Alexander Greenhill (1814–94: *DNB*), physician, the nameless "old pupil"—"(B.)," identified in *DNB*—to whom several letters are printed in Stanley. Mrs Ward was apprehensive about the marriage, as Mary Penrose Arnold, her sister-in-law, wrote to another sister-in-law. "She does not know Dr Greenhill half so well as we do, for Laura has principally made her acquaintance with him here & at the Prices—& I think her principal satisfaction is in our thinking so highly of him. There certainly are some points about which I shall be anxious, for Dr Pusey has through his affections got such a strong influence over him, that he is perhaps more inclined to his opinions than is to be desired when his wife who is very decided in her own judgement & opinions will have so little sympathy with him, & he is of so sensitive a nature that my anxiety will be how he may agree to differ—With Laura I do not feel this for where she feels that the great views & principles are the same, she would hear any quantity of discussion without being worried by it—being very unlike her Aunt Arnold in that respect" (to Susanna Brooke Penrose, Aug. 29, 1840; MS Brotherton Collection).

3. Edward Hawkins (1789–1882: *DNB*) was the provost of Oriel College (where in 1815 he had known Arnold as a fellow) from 1828 to 1874 and was crucially involved at every stage in the appointment to Rugby (see Wymer, pp. 83–87). The vice-chancellor was Philip Wynter (1793–1871), president of St John's College, "serene, indifferent, handsome—'St John's Head on a charger' men called him as he went out for his daily ride" (Tuckwell, p. 151). Richard Jenkyns (1782–1854: *DNB*) was the great master of Balliol. Thomas Edward Bridges (c. 1773–1843), an old Wykehamist, was president of Corpus Christi College 1823–43. B. Fellowes, of Ludgate Street, publisher of Dr Arnold's *Postscript to Principles of Church Reform, Christian Life its course, its hindrances, and its help. Sermons, preached mostly in the chapel of Rugby School, History of Rome* and, later, of Stanley, and of Arnold's *The Strayed Reveller.*

4. "He was certainly for most of his time the most distinguished undergraduate in Oxford" (Katherine Lake, *Memorials of William Charles Lake*, p. 31). See below p. 53 n. 10.

To Archibald Campbell Tait[1]

Fox: How

My dear Sir   Saturday, [August 3, 1842]

I am very glad that I delayed so long to thank you for your very kind Letter, as it enables me to congratulate you, which I do very sincerely, on your appointment to Rugby. From the very beginning when we found that Archdeacon Hare[2] would not stand, I heartily wisht for your success: as my first feeling was that the one Point of paramount importance was to provide for the efficient government and firm and consistent management of the school: which seemed to me far the most necessary Requisite in the Election, and one that there was some danger of neglecting. I feel so confident that if you have a school wisely and firmly governed, and boys and masters alike impresst with the conviction that their main object should be to *unite* their efforts in making and keeping the Place a Christian School, all the intellectual Proficiency which is so apt to be the first thing considered, will be sure to follow as a matter of course. And the great danger seemed to be, that this Rule does not apply equally in both cases: that you might very well have the intellectual Part of a school exceedingly good, and yet be ruined for want of a wise and consistent firmness in the other. And I felt sure that you would labour to prevent the one Principle from gaining an undue Predominance: and by zealously maintaining the other still preserve at Rugby that spirit which it was my Father's first anxiety and chief greatness to inspire.

I am sure you will excuse my troubling you will all this, but I wisht to explain to you the grounds on which I had been so anxious for your Election: I will now thank you for your kindness in writing to me. I hope if possible to get through my Histories in the course of this vacation: yet I cannot but feel that the great trial will be the complete alteration of habits when I return to Oxford. You have so many Rugby friends that I suppose you will learn everything that may be necessary from them: but if there is any Information about the School House itself that we could give you, I am sure we should be very glad to do so.—

    Believe me, my dear Sir,   Yours very faithfully

M. Arnold.—

Saturday Morning.

MS. Lambeth Palace Library.

1. Archibald Campbell Tait (1811–82: *DNB*), who entered Balliol College in 1830 (B.A. 1833), where he became fellow, junior dean, tutor, and lecturer, was Dr Arnold's successor as headmaster of Rugby School.

"Dr. Arnold died on Sunday, June 12th, 1842, and, ten days later, Archibald Tait, mainly at the instigation of Lake and Stanley, declared himself a candidate for the vacant post" (Randall Thomas Davidson and William Benham, *Life of Archibald Campbell Tait*, 1: 110). Rival candidates were C. J. Vaughan, Bonamy Price, Charles Merivale, Herbert Kynaston, J. W. Blakesley. "The news of his election did not reach him till July 29th . . . . it was largely at the instigation of Arthur Stanley that he had resolved to become a candidate for the Head-mastership. But in the weeks which followed, Stanley seems to have felt it impossible to recommend any one as really fit to take Dr. Arnold's place, and before the actual election took place he had practically ceased to suppport Tait's candidature" (pp. 111–13).

After the headmastership of Rugby School (1842–50), Tait became dean of Carlisle till 1856, when he was appointed bishop of London, and became archbishop of Canterbury in 1869 (*VF*, 12/25/69, Coïde [Tissot]).

2. Julius Charles Hare (1795–1855: *DNB*), archdeacon of Lewes since 1840, "was first distinguished in the literary world as one of the translators of Niebuhr's History of Rome, in conjunction with Mr. Connop Thirlwall. Since this publication a vast number

of works, professional and critical, have proceded from the Archdeacon's pen and have been received with the highest approbation; for he was a most original and profound thinker, and in his controversial writings always preserved a just candour and impartiality" (obituary, *Annual Register*). The prescriptive pieties having been observed, one ought to point out that Hare was in fact hotly partisan in defense of liberal Anglican causes, and very close to Dr Arnold's own positions. He figures in Carlyle's *Life of Sterling* from the first sentence (Sterling was Hare's curate at Hurstmonceaux, and Hare was, with Carlyle, Sterling's literary executor).

To John Duke Coleridge[1]

Fox How

My dear Coleridge   Sunday Night, January 8, 1843

If all your intimate Friends (whose name is Legion)[2] repay your exertions with as great a Promptitude as I am doing, I think you will have no cause to complain. I call your attention to this, merely in consequence of the suspicion implied in the last line of your letter: "Mind you write," &c: not, "Mind you write *soon*": but conveying the very injurious impression, that you believed me to be in the habit of abstaining from answering letters altogether. However this will undeceive you: and as you are not coming back I think till the 28th I shall really expect you to let me hear again from you in the course of the next three weeks.

—Your letter was in all respects most welcome: in one most especially, that of giving me some information as to the literature of the day. For as we do not even see newspapers I had heard nothing whatever of the new Quarterly[3] or of Thirlwall's charge:[4] and about the charge my curiosity had been raised, as it appeared to have attracted Hawker's attention,[5] who generally neglects such things. Still, though it seems most ungrateful to complain, I do not approve of your omitting your own Proceedings so entirely. It is too bad if, in a letter at least, one may not transgress Lake's Rule and talk about one-self.[6] As "a great relative of your own" [7] up here observed to Price on another subject, "What do I care for Society? I am all for the individual Citizen"— so I have always thought that no Letter on Earth can be long enough to discuss the Literature of the day, and that the subject is better reserved for future conversations; in order that your own undiluted self may have room to give an account of its Proceedings:—I own that it is very thankless in me to appear discontented with what I have got: but I hope that you will draw from what I have said the complimentary Inference which Mackarness[8] would not fail to detect, that my Interest in your own Pursuits makes me willing to forego much very pleasant and profitable Instruction.—I am indignant at the contemptuous confidence with which you and Brodie[9] dismiss Homeopathy. If all the rest must perish, I will at least make an effort to rescue Nux Vomica and Sulphur from the general Ruin. As for the Case of poor Lady Denbigh, I cannot conceive any system in the world preventing the formation of a tumour on the brain: and this, I believe, caused her death. But the general defence of Homeopathy I cannot undertake: and I am willing to confess that even my admiration for my two favourites, is, more meo, rather an unreasoning one.

—If I am to apply my ⟨own⟩ Principle of individualising letter writing (the Expression is Lakean) to my own Practice, I shall very soon have exhausted myself. I have been living in perfect quietness: my chief occupation having been abuse of the weather,—and my idleness having been considerable: and there seems to be no Prospect of any change of condition before the 21st. When I add that I am perfectly well, and that it is now freezing hard, I have really told you everything. But you—living in the midst of London & the heart of literary Society, have no Excuse for not detailing to me the sayings that have been uttered and the People that you have seen.

—As to the Proceedings of the Committee, I own we are all somewhat disappointed. Stanley's[10] unproposed Plan of a scholarship at Oxford for all boys from all schools, or men who have not completed their second term, to be held like a University Scholarship seems preferable to any other I have heard. The scholarships at Rugby will merely relieve the Masters from those which they give at present: and which I do not think they feel to be any great burden. What you say about the connection of my Father's name with Rugby has far more weight in it: only I think that if the School continues as it is at present, his name will be of necessity bound up with it, as having almost created it anew: and if it goes down, the money will be completely thrown away. You have my crude notions on the subject—and I cannot see any definite Reasons for changing them: in fact the Reason you give was the first that I had heard: except the old objection as to the Scholarship at Oxford not being accepted: which Hawkins' mysterious disclosures appear by Stanley's account, to have cleared away.

—I am extremely glad that you like the sermons:[11] I always wisht that you should read them: they seem to me the most delightful & the most satisfactory to read, of all his writings. The last Sermon but two, in the last volume, preacht on Whitsunday, is, I think, the most beautiful of all of them. I neither expect nor desire that they should change your admiration for Newman. I should be very unwilling to think they did so in my own case. But owing to my utter want of *Prejudice,* (you remember your slander) I find it perfectly possible to admire them both. You cannot expect that very detailed and complete controversial sermons, going at once to the root of all the subjects in dispute, should be preacht to a congregation of Boys: it would be very unfit that they should. The peculiar Nature of Newman's Congregation gives him, I think, a great advantage, in enabling him to state his views, & to dwell on them, in all their completeness. But I speak on these matters with a consciousness of much ignorance.

—Faber is up here & is just going away: he is still very clever, very amiable, and very absurd. His farewell sermon to-night was absolutely shocking from the Egotism that ran through every line of it even when discussing the most sacred subjects. When he drops himself altogether, I have heard him very good. He has positively gone so far as to present me with his Poems: many of them weak & ridiculous enough. It is a nice point of morality how far an action of this kind binds one over to keep the Peace towards a man in speaking of his writings and himself. It must be owned that Faber's Peculiarities are very tempting.—[12]

—Do not believe, from my "frivolous criticism," (I must again refer you to Lake), that I am not very much interested by your letter & very much delighted to receive it. I only hope that you will not disappoint me: and write me another, which shall combine with the information your present one conveys to me an accurate Record of your sayings and doings in the last month.

—Will you give my respects to your Father[13] and remember me very kindly to your brother & believe me to remain   Yours affectionately,

M. Arnold.—

MS. Lord Coleridge.

1. John Duke Coleridge (1820–94: *DNB*; *VF*, 4/30/70; 3/5/87), later Baron Coleridge and Lord Chief Justice, was Arnold's friend longer than any correspondent in these volumes outside his family, and there are more letters to him than to any other friend except Clough (with whom, at the current tally, he runs a dead heat), Lady de Rothschild, and George Smith.

It was a special relationship. Their fathers had been at Oxford (Corpus Christi) at the same time and remained close friends; Coleridge was the son, Arnold the son-in-law, of a judge, and both acted as marshals; they had been at Laleham together for a few months in 1831, and Coleridge twice recalls that "a bright little fellow was put upon a table in a room full of people at Laleham, and recited with intelligence and effect Mr. Burke's magnificent description of Hyder Ali's ferocious desolation of the Carnatic" (*The Times*, Nov. 2, 1891, reprinted in W. P. Fishback's *Recollections of Lord Coleridge*, slightly different in the memorial article in the *New Review*, July, Aug. 1889); Coleridge had known and loved Fox How almost as long as Arnold himself; both were profoundly influenced by Newman, with whom their fathers were at odds, and a brother of each converted to Roman Catholicism; and, moreover, their wives and families were friends and exchanged visits with some frequency. Except in religion, Coleridge was always far more egalitarian than Arnold, and he never repudiated Gladstone. And, finally, on Arnold's death, it was to Coleridge that his widow turned for advice and help with *Essays in Criticism, Second Series*, to which he contributed a brief Prefatory Note (Super, 11:383–84). (This sketch is adapted from *Album*, pp. 108–9.)

2. Matthew 5:9, Luke 8:30.

3. The allusion, unclear, is possibly to the *English Review, or Quarterly Journal of Ecclesiastical and General Literature*, which began publication in 1844.

4. Connop Thirlwall (1797–1875: *DNB*), historian and (1840) bishop of St David's.

5. John Manley Hawker (c. 1820–84 or 1885), son of William Henry Hawker, curate of Charles' Chapel, Tavistock Place, Plymouth; Balliol B.A. 1842; prebendary and treasurer of Exeter Cathedral 1871, rector of Ideford "1856 until his death in 1885" (Foster; William White, *History, Gazetteer and Directory of Devonshire*, 1850).

6. William Charles Lake (1817–97: *DNB*). Of Rugby (see above p. 11) and Balliol; dean of Durham, 1869–94. Tuckwell (pp. 206–12): "He was not liked either as Tutor or as Proctor. His manner was cold, sarcastic, sneering; and a certain slyness earned him the nickname of 'Serpent,' applied originally at Rugby in reference to his sinuous shuffling walk, and retained by Balliol undergraduates as characterising his methods of College discipline" (p. 206). John Connington: "Do you know, Lake, that the men call you Puddle?" (p. 207). "In 1858 he took the College living of Huntspill . . . a secluded, unhealthy, stagnant village in the Bristol Channel marches. He was not a man to spend there much of his time: he kept a capable curate . . . and lived mostly in London, enjoying club life at the Athenæum, and labouring for a long time on the Duke of Newcastle's Education Commission. I remember when one of his principal farmers came up and said, 'We don't see much of you at Huntspill, Mr. Lake.' 'You may depend upon it,' said the faithful herdman, 'that you won't see more of me than I can help.' . . . None the less, at every period of his life, he showed himself extraordinarily capable. His Rugby schooldays placed him in the inner circle of Arnold's best beloved and cherished pupils. . . . He was not always *facile à vivre*: many persons noted, and still recall him as cold, stern, masterful. . . . But with intimates he was cordial, trustful, staunch, affectionate; and he never forgot old friends. In the company of such he was a very charming talker. . . . He was in his last days every inch a Dean. His tall figure and authoritative diction suited the hieratic consequence of gaiters and apron." Arnold speaks in 1873 of his "bitter tongue" but was touched by his memorial tribute in the *Guardian* on Mrs Arnold's death and the sermon he preached on her in Rydal Church.

7. Hartley Coleridge (1796–1849: *DNB*), oldest son of the poet and first cousin of John Duke Coleridge's father. He was a lovable sot, whose charm was legendary. See Earl Leslie Griggs, *Hartley Coleridge, His Life and Work*.

8. John Fielder Mackarness (1820–89: *DNB*), of Eton (with John Duke Coleridge, whose sister Alethea he married in 1849) and Merton, and, like Coleridge, a fellow of Exeter College, 1844–46. In 1870 he was consecrated bishop of Oxford (Gladstone's letter in Coleridge, 2:165–66, deftly demonstrates that the appointment both was and was not a "family arrangement").

9. Benjamin Collins Brodie (1817–80: *DNB*, succeeded as 2d baronet 1862), at Balliol 1834–38 and a member of the Decade, was a chemist and in 1865 appointed professor of chemistry at Oxford. Lady Denbigh, wife of the 7th earl (chairman of the trustees of Rugby School), died Dec. 16, 1842, from a "disease of the brain," not (as was rumored and reported) from "fright occasioned by witnessing" an accident; a number of Rugbeians, including Tait, were present at her funeral (*The Times*, Dec. 20, 24, 27, pp. 4, 4, 5).

Nux Vomica (the word *strychnine* was a neologism) and sulphur were both laxatives, and Arnold may be only half playful.

10. Arthur Penrhyn Stanley (1815–81: *DNB*; *VF*, 9/21/72), dean of Westminster from 1864 till his death, son of a bishop and nephew of Lord Stanley of Alderley, had been at Rugby under Arnold and then at Balliol and was at this time a fellow of University College (tutor 1843–51). He was always close to the Arnold family and to Matthew Arnold personally, and his name occurs often in these letters, not merely for his life of Dr Arnold. Arnold was "quite as fond" of Stanley as of Clough (see below his letter to Coleridge, Jan. 10. 1882, about his elegy on Stanley, "Westminster Abbey"—Allott, p. 595).

Stanley's charm (like his atrocious handwriting) was celebrated. W. C. Lake "used to say that Stanley never was a boy; he left school as he entered it, something between a girl and a man," and Jenny Lind reported that "he had no ear and hated music, or at least was bored by it, [and] usually left the room when she warbled," his favorite instrument being the drum (Tuckwell, pp. 196, 80). Of this "child of light," as Arnold called him, F. W. Farrar wrote: "His was the purest, most childlike, most beautiful spirit I have ever known" (*Men I Have Known*, p. 125). See also *Album*, pp. 90, 100–101, and above p. 46 and n. 4.

11. *Two Sermons on the Interpretation of Prophecy* 1839. *The Christian Life: its hopes, its fears, and its close*, ed. M. Arnold, 1842, 1845; 1878, 3d edn ed. Jane Arnold Forster, as vol. 5 of *Sermons*.

12. Frederick William Faber (1814–63: *DNB*), at Balliol (Newdigate prizeman) a decade before Arnold and, from 1837 to the date of this letter, a figure in Ambleside, which he was now quitting to become rector at Elton, Hunts., was a preacher, theologian, and author of hymns mainly used by the church that, in Newman's steps, he abandoned in 1845. His volume was *The Styrian Lake and Other Poems* (1843).

13. Sir John Taylor Coleridge (1790–1876: *DNB*), nephew of the poet and justice of the King's Bench from 1835 (resigned 1858).

Henry James Coleridge (1822–93: *DNB*), Eton and Trinity College, Oxford, and a fellow of Oriel College. Ordained an Anglican, he converted to Roman Catholicism in 1852 and became a Jesuit priest. In the 1860s he moved from Wales to Farm Street, London, where Arnold sometimes heard him preach in the church there.

To John Duke Coleridge

Fox How

My dear Coleridge   Tuesday, [April 11, 1843][1]

I was glad to find by a quotation from your letter to Stanley about a week or ten days ago that like a discerning Person you had hit upon the right reason for my silence and not had recourse to those miserable Insinuations about Laziness Carelessness and so on which too many of my friends are apt to indulge in on similar occasions. But your Letter certainly deserves an answer: tho: I shall see you again I hope so soon, that I had many doubts about writing. Also I must premise that I use the word answer in it's most general and extended Sense, as I have left your Letter behind me at Oxford, and it is rather a hopeless business to take Shots at what I believe you to have said. One thing I do remember: tho: not the exact expressions you used, in all their original Pointedness: however ⟨the⟩ it was to the effect that I was slow in writing, which is the melancholy Truth: though melancholy, I believe, more because it adds to one's Trouble, than because what one writes suffers by it. It is certainly possible to be too slow: that is to go on for ever with a Pen in your hand, never able to set oneself steadily to the work before one: but if one is really working, and delayed merely by being unable to satisfy oneself easily, I cannot think that the Time is wasted. As a boy I used to write very quickly: and I declare that at first it was with an effort that I compelled myself to write more slowly and carefully: though I am ready to confess that now I could not write quicker if I would. So that if, as I believe, you did me the honour to associate me with yourself in this defect, I think we may both console ourselves with the Reflection that all we write ought to be the better for it: whether it is or no. One gets more and more incredulous too, as to those prodigies of intellectual Exertion, by which works that are to endure for centuries are thrown off in a month: tho: of course this extreme rapidity did once seem very fine to us and very much to be envied.

But if People are to be allowed to write very slow, they ought I confess to write very constantly, or there is a great stiffness about their Productions when they are complete. This is a great fault in my Poem,[2] and is ludicrously enough united with the fault of over Rapidity in the last Part which I had to finish in two or three days. However some of it, I think, is fairly good: though it's chance of winning is of the smallest. There are faults in the construction which alarm Stanley terribly: and I should think the construction of a Prize Poem ought to be conducted on certain fixt Principles: and would be, and very fairly, made a Point of great Importance. But I should think you were beginning to feel that you had had nearly enough on this subject.—

—I came up here in the full expectation of being able to devote myself to the great delight of the year, fly-fishing: but we have had January weather, and the ground last night and this morning has been covered with Snow. You cannot conceive the delight I find in my solitary fishing among the mountains here: indeed I am glad you cannot or you would certainly regard it with the same lordly Contempt, with which Hawker complains that you look upon his Attachment to Coaches. Tho: indeed I am bound to consider my Taste as the superior one of the two: so much so that it is absolutely above contempt. I do not think I should care so much for it any where else: tho: on Dartmoor I do not see what else will be left for me to do: tho: Hawker would tell you that he had a catalogue of amusements and occupations sufficient to absorb every hour of our stay down there.[3] However the only definite ones appear to be, playing cricket with some club twelve Miles off: and

I have not the slightest idea of exhibiting myself in this capacity: and of riding Devonshire Ponies up and down ascents and declivities which he himself owns to be covered with Masses of Granite, tho: he asserts the Turf itself to be of the most Exquisite Softness when you get upon it: and for exploits of this kind I have not yet acquired sufficient Taste, or I am afraid sufficient Nerve.

How gloriously beautiful North Leach Church is! You must know it, I suppose, being architectural, by Pictures if not by having actually seen it. Even I, who am profoundly ignorant on the subject, was perfectly astonisht that I had never heard of it. It reminded me extremely of a Cathedral Church I had seen in the North of France, at Mantes. I did not expect to have arrived at crossing, so must come to an abrupt conclusion. Will you make my respects to your Father, and remember me very kindly to your brothers and believe me to remain   affectionately your's

M. Arnold.—

MS. Lord Coleridge.

1. Imaginatively dated Mar. 2, 1843 (without brackets) in Coleridge, 1 : 123. London had a "heavy fall of snow towards daylight" with temperatures from 36 to 45 degrees F on Apr. 13 (*The Times*, Apr. 14, p. 6; "Meteorological Diary," *Gentleman's Magazine*, May). No other snow is recorded after Feb. 17, Mar. 2 fell on Thursday, and Arnold would not have gone to Westmorland for fly-fishing in term.

2. "Cromwell" (Allott, p. 13).

3. Brimpts, Ashburton, Devonshire.

To Laura Ward Greenhill

My dear Laura   Thursday, [? June 15, 1843]

I am afraid it is really impossible for me to dine out again before Collections: for I am actually loaded with work, and I have to dine out to night: to: morrow Evening too is always my busiest one, as we have an Essay to do. I shall probably not go down till Monday week, so that I shall see you two or three times before I go.   Your's very affectionately

M. Arnold.—

MS. Bodleian Library.

1. Collections are the college examinations at the end of any term. In Dec. 1842 Collections were Dec. 10–14; in 1843 Mar. 29–31 and June 22–24. Kenny (p. 231) notes an English Essay and Latin Essay for June 14 and 15, and on the 14th "Prizes Mat.," apparently the Newdigate Prize for "Cromwell," which was to be recited at Commemoration on June 28. If Arnold had gone down on "Monday week" as he said, the date would have been Monday, June 26. In any case he left Oxford on Thursday or Friday,

June 29 or 30, with J. Manley Hawker to visit Hawker at Brimpts, Devonshire (Coleridge, I : 128 – 29). See Warren Anderson, "Arnold's Undergraduate Syllabus," *The Arnoldian* 6 (Winter 1979):2 – 6.

John Manley Hawker to John Duke Coleridge

Brimpts
July 3, 1843

We arrived here on Friday evening after sundry displays of the most consummate coolness on the part of our friend Matt, who pleasantly induced a belief into the passengers of the coach that I was a poor mad gentleman, and that he was my keeper. In Exeter we saw Waite, Mackarness, Farrer, and your brother, for a few minutes, just as they were starting—Mackarness very pleasant and lordly! Arnold, at present, hardly acknowledges that there is anything to admire in the glorious scenery about here, and says that the hills are lumpy. I have never seen the Lake country, therefore cannot enter the lists of comparison, but I cannot think that it is so much more beautiful than Devonshire. This is a stupid epistle, but Arnold has been bothering me in the early part of it, and it is past bedtime now (ten o'clock). So good-night![1]

Text: Coleridge, 1 : 29.

1. "In another letter dated August 12, he reverts to Arnold's depreciation of Devonshire. 'I am fully prepared to do justice to Westmoreland, but I must confess that the one-sided views of our friend Matt. would urge one very strongly to retaliate in his own coin. It certainly is most trying to hear a man say of a county which you have for years been accustomed to admire in every shape and under aspect, "This is nice, *when* it has the sun upon it," in a sort of patronising concession to me' " (Coleridge, I : 129n).

To John Duke Coleridge

Brimpts, Ashburton
My dear Coleridge   Friday, [August 4, 1843]

If I did not answer your letter by return of Post you would scarcely get an answer before I left the country: for my original Plan of staying here six weeks was altered by finding that my Brothers went back to Rugby on the 12th,[1] and that I must cut my time here shorter in order to catch them at Fox: How: and one of them whom I have not seen for a year I was particularly anxious not to miss. Therefore I leave Ashburton on Sunday next (Sunday travelling, to judge from the Coaches we see, appears to be a Devonshire Custom), sleep in Exeter that night, and go straight on the next day, arriving at Ambleside on Tuesday morning, and so home. I am really very sorry that I cannot come to you: but I think from what you say, that even if I had stayed here as long as I at first intended, our times would scarcely have suited if you had to go the last Part of the Circuit. If you are so near us as Teignmouth, I do not see why you should not rush over the intervening Moor, and appear here on Sunday morning, just in time to witness the touching Sorrow of our little Circle at the first Parting, and to attend the Performance of a most extraordinary Individual in Ashburton—Individual, who has already electri-fied us for two Sundays. The journey of twenty one miles too in the bracing air of these wild and picturesque Moors (guidebook style) would do you the greatest good: and your sadly luxurious tastes would not be, I think, intoler-ably shockt, by a single day's Experience of our rigid simplicity of living.—

—I do really think that I should have written to you without waiting for your letter if I had known earlier of your illness: but being a sadly irregular letter writer, I always expect my Correspondents, unreasonably perhaps, to stimulate me by their expressions of doubt and distrust in their own first letters, to astonish them by a speedy and immediate Reply. I really hoped you had got perfectly rid of your illness: and certainly you managed to con-ceal it well enough at Oxford, as I who imagine myself to be an observer of faces never conceived that there was anything the matter with you, except that you were a great deal worried by having many things to do. And this reminds me that I have never congratulated you on the Result of the chief among these many things to do: your Election at Exeter.[2] After your disap-pointments by illness, I am extremely glad that you have finisht with that most pleasant and graceful Conclusion of an Oxford Life, an open Fellow-ship: and I need not say how pleasant it will be to have you for an additional year in Oxford, on my own account: and on your's too, if you think it will really be for your happiness to spend one year more in Oxford with no par-ticular Employment, before you proceed to set to work in earnest at what you intend to be an actual business in Life. But I grow didactic.

I am sure I am very glad if you are pleased with the Results of the Archbishops's letter; and Mr Richard Greswell's Conduct,[3] (of the gentleman himself I am entirely ignorant) seems worthy of all admiration. I had the high Privilege of becoming pretty intimately acquainted with the contents of the letter, as I happened to hear it read no less than three times: with the accom-panying Privilege of assisting at the Collection. But I cannot think so highly and hopefully as you do of a scheme, however nobly supported, which is no more than a scheme of authorized subscription, and a scheme which builds churches instead of endowing clergymen.—

—See what it is to say rash things: I had quite forgotten my unfortunate assertion that Devonshire was overpraised: and you now bring it forward to throw suspicion on my judgement. But of my judgement I abate nothing: the Rivers and Valleys are fine, and Holne Chase is beautiful: but the hills seem to me worth very little except for the sake of that sublimest of stones, granite, of which they are composed. But I must be altogether wrong about Devonshire: for dining the other Evening with the Revd Hamilton South-combe, our Curate,[4] he and a man of the name of Grainger[5] (so I took it) decided positively and authoritatively that Devonshire was pre-eminent in beauty among the English Counties, and teemed with great Men: and re-markt at the same time with great force and shrewdness on the singular In-sensibility of Devonshire Men to their own merits and their County's, and the very reprehensible silence they maintained on the subject. Undoubtedly they must know being Devonshire Men: & so of course I must have been quite wrong.—

Pray come here, or write: if you do not write at once, direct to me at Fox: How.   Ever affectionately yours,

M. Arnold.—

MS. Lord Coleridge.

1. Edward and William.
2. He was "elected to a Fellowship at Exeter College" on June 30 (Coleridge, 1:118).
3. Unaccountably, the paragraph was silently omitted in Coleridge, 1:132. Richard Greswell (1800–1881: *DNB*), for thirty years fellow and tutor of Worcester College, Oxford, is remembered as the man who infused new life into the National Society for Promoting the Education of the Poor in the Principles of the Established Church: "In 1843 he opened a subscription on behalf of national education, with a donation of 1,000£, and ultimately raised 250,000£ for the funds of the National Society" (*DNB*). The long letter of the archbishop of Canterbury, William Howley (1766–1848: *DNB*), president of the National Society, was dated July 5 and published in the *Record*, Aug. 10, p. [3]. Later in the year he recharged the fund-raising campaign year with a letter from the queen soliciting support to be read at every service from every pulpit (*The Times*, Dec. 9, 1843, p. 5). See Arnold's late essay "Schools in the Reign of Queen Victoria" (Super, 11:210–45).
4. The Rev. J. L. Hamilton Southcombe (born c. 1818), from Honiton House, Devon, matriculated from All Souls' College in 1836, age 18, took a B.A. in 1840. White's *Devonshire* identifies him as curate at the Vicarage, Dunsford.
5. Probably *Granger*, the usual Devonshire spelling, and perhaps (*faute de mieux*) the Rev. Thomas Granger, Maddocks Row, Exeter (White, *Devonshire*, p. 129). At least three Southcombes had Granger as a middle name. Foster lists no Grainger from Devonshire or thereabouts (none from elsewhere who would fit here) and three Grangers from Devon-shire, one from Dorset, all 18th c.

To Mary Penrose Arnold

Balliol

My dearest Mother   Sunday, [*c.* June 1844]

If I had seen before yesterday your letter to Mary, in which you said that having had a great deal of writing lately you should wait for me to write again before you wrote, this week should not have past without it's due letter. But remembering that your letter which I got on the morning of last Wednesday week, was but the answer due to my letter of the Tuesday week before, I had indignantly waited for nine days expecting an answer to my last letter, and finding none. I have not been regular to my day this term, but I am sure a week has never passed without it's letter, and as for Tom I have seen some of his letters as he wrote them, not their contents but their size, and I am sure they seldom contain more than half the writing of mine, some of which too have been double ones. However while I repel complaints, I confess that I would have written in a moment if I could have known that you wished and waited for it, or even if I had known that you wished me to speak about the Memoir, beyond what you had heard me say at Fox: How.[1]

—There is not much for me to say—except as to the body of letters which I had not seen and which delight me: I did not know, even if I may have thought, that he had felt or entered upon many of the difficulties there discussed: and on whatever subjects he touches he seems in these letters, above all other Places, to have got a free full expression of himself: the compass of a letter constrains him to be pithy, and the writing to one man instead of to the world lets him open his heart as wide as he likes. It often does happen that the rough sketch a man throws off says more about him than the same sketch filled up and transferred in all it's fulness into a book: but with him it is not only more characteristic, but infinitely more pregnant with meaning: to us particularly who can supply what is absolutely necessary, from having known him, and no more than we want, on questions of Church, and of religious belief, (wishing only that he had sometimes begun a little farther back) I could not have believed I should find anything to enjoy so fully and so fully to go along with. What I have always thought clean conclusive, as he would have said, against the completeness of Newman's system, making it impossible that it should ever satisfy the whole of any man's nature, and which I have no doubt now I may have heard him say, is most characteristically put out in the cxxxth Letter.[2] As to other People, it seems to give no offence, or rather the offence is absorbed in the Interest: I believe so, really: Stanley is not much mentioned; I have heard him praised for the School-chapter: he himself is well content that it should be so; he says People want more anecdote which he can give in a second Edition. Coleridge abused one or two Parts, but his Criticism is generally sad stuff: and admired the school teaching open-mouthed, especially by contrast with Hawtrey's.[3] I think myself there is a little Repetition in the Letters: so many on the same subject, for which things said and done by him might well be substituted. The sale in Oxford seems to have been very good: but Stanley has heard nothing from Fellowes about this.[4] It has cost Bloxham[5] and a Fellow of Magdalen or two, sleepless nights. Men whose names you do not know, and who knew his works but little, or gathered little of his Greatness from them, speak, I believe, most warmly: I of course, hear less than others. Temple,[6] a fellow and Tutor here, says he discovers in this Book the substance of all he has ever heard any Rugby man ever say. You have seen Moberly's letter, I believe.—I will not delay to send this now: but I will continue on other subjects this evening: only let me ask for my allowance to be paid as soon as possible: you shall have my exhibition before June ends. I am in an awful state of want: with absolutely only one shilling and six Pence in the world, and [?]Daman staring me in the Face.[7] For my rooms I get nothing till the end of next Term, so there is no present Relief from them. However the throats of all my great old Debts, Giants, Pope & Pagan,[8] are well cut. Prevail on the children to remember me by constant Pinches, and remember me to Henrietta,[9] who I know admires my Beauty on Trust. I am very kind to Mary.   Ever your most loving Son

M. Arnold.—

MS. Balliol College.

1. Stanley, published May 31, 1844 (Honan, p. 71).
2. To Sir Thomas Pasley, Dec. 14, 1836, in the first edition. (This letter became no. 148 in the second and third editions, no. 152 in the fourth and fifth.)
3. Edward Craven Hawtrey (1789–1862: *DNB*), headmaster at Eton, but later (1852–62) provost.
4. For Fellowes see above p. 47 n. 3.
5. John Rouse Bloxam (1807–91: *DNB*) maintained an improbable equilibrium between extremes of Rugbeianism and Tractarianism. He, his father (a master at Rugby School for 38 years), and his five brothers were all old Rugbeians; and he was not only a fellow (as well as dean of the arts, bursar, vice-president, etc.) of Magdalen College, Oxford, but also for several years Newman's curate at Littlemore, the "incarnation of all that was ideal in the College, its mediævalism, sentiment, piety . . . [and] the first man to appear in Oxford wearing the long collarless coat, white stock, high waistcoat, which form nowadays the inartistic clerical uniform" (Tuckwell, p. 165).
6. Frederick Temple (1821–1902: *DNB*; *VF*, 11/6/69) moved onward and upward—see below p. 118 n.
7. Probably Charles Daman (born c. 1802), fellow Oriel, 1836–42, tutor 1837–66 (Foster).
8. Bunyan, *The Pilgrim's Progress.*
9. Henrietta Whately (see below pp. 74 n. 1, 166 n. 17).

To John Duke Coleridge

Patterdale

My dear Coleridge   July 28, [1844]

It is difficult for me to know in what terms to express myself after your last letter: so completely is it penetrated with that unfortunate error as to my want of Interest in my Friends which you say thay have begun to attribute to me. It is an old subject which I need not discuss over again with you: the accusation, as you say, is not true: I laugh too much, and they make one's laughter mean too much. However the Result is that when one wishes to be serious one cannot but fear a half suspicion on one's Friends' Parts that one is laughing: and so the difficulty gets worse and worse: so much so that it is impossible for me to say more about your marriage than that I congratulate you, which I do very sincerely.[1] I know you are shaking your Head. You told it me, you know, as briefly as you could, and as late as you could, and it is a delicate subject at best. If it had been left, though, for some of your Friends to tell me, the Congratulation would have been left for a personal Interview: for I was not likely to hear of it in this deep seclusion, and should have gone back to Oxford in Ignorance. It was a great surprise: I had heard you speculate too in so disengaged a way, but a few months before, on the Desirableness of Marriage. Mais nous avons changé tout cela.[2] I see I shall be incurring fresh Suspicions, so I shall quit the subject: I could speak on it more freely than I can write.—

—For the Poems I have to thank you, too. I should have been very sorry if these same unworthy Suspicions had restrained you from sending them to me. I certainly do not value them most as a Bibliomaniac; you knew that I should be very much interested in reading them. Some I found I had read before in the Eton Bureau,[3] and those some of the longest: I think you told me the authorship of each as it came out. I like some of the new ones best: best of all some Stanzas which I think are to Prichard[4] beginning "I reverence thee." This I like very much: some of the earlier Poems to young Gentlemen puzzled me in naming their objects. The printing them publicly could have shocked nobody: but I am glad that being in some sort a Revelation of the Spirit, as your Uncle[5] says, you set an Example of printing such things privately. Though he says it of Milton, and no one less: so it is no Reproach: and, generally, your's do fall into the great class headed by Milton as opposed to the other class headed by Shakespeare tho: both he & you are votaries of the "imaginative Passion": our Friend young [?]Germany would express the two classes by two words, which I hold myself bound, till my degree is taken, to abstain from.[6]—I have not written as I could have wished, but the Reproaches of your letter marred the Frankness of mine. Will you tell me when you shall be called to the Bar, and if you come back next Term?[7] Will you also make my best Respects to your Father, & believe me,   ever your's affectionately

M. Arnold.—

Clough & Walrond send their best Congratulations.

MS. Lord Coleridge.

1. On Aug. 11, 1846, Coleridge married Jane Fortescue Seymour, sister of his Eton and Balliol friend John Billingsley Seymour, son of the Rev. George Turner Seymour, of Farringford, Isle of Wight, where the wedding took place.

2. Molière, *Le Médecin malgré lui* 2.6.

3. "Between November 1842 and November 1843, seven numbers [of the *Eton Bureau*] were issued. Coleridge contributed at least six prose and some fifteen or more pieces of verse. He reprinted the poetry, or most of it, in *Memorials of Oxford,* a booklet printed, but 'not published,' in 1844, and which forms the first part of *Verses during Forty Years,* a larger volume, printed for private circulation in 1879" (Coleridge, 1 : 105).

4. Constantine Estlin Prichard (c. 1820–69), Balliol College, B.A. 1841, fellow 1842–54, M.A. 1845, vice-principal Wells College 1847, prebend Wells 1852, rector of South Luffenham, Lincoln, 1854–69 (Foster). He was one of Coleridge's "most intimate friends" (Coleridge, 1 : 50n).

5. Samuel Taylor Coleridge, his great-uncle: "In the Paradise Lost the sublimest parts are the revelations of Milton's own mind, producing itself and evolving its own greatness" (Lecture 10, *A Course of Lectures* in *Literary Remains*).

6. The meaning is not certain. The transcription (helplessly) follows E. H. Coleridge (1 : 146), who glosses it: "'Objective' and 'Subjective,' one may suppose." For "Young Germany" see below p. 148 n. 1.

7. Coleridge did *not* return to Exeter College; he was called to the bar in November.

To Arthur Hugh Clough

[?Fox How] [? December, 1844][1]

Ye too, who stand beside the hoary Throne,
Where Time, else dumb, hath signified his Sway,
  To the blind slaves of Power to make it known
Material Grandeurs do in Heaven decay,
  —Keep all, o keep, continual holiday!
And let—&c[2]

—wch whence it proceeds you do not know: You mean INDIANA'S LET-TER, without which I think the book not preeminent among the Author's other novels. "Believe me," (I quote from Memory)—"if a Being so vast deigned to take any Part in our miserable Interests, it would be to raise up the weak, and to beat down the strong:—it would be to pass his heavy hand over our heads, and to level them like the waters of the Sea:—to say to the Slave, 'Throw away thy chain,'—and to the Strong, 'Bear thy Brother's bur-den: for I have given him strength and wisdom, and thou shalt oppress him no longer.'[3]—And the correspondence of Jacques & Sylvia—the Sunday Shoes letter you remember. But never without a Pang do I hear of the grow-ing Popularity of a strong minded writer. Then I know what hideosities[4] what Solecisms, what Lies, what crudities, what distortions, what Grimaces, what affectations, what disown[m]ents of that Trimmer-X-Hannah-More-typed[5] spirit they are of, I shall hear and see amongst the born-to-be-tight-laced of my friends and acquaintance: then I know the strong minded writer will lose his self-knowledge, and talk of his usefulness and imagine himself a Reformer, instead of an Exhibition. Rightly considered, a Code-G.-Sand[6] would make G. Sands impossible. The true world for my love to live in is, a general Torpor, with here & there a laughing or a crying Philosopher. And whilst my misguided Relation[7] exchanges the decency God dressed his Features in for the déshabille of an Emotee, we, my love, lovers of one another and fellow worshippers of Isis, while we believe in the Universality of Passion as Passion, will keep pure our Æsthetics by remembering its one-sidedness as doctrine. Oh my love suffer me to stop a little.—Very much later, almost night. Oh my love, goodnight.

M. Arnold.—[8]

MS. Yale University

1. Lowry (p. 58) suggested something like Feb.-Mar. 1845 from Rugby.

2. Allott, p. 645. The speaker may be Mycerinus.

3. The relevant excerpts from George Sand's novels *Indiana* (1831) and *Jacques* (1834) are printed by Lowry, pp. 167–68.

4. "Hideosity," *OED* 1856; "Emotee," below, not in *OED*.

5. Mrs Sarah Trimmer (1741–1810: *DNB*), author of children's books, exemplary tales, and edifying works: "Of Mrs Trimmer's books on education," Byron, *Don Juan* 1.123. Hannah More (1745–1843: *DNB*), author of moral and religious treaties: "'Coeleb's Wife' set out in quest of lovers," *Don Juan* 1.124 (her most popular work was *Coelebs in Search of a Wife*, 1809).

6. Cf. Code Napoléon, Code civile: "George Sand's fresh and living views of society, if hardened into law, would . . . lose their vital freedom and play" (Lowry, p. 59).

7. Tom Arnold is presumably the "misguided Relation."

8. Following the signature are what may be three reversed, angled, marching uppercase letter Rs, a scribbled irregular arabesque, and another symbol somewhat like a footed uppercase A.

William Wordsworth to Isabella Fenwick

[Saturday,] January 25, 1845

Did we tell you that Mr Robinson and some of the Arnolds were present when Mrs Winyard performed upon Jane. Mary Arnold has taken most accurate memorandums of all that occurred, and you may see them yourself, but it should seem that nothing at all decisive happened, except that when the organ of veneration was touched the sleeper assumed an attitude and expression of devotion more beautiful than anything he, Mr R, ever beheld.

When Miss M[artineau] drank tea at Mrs Arnold's on *Thursday*, Mrs Wynyard could not be of the Party, because Jane was by all means to be mesmerised on *that* day, it being *Thursday*, and on Thursdays the effects are always the *most striking*.

Text. *The Letters of William and Dorothy Wordsworth*, ed. Ernest de Selincourt, rev. Alan G. Hill, 7: 654 (extract).

To Arthur Hugh Clough

Rugby
My dear Clough   Wednesday, [?March 5, 1845][1]
     Your letters touched on business, and therefore tho: one is lost, I will try and say something. First my love to Walrond, with a reference to the Corner of the 11th Page of my 7th Tract—where he will find that "the Rewards of intellectual ambition are at best transitory: but a quiet Conscience is an unfailing Friend."[2] He being thus soothed, and Tom being waived; as surely written in my heart, and Pits,[3] as surely soon to be written to with Paper and Ink, let me say that a faint Image of my present Labours may be shadowed forth under the Figure of Satan, perambulating under the most unfavourable circumstances, a populous neighbourhood thro: which I have lately passed distributing Tracts: which reminds me that I do not give satisfaction at the Master's Meetings. For the other day when Tait had well observed that strict Calvinism devoted 1000s of mankind to be eternally,—and paused—I, with, I trust the true Xtian Simplicity suggested "———", Which was yet nothing to that plainer saying of P. Arnold's[4] at the same meeting, when, disparaging the Qualifications of Mayor as a Master,[5] and ungenerously taunting him with an inborn stiffness of carriage, he remarked that "Hell fire would not make him dance."
     —But you are not to suppose that these Druidical Remains,[6] these touches, if I may so speak, of the aboriginal Briton, are found often among the stately Edifices of our Magistracy: nor yet are you not to suppose that it is so late at night that this licentious Pen wanders whither it will. True, I give satisfaction—but to whom? True, I have yet been late on no Morning, but do I come behind in no thing? True, I search the Exercises, but the Spirits?—For which Reason it seems not clear why I should stand at Oriel: for wisdom I have not, nor skilfulness—after the Flesh—no, nor yet Learning: and wh[o] will see a delicate Spirit tossed on Earth, opossumlike, with the down fresh upon him, from the maternal Pouches of nature,[7] in the grimed and rusty coalheaver, sweating and grunting

> with the Burden of an honour
> Unto which he was not born.—[8]

I have other ways to go. But you may tell Congreve[9] as to the stabling—that is not the business: but the Business is between us two, and I feel his kindness. I hear a huge form, the Lower 5th. He will get a hundred Pounds from Easter till June. He is free on the 28th of June. Till then he lodges not takes Possession: would the Varlet push dying Men from their stools?[10] And the same to you.

—But, my dear Clough, have you a great Force of Character? That is the true Question. For me, I am a reed, a very whoreson Bullrush: yet such as I am, I give satisfaction. Which you will find to be nothing—nor yet is a patent Simulation[11] open to all men, nor to all satisfactory. But to be listless when you should be on Fire: to be full of headaches when you should slap your Thigh: to be rolling Paper Balls when you should be weaving fifty Spirits into one: to be raining when you had been better thundering: to be damped with a dull ditchwater,[12] while in one school near you sputters and explodes a fiery tailed Rocket, and in the rest patent Simulators ceaselessly revolve: to be all this, and to know it—O my Clough—, in the [?this] house they find the Lodger in Apricot Marmalade for two meals a day—and yet?— But, my love, the clock reminds me that I long since sung,

"Night comes:—with night comes Silence, hand in hand:—
With night comes Silence, & with that, Repose:—
And pillows on her frozen breast, and locks
Within the Marble Prison of her arms
The 'Usher's' rash & feverish Melancholy:
Cuts short the Feignings of fantastic Grief,
Freezes the sweet strain on the parted Lips,
And steals the honied Music of his Tongue—["][13]

—Which last two Lines, I perceive, hang loosely around the Point. In drowsiness and heaviness, Goodnight, and love to all.   ever your's lovingly

M. Arnold.—

MS. *Yale University.*

1. Arnold left Fox How on Jan. 20 for Oxford, where he remained till Feb. 24, was at Rugby till Mar. 22, and then returned to Oxford for exactly a week. He got the Oriel fellowship on Mar. 28.

Lowry dated the letter "shortly before March 28." The last date possible is the Wednesday before Easter (Mar. 23), but Arnold says "I have yet been late [for prayers] on no Morning," a claim he could not truthfully have made after Mar. 6 (he was also late on Mar. 12 and 18) (MS diary, Yale).

2. Untraced. Perhaps Arnold's own.
3. Unidentified, probably a nickname.
4. Plug Arnold, the Rev. Charles Thomas Arnold (1817–78), son of the Rev.

Aldous Arnold, of Ellough, Beccles, Suffolk, entered Rugby in Oct. 1831; Balliol 1836; scholar of Magdalen Hall, B A., second class in classics 1840, M.A. 1843. He became an assistant master at Rugby under Dr. Arnold in 1841 and remained there till his death (Rome, May 9, 1878), and according to Tait (quoted in Knight, *Principal Shairp and His Friends*, p. 130) he was specially interested in German literature. In 1841 Clough wrote (Mulhauser, 1:113) "Pfl. [for *Pfropf*, plug?] Arnold is going to be married." He was ordained by the bishop of Worcester in 1842. See below p. 117 n. 3.

5. Charles Mayor (c. 1815–1846, Aug. 31). "Son of the Rev. J. Mayor, Collingham, Notts. Exhibitioner 1833. Trinity College, Cambridge. B.A. Fourth Classic, 1837. Assistant Master at Rugby, 1840–46. Died 31 August 1846. A Memorial Inscription written by the Rev. Charles Arnold is in the School Chapel" (Rugby, p. 238).

6. *OED* 1879.

7. "Are we Opossums; have we natural Pouches, like the Kangaroo?" (Carlyle, "Pure Reason," *Sartor Resartus*).

8. Tennyson, "The Lord of Burleigh," ll. 79–80.

9. Richard Congreve (1818–99: *DNB*), Rugby and Wadham College, Oxford, an English Positivist, was assistant master at Rugby in 1845. "Third son of Thomas Congreve, Esq. Combe, Warwickshire. . . . Editor of Aristotle's Politics and of several Essays and Publications, of which 'Human Catholicism' is the best known. Died 7 July 1899 (Rugby). Lowry cites Frederic Harrison, *Autobiographic Memoirs*, 1:83 ff. for "an interesting appreciation of his ability as a teacher."

10. *Macbeth* 3.482.

11. Carlylese, perhaps a variant of his "Patent Digester" in *Sartor Resartus* ("Incident in Modern History") and *Past and Present* ("Working Aristocracy," last sentence).

12. "Dull as ditchwater (*OED* 1844).

13. Lowry, p. 57: "a partial burlesque of one of Arnold's own early verses that appears among a collection of notes towards his poems, the manuscript of which is in possession of Professor C.B. Tinker, of Yale University" (printed in Allott, p. 639, and Ullman, *Yale Manuscript*, 63 [facsimile]-65). I do not think it is a burlesque, here or in Yale MS. It may derive from Shelley's "Alastor," esp. ll. 129–91 (Arab maiden).

To Thomas Trevenen Penrose[1]

Rugby

My dear Uncle Trevenen   Tuesday, April 8, [1845]

Since I heard from you in December I have never ceased intending to write & thank you for what you then said: but at the time I did not well know what to say. And I do not know why the getting this Fellowship should increase my Confidence: for tho: it may in some measure atone for the discredit of a second class in the Eyes of those who felt most the discredit of it, yet in real truth it leaves me, as to my reading, very much where I was before: and the truth is that the Examination was different, not that I deserved in April much more of a literary success than in November. But I know that you will be glad on many accounts for my good Fortune, tho: it was not the discredit of my class that would have most grieved you: and at all events I am glad it gives me an occasion to write, that I may say, tho: late, how much I felt the kindness of your letter in December.

I am exceedingly glad that the Election is one the Circumstances of which will delight them so much at home: besides that the College was Oriel, the time was the 30th Anniversary exactly from the day Papa was elected at Oriel. We had nothing but modern Prayerbooks at hand in my rooms, which did not give the dates of Easter so far back as 1815:[2] so Tom went thro: an elaborate Computation, and discovered that Easter in that year fell within a day or two of Easter 1845: and the time of Election is always the same. I myself too am very glad that it gives me a certain Prospect of relieving Mamma of myself, tho: it is certainly not the first subject for delight that occurs to her: but there was much that made it wrong for me to go on after my degree doing nothing for myself, and as Pupils avoided me as a suspected Person, I was by no means safe of a livelihood without a Fellowship.—

I am glad that all Charles Penrose's former disappointments are so thoroughly justified: what could have been worse luck, as he can see it now, than his getting Fleetwood or Cheltenham,—Meanwhile John has been one of the authors of a disturbance here, which you may have heard of, now happily concluded.[3] Tait wished to put Congreve into Grenfell's Place as to Form as well as House: and all those whose heads he was raised over, fiercely resented the affront. Tait certainly managed the matter clumsily, and in a cowardly manner: but the difference between the Lower 5th and the Forms beneath it is so small as to make the disturbance for the sake of such small gains, almost ridiculous. The protesting masters thought that the step would lower them first in the Estimation of the world at large, and then, more particularly, in that of the parents of their Pupils: whereas, from all I can learn, the Parents would hardly have heard of so slight a Proceeding, and if they had heard, would not have cared two straws. It is settled now by Tait's making concessions equal to the Injury he inflicts: but none of them come out of it, I think, very greatly: and the fuss in school & Town has been prodigious. With all this I have little to do: for I leave Rugby, I hope, on Wednesday week, to reside for my Probationary year at Oxford: and tho: I have got on pretty well, and tho: the little Boys give me the greatest delight, yet the work is certainly too hard, and I should make but a very poor Schoolmaster. But on the whole I am glad to have been here these six weeks, & they are very glad of it, I think, at home.—With all love to my Aunt believe me   ever your's
                                                                M. Arnold.—

MS. Balliol College.

1. Thomas Trevenen Penrose (1793–1862), attended Corpus Christi College, Oxford, where he knew both John Keble and Thomas Arnold (who married his sister, Mary Penrose), both friends for life. In 1824 he married Susanna Brooke. He became vicar of

Coleby, Lincs, in 1828, and rector of Weston, Notts, in 1834. "From his earliest childhood he was the darling, as he was the youngest, of his large family. As a boy, and as a young man, he everywhere had a blameless name. Simple, manly, affectionate and gay, he won the love and respect of old and young alike. And what he was in youth he continued to be in manhood. It is not eary to convey the indescribable charm that made him so lovable. The mingled tenderness and strength of his character were marked characteristics" (Frances Arnold, his niece, in Baldwin, pp. 124–25). His sister "Jane Penrose . . . lived beside him in 'The Cottage' [at Coleby], and . . . survived him ten years, and died [in 1871] at the age of 87" (p. 127), but The Cottage also harbored his Aunt Peggy (d. 1834) and two other sisters, Elizabeth (d. 1831) and Lydia (d. 1842). A sketch of him, by the latter, in the pulpit at Coleby is on p. 95.

2. In 1815 Easter fell on Mar. 26, in 1845 on Mar. 23.

3. Charles Penrose (1816–68) and John Penrose (1815–88) were sons of Thomas Trevenen Penrose's brother John Penrose (1778–1859), vicar of Bracebridge. Charles (Rugby, Trinity College, Cambridge, B.A. 1836), headmaster of Grosvenor School, Bath, 1843–45, was headmaster of Sherborne School, 1845–55 (the justification referred to), curate of North Hykeham (near Bracebridge and Lincoln) 1856 and perpetual curate from 1857. He edited *Select Private Orations of Demosthenes with English Notes* (1843) and published *Eight Village Sermons* (1858). Lowry prints a letter from him to Arnold written Mar. 5, 1861.

Of the Rev. John Penrose we know less. According to Rugby, I:xix, he was educated at Winchester College (unlisted in Kirby's *Winchester Scholars*). He matriculated from Balliol College in July 1832 and was a fellow of Lincoln College 1837–43 (Foster); he was assistant master at Rugby 1839–46 (33, Bilton Road) and master of a school at Exmouth 1846–72. "Accounts of the school and of its discipline vary very much. Some distinguished men, whose earliest school years were spent there, speak of Mr. Penrose's severity, and of the Spartan regime which offered few of the amenities of life. All were agreed that Mr. Penrose was an exceptional man, and an exceptional teacher of classics and history, and it is fair to say that many of his pupils, including Oakeley Arnold-Forster himself, looked back with kindly and tolerant memories to the school, and with real affection and esteem for the able man who conducted it" (*The Right Honourable Hugh Oakeley Arnold-Forster: A Memoir by His Wife*, pp. 22–23). Penrose died in Norway on June 20, 1888.

To Susanna Elizabeth Lydia Arnold

My dearest Susy   [June, 1845][1]
  It is quite true that your answer was much more than my note deserved, is it possible you directed the Gun-case to MISS Westley Richards? I roared for half an hour, at the bare imagination of it. Thank you very much—I have heard from the Man, and it is all right. I must repeat what I said about Ruby—pray do not let Robin Clark overfeed her: I hate her being fat & it is very bad for her—a very little vegetable food is all she should have this weather. You will pay you know for this heat by a wet July.
  Your teeth indeed but think of mine—such agonies, O my. On Mon-

day the one Relief from the sure hand of Cartwright. Allow me to say my dear if you really suffer pain from a tooth, Bell[2] is quite fit to draw it: a girl's tooth or a woman's is just what those People can draw as well as Cartwright. His supernatural strength is only for the largest & firmest teeth: he is not particularly skilful. But when he pulls it comes. I shall begin to mumble soon. I will be bound you have been going on with our Grandmamma's Remedy for Camphorated spirits: take my profound experience for it my dear, you might as well use a little cotton wool wrapped round the point of a pen dipped into it, & thrust it into the hole—either leaving it there or not as you like. The advance on Kreosote is Oil of Cloves—mind that—do not let me speak in vain—applied in the same way—if that, wch is the strongest Remedy, fails, there is no remedy but an opiate: which I hope your Mother will not let you take. I had the strength of mind to resist it the other night: it brings on fever, [4 or 5 words inked over]

—So much for the Teeth. I will leave the subject now, adding that I have another old complaint, and another Inflammation of the Ear. Life is full of these agreeable surprizes. I always expect to wake with some new part gone wrong.

—After hunting Walter all over Oxford on Wednesday, Tom having taken charge of him, and removed him somewhere beyond all human sight, I heard the tramping as of a young cart horse behind me in the street towards evening: and turning round beheld Walter, with his hair parted in the middle by Edward's [?]case [?care ?cane] and fresh from bathing. He dined with me and his brothers in my rooms. I was surprized he did not seem more to regret leaving Harnish—he regarded the presents he had received pretty much as things to be expected. But the testimony to the excellence of the Place is that holidays after holidays one sees him unchanged—as easily moved as ever—and suspecting nothing & nobody. I trust he was not made ill at dinner: I looked after him—the next morning I was in bed with a night of toothache when he went away. Tell Mamma his cloth jackets are a hideous cruelty in this weather, poor child.

Edward I dare say as usual made a mountain out of a Molehill. I believe I shall go abroad this summer, which will do me good, I think & hope. John Penrose has offered to come to Auvergne with me: and to leave me in about a fortnight. This will save you my dear from about 3 Oxford Parties in the neighbourhood, the tutors to which I know, and must have asked, I fear. Love to Mamma and all. Lake is here, much better.   ever your loving brother—

M. Arnold.—

MS. Frederick Whitridge.

1. This is the only June when Edward, Thomas, and Matthew Arnold were in Oxford at the same time, and June was the only hot month before July—the thermometer reached 90 degrees.
2. Probably Thomas Bell, chemist and druggist, Ambleside (Martineau).

To William Henry Lucas

[Oriel College, ?October, 1846][1]

Dear Lucas

Have you a fourth? At 7 I will come or a little before. But mind, I cannot get a fourth.   In great haste

M. Arnold.

Bless you.

Text. Kenneth Allott, 'Matthew Arnold: Two Unpublished Letters,' Notes and Queries, Aug. 1955, p. 357.

1. This note, Lucas's invitation, and a later letter to Lucas (below p. 354) were published in "Matthew Arnold: Two Unpublished Letters," *Notes and Queries*, Aug. 1955, pp. 356–57, by Kenneth Allott, who dated the two whist notes "almost certainly between 28 March 1845, when Arnold was elected a Probationary Fellow of Oriel, and early December 1847, when he was already settled in London as private secretary to Lord Lansdowne." My date, neither more nor less reliable than any other specific possibility in Allott's limits (Sundays and vacations being excluded), is whimsical and sentimental; there is no other letter for 1846; and he lost £2 at whist in the "October term" (MS diary, Yale). As evidence, this is all but worthless, for Arnold, possibly the most scrupulous financial accountant in English poetry (sometimes with a basic version of double-entry bookkeeping), itemizes and tots up other whist losses and gains.

William Henry Lucas (1821–1919), "sometime canon of Winchester, who matriculated at Oxford in 1839, graduated in 1843 and was subsequently a fellow of Brasenose until 1852. After this date he held various curacies until he became Vicar of Sopley (Hants) in 1866. He knew Tom . . . more intimately than he knew Matthew Arnold" (Allott, *Notes and Queries*, p. 356). Arnold's note replies to Lucas's invitation, addressed "M. Arnold Esq—/ Oriel Coll:"—"Dear Arnold / Turner and I are alone in the Common room and longing for whist—come and take pity upon our forlorn condition—as soon as you like. / Yours very truly, / W. H. Lucas." Edward Tindal Turner (born c. 1822) was also a fellow of Brasenose and later vice-principal and, in 1870, registrar of the university.

Arthur Hugh Clough to John Campbell Shairp

My dear Shairp   [February 22, 1847]
. . . Matt is full of Parisianism; theatres in general, and Rachel in special: he enters the room with a chanson of Beranger's on his lips—for the sake of French words almost conscious of tune; his carriage shows him in fancy pa-

rading the rue de Rivoli;—and his hair is guiltless of English scissors: he breakfasts at twelve, and never dines in Hall, and in the week or 8 days rather (for 2 Sundays must be included) he has been to Chapel *once.*

Text: Mulhauser, 1:178–79.

Baron Bunsen to Mary Penrose Arnold

4 Carlton Terrace

My dear friend   28 April 1847

My oldest Son's wedding,[1] & then a long deferred visit to my second son, whence I returned only the night before last, have prevented me from wishing you joy directly for the happy event in your dear family. Allow me to do so now! We have already made attempts to secure seeing Mrs Twining, but found she was not yet in town.[2]

Now I must tell you what Lord Grey told me this morning, at the Queen's Levee, when I enquired after your excellent Son Tom. He said he had given him 3 or 4 difficult tasks, & he had done himself *great honour.* Among others he had given him an abstract to make of a great heap of papers, referring to that very complicated question, the property of the land to New Zealand, and he had made a capital report on the subject.[3]

When we were speaking on this subject, the Marquess of Lansdowne joined our conversation by saying: "That the eldest is with me as private Secretary, and does very well." I was very glad to hear this, to me new, piece of intelligence, for a confidential place like that of private Secretary to Lord L. is exactly a place where a young man of talents & acquirements can distinguish himself, & find that sort of steady intellectual employment, which I always thought so particularly desirable for your eldest Son.[4]

I am sure it will be gratifying to you to hear what those two Ministers said about your Sons: both are honest admirers of your great husband. We are expecting a visit from our Son Henry & his bride to-morrow. He will proceed to Lilleshall, as soon as a sprained arch will allow him to go about.

My two daughters in law are all I could ever pray for.

Frances hopes to be here before [the] end of May. They are at present at Venice. I hope George will accompany them: his eyes are still weak, & I want him to take care of them.[5]

With our united kindest regards, to all you dear ones,   Ever, my dear friend   Yours affectionately

Bunsen

MS. Balliol College.

1. "Bunsen, with his wife and the whole family, accompanied by the Prince Löwenstein, Prussian Secretary of the Legation, who was the 'best man' on the occasion, went to Stoke Park on April 14, in order to be present at the marriage of his eldest son, Henry, to Mary Louisa Harford-Battersby, which was celebrated on April 15, by Dr. Monk, Bishop of Gloucester and Bristol, previous to Henry Bunsen's institution to the vicarage of Lilleshall in Shropshire, to which he had been presented by the Duke of Sutherland" (Frances Baroness Bunsen, *Memoirs of Baron Bunsen*, 2d edn, abridged and corrected, 1869, 2:78).

2. Mary Arnold, who married William Aldred Twining, on Apr. 8, at Rydal (*Annual Register*).

3. "Mrs. Arnold used her influence to help him [Tom Arnold] to a post as préciswriter in the Colonial Office: here he was well-liked, and might soon have built himself a successful career" (*Letters of Thomas Arnold the Younger 1850–1900*, ed. James Bertram, p. xvii). Henry George Grey (1802–94: *DNB*), 3d earl, was secretary for the colonies 1846–52.

4. "Matthew Arnold had just become, to the surprise and slight scandal of his family, private secretary to Lord Lansdowne, then Lord President of the Council" (Bertram, p. 2n)

5. Bunsen had five sons and five daughters. The sons (see *DNB*): Henry (1818–55); Ernest (1819–1903) m. Elizabeth Gurney Aug. 5, 1845; Karl (1821–87); George (1824–96); Theodor (1832–92). The daughters (see Augustus J. C. Hare, *The Life and Letters of Baroness Bunsen*): Frances (b. 1826); Emilia (b. 1827); Mary Charlotte Elizabeth (b. 1829); Theodora (1832); and Augusta Matilda (b. 1837).

Edward Penrose Arnold to Mary Penrose Arnold[1]

Oxford

My Dearest Mother,   Wednesday, November 24, 1847

It is but a duty to write & tell you, were it not besides a great pleasure, of the last news of Tom, especially as I was the last of any of the family who saw him. On Saturday I went to London with the Master's leave to see Tom off thinking that he was going to sail on Sunday. That evening, he, Matt, Clough, Walrond and myself went to the Lyceum, where he was in very good spirits & laughed at part of the play a great deal. On Sunday we all went down to the London Docks together, calling by the way at Bedford Place, but K was out. After walking through some of the most intricate & poor parts of Wapping, we came to Shadwell Basin, & went on board the *John Wicliffe*. After a little delay we got into Tom's Cabin. He has it with another man, whose Berth is above Tom's. Matt joked a great deal about the smallness & closeness of the hold, but Tom did not in the least mind it. Clough indeed says, that it is a good-sized one for an emigrant ship, & that Tom is very lucky. I did not like to laugh at what was so serious a matter to Tom, but my firm conviction was that *I* could not live out a voyage of 5 months there. . . . [2]

We went all over the ship & then, after walking through the Thames Tunnel, & coming back in a boat to Execution Dock we went back in a Steamer to Westminster. In the evening I went to tea, & found Furnevall (a Lincoln's Inn man) & Edward Whately there[3] . . . . On Monday he (Tom), Clough, Willy & I dined together at Long's. Matt came in the middle of dinner to say he could not come, as Lansdowne was keeping him about the Speech. He gave Clough & me however tickets for the Princess's Theatre, as he could not go himself, & we saw Macready act in Philip van Artevelde for the first time.[4] The scenery was beautiful and Macready acted very well; but the play is too long in itself though curtailed immensely & essentially slow for acting. I sat next to Crabb Robinson, who is coming northwards before Christmas. . . .[5]

On Tuesday morning I breakfasted with Tom, & Clough went back to Oxford by the Express. After breakfast I went to Long's [6] & waited there till 1 for Matt who said that he would follow Tom with me to Gravesend. But then he found he must be with Lanny at 4, so that was impossible. We then went to Tom's Room. He had been gone 10 minutes, so we bolted into a Cab & set off for London Bridge as hard as we could. Just as we got there, we saw Tom with his luggage standing in the street. So we walked altogether with 3 porters & the luggage to the Station & went by rail to Blackwall. Here Matt was obliged to leave it being 3 o'clock, but as I found it was just possible to go to Gravesend & still be in time for the Great Western at 9 I determined to go on. When we got out on the Quay at Blackwall, Tom's spirits quite rose. After leaving the smoke & dirt of London here was the River with vessels of all shapes & sizes & a blood-red sun going down over London— the very image as Tom remarked of Turner's picture of the Old Temeraire. Tom was rather affected at leaving Matt. From the steam-boat he watched him till he disappeared in the Station & then I saw the tears in his eyes, as he leant over the Gunwale to look at the water. About 5 minutes after 3 we started, & thought it was very cold, yet it was a brilliant sunset, & the river with all its shipping is always beautiful, besides the banks above Erith & Greenhithe are very pretty. We paced the Deck talking till we arrived at Gravesend at ¼ to 5. I asked him if he felt the least inclination to change his mind were it possible. He said, not the least, that when he had made up his mind fully, he looked upon the thing as inevitable, besides that his wish to go was as strong as ever. The last I saw of him was his being pulled in a boat with his luggage out to the *John Wicliffe*, sitting in the stern, & then in the dusk I could see a light hung over the ship when the boat was alongside, & he went on board his home for the next 5 months. In 10 minutes I had to start back again: it was a lovely night: an almost full moon shining on the water & the ghostly ships which flow silent past us. I got to Blackwall at 20 minutes past 7, in Long's at ½ past 8 & to the station exactly in time, & was in my own rooms at ½ past 11 where I found a letter from you & Uncle. Oh how I love you.   Your fond son,

E. P. Arnold

I am very glad about Willy.[7]

Text: Hopkinson, pp. 23–25.

1. Edward Penrose Arnold was an undergraduate at Balliol College, under Richard Jenkyns as master.

2. Tom Arnold's reasons for emigrating to New Zealand were complex. His "conscious reasons," as Kenneth Allott put it, "were two: first, to discover a freer, happier, and more equitable social order than he saw around him in England in 1847; second, to discover his real self in independent isolation" (quoted in Introduction to Bertram, p. xxxii). Bertram points out (pp. xxviii-xxx) that in 1839 Dr Arnold, himself with dreams of emigration, "had invested in the New Zealand Company, acquiring what turned out to be two country sections of 100 acres each, and a town section" and adds that Tom Arnold, disillusioned with society and distrustful of self, was also disappointed in love, having been rejected by Henrietta Whately, daughter of the archbishop of Dublin; she was the sister of Tom's special friend Edward, named below.

3. Frederick James Furnivall (1825–1910: *DNB*), later famous as a scholar, editor, founder of literary societies (Early English Text, Chaucer, Ballad, New Shakspere, Wiclif, Shelley, Browning) and polemicist, had entered as a student at Lincoln's Inn in 1846 and was called to the bar at Gray's Inn three years later. He was one of the founding fathers of what is now the *OED*.

Edward William Whately (1823–1892), an amiable mediocrity whom Trollope would have relished, entered Rugby at the same time as Matthew Arnold, went on to Christ Church, and became archdeacon of Grandelagh in 1862, chancellor of St. Patrick's Cathedral 1862–71, and rector of Littleton, Middlesex, 1872–92. Tom Arnold, who traveled on the continent with the family in the summer 1839, and again in July 1846 (and mentions neither journey in *Passages in a Wandering Life*), maintained his friendship with Edward if not with his sister: "It was very nice of dear old Edward Whately to go to Oxford to see you," Tom Arnold wrote to his wife in 1887 (E. Jane Whately, *Life and Correspondence of Richard Whately*, 2:105–6; Boase; Bertram, p. 216).

4. At the Lyceum they saw John Maddison Morton's *Box and Cox*, at the Princess's Henry Taylor's *Philip van Artevelde*.

5. Henry Crabb Robinson (1775–1867: *DNB*), the diarist, formerly a foreign correspondent for *The Times*, was a man-about-town and friend of the great and famous (Wordsworth's "Companion! by whose buoyant Spirit cheered").

6. Long's Hotel Limited (Family), 15 and 16 New Bond Street.

7. William Delafield Arnold (*DNB*) sailed for India early in 1848 to become a cadet in the army of the East India Company, an experience that resulted in his novel *Oakfield* (1853). He died at Gibraltar on his way home in 1859 (see Matthew Arnold's poems "Stanzas from Carnac" and "A Southern Night"), and his four children were adopted by the William Forsters and took the name Arnold-Forster.

To Arthur Hugh Clough

London
Dear Clough   Wednesday, [? December 1, 1847]
Till Tuesday in next week I shall certainly be here, & probably
longer.—Blackett[1] wants me to pass the Nativity of our B. L. with him and
his sister at Brighton—But I am not earnestly bent on this.—You talked of
coming here on the 7th—Why not now till Saturday?—Everything in its
own order as Paul or Peter observes.[2] The 7 Spirits Poem[3] does well what it
attempts to do I think. Tho: I still ask why 7. This is the worst of the alle-
gorical—it instantly involves you in the unnecessary—and the unnecessary
is necessarily unpoetical.[4] Goly what a !!!Shite's!!! oracle! But profoundly
true.—Besides its trueness to its purpose, or constituting this, the feeling is
deep in the Poem, & simul[taneously] runs clear. Farewell David. Had I the
skill I had e'er Rudge flitted wormwards I would limn Bathsheba washing
herself.—Bring up my gold in the paniers of an ass. I spell *paniers* so.

M. Arnold

MS. Yale University.

1. John Fenwick Burgoyne Blackett (1821–56), of Wylam, Northumberland, and
of Marylebone, London, matriculated from Christ Church in May 1838, B.A. 1842, was
a fellow of Merton College, M.A. 1845, of Lincoln's Inn from June 1842; M.P. from
Newcastle-on-Tyne from 1852 to Jan. 1856. He wrote for the *Globe* (Foster; Lowry,
p. 118) He was very much in Arnold's inner circle of affectionate friends—Arnold borrowed money from him as freely as from Walrond or the family circle, as the 1851 Diary
reveals, and he was present at Arnold's wedding. He died Apr. 25, 1856, at Villeneuve sur
Yonne (for Arnold's response to the news of his death see below p. 337 (*Landed; Annual
Register*). Blackett's sister Frances Mary (Fanny du Quaire) became one of Arnold's closest
friends (see below p. 384 n. 1).
2. Paul—1 Corinthians 15:23.
3. "The Questioning Spirit," the opening poem of *Ambarvalia*; in manuscript the
first words (now "The human spirits") were "Seven human spirits" (*The Poems of Arthur
Hugh Clough*, 2d edn, ed. F.L. Mulhauser, p. 564).
4. The sense of the rest of the letter is not obvious. Arnold seems to mean that in
Clough's poem "the voice" (l. 26, the "questioning spirit," l. 38), though agnostic ("I also
know not, and I need not know"), is oracular because it enjoins duty, hope, and belief
without knowing why. This profound truth is unpleasant and the oracle is a therefore a
shite. ("Shites" is surrounded by curly lines and flanked by six exclamation points.)
David ("beloved") implies Jonathan: "The soul of Jonathan was knit with the soul
of David, and Jonathan loved him as his own soul" (1 Samuel 18:1). David ogles Bathsheba "washing herself" in 2 Samuel 11:3; Honan (p. 117) suggests that Arnold alludes to
an anecdote recorded in 1859: "Lord Lansdowne said that in his youth he had known the
famous beauty Mme. Taille. . . . Once she observed that he was looking at her and said,

"Vous croyez que je rougis, je vous prouverai le contraire," and she rang for a basin of water and a towel and washed herself before him" (Charles Lacaita, *An Italian Englishman, Sir James Lacaita*, p. 130).

Barnaby Rudge is hanged in ch. 77. "Bring up my gold" is unclear. (Perhaps Clough had borrowed money of Arnold?) "Paniers" (one *n*) is the French spelling.

To Arthur Hugh Clough

[London]

My dear Clough   [early December, 1847]

I have had so much reluctance to read these, which I now return that I surely must be destined to receive some good from them.[1]

—I have never been reminded of Wordsworth in reading them by rhythms or expressions: but of Tennyson sometimes & repeatedly of Milton—Little hast thou bested &c, e.g, sounds to me Miltonically thought & expressed.[2]

I have abstained from all general criticism, but here & there put a word agst an expression: but as it was done at a first reading, these are to be very slightly attended to.—It would amuse you to see how treatments differ, if you saw some things in which I have come on the same topics as you: those of your 4th poem. 1st vol.e.g.[3]

—The 2nd Poem in the 1st volume[4] I do not think—valuable—worthy of you—what is the word?

—And as a metrical curiosity the one about 2 musics does not seem to me happy.[5]

But on the whole I think they will stand very grandly, with Burbidge's "barbaric ruins" smirking around them.[6] I think too that they will give the warmest satisfaction to your friends who want to see something of your's. Stanley will have the "calf" one by heart the day it appears.[7] If I cannot come & see you, I will try to write.   Your's

                                                    M. Arnold.

Yale University.

1. "Arnold refers to two manuscript note-books in the present Clough collection. One of them contains fair copies of poems written from 1839 to 1842, the other, later verses" (Lowry, p. 61.)

2. From "In a Lecture-Room" (Lowry).

3. "Like a child / In some strange garden left awhile alone" (Lowry).

4. "Enough, small Room" (Lowry).

5. "The Music of the World and of the Soul" (Lowry).

6. Thomas Burbidge (1816–92), co-author with Clough of *Ambarvalia*, was at Rugby under Dr Arnold and then at Trinity College, Cambridge. In 1848 he married an Italian wife—"a very nice simple, lively and affectionate little body," according to

Clough—and he seems to have offended some with his language: "I think you people are making great donkeys of yourselves about Burbidge's freedom of speech," Clough wrote (Mulhauser, 2:224,245). From 1851 to 1857 he was master of Leamington College and thereafter chaplain at Trieste, Malta, and Palermo, and was canon of Gibraltar, 1868. ("Barbaric ruins": unidentified).

7. "The New Sinai."

To Arthur Hugh Clough

[London]

My dear Clough   [shortly after December 6, 1847]

I sent you a beastly vile note the other day:[1] but I was all rasped by influenza and a thousand other bodily discomforts.[2] Upon this came all the exacerbation produced by your apostrophes to duty:[3] and put me quite wrong: so that I did not at all do justice to the great precision and force you have attained in those inward ways. I do think however that rare as individuality is you have to be on your guard against it—you particularly:-tho: indeed I do not really know that I think so. Shakspeare says that if imagination would apprehend some joy it comprehends some bringer of that joy:[4] and this latter operation which makes palatable the bitterest or most arbitrary original apprehension you seem to me to despise. Yet to *solve* the universe[5] as you try to do it is as irritating as Tennyson's dawdling with its painted shell is fatiguing to me to witness: and yet I own that to *re-construct* the Universe is not a satisfactory attempt either—I keep saying Shakspeare, Shakspeare, you are as obscure as life is: yet this unsatisfactoriness goes against the poetic office in general: for this must I think certainly be its end. But have I been inside you, or Shakspeare? Never. Therefore heed me not, but come to what you can. Still my first note was cynical and beastly-vile. To compensate it, I have got you the Paris diamond edition of Beranger,[6] like mine. Tell me when you are coming up hither. I think it possible Tom may have trotted into Arthur's Bosom in some of the late storms;[7] which would have been a pity as he meant to enjoy himself in New Zealand. It is like your noble abstemiousness not to have shown him the Calf Poem: he would have worshipped like the children of Israel. Farewell.   Your's most truly

M. Arnold.

MS. Yale University.

1. The preceding letter (Lowry).
2. With a nod to *Hamlet* 3.1.62–63.
3. Lowry (p. 63) says that Clough's "apostrophes to duty" were the verses beginning "Duty—that's to say complying," but more probably the phrase includes "The Questioning Spirit" and "Thought may well be ever ranging" as well.

4. *A Midsummer Night's Dream* 5.1.18–20.

5. David DeLaura has pointed out to the editor that this comes from Goethe's *Conversations with Eckerman and Soret*, Oct. 15, 1825 (Oxenford's tr., new edn, 1874, p. 161): "Man is born not to solve the problems of the universe, but to find out where the problem begins, and then to restrain himself within the limits of the comprehensible."

6. Pierre Jean Béranger (1780–1857), French poet, famous for *chansons*, especially "Le Roi d'Yvetot").

7. *Henry V* 2.3.10–11. "One of the worst hurricanes that ever swept England played havoc with all shipping from Saturday, December 4, until the middle of the following week" (Lowry, p. 62).

To Arthur Hugh Clough

London[1]

My dearest Clough   Tuesday, [December 1847 or early 1848]

My heart warms to the kindness of your letter: it is necessity not inclination indeed that ever repels me from you.

I forget what I said to provoke your explosion about Burbidge: au reste, I have formed my opinion of him, as Nelson said of Mack.[2] One does not always remember that one of the signs of the Decadence of a literature, one of the factors of its decadent condition indeed, is this—that new authors attach themselves to the poetic expression the founders of a literature have flowered into, which may be *learned* by a sensitive person, to the neglect of an inward poetic life. The strength of the German literature consists in this— that having no national models from whence to get an idea of *style* as half the work, they were thrown upon themselves, and driven to make the fulness of the content of a work atone for deficiencies of form. Even Goethe at the end of his life has not the inversions, the taking tourmenté style[3] we admire in the Latins, in some of the Greeks, & in the great French & English authors. And had Shakspeare & Milton lived in the atmosphere of modern feeling, had they had the multitude of new thoughts & feelings to deal with a modern has, I think it likely the style of each would have been far less *curious & exquisite*. For in a *man* style is the saying in the best way *what you have to say*. The *what you have to say* depends on your age. In the 17th century it was *a smaller harvest than now*, & sooner to be reaped: & therefore to its reaper was left time to stow it more finely & curiously. Still more was this the case in the ancient world. The poet's matter being *the hitherto experience of the world, & his own*, increases with every century. Burbidge lives quite beside the true poetical life, under a little gourd.[4] So much for him. For me you may often hear my sinews cracking under the effort to unite matter. . . . [5]

MS. Yale University.

1. This letter (which ends abruptly, with no punctuation after "effort to unite matter") and the one below (p. 82) (which begins abruptly), each two pages on a single leaf, may be parts of a single letter. See Lowry's note pp. 64–65, and R.H. Super's in *The Time-Spirit of Matthew Arnold*, pp. 94–95.

2. "General Mack was at the head of the Neapolitan troops;—all that is now doubtful concerning this man is, whether he was a coward or a traitor,—at that time he was assiduously extolled as a most consummate commander to whom Europe might look for deliverance . . . but when the general, at a review, so directed the operations of a mock fight, that, by an unhappy blunder, his own troops were surrounded instead of those of the enemy, he [Nelson] turned to his friends and exclaimed, with bitterness, that the fellow did not understand his business. . . . 'General Mack,' said he, in one of his letters, 'cannot move without five carriages! I have formed my opinion. I heartily pray I may be mistaken'" (Lowry, p. 65, quoted from Southey's *Life of Nelson*, ch. 6).

3. Used in *On Translating Homer* (Super, 1:116).

4. Jonah 4:5–6.

5. *Tempest* 3.1.26, Ferdinand to Miranda, "I had rather crack my sinews, abreak my back," but probably not echoed here.

To Mary Penrose Arnold*

My dearest Mother   Sunday, January 2, 1848

I write this in my stage between Laleham and Bowood:[1] to say that I hope to come home in about a week from this time: tomorrow week, perhaps. I go to Bowood by the 2 P. M. train tomorrow, to arrive by dinnertime. I do not expect I shall know a soul there.

Last Monday I went to Laleham. I found Aunt[2] in her room and looking very feverish & unwell: but she improved every day I was there. It was nearly dark when I left the Weybridge station, but I could make out the wide sheet of the grey Thames gleaming through the general dusk as I came out on Chertsey bridge: ⟨and⟩ I never go along that shelving gravelly road up towards Laleham without interest; from Chertsey Lock to the turn where the Drunken Man lay. Today after morning church I went up to Pentonhook: and found the stream with the old volume, width, shine, rapid fulness, Kempshott and swans, unchanged & unequalled—to my partial and remembering eyes at least. On the Hook itself they have been draining and cutting a little: but the old paved part of the barge road on the Laleham side of the Lock house is all as it was: and the campanulas they told me grow as much as ever there in summer. Yesterday I was at Chertsey, the poetic town of our childhood as opposed to the practical historical Staines: it is *across* the river, reached by no bridges and roads, but by the primitive ferry the meadow path the Abbey river with its wooden bridge and the narrow lane by the old wall:[3] and itself the stillest of country towns backed by St Ann's leads nowhere, but to the heaths and pines of Surrey. How unlike the journey to Staines, and the great road through the flat drained Middlesex plain with its single standing pollarded elms.

Jane is the only one I connect with Laleham & her I do at every point. Only I am afraid she falls more and more out of sympathy with the Bucklands, while I blend them more & more with the place: and with persons as well as things grow to venerate the tie of attachment in preference to that of passion, admiration or common interests. I am at perfect peace with them and their truly unchanged house with its old clean bitter smell. The only jar I received was from a visit to the Lambarts at Hampton.[4]

I was yesterday at the old House and under the cedars and by the old pink acacia. I went to see Mrs Powell and Mrs Nokes: the first of whom at 80 recalls her charwoman days, and her puff paste that did not give satisfaction because Mr Buckland preferred short paste—and thanks the dear Lord that she can still do for herself. The second is in extreme feebleness but she too remembered the Whitmonday on which that nice man Mr Arnold, when no one came over from Staines took the duty himself &c. &c.

I must stop—goodnight with love to all   ever your affectionate

M. Arnold.—

MS. Balliol College.

1. Lansdowne's seat in Wiltshire, near Calne.
2. Dr Arnold's sister Frances (d. 1863), who married the Rev. John Buckland (1785–1859: Boase) in 1816 and helped him run the Laleham school.
3. The language suggests "Stanzas from the Grande Chartreuse," ll. 169 ff.
4. Oliver William Matthew Lambart (1822–63) was the third son of the 7th earl of Cavan, whose second wife was Lydia Arnold (d. 1862), sister of Thomas Arnold. Oliver Lambart was thus Matthew Arnold's first cousin; his wife (m. 1844) was Anne Elizabeth Willes (d. 1881). Why the visit was a "jar" is not known, but some evidence, mostly a palpable silence, suggests a relationship with the Lambarts, titled and untitled, of imperfect sympathy. See below p. 350–51 and n. 1.

Jane Martha Arnold to William Delafield Arnold

January, 1848

Matt has enlarged to you upon the felicities of the after part of your voyage, when you come in sight of India—and upon the reverence with which you must look at the Cocoa Groves and the whitebearded Brahmins and carry back your thoughts thousands of years to the time when ancestral Brahmins sitting in ancestral groves pondered earnestly—where shall wisdom be found and where is the place of understanding.

Text: W. D. Arnold, Oakfield, with an Introduction by Kenneth Allott (1973), p. 36.

Jane Martha Arnold to Thomas Arnold

Fox How
My dearest Tom   Monday, January 17, 1848
[Half a page omitted] We very often look at your picture, the Daguerrotype I mean, and very often talk about you, and I tell Mamma the history
of all my visits to your lodgings, and of our expedition to the John Wickliffe,
of which as you may suppose she is never tired of hearing, and then Edward
and Matt begin to torment her by telling her what miserable accommoda-
tions you had, and thank their stars that they are not in your place, but I do
not think they succeed in making her think that you will be very unhappy at
the lack of creature comforts. Since you and Walter have been gone, our
conversation certainly has taken in a very large sweep of subjects. . . . [18
lines omitted] We had three delightful letters yesterday from Walter to
Mamma & Fan & Rowland, in which he gives all the details [about the wreck
of the *Avenger* off the northern coast of Africa on December 20] that had
reached him, but he did not say much about his own feelings on the matter.
He seems to be very happy on the S. Vincent, and thoroughly interested in
his work, the study of navigation, &c. The feeling which seems to prevail on
this head on board the S. Vincent curiously confirms what Papa says in one
of his sermons, that school is the only place where it is thought a disgrace &
a ridiculous thing to do your proper work diligently. When I contrast Walter's way of speaking about his nautical studies, even the driest of them, with
the way in which Edward & Willy have always spoken of their school &
college work, I do feel unspeakably thankful that dearest Walter is in a profession which calls for such manly qualities. The dear little man takes it very
much to heart about Willy's going to India, & especially laments that a
brother of his should run a risk of dying by the sword of a Barbarian & not a
civilised man. So you see he will consider it a blot on the family escutcheon
for ever, if you come to harm in any skirmish with the natives.

Matt and Edward & Willy have been amusing themselves since dinner
by dancing the Polka, & Mary is probably reading Manning's Sermons,
which Matt has given her and which are very great favourites with both her
& me. Susy is sitting by my side copying out Walter's last letters, and Mamma
& Fan are sitting over the fire reading. Outside the world does not look very
cheerful. . . . [9 lines omitted] Mamma has bought the *Memorial* trees for you
& Willy & Walter, and they are all planted—Walter's oak in the field near
the birch copse, your Weymouth Pine upon my rock, and Willy's holly on
the other rock. [3 lines and final page omitted]

MS. Brotherton Collection.

To Arthur Hugh Clough

[London][1]

[c. February 24, 1848]

A growing sense of the deficiency of the *beautiful* in your poems, and of this alone being properly *poetical* as distinguished from rhetorical, devotional or metaphysical, made me speak as I did. But your line is a line: and you have most of the promising English verse-writers with you now: Festus for instance.[2] Still, problem as the production of the beautiful remains still to me, I will die protesting against the world that the other is false & JARRING.

No—I doubt your being an ARTIST: but have you read Novalis?[3] He certainly is not one either: but in the way of direct communication, insight, & report, his tendency has often reminded me of your's, though tenderer & less systematic than you. And there are the sciences: in which I think the passion for truth, not special curiosities about birds & beasts, makes the great professor.—

—Later news than any of the papers have, is, that the National Guard have declared against a Republic, and were on the brink of a collision with the people when the Express came away.[4]

—I trust in God that feudal industrial class as the French call it, you worship, will be clean trodden under. Have you seen Michelet's characterization (superb) of your brothers—"La dure inintelligence des Anglo-Americains."[5]

—Tell Edward I shall be ready to take flight with him the very moment the French land, & have engaged a Hansom to convey us both from the possible scene of carnage.   your's

M. A.

MS. Yale University.

1. See note above p. 79 n. 1.

2. The long, popular poem by Philip James Bailey (1816–1902), first published (anonymously) in 1839 and, lengthening, in several editions thereafter. Arnold said in Nov. 1873 that he had read it "some five and thirty years ago." See also below p. 107 and n. 2.

3. Novalis, pseudonym of Friedrich Leopold von Hardenberg (1772–1801), German romantic poet and novelist, was the subject of an essay by Carlyle in 1829 (reprinted in *Miscellaneous Essays*); Honan (pp. 157–58) associates Arnold's interest in him with Mary Claude.

4. Louis Philippe abdicated in the early afternoon of Feb. 24. "The electric telegraph of the same day announced that the National Guards had sided with the people" (*Annual Register*). The "express" is the "Govt messenger" of p. 87 below.

5. Jules Michelet's *Le Peuple* (1846), pt 2, ch. 9, a book important to Arnold to which he never alludes by name. Michelet (see below p. 99), speaking of the extermi-

nation of a people (Scottish Highlanders, North American Indians), wrote: "Les Anglais d'Amérique, marchands, puritains, dans leur dure inintelligence, ont refoulé, affamé, anéanti tout à l'heure ces races héroiques, qui laissent une place vide à jamais sur le globe, un regret au genre humain." In 1877 Arnold jotted down part of it (*The Note-books of Matthew Arnold*, ed. Lowry, Young, and Dunn, p. 276), and quoted it in the essay "A Word about America" (Super, 10:14) in 1882. The preface to this book, "A M. Edgar Quinet," probably contributed to passages of "Resignation" and, almost certainly, *Culture and Anarchy* ("*barbares* . . . pleins d'une sève, nouvelle, vivante et rajeunissante," etc.).

To Thomas Arnold

Lansdowne House[1]

My dearest Tom   February 28, 1848

Here I sit, opposite a marble group of Romulus & Remus & the wolf, the two children fighting like mad, and the limp-uddered she-wolf affectionately snarling at the little demons struggling on her back. Above it a great picture, the Jewish Exiles,[2] which would do for Consuelo and Albert resting in one of their wanderings worn out upon a wild stony heath sloping to the Baltic—she leaning over her two children who sleep in their torn rags at her feet. Behind me a most musical clock, marking now 24 minutes past 1, P. M. On my left two great windows looking out on the court in front of the house, through one of which slightly opened comes in by gushes the soft damp breath with a tone of spring-life in it which the close of an English February sometimes brings—so different from a November mildness. The green lawn[3] which occupies nearly half the court is studded over with crocuses of all colours—growing out of the grass, for there are no flowerbeds, delightful for the large still-faced whiterobed babies whom their nurses carry up and down on the gravel court where it skirts the green. And from the square and the neighbouring streets, through the open door whereat the civil porter moves to and fro, come sounds of vehicles and men in all gradations some from near & some from far, but mellowed by the time they reach this backstanding lordly mansion. But above all cries comes one whereat every stone in this & other lordly mansions may totter and quake for fear— Se____c____ond Edition of the Morning Herald—L____a____test news from Paris:—arrival of the King of the French."[4]—I have gone out and bought the said portentous Herald, and send it herewith, that you may read and know. As the human race for ever stumbles on its great steps, so is it now. You remember the Reform Banquets last summer:[5]—well—the diners omitted the King's health, and abused Guizot's[6] majority as corrupt and servile: the majority and the King grew excited; the Government forbade to continue the Banquets. The king met the Chamber with the words "passions ennemies et aveugles" to characterise the dispositions of the Banqueters: and Guizot grandly declaimed against the spirit of Revolutions all over the world. His practice suited his words, or seemed to suit it: for both in Switzerland and Italy, the French Government incurred the charge of siding against the Liberals. Add to this the corruption cases you remember, the Praslin murder,[7] and later events which powerfully stimulated the disgust (moral indignation that People does not feel) entertained by the lower against the governing class. Thiers,[8] seeing the breeze rising, & hoping to use it, made most telling speeches in the debate on the Address, clearly defining the crisis as a question between revolution & counter-revolution and declaring enthusiastically for the former. Lamartine[9] and others, the sentimental & the plain honest were very damaging on the same side. The Government were harsh—abrupt—almost scornful. They would not yield—would not permit banquets: would give no Reform till they chose. Guizot (alone in the Chamber I think) [spoke] to this effect but still noble. With decreasing Majorities the Government carried the different clauses of the address: amidst furious scenes, opposition members crying that they were worse than Polignac.[10] It was resolved to hold an opposition banquet in Paris in spite of the Government last Tuesday, the 22nd. In the week between the close of the debate and this day there was a profound uneasy excitement, but nothing I think to appal the rulers. They had the fortifications: all kinds [paper torn: of] stores, & 100,000 troops of the line. To be qui[te] secure however, they determined to take a formal legal objection to the banquet at the doors, not to prevent the procession thereto. But the opposition published a proclamation inviting the National Guard who sympathized to form part of the procession in Uniform. Then the Government forbade the meeting altogether—absolutely—& the opposition resigned themselves to try the case in a Court of Law. So did not the People. They gathered all over Paris: the National Guard, whom Ministers did not trust were not called out: the Line checked & dispersed the mob on all points. But next day the mob were there again. The Ministers in a constitutional fright called out the National Guard: a body of these hard by the Opera refused to clear the street: they joined the people. Troops were brought up: the Mob & the Nat: Guard refused to give them passage down the Rue Lepelletier they occupied: after a moment's hesitation they were marched on along the Boulevard. This settled the matter. Everywhere the National Guard fraternized with the people: the troops stood indifferent; the King dismissed the Ministers: he sent for Molé,[11] a shade better: not enough: he sent for Thiers—a pause: this was several shades better—still not enough: meanwhile the crowd continued & attacks on different posts with slight bloodshed, increased the excitement: the King abdicated in favour of the Count of Paris[12] & fled. The Count of Paris was taken by his mother to the Chamber—the people broke in: too late—not enough:—a republic—an appeal to the people. The royal family escaped to all parts, Belgium, EU, England: a Prov: Govt named. You will see how they stand: they have adopted the last measures of Revolution.—News has just come that the National Guard have declared against a Republic, & that a collision is inevitable. If possible I will write by the next mail & send you a later paper than the Herald by this mail.   Your truly affectionate, dearest Tom,

M. Arnold.

MS. Balliol College.

1. Addressed: T. Arnold Esqre / Wellington / New Zealand / Viâ Sydney. Postmarked: WELLINGTON / NEW ZEALAND / AU20 / 1848 / A. Another ptmk, illegible on photocopy, written over in ink: pd / PN—. Docketed [by TA? a small, neat hand]: M.A. / Feb. 28 / Recd August 22/48. Stamp: T.P. / MOUNT *StG [superscript letter illeg.] Arnold lived on the south side of Mount Street, "over the seamstress shop of a Mrs Boag," and "headed letters, 'Boag's Baby-linen Warehouse, Mount-street' " (Honan, p. 119, quoting Tom Arnold's "Matthew Arnold (By One Who Knew Him)."

2. Pauline Steinhäuser's large oil painting on canvas "Polish Exiles" is no. 251 in *Catalogue of the Collection of Pictures Belonging to The Marquess of Lansdowne, K. G., at Lansdowne House, London, and Bowood, Wilts.* (1897), and there is a little eulogy of it in G. F. Waagen, *Treasures of Art in Great Britain* (1854), 2:152. (It was "given to a local School of Art in Wiltshire" in 1910 or earlier, according to Ward, 1:64–66, whose transcription of part of this letter reads "Rembrandt's Jewish Exiles.") The "marble group of Romulus & Remus," now at Bowood but still "on top of the bookcase" in 1910, is not listed in Michaelis, *Ancient Marbles in Great Britain*, 1882, *s.v.* Lansdowne House, and is presumably not ancient (Ward, 1:64). In George Sand's novel *Consuelo* (1842–43) Albert and Consuelo, together, never come near the Baltic (though Albert's youthful travels had included Prussia, Poland, and Lithuania); clearly it is the *Polish* Exiles who are "resting." Mrs Ward (Tom Arnold's daughter) notes (1:16): "There are many allusions of many dates in the letters of my father and uncle to each other, as to their common Oxford passion for George Sand. *Consuelo*, in particular, was a revelation to the two young men brought up under the "earnest" influence of Rugby. It seemed to open to them a world of artistic beauty and joy of which they had never dreamed; and to loosen the bands of an austere conception of life, which began to appear to them too narrow for the facts of life."

3. Berkeley Square.

4. Not so. Louis Philippe arrived in Newhaven from Honfleur in the early morning, Mar. 3.

5. "During the autumn, a number of reform banquets, as they were called, were held in different parts of France, when the most violent language was held against the ministry, which had become exceedingly unpopular in the country" (*Annual Register*, p. 329).

6. François Guizot (1787–1874), before this date and after it an important historian (parts of his *Histoire de la révolution d'Angleterre* were studied at Rugby), was now an important statesman, in fact, foreign minister and, briefly, prime minister, "brought down, at the end, by his own inflexible conservatism." As minister of public instruction, he was responsible for "la loi Guizot" in 1833, which "established and organized primary edu-

cation in France," and it was in this capacity that Arnold sought him out in Paris in 1859. See *Album*, pp. 117–18, and below pp. 422–23.

7. The duchess of Praslin was found in her Paris apartment "horribly mutilated and dying of her wounds" on Aug. 18, 1847. The duke was arrested, took poison, and died (*Annual Register*, pp. 103–10).

8. Adolphe Thiers (1797–1877; *VF*, 1/6/72) was also an important historian and statesman.

9. Alphonse de Lamartine (1790–1869), the romantic poet, romantic historian, and romantic politician, was minister of foreign affairs in the Provisional Government, which had just proclaimed the Republic.

10. Jules Armand, prince de Polignac (1780–1847), politician and diplomat, was the most Royalist, Catholic, and reactionary of them all.

11. Louis Matthieu Molé (1781–1855) had been prime minister under Louis Philippe from 1836 to 1839 but could not form a ministry now.

12. Louis Philippe Albert d'Orléans (1838–94), comte de Paris, grandson of Louis Philippe, in fact fled to the United States, fought in the Civil War (for the Union), and wrote a history of it in four volumes.

To Arthur Hugh Clough

London
My dear Clough   Wednesday, [March 1, 1848]

I received yours just now, as I was beginning to drop into a slight doze over the works & days of the respectable Hesiod: a result however I attribute not so much to that writer, as to one St Marc Girardin,[1] a lecture of whom upon "le Caractère du Père dans la Comédie"—I had just previously closed, one of my painfullest follies being the itch to read thro: a book whereof I need a small part.

As to my news Lord L[ansdowne] told it me, & it came from a Govt messenger[2]—who seems however to have shared the cock-&-bull-prolific excitement of common men at these moments. Yesterday I taxed the hoary Communicator: & he owned that the assertion was premature: but declared that numbers of Gig-owners[3] were entering the N[ational] G[uard] in that view: & instanced the duc de Guiche.[4] However I think Gig-owning has received a severe, tho: please God, momentary blow: also, Gig-owning keeps better than it re-begins. Certainly the present spectacle in France is a fine one; mostly so indeed to the historical swift-kindling man, who is not over-haunted by the pale thought,[5] that, after all man's shiftings of posture, restat vivere. Even to such a man revolutions & bodily illnesses are fine anodynes when he is agent or patient therein: but when he is a spectator only, their kind effect is transitory.

—Don't you think the eternal relations between labour & capital the Times twaddles so of have small existence for a *whole society* that has resolved no longer to live by bread alone.[6] What are called the *fair profits* of capital which if it does not realize it will leave it's seat & go elsewhere, have surely no absolute amount, but depend on the view the capitalist takes of the matter. If the rule is—everyone must get all he can—the capitalist understands by *fair profits* such as will enable him to live like a colossal Nob: & Lancashire artisans knowing if they will not let him make these, Yorkshire artisans will, tacent & sweat. But an apostolic capitalist willing to live as an artisan among artisans may surely divide profits on a scale undreamed of Capitalisto nobefacturo. And in a country all whose capitalists were apostolic, the confusion a solitary apostle would make, could not exist.

—Answer me that. If there is necessity anywhere, it is in the Corruption of man, as Tom might say, only.—

—Burns is certainly an artist *im*plicitly—fury is not incompatible with artistic form but it becomes *lyric* fury (Eh?) only when combined with the gift for this. And Beranger both in—& ex. They accuse him by his finisht classicality of having banished the old native French Forms. O, you must like him.

I wish you could have heard me and my man sneering at the vulgar officiousness of that vulgar fussy Yankee Minister at Paris.[7] My man remarks that Poets should hold up their heads now a Poet is at the head of France.[8] More clergyman than Poet, tho:, & a good deal of cambric handkerchief about that. No Parson Adams.[9]

—I am disappointed the Oriental wisdom,[10] God grant it were mine, pleased you not. To the Greeks, foolishness.   Your's

M. A.

MS. Yale University.

1. Marc Girardin, known as Saint-Marc Girardin (1801–73), a highly respected and popular critic and lecturer ("partly a university man, partly a man of the world, a pedantic, intelligent, and foppish personage," *Athenæum*, Apr. 19, 1873), was professor of French poetry at the Sorbonne. His *Cours de littérature dramatique* (5 vols, 1843–68) included as Lecture 12 "Du Caractère paternel dans la comédie." But, though Arnold dozed, "the itch to read" as usual resulted in an itch to write; see Kenneth Allott's "Matthew Arnold's 'Stagirius' and Saint-Marc Girardin," *Review of English Studies* 9 (1958): 286–92, cited in Allott, p. 34, and Honan, p. 140. See also Arnold to Macmillan Oct. 12, 1864, and note.

2. The "express" (above, p. 82).

3. Carlylese—used not "as symbolic of aristocrats" (Lowry, p. 69) but as symbolic of smug middle-class respectability ("Jean Paul Friedrich Richter," *Sartor Resartus*, "Boswell's Life of Johnson," *The Diamond Necklace, The French Revolution*).

4. Antoine Alfred Agénor de Gramont (1819–80), duc de Guiche, who had resigned his commission in the artillery in 1841, entered the National Guard in 1848. (He succeeded as duc de Gramont and prince de Binache on the death of his father in 1854.)

5. An echo of *Hamlet* 3.1.85.

6. Deuteronomy 8 : 3 (etc.). Lowry (p. 169) quotes from a leading article in *The Times*, Mar. 1.

7. Lansdowne ("My man") and Richard Rush (1780–1859), "who, on February 28, made an address to the new Government at the Hôtel de Ville. Finding himself, as he said, at too great a distance to await instructions from Washington, he took the liberty of congratulating the new régime. He pointed out his joy that American principles were now to have trial in France, quoted from George Washington, and made a profound impression on the French people who were delighted by this formal recognition of their republic" (Lowry, p. 70, citing *The Times*, Feb. 29, p. 6, and Mar. 2, p. 5).

But there is more here than meets the eye—perhaps more than met Arnold's. Rush grew up in Philadelphia in "a cultivated household" very like Arnold's own and had a distinguished career in government. As minister to Great Britain 1817–25, he "was undoubtedly amongst the most efficient and amongst the best liked of American ministers to the Court of St. James. A man of high breeding, emphatically a gentleman, he moved with ease in the British society of his period, and his genuine regard for the British people, coupled with wide intellectual interests and a tact that was almost unfailing, gave him a wide measure of success" (*DAB*). He knew Lansdowne personally and officially and dined several times at Lansdowne House. They were adversaries in a diplomatic incident in 1824 in which Lansdowne came off second best.

In 1847 President Polk appointed him (now, like Lansdowne, aged 67) minister to France, where he arrived "in the closing days of the July monarchy, and was a witness to the stirring events of the February revolution, which he described with much skill (*Occasional Productions*, pp. 355–82). After a brief period of reflection, he decided to recognize the republic then set up, without waiting for instructions from Washington, and despite the reserve of all the other members of the diplomatic corps. He followed with obvious mistrust the course of the red republican revolt of July, but seems to have witnessed without extravagant regret the election of Louis Napoleon as president in December 1848" (*DAB*). See also Rush's *Memoranda of a Residence at the Court of London* (in several editions from 1833 to 1873) and J. H. Powell's *Richard Rush, Republican Diplomat* (1942).

8. Lamartine was effectively head of government.

9. In Fielding's novel *Joseph Andrews*.

10. *Bhagavad Gita*. It is perhaps relevant that William Arnold, who had spent his last month with Matthew Arnold in the Mount Street flat (and referred to him affectionately as "the rich old Villain"), sailed for India on this very date (Woodward, p. 188; Ward, 1 : 88).

To Arthur Hugh Clough

[London]

Dear Clough   Saturday, [March 4, 1848]

I did not at first answer your question because I wanted to consider a little: which I do best as I walk past the shops in the street: I think the double columned large 8vo advantageous in itself—but it does not do so well for a first publication as it seems to imply a large sale & among the people. I think therefore you are almost forced by the decencies to begin in the 12mo.[1]

It seems as if the French Government might fall into the relaxation naturally consequent on great tension and trust to routine like other people: in which case they will infallibly be done for: nothing but a perennial enthusiasm can now work France—which may or may not be impossible. They cannot be Americans thank God if they would.

If you do not see the difference between Rush's step & that of his bated imitators I quit the subject.

The Indians distinguish between meditation or absorption—and knowledge: and between abandoning practice, & abandoning the fruits of action & all respect thereto. This last is a supreme step, & dilated on throughout the Poem.[2] A man sits waiting for me. Goodbye

M. Arnold.—

MS. *Yale University.*

1. It is in fact a 16mo in 8s (Professor David Vander Meulen).
2. The *Bhagavad Gita.* Lowry (p. 71) adds: "Much of it, I am inclined to think, heavily influenced Arnold's own *Resignation* and other early poems." See Connell, pp. 26–30, Honan, pp. 98–100, Ullman, *The Yale Manuscript*, pp. 84–87.

To Arthur Hugh Clough

L[ansdowne] House
My dear Clough   Monday, [March 6, 1848]

You must come this week if you come but on my conscience I do not think it is worth while. The squalor of the place, the faint earthy orange smell, the dimness of the light, the ghostly ineffectualness of the sub-actors, the self-consciousness of Fanny Kemble, the harshness of Macready, the unconquerable difficulty of the play, altogether gave me sensations of wretchedness during the performance of Othello the other night I am sure you would have shared with me had you been there.[1] I go no more, except to accompany you. But what are your plans about coming to town, any way?

You have seen Lamartine's circular.[2] The Austrian & English aristocracies to whom it comes the latter particularly will simply not understand it. Vague theorizing out of his "Girondins" they will say here. Yet no more will the *people* here than their rulers. Therefore while I own that the riding class[3] here are incapable of distilling the oil you speak of, let us add that the people would be at any rate insensible to it. It is this—this *wide & deepspread intelligence*[4] that makes the French seem to themselves in the van of Europe. People compare a class here with a class there the best in each, & then wonder at Michelet's or Guizot's vanity. I don't think you have done them justice in this respect. Do you remember your pooh-poohing the revue des deux mondes, & my expostulating that the final expression up to the present time of European opinion, without fantastic individual admixture, was *current* there: not emergent here & there in a great writer,—but the *atmosphere* of the commonplace man as well as of the Genius. This is the secret of their power: our weakness is that in an age where all tends to the triumph of the logical absolute reason we neither courageously have thrown ourselves into this movement like the French: nor yet have driven our feet into the solid ground of our individuality, as spiritual, poetic, profound *persons*. Instead of this we have stood *up* hesitating: seeming to refuse the first line on the ground that the second is our *natural* one—yet not taking this. How long halt ye between two opinions:[5] woe to the modern nation, which will neither be philosophe nor philosopher. Eh?   Your's with apologies for longueurs[6]

M. Arnold.

Yet it is something for a nation to feel that the only true line is its natural one?

MS. Yale University.

1. "On February 21, William Charles Macready and Fanny Kemble Butler had begun an engagement of eight Shakespearian plays at the Princess's Theatre. The performance of *Othello* that Arnold saw was doubtless that of February 25" (Lowry, p. 73, who cites Macready's *Diaries*). In 1882, after another visit to the same theater, Arnold wrote in *The Pall Mall Gazette*: "I am a sexagenarian who used to go much to the Princess's some five-and-thirty years ago, when Macready had an engagement there. I remember it as if it were yesterday. In spite of his faults and his mannerism, Macready brought to his work so much intellect, study, energy, and power, that one admired him when he was living, and remembers him now he is dead. During the engagement I speak of, Macready acted, I think, all his great Shakespearian parts. But he was ill supported, the house was shabby and dingy, and by no means full, there was something melancholy about the whole thing. You had before you great pieces and a powerful actor; but the theatre needs the glow of public and popular interest to brighten it, and in England the theatre was at that time not in fashion" (Super, 10:94, and notes pp. 480–81).

2. "In order to quiet the apprehensions of foreign Governments and indicate the policy of the new Republic, M. de Lamartine, in his capacity of Minister of Foreign Affairs, issued a very able circular or manifesto to the diplomatic agents of France throughout Europe. In this he said—'The proclamation of the French Republic is not an act of aggression against any form of government in the world. . . . War, then, is not the principle of the French Republic, as it became the fatal and glorious necessity of the Republic in 1792. . . . The French Republic will, then, not make war on any one . . . . One only question of war was mooted, a year ago, between England and France. It was not Republican France which started that question of war; it was the dynasty. The dynasty carries away with it that danger of war which it had given rise to for Europe by the entirely personal ambition of its family alliances in Spain. . . . The Republic has no ambition. The Republic has no nepotism. It inherits not the pretensions of a family.' " (*Annual Register*, pp. 246–49). Lamartine's *Histoire des Girondins*, a poeticized, romanticized account of the French Revolution, appeared in 1847.

3. Presumably, "Gig-owners" (see above p. 86 n. 3). (Arnold did not write "ruling class.")

4. A rendering of Sainte-Beuve's "intelligence ouverte et traversée" (see Bonnerot, pp. 518–19n and below p. 481).

5. I Kings 18:21.

6. Misread by Lowry as "longness" but later corrected.

To Mary Penrose Arnold*

Dear Mamma   Tuesday, [March 7, 1848]

You need not return the National.[1]

I send you the Examiner with an article of Carlyle's[2]—How deeply restful it comes upon one, amidst the hot dizzy trash one reads about these changes everywhere.

I send Price's[3] letter to Coleby. I think I thought much the same about the decisive point of ruin [?gain] to the King's affairs. As for his conscience, I incline to think he was only old and nervous.

Certainly taken individually the French people no more than our own are up to the measure of the ideal citizen they seem to propose to themselves; this thought constantly presses on me: but the question to be tried is whether the proclamation of this ideal city & public recognition of it may not bring a nation nearer to that measure than the professedly unbelieving governments hitherto for some time in force everywhere. The source of repose in Carlyle's article is that he alone puts aside the din & whirl and brutality which envelope a movement of the masses to fix his thoughts on its ideal invisible character.

—I was in the great mob in Trafalgar square yesterday, whereof the papers will instruct you: but they did not seem dangerous, & the police are always I think needlessly rough in *manner*—English officials too often are. It will be *rioting* here, only: still the hour of the hereditary peerage & eldest sonship and immense properties has I am convinced, as Lamartine would say, struck. You know I think Papa would by this time have been a kind of Saint Martin[4]—the writer, not the saint proper. But I do not think England will be liveable in just yet. I see a wave of more than American *vulgarity* moral intellectual & social preparing to break over us. In a few years people will understand better why the French are the most civilized of European peoples: when they see how fictitious our manners & civility have been—how little inbred in the race. Ever your's

             M. Arnold.—

MS. Balliol College.

1. *Le National*, the Parisian daily published from 1830 to 1851, not the *National*, a London weekly from Mar. 1846 to Mar. 1849 (see below p. 101).

2. "Louis Philippe," *Examiner*, Mar. 4, 1848, reprinted in *Rescued Essays of Thomas Carlyle*, ed. Percy Newberry, 1892. Carlyle wrote, for example: "Sophist Guizot, Sham-King Louis Philippe and the host of quacks, of obscene spectral nightmares, under which France lay writhing, are fled" (p. 4). "Egalité Fils, after a long painful life-voyage, has ended no better than Egalité Père did. It is a tragedy equal to that of the sons of Atreus" (p. 9). "Thrones founded on iniquity, on hypocrisy, and the appeal to human baseness, cannot end otherwise" (p. 12).

3. Bonamy Price (see above p. 4). The letter was sent to Thomas Trevenen Penrose, vicar of Coleby (see above pp. 17, 67–68).

4. Louis Claude de Saint-Martin (1743–1843), French philosopher and mystic, an obscure and difficult writer, who somehow seems the very antithesis of Dr Arnold. Saint-Martin influenced Senancour, as Iris Sells points out (*Matthew Arnold and France*, p. 44, citing Joachim Merlant, *Sénancour*), and one of his books is named in Lettre 85 of *Obermann*: "Depuis ce déjeûner j'ai remis sur ma table *De l'Esprit des choses*, et j'en ai lu un volume presque entier."

To Arthur Hugh Clough

L[ansdowne] House

Dear Clough   Ash Wednesday, [March 8, 1848]

Come this week if possible for as the season advances I keep hoping to get away to Oxford myself if possible. You cannot be sure beforehand of what you will see. Macbeth is the best—or Wolsey.[1]

I have been a constant attender on the emeutes here—endeavouring to impress on the mob that not royalty but aristocracy—primogeniture—large land and mill-owners were their true enemies here. But they draw it very mild at present.[2]

By trivialities do you mean novels as opposed to Comte[3] & them of that kidney—Figaro as opposed to the Contrat Social. For amongst a *people* of readers the litterature is a greater engine than the philosophy. Which last they change very fast—oh said a F[renc]hman[4] to me the other day—Comte—Comte has been quite passé these 10 years.

Besides in the Revue[5] one has the *applied* ideas on all points:—of litterature, of politics—Polish—Irish—Italian. The value of the F[renc]h movement being always not absolute but relative I prefer to read their relative not their absolute litterature. Which last is tiresome what I have seen of it.

Seditious songs have nourished the F[renc]h people much more than the Socialist: philosophers: though they may formulize[6] their wants through the mouths of these.[7]

—Well but come—

The Prov[isional] Gov[ernment] is said to be divided—Garnier Pages Cremieux & Marie versus Ledru Rollin, Flocon—& Louis Blanc.[8] Lamartine neutral—inclining to the first set. Not a bad electoral scheme, as they are?

The Examiner article is by Carlyle—& how solemn, how deeply *restful* it strikes on one amidst the heat & vain words that are everywhere just now—Yet the thoughts extracted & abstractedly stated, are every newspaper's: it is the *style* & feeling by which the beloved man appears. Apply this Infidel to the Oriental Poem. How short could Mill write Job?[9]

Carlyle says, I am told—"The human race has now arrived at the last stage of Jack assification."   Your's

M. Arnold.—

MS. Yale University.

1. Macready's Shakespearean productions at the Princess's Theatre (see above p. 89 and n. 1).

2. "The triumph of the populace of Paris was the signal for disturbances in every part of Europe. London was not exempt from the scourge; but, fortunately, the nature of the proceedings of the mob were eminently calculated to bring popular émeutes into contempt. On Monday, the 6th of March, Trafalgar Square and Charing Cross were the scene of one of these burlesque émeutes. . . . By one o'clock 10,000 persons were gathered in the square; and mob-mischief of a playful sort—'bonneting,' and pushing people into the fountains—filled up the time. A few orators then appeared, and made inflammatory allusions to the revolution in Paris. By the time the speeches were over, the crowd had increased to some 15,000—artisans and labourers out of work, idle spectators, and thieves. . . . Occasionally were heard shouts of ' *Vive la République*'! . . . For some days afterwards these disturbances were renewed, chiefly by the parade of a few hundreds of ragamuffin boys, whose chief object seemed to be the fun of stealthily smashing valuable panes of glass in the shop windows" (*Annual Register*, which also reports rioting in Manchester, Glasgow, Edinburgh, Newcastle, "and other places").

3. Auguste Comte (1798–1857), the Positivist philosopher, and Rousseau's *Du Contrat social* (1762) contrasted with the frivolity of Beaumarchais's clever and comic rogue in *Le Barbier de Séville* (1775) and *Le Mariage de Figaro* (1784). (*Le Figaro*, the newspaper, was at this time a small, unimportant weekly.)

4. Probably, Philarète Chasles (1798–1873), a cosmopolitan critic and man of letters thoroughly anglicized (he fled to England in 1817 and lived there for seven or eight years). Apparently acquainted with everyone in England and France, he introduced Arnold to Michelet in Feb. 1847, and may have introduced him to Sainte-Beuve also ("I knew him well, and from his youth to his latter age we were—I do not say friends, he had none—but admirably *bien ensemble*," Chasles wrote in a brief epitaph in "Notes from Paris," *Athenæum*, Apr. 19, 1873, p. 505). He was now professor at the Collège de France: "a chair in Germanic Languages and Literatures was created for him. . . . Since he had never obtained any sort of university degree he was permitted to acquire, within twenty-four hours, the bachelor's, *licencié's*, and doctor's degrees at the *Faculté des lettres de Paris*," one of his examiners being Saint-Marc Girardin (A. Levin, *The Legacy of Philarète Chasles*, 1:xxi, 228). He was a steady contributor to the *Journal des débats* (in which he had written on *Obermann*) and, from 1834 to 1849, to the *Revue des deux mondes*, and "for fully forty years" he wrote "letters and articles from Paris" for the *Athenæum*, where an obituary appeared July 26, 1873, p. 113. (*The Illustrated London News* printed an article on him, with a photograph by Nadar, on Apr. 14, 1860, pp. 361–62.)

5. *La Revue des deux mondes*, founded in 1829, is cited in *The Note-books of Matthew Arnold* more than any other periodical, including *The Times*. Published fortnightly, it had already run articles on Italy (two) and Poland by this date in 1848 and printed an incisive paragraph on Ireland ("dans laquelle régnait une terreur qui rappelait les temps barbares"). A long article on Ireland appeared in Sept. 1847.

6. Béranger has been more nourishing than Comte or Saint-Simon. "Formulize": *OED* dates the first occurrence 1851.

7. These politicians (all listed in *Petit Robert*, etc.) are Louis Antoine Garnier-Pagès (1803–78), Isaac Moise (Adolphe) Crémieux (1796–1880), Pierre Thomas Marie de Saint-Georges (1795–1870), Alexandre Auguste Ledru-Rollin (1807–74), Ferdinand Flocon (1800–1866), and Louis Blanc (1811–82: *VF*, 12/20/79).

8. "The heightening by which the poem [*Bhagavad Gita*, which Arnold read in Wilkins's translation] attains distinction is akin to that which Carlyle gains. The Book of Job could be reduced to a logical skeleton by John Stuart Mill, whereby it would lose its power and charm" (Lowry, p. 75).

To Jane Martha Arnold*

L[ansdowne] House

My dearest K   Friday, March 10, 1848

My excuse for not answering you, dear child, must be that not having been privately disposed lately, it mattered little I thought to whom my public general chronicles or remarks were addressed.—Now—before I go further let me ask what I have meant to ask depuis longtemps: has not this French excitement roused & benefitted Mary?[1] Let someone answer this, pray. Would that I were coming home as she leaves it. It is so hard to sequester oneself here from the rush of public changes and talk, and yet so unprofitable to attend to it. I was myself tempted to attempt some political writing the other day: but in the watches of the night[2] I seemed to feel that in that direction I had some enthusiasm of the head perhaps, but no profound stirring. So I desisted: and have only poured forth a little to Clough, we two agreeing like two lambs in a world of wolves[3]—I think you would have liked to see the correspondence.

What agitates me is this: if the new state of things succeeds in France, social changes are *inevitable* here & elsewhere—for no one looks on seeing his neighbour mending without asking himself if he cannot mend in the same way:—but without waiting for the result, the spectacle of France is likely to breed great agitation here: and such is the state of our masses that their movements now *can* only be brutal plundering and destroying. And if they wait, there is no one, as far as one sees, to train them to conquer by their attitude and superior conviction: the deep ignorance of the middle & upper classes, and their feebleness of vision becoming if possible daily more apparent.—

You must by this time begin to see what people mean by placing France *politically* in the van of Europe: it is the *intelligence* of their *idea-moved masses* which makes them politically as far superior to the *insensible masses* of England as to the Russian Serfs.[4]—And at the same time they do not threaten the educated world with the intolerable *laideur* of the well-fed American masses, so deeply antipathetic to continental Europe. Remark this to Miss Martineau cursorily.[5]

But I do not say that these people in France have much dreamed of the deepest wants of man—or are likely to enlighten the world much on the subject: and I do not wonder at Guizot, who is an austerely serious man rather despising them. Indeed I believe he had got with the spectacle of corruption & meanness round him to despise the whole human race pretty roundly: and as, tho: he never took bribes, he let his creatures bribe others, so tho: he would have never lied to his own soul he passed on a lie from the king to others now & then with a sardonic indifference. This is all he is accused of in the Spanish affair: the king lied to him at first, and when he found it out, instead of leaving office, he brazened out the affair. You know he must have despised such an ineffectual set as Lord Normanby[6] & the English Govt: men who between them all never had a thought in their lives. He lives quite retired here they say, not even seeing the king.[7] I cannot help thinking of Lucan's famous line— *Victrix causa Deis placuit—sed victa Catoni.*[8]—Be kind to the neighbours, "this is all we can."[9]   ever your's

M. Arnold.

MS. Frederick Whitridge.

1. Mary Arnold Twining, Arnold's "most worldly sister," "the frankest, most outspoken of the four Arnold sisters, she studied Christian Socialism in London" (Honan, pp. 151, 427). She had been at Fox How since December—"so changed—" wrote Mary Wordsworth, "so thin and pale! It was deemed quite necessary on every account that, however unwillingly, she should come home—and a hard trial it must be for her. They do not speak openly of the afflicted *state* to her Husband, only that it is quite improper that he should see her, or his family—Paralysis of the Brain—and extreme weakness is the state in which he is, as far as we can gather. Yet we understand that he has muscular strength that enables him to walk in a considerable way. This, as it appears that there is not the slightest hope of recovery, is to be lamented—as causing fear of a long continuance in so very distressing a state" (*The Letters of Mary Wordsworth*, selected and edited by Mary E. Burton, p. 290). Twining died in Nov.

2. Adapted from Psalm 63:6.

3. Luke 10:3.

4. See below p. 107.

5. Harriet Martineau (1802–76: *DNB*), the writer, had built a house, The Knoll, at Ambleside in 1846 and was thus a neighbor of the Arnolds. At this point she had written two books on America, *Society in America* (3 vols, 1837) and *A Retrospect of Western Travel* (3 vols, 1838). She and Arnold, as will be seen in these letters, never really liked or ap-

proved of each other. She was ear-trumpet deaf, dogmatic, earnest, radical, and, in his view, superficial; he was flippant, conservative, foppish, insincere, and, in her view, superficial. In 1855 he devoted thirty-odd lines of "Haworth Churchyard" to her and twenty years later excised them all.

6. Constantine Henry Phipps (1797–1863: *DNB*), first marquis of Normanby, ambassador at Paris 1846–52 (his Paris journal for 1848 was published in 1857 as *A Year of Revolution*) and minister at Florence 1854–58, "in which posts he mingled too much in the politics of foreign states" (*Concise DNB*).

7. Guizot had taken refuge in London (Pelham Crescent, Brompton) on Mar. 3. In 1846, in a sort of quasi miniwar of Spanish Succession, amidst a maelstrom of intrigue and counter-intrigue, Isabella II of Spain (aged 16) was maneuvered into marriage with Francisco de Assisi de Bourbon, her first cousin, and on the same day her sister married the Duc de Montpensier, son of Louis Philippe—all this under the influence of the French king and Guizot and in the teeth of understandings with the English government, which viewed the affair as typical of *la perfide Gaule*. (This is but the first act of a fascinating drama in which Arnold became involved personally, if peripherally, twenty-two years later when Tommaso Alberto Vittorio, second Duke of Genoa, then living with the Arnolds at Harrow, was offered the throne that Isabella, a foolish, wayward woman, abdicated (see below Bulwer-Lytton's letter to Arnold May 16, 1869).

8. Lucan, *Works* (tr. Ridley), 1:28: "The conquering cause was pleasing to the Gods—but the conquered one to Cato." Arnold used it in "On the Study of Celtic Literature" (Super, 3:305).

9. Unidentified.

Theodore Walrond to Thomas Arnold

Rugby

My dear Tom   March 21, 1848

Shairp tells me that there is a budget forming for you—I should be sorry to let it go without a line from me. Although indeed I do not know that I have anything to say which could interest you. At such a distance, the common ἀγωνίσματα ἐς τὸ παραχρῆμα ἀκούειν in the shape of views on questions of the day, French Revolutions, Changes of Ministry, Chartist Demonstrations, & Repeal Seditions, would lose their savour. And for κτῆμα ἐς ἀεὶ, I doubt whether your thoughts & mine travel enough in the same line, to make it possible for me to "add anything" to you. But I must tell you, with what deep interest I read your long letter to Shairp—from the feeling I had in reading it I claim the right to call you my friend in the truest sense: not as agreeing with every word you say, or having felt, or even being able to imagine, all that you have felt, but as feeling, with a thrill of elevating pleasure, that our feet are on the same ground & our eyes looking up toward the same sun. I never understood you thoroughly at Oxford, nor you, I think, me: but this is only one of the many cases in which we value not, until we lose.

I daresay Shairp has told you all about Tait's illness—He was despaired of for several days but is now recovering. I am here meantime as hack, not unwilling: for I am fond of the old place, & like seeing Price, Cotton, Bradley, Shairp—especially the last:—and, perhaps more than all, I *like* being in the fresh atmosphere of boys, instead of the stale & fusty one of Dons & half-men. I think I shall very likely take to it as my Life's work. It is more direct good-doing, than any other lines open to me and for a man with no very strong original instincts to help him out with a view of his own, but rather a turn for making what he can out of existing circumstances, such a line as this is the most that can be hoped.—So much for myself. It is the only subject I can write of, knowing absolutely nothing of you, & taking for granted that the public news will have reached you through the Papers or other means. Do the same to me, if you can find time to write—tell me especially about the Country & whether it disappoints you at all. I should dislike the want of long kingly rivers—but perhaps the mountains make up. Shairp & I often study the map of New Zealand, & his vivid imagination only wants a very few data from your pen to picture it all.

I know nothing special about your family, but of course they speak for themselves. There are rumours of a Change of Ministry, but whether that wd affect Matt I know not. But no cat is surer to fall upon his legs.—In a few weeks I trust to hear Jenny Lind again. It is strange that Stanley & I, so unlike, agree in looking to Jenny Lind & your Father as the two beings who have most powerfully testified to us the presence of a Deity in the World. Have you not something of the same feelings? Enough.   Your affection-ate friend

Theodore Walrond

MS. Balliol College.

To Jane Martha Arnold*

L[ansdowne] House
My own dearest K   Tuesday, [March 28, 1848]
    I am waiting here, (6¼ P. M.) till Ld L[ansdowne] comes back from the House—but if he does not arrive by 6½ he begged me to go. I have not opened my great F[renc]h.[1] table to write to you—but I have set my paper on an account of Scinde,[2] & hold this on my knee: it is beginning to grow dusk—but it has been a sweet day, with sun & a playing wind and a softly broken sky. The crocusses which have long starred the lawn in front of the windows, growing like daisies out of the turf, have nearly vanished—but the lilacs that border the court are thrusting their leaves out to make amends.

"The clouds of sickness cast no stain upon
"Her vallies & blue hills:
"The Doubt, that assails all things, never won
"This faithful impulse of unfaithful wills"—[3]

—It gets more & more grey and indistinct, and the musical clock behind me is quickening its pace in preparation for its half hour peal—I shut this up & go.

Wednesday

—After all my dressing when I arrived at the Bunsens last night pursuant to invitation the servant told me they had put off their parties, the Prince of Prussia[4] having just arrived: so back I trundled: walked the streets a little while, tried to read a grammar, even a novel—found myself too feverish—& actually went to bed at 10¼—slept like a top till 9½—and am better today. So I avoid all medicine.

—How plain it is now, though an attention to the comparative litteratures for the last 50 years might have instructed anyone of it that England is in a certain sense *far behind* the Continent. In conversation in the newspapers one is so struck with the fact of the utter insensibility one may say of people to the number of ideas & schemes now ventilated on the Continent—not because they have judged them or seen beyond them, but, from sheer habitual want of wide reading & thinking. Like a child's intellectual attitude vis a vis of[5] the proposition that Saturn's apparent diameter subtends an angle of about 18″.[6] Our practical virtues never certainly revealed more clearly their isolation. I am not sure but I agree in Lamartine's prophecy that 100 years hence the Continent will be a great united Federal Republic, and England all her colonies gone in a dull steady decay.[7]

M. A.

MS. Frederick Whitridge.

   1. Russell, not understanding the abbreviation, omitted it. See above p. xxvi.

   2. William Francis Patrick Napier, *The Conquest of Scinde* (1844–46).

   3. Allott, p. 646.

   4. Wilhelm I (1797–1888: *VF*, 9/24/70), the heir presumptive (emperor of Germany 1871–88), *fled* to England. "At this time he was the best-hated man in Germany, the mass of the Prussian people believing him to be a vehement supporter of an absolutist and reactionary policy. He was even held responsible for the blood shed in Berlin on the 18th of March, and was nicknamed the 'Cartridge Prince.' . . . So bitter was the feeling against him that the king entreated him to leave the country for some time" (*Encyclopædia Britannica*, 11th edn, 28:666).

   "On the morning of March 27, at eight o'clock, his Royal Highness the Prince of Prussia arrived at No. 4 Carlton Terrace, unannounced, and causing as much surprise as if, on reading the notice in the papers two days before his having retired from Berlin, the possibility of his directing his course towards England had not occurred to Bunsen. . . .

"One great business on Monday was making out the list of persons to be sent to, and put off—as we had made invitations for a series of Tuesday evenings" (Frances Baroness Bunsen, *Memoirs of Baron Bunsen* (2 vols., Philadelphia, 2d edn, abridged and corrected, 2:102,104).

5. The idiom (with *of*) is French, not English.

6. This could have come from Newton, Laplace, Lalande, any subsequent astronomer, or an encyclopædia; this sentence from John F. W. Herschel's *Outlines of Astronomy* (1849), section 514, will serve: "A still more wonderful, and, as it may be termed, elaborately artificial mechanism, is displayed in Saturn, the next in order of remoteness to Jupiter, to which it is not much inferior in magnitude, being about 79,000 miles in diameter, nearly 1000 times exceeding the earth in bulk, and subtending an apparent angular diameter at the earth, of about 18" at its mean distance."

7. Untraced.

To Jules Michelet[1]

Londres

Monsieur   le 7 avril, 1848

Le souvenir de l'accueil bienveillant que vous m'êtes fait il y a un an environ lorsque j'eus l'honneur de vous être présenté par l'entremise de M. Philarète Chasles,[2] m'enhardit à vous demander la permission de vous présenter un de mes amis, M. Stanley, professeur de l'Université d'Oxford, qui a rendu depuis longtemps un respect et un hommage des plus sincères à votre admirable talent et à vos travaux historiques, et qui desire vivement vous être connu.[3]

Bien que jeune encore, M. Stanley s'est déjà fait distinguer par un ouvrage fort remarquable sur le premier siècle du Christianisme,[4] entres tous les theologiens Anglais de la nouvelle école liberale.

J'ose espérer, Monsieur que M. Stanley vous priera au nom de tous les étudiants anglais de ne pas cesser à travailler au milieu même des distractions politiques dans ce champs vénérable de l'histoire et du passé où personne ne saurait vous remplacer.

Agréez Monsieur l'assurance de ma considération la plus distinguée.

M. Arnold.

MS. Bibliothèque Historique de la Ville de Paris.

1. Jules Michelet (1798–1874), perhaps the most famous, most loved, and most Gallic of all French historians, had by this date already written six volumes of *Histoire de France* (1833–43) and numerous other works, including *Le Peuple* (see above p. 82 n. 5) and the first volume of *La Révolution française* (1847). From 1838 to Jan. 1848 he occupied the chair of history at the Collège de France, was suspended, and then, reinstated in the revolutionary fervor of Mar. 1848, remained there till the *coup d'état* of Napoleon III in Dec. 1851. Arnold met him in Paris in 1847, and, as will be seen later, called on him again in 1859 (see below p. 442).

2. See above p. 93 n. 2.

3. "The news of the French Revolution threw Stanley into a fever of excitement. . . . On Saturday, April 8th, the party, consisting of Stanley, Jowett, F. Palgrave, and [Robert] Morier . . . left Folkestone for Boulogne" (Stanley, 1 : 390–91).

4. *Sermons and Essays on the Apostolical Age* (Oxford, 1847).

To Arthur Hugh Clough

[London]

Dear Clough   4¾ Monday, [April 10, 1848]

I am not sure of having time to send you a paper: I am only just come from my man—but all is perfectly quiet—The Chartists gave up at once in the greatest fright at seeing the preparations: braggarts as they are, says my man: & Fergus O'Connor and Co.[1]—after giving themselves into custody expressed the greatest thankfulness to the Government that their polite offer was not taken advantage of on condition of their making the crowd disperse.—Then came ½ an hour after, the hard rain.

—The petition is quietly progressing in cabs, unattended, to Westminster.

—There may be a little row in the evening, from the congregated pickpockets &c.—but nothing much I think certainly.   Your's

M. A.

F. W. N.	Paris [?]Ls
B. C. B.	Lon Oxford May 21st
R. W. E.	don [?][Lenkr.]
Chapman & Hall	L'p'l June 15
Wigglesworth	
Bank.	
Passport[2]	

MS. Yale University.

1. Feargus O'Connor (1794–1855: *DNB*), the Chartist leader, was M.P. from Nottingham. The demonstration, staged for the sake of presenting to Parliament a gigantic petition for the enactment of the six points of the People's Charter, fizzled out when O'Connor "engaged for its peaceable character" (*Annual Register*, pp. 50–54). Recent historians have stringently revised the received Establishment views (including those of Lansdowne, Arnold, Kingsley's novel *Alton Locke, Annual Register,* and *DNB*) of O'Connor, Chartism in general, and Apr. 10 in particular: see James Epstein, *The Lion of Freedom: Feargus O'Connor and the Chartist Movement, 1832–1842* (1982), Henry Weisser, *April 10 Challenge and Response in England in 1848* (1983), and especially John Saville, *1848: The British State and the Chartist Movement* (1987).

2. Clough's notations: Francis William Newman, Benjamin Collins Brodie, Ralph

Waldo Emerson, Wigglesworth, Yorkshire, near Settle; "Paris Ls" may be "Paris £s"(or possibly Paris L[ondo]n; "Lenkr." remains elusive; and "L'p'l" is of course Liverpool.

To Mary Penrose Arnold*

Dear Mamma   Wednesday, [April 12, 1848]
    Don't trouble yourself to send me papers—for I see all papers at clubs and so forth. Thank you very much, dear, nevertheless for the Economist. That article is said here to be Wilson's not Greg's.[1] How is this? To say the truth the responsibility of sending back a paper weighs on my mind.
    The National[2] of yesterday reports that London was *en pleine insurrection*. Do you wish for the National always or only when I think it interesting? This question I asked before and received no answer.
    I saw Emerson the other day and had a very pleasant interview.[3] I did not think him just to Wordsworth—he had a very just appreciation of Miss Martineau which indeed no man of a certain delicacy of intellectual organization can fail to have. He said Carlyle was much agitated by the course of things: he had known he said a European revolution was inevitable, but had expected the old state of things to last out his time. He gives our institutions as they are called—aristocracy—Church—&c. five years, I heard last night: long enough certainly for patients already at death's door to have to die in. I was at the Chartist convention the other night—and was much struck with the ability of the speakers.[4] However I should be sorry to live under their Government—nor do I intend to: though Nemesis would rejoice at their triumph—The ridiculous terror of people here is beyond belief—and yet it is not likely I fear to lead to any good results.
    Tell Miss Martineau it is said here that M. Milnes[5] refused to be sworn in a special constable, that he might be free to assume the post of President of the Republic at a moment's notice. Edward are my fishing books at home?   ever yours

                                                            M. Arnold

MS. Balliol College.

    1. Without more information the article is unidentifiable but might have been the substantial opening essay in the number for Apr. 1, "The Fermentation of Europe" (pp. 365–68), of which the closing sentence reads: "The wise course for England and Europe to pursue throughout the present crisis, seems to us both obvious and simple. We must regard France as suffering in the paroxysm of a strange disease and draw a cordon sanitaire around her, till the violence of the malady shall have spent itself, and the danger of contagion shall be past." This article was reprinted in Greg's *Essays on Political and Social Science* (1853), 2:1–62.

James Wilson (1805–60: *DNB*), politician and political economist, established the *Economist*, a weekly (later edited by his son-in-law Walter Bagehot), in 1843; in 1847 he was elected to Parliament from Westbury, Wilts, and later became an important figure in government. See "Memoir of the Right Hon. James Wilson" (reprinted from the *Economist*) in Walter Bagehot's *Literary Studies*.

William Rathbone Greg (1809–81: *DNB*), essayist, who had settled in the Lake Country in 1842, was a neighbor of Southey, Harriet Martineau, Wordsworth, and Hartley Coleridge as well as of "the Speddings, the Arnolds at Fox How, the Davys at Ambleside, the Fletchers at Lancrig," as John Morley writes. His second wife (m. 1874), was a daughter of James Wilson. Greg's *Literary and Social Judgments* (1868) included essays on Madame de Staël, French Fiction (on George Sand, among others), Chateaubriand, and Tocqueville, as well as English fiction ("False Morality of Lady Novelists"), "Why Are Women Redundant?," and "The Doom of the Negro Race." See John Morley's "W. R. Greg: A Sketch" in *Critical Miscellanies*.

2. *Le National* (see above p. 91).

3. This was the second European tour of Ralph Waldo Emerson (1803–82: *DAB*), whom Arnold met in London with Clough on Sunday, Apr. 9 (Kenny, p. 240). Most of what is known about the meeting (and all in Rusk's biography of Emerson) comes from this letter, and Arnold did not allude to it in his lecture on Emerson in 1883 (Super, 10: 165–86). Carlyle's essay "Chartism" appeared in 1839.

4. The National Convention sat from Tuesday, Apr. 4, till Saturday, Apr. 8, at the Library Institute, John Street, Fitzroy Square (Saville, *1848*, pp. 103–5).

5. Richard Monckton Milnes (1809–85: *DNB*; *VF*, 9/3/70), later Lord Houghton, far more conspicuous in Tennyson, Swinburne, and most other circles than in Arnold's, was later on a renowned host and collector of celebrities, *objets d'art*, and erotica. In 1848 he was M.P. from Pontrefact and, already author of several volumes of poetry and books of travel, acquired more fame as the author of the very important *Life, Letters and Literary Remains of John Keats*. published in August. A letter from Houghton to Arnold, 1878, is printed in *Album*, pp. 47, 113–14.

To Arthur Hugh Clough

[London]

Dear Clough   Friday, [? April 14, 1848][1]

Receipt takes a p.

I would not say *unworthily*—for that sounds like conscious peculation.[2]

And perhaps the second Paragraph is a little obscure & heavy. But the general thing is right, I think—though I would have had it shorter. Quite right to wait about signing it. I care very little about it—except that it is one of the few changes I think *clearly desirable* as well as *necessary*.

And to know that there are traitors within the place mightily enheartens the attaquers.

Tell me when you have fixed on your line, & I will write to Stanley.

—I hear Cobden's slip about the American Consul has done him great harm: the House firmly believing he told a lie.[3] I cannot say how it was with him: but by Yorkshire & Lancashire eo perventum est[4] that such a feat in their champion would not much shock them.

—A friend of Morris's[5] says—now is the time to preach Christ to France—Germany cannot do it, England must.—I like the king of Prussia, but he is misdated & misplaced, I fear, even in Germany.[6]

—I was glad to see you the other day, and spiritually to shake hands. Do not let us forsake one another: we have the common quality, now rare, of being unambitious, I think. Some must be contented not to be at the top.

I have G. Sand's letter[7]—do you want it? I do not like it so well as at first. For my soul I cannot *understand* this violent praise of the people. I praise a fagot whereof the several twigs are nought: but a *people*?   your's

M. Arnold.—

MS. *Yale University.*

1. Lowry's date, Mar. 24, is too early, since Arnold could not have read George Sand's letter before Saturday, Apr. 1 (see note 7, below).

2. "Arnold . . . is apparently discussing a draft of formal resignation, and expresses his conviction that revolt within the colleges against the Articles will encourage those who might like to see Oxford disassociated from them" (Lowry, p. 76). See Mulhauser, 1:219–22.

3. Richard Cobden (1804–65: *DNB*), statesman and M.P. from the West Riding, Yorkshire, did not literally *prevaricate*, but he allowed the House to believe that a conversation with the American consul at Malta in 1836–37 had in fact taken place recently. This deviousness was exposed in the House on Mar. 20, and there was a censorious editorial in *The Times* next day and a "severe leading article" on Apr. 7. See Lowry, pp. 170–71. In 1864 Arnold had some correspondence with Cobden, who has been called the "most important nineteenth century British politician never to have held national government office" (Nicholas Edsall, *Richard Cobden: Independent Radical*, p. vii).

4. It has got to the point.

5. John Brande ("Jack") Morris (1812–80: Boase), at Balliol from 1830 to 1834 (B.A.) and then a fellow of Exeter College from 1837 to 1846, when he resigned because of his conversion to Roman Catholicism, an ardent and "learned Newmanist" (Mulhauser, 1:82, 168) and Hebrew lecturer, was the author of *Nature a Parable; a Poem* (1842) and *Essay towards the Conversion of Learned and Philosophical Hindoos* (1843) and, later, of other religious works. (See also Allibone; Tuckwell, p. 151.)

6. Arnold is thinking of Friedrich Wilhelm IV (1795–1861), king of Prussia, in contrast to Ludwig of Bavaria (who, besotted with Lola Montez, had just abdicated in favor of his son) and the heads of the other German states. See the excellent summary in *Annual Register*, pp. 355–94 and Lowry's note, p. 77.

7. George Sand's two *Lettres au peuple*, "Hier et aujourd'hui" and "Aujourd'hui et demain," dated (as Lowry noted) Mar. 7 and 19, were first *published*, by Hetzel, on Apr. 1 and 8 (and then reprinted in her journal, *La Cause du peuple*, on Apr. 9 and 16), according to Spoelberch, pp. 26–27). Arnold had apparently seen only the first letter.

Clough had been in London with Arnold on Saturday and Sunday, Mar. 18 and 19, and saw him there again on Thursday, Apr. 5, and Friday, Apr. 21 (Kenny, pp. 245–46).

Edward Penrose Arnold to Mary Penrose Arnold

Sandgate

My dearest Mamma   Sunday, April 15, [1848]

It is some time since I have written, but when you hear the reason you will not wonder. *I have been at Paris.* The Aldersons determined to go a 4 day's trip to France, and I went with them. On Tuesday we started by the boat for Boulogne at 11.30, and started by the evening train at 8 o'clock for Paris: We rolled a great deal in crossing, but though I was very uncomfortable, yet I was not outright sick. The passage was only 2 hours & 10 minutes. The railway journey was frightfully tinny, and I did not sleep a wink all night. The party exactly filled a carriage, and consisted of the Baron & Lady Alderson,[1] the two eldest sons & daughters, Mr Dodsworth who joined us at Folkestone, and myself,—8 in all. We got to Paris by 5 in the morning, and went off directly to Meurice's in a Bus. We passed Prudhomme's newspaper office, and at that hour the street was crowded with people waiting for that horrible revolutionary trash which the "Peuple" disseminates. We did not go to bed, but washed & then sallied forth. Our Salon was very high up, au cinquième, but it looked over the Tuilleries Garden, and the trees were all quite out, being mostly as you know horse-chestnuts & lindens.—But oh, the dream that these two days in Paris have been! Wednesday and Thursday we spent there, and on Friday we got to Amiens by 12 o'clock and stayed there till Saturday (yesterday) morning, when we came back to Boulogne and crossed over at 2 in the afternoon. There was a great swell, and I was dreadfully ill all the time: the boat was crowded with the English deputation returning, the most awful set of snobs & vulgar people that you can imagine. There was also a dreadful smell of paint, which the hot sun brought out insufferably. This afternoon I am stopping home from church, as I really am not quite recovered enough to go again, and in Hyth church this morning I was still feeling sick.—The whirl of these last 4 days renders it impossible to know where to begin describing: but I have begun a journal, which you shall see directly it is finished. But the things that produced the greatest impression on one were the Champs Elysees at ½ past 4 o'clock on Thursday afternoon, a lovely summer day, and crowded as it was with people and carriages:—The Cathedral at Amiens which I shall never forget, the general state of fear and anxiety in which everybody seemed to be living as though Paris were a volcano which might blow up tomorrow,—the enormous number of troops everywhere, for there are more than 50,000 troops of the line & nearly 200,000 National Guards in Paris; and so on: for I find that everything was entirely new & everything made a great impression: which never can be entirely effaced, however often I may in future go to the Continent. I can hardly believe that so much has happened within a week, and yet my head is full of nothing else.—Thanks for your letter which I found yesterday. When shall I see you all. I have sent to Walrond to send my letters to Long's so that I can answer Mr Burg's [?Bury's] a day sooner at all events. Love to all the darlings from your most loving & devoted Son

E P Arnold.

MS. Balliol College.

1. Sir Edward Hall Alderson (1787–1857: *DNB*; knt 1830), judge, baron of Court of Exchequer 1834–57. He married Georgina Drewe (d. 1871) in 1823, and they were a "large family" (*Annual Register*); his two older sons, Edward Pakenham (d. 1876), whom Arnold thought "rather a young ass" (see below p. 342) and Charles Henry (1831–1913: *WWW*), who became a school inspector (see below p. 383n), appear to have been widely known. See Hopkinson, pp. 27–30.

To Arthur Hugh Clough

[London]

Dear Clough   [? mid-April, 1848]

I had used the same words almost to Blackett about Cobden & the H[ouse] of C[ommons].[1]

—And the newspapers—my God!—But they & the H. of C. represent England at the present moment very fairly.

I cannot believe that the mass of people here would see much bloodshed in Ireland without asking themselves what they were shedding it to *uphold*. And when the answer came—1. a chimerical Theory about some possible dangerous foreign alliances with independent Ireland: 2. a body of Saxon landlords—3. a Saxon Ch[urch] Estab[lishmen]t their consciences must smite them. I think I told you that the performance of Polyeucte[2] suggested to me the right of large bodies of men to have what article they liked produced for them. The Irish article is not to my taste: still we have no really superiour article to offer them, which alone can justify the violence offered by a Lycurgus or a Cromwell to a foolish nation, as unto Children.[3]—It makes me sick to hear Ld Clarendon praised so;[4] as if he was doing anything but cleverly managing the details of an imposture.

I do not want England to attack Russia: she has no real share in this movement: & there is no good in her having an apparent one.[5] Expectandum est.[6]—I send G. S.[7]   Your's

M. A.

MS. Yale University.

1. See above p. 103 n. 2 and, for Blackett, above p. 75.

2. Arnold, who saw Corneille's play in Paris in June and again in Dec. 1846, seems to refer to the conversion of Romans and Armenians (Néarque, Polyeucte, Pauline, Félix and perhaps Sévère) to Christianity.

3. Deuteronomy 32:21 or Romans 10:19 plus Hebrews 12:5.

4. George William Frederick Villiers (1800–1870: *DNB*; *VF*, 4/24/69), 4th earl of Clarendon, was Lord-Lieutenant of Ireland 1847–52. The coercive Crown and Government Security bill (treason-felony), introduced on Apr. 7, became law on Apr. 22. "Dangerous foreign alliances" refers to Lamartine's pro forma reception and, in a playlet approved by Lord Normanby, suave rebuff on Apr. 3 of an Irish mission seeking support. "Saxon" comprises the British in Great Britain and the protestants in Ireland, and Arnold is referring to tenant-right agitation and the Encumbered Estates Bill, mere fingers in the dike, which was finally passed at the end of July. See *Annual Register*, pp. 114–22, and Kevin B. Nowlan's excellent article "The Political Background," in *The Great Famine Studies in Irish History 1845–52*, ed. R. Dudley Edwards and T. Desmond Williams, pp. 192–94.)

5. Attack *verbally* or *diplomatically*, for there was never any question of an armed attack, and Arnold was not an alarmist. Because of the revolution in France the Russian emperor had rattled sabers by strengthening his border forces and, on Mar. 26, issuing a ringing manifesto (printed in *The Times* on Apr. 6, reprinted in the *Annual Register*, pp. 372–74). Lowry's long note (pp. 171–72) takes the fulminations in the House of Thomas Chisholm Anstey (1816–73: *DNB*), M.P. for Youghal and radical of radicals, more seriously than Anstey's colleagues took them: his anti-Russia motion made and seconded, the House adjourned for lack of a quorum.

6. It is necessary to wait and see.

7. See above p. 103 n. 7.

Francis Turner Palgrave to Thomas Arnold

Hampstead
April 28, 1848

Clough is about to go to Paris—with R. W. Emerson, whom he and I, and Stanley and others, made acquaintance with very agreeably (I thought often of you and wished you were there) at Oxford. I have just returned from Paris, after a fortnight spent there very agreeably, with Stanley, Jowett, and fat old Morier of Balliol. We saw great views of 300,000 troops, and attended various clubs. Their prospects are rather dark, from financial difficulties— but we were much struck with the good sense and sobriety (mental as well as bodily) of the *blouses*—whilst the noblesse, by cutting the place nearly to a man, no cry of à bas les aristocrats having been raised, show that they at least, are unfit to reign. I *long* to hear how you like your life—feeling dismally unsettled about my own (do not repeat this)—although at present I expect to be fixed for some time with Temple of Balliol in a Govt School. Farewell! with best love and most frequent remembrance

Yrs F. T. Palgrave.

MS. Balliol College.

To Jane Martha Arnold

London

My dearest K May 11, 1848[1]

How did you get hold of Festus?[2] I can imagine it a book Miss Martineau worships. The man wrote it between 1 & 3 & 20: and it shews a remarkable person no doubt. Whether a remarkable poet is another thing. The book like Kingsley's play[3] is cramm'd with passages & pervaded by a tone which in persons of much less power perhaps (as Gray) but of a strictly poetical turn, could by no possibility occur. There is perhaps a kind of free masonry as to detecting the absence or presence of this tone: I miss it in Clough and find it even in Heber.[4] If united with a very low degree of intellectural energy, or if found in a man whose circumstances are unfavorable to its developement, it may not by itself preserve poetry, as thousands of vers de societé in which it was present have been lost: but no intellectual energy can compensate for its absence. The world, which does not clearly know what it wants but which is yet no more allowed to feed permanently on what is not sound than cows are allowed to feed on nightshade, always lets *unpoetical* poems drop after a time. I suspect Faust & Festus compared would shew the difference between a poet's treatment of a perilous subject & a vigorous able imaginative man's, not properly a poet: I say a perilous subject, for so it is: & the Greeks are eternally interesting because they have nothing to do with such, but keep nearer to the *facts* of human life. And also Faust which was in its time in 1790 is not in its time in 1845.[*sic*] Goethe in his old age was imploring constantly the young poets to remember that attempts which were inevitable in his youth, were in the then state of the world & of literature out of place.[5] However England has fallen intellectually so far behind the continent that we cannot expect to see her assisting to carry on the intellectual work of the world from the point to which it is now arrived: for to what point it is arrived not 20 English people know: so profoundly has activity in this country extirpated reflexion.[6] So we may expect to see English people doing things which have long been done, & re-discovering[7] what has been discovered & used up elsewhere, like Faustism. Meanwhile I shall proceed on my way, thankful for the circumstances that have made me awake to the necessity of somehow getting my head above the present English atmosphere in order to accomplish anything permanent. You are wrong about Goethe I am quite sure, but I will not dispute.

I don't think the Ministry are even yet quite secure.

Your affectionate

M. A.

MS. Balliol College.

1. Since S. O. A. Ullman dates this letter "[1850]" in *Matthew Arnold: The Yale Manuscript*, 1989, pp. 143, 200), it is necessary to point out that in Arnold's date ("May 11/48") the last two numbers are so obscured by cross-writing that certainty of transcription is not possible. My date is based on internal evidence alone.

2. A revised edition of Bailey's *Festus* was issued early in 1848 and was discussed not only by Arnold and Clough (see above, p. 82) but also by Tennyson and Emerson (Tennyson 1:283, 285). The next edition of *Festus* was in 1852.

3. *The Saint's Tragedy*, the only play of Charles Kingsley (1819–75: *DNB*; *VF*, 3/30/72), novelist, Christian Socialist, and for nearly a decade Regius Professor of Modern History at Cambridge, was published in Jan. 1848. Another Arnold sister, Mary Twining, was reading it in the summer, as Clough reported to Tom Arnold (Mulhauser, 1:216).

4. Reginald Heber (1723–1826: *DNB*), bishop of Calcutta and poet, is remembered as a hymnwriter ("From Greenland's Icy Mountains," "Holy, Holy, Holy," "The Son of God Goes Forth to War," and others), treasured perhaps for reasons other than their "strictly poetical turn."

5. See below, pp. 114–15. Lowry (p. 87) identifies the source as Goethe's "Homer noch einmal" in *Schriften zur Literatur*, pt 3.

6. See above p. 95.

7. Transcribed by Ullman (p. 143) as "see discovering."

To Arthur Hugh Clough[1]

London

Dear Clough   Wednesday, [May 24, 1848]

Thanks for all favours.

I broke my anti-journal rule to see what was become of Hume's Motion this morning, and find it put off—with a stinging speech from Cobden at O'Connor—an unfortunate declaration (I think) from Lord John which Hume turns to account in his address to the people and perhaps more remarkable than any, a speech from Milner Gibson, who has got quite clear now.[2]

What you say about France is just about the impression I get from the accounts of things there—it must be disheartening to the believers in progress—or at least in any progress but progress en ligne spirale which Goethe allows man[3]—tho: from him I scarcely understand this concession. If you remember it is exactly Wordsworth's account of the matter in his letter in the 'friend'[4]—wch is curious—but this you don't much want to hear.

—There was a report here the other day that George Sand was arrested—not true I suppose—but how charming the beginning of F.[rancois] le Champi is and how did you like Teverino—Her true style now, indeed?[5] Milnes perhaps you find very pleasant alone or where there is no necessity for him briller: it is that fatal need which unsexes quite the sweetest-natured perhaps who are not at the same time philosophers.[6]

A sudden thought strikes me—is my man going to the Derby—for at the door stands a brougham with a postillion and pair. . . . [7]

I met Martin the American Chargé d'affaires to Rome[8] the other day— such a contrast—so exuberant jolly and all-permitting—praying for the stability of this country, looking on the American revolution as a mere political developement against the will of a Tory govt.: and being, not a triumph over the England nation—and equally disliking and despising the Yankees. From the south therefore—a strong head and face, and truly genial—he only said, Sir and Ma'am that was wrong—alas, the Children of this world etc.—

Last night I met R. Palmer[9] who worded me like the Devil. however I praised him for his votes and attitude in Parliament. Have you seen an article in the Examiner signed M. in answer to Carlyle on Ireland. Mill's, they say.[10]—Mithridate was a young man's effort—but you know you are a mere d—d depth hunter in poetry and therefore exclusive furiously. You might write a speech in Phèdre—Phedra loquitur—but you could not write Phèdre.[11] And when you adopt this or that form you must sacrifice much to the ensemble, and that form in return for admirable effects demands immense sacrifices and precisely in that quarter where your nature will not allow you to make them. Have you read Andromaque, and what do you think of Rachel—greater in what she is than in her creativity, eh? exactly the converse of Jenny Lind.[12] By the way what an enormous obverse that young woman and excellent singer has.

Farewell—Farewell—your judgement cannot allow you to get the common slow picture of Beethoven.[13] I have got a good Goethe—the og.German—quite by accident.

M. A.

I've a great mind to send you Bohn's Catalogue[14] with this by post and not to affranchir.

Text. Lowry, pp. 80–81.

1. The location of the manuscript of this letter, unrevealed by Lowry, remains unknown, and the ellipsis below, after "postilion and pair," remains unexplained (see above p. xxiv).

2. Joseph Hume (1777–1855: *DNB*) was M.P. for Montrose; Lord John Russell (1792–1878: *DNB*; *VF*, 6/5/69), the great Whig leader, third son of the 6th duke of Bedford and raised to the peerage himself in 1861 as Earl Russell and Viscount Amberley, prime minister since 1846; Thomas Milner-Gibson (1806–84: *DNB*), M.P. for Manchester, was vice-president of the board of trade under Russell (and a privy councillor) but had left office in Apr. ("got quite clear now").

"Joseph Hume's motion for extending the electoral franchise was put off at 11.15 p.m. until June 20. O'Connor, the Chartist leader, claimed that this postponement was only added evidence of the attempt of the middle classes further to trifle with the working men. Cobden, in turn, severely rebuked O'Connor for setting the masses always against any movement that could really help them. Lord John Russell, in course of the debate, said he believed the middle and working classes generally wanted neither the Charter nor Hume's reforms. On the principal page of *The Times* next morning, Hume called attention to Lord John's remark and asked his supporters now to let there be no doubt as to their convictions (*Times*, May 24, 1848, pp. 2–4). Milner Gibson's speech was a strong protest against the way the House could trifle time on empty matters, and a sharp reply to George Bentinck's attack upon free trade" (Lowry, pp. 81–82).

3. In Goethe's "Materialien zur Geschichte der Farbenlehre" ("Einleitung," par. 3), as Lowry notes (p. 82). The French phrase "en ligne spirale" does not suggest that Arnold read "The Theory of Colors" in French, for it had apparently not been translated into French at this date and moreover for Goethe's "Spiralbewegung" the French idiom would be simply "en spirale."

4. Wordsworth's "Reply to Mathetes," *The Friend*, Dec. 14, 1809, Jan. 4, 1810, was often reprinted and included in collected editions.

5. George Sand's novel *François le champi* (1850), reviewed in the *Athenæum* in May, had appeared in the *Journal des débats*, Dec. 31, 1847-Mar. 14, 1848 (and also in *Le Courier belge* in Feb.-Mar.), and there were several unauthorized editions of it in Brussels in 1848. The charming "beginning" must be the "Avant-propos." *Teverino* was published in 1845. "The rumour of her arrest was reported in *The Times* of Monday, May 22" (Lowry, p. 82) and circulated in Paris, though in fact she had left Paris for Nohant on May 17: "Je ne suis cependant partie que le 17 au soir, parce qu'on me disait que je devais être arrêtée" (George Sand, *Correspondance*, ed. Georges Lubin, 8:461).

6. Richard Monckton Milnes, very much the man about town in Paris as in London, "set off to observe what was happening there for himself. In Paris he was found by Mr. [W. E.] Forster, who was also attracted to the spot, staying at Meurice's Hotel, "fraternising with everybody," and making himself equally at home in the salons of the Legitimists and the soirées of the Communists. It added of course immensely to his interest in the movements in Paris that he was on terms of personal intimacy with most of the leading men in the France of that day, from the King downwards. His curiosity was insatiable, and was in no degree limited by his likes or dislikes" (Reid, 1:404).

7. In attendance at the Derby on this date were three dukes, three marquises, twelve earls, and two dozen additional titles, but Lansdowne was not among them (*The Times*, May 26, p. 6).

8. "Mr. Jacob L. Martin, Chargé d'Affaires at Paris from Oct. 1, 1846, to June 28,

1847, was given [a] similar appointment to the Papal States in Apr. 1848. He was in England during the spring of 1848 for his health. He left England for Rome on July 17, 1848, dying little more than a month later from apoplexy. (Record furnished by courtesy of the Department of State, Washington.)" (Lowry, p. 82).

9. Roundell Palmer (1812–95: *DNB*; cr. earl of Selborne, 1882; *VF*, 3/16/72), of Rugby (before Dr Arnold, whom he later knew well and who introduced him to Stanley), Winchester, Christ Church and Trinity, Oxford, and then a fellow of Magdalen College, 1834–48. From 1847 to 1857 he was Member for Plymouth and from 1861 to 1872 for Richmond. A High Church conservative who gradually became a liberal, he was twice Lord Chancellor under Gladstone, though he broke with him over Home Rule. His "votes and attitude in Parliament" may have had to do partly with the reform of the Examination Statute at Oxford (see Jowett, 1 : 174).

10. Carlyle's "The Repeal of the Union" (advocating force against anarchy in Ireland) was in the *Examiner*, Apr. 29, 1848 (rpt in *Rescued Essays*, pp. 15–52); the reply of John Stuart Mill (1806–73: *DNB*) in the *Examiner*, May 13, pp. 307–8 (rpt in *Collected Works of John Stuart Mill*, vol. 25, *Newspaper Writings*, ed. Ann P. Robson and John M. Robson, pp. 1095–1100) was of course an "unqualified dissent."

11. In Paris Clough saw Rachel in Racine's *Phèdre* at the Théâtre de la République on May 9 and 11 and *Mithridate* on May 18 (Kenny, p. 248).

12. Jenny Lind (1820–87: *DNB*: naturalized a British subject in 1859), the Swedish singer, whom Clough had heard in London a year earlier and was to hear again in 1849 (Mulhauser, 1 : 181, 183, 243, 245) was singing in London at Her Majesty's Theatre. Arnold's phrase "enormous obverse" is perhaps, as Honan (p. 121) wickedly implies, a deliberate counterthrust to Tom Arnold's "supersensual" and "superhuman" (Mulhauser, 1 : 183).

Her popularity was a national mania, and Oxford (where she was "Stanley's guest, having stayed with his father [the Bishop] at the Palace when she sang at Norwich") went "crazy" over her in December (Tuckwell, p. 79; see also *A Victorian Dean, a Memoir of Arthur Stanley*, ed. the dean of Windsor and Hector Bolitho, pp. 45–46).

13. The allusion is not clear.

14. Henry George Bohn, *A Catalogue of Books* (1841), known as the "Guinea Catalogue," which weighed nearly seven pounds, contained 1,948 pages, 23,000 articles, and a list of 300,000 books. See Francesco Cordasco, *The Bohn Libraries: A History and a Checklist*, 1951, p. 104.

To Arthur Hugh Clough

London
Dear Clough   Thursday, [? June 29, 1848]
Do you know that Ld Lovelace's son's tutorship is again open?[1]

Or do you indeed as you suggested mean to become one of those "misanthropical hermits who are incapable of seeing that the Muse willingly *accompanies* life but that in no wise does she understand to *guide* it?"[2]

I spare you the rest about "nimbly recovering oneself" &c. of which you will guess the to you quite alien author.

—I am divided between a desire to see those cursed poltroons the Lombards well kicked—and to have so ugly a race as the Germans removed from Italy. I suppose for travellers it is desirable that the Germans should remain as police & the useful arts generally are unknown to the Italians.[3]

What a nice state of things in France.[4] The New Gospel is adjourned for this bout. If one had ever hoped any thing from such a set of d____d grimacing liars as their prophets one would be very sick just now. I returned & saw under the sun &c—but time & chance happeneth unto all.[5]

—If you mean to do nothing why not emigrate? Shake yourself[6]—it is easier to discover what we *can* do than our vanity lets us think. For God's sake don't mope, for from that no good can come.

I have not even begun the work you allude to in your last.

Your friend—

M. A.

MS. Yale University.

1. Lovelace was William King, later King-Noel (1805–93), who succeeded as Baron King and Ockham in 1833 and was created earl of Lovelace in 1838. In 1835 he married Byron's daughter Ada (d. 1852), and of their two children the younger son, Ralph Gordon Noel King [Milbanke] (1839–1906: *DNB*), who became Baron Wentworth on the death in 1862 of his older brother (Byron Noel, a pathetic victim of paternal tyranny) and succeeded as 2d earl of Lovelace, is referred to here. Brought up by his grandmother, Lady Byron, widow of the poet, "He was isolated from boys and girls of his own age, and his only contact with the male sex was in the persons of a dreary succession of tutors, only one or two of whom seemed to be at all fitted for their office" (Mary countess of Lovelace, *Ralph Earl of Lovelace*, 1920, pp. 3–4). In 1905 his *Astarte*, an attempted vindication of his grandmother, stirred up a storm that blows even now. (See below letter to Bagehot, Jan. 19, 1876.)

2. Goethe's *Zahme Xenien* [Tame Epigrams] 8:
   Jüngling, merke dir, in Zeiten,
   Wo sich Geist und Sinn erhöht:
   Dass die Muse zu *begleiten*,
   Doch zu *leiten* nicht versteht.

(This passage was identified by Lowry in the margin of a corrected copy at the College of Wooster.)

The substitution of "misanthropical hermits" for Goethe's "Jüngling" suggests connections with "The Scholar-Gipsy" and "Thyrsis" as well as with "Empedocles on Etna."

3. "In the latter part of June the Austrians captured both Padua and Palma Nuova, and their communications with Vienna, through the passes of the Tyrol, were now undisturbed by the presence of an enemy" (*Annual Register*, p. 324).

4. The four days of June, a revolution within a revolution: "The masses of unemployed workmen in Paris, who must either support themselves on the pittance doled out in the *Ateliers Nationaux* or starve, were ripe for a revolt," and on June 23 they manned the barricades against the National Guard in three or four days of civil war. "Paris was declared to be in a state of siege," and all the Executive powers were delegated to General

Cavaignac, who functioned as military dictator until June 28, when he became president of the Council and formed a cabinet. (*Annual Register*, pp. 282–89) See Clough's letter to Tom Arnold on July 16, and his comment: "Matt was at one time really heated to a very fervid enthusiasm, but he has become sadly cynical again of late" (Mulhauser, 1:214–15). "New Gospel" is not clear.

    5. Ecclesiastes 9:11.
    6. Echoing *Paradise Lost* 1.330.

To Arthur Hugh Clough

[London]
Dear Clough   Lundi, [July, 1848] [1]
    Did I ever say to you a fragment—

        "this little which we are
        "Swims on an obscure much we might have been" [2]

    I do not say I discern the *right* way for you: have we one? but such a way as the βουλή & νόος of man can shape out, pace Fato, that I tried to discern. [3] This β & ν do not talk of *the* absolutely right but of *a* promising method with ourselves. If you do nothing I see some dangers for you: & I suggest what precaution prudence suggests. But I dare say you will not be satisfied till you have tried your own way: if you think you have any absolute one I am sure you will not. follow it therefore—you will remember ὁ μὴ δαρεὶς ἄνθρωπος οὐ παιδεύεται. [4]

    Tell me what you are doing—and do not suppose I make pretension to *know* you or anybody.

    When do you publish? [5] do you go on writing? You see your [?]revived journal. Those Lombard republicans are S—s, [6] If ever such there were.   Your's

                                       M. A.

would I were hence,

MS. Yale University.

    1. Lowry's date, *faute de mieux* (the small sheet, 3¾" x 3," not seen before, is used later), and similarities of subject (especially "fragment") and handwriting suggest the letter to K, below pp. 143–44.
    2. Allott, p. 646. Arnold wrote this fragment and signed it (presumably to someone and possibly with the photograph framed with it) on Dec. 2, 1883 (Ulysses Catalogue no. 30, [Spring 1994], Lot 20), when he and his wife were staying with Charles Eliot Norton in Cambridge, "in whose house Clough passed 2 months" (letter to Thomas Arnold, Nov. 30, 1883).
    3. " 'Will (reason)' and 'perceptive intelligence' " (Lowry, p. 85n).

4. "'The man who has not been thrashed has not been disciplined.' A common Greek proverb" (Lowry, p. 85n).
5. *Ambarvalia* appeared in Jan. 1849.
6. See above p. 75.

Mary Penrose Arnold to Thomas Arnold

July 17, 1848

I heard from Matt yesterday after long silence, and in case he should not write regularly himself, I will tell you what he says about his language preparations for his tour abroad. "It is now said that Parliament will be up in the middle of August, instead of at the end, in which case I shall have *some longer days for Switzerland*, which I desire often. I shall have to speak German a little and Italian too—in the latter I am going to take twelve lessons, the former almost breaking my heart, because I cannot get to read it like French, though I work at it with fury. They are lumbering old cart-horses, the Germans, and that is the truth. Their endless chatter about minutiae and attempts to construct theories on insufficient evidence would make me furious, if I did not remember that they have had recourse to this because they have no practical life as in France and England, and the mind must be occupied. And in England there is too exclusive a practical life: however, I must say I think this extreme does not so confuse and tire out the mind and [*for* as] unfit it for the perception of the truth as the German one."

Text. Fox How after Dr Arnold's Death (Brotherton Collection).

To Arthur Hugh Clough

London

My dear Clough   July 20, [1848]

Goethe says somewhere that the Zeitgeist when he was young caused everyone to adopt the Wolfian theories about Homer, himself included:[1] and that when he was in middle age the same Zeitgeist caused them to leave these theories for the hypothesis of one poem & one author: inferring that in these matters there is no certainty, but alternating dispositions. This view, as congenial to me as uncongenial, I suspect, to you, causes me, while I confess that productions like your Adam & Eve[2] are not suited to me at present, yet to feel no confidence that they may not be quite right & calculated to suit others. The good feature in all your poems is the sincerity that is evident in them:

which always produces a powerful effect on the reader—and which most people with the best intentions lose totally when they sit down to write. The spectacle of a writer striving evidently to get breast to breast with reality is always full of instruction and very invigorating—and here I always feel you have the advantage of me: "much may be seen, tho: nothing can be solved"³—weighs upon me in writing. However it must be continued to tread the winepress alone.⁴

Ewald has just published a final volume:⁵ Stanley says he is not at all offensive like Newman,⁶ looking on Judaism as a religion: but that poor Newman being insane should not be judged harshly. Ewald judges the new revolutions very harshly tho:—and rates the Germans soundly for their imitations of the French—that shallow and Godless people, he says.

I have told Stanley of your intention to resign your fellowship—& Walrond: & I think Blackett—but no one else, and shall I think have strength given me to let it go no further.

But we are not in our own hands and can only watch & pray.⁷

God bless you: there is a God, but he is not well-conceived of by all.   Your affectionate

Matthew Arnold.—

MS. Yale University.

1. "Homer noch Einmal" in "Griechische und Römische Literatur," *Schriften zu Literatur und Theater* (Lowry, p. 87); the theories of Friedrich Wolf in *Prologomena ad Homerum* (1795) held "that the Homeric poems as we know them were a rather late blending of unconnected ancient lays handed down by oral recitation" (Super, 1:239).

2. Mulhauser, pp. 165–87; published in 1869 as "The Mystery of the Fall."

3. Unidentified.

4. Isaiah 63:3.

5. "Georg Heinrich August von Ewald (1803–75), the German scholar and theologian, whose study of the Hebrew origins was attracting wide interest" (Lowry, p. 86); the reference is to his *Alterthümer des Volkes Israels* (1848). Stanley (1:329–30) had met him in Dresden in 1844.

6. Francis William Newman (1805–97: *DNB*), younger brother of John Henry Newman, formerly (1826–30) a fellow of Balliol College, now professor of Latin at University College, London, and (from Feb. to Nov.) principal of University Hall, Gordon Square. (His successor was Clough.) On the very day of this letter he was present at the laying of the foundation stone on which his name was inscribed. See Newman's letter to Clough (Mulhauser, 1:187–90) in Dec. 1847. Arnold refers to Newman's *History of the Hebrew Monarchy* (1847). The hapless Newman reenters below p. 172 and later. See William Robbins, *The Newman Brothers*, pp. 169–72. Tuckwell (p. 205) remarks that in company Newman "did not so much converse as emit pilulous dogmas from his thin lips in a prim, didactic, authoritative tone."

7. Matthew 26:31, Mark 13:33, 14:38.

To Jane Martha Arnold

[July 31, 1848][1]
it is also true for everyone else in the world: to ask for no more than an
absolute conviction for ourselves without troubling ourselves with questions
we can never answer as to the existence of one same rule for all the world.
But generally we consider mere individual belief as only opinion and will not
act steadily on it: and have to become fanatics that is to impose one rule on
all the world before we can believe it ourselves. I send you as a birthday
present a sonnet ['Religious Isolation,' enclosed] on this subject addressed to
Clough a great *social* fanatic—

MS. *Balliol College (fragment).*

1. Allott cites the letter and says it is dated "31 July 1848"; Honan (p. 449) dates it
"[31 July 1848]." It was quoted by Alan Harris, without date, in "Matthew Arnold: The
Unknown Years," *Nineteenth Century,* Apr. 1933, p. 500. The sonnet was "Religious Isolation" (Allott, p. 109).

To Arthur Hugh Clough

London
Dear Clough   Thursday, [July–early August, 1848]
I had lost your note and was purposing to send all your papers to Liv-
erpool—but I have found it again & send them to the address you desired.
I have done you no harm by telling—I have told no one else: Stanley
inferred you were certainly *going* to have told him: no doubt said I. Redcar,
Yorkshire my family are at—but to Fox How with a "to be forwarded"
would have found them thoughtless villain.
—I meant to say that your treatment of Adam & Eve's story[1] rather
offended me: but then I was quite in another way just now.
The Gregs[2] are just the thing for you as a family—without pretension,
intelligent &c. 150£ is little certainly, but it means living in the house I conclude. But I should make plug[3] represent to them that a real graduated experienced well-known Oxford top-sawyer would snuff disdainfully *in his
opinion* at such a price: they must have been thinking of some inferior dis-
senting-made article. But if they excused their poverty (as they are embarrassed just now) I should say the family & the Lake Country made up for an
extra £50. You have £50 a year of your own at least—and God knows you
have few expenses as to dress &c. Still I should use jackall plug[4] to some

extent to feel & smell about. What do you want to write to my people about.   Your's ever

M. A.

MS. Yale University.

1. See above p. 115 and n. 2.
2. See above p. 102. Clough was at "Windermere, August 15 chez Greg" (Lowry, p. 88; Kenny, p. 254).
3. The Rev. Charles Thomas Arnold, Clough's friend (see above pp. 65–66n).
4. "A person who acts like a jackal, *esp.* one who does subordinate preparatory work or drudgery for another, or ministers to his requirements" (*OED*).

To Arthur Hugh Clough

London

My dear Love   August 12, 1848

"By our own spirits &c &c." [1]

I desire you should have some occupation—I think it desirable for everyone—very much so for you. Besides since the Baconian era wisdom is not found in desarts: and you again especially need the world & yet will not be absorbed by any quantity of it.—That Greg's £150 is monstrous:[2] probably the natural history is no more than would be most beneficial for you to learn & most healthful—you poor subjective, you—do you not care to know quo sidere &c.[3] But a person like you might probably soon turn the education your own way. And Esher is a heaven upon earth for beauty.

—I have been thinking about you for the Co-Examinership with Lingen:[4] it is the mathematical one—Temple says it would take you from 6 to 7 hours pr diem from now at mathematics to be up to the mark by Xmas when the appointment is made.—Eh? Altogether I don't think you'd stand that— and when you have begun the work is very hard—it is possible too Lingen might wish a less extraordinary colleague: but efforts might be made if you liked: £500 a year, & no oaths.—But considering Esher & all other things, I am for Ld King.[5] Why did you not tell me or some one who might have remonstrated before you answered Stanley in the negative, who weeps and answers not.[6] He is in Scotland—knowest thou where? I know not.—What are you doing—reading? writing?

M. A.

MS. Yale University.

1. Wordsworth, "Resolution and Independence," l. 47.
2. See above p. 102.

3. Virgil, *Georgics* 1.1, "At what season [it is well to till the soil]."

4. Ralph Robert Wheeler Lingen (1819–1905: *DNB*) after Trinity College, Oxford, became a fellow of Balliol, where he was Arnold's tutor, a relationship that shadowed them both thereafter. (Lowry's note p. 143 is off the mark: see below p. 273.) In 1847 he entered the Education Office and in 1849, precociously, became secretary, an office he held for twenty years. He was thus Arnold's superior and his name appears frequently in these letters, often subacidly. In 1869 he became permanent secretary to the Treasury, was made K.C.B. in 1878, created baron in 1885. He was an important civil servant—and a self-important bureaucrat, a stickler for rules, long on efficiency and self-righteousness, short on compassion and charm. See an excellent, long article by A. S. Bishop, "Ralph Lingen, Secretary to the Education Department 1849–1870," *British Journal of Educational Studies* 16, no. 2 (1968):138–63. See below p. 273.

"Two officials, with the title of 'Examiner,' whose function would be to scrutinize the reports of H. M. I[nspector]s and make recommendations on them, were engaged on a temporary basis. Lingen was made Chief Examiner, the other position going to a young cleric, the Rev. Frederick Temple, who was waiting to take up his duties as the first Principal of Kneller Hall, the proposed training college for workhouse schoolmasters" (A. S. Bishop, "Ralph Lingen," p. 139).

Frederick Temple (see above p. 60), having been a fellow, tutor, and junior dean of Balliol, was on the threshold of the illustrious career for which he was manifestly destined: headmaster of Rugby School, bishop of Exeter (see Arnold's congratulatory letter Oct. 12, 1869), bishop of London, and archbishop of Canterbury, 1896–1902. See E. G. Sandford, ed., *Memoirs of Archbishop Temple* (1906) and Tuckwell, pp. 216–21.

5. Courtesy title of the younger son of the earl of Lovelace, who lived at Esher with his grandmother (see above p. 112 n. 1).

6. Job 35:12?

To Arthur Hugh Clough

L[ansdowne] H[ouse]

Dear Clough   Friday, [August or September, 1848]

The exercise of the intellect is to you not grievous but pleasant: therefore I send you Edward's questions which I am incapable of fitly answering, and which if you will solve & send to Redcar to him it were well.[1] I know you can do this without book—so wonderful a thing is practice.

I have been reading with equal surprize & profit lately the short work—

> "Of that lame slave who in Nicopolis
> "Taught Arrian, when Vespasian's brutal son
> "Cleared Rome of what most sham'd him— [2]

There's for you but this style is not hard tho: rather taking. What dispute is now going on

> "Where young Archestes doth with Ister join,
> Ister, Tethys & Ocean's sixth-born son."[3]

—But the difference between Herodotus & Sophocles is that the former sought over all the world's surface for that interest the latter found within man.   Your's affectionately

M. Arnold.

MS. Yale University.

1. Edward Penrose Arnold was at Redcar, Yorkshire, preparing for the examinations for his B.A. degree (see below p. 127 n. 2).
2. "The first draft of the tribute to Epictetus in Arnold's early sonnet, *To a Friend.* The 'short work' is the *Enchiridion*" (Lowry, p. 90).
3. Lowry (p. 90): "Ister, in Hesiod and Sophocles, and generally in classical literature, is the name of the present Danube. A long search . . . has failed, however, to find the word 'Archestes'. [Allott, p. 646, reads "Anchestes."] Apparently it refers to some tributary of the Danube. . . . Arnold is doubtless thinking of the trouble in the Danube valley that marked the general European crises of 1848." *The Times* in July and Aug. had many reports on the "Danubian Principalities."

To Arthur Hugh Clough[1]

Baths of Leuk
My dear Clough   September 29, 1848

A woodfire is burning in the grate and I have been forced to drink champagne to guard against the cold and the café noir is about to arrive, to enable me to write a little. For I am all alone in this vast hotel: and the weather having been furious rain for the last few days, has tonight turned itself towards frost.[2] Tomorrow I repass the Gemmi and get to Thun: linger one day at the Hotel Bellevue for the sake of the blue eyes of one of its inmates:[3] and then proceed by slow stages down the Rhine to Cologne, thence to Amiens and Boulogne and England.

The day before yesterday I passed the Simplon—and yesterday I repassed it. The day before yesterday I lay at Domo d'Ossola and yesterday morning the old man within me[4] and the guide were strong for proceeding to the Lago Maggiore: but no, I said, first impressions must not be trifled with: I have but 3 days and they according to the public voice will be days of rain: coupons court à notre voyage—revenons en Suisse—So I ordered a char yesterday morning to remount the Simplon. It rained still . . . here and there was something unblurred by rain. Précisons: I have noticed in Italy— the chestnuts: the vines: the courtliness and kingliness of buildings and people as opposed to this land of a republican peasantry: and one or two things more: but d—n description. My guide assures me he saw one or two 'superbes filles' in Domo d'Ossola (nothing improper): but I rose late and disheartened by the furious rain, and saw nothing but what I saw from the carriage. So Italy remains for a second entry. From Isella to Simplon the road is glory to God. In these rains maps and guides have suffered more or less: but your Keller very little:[5] I travel with a live guide as well as Murray:[6] an expensive luxury: but if he is a good Xtian and a family man like mine, a true comfort. I gave him today a foulard[7] for his daughter who is learning French at Neufchatel to qualify her first for the place of fille de chambre in a hotel and afterwards for that of soubrette in a private family. I love gossip and the small-wood of humanity generally among these raw mammoth-belched half-delightful objects the Swiss Alps. The lime stone is terribly gingerbready: the pines terribly larchy:[8] and above all the grand views being ungifted with self-controul almost invariably desinunt in piscem.[9] And the curse of the dirty water—the real pain it occasions to one who looks upon water as the Mediator between the inanimate and man[10] is not to be described.—I have seen clean water in parts of the lake of Geneva (wch whole locality is spoiled by the omnipresence there of that furiously flaring bethiefed rushlight,[11] the vulgar Byron): in the Aar at the exit of the Lac de Thoune: and in the little stream's beginnings on the Italian side of the Simplon. I have however done very little, having been baffled in two main wishes—the Tschingel Glacier and the Monte Moro, by the weather. My golies, how jealous you would have been of the first: 'we fools accounted his calves meagre, and his legs to be without honor'.[12] All I have done however is to ascend the Faulhorn—8300 above the sea,[13] my duck. This people, the Swiss, are on the whole what they should be; so I am satisfied.—L'homme sage ne cherche point le sentiment parmi les habitans des montagnes: ils ont quelque chose de mieux—le bonheur.[14] That is but indifferent French though. For their extortion, it is all right I think—as the wise man pumpeth the fool, who is made for to be pumped.[15]

I have with me only Beranger and Epictetus: the latter tho: familiar to me, yet being Greek, when tired I am, is not much read by me:[16] of the former I am getting tired. Horace whom he resembles had to write only for a circle of highly cultivated desillusionés roués, in a sceptical age: we have the sceptical age, but a far different and wider audience: voilà pourquoi, with all his genius, there is something 'fade' about Beranger's Epicureanism. Perhaps you don't see the pourquoi, but I think my love does and the paper draws to an end. In the reste, I am glad to be tired of an author: one link in the immense series of cognoscenda et indagenda[17] despatched. More particularly is this my feeling with regard to (I hate the word) women. We know beforehand all they can teach us: yet we are obliged to learn it directly from them. Why here is a marvellous thing. The following is curious—

'Say this of her:
The day was, thou wert not: the day will be,
Thou wilt be most unlovely: shall I chuse
Thy little moment life of loveliness
Betwixt blank nothing and abhorred decay
To glue my fruitless gaze on, and to pine,
Sooner than those twin reaches of great time,
When thou art either nought, and so not loved,
Or somewhat, but that most unloveable,
That preface, and post-scribe thee?'— [18]

Farewell, my love, to meet I hope at Oxford: not alas in Heaven: tho: thus much I cannot but think: that our spirits retain their conquests: that from the height they succeed in raising themselves to, they can never fall. Tho: this uti possedetes [19] principle may be compatible with entire loss of individuality and of the power to recognize one another. Therefore, my well-known love, accept my heartiest greeting and farewell, while it is called today.   Yours,

M. Arnold

Text. Lowry, pp. 91–93.

1. Lowry's transcription is the only source of this text, perhaps the best letter Arnold ever wrote. He did not reveal the location of the original or account for the ellipsis (after "It rained still") in the second paragraph. See Introduction, p. xxiv.

2. With overtones of Coleridge's poem "Frost at Midnight?"

3. These fateful nineteen words gave rise to an industry that still thrives—the identification of the possessor of the blue eyes, associated with Arnold's Marguerite poems. See Park Honan's "Mary Claude's Blue Eyes" (*Author's Lives*, pp. 144–58) with the reference to "discussions of the biographical evidence" in "Miriam Allott's lively essay" and Honan's reply in *Victorian Poetry* 23 (Summer 1985):125–43,145–59. See also Introduction p. xxiv and below p. 124 and n. 6.

4. For "the old man within?" "old man with me?" A misreading or an omission.

5. *Original von Keller's Zweiter Reisekarte des Schweiz* (1844)—described by Ruskin (*Praeterita*, 2. xi) as "the only map of Switzerland which has ever been executed with commonsense and intelligence." See below pp. 134, 357.

6. Murray's *Handbook for Travellers in Switzerland.*

7. *OED*'s earliest example is dated 1864. Arnold mentions Marguerite's "lilac kerchief" in "A Memory Picture," her "soft, enkerchiefed hair" in "Meeting," and "The kerchief that enwound thy hair" in "The Terrace at Berne."

8. Gingerbready (*OED*, 1867); larchy (no instance recorded).

9. End in the shape of a fish—that is, does not fulfil the promise of the beginning, as in Horace *Ars Poetica* l. 4. The phrase occurs also in Virgil, Seneca, Pliny, but Arnold's reference here suggests not only Horace but also Ovid's *Metamorphoses* 4: 727, in which the monster (belua) belches forth waters mixed with purple blood, as Perseus slays the dragon (Loeb).

10. Adapted from 1 Timothy 2:5.

11. "Bethiefed": from "thief," "'An excrescence in the snuff of a candle (J.)' which causes it to gutter and waste" (*OED*). ("Stranger" in Coleridge's note to "Frost at Midnight" is the same but is "supposed to portend the arrival of some absent friend.")

12. Unidentified.

13. Possibly a misreading: 8,805, if he went to the top.

14. Untraced.

15. "Marcus Cato," 9.4, in Plutarch's *Lives*.

16. "The *Enchiridion of Epictetus* I had ever with me, often as my sole rational companion; and regret to mention that the nourishment it yielded was trifling" ("Sorrows of Teufelsdröckh," *Sartor Resartus*).

17. "Things to be known and to be investigated." (He must have written "indaganda.")

18. Allott (p. 639) says the "Lines are anti-pyretic for his reluctant romantic excitement."

19. "As you possess"—property remains with the possessor (Justinian, *Institutes* 4.154). Arnold must have written "possedit*is*."

Jane Martha Arnold to Thomas Arnold[1]

Fox How

My dearest Tom   Thursday, October 26, 1848

Mamma and Matt have this day sent off a letter to the care of Mr Harrington[2] for you. I suppose it will reach you sooner than this, which is to go ⟨round⟩ by the Sydney Mail; though really I do not know, for I should think letters might go round the globe and back again in less time than they take in getting to & from New Zealand. . . . [2 pages omitted] But Ireland is a problem which all the world resolves is too difficult to be solved, so I need not perplex my brains or try your patience with any more lucubrations on the subject. Mamma and Mary Fan & Susy are gone to bed, dear old Matt is still reading Alison by my side,[3] but as our fire is just out, and there is some sharpness in the air this October night, I shall not sit up any longer, not even to flatter myself into the thought that I am having one of our old fireside talks together, you dear, beloved boy, so I wish you goodnight and proceed to wind up my watch, give Matt a parting nod & retire to my dressing room.

Sunday evening October 29th.

The second bell for tea has rung, my dearest Tom, and Mamma has already made tea, but I will spend the next few minutes in writing to you. Fancy the tea table then spread in the dining room, with the lamp standing in the middle, a brown & white loaf, as in old days, on either side, and Rowland just coming in to know whether she is to send in Damson or Gooseberry jam for our *Sunday treat*. At the Piano sits dear Susy, playing some chants, I think, with little Jamie Hearn[4] listening by her side, and before the fire sits Mary, reading a book of Hymns, on the rug sits Boadicea scratching herself with an air of inexpressible contentment. And now the party is increased, & dear old Matt comes down dressed for tea, and seats himself at the bottom of the table to amuse himself with the Spectator till Mamma comes in—a moment now beginning to be rather anxiously waited for—and Fan too, the little delinquent has not yet appeared; but we shall not pay her the compliment of waiting for her. And now here comes dearest Mother—how I wish you could see her dear face as I do at this minute, looking, thank God so well—and she so comfortable in one of her endless grey shawls. They will not allow me to write any longer in peace, so I must continue my letter after tea.—We have had Matt at home with us about a fortnight, and I am afraid that he will have to leave us again this week; much to his disgust as well as ours. He and I have had some very pleasant walks together, on Loughrigg & into Scandale &c and he has repeated to me a good deal of his poetry, which I think very beautiful, and wonderfully improved both in simplicity and vigour since I last heard any of it, which was I believe at Allonby. He seems at present to be inspired by ancient art & poetry, and some of his most wonderful poems are in this direction, one especially which I wanted him to send you, is in a choral metre (too difficult I tell him for anyone to read, but when repeated by him it is harmony itself) and describes most beautifully the [?]⟨travail & pain⟩ different conditions upon which the immortal Gods & the mortal poet or seer enjoy their privelege[*sic*] of seeing & knowing more than other men.[5] But I hope you will see the Poem some day and therefore I will not spoil it by description. Matt sometimes talks of publishing, but I do not think he will do so yet. Though not much of a judge, I cannot but think that these poems would attract a great deal of attention, and do much to improve the poetical taste of the country, but that they would ever become very popular or deeply impress the mind of the country I cannot help doubting— and for this reason, because Matt's philosophy holds out no help in the deep questions which are stirring in every heart in the life & death struggle in which the world is every year engaged more deeply, and poetry which does not do this may charm the taste, excite & gratify the intellect but not, I think take lasting possession of the heart. Wordsworth's poetry, it seems to me, did ⟨do this for his gen⟩ speak the word which was needed by his generation in a most artificial age, he led men back to nature, and through nature & the natural piety of the heart, to Him who is the source of both. But now we seem to want something more direct still, surrounded by tumults & perplexities without & within, we want to know the spell which shall evoke a righteous and peaceful order from this chaos, and what but our Christian Faith can give us this? I do not, of course, mean that poems must turn into Sermons, but while men are struggling for their own life & their neighbours, whether [it] is spiritual, social or political life—and conscious that they must sink unless they can find some Mighty Helper, surely language which tells them of a dumb inalterable order of the universe and of the vanity of the labours in which they are vexing, will seem too unreal & far too hopeless for them to listen to. Dear Matt has a good deal of the Eastern Philosopher about him at present, which does not suit the European mind. But he is a dear, dear boy, and I cannot say how much pleasure it gives me to have him at home, so loving as he is and surely the time will come when he will find that nothing but the faith of a little child in Him who has united together Heaven & Earth, Christ, our Lord and our God, can avail to guide him through the "waves of this troublesome world"—I know he wrote to you the other day and how glad I shall be when you get well settled in New Zealand and can write to him and all of us, long letters. About this time I think you will get the letter in which I told you of our expedition up the Hill Bell on the 1st of May—and soon surely we shall hear from Wellington.

This winter I am going to help Miss Claude[6] in a weekly evening school for young girls who are in service or otherwise too much occupied to get any instruction in the day time. Every Thursday Evening we meet in the National School at 5 oclock, and teach reading writing & Arithmetic till 7. We began last Thursday and the girls themselves seem so anxious to improve themselves that it is very interesting to teach them, and as some of them are very advanced scholars I shall have to improve *myself too.* . . . Monday Morning. . . . [one page omitted].

As you may not get our letters in the regular order in which they are written, & this may possibly reach you before the one Mamma & Matt sent a week ago, I will tell you where all the family are at present. To begin with home. We have not yet had breakfast, and yet I have written all this page, and Matt has all the time been sitting over the fire with his Novalis in his hand & his German Dictionary, instructing his inner man, & comforting his outer man by the warmth of a roaring fire which suits well this sharp October morning. Mamma & Fan have been reading in the diningroom—the lazy Susy has not yet come down, nor Mary, but I believe she is up, and little Jamie is late this morning, as he was sent to bed last night almost in a fit of hysterics. He is a very excitable child, and some some facetiae of Matt's were quite too much for his nerves. Considering the state his father is in, I should be rather anxious about Jamie, as he grows up. . . . [seven lines omitted] By the description that I have given you of our before breakfast occupation you will see that we have rather improved as to early habits—it must be confessed however that breakfast was rather later than usual, as bread had to be fetched from Ambleside.—Edward is at Oxford expecting very soon to go in for his degree, if he gets a fourth class it is as much as we expect, he has really read so very little, and now his health is against him too, though he is better than when he left us in the beginning of the month. Then his face was so bad that he wanted to go abroad directly, and Erasmus Wilson[7] whom he consulted in London advised him to winter at Rome; but now his face is well again, and we shall probably have him at home as usual at Christmas—indeed I hope we shall, otherwise we should have no brother at all with us at Christmas—Matt says he will not be able to come, & only think how sad it would seem for Mamma Susy Fan & I to sit down to our Christmas dinner alone, at this table once so well filled. I am sure the Turkey would walk out of the dish & refuse the countenance of his presence to such degeneracy but I have good hopes that Master Ned will "come trundling home" as usual. Walter is still with the St Vincent at Portsmouth, and I fear will be there all the winter—he got a few days leave the other day & went to Oxford with Matt & Edward, and dined in Hall at Balliol in his uniform. We have not had any letters from Willy this month—his last packet was delightful so thoughtful & so loving towards home. Thus far his going to India seems to have had a most blessed effect upon him, though he does not seem to find much happiness in his profession. It is dull work staying at Dinapore, and the society of the mess he describes as worse than the worst to be met with at public schools. What do you think of this? It seems there is one officer in the regiment who is a religious man, and the mess is trying to buy him out into another regiment!—Willy's letters are really very interesting in themselves, he describes Indian scenery & Indian life so well, and enables us to live with him his Barracks life. . . . [1¼ pages omitted] Do not say anything (in allusion to what I have said about Matt) in your letters, unless you think he would like it, because you must not forget that he has repeated his poetry & talked it over to me *only*—and would not like it to be a subject of public discussion in the family. I do not scruple to say to you what I have said to him, because I know if you were at home he would talk about it all to you more than to me—but you will be discreet in your comments, my dearest. . . . [3/4 page omitted, including a 27-line letter by Frances Arnold and a 9-line note by Mary Rowland].

MS. Balliol College.

1. Two long excerpts from this extraordinary and important letter were quoted in *Fox How after Dr Arnold's Death* (misdated 1850, because of a misreading of "27" for "29" on p. 2—"Sunday Evening, October 29th"). It was correctly dated by Connell, pp. 26–27 and note.
    2. Unidentified.
    3. Archibald Alison (1792–1867: *DNB*), historian—probably his extremely popular *History of Europe* (10 vols, 1839–42), of which there were many editions, but conceivably his *Life of the Duke of Marlborough* (1847) or other titles.
    4. James Seckerson Hearn (c. 1841-?], son of James Hearn (c.1785–1864), rector of

Hatford, Berks, from 1836, but curate at Laleham in the 1820s. Godson of Mary Penrose Arnold, Jamie lived at Fox How from May 1848 till Jan. 1850, during his father's illness. He matriculated from Worcester College in Mar. 1859, age 18. Among the dozen or so letters from various Arnolds to his mother or himself in the library of the University of Rochester, one (dated Oct. 27, 1873) from Frances Arnold to his mother (on the death of her own mother) says: "We often used to speak together of the times when your Jamie was with us. How little we could have dreamt that she would survive him so many years." See Stanley, p. 44; Wymer, p. 57; McCrum, *Thomas Arnold Head Master*, p. 90.

    5. "The Strayed Reveller" (Allott, p. 67).

    6. This passage does not suggest that Mary Claude, a neighbor, was the possessor of the famous "blue eyes" of "Marguerite" at the Hotel Bellevue in Thun, Switzerland, one month earlier. See above p. 119 and n. 3.

    7. William James Erasmus Wilson (1809–84: *DNB*), surgeon and author of a "Treatise on Diseases of the Skin" (1842).

To Arthur Hugh Clough

London
My dear Clough   Wednesday, [?November 29, 1848][1]

    Who had the clearest insight into the way in which business proceeded in the schools?[2] That you, who have never had or acquired the art of correcting your individual judgement of merit by an appreciation of the circumstances that weigh with the world, in matters where the result is in the world's hands, should have so erred, does not surprise me: but that Walrond who, being more worldly than you, should have some tact, coincided with you in so monstrous a notion as your's, surprized, nay nettled me to a degree that required all the self-controul I muster when really nettled to conceal. Tell him this: and beg him to cultivate that finesse in his judgements, which it is so easy to lose. I hear from Landon[3] thro: Shephard that Edward's Ethics paper was marked with the first class mark. Nor does this surprise me, though I do not account him therefore a philosopher.

    —I have been at Oxford the last two days and hearing Sellar[4] and the rest of that clique who know neither life nor themselves rave about your poem gave me a strong almost bitter feeling with respect to them, the age, the poem, even you.[5] Yes I said to myself something tells me I can, if need be, at last dispense with them all, even with him: better that, than be sucked for an hour even into the Time Stream in which they and he plunge and bellow. I became calm in spirit, but uncompromising, almost stern. More English than European, I said finally, more American than English: and took up Obermann, and refuged myself with him in his forest against your Zeit Geist.[6]

    —But in another way I am glad to be able to say that Macpherson gave a very good account of the sale: & that, tho: opinions differed, I found what I thought the best such as Riddell's[7] and Blackett's in favor of the metre strongly: the opinion of the first has a scientific that of the second an aesthetic value. Stanley thought him [*sic for* his? them?] the best Hexameters he had seen in the modern languages. My people at home could not manage the metre, but thought there was humour & pathos enough in the poem to stock a dozen ordinary poems. I was surprized to see no notice in any Sunday papers: but next Sunday, I suppose. You will be glad to hear Conington intends to review it.[8] I bantered him gently about a discovery he had made in one of your lyrics of a resemblance to one of Tennyson's, which I never saw, and I do not think you either. Say to Shairp I have seen a copy of Visconti[9] just like mine: same price: £4–4s. does he want it? If not he does Walrond. Let me know pray. When are you coming up hither love? My man has the gout at Bowood.   Your's ever

M. A.

MS. Yale University.

1. As Lowry, who dates the letter "(15, 22, or 29?)," points out (p. 94), "Lansdowne left London for Bowood Park . . . on November 13, and returned to town on Wednesday, December 6." Arnold was at Rugby with Clough and Walrond "for ten days," about Nov. 13–23 (Mulhauser, 1:224).

2. The phrase "in the schools" refers to "the periodical examinations for the degree of B.A." (*OED*); see Hughes's *Tom Brown at Oxford*, ch. 24, "The Schools." The "rather mysterious first paragraph" of this letter (Lowry, p. 94) surely refers not to Stanley or Clough but to Edward Arnold's receiving "only a third class *in literis humanioribus* for Michaelmas term," announced in *The Times*, Nov. 29 (Lowry, p. 95n).

3. Lowry's misreading was first corrected by J. C. Maxwell in *Notes and Queries*, Oct. 1953, p. 440. The examiners were Osborne Gordon (*DNB*) of Christ Church, Mark Pattison (*DNB*) of Lincoln, Rowland Mucklestone of Worcester, and James Timothy Bainbridge Landon (a Rugbeian) of Magdalen (*Annual Register*). Thomas Henry Sheppard (1814–88), also a Rugbeian, from Oriel, in 1851 became a fellow and chaplain of Exeter College, where he remained till his death, a week before Arnold's. In 1865 he was the "main agent" in unseating Gladstone as the representative of the University of Oxford, and he was a subeditor of the *New English Dictionary* for the letters *u* and *v* (Boase).

4. William Young Sellar (1825–90: *DNB*) had studied at Glasgow under Tennyson's brother-in-law Edmund Lushington and entered Balliol in 1842, where "along with Alexander Grant, Palgrave, Robert Morier, and others, he was one of Jowett's coterie of idolaters" (Tennyson, 2:67n). "He had crowned a brilliant Oxford career by taking an open fellowship at Oriel" in 1848 (Jowett, 1:126) and went on to a distinguished academic career at Glasgow, St Andrews, and, from 1863, the University of Edinburgh. See below p. 347 n. 4 and also E. M. Sellar, *Recollections and Impressions,* pp. 151–52, 156, and J. M. Barrie's *An Edinburgh Eleven.*

5. Clough's poem *The Bothie of Toper-na-Fuosich* (later *Tober-na-Vuolich*) had just been published by Francis Macpherson of Oxford.

6. *OED* cites this sentence, but it was used by Carlyle (as German, translated) in "Characteristics" (1831) and in "Genesis," *Sartor Resartus*, in 1833–34.

7. James Riddell (1823–66: *DNB*), an exact contemporary of Arnold's at Balliol, was a fellow and then lecturer or tutor till his death, having got his start there tutored by Jowett: "The honours gained by James Riddell and Edwin Palmer, both in 1845, mark the commencement of a fresh series of Balliol successes" (Jowett, 1:89). A member of the Decade and later a notable classicist, he was caught up in Balliol in-fighting and, strangely, instrumental in 1854 in electing Robert Scott, a mediocrity, as master over Jowett (Tuckwell, p. 202), a victory for which the College suffered during sixteen years.

8. John Conington (1825–69: *DNB*), an old Rugbeian, was a classicist especially distinguished, later, for his edition of Virgil. At this time he was a fellow of University College; in 1854 he became Corpus Professor of Latin Literature and in 1856 a fellow of Corpus Christi. More memorable alive than dead, he was a man, as Tuckwell writes (p. 104), "whose extraordinary visage, with its green-cheese hue, gleaming spectacles, quivering protrusive lips, might be encountered every day at 2 o'clock on his way to a constitutional." He was known among the undergraduates as "the Sick Vulture" (p. 207). See Tennyson, 2:416n, Jowett, 1:176, 249, and below p. 273.

9. Filippo Aurelio Visconti's *Musée Chiaramonti* (Milan, 1818–22) is listed in Bohn, 1:1856 (p. 174) at exactly this price. See letter to Craik below, Feb. 21, 1878.

To Arthur Hugh Clough

London
My dearest Clough   Monday, [?early December 1848]
What a brute you were to tell me to read Keats' Letters.[1] However it is over now: and reflexion resumes her power over agitation.

What harm he has done in English Poetry. As Browning[2] is a man with a moderate gift passionately desiring movement & fulness, and obtaining but a confused multitudinousness, so Keats with a very high gift, is yet also consumed by this desire: & cannot produce the truly living & moving, as his conscience keeps telling him. They will not be patient—neither understand that they must begin with an Idea of the world in order not to be prevailed over by the world's multitudinousness: or if they cannot get that, at least with isolated ideas: & all other things shall (perhaps) be added unto them.[3]

—I recommend you to follow up these letters with the Laocoon of Lessing: it is not quite satisfactory, & a little mare's nesty—but very searching.[4]

—I have had that desire of fulness without respect of the means, which may become almost maniacal: but nature had placed a bar thereto not only in the conscience (as with all men) but in a great numbness in that direction. But what perplexity Keats Tennyson et id genus omne[5] must occasion to young writers of the ὁπλίτης[6] sort: yes & those d____d Elizabethan poets generally. Those who cannot read G[ree]k sh[ou]ld read nothing but Milton & parts of Wordsworth: the state should see to it: for the failures of the στάσιμοι[7] may leave them good citizens enough, as Trench:[8] but the others go to the dogs failing or succeeding.

So much for this inspired "cheeper" as they are saying on the moors.[9]
My own good man farewell.

M. A.

MS. Yale University.

1. Clough was reading Milnes's *Life, Letters and Literary Remains of John Keats*, just published, on Aug. 15 (Kenny, p. 255).
2. Arnold's first allusion to Robert Browning (1812–89) perhaps suggests *Sordello* (1840) and *Bells and Pomegranates*, especially *Dramatic Lyrics* (1842) or *Dramatic Romances and Lyrics* (1845). Clough mentions the latter ("a series of cheap numbers") in Dec. 1847 and Tom Arnold in Dec. 1849 ("some of Browning's plays that I have read," Bertram, p. 164).
3. Matthew 6:33.
4. Arnold's poem "Epilogue to Lessing's Laocoön" (Allott, p. 550), written apparently in the early sixties, was published in 1867.
5. And all of that sort.
6. Hoplites.
7. "Steady sort of men": Lowry's misreading and misinterpretation were corrected by Super in Allott-Super, pp. 281, 565.
8. The allusion is puzzling. Richard (Chenevix) Trench (1807–86: *DNB*), who attended Trinity College, Cambridge, and was an Apostle, with Tennyson, Hallam, and the others, later became dean of Westminster (1856) and archbishop of Dublin (1864) and wrote or edited many books on theology, philology, etc. At this time he was a minor poet, author of several minor works on religious subjects, and professor of divinity at King's College, London. But Arnold perhaps meant the older brother, Francis Chenevix Trench (1806–86: *DNB*) of Harrow and then Oriel College (B.A. 1834) who was perpetual curate of St John's, Reading, and the author of a few books. Moreover, Boase lists William Steuart Trench (1808–72), who became "agent to estates of marquess of Lansdowne in Kerry Dec. 1849 to death."
9. Super's correction of Lowry's "moon": cheepers are "the chicks of partridge and grouse" and Arnold's meaning, still not obvious, may be in one of the illustrative citations—the cheeper's "cry of alarm is acuter than that of the full grown bird" (*OED*). Wright's *English Dialect Dictionary* lists "a soft, light kiss without noise," or ("cheep") "word, hint, least mention" and ("to cheep") "disclose a secret, mention, tell only a little."

To Frederick Temple[1]

The *Revd F. Temple.*   Bowood, Calne
My dear Sir   December 22, 1848
   I am desired by Lord Lansdowne who is still from a sudden return of gout under great difficulty in writing himself as he has been suffering acute pain from it, to acknowledge your communications, and to say he is much obliged to you for the great attention you have given to the business of the office which he is aware must have proved very laborious to you. He returns the Tabular Statements approved, and after looking through them sees no

reason for directing any of the proposed apprenticeships to be suspended, or for not confirming the rejections on the grounds stated.

He is at the same time desirous as he has on other occasions stated that when any apprenticeship is rejected solely on the score of deficiency in the Schoolmaster, or, as in this instance, Schoolmistress, care should be taken to accompany it with some notice and encouragement to the pupil whose merit may probably be the greater from that very circumstance.

Lord Lansdowne has received a letter from Mr Shuttleworth who describes himself as essentially better—but he had before earnestly pressed upon him through Mrs Shuttleworth[2] to abstain from all attention to details of business.

Lord Lansdowne will probably be in town before the end of the second week in January, but in the meanwhile will look through and return any book of agenda you send him. I remain, my dear Sir,   your faithful servant,

M. Arnold.—

MS. Texas A&M University.

1. See above p. 118 n. 4.
2. James Kay Shuttleworth (1804–77: *DNB*; cr. bt 1849), born Kay, in 1842 married Janet Shuttleworth (d. 1872) and added her name to his. He was the first secretary of the Committee of Council on Education (1839–49), and is remembered, even revered (by Arnold and others), not for his two novels but as the "founder of English popular education."

To Arthur Hugh Clough

L[ansdowne] H[ouse]

My dear Clough   Friday, [early February, 1849]

If I were to say the real truth as to your poems in general, as they impress me—it would be this—that they are not *natural*.[1]

Many persons with far lower gifts than yours yet seem to find their natural mode of expression in poetry, and tho: the contents may not be very valuable they appeal with justice from the judgement of the mere thinker to the world's general appreciation of naturalness—i.e.—an absolute propriety—of form, as the sole *necessary* of Poetry as such: whereas the greatest wealth & depth of matter is merely a superfluity in the Poet *as such*.

—Form of conception comes by nature certainly, but is generally developed late: but this lower form, of expression, is found from the beginning amongst all born poets, even feeble thinkers, and in an unpoetical age: as Collins, Green[2] and fifty more, in England only.

The question is not of congruity between conception & expression: which when both are poetical, is the poet's highest result:—you say what you mean to say: but in such a way as to leave it doubtful whether your mode of expression is not quite arbitrarily adopted.

I often think that even a slight gift of poetical expression which in a common person might have developed itself easily & naturally, is overlaid and crushed in a profound thinker so as to be of no use to him to help him to express himself.—The trying to go into & to the bottom of an object instead of grouping *objects* is as fatal to the sensuousnesss of poetry, as the mere painting, (for, *in Poetry*, this is not *grouping*) is to its airy & rapidly-moving life.

"Not deep the Poet sees, but wide":[3]—think of this as you gaze from the Cumner Hill toward Cirencester & Cheltenham.—You succeed best you see, in fact, in the hymn,[4] where man, his deepest personal feelings being in play, finds poetical expression as *man* only, not as artist:—but consider whether you attain the *beautiful*, & whether your product gives *pleasure*, not excites curiosity & reflexion. Forgive me all this: but I am always prepared myself to give up the attempt, on conviction: & so, I know, are you: & I only urge you to reflect whether you are advancing. Reflect too, as I cannot but do here more & more, in spite of all the nonsense some people talk, how deeply *unpoetical* the age & all one's surroundings are. Not unprofound, not ungrand, not unmoving:—but un*poetical*.[5]   Ever your's

M. A.

MS. Yale University.

1. Presumably, a reference to *Ambarvalia*, published in the latter half of January.
2. *Sic*, but Arnold surely meant Thomas Gray.
3. "Resignation," l. 214 (Allott, p. 88).
4. Clough's "Qui Laborat, Orat" (his poem "ὕμνος ἄυμνος" was not yet written).
5. Super's (significant) correction of Lowry's *unpoetical*.

To Arthur Hugh Clough

[c. February 28, 1849]

If you can, get the Guardian of this week, to see a notice of some poems by that Skeffington who was at Worcester, & always at the Union & who afterwards died at Rome at 22.[1] There is one on the Etruscan tombs of

Perugia & Chiusi in which the following lines occur respecting the old Etruscans.

"Is all silent? know we nothing? Can Philosophy not rear
Some dim theoretic ages from the social fossils here?
And, amid the frightful clashing of her after-ages wild,
Hath the old world clean forgotten those who tended her, a child?
They are gone!—like sea-shore footsteps when the tide flows,—they
    are gone!
Swept by Heaven-won Regillus, swept by fatal Vadimon.
Swept, poor prisoners of Sorrow, to the doubtful dusk of death,
That another generation might be told the name of Faith.
Ah! for grief! what anguish took them when the fetter'd soul look'd
    out,
Straining aching eye in vain to pierce the curtain of their doubt!
Ah! for grief! what longing seiz'd it, to have wings & wander hence,
As the torn soul in its frenzy batter'd on the seas of sense!
Ah! for grief! what curse was knowledge! what a burden was the mind!
Better be a beast—go, fat thee, feed, & propagate thy kind!" &c. &c.

—I have abridged: whereby it gains: but what a true fire! although the union of a freedom from all desire to subjugate destiny with the natural fire of youth produces a state in which astonishing results can be produced compared with what can be produced early by the unintoxicated honest. He is a rapturous Xtian.[2]

MS. Yale University.

1. Lowry (pp. 101–2): "The *Guardian* for the week of February 28, 1849 (pp. 145–46), contained a testimonial of a volume of poems by the Hon. Henry Robert Skeffington. The review gives the facts of the poet's life. The eighth child of the late Viscount Ferrard, he became a commoner of Worcester College, Oxford, in 1841, and was graduated in 1843. He died at Rome, February 17, 1846, in his twenty-second year." In fact, Skeffington, born in 1820, died on Feb. 20, in his twenty-seventh year. His volume *A Testimony: Poems* was published by W. D. Biden, Kingston-upon-Thames, in 1848. Of Skeffington's forty-four lines in "The Etruscan Tombs at Perugia and Chiusi" Arnold here transcribes 11. 23–28, 31–36, 39–40, but the whole (printed in the *Guardian* and reprinted below Appendix C) is far more compelling than the sum of these parts, for unquestionably it suffuses "Stanzas from the Grande Chartreuse" (Allott, p. 301). Skeffington also wrote "The Grave of Alaric—The Visigoth's Lament" and "Cromwell."

2. "Subjugate destiny" (as Lowry observes) is used also in the letter to Clough p. 135. A "rapturous Xtian" could not have desired to "subjugate destiny"; "unintoxicated honest" perhaps implies a reproof of Clough.

To Arthur Hugh Clough

Dear Clough   [c. March 1, 1849]

The Iliad translation is better, but not Anglicised enough I think. I am told that Germans who are ignorant of the original complain that they cannot understand Voss. Carlyle's Dante seemed to me clearer.[1]

—It is true about form: something of the same sort is in my letter which crossed your's on the road. On the other hand, there are two offices of Poetry—one to add to one's store of thoughts & feelings—another to compose & elevate the mind by a sustained tone, numerous allusions, and a grand style.[2] What other process is Milton's than this last, in Comus for instance. There is no fruitful analysis of character: but a great effect is produced. What is Keats? A style & form-seeker, & this with an impetuosity that heightens the effect of his style almost painfully. Nay in Sophocles what is valuable is not so much his contributions to psychology & the anatomy of sentiment, as the grand moral effects produced by *style*. For the style is the expression of the nobility of the poet's character, as the matter is the expression of the richness of his mind: but on men character produces as great an effect as mind.

This however does not save Burbidge who planes & polishes to the forgetting of matter without ever arriving at style. But my Antigone[3] supports me & in some degree subjugates destiny.

—I have had a very enthusiastic letter from Brodie and from John Coleridge, to my surprize. These are all I have heard from. Shairp is δεξιά.[4]   Your's

                                                        M. A.

MS. Yale University.

1. Clough's translations of *The Iliad* are listed (pp. 539–40) and partially reprinted (pp. 513–29) in *The Poems of Arthur Hugh Clough*, 2d edn, ed. Mulhauser. For Arnold's mature opinion ("too odd and uncouth") see the letter to Whewell, Apr. 27, 1862. Johann Heinrich Voss (1751–1826), German poet, translated both *The Odyssey* (1781) and *The Iliad* (1793) in hexameters. Thomas Carlyle's younger brother John Aitken Carlyle (1801–79: *DNB*) published *The Inferno: A Literal Prose Translation* in 1848, in the latter half of December (*Publishers' Circular*). Clough was reading it on Feb. 20 (Mulhauser, 1:245).

2. Arnold's first use of this famous phrase, which became his own and a bludgeon against Francis Newman in *On Translating Homer* (1861), where it is used repeatedly (*OED* 1868, citing James Russell Lowell—who was adapting Arnold). See below p. 172.

3. "Fragment of an Antigone" (Allott, p. 61), in *The Strayed Reveller, and Other Poems*. The phrase "subjugate destiny" is used above p. 132.

4. On the right side (Lowry).

To Arthur Hugh Clough

Dear Clough—   Saturday, [March, 1849]

First for your matters. I do not know the Iliad sufficiently well to give an opinion as to translating a portion: but before the end of April I shall know it well I hope.

—Your passage today is plainer: but not, I think, quite the thing, somehow. It is still too hard. Even things like *ordainer* Zeus would not be relished. You somehow keep too near the Greek sentence-form. Read the Bible: Isaiah, Job &c.

—I should print in lines, as it makes it look easier: without the least scruple about placing opposite a Greek line an English one great part of which belonged to some other Greek line: if it is to be more than a *cab*,[1] you must *Anglicisé*, and this in the *form* above all. It is quite consistent with literalness so to do. And put paragraphs as often as they occur in Dindorf.[2] This too conduces to plainness.

—As to "anger fierce" I think the rule is to use English inversions & not G[ree]k ones. The inversion in question is I think a G[ree]k one. But there is no lack of them in English. Again consult the Bible. Milton uses Greek & Latin structures for sentences, but then these sentences are comprehended within an *English metre-form*, which saves the impression of the *whole* from being foreign. But in prose you have no such counterbalance-means to a system of UnEnglishly constructed sentences.

—βοῶπις, large or full eyed: because we do not use the image in England: saucer-eyed & other-eyeds there are, amongst which you may perhaps find one that serves. For large-eyed is a shirking the word: though ox-eyed is unallowable as not English.[3]—Drat Hexameters. Try a bit in the metre I took for the sick king.[4]

—For myself: Cumin[5] also advises a running commentary for the New Sirens: & Shairp[6] finds them cloudy & obscure: and they are, what you called them, a mumble.

—*Yet* would be better than *Ah* in the passage you mention. It *expresses* the connection, which is now left to be perceived.[7]

I must hear some day how you feel about Resignation. Tell me freely if you do not like it.

Goldwin Smith[8] likes the classical ones: but they hinder females from liking the book: and Shairp urges me to speak more from myself: which I less & less have the inclination to do: or even the power.   your's sincerely,

M. Arnold.

MS. Yale University.

1. Crib (*OED* 1876, citing *Academy*).

2. Wilhelm Dindorf (1802–83), German classical scholar, editor of Aristophanes, Æschylus, Sophocles, Homer, etc., and, with his brother, *Thesaurus Græcæ Linguæ*.

3. "Ordainer Zeus" and "anger fierce" are not in the translations printed by Mulhauser; "ox-eyes" and "ox-eyed" (*Iliad* 1.551, 568) are on pp. 526–27.

4. "The Sick King in Bokhara" (Allott, p. 79), in iambic tetrameter; for "The New Sirens" (Allott, p. 47) Arnold provides an argument in the next letter; see also below p. 153 n. 1. For "Resignation" (Allott p. 88) see above p. 83 n. 5.

5. Patrick Cumin (1824–90: C.B. 1886), at Balliol with Arnold and then a student at the Inner Temple (called to the bar in 1855); he was Macaulay's secretary for two years (Coleridge, 2:260) and, like Arnold, was appointed to the Newcastle Commission in 1858. He edited the *London Review and Weekly Journal* from Apr. 1862 (Boase; Super, 2: 364–65). He was in the Education Department from 1868 and became secretary in May 1884, and was always on friendly terms with Arnold, socially as well as professionally.

6. John Campbell Shairp (1819–85: *DNB*), Scottish by birth, in life, and at death, was at Glasgow and then (1840) Balliol, where, along with Coleridge, Arnold, Clough, Walrond, and the others, he was a member of the Decade, about which Coleridge wrote so feelingly in his memorial notice of Shairp: "We discussed all things human and divine—we thought we stripped things to the very bone—we believed we dragged recondite truths into the light of common day and subjected them to the scrutiny of what we were pleased to call our minds. We fought to the very stumps of our intellects" (William Knight, *Principal Shairp and His Friends*, p. 412). Shairp won the Newdigate prize in 1842 (a year before Arnold), became an assistant master at Rugby, went on to Glasgow and then to St Andrews, where he was professor of Latin and principal of the United College.

7. A tantalizing puzzle, since no manuscript is known of the poem. "Yet" begins lines 17, 91, 195 and would be preferable to "Ah" in all three; the last read "But" in the first edition. "Ah" begins lines 57 and 63; the former read "Come" in the first edition, and "Yet" (impossible in 63) would be acceptable.

8. Goldwin Smith (1823–1910: *DNB*), critic, reviewer (*Saturday Review*), historian, polemicist, and a learned, vigorous, witty writer in no way crippled by self-doubt. At this point he was Stowell Law Fellow at University College, Oxford, and in 1858 became Regius Professor of Modern History, moved to Cornell University in 1868 and thence to Toronto in 1871, where (already well-to-do) he married money and lived happily till his death. There Arnold saw him in 1884. Tennyson, who cared little for wit at his own expense, smarted under Smith's review of *Maud*, and Smith's view of Tennyson (see Tennyson, 2:139–41) seems to have been pretty much what Arnold's was later on of Ruskin. Smith and Arnold, on the other hand, were siblings culturally and intellectually, sharing friends, clubs, and religious and political attitudes, as well as an inability to grow past a certain point, and they treated each other with wary respect. See Super's excellent notes on Smith, especially 2:352–53, 3:467, 5:387, 8:425, 10:528–29. Goldwin Smith's *Reminiscences* (1910), ed. Arnold Haultain, are worth reading.

Thomas Arnold to Jane Martha Arnold[1]

[August 10, 1849]

So dearest Matt was to publish the volume of poems in February. I cannot and will not believe that he would forget to send a copy to me, than whom no human being in the world will read them with a deeper interest; but if he does, do you, my dear K, have them sent to me, that's a darling. Let him not mind what the rascally reviewers say; the circle which finally awards the wreath of Fame is very small, as he well knows, and always 'approfondit' before it criticises. Emerson says that there are but about a dozen persons in a generation who can understand Plato; but that for these dozen his works come down from age to age as regularly as clockwork. I have only had a few lines from Matt this time, in Mother's letter of December 28th, but these few, though rather wicked, delighted me, they were so entirely Mattish. In them he spoke of his feelings about Clough. The last sentence might be worthily placed among the Apothegms of Goethe; shews indeed, I think, that the German sage has made a great impression on our Matt; and no wonder. "He who has no energy grows stupid unless he is born with finesse."

Text. Bertram, pp. 127–28.

1. This and the next letter are deliberately placed here.

Thomas Arnold to Mary Penrose Arnold

September 2, 1848

I have said nothing as yet about the Strayed Reveller, or Ambarvalia or the 'Bothie'; though, as you may imagine, I have read them all through. I must write to dear old Matt himself. It was very pleasant to recognize old friends; especially the 'New Sirens.' Does Fausta mean K, and is the walk, 'ten years ago' alluded to in 'Resignation', that which we took over Wythburn Fells to Keswick with Capt. Hamilton? Or was no particular walk intended: the 'Bothie' greatly surpasses my expectations. With a vein of coarseness cropping out here and there, it is yet on the whole a noble poem, well held together, clear, full of purpose, and full of promise. With joy I see the old fellow bestirring himself, 'awakening like a strong man out of sleep, and shaking his invincible locks'; and if he remains true and works, I think there is nothing too high and great to be expected from him. I do not think Matt was right in saying that Clough 'had no vocation for literature'.

Text. Bertram, pp. 135–36.

To Arthur Hugh Clough

Saturday, [*c.* March, 1849]

Much better, I think. Be easy, easy. Επι ξυροῦ ἀκμῆς has not an English equivalent—literal, as you put it.[1] Think of something else. "Gerenian horseman" is a bad *style* of thing—Put articles

—The horseman of Gerenia, I should say, to avoid obscurity. *A single thing* is not *strown.* "Yes in all this &c." is a truly Cloughian line: a little too much so.   Your's

M. Arnold

MS. *Yale University.*

1. "On the razor's edge" (i.e., at the critical moment), *Iliad* 10.173 (proverbial). "Horsemen of Gerenia" is from *Iliad* 10.168.

To Arthur Hugh Clough

[March, 1849][1]

The *New* Sirens

A lawn stretching away in front of the palace of the New Sirens, dotted with pines & cedars, & with glimpses to the right & left over the open country. Time evening.

. . . .

The speaker (one of a band of poets) stands under a cedar, newly awakened from a sleep: the New Sirens are seen round about in their bowers in the garden, dejected.

He addresses them, saying he has dreamed they were=the Sirens the fierce sensual lovers of antiquity.

Yet, he says, this romantic place, and the multitude & distinction of your worshippers some of them attracted from the service of the spirit by you, seem to indicate a higher worth in you. Are you then really something better & more lawfully attractive than the old Sirens?

—oh, he continues, I perceive the change that gives you an advantage over them. Your love is romantic, and claims to be a satisfying of the spirit.

And, he says, I cannot argue against you: for when about to do so, the remembrance of your beauty & life as I witnessed it at sunrise on these lawns occupies my mind, & stops my mouth.

Yes, he continues, that was glorious: and if that could have lasted, or if we were so made as not to feel that it did not last—(aposiopesis).

—But, soon after the life & enjoyment I witnessed in you at day-break, a languor fell upon you as the day advanced: the weather clouded, your happy groups were broken up, and in lassitude & ennui you dispersed yourselves thro: the gardens, and threw yourselves dispiritedly down in your bowers where at evening I now see you.

—Does the remembrance of your vivacity of this morning suffice to console you in the void & weariness of the afternoon & evening? or do your thoughts revert to that life of the spirit to which, like me, you were once attracted, but which, finding it hard & solitary, you soon abandoned for the vehement emotional life of passion as 'the New Sirens'?

What, he says, without reply, I see you rise & leave your bowers, & re-enter your palace. And yet do not be angry with me: for I would gladly find you in the right & myself, with my conscientious regrets after the spiritual life, wrong.

(They have re-entered the palace, & night falls)

—That is right, he continues, away with ennui, & let joy revive amidst light & dancing.

—But, (after a pause he continues), I, remaining in the dark & cold under my cedar, & seeing the blaze of your revel in the distance, do not share your illusions: & ask myself whether this *alternation* of ennui & excitement is worth much? whether it is in truth a very desirable life?

And, he goes on, were this *alternation* of ennui & excitement the best discoverable existence, yet it cannot last: time will destroy it: the time will come, when the elasticity of the spirits will be worn out, & nothing left but the weariness.

(This epoch is described under the figure of morning but all this latter part you say is clear to you.)

I have thus, my love, ventured to trouble you with a sort of argument to the poem, thanking you for the trouble you seem to have bestowed on it.

But your word is quite just—it is exactly a mumble[2]—& I have doctored it so much & looked at it so long that I am now powerless respecting it.

I believe you are right about the shuttle also: but I will look in the technological dict: one is sadly loose by default of experience, about spinning & weaving, with a great poetical interest in both occupations.[3]

Brodie's letter pleased me very much: Wall[4] tells me he thinks the poems really very pretty—especially (notwithstanding its odd title) the Merman.[5]

Goodbye my love

M. Arnold.—

MS. Yale University.

1. This letter is clearly the "running commentary" recommended by Clough, Cumin, and apparently others (see above p. 136).

2. *OED* (as substantive) 1902.

3. In line 96 "shuttle falls" was emended to "spindle drops" in *Poems*, 2 vols, 1869.

4. Henry Wall (1810–73), son of Richard Wall, of Barbados. He was at St Alban Hall, Oxford (B.A. 1833), was vice-principal 1837–51 and a fellow of Balliol 1839–71 and also chaplain; professor of logic 1849–73 (*Balliol College Register*). Tuckwell (pp. 203–4) has a delicious sketch of him worth more than all these facts: e.g. "He was an undesirable dinner guest, starting questions which he seemed to have prepared beforehand for the pleasure of showing off his dexterity in word fence, rousing temper, and spoiling conversational amenities."

5. "The Forsaken Merman" (Allott, p. 100).

To Mary Penrose Arnold

London
Dearest Mamma   Wednesday, [March 7, 1849]

I think I write very often. I have somehow a notion that I write oftener than I hear. I was truly sorry to hear of your alarm about Willy: but all the children exaggerate their ailments & are easily frightened about themselves as their poor dear father was. I have symptoms of cholera:[1] sinking in the region of the abdomen, debility in the limbs, want of appetite, slight diarrhœa &c. &c.: however I shall get through I expect. Tell Edward the Aldersons have asked me to dinner, and I have called there, & like Lady Alderson: the girls I have not yet seen except at parties, consequently I don't know them to speak to. I have also called on the Bunsens and left my book.[2] I want Edward to bring me Keller's Map[3] of Switzerland from home: unless he wants it for himself. Will you tell Walter[5] when you write that the copy of Don Quixote he read out of in my lodgings when in town the other day is a present for him. I have got another copy and am keeping that as a present for him. I have got no books scarcely lately: which I am glad to find, as I was afraid I should not stop when I had supplied what seemed to me to be my real wants. I dined last night with a Mr Grove[4] a celebrated man of science: his wife is pretty & agreeable, but most on a first interview. The husband & I agree wonderfully in some points—he is a bad sleeper, and hardly ever free from headache: he equally dislikes & disapproves of modern English existence, & the state of excitement in which everybody lives: & he sighs after a paternal despotism & the calm existence of a Russian or Asiatic. He shewed me a picture of Faraday,[5] which is wonderfully fine: I am almost inclined to get it: it has a curious likeness to Keble,[6] only with a calm earnest look unlike the latter's Flibbertigibbet[7] fanatical twinkling expression. It is one of the pictures done from a daguerrotype, & the only satisfactory one I have seen. I

hate daguerrotypes more & more. Don't let Swiny[8] forget about the Map—
& fishing things: let me know when the loathsome donkey hears from
Ld H.[9] & means to come here. If it comes in K's way tell her to read the
biography of Collins the painter,[10] just published: especially as she likes religious ones.

I hope Edward's fear of coming southward to the Cholera will not make
him give up his engagement.   Your's

M. A.

MS. Balliol College.

1. Edward caught it (see below p. 149), and the cholera was in fact epidemic: "In
October, 1848, the Asiatic cholera was ascertained to be among us, and in the Spring
quarter of 1849, it was committing noticeable ravages in London, Liverpool, and other
places." The mortality rate was up by 3 percent, an increase of 60,492 deaths, "an excess
caused almost entirely by cholera. . . . The pestilence appears to have exhausted its viru-
lence in the summer quarter" (*Annual Register*, pp. 449, 456−57).

2. *The Strayed Reveller, and Other Poems*, just published (Feb. 1849).

3. See above p. 121.

4. William Robert Grove (1811−96: *DNB*; knt 1872), scientist (inventer of a gas
voltaic battery) and judge. In 1837 he married Emma Maria Powles (d. 1879).

5. Michael Faraday (1791−1867: *DNB*), the noted physicist and chemist—"our
honoured and justly honoured Faraday" (*Culture and Anarchy*); "great and admirable master of natural knowledge," *Literature and Science* (Super 5:184, 439; 10:65, 489).

6. John Keble (1792−1866: *DNB*), divine and poet, initiator of the Oxford Movement with his sermon on national apostasy, and Arnold's godfather. He was at Corpus
Christi with Thomas Arnold and also with John Taylor Coleridge, who wrote of him as
"our senior among the under-graduates, though my junior in years, the author of the
Christian Year, who came fresh from the single teaching of his venerable father, and
achieved the highest honours of the University at an age when others are frequently but
on her threshold" (Stanley, p. 32). Later, he was a fellow of Oriel and then tutor, overlap-
ping briefly with Newman and Pusey, both *his* juniors. He was Professor of Poetry at
Oxford, 1831−41, and Keble College was founded in his memory soon after his death.

7. Like Dick Sludge in *Kenilworth*, chs. 7−10 (not *King Lear* 3.4.120).

8. His brother Edward.

9. Dudley Ryder (1798−1882: *DNB*; *VF*, 4/8/71), 2d earl of Harrowby, whose
son, Dudley Francis Stuart Ryder (1831−1900: *DNB*; *VF*, 11/28/85), Viscount Sandon
(later 3d earl), Edward was to tutor. See below p. 150n and letters to Thomas Arnold and
Lady de Rothschild, Feb. 1, 1875, Nov. 3, 1875.

10. William Wilkie Collins, *Memoirs of the Life of William Collins, R.A.* (2 vols)
appeared in the first half of Nov. 1848 (*Publishers' Circular*).

To Jane Martha Arnold

London
Dearest K　　　　　　　　　　　　Wednesday, [? March 7, 1849]
I must now write a line to you, tho: I must begin it by answering Mamma's note. I do not know how far Edward would be prevented from taking orders by this pupil.[1] Has he then hitherto attended no lectures? He might easily manage to attend enough of those most frivolous things to get ordained when old enough. If possible I am in favor of his taking the pupil. Hawkes is one of Pearson's curates:[2] I need not say how pleasant it would be for both of them.

I have not heard from you my darling since you got my book, which I hoped to have done, seeing your intimacy with it and me. I will say a little about it. I hear from Fellowes that it is selling very well: and from a good many quarters I hear interest expressed about it, though everyone likes something different (except that everyone likes the Merman) and most people would have this & would have that which they do not find. At Oxford particularly many complain that the subjects treated do not interest them. But as I feel rather as a reformer in poetical matters I am glad of this opposition. If I have health & opportunity to go on I will shake the present methods till they go down, see if I don't. More and more I feel bent against the modern English habit (too much encouraged by Wordsworth) of using poetry as a channel for thinking aloud, instead of *making* anything.

Has Miss Martineau seen them—or have the Fletchers[3] or Mrs Whately or uncle[4] said anything about them. Most middle-aged people wait I suspect to see a review or newspaper notice of some sort before they commit themselves.—You need not tell Miss Martineau that I think her friend Knight[5] a tiresome coxcomb in his writings about Shakspeare. Goodbye—I send the letters I missed sending the other day.　　　ever your affectionate
　　　　　　　　　　　　　　　　　　　　　　　　　　M. Arnold—

You know Sir C. Napier[6] is going out to India.

MS. Frederick Whitridge.

1. Possibly Viscount Sandon (see above p. 141).
2. John Hawkes (c. 1820–1908), from St Mary's, Shandon, co. Cork, who entered Balliol in 1838 (B.A. 1843, M.A. 1845) and was perpetual curate at Redhill, Havant, Hants, 1850–56, and rector of Cotleigh, Devon, 1875–79 (Foster). Hugh Pearson (1817–82: *DNB*), Balliol (B.A. 1839, M.A. 1841), the "most beloved of country clergymen," was vicar of Sonning, Berks, from 1841 till his death (Arnold attended his funeral there on Apr. 13, the sermon preached by Jowett) and canon of Windsor from 1876. He was

Stanley's own familiar friend and there are many references to him in Prothero's *Life and Correspondence* of Stanley. See also Coleridge, 2:311, and Jowett, 2:194.

    3. Neighbors—Eliza Fletcher (1770–1858: *DNB*), widow of Archibald Fletcher (1746–1828: *DNB*). "Resolving to settle in the Lake District, Mrs Fletcher took up her quarters at Thorney How, a small house on the south-western flank of Helm Crag, looking up the mysterious glen of Easedale. After a time she removed to the house not far off which she had built at Lancrigg. Her daughter Mary married Sir John Richardson, well known as the Dr Richardson of Franklin's 'Voyages.' Another of her daughters [Margaret] married Dr [John] Davy [1790–1868: *DNB*], the brother and biographer of Sir Humphry. The Davys built a house—Lesketh How—near Ambleside, between which and Fox How there was constant coming and going for many years" (Thomas Arnold, *Passages in a Wandering Life*, p. 52). "Eliza Fletcher's charm and beauty, in age as in youth, were notable. Her *Autobiography* was privately printed in Carlisle, 1874, and published in Edinburgh in 1875" (Tennyson, 1:338).

    4. Thomas Treveneen Penrose.

    5. Charles Knight (1791–1823: *DNB*), author and publisher. Arnold refers to *Pictorial Edition of the Works of Shakespeare* (8 vols, 1838–43). Knight had published Harriet Martineau's *Tales* in his "Weekly Volumes" series, edited a periodical, *The Voice of the People*, to which she contributed, and begun *A History of the Thirty Years' Peace, 1815–45*, which she completed.

    6. Sir Charles James Napier (1782–1853: *DNB*), military hero, conqueror of Sind (1844), had returned to England in 1848, and on Mar. 24, 1849, left to return to India.

Mary Penrose Arnold to Thomas Arnold (extract)

March 14, [1849

But the little volume of Poems! That is indeed a subject of new & very great interest—By degrees we hear more of public opinion concerning them and I am very much mistaken if their power both in thought & in execution are not much more felt & acknowledged. I had a letter from dear Miss Fenwick to-day whose first impressions were that they were by *you* or by Jane—for it seems she had heard of the volume as much admired & as by one of the family, and she had hardly thought it would be by one so moving in the busy haunts of men as dear Matt. He has sent us some of the letters he has received—and to-day forwarded to me one he had got from Mrs Whately of which he says "she shines preeminent among all the writers of letters to me as usual." It is indeed a striking letter & gratifies me very much for there is no hardness even where she finds most to jar—a perfect freedom in giving out her thoughts & criticism & an old affection running through all which it is affecting to me to see. Intellectually too I think her very striking, & they will weigh with him the more—from her cordial appreciation of the beauty & passion which I should have feared she might hardly have been [?]willing fully to recognise—Matt himself says "I have learned a good deal as to what is *practicable* from the objections of people even when I thought them not reasonable, and in some degree they may determine my course as to publishing—e.g. I have thought of publishing another volume of short poems next spring, and a tragedy I have long had in my head[1]—the spring after; at present I shall leave the short poems to take their chance, only writing them when I cannot help it, & try to get on with my Tragedy, which however will not be a very quick affair. But as that must be in a regular & usual form it may perhaps, if it succeeds, enable me to use metres in short poems which seem proper to myself, whether they suit the habits of readers at first sight or not—But all this is rather vague at present xx—I think I am getting quite indifferent about the book. I have given away the only copy I had and now never look at them. The most enthusiastic people about them are Young Men of course—but I have heard of one or two people who found pleasure in resignation & poems of that stamp which is what I like."

MS. Balliol College.

    1. *Empedocles on Etna and Other Poems*, published in Oct. 1852, and "Lucretius."

To Jane Martha Arnold

London

My dearest K   Saturday, [March 17, 1849]

    The parcel shall be carried to Miss Coltman[1] when it arrives.

    Fret not yourself to make my poems square in all their parts, but like what you can my darling. The true reason why parts suit you while others do not is that my poems are fragments i.e. that I am fragments, while you are a whole; the whole effect of my poems is quite vague & indeterminate: this is their weakness: a person therefore who endeavoured to make them accord would only lose his labour: and a person who has any inward completeness can at best only like parts of them: in fact such a person stands firmly and knows what he is about while the poems stagger weakly & are at their wits end. I shall do better some day I hope. Meanwhile change nothing, resign nothing that you have in deference to me or my oracles: & do not plague yourself to find a consistent meaning for these last, which in fact they do not possess through my weakness.

    There—I would not be so frank as that with everyone.

    I am a wicked wicked beast about the Spectator:[2] you shall have last week's—it has been lying on my sopha all this week: but I have been putting a bookcase up & changing servants. I must try & get up at 5 in the morning. I quite agree about Rome, only there is a certain excuse for the French in their not bad intentions at first. When once beaten, one does not like to give in before trying to set oneself right.[3]   Your's,

M. A.

I cannot after all find last week's *Spectator.*

MS. *Frederick Whitridge.*

    1. Unidentified, but perhaps a relative of the Rev. George Coltman (1812-83), who was at Brasenose College 1829-33 and then "rural dean at Hagnaby and rector of Stickney, in the Tennysonian parts of Lincolnshire" (Tennyson, 1:216n; see also 249, 318n, 3.152), a canon of Lincoln, and a member of the Hanover Square Club (*Upper Ten Thousand*). His older brother, Thomas, also of Brasenose, is a possibility, as is Judge Sir Thomas Coltman (c. 1781-1849), of Rugby and Brasenose (Foster).
    2. *The Strayed Reveller* was reviewed in the *Spectator* 22 (Mar. 10, 1849):231.
    3. "On the 8th of March a discussion arose in the National Assembly on the foreign policy of the Republic, and chiefly with reference to the conduct and intentions of France in respect of the Italian question . . . . Instead of fraternally receiving the envoys of the Roman Republic, the French Government obstinately refused to recognise any other envoy than the nuncio of the Pope, whose power had ceased to exist" (*Annual Register,* pp. 229-30).

To Mary Penrose Arnold

London

Dearest Mother   Thursday, [March 22, 1849]
    The best things come late: Price is a good pendant to Mrs Whately. There is a great deal of truth in what he says—but are we our own masters to write cheerfully or not: though we are, not to write sulkily. But I must say that these letters may well be a profound satisfaction to me, as to praise & appreciation, tho: one's vanity might desire instant trumpet-blares in all the newspapers, yet when one considers the slow growth of the reputations of those poets who composed before the invention of printing, & how little outward acceptance they found (except perhaps in extreme old age) owing to their poetry, one may rest well contented with all these kind letters within a month after publication, and when one is but 26 years old. And one would wish to justify these people's kindness by going on to do something *well*: to which reviewing will not help one by any means. There is a little notice in the Literary Gazette:[1] it says that the author had no need to seek an incognito: it goes on to say that the poems shew skill rather than feeling: in fact just the opposite of the Spectator. I think from the page or two they read in order to review the book, they do not well know what to make of it.—I know you like to hear what is said about the book, so I tell you.
    Froude's appointment in V. Diemen's land is cancelled: so he will come,

I fear, to live in town:[2] I only half like him & he comes & hangs about people, Blackett says, who is dreadfully frightened of being interrupted by him. His book is unpleasant: but for all this shrieking & cursing at him I have the profoundest contempt.—Ah how beautiful the daffodills must be in this mild weather: if they are not over, that is: & the double ones are not. Price talks about cheerfulness & elasticity—their place [*short wd illeg.*] in the country. Bless you darling, and love to all my darling darling children.

What *has* become of Tom. Tell me when you want my book for him. I write scraps but they come very often You none of you write *much*: tho: Jane, when she does write, writes a good deal.   Your's

M. A.

MS. Balliol College.

1. *Literary Gazette and Journal of Belles Lettres, Arts, Sciences*, Mar. 17, 1849: "*The Strayed Reveller. By A____.* Fellowes, pp. 128. 'A.', though the first letter in the alphabet, is a modest incog., and yet the writer need not have feared to give his name. The miscellaneous contents are, in our judgment, drawn more from classic than from natural founts; but many of the pieces are tastefully constructed, and display accomplishment if not deep feeling."

2. James Anthony Froude (1818–94: *DNB*; *VF*, 1/27/72), historian, editor of *Fraser's Magazine* 1860–74, and man of letters, was an undergraduate at Oriel College 1835–42, where he fell under the spell of Newman, and then a fellow of Exeter till 1849, when, his "novel" *The Nemesis of Faith* having been torn up and thrown in the fire by a lecturer, William Sewell (nicknamed "Suculus," little pig, because, though sympathetic to Newmanism, he wouldn't go the whole hog), he resigned to take up the headmastership of a school at Hobart, Tasmania (Van Diemen's Land), which he also resigned (before taking it up). In June 1849 he met and fell under the spell of Carlyle, and whatever reputation remains to him probably derives from this association, for he became Carlyle's literary executor and published several volumes on the Carlyles, including the notorious *Reminiscences* (1881), *Letters and Memorials of Jane Welsh Carlyle* (1883), and a four-volume biography. As a historian, he is (in responsible quarters, always has been) discredited, though as a prose stylist and narrative artist he is memorable. Ironically, when he told the truth, as in his novel and the books on the Carlyles, he was reviled, and when he sophisticated it, as in his histories, he was praised. (Like Arnold, he was a member of the Athenæum and The Club, though not of Grillion's; two letters from Froude to Arnold are in *Album*.)

Mary Arnold Twining to [?]Thomas Arnold

[March, 1849]

I have been in London for several months this year, and I have seen a good deal of Matt, considering the very different lives we lead. I used to breakfast with him sometimes, and then his Poems seemed to make me know Matt so much better than I had ever done before. Indeed it was almost like a new Introduction to him. I do not think those Poems could be read—quite independently of their poetical power—without leading one to expect a great deal from Matt; without raising I mean the kind of expectation one has from and for those who have in some way or other, come face to face with life and asked it, in real earnest, what it means. I felt there was so much more of this practical questioning in Matt's book than I was at all prepared for; in fact that it showed a knowledge of life and conflict which was *strangely like experience* if it was not the thing itself; and this with all Matt's great power I should not have looked for. I do not yet know the book well, but I think that "Mycerinus" struck me most, perhaps, as illustrating what I have been speaking of.

Text. Ward, 1:58–59.

Mary Arnold Twining to "another member of the family"

[?March, 1849]

It is the moral strength, or, at any rate, the *moral consciousness* which struck and surprised me so much in the poems. I could have been prepared for any degree of poetical power, for there being a great deal more than I could at all appreciate; but there is something altogether different from this, something which such a man as Clough has, for instance, which I did not expect to find in Matt; but it is there. Of course when I speak of his Poems I only speak of the impression received from those I understand. Some are perfect riddles to me, such as that to the Child at Douglas, which is surely more poetical than true.

Text. Ward, 1:59–60.

1. "To a Gipsy Child by the Sea-shore" (Allott, p. 22), published in *The Strayed Reveller, and Other Poems.*

To Mary Penrose Arnold

London

My dearest Mother   April 10, 1849

I am still here, Lord Lansdowne having gone out of town on Friday, & returning today. It was not worth my while to go to Oxford or Rugby for a day or two, as I must go to Oxford tonight to be present at the important part of the Oriel election:[1] & with the Ministry in so shaky a position I must take care of my resources. I came home for a week last Easter: & would gladly do so again—but you see it is impossible. My holidays, broken by Lord L's return today, end altogether on Saturday morning. Then, if the Ministry continue in office, town again till the middle of August.

Is Mrs Hull dead?[2]

I observe I have neglected to send you the Spectator, about which I am for ever forgetting. However this week & last it has been very stupid. Only there is a good character of the Ministry this week.

I am still not very well: but it is not much, and the sun always puts me right again.

I do not hear much of my book to tell you. I don't think, whatever Fellowes says, it écoules much: anonymousness—miscellaneousness—& the weariness of modern poetry—felt generally, are all against it. There is a destiny in these things: I mean a set of circumstances against which a merit twenty times greater than mine would be quite in vain. Sooner or later perhaps: but who can say how much good or *promising fragmentary* poetry[3] time has swallowed? tho: not perhaps since the invention of poetry [*for* printing?] any great poems. Sometimes I feel disheartened by the universal indifference: sometimes I think it good for me. However time will shew.

—I have Copley Fielding's[4] autograph for Walter's book. I will send the Times when the Indian news comes.[5]   Ever your's

M. A.

MS. Balliol College.

1. Thomas Collett Sandars (1825–94: *DNB*) and Alexander Grant (1826–84: *DNB*), both scholars of Balliol (Sandars of Rugby as well) and both disciples of Jowett, were elected to Oriel fellowships (*The Times*, Apr. 14, 1849, p. 8).

2. The first of three wives (see above p. 32 n. 2). The Hulls, having left Tavistock Square in 1846, were now living (and dying) at Tickwood, near Wenlock, Shropshire.

3. See above p. 32.

4. Antony Vandyke Copley Fielding (1787–1855: *DNB*), the watercolor painter, was president of the Water-Colour Society 1831–55.

5. At the battle of Goojerat on Feb. 21 British forces led by Lord Gough defeated the Sikh and Afghan army, a victory that led forthwith to the "annexation of the Punjab to the British Empire in India" (*Annual Register*, pp. 381 ff., 42–43); the news (based on a dispatch from Bombay on Mar. 17) was reported in *The Times* on Apr. 18.

To Mary Penrose Arnold*

London
My dearest Mamma   May 7, [1849]

Tho: I believe the balance of correspondence is in my favor at present, I will write to you a few lines instead of sitting idle till Ld L[ansdowne] summons me. I have just finished a German book I brought with me here: a mixture of poems & travelling journal by Heinrich Heine, the most famous of the Young German literary set.[1] He has a good deal of power, though more trick: however he has thoroughly disgusted me. The Byronism of a German, of a man trying to be gloomy cynical impassioned moqueur &c. all à la fois, with their [?]tourist bonhommistic[2] language & total want of experience of the kind that Lord Byron an English peer with access everywhere possessed, is the most ridiculous thing in the world. Goethe wisely said the Germans could not have a national comedy because they had no social life: he meant the social life of highly civilized corrupt communities like Athens Paris or London:[3] & for the same reason they cannot have a Byronic poetry. I see the French call this Heine a "Voltaire au clair de lune," which is very happy.[4]

I have been returning to Goethe's life & think higher of him than ever. His throrough sincerity—writing about nothing that he had not experienced—is in modern literature almost unrivalled. Wordsworth resembles him in this respect: but the difference between the range of their two experiences is immense, & not in the Englishman's favor.

—I have also been again reading Las Cases,[5] & been penetrated with admiration for Napoleon, though his southern recklessness of assertion is sometimes staggering. But the astonishing clearness & width of his views on almost all subjects, & when he comes to practise his energy & precision in arranging details, never struck me so much as now. His contest with England is in the highest degree tragic. The inability of the English of that time in any way to comprehend him, & yet their triumph over him—& the sense of this contrast in his own mind—there lies the point of the tragedy. The number of ideas in his head which "were not dreamed of in their philosophy,"[6] on government & the *future of Europe*, and yet their crushing him, really *with the best intentions*—but a total ignorance of him—what a subject! But it is too near at hand to be treated, I am afraid. To one who knew the English, his fate must have seemed inevitable: & therefore his plans must have seemed imperfect: but what foreigner could divine the union of invincibility & speculative dulness in England?   Ever your's

M. A.

MS. Balliol College.

1. "Young Germany" (c. 1830–50) was an antiromantic revolt, social and literary, defined as a school or movement largely by a decree suppressing it. Heinrich Heine (1797–1856), the lyric and satiric poet, remains its best-known adherent, and the book is the *Reisebilder* or at least the first part, *Die Harzreise* (1826). Later, Arnold published an essay on Heine in *Essays in Criticism* (Super, 3:107–31) and a poem, "Heine's Grave" (Allott, p. 507). See above p. 61 n. 6.

2. Not in *OED*—a barbarous and presumably humorous coinage.

3. Goethe said that "Byron had too much *empeiria*" (experience, worldliness) and also that his superiority to Schiller lay in his "knowledge of the world" (Eckermann, *Gespräche mit Goethe*, July 26, 1826, Jan. 18, 1827).

4. It was happier than Arnold's (unidiomatic) misrepresentation. The Heine references are "translations from memory, and a condensed quotation, of passages from Gérard de Nerval's 'Les Poésies de Henri Heine,' " published in the *Revue des deux mondes* in July and Sept. 1848, and Nerval's allusions to Byron ("ce Byron d'Allemagne à qui il n'a manqué, pour être aussi populaire en France, que le titre de lord") and Voltaire ("Henri Heine est . . . un Voltaire pittoresque et sentimental, un sceptique du XVIIIe siècle, argenté par les doux rayons du clair de lune allemand") are appreciative (V. E. Horn, *Notes and Queries* 216 [July 1971]:248–49). Arnold ought to have written "au clair de la lune" or (like Nerval) "du clair de lune Allemand."

5. Emmanuel Augustin Dieudonné, comte de Las Cases (1766–1842), served under Napoleon and accompanied him to Saint Helena, where he functioned as a Boswell or Eckermann for eighteen months, before his expulsion by Hudson Lowe. His *Mémorial de Sainte-Hélène* (1822–23) contributed a good deal to the Napoleonic myth, some of which is refracted here. Goethe, whose admiration for Napoleon exceeded even Arnold's, said pretty much the same things to Eckermann (*Gespräche mit Goethe*, Mar. 11, 1828, Apr. 7, 1829, Feb. 10, 1830).

6. *Hamlet* 1.5.167.

To Mary Penrose Arnold

London

My dearest Mamma   Thursday, [? May 17, 1849][1]

Edward went on Tuesday evening—He had a rather bad attack of cholera or something like it on Monday, being sick, & looking at one time very ill. Howbeit he recovered, and has now perhaps satisfied Destiny for this term: so that he may safely go to Paris.[2] He left his keys behind him as usual. I am going to send them to him at Bordeaux. I think his journey will be very good for him in all respects: and probably after this he would have no difficulty in obtaining *travelling* pupils to any amount, should his health make it desirable. I hope however he will not deceive himself as to the amount of money he will probably get by the business: there is nothing like a fixed rule in these matters: but £100 is the very most he will get, & I should not wonder if he got no more than £50.

You will lend me £20 or £25 in August again for two or three months if I want it to go abroad with, won't you. I have prospects of not needing to borrow next year if I go, for I am beginning to be in a position to save a little money—a very little, merely for extraordinary emergencies such as journeys: to save money generally I think wrong except you have a family to provide for after your death. I should be glad to hear how the state of Railways affects you:[3] & whether you have yet begun to feel the benefit of the boys being off your hands to some extent.

—I want to write to Walter: do I remember that you said it would be useless to do so after the 18th? If so why? Love to my darling K. Tell Mary I talked to Mrs Coleridge's daughter last night and ceased to admire her.[4] I never see anyone I like beyond a certain point. Little Toddy Burgoyne[5] I like best: but she will outgrow what there is truly attractive in her like the rest of them.

—Henry Bunsen called on me the other day: O I am going to Carlton Terrace this evening.   Your's

M. A.

MS. Balliol College.

1. The date is wishful, though probably close.
2. As tutor to Lord Sandon.
3. Financial scandals about the profiteering, peculation, and mismanagement of railway funds by George Hudson, beginning in the last days of February and continuing for several months. Three Committees of Investigation were producing reports with "more and more lurid details of Hudson's delinquencies" (Richard S. Lambert, *The Railway King 1800–1871: A Study of George Hudson and the Business Morals of His Time,* p. 264), and Hudson was summoned before the House of Commons on May 17. (Carlyle's essay "Hudson's Statue," one of the *Latter-Day Pamphlets,* appeared in July 1850, and in the same month Judge Wightman—not yet Arnold's father-in-law—presided at York over a libel suit directly relating to the affair.)
4. Edith Coleridge (b. 1832), daughter of Henry Nelson Coleridge (1798–1843: *DNB*) and Sara Coleridge (1802–52: *DNB*), nephew and daughter of the poet, published *Memoir and Letters of Sara Coleridge* in two volumes in 1873.
5. Mary Caroline, daughter of Sir John Montagu Burgoyne, of 7 Lowndes Square, relations of the Blacketts (see below p. 450 n. 2).

To Jane Martha Arnold

London

My dearest K   Monday, [? May, 1849]

x x x More & more I think ill of the great people here:[1] that is their two capital faults, stupidity & hardness of heart become more & more clear to me. Their faults of character seem to me, as I watch the people in the park, to be the grand impairers of English beauty. In the men certainly: for the faces of the handsomest express either a stupid pride, or the stupidity without the pride & the half alive look of many pretty faces among the women, so different from the Southern languor, points to something very like stupidity. And a proud looking Englishwoman is the *hardest* looking thing I know in the world. So I should not be sorry to get away: but I still accustom myself to feel that we should pity these people rather than be angry with them.

I do not think any *fruitful* revolution can come in my time; and meanwhile, thank God, there are many honest people on earth, and the month of May comes every year.

x x Goodbye: this is rather a sombre letter, but I have not breakfasted & it is 11½, which is perhaps the reason.

I have many poetical schemes; but am fermenting too much about poetry in general to do anything satisfactory. My last volume I have got absolutely to *dislike*.   Ever yours

M. A.

Text. Transcript (by ?Jane Martha Arnold), Balliol College.

   1. Lansdowne House?

To Jane Martha Arnold

Thursday

Dear K   [? May 1849][1]

I return Willy's letter, with which I am deeply interested. I send you the above which I wrote the other day lying in a favorite glade of mine in Kensington Gardens, & which I hope may give you a feeling of the place & time. I write a good deal easier than I did—tho: not much in quantity. I think there is nothing obscure in these—love to all—   your's

M. A.

Written in Kensington Gardens[2]

In this cool open glade I lie
Screen'd by dark trees on either hand:
While at its head, to stop the eye,
Those dark-topp'd red-bol'd pinetrees stand.

The clouded sky is still and grey,
Through silken rifts soft peers the sun:
Light the clear-foliag'd chestnuts play,
The massier elms stand grave and dun.

The birds sing sweetly in these trees
Across the girdling City's hum.
How green under the boughs it is!
How thick the tremulous sheep-cries come!

Here where I lie what marvels pass!
What active endless life is here!
Buttercups, daisies, clover, grass,
An air-stirr'd forest, fresh and clear.

No fresher is the mountain sod
Where the tired angler lies, stretch'd out,
And, eas'd of basket & of rod,
Counts his day's spoil, the spotted trout.

The child who runs across the glade
Takes to his nurse his broken toy;
The brown thrush crosses overhead,
Deep in her unknown day's employ.

I, on men's impious uproar hurl'd,
Think sometimes, as I hear them rave,
That Peace has left the upper world,
And now keeps only in the grave.

But here is peace for ever new.
When I, who watch them, am away,
Still all things in this glade go through
The stages of their quiet day.

Then to their happy rest they pass.
The flowers close, the birds are fed,
The night comes down upon the grass,
The child sleeps warmly in his bed.

In the brick world, which rumbles nigh,
Be others happy, if they can.
But in my helpless cradle I
Was look'd on by the rural Pan.

Calm Soul of all things! make it mine
To feel, amid the city's jar,
That there abides a peace of thine
Man did not make, & cannot mar.

The will to neither strive nor cry,
The power to feel with others give.
Calm, calm me more: nor let me die,
Before I have begun to live.

MS. Balliol College.

1. Date determined by the obvious connection of this letter with "The New Sirens" (also perhaps set in Kensington Gardens), both poem and "argument" (above p. 139), in language, *mise-en-scène*, and theme.

2. "Written in Kensington Gardens" (Allott, p. 269), published in *Empedocles on Etna, and Other Poems*, 1852. An earlier draft was printed by Tinker and Lowry, pp. 196–98, and (more accurately) by Ullman, *The Yale Manuscript*, pp. 131–32.

To Mary Penrose Arnold*

London
My dearest Mamma   Sunday, [July 29, 1849]

I send you Tom's letter: I should have sent it before: but I had a long letter [?]a preparing to go with it which is at L[ansdowne] House & not finished: however I will not keep Tom's any longer. I am going at 4 o'clock to Laleham to dine as I half promised I would do.[1] I have been out very little the last week, as nearly every one I know is out of town. There was a sonnet of mine in last week's Examiner, "To the Hungarian Nation"[2] but as it was not worth much I don't send it. Tell dearest K that I shall not forget her on Wednesday. I give her the new 1 vol. edition of Lockhart's Life of Scott— but it must wait for Edward or me to bring it as it is too big a book for the new postal arrangements. What a book—what a man.—I have read a good deal of biography lately—Byron—Scott—Napoleon—Goethe—Burns[3]— the 29th of August this year is the centenary of Goethe's birth.—Let me add that I have finished the Iliad, going straight thro: it that is: I have within this year read thro: all Homer's works & all those ascribed to him. But I have done little tho: more than most years, tho: I am getting more of a distinct feeling as to what I want to read: however this though a great step is not enough without strong command over oneself to make oneself follow one's rule: conviction as the Westminster divines[4] say must precede conversion but does not imply it.—I cannot yet speak positively about coming to Filey[5]— but things look like my going abroad. However you shall hear before I go, at any rate. Love to all.   Your's, a thousand times

M. A.

I shall certainly follow your suggestion about the Wordsworths.

MS. Balliol College

1. Where the Bucklands lived.

2. "To the Hungarian Nation" (Allott, p. 120), published in the *Examiner*, July 21, 1849 (not reprinted by Arnold).

3. Probably either J. G. Lockhart's *Life of Robert Burns* (1828, 5th edn 1847) or Allan Cunningham's edition of Burns's *Works* with a *Life* and with notes by Scott, Campbell, Wordsworth, and Lockhart (Bohn, 1847); Thomas Moore's one-volume *Life* of Byron

(1847); Goethe's *Dichtung und Wahrheit* and of course Las Cases's *Mémorial de Sainte-Hélène* (see above p. 148).

4. The Westminster Assembly of Divines (1643), convoked to advise Parliament as to church government, produced the Westminster *Confession, Directory of Public Worship,* and *Catechisms*—all associated now with Scottish Presbyterianism. There is much about it in Arnold's *St Paul and Protestantism.*

5. A coastal village near Scarborough, Yorks, with a fine beach and a spa with a "reputation for cases of scrofula, dyspepsia, and nervousness" (*Imperial Gazetteer*).

To Frances Bunsen Trevenen Whately Arnold

London [*for* Bournemouth]

My dearest Fan   Wednesday, [? August 1, 1849]

Thank you for your letter. When you come to Rugby I shall try and get there to see you for a day. On Sunday afternoon I went to Laleham, which you have never seen. In the afternoon I went to Pentonhook with Uncle Buckland, Fan and Martha, and all the school following behind, just as I used to follow along the same river bank eighteen years ago. It changes less than any place I ever go to. I should like to go there with your sister Jane. Tell her the horse-chestnuts on the lawn before the Hartwells looking to the river and Chertsey were just going out of bloom.[1] On Monday morning I got up at half-past six, and bathed with Hughes[2] in the Thames, having a header off the "kempshott" where the lane from the village comes down on the river, and at seven I was swimming in the Thames with the swans looking at me.

Bournemouth on the Sea[3] is a very stupid place; a great moorland covered with furze and low pine woods comes down to the sea-shore, and breaks down towards it in a long sweep of cliff, half sand, half mud. There are no little bays and ins and outs as in the Isle of Man, but to the right and left you see one immense, gradually-curving line till the coast ends in two ordinary headlands at great distances on each side of you. A little brook runs into the sea here, and my great amusement was to hang upon the bridge and watch two little girls who had laid a plank across the stream below me, almost touching the water, the banks being on a level with it, and kept running across it by turns, splashing themselves by the jigging of the plank. Seeing me watch them always made them go faster and faster, till at last they were nearly wet through, and went home to change.   Yours,

M. A.

Text. Russell, 1 : 13—14.

1. See above p. 79. Francis Hartwell, of Boulogne and Laleham, was an old neighbor whose eldest son, Francis Grant Hartwell, attended Rugby and then entered Oxford (Exeter), just a year before Arnold. See below p. 193 n. 1.

2. Thomas Hughes (1822–96: *DNB*; *VF*, 6/8/72) is forever identified with romantic idealism, in life as in fiction—Tom Brown, Dr Arnold, Rugby School, muscular Christianity, and Rugby, Tennessee. (The sentence is paraphrased, without acknowledgment, in Edward C. Mack and W. H. G. Armytage, *Thomas Hughes: The Life of the Author of Tom Brown's Schooldays*, pp. 62–63.)

3. At this time a new watering place, with a population of about 500.

Francis Turner Palgrave to Thomas Arnold

Privy Council Office
September 14, 1849

I am reading "Mauprat" with intense interest, and have much to write to you about G. Sand. I wish you would name any book that I might send you. I have had to takes shots, and send you the "Princess."[1] If I have not delayed too long, it will go from Fellowes in a box sent by your Mother. Have you all G. Sand? Would you like Carlyle's Cromwell?

MS. Balliol College.

1. Tennyson's poem, published Dec. 1847.

To Arthur Hugh Clough

Thun

My dear Clough   Sunday, September 23, [1849]

I wrote to you from this place last year.[1] It is long since I have communicated with you and I often think of you among the untoward generation with whom I live and of whom all I read testifies.[2] With me it is curious at present: I am getting to feel more independent & unaffectible as to all intellectual & poetical performance the impatience at being faussé[3] in which drove me some time since so strongly into myself, and more snuffing after a moral atmosphere to respire in than ever before in my life. Marvel not that I say unto you, ye must be born again.[4] While I will not much talk of these things,[5] yet the considering of them has led me constantly to you the only living one almost that I know of of

> The children of the second birth
> Whom the world could not tame—[6]

for my dear Tom has not sufficient besonnenheit[7] for it to be any *rest* to think of him any more than it is a *rest* to think of mystics & such cattle—not that Tom is in any sense cattle or even a mystic but he has not "a still, considerate mind."[8]

What I must tell you is that I have never yet succeeded in any one great occasion in consciously mastering myself:[9] I can go thro: the imaginary process of mastering myself & see the whole affair as it would then stand, but at the critical point I am too apt to hoist up the mainsail to the wind & let her drive. However as I get more awake to this it will I hope mend for I find that with me a clear almost palpable intuition (damn the logical senses of the word) is necessary before I get into praxis:[10] unlike many people who set to work at their duty self-denial &c. like furies in the dark hoping to be gradually illuminated as they persist in this course.[11] Who also perhaps may be sheep but not of my fold,[12] whose one natural craving is not for profound thoughts, mighty spiritual workings &c. &c.[13] but a distinct seeing of my way as far as my own nature is concerned: which I believe to be the reason why the mathematics were ever foolishness to me.[14]

—I am here in a curious & not altogether comfortable state: however tomorrow I carry my aching head to the mountains & to my cousin the Blümlis Alp.[15]

> Fast, fast by my window
> The rushing winds go
> Towards the ice-cumber'd gorges,
> The vast fields of snow.
> There the torrents drive upward
> Their rock strangled hum,
> And the avalanche thunders
> The hoarse torrent dumb.
> I come, O ye mountains—
> Ye torrents, I come,

Yes, I come, but in three or four days I shall be back here, & then I must try how soon I can ferociously turn towards England.

My dearest Clough these are damned times—everything is against one—the height to which knowledge is come, the spread of luxury, our physical enervation, the absence of great *natures*, the unavoidable contact with millions of small ones, newspapers, cities, light profligate friends, moral desperadoes like Carlyle, our own selves, and the sickening consciousness of our difficulties: but for God's sake let us neither be fanatics nor yet chalf[16] blown by the wind but let us be ὡς φρονιμος διαρισειεν and not as any one else διαρισειεν.[17] When I come to town I tell you beforehand I will have a real effort at managing myself as to newspapers & the talk of the day. Why the devil do I read about Ld. Grey's sending convicts to the Cape,[18] & excite myself thereby, when I can thereby produce no possible good. But public opinion consists in a multitude of such excitements. Thou fool[19]—that which is morally worthless remains so, & undesired by Heaven, whatever results flow from it: & which of the units which has felt the excitement caused by reading of Lord Grey's conduct has been made one iota a better man thereby, or can honestly call his excitement a *moral* feeling.

You will not I know forget me. You cannot answer this letter for I know not how I come home.   Your's faithfully,

M. A.

MS. Yale University.

1. See above p. 155.
2. Acts 2:40.
3. Strained, warped.
4. John 3:3, 7.
5. John 14:30.
6. "Stanzas in Memory of the Author of 'Obermann' " (Allott p. 135), ll. 143–44.
7. Prudence or perhaps self-possession.
8. Unidentified.
9. Suggesting a much-loved quotation from Eckermann's *Gespräche mit Goethe* (Mar. 21 1830), recorded five times in Arnold's *Note-books* (see p. 38): "Die Hauptsache ist dass man lerne sich selbst zu beherrschen."
10. "Prayer" in all previous printings. See Introduction, p. xxiii.
11. A farrago of passages from *Paradise Lost*—1.22–23 ("what in me is dark / Illumine"), 2.406 ("palpable obscure"), 2.670–71 ("black it stood as Night, / Fierce as ten Furies").
12. John 10:16.
13. Keats, Second Sonnet to Hayden, "hum / Of mighty workings?"
14. 1 Corinthians 2:14.
15. Suggesting St Francis's *Canticle of the Sun,* translated by Arnold in his 1864 essay "Pagan and Medieval Religious Sentiment" (Super, 3:212–31, esp. pp. 224–25). Lowry (p. 110) read "Bhunlis Alp." The verses were included in "Parting" (Allott, p. 123).
16. Psalms 1:34, 35:5.
17. " 'As the man of practical wisdom would define it,' the standard for judging virtue in Aristotle's *Nicomachean Ethics* 2.vii.1107a" (R. H. Super, *Matthew Arnold,* The Oxford Authors, p. 566).
18. "In consequence of a plan formed by Earl Grey, the Colonial Minister, to distribute the better class of convicts amongst various settlements of the British Crown, for the double purpose of reforming the convicts and supplying the colonists with labourers, an Order in Council was issued on the 4th of September, 1848, in which, amongst other places, the Cape of Good Hope was named as one of the stations where convicts under the new system were to be received. When the news of this reached the Cape, the inhabitants loudly expressed their dissatisfaction, and the strongest feeling was displayead against what was considered an attempt to degrade a free colony into a penal settlement" (*Annual Register,* 1849).
19. Luke 12:20, 1 Corinthians 15:36.

Jane Martha Arnold to Thomas Arnold[1]

Fox How

My own dearest Tom   Friday, November 23 [and 30], 1849

It is just 8 o'clock, but these November mornings are so dark that I can still hardly see to write—however before Susy & Fan come down to our lesson in Ollendorff,[2] Titlings[3] will have time to give herself a few more finishing licks on the rug, and I shall at least make a beginning of my letter. Many of my thoughts have been with you already this morning dearest, as I was dressing in my little room, once yours—and whiling away that, to me, most tiresome operation, by reading between the intervals Buxton's life[4]—the third time of reading I believe, for it is a book after my own heart; and Susy Fan & I have bought between us the new edition which is just come out.—Well, Susy & Fan soon entered, and we have now hobbled through our German lesson—about which we are most virtuously persevering though we have none of us much turn for grammar—and now I hear the rattling of the breakfast things in the diningroom, and expect soon to hear the prayerbell. Now appears old Banks[5] at the window to speak about a grand piece of work which we are doing for the benefit of Fox How—making a feasible entrance into our field at the corner by Mr Roughsedge's gate, so that the hay-cart need no longer come over the lawn. It will be a great improvement, and gives employment to people at a very dead time of year, which is another good thing.—Another interruption; this time it is the Postman's horn (You see that we get our letters much earlier now—) and he brings no letter from New Zealand alas, nor from Walter as we hoped—but a long chatty one ⟨from⟩ to me from Mrs Hill, & another from Carly—and a bill for Master Ned (his old tricks,[6] you see) Then there comes a letter to Susy from Miss Spooner—and to Mamma one from dear Aunt Ward in answer to a proposal of Mother's to contribute £15 a year to Elvy: Watkin's support, if any comfortable home can be found for her—if the Bucklands would do the same, she might at once retire into peace & quiet, poor thing! which would be a comfort to the Wards too, for she is very fretful & hypochondriacal I am afraid—but after a life so wearing to the health & spirits as hers has been, it is not wonderful.[7]

The last letter is from dear old Matt, in answer to a question Mamma had asked him about giving Mr Gell[8] a sort of indirect testimonial to the Trustees—but this subject of the election to Rugby is too interesting to be entered upon at this minute—and besides at last breakfast is ready, and I must cease my gossiping.

Friday. November 30th.

Your birthday, my darling Tom! only think of its being the *third* that has past since we saw you—for if you remember you had left home, and were even, I think on board the John Wickliffe before the 30th of November 1847. And how many more will pass before we set eyes on your beloved face again? Your last letters have indeed spoken of your return as possibly nearer than we had supposed—but the future must be very uncertain; and if you were to become interested in any work in New Zealand, you might still wish to remain there; indeed there seems so much uncertainty about your plans, that we are quite baffled in looking forward—and in not knowing when I shall be able to kiss *you*! I have consoled myself this morning by kissing your picture—that dear picture which I saw taken in London, and which, though a little faded, is one of the greatest treasures we have. We put it on the breakfast-table this morning, along with the tall cake by which your birthday was duly honoured, indeed, Mrs Pritchard,[9] in her desire to honour you, has made the cake so gigantic that we see no prospect of being able to demolish it with our diminished forces, and now that Matt, who helped us handsomely through Edward's, is gone.—So now the *three elder ones* have reached the venerable ages of 26, 27, and 28—or will on Matt's birthday. I wonder whether the last two or three years have seemed such an advance in life to you, as they have to me. I need not ask though, because at my age a woman feels the difference of a few years much more than a man—a man has something young about him till after 30—whereas a woman when she has once passed youth experiences little change of feeling till the time when the vigour of life begins to decline—so here I am feeling all the sobriety and self-possession of 40—and philosophizing to girls, about the feelings I used to have at their age, &c &c. You need not be frightened at me, however, dear. I hope that I am not yet very stiff & formal—indeed I feel that the stiffness & harshness to which my character has a natural tendency, are rather lessening than encreasing as I grow older (don't think me conceited)—though slowly indeed & not without much labour. But if it is often true that "the old man clogs our earlier years"—I hope it will be true also, that

"Simple childhood comes the last."[10]

But I have wandered from you to myself and perhaps you will not be sorry for me to cut short my reflections altogether and come to a few facts.—May God bless you dearest Tom, always—& in all your works. What a comforting thought it is that at this very moment when we are vainly wishing to be near you, & perplexing ourselves with a thousand anxieties—*His* eye is upon you, & upon us together. His ear hears the prayer which we offer for you, and His love pauses not to fulfil it, if only His wisdom sees it to be good—Yet it is indeed a blessed thought that He does not forget His children whom He has adopted & 'accepted in the Beloved'—that His love follows them through all their wanderings, and that by sorrow or joy, by solitude or friendship, by success or disappointment He is still striving to purify them, and lead them home to Himself.

We shall be a very small party at home this Christmas. Matt will probably have to go to Bowood. Mary will be staying with the Hulls,[11] and so Edward will be the only addition to our present party. It is possible that his friend Alderson may come with him, and Lucy O'Brien[12] talks of paying Susy a visit. Susy & Edward will, I suppose go to Armathwaite[13] in the course of the holidays & these will be our only gaieties, with the exception of a Christmas tree which Fan is going to have for the entertainment of all the Rydal school children, & to which the Crewdsons[14] are invited, by her particular request. Fan is teaching the children some songs for the occasion, and there is a present on the Tree for each of them—so I hope it will be a happy evening for the dear little things.

Do you often think of the Christmas you spent at Norwich? The palace will be desolate enough this Christmas, for Dr Hinds does not go there for some months, and the Stanleys leave it tomorrow morning.[15]—I think you will be interested in what Stanley says about it in a letter Mamma had from him yesterday—"My Mother & sisters will live in London—the centre of their friends—probably in Eaton Square, if the house in Brook Street can be sold. They are all well, but the anxiety about a new house, as well as the toils of departure, are very trying at times to my dearest Mother: though on the whole I think that the *local* separation occasions her but little pain. She lived here for *him*, and now that that interest is gone, I believe that the only spot for which she really cares, is the centre of the nave, where the black marble slab reflects in its deep mirror, the western window, which will be, as I think I told you, his only monument. Catherine too feels the same, or nearly so. But to poor Mary the pang is terrible. Norwich had become to her more than a second Alderley, she was devoted to him—through him she became devoted to the place, & the place became to her what I fear no other place can ever become again—an immense sphere of usefulness of which she could be the head, without ostentation, and without stepping in the slightest degree from her position. Long & deeply, I believe, she will be lamented, as he will be, in all classes,x x

Think what a whirl I shall find myself in in Oxford on Sunday next, after this long seclusion. Think of us too in the sad hours of Saturday morning—and think too how strangely with all these feelings of sorrow & separation, is again blended, as in 1842, the trouble of the vacancy at Rugby"—

You may suppose that we like Stanley, are full of anxiety about the new election. Dr Tait becomes Dean of Carlisle. Dr Hinds becomes Bishop of Norwich—both good appointments, but neither of them such important positions as Rugby—and the choice of candidates for that is mostly deplorable—Lake! Mr Cotton, Mr Simpkinson, Mr Goulburn, Dr Kennedy &c.[16] and lastly Gell, whom we all wish to succeed. We have known nothing of him lately it is true, but we know that he *had* qualities which well fitted him for the post—and a man's whole character is not likely to change—one note he wrote to Mamma the other day was so beautiful, & showed such generosity & real greatness, that it alone would have made me wish for him. But I am afraid he has little chance—his scholarship is said to be very bad, which of course is a great objection, & decisive against him if there were any other candidate tolerably suited for Rugby in character—but if you must choose between a want of scholarship, & a want of judgement, a want of vigour & strength, a want of temper & calmness &c there can be no doubt which can be best dispensed with—almost all the old Rubgy men support Lake, which I am amazed at, for I think he is nearly the worst of the lot—I cannot think of a single quality he has, good or bad, which would not be misplaced at Rugby—I will copy for you a few lines received from Matt today. 'Lake is— like most people who have lived at Oxford all their lives without being born philosophers—a perfect child—if all does not go as he wishes it, he can neither keep his temper, nor conceal that he has lost it. He would be as unfit as possible, I think. Clough thinks so too, and is still convinced (I saw him last night) that Gell, though far from perfect, is the best they can have. And I think so too. And Walrond comes here on Saturday, whom we shall persuade, no doubt, and he will persuade Shairp & influence others at Rugby. Price wants to spoil every body's hand that he may be left to make his own— x x x Willy would give up his commission I suppose, if he took the school. I dare say he would do it well enough—for no great learning can be wanted there. It is good for his health, & a fixed occupation to divert him from dwelling on the sins of India. If left in the army he will some day mount a tub in the barrack yard, & prophesy to his regiment & the Government of India, all the judgements he thinks they deserve. Love to all my little ones.
Ever yours affecly

M. A."—

I do not know whether Mamma has told you enough about Willy to explain to you Matt's allusion, and I see that his own letter to you says nothing about it. Soon after he went to the hills he undertook, in an emergency to assist a man there in his school, & accordingly for some time, in spite of much ridicule of an 'Ensign turned School-master' he taught there three or four hours daily. This was nothing but good for all parties—but the Master a Mr Maddocks, has got more out of Willy on one pretence or another till Willy has now actually the whole charge of the school upon his hands, & is with the boys almost all day. Mr Maddocks has some other appointment & now proposes to Willy that he should resign his commission & take the school, and Willy, who has a great idea of the good that is to be effected in India through these hill schools, has not altogether declined, but waits partly to hear from us—though I think he inclines against the change. For my part I should hate Willy's having anything to do with that man or his school—for I am sure he would get him into some trouble—he is such an unscrupulous, grasping man, considering no one's convenience but his own. It is quite evident to me that dear Willy is deceived in him—and though I love him ten thousand times better for his readiness to be useful at any cost to himself— which he has proved in spite of ridicule & labour—I should like him to begin any new profession under better auspices than that man's—However, having tried to put the dear boy on his guard in this respect, I do not think we should attempt to influence him much—he is so simply desirous to do right, that I am sure he cannot go far wrong—if only he does not act in a hurry, & under false impressions of the man he has to deal with.—I am glad to think that Willy has two or three friends at Landour, who will give him both wise & Christian advice—but the dear boy is not—it must be confessed—the kind of person to take advice—it is a family failing. Meantime whatever he does, & wherever he is, he is a subject of the deepest thankfulness to us—and if I had formed any ambitious hopes for him, I can truly say that so far as they had any tincture of worldliness in them, I am glad they should be mortified as long as Willy is living only to serve God, one ought not to have a moment's care whether it is in a more humble, or more distinguished sphere. You will be touched by dearest Willy's letter to you, I am sure—he feels such strong affection for all his brothers, and seems to have such a longing for your counsel & sympathy. Matt wrote him such a good letter when he was at home, advising him against withdrawing from the world & pointing out how effective Papa was beyond mere thinkers & recluses, just because ⟨he did his⟩ worldly men saw that in the mere business of life he met them & beat them on their own ground.

It is turning out a beautiful afternoon, and we must soon go out. I meant to have told you about some of the books (though they are few enough) that we have been reading—of public events I can tell you nothing because we see no newspapers & now that Miss Martineau & Mr Greg are away—hear nothing. Of our home life too, I have little to say—it is so perfectly uniform—the only change is that we get more & more interested in the schools & such things, and encrease our knowledge of the poor people—

to our mutual good, I hope. Even the list of our friends I ransack in vain for any news. We are to drink tea tomorrow at "Friend Ball's"—and the singing lessons have brought about a good deal more intercourse with the Quillinans—poor Mr Roughsedge is always ill with the gout, & Mrs Roughsedge always nursing. Kate Southey is now staying at the Mount—much aged since I last saw her—the 1st Vol of her Father's life by Cuthbert is just out—the early letters, about the scheme for emigrating to America, are very fresh & delightful—. Mr Rollestone, the new curate at Rydal, being a young man, of course affords a certain amount of conversation for the young ladies in the neighbourhood—but is no great acquisition, I think. The Fletcher Flemings are as much attached to the family as ever—and Matt *comes the popular* man so strong when he is in the valley, that he involves us in all sorts of invitations—. We have not heard much from the Whately's lately—poor Jane is very unwell still. The Wales have been staying at Redesdale for many months, as he has given up his profession & they are going to live on their estate in Norfolk. Mr Wale had a short but most alarming illness the other day—but he is well again, and the baby, my godchild, is of course the admiration of the family.[17]

I suppose we shall see something of the Taits when they are at Carlisle—of Rugby, when they are gone, & the Prices, we shall hear less than ever—. By the bye, about Mr Price, Matt means I suppose that he wants to have the mastership *offered* to him as the only eligible man—but I hope that will not be.

And so you have taken to smoking—and we can no longer boast that *none* of our brothers make themselves a nuisance by that most unpleasant habit. Well, you shall smoke in *Banks' hole* when you come home—but no where else. I wonder whether the Canterbury settlement will take out any one you will like. It will bring more books at least into the settlement—but I am afraid they will be rather a *Churchy* set.—If you do not like the books we have sent you, you must blame Matt & Stanley who made the choice. I wish we could send you more—but as for your saying in one of your last letters that 'you think you were formed for a literary life'—I must be so bold as to say that I think you were never more mistaken in your life—just consider how totally different has been your natural bent, whenever it has had an opportunity of manifesting itself ever since boyhood—. The absence of literature & literary tastes in the colony, gives them an exaggerated ⟨value⟩ charm in your eyes, and as you have a real taste for them, makes you fancy you would find them more sufficient than you would. I am sure dear, that you would not have followed books or writing, as your profession, for a year, before you would be sick to death of them—and long to be among men & actions—Only think what a different character a man must have from yours, who could spend his life contentedly in his study: while such social & political questions as our time presents, are struggling to a solution—I know that the man sitting in his study may help this solution forward more than any one—but there is nothing I am more certain of than that you are not formed for that part—You are formed for action, for government—& because this seems debarred you, do not be seduced into throwing yourself into another kind of life—whether in New Zealand or here; if you are wise you will have some active, practical life—at least this is my theory—but it amuses me to think how many wise lectures I waste upon you. My dearest—tell us how your school goes on—   Your most loving sister,

JM Arnold

You may conclude that news & remarks do not get quite correctly from New Zealand to India & back again—so you need not suppose that I have been *blacking* you to Willy.

MS. *Balliol College.*

1. This compendious letter (comprising part of one from Matthew Arnold) is printed complete for the sake of its picture of life at Fox How.

2. Heinrich Gottfried Ollendorff (1803–65), a London resident, had popularized a series of books for teaching various languages widely used in Great Britain and the United States; here, *Ollendorff's New Method of Learning to Read, Write, and Speak the German Language*, first issued in 1838, all with the usual exercises and questions in a special language never spoken on land or sea—e.g., "Whither do you wish to go?" "Is the friend of the Spaniard able to carry provisions?" "What is your pleasure, Sir?"—pp. 68, 69, 183.

3. "Titlings and Boadicea are in excellent health and spirits. Titlings has lately taken up her abode on the stool beside the fire and is rarely absent, except at meal times. Boadicea is as lovely and wicked as ever" (Frances Arnold to Tom, Jan. 1849, in Bertram, p. 67).

4. Charles Buxton's *Memoirs of Sir Thomas Fowell Buxton, Baronet* (1848), second and third editions in 1849. Sir Fowell, philanthropist and emancipationist, was, though not technically a Quaker, associated with the Society of Friends; his sister Anna (d. 1855) was the mother of William E. Forster.

5. Banks, who died in Aug. 1865, was the gardener. Hornby Roughsedge, J. P., and his wife, often mentioned in the Wordsworth letters, lived at Fox Ghyll nearby, which was bought by the Forsters in 1873. Roughsedge's first name comes from Martineau, p. 23.

6. Herbert Hill (see above p. 17 n. 2) had been an assistant master at Rugby (1836–39) and was now headmaster of King's School, Warwick. "Carly" remains unidentified (perhaps their cousin, Caroline, daughter of John Ward? Her name occurs in Bertram, p. 156). Master Ned is Edward Penrose Arnold.

7. Miss Spooner was perhaps a sister of Catherine Tait (*née* Spooner), wife of A. C. Tait, or possibly an aunt of William Archibald Spooner (1844–1930: *DNB*; *VF*, 4/21/98), later warden of New College, Oxford (remembered for "Spoonerisms"), who was buried in Grasmere, "where his wife's house, How Foot, had been for many years a beloved holiday home." For Aunt Ward, Dr Arnold's sister Martha, see above p. 22 n. 6. Watkin has not been identified.

8. John Philip Gell (1816–98) was at Rugby 1830–35, where he became Clough's friend (and taught him to shave and "until he was proficient at it shaved him himself") and Dr Arnold's disciple, and afterwards at Trinity College, Cambridge (B.A. 1839). Dr Arnold nominated him in 1839 as "Head Master of a great school in Van Diemen's Land" (Stanley, p. 336), where he went and remained for nearly ten years. In 1849 he married Eleanor Franklin, daughter of Sir John Franklin (d. 1847, but Lieutenant Governor of Van Diemen's Land, when Gell went out). See Woodward, pp. 73–126, and the letter of consolation to the widow which concluded the *Life* (Stanley, pp. 435–37).

9. A domestic servant.

10. Unidentified.

11. The Winstanley Hulls (see above p. 32 n. 21).

12. Unidentified, but perhaps a daughter of Donough O'Brien, of Rugby, who entered two sons in the school in 1847.

13. Probably, Armathwaite Hall, Cumberland, the seat of Sir Henry Vane (1830–1908; 4th bt). He succeeded his father in 1842, but married only in 1871, and his mother dispensed hospitality. Mrs Arnold wrote to Jamie Hearn (see below p. 125 n. 4) on Jan. 20, 1850: "Susy is come back from Armathwaite [where she had passed a fortnight or so for Vane's birthday festivities]. . . . The Lake was so hard frozen at Armathwaite that Lady Vane gave a deer which was roasted whole on the shore and hundreds of people assembled to partake of it in tents—and there were races in skating on the ice and the people were exceedingly pleased and as you will [?imagine] between drank Sir Henry Vane's health who went down to dine with them" (MS. Rochester).

14. The family of William Dillworth Crewdson (1774–1851), a Kendal banker, Quaker, and friend of the Wordsworths.

15. Samuel Hinds (1793–1872: *DNB*), named bishop of Norwich on the death of Edward Stanley (1779–1849: *DNB*), father of A. P. Stanley, who died in September.

16. Nearly two dozen candidates for the Rugby headmastership are listed in *The Times*, Dec. 11, p. 5. For Goulburn see below p. 169 n. 4. George Edward Lynch Cotton (1813–66: *DNB*), of Westminster and Trinity College, Cambridge, a housemaster at Rugby School 1837–52 (the "young master" in *Tom Brown's Schooldays*), headmaster of Marlborough 1852–58, and then bishop of Calcutta. He drowned in the Ganges "while disembarking from a steam-boat" (*Annual Register*), but he is remembered in Arnoldian circles because of his broken engagement in 1842 to the writer of this letter. The breach was healed, however, and in 1858 he visited Fox How just before leaving for India and in 1859 in Calcutta William Arnold visited *him* just before leaving for England (Mulhauser, 2:555, and Woodward, p. 223). See the sketch by J. C. Shairp in *Portraits of Friends*, pp. 114–38, and Arnold's letter to his mother Nov. 3, 1866.

John Nassau Simpkinson (1817–94), of Rugby and Trinity College, Cambridge, was an assistant master at Harrow 1845–55 and then rector of Brington, Northants, and North Creake, Norfolk, and also a contributor to the *Edinburgh Review* (Rugby; Harrow).

Benjamin Hall Kennedy (1804–89: *DNB*), of Shrewsbury and St John's College, Cambridge, was an assistant master at Harrow 1830–36 (Harrow), and then head of Shrewsbury for thirty years (1836–66) before becoming Regius Professor of Greek at Cambridge, 1867–89.

17. William Ball (1801–78), a former solicitor and author of nine volumes of verse, at Glen Rothay, where "Wordsworth met many of his Quaker friends" (*Letters of William and Dorothy Wordsworth*, 2d edn, rev. Alan G. Hill, 6:264–65n).

Edward Quillinan (1791–1851: *DNB*), husband of Dora Wordsworth (d. 1847) and (by his first wife) father of Jemima (1819–91) and Rotha (d. 1876); see Arnold's poem "Stanzas in Memory of Edward Quillinan" (Allott, p. 257).

Kate Southey was the poet's youngest daughter; Cuthbert Southey (1819–88), her brother, brought out *The Life and Correspondence of the Late Robert Southey*, 6 vols, 1849–50.

Mr "Rollestone" was probably Robert Rolleston (c. 1820-??), University College, Oxford, B.A. 1842, ordained deacon a year after, and priest in 1844, later perpetual curate at Seathwaite, Lancs, and (1860–63) Holy Trinity, Warrington, and in 1868 rector of Sandford Rivers (Foster; Crockford).

Fletcher Fleming (1795–1876), perpetual curate of Rydal and Loughrigg 1825–57 and rector of Grasmere from 1857, was one of the eight sons of Wordsworth's old school friend John Fleming of Rayrigg, rector of Bootle, near Millom, and the name occurs often in the Wordsworth letters.

Charles Brent Wale (1817–64), a lawyer, in Sept. 1848 married Archbishop Whately's daughter, Henrietta (d. 1908), who had rejected Tom Arnold's proposal of marriage ("my heart is much deadened both to pain and pleasure"). "Redesdale" was the Whately's country house in Ireland. The godchild was Elizabeth Branch Wale—not, alas, her younger sister Henrietta, who in 1877 married Tom Arnold's oldest son, W. T. Arnold. (See the excellent summary in Bertram, pp. xxix-xxxii; *Landed*; Venn.) Elizabeth Jane Whately (1822–93: identified in *DNB* only as "female issue"), the archbishop's oldest daughter, "was an active worker among the poor during the Irish famine; conducted a mission in Madrid in 1872, and afterwards established a school in Cairo for European children" (Allibone, listing twenty-one titles).

Mary Arnold Twining to Thomas Arnold

December 1, [1849]

One day in conversation with Matt he [Wordsworth] talked very openly about Goethe—I will copy what I wrote down "Speaking of Goethe he said that he wrote too artistically—the arts were too obvious—his writings were more deduced from these than the arts deducible from his writings—Thus he could never be a truly great dramatic genius—he was not driven inevitably upon the drama because he cd not help it—he said no man cd be placed in worse circumstances than Goethe was—there *could* be nothing worse than for a Man to spend his life in one of these small mechanical German Courts—he spoke strongly of Goethe's want of Interest in Politics—that it was a great discredit to him that he was not more of a citizen— he *ought* to have cared more for these things—also he considered it a "deep disgrace" to Goethe that he never came to England—the great mistake he made in thinking he could gain all he wanted without it—that Italy cd furnish everything.

MS. Balliol College.

To Arthur Hugh Clough

Dear Clough   [Rugby, c.December 15, 1849][1]
Lawley called[2]—stayed a vast while—and hindered my coming to wish you goodbye.

I have been to Thurleston with Walrond today[3]—to Kenilworth tomorrow—don't you envy me.

I shall go to Bowood most likely at the begining of next month. I will let you know when I am about to come thro: town.

They are very bitter agst Lake some of them: Price above all. Goulburn they say will be elected:[4] the boys will blow their nose in his coat tails as he walks thro: the 4gle.[5]   Your's in great haste

                                                                    M. A.

Down again dressed for dinner after dinner to the Price's—but thou'dst not think, Horatio, how ill it is here—[6]

I said a lovely poem to that fool Shairp today which he was incapable of taking in. He is losing his hair. Tom has had an offer of the Inspectorship of schools in V. Diemen's land.[7] £400 a year & his expenses: we hear from the Colonial office that this offer has been made by the Governor of V. Diemen's land. Whether accepted or not we don't know. I shouldn't wonder if he took it. I think I shall emigrate: why the devil don't you.

I will send you the Homer travestied someday.[8]

                                                                    M. A.

MS. Yale University.

1. Lowry, perhaps misreading his own handwriting, dated this letter one month too early.

2. Probably *Frank* Lawley (*pace* Lowry), in London. The two Lawley brothers, one charming and bad, the other dull and good, are sometimes confused. Stephen Willoughby Lawley (1823–1905), third son of 1st Baron Wenlock, at Rugby and then (1841–45) Balliol, became rector of Escrick, Yorks, 1848–68, and sub-dean of York 1852–62. He is mentioned half-a-dozen times in Kenny (Clough tutored both); in 1897 Tom Arnold described him as "the dear, the excellent Stephen" (*The Letters of Thomas Arnold the Younger*, ed. Bertram, p. 238). His younger brother Francis Charles Lawley (1825–1901: *DNB*), also of Rugby and then (1844–48) Balliol, with (like his brother) a Second in Classics, was much more colorful—indeed, *too* colorful, for after an All Souls' fellowship and a two-year stint as M.P. for Beverley, he became Gladstone's private secretary, gambled disastrously in horse-racing, and, charged with unethical use of privileged information ("insider trading") on the stock exchange, lost his appointment as governor of South Australia (see below p. 291). He retreated to the United States and was correspondent for *The Times* during the Civil War, teaming up for a while with Col. Garnet Wolseley (see W. S. Hoole, *Lawley Covers the Confederacy*, 1964, with a portrait,

which lists his dispatches). After his return in 1865 Arnold (who kept his distance) saw him from time to time in London (see below p. 288, and letters to him Nov. 19, 1878, Mar. 7, 1880). In 1897 Tom Arnold described him as "not a very satisfactory person," but he earned a favorable notice in the *DNB* ("handsome presence," "courtly demeanour," "fascinating companion"), whereas "the dear, the excellent Stephen," a shadow among shadows, disdained by Boase, *The Times*, and the *Annual Register*, is remembered only by his University (Foster) and his Church (Crockford) wailing at the impassable streams of (in Chatham's phrase) the insignificance for which God and Nature alike designed him.

3. Theodore ("Todo") Walrond (1824–87) entered Rugby in 1834, in 1840 became captain or head boy, and in 1842, tutored by Clough, won the scholarship to Balliol, where he became as he remained one of the innermost of the inner circle: a Jowett disciple and one of the Decade, a guest at Arnold's wedding, godfather to Budge Arnold, namesake of Tom Arnold's son Theodore, author of the life of Dr Arnold for the *DNB* (he had begun editing the life and letters of A. P. Stanley, with whom he had traveled in the Near East—they bumped into William Arnold in a Cairo hotel in Dec. 1852!), and much else. From Oxford he went back to Rugby for three years as assistant master and from Rugby went once again, in 1851, to Balliol, this time as fellow and tutor. In 1856 he was "appointed Examiner to the newly created Civil Service Commission . . . [where] he remained until his death, filling successively the posts of Secretary and [in 1875] Commissioner" (*Annual Register*).

In 1859, as money and society, like love (in Lawrence's phrase), seek "a perfect communion of oneness," he married Charlotte Grenfell, daughter of a director of the Bank of England, thereby becoming Max Mueller's brother-in-law and uncle-by-marriage of Charles Kingsley and J. A. Froude, and on her death married her cousin in 1876. He stood for the headmastership of Rugby in 1869 but failed partly because Rugby was still purging itself of Dr Arnold and partly because he was a layman. (Matthew Arnold himself initially supported F. W. Farrar, who withdrew, and then wrote a testimonial for Walrond—see below Arnold to his mother in 1869, Oct. 23 and Nov. 21, 27.) Walrond was made C.B. in 1871.

He and Arnold were always close friends—in fact, he was one of Arnold's trustees—but he remains the most obscure by far of what Tom Arnold called the "little interior company" (*Passages in a Wandering Life*, p. 58). He was the best athlete of the lot (cricket, football, diving, and "one of the best oars in the University" (Thomas Hughes's obituary in the *Annual Register*) and possibly, with a First in Classics, the best scholar—"In lore of Hellas scholar without peer," according to J. C. Shairp's poem "Balliol Scholars 1840–43." Kenny, saying that Clough was "clearly in love with Walrond," thinks it "unlikely that there was overtly sexual expression of affection between them" and adds that Clough "who agonized so much over masturbation, would have been tormented with guilt by sodomy" (p. lxiii). Walrond's purity and probity are affirmed by all who knew him: "That sweet face," says Shairp, was "by no rude thought defiled." Nature made him and then broke the mold. "From the very first to the very last, in the power of doing thoroughly well the work set before him, in scrupulous fidelity, in high-toned integrity, in calm and righteous judgment, in practical and sound sense, and, not least of all, in hearty appreciation of all that was best in literature as well as in life, his friends will, I feel sure, unite in saying that they have rarely known his equal" (G. G. Bradley, cited in John Curgenven, "Theodore Walrond: Friend of Arnold and Clough," *Durham University Journal* 44 (Mar. 1952):56–61). And Curgenven, who knew Walrond's daughter, assures us that he was "a devoted husband and father." One has to conclude that he *courted* obscurity and, like some real life Michael Henchard, deliberately willed his own oblivion by order-ing the destruction, at his death, of "a large number of letters from both Arnold and Clough" (Curgenven, p, 56); no letter to him from either is recorded. He remains un-known and unknowable, and, for these reasons, uninteresting. (Kathleen Tillotson's ex-cellent essay "Rugby 1850: Arnold, Clough, Walrond and *In Memoriam*," *Review of En-glish Studies*, Apr. 1953, reprinted in *Mid-Victorian Studies*, 1965, is by all odds the best thing written on Walrond. See also Boase; *Landed; Upper Ten Thousand;* and the obituary in the *Annual Register*, June 1887.)

4. Edward Meyrick Goulburn (1818–97: *DNB*), of Eton and (1834–39) Balliol; from 1841 to 1846 he was fellow and then tutor and dean of Merton College. Staunchly conservative, he took two steps backward if the Zeitgeist took one forward though otherwise remained stationary, and on Dec. 17, 1849, he was elected headmaster over W. C. Lake, because the Trustees wanted to move away from Dr Arnold as far as possible as rapidly as possible. The momentum of the Arnoldian tradition was still too great, how-ever, and Goulburn and the school were set on a collision course that damaged both: the school lost students, Goulburn his job (see *Memoirs of Archbishop Temple*, ed. Sandford, 1:151–55). After marking time for nine years, first at Quebec Chapel, Marylebone, and then at St John's, Paddington, he accepted the deanship of Norwich, where he remained till 1889, when he resigned to retire to Tunbridge Wells and write an "unreadable" book (see Tuckwell, especially pp. 217,269–74).

5. "He used . . . to go out to dinner in his cassock, and never appeared without it among us boys" (Tuckwell, p. 272).

6. *Hamlet* 5.2.222–23.

7. "Towards the end of October 1848 I received a letter from Sir William Denison [1804–71: *DNB*], offering me the post of Inspector of Schools in the Colony of Tas-mania" (Thomas Arnold, *Passages in a Wandering Life*, p. 113).

8. Unidentified.

To Wyndham Slade * [1]

Dear Slade   *Le Samedi matin,* [1850] [2]

I forgot to say last night that you must breakfast here to-morrow, Sun-day, at 10 *pas plus tôt*, because Blackett [3] is coming, who wishes to meet you. Ridiculous as such a desire is, it is too unimportant for me to refuse to gratify it.   Your faithful servant,

Matthew Arnold.

Text. Russell, 1:14–15.

1. Wyndham Slade (1826–1910), from the West Country (Montys Court, Taun-ton), Eton, and Balliol (B.A. 1848), son (and later son-in-law) of a baronet, a student at the Inner Temple from Jan. 1847 and called to the bar on Nov. 22, 1850—unmistakably a route to John Duke Coleridge and thence to Arnold. Slade had traveled with Arnold in the Tyrol in 1849, had visited Arnold in the Lake Country in 1850 and (with "some of his family") traveled with the Arnolds in Switzerland in Aug. 1857; he stood as godfather to Lucy Arnold in 1859, and Arnold saw him in Paris later the same year. In 1863 he married

Cicely Neave, and the Arnolds and Slades remained on friendly, familiar terms. Slade became a Revising Barrister in 1865 and from 1877 till 1901 was a Metropolitan Police Magistrate. He shared Arnold's passion for hunting and fishing and in general seems a debonair and well-heeled friend and companion (*WWW*; *Landed*; *County Families*).

    2. The date is Russell's.

    3. See above p. 75 n. 1. Russell has "John Blackett"; the first name was deleted by Kenneth Allott, who saw the MS.

To Drummond Rawnsley[1]

Revd Drummond Rawnsley.   London
My dear Sir   January 21, 1850
    I have received your letter with the promised autograph on my return to town and am very much obliged to you for it.

    You must have had as cold a journey home as you had the morning we left Reading together. They say here that the Thames is going to be frozen.[2]

    I am, my dear Sir,   Your's very faithfully

M. Arnold.—

MS. University of Virginia.

    1. Drummond Rawnsley (1817–82), of an old Lincolnshire county family and re-membered now only because, man and boy, Tennyson loved him, was "The Vicar of Shiplake" from whose house Tennyson was married in June 1850 and to whom Tennyson addressed the poem of that title. But he had been at Rugby under Dr Arnold and after-wards at Brasenose. The "promised autograph" must be Tennyson's; the two poets first met, months later, on Oct. 14, 1850, when the Tennysons, according to an entry in Emily Tennyson's manuscript journal (a latter-day redaction of the original), left Coniston "for Cheltenham and travelled with Mr Matthew Arnold, then in the hey-day of youth to Crewe."

    2. Arnold had been home at Fox How for Christmas. On Jan. 11 Frances Arnold wrote to Jamie Hearn (MS. Rochester): "At 2 o'clock [on Monday, Jan. 7] I went down to the Station [at Bowness] and found Matt and Edward. Edward was going as far as Kendal that he might have something done to his teeth and I went with them. We went all together as far as Kendal and then Edward and I said goodbye to dear Matt, & went up into town."

Mary Arnold Twining to Thomas Arnold (extract)

Tickwood
January 31, 1850
    Matt's Poems wd be something like a familiar Epistle to you in which you wd perhaps trace your way back into old days and conversations, and mental passages more or less connected with other's.

MS. Balliol College.

To Jane Martha Arnold[1]

London
My dearest K   Tuesday, [? May, 1850]
I must write again before I see Mr Forster[2]—I have been in a kind of
spiritual lethargy for some time past, partly from headache partly from other
causes which has made it difficult for me to approfondir any matter of feeling—but I feel quite sure my darling that when I can sink myself well down,
into the consideration of you & your circumstances as they really are then
will you be truly set right in my mind in respect of your engagement. This I
say not to please you but because I really feel it to be the truth [;] at present
my objections are not based in *reality*, that I feel.

I am subject to these periods of spiritual eastwind when I can lay hold
only of the outside of events or words—the material eastwind which now
prevails has something to do with it, and also the state of strain & uneasiness
in which in these days & in London it is so hard not to live. You my darling
have been a refreshing thought to me in my dryest periods: I may say that
you have been one of the most faithful witnesses (almost the only one after
papa) among those with whom I have lived & spoken of the reality & possibility of that abiding inward life which we all desire most of us talk about
& few possess—and I have a confidence in you & in this so great that I know
you will never be false to yourself: and everything merely fanciful & romantic
should be sacrificed to truth. [lower 4/5 of page torn off] & said quite seriously—["]I congratulate you Mr Arnold—your sister is going to marry
a cousin of mine."—quelle bêtise! However, they are very pleased. [lower
4/5 of page torn off] Spanish, & going to Spain this summer.[3] Mary[4] was at
the Bunsens—very quiet in manner—but the Gods as Schiller says[5] have
fastened an iron ring round her forehead—and this gives her a *separated* look
in company, poor poor thing. I shall some day try if I cannot be of help to
her. I sometimes think I might—love to all.   adieu, darling
                                                          M. A.

MS. Balliol College.

1. About four-fifths of p. 3 (and therefore of p. 4) of this extraordinary letter have
been cut off—manifestly censored (the closing lines and signature are written in the margin and across the top of p. 1) and possibly written on the same day as the letter to Clough,
following. It echoes "Memorial Verses" especially ll. 46, 55–56, and possibly also Matthew 26, especially verses 33, 35, 59 ("Yet will I never be offended," "Yet will I not deny
thee," "sought false witness") and Ezekiel 17:10, 19:12 ("east wind . . . wither," "east
wind dried up") as well as *Hamlet* 1.3.78 ("To thine own self be true").

2. William Edward Forster (1818–86: *DNB*; *VF*, 3/6/69), whom she married on
Aug. 15, 1850, at Rydal Church. See Introduction, p. xxxii, Reid—Patrick Jackson is writ-

ing a much-needed new biography—and the excellent *Irish Journal* of Florence Arnold-Forster, his niece and adopted daughter. See below p. 207 n. 2.

    3. Slade was brushing up his Spanish. See below pp. 173–74.

    4. Probably his sister Mary Twining but possibly Mary Bunsen, married on Apr. 4 to John B. Harford, of Stoke, near Bristol (*Memoirs of Baron Bunsen*, 2:164).

    5. Untraced.

To Arthur Hugh Clough

Dear Clough   Tuesday, [May 1850]

    Or my memory bewrayeth me[1] or thou promisedst to come & breakfast with me tomorrow morning. Maskelyne[2] has offered himself for that day: & two is to my mind naught at breakfast—besides thou lovest not that young man. Forster wants to see you: come therefore on Friday at 9¼ & you shall meet him. I am engaged the evenings of this week: still I would fain see thee as I have at Quillinan's sollicitation dirged W. W. *in the grand style* & need thy rapture therewith.[3]

    F. Newman's book I saw yestern at our ouse.[4] He seems to have written himself down an hass. It is a display of the theological mind, which I am accustomed to regard as a suffetation, existing in a man from the beginning, colouring his whole being, and being him in short. One would think to read him that enquiries into articles, biblical inspiration, &c. &c. were as much the natural functions of a man as to eat & copulate. This sort of man is only possible in Great Britain & North Germany, thanks be to God for it. Ireland even spews him out.[5]

    The world in general has always stood towards religions & their doctors in the attitude of a half-astonished clown acquiescingly ducking at their grand words & thinking it must be very fine, but for its soul not being able to make out what it is all about. This beast talks of such matters as if they were meat & drink. What a miserable place Oxford & the society of the serious middle classes must have been 20 years ago. He bepaws the religious sentiment so much that he quite effaces it to me. This sentiment now, I think, is best not regarded alone, but considered in conjunction with the grandeur of the world, love of kindred, love, gratitude &c. &c.

    Il faut feuilleter seulement cet ouvrage: wenn man es durchlesen sollte, so wäre es gar zu eckelhaft.[6]   your's dear

                                              M. A.

MS. Yale University.

    1. Echoing Matthew 26:73

    2. Mervyn Herbert Nevil Story-Maskelyne (1823–1911: *DNB*) entered Wadham College in Nov. 1840 (B.A., with a second class in mathematics, 1845). He dabbled in law

but, abandoning it for science, became in 1856 professor of mineralogy at Oxford and in 1857 keeper of minerals at the British Museum. On the death of his father in 1879 he settled down as a country gentleman and spent twelve years in the House of Commons. In 1884 his second daughter, Mary Lucy, married Arnold's nephew, Hugh Oakeley Arnold-Forster (see below p. 267 n. 8), and in 1910 published *The Right Honourable Hugh Oakeley Arnold-Forster: A Memoir.*

3. "Memorial Verses" (Allott, p. 239). Wordsworth died on Apr. 23; the poem is dated Apr. 27, the day of burial; it was published in *Fraser's Magazine* in June. Lowry (p. 114) misleadingly quotes a letter from Edward Quillinan to Crabb Robinson, "asking him to call on Arnold at 101 Mount Street . . . and see "a very clever little poem on 'The Death of Wordsworth.' . . . It is very classical or it would not be M.A.'s. . . . It is a triple Epicede on your Friends Wordsworth and Goethe, and on Byron who, I think, leaving other objections out of the question, is not tall enough for the other two;—and you, who have no taste for tri-unities will hardly approve this. But M. Arnold has a good deal of poetry in him; and it will come out in spite of all the heathen Gods and goddesses that hold him in enchantment" (Crabb Robinson, *Correspondence with the Wordsworth Circle*, 2:769). But Quillinan's letter is dated Jan. 16, 1851. For "grand style" see above p. 135 n. 2.

4. Francis William Newman (see above p. 115 n. 6) had just published (advertised in *The Times* on May 6) his *Phases of Faith; or, Passages from the History of My Creed* (the titlepage identifies him as "Formerly Fellow of Balliol College, Oxford"). The rationalist approach to theology, the bad prose, the self-righteousness of the "dialogue of the mind with itself," and conceivably Jane Arnold's engagement to a prig adequately account for Arnold's strictures. "Our ouse" means of course Fox How, where Arnold had been for Wordsworth's burial ("We stand to-day by Wordsworth's tomb") and where he no doubt first heard of his sister's engagement to Forster. "Suffetation" (not in *OED*) perhaps means "superfetation."

5. Possibly an echo of *Inferno* 3.34–42?

6. "It's just a book to leaf through; if you had to read it through, it would just be too awful."

To Wyndham Slade

London
My dear Slade   Wednesday, [late spring or summer, 1850]
    Last night for the 5th time the deities interposed: I was asked specially to meet the young lady [1]—my wheels burned the pavement—I mounted the stairs like a wounded quaggha, the pulsations of my heart shook all Park Crescent [2]—my eyes devoured every countenance in the room in a moment of time: she was at the opera, and could not come. At the last moment her mother had had tickets sent her, and sent a note of excuse.

    I suffer from great dejection and lassitude this morning—having shown a Spartan fortitude on hearing the news last evening.

    That I shall go abroad is not doubtful to me—I confess however, my love, that Spain is a little so. I find that they want me at once the 14th or 15th of October: now the *whole* of that month is wanted for Spain, September being still too hot. Then it *is* very expensive: young Wolff[3] was told to take £100 for eight weeks—and has done so—then a whole herd of people is going there. Then we neither of us know the language so well as we shall next year, or should—in fact we know it quite too imperfectly for real amusement with the natives.[4] Also next year there is an Oriel election in Easter week: therefore I shall then go there & have the autumn free.

However let nothing hinder our going somewhere together—the Pyrenees—or Savoy and the Italian lakes which I confess I should prefer—but I put myself in your hands.

Let me have a line to say when you come.

£60 or £70 is about the figure I am desirous my foreign expenditure should this year amount to.

How strange about die unerreichbare schöne![5] To have met her to have found something abstossend, and to have been freed from all disquietude on her account, voilà comment je comprends a matter of this kind. But all the oppositiveness & wilfulness in the human breast is agacée by a succession of these perverse disappointments. farewell. denke mein

M. Arnold.

Text. Tinker and Lowry, pp. 169–70.

1. Frances Lucy Wightman (1825–1901), third of the four living daughters of Sir William and Lady Wightman, of 38 Eaton Place, Belgravia. She and Arnold married on June 10, 1851 (see below p. 211n). The best source of information about the Wightmans, including a family tree, is Harding. The quagga (Arnold misspells it) was a zebralike South African animal, now extinct; the language is that of the mating ritual (see 1851 diary in early May 1851).

2. Sir John and John Duke Coleridge lived at 26 Park Crescent.

3. Henry Drummond Charles Wolff (1830–1908: *DNB*; K.C.B. 1879), politician and diplomat, always in the Conservative ranks. "Owing to my having been at Rugby [under Tait], though younger than himself, I knew Mr. Matthew Arnold very well in later life, and had the greatest possible regard and admiration for him" (Wolff's aptly named *Rambling Recollections*, 1:22). His Spanish holiday in May (recounted in ch. 10) was well worth his £100, for he climaxed a long career in the House of Commons and the Foreign Service with the ambassadorship to Spain, 1892–1900. From 1859 Arnold would have seen him frequently at the Athenæum, where Wolff collected many of the anecdotes that enliven his autobiography. He was caricatured by Ape in *Vanity Fair*, Sept. 5, 1874—not (*DNB*) by Spy in 1881. He reenters Arnold's life again in 1869 (see Arnold's letter to him on Apr. 21 in that year).

4. Forsooth! The *Note-books* contain no quotation in Spanish, have no Spanish author in the "Lists of Reading."

5. "How strange about the unattainable beauty! . . . something repugnant . . . farewell. think of me." Wyndham Slade "noted on the letter: 'the unerreichbare schöne was the lady who afterwards became his wife' " (Tinker and Lowry, p. 170).

Mary Arnold Twining to Thomas Arnold

Fox How
August 30, [1850]

I do not feel sure that you have had an account of K's wedding, so I will try to give you a brief one—picture to yourself a glorious summer day—the 15th of Augst, 1850[1]—one of the very brightest & most beautiful days of the year—Look into the dining room at the usual breakfast hour, and you will see the table at its usual size, with the old green & white china, and the bread & butter, and no remarkable signs of festivity except a large white cake of that peculiar aspect wch belongs to one occasion—the cake, however, is uncut—and the small party, consisting of Mamma and your four Sisters, Edward, and one other who tho' not related seems to have some near & very significant claim are gathered round the table just or nearly as you might have seen them on many previous days—After breakfast however, things do not quite take their usual course—something different from common is astir for the Sisters go up stairs and there is some special dressing—it is a very simple affair however—no maids are in attendance—but K's little dressing room door is shut, and something is going on within—presently the door opens, and the dear K comes out dressed differently indeed—very differently from usual but scarcely less simply—so gracefully becoming is the plain white silk dress and the lace veil which entirely covers, tho' it does not conceal the sweet modest face & head with its wreath of orange flowers & myrtle. . . . but I should like to tell you a little more about K's marriage— about 10 o'clock, in three carriages only, we went to Rydal Chapel—William went first with Edward, then Susy & Fan (the two bridesmaids), & Rowland and I followed—and Mamma and K came last. Some little girls, the children of Dr. Christopher Wordsworth, were dressed in white and scattering flowers in the churchyard. Edward waited at the gate to lead K into church it was nearly filled with people, and I believe if ever true & cordial interest was allied to human curiosity it was in this case. I cd not easily tell you how deep an impression, grown up with many years of Residence, I believe K has made in the Valley—quietly she has gone on, working diligently in the path allotted to her—living for the day, thus making her own 'steps clear', she has been enabled to shed light around those of others, and to guide & instruct & refresh them on their way to K's history. . . .

MS. Balliol College.

1. In the description of the wedding of Jane Arnold and W. E. Forster (printed by Honan, p. 214) the remarkable thing is the absence of Matthew Arnold's name in this

letter of eight closely written pages. On July 23 Clough wrote to Tom: "This is Tuesday, and on Thursday I start for Antwerp, to get a holiday on the Continent somewhere. Matt comes to Switzld in a month, after your sister's wedding. He is himself deep in a flirtation with Miss Wightman, d[aughte]r of the Judge. It is thought it will come to something, for he has actually been to Church to meet her" (Mulhauser, 1:286).

Tom Arnold, in a memorial notice called "Matthew Arnold. (By One Who Knew Him Well)," in the *Manchester Guardian* (May 18, 1888), commented: "It was not all prosperous sailing in his love, any more than is the case with ordinary mortals, and of one such counterblast which drove him out of England and towards the Alps the lovely stanzas 'Vain is the effort to forget' ['On the Rhine'] are the record." (The "counterblast" was Wightman's prohibition against further meetings.) The poems composed during August (Allott, pp. 243–52) supply the only details available about this blank period in Arnold's life—"The River" (gliding down the Thames in August with Miss Wightman), "Separation," "Calais Sands," "Longing," etc.

To Arthur Hugh Clough

Rugby
Dear Clough   October 23, 1850

So you are come back—I came to Rugby too late on Monday to find you.

Of your letters I naturally saw nothing—not having been at Geneva. I hope they were characterized by your usual laconism, & then the loss is the less. I could not write to you for ignorance of your orbit—nor did I want to much: I have often thought of you, however.

Walrond seems to have learned nothing of your late goings on: tell me what they have been—what you have chiefly meditated or performed—in what spirits you are and health, quod rerum omnium est primum, muth veloren alles verloren.[1] In all religions the supreme Being is represented as eternally rejoicing.

I thought of you in a letter of Jacobi's the other day—now for my best hand—Der ich ward der bin ich, gequält von meiner Kindheit an mit einem heimlichen unuberwindlichen Eckel an mir selbst, dem Menschen; so dass ich, immer mehr verarmt an Hoffnung, oft es kaum ertrage, so ein Ding zu seyn: eine Luge, unter lauter Lugen; ein Getraume, von Getraumten; und wenn ich meine wach zu seyn noch weniger als dass.[2]

I communicate this on the strength of Pliny's adage quoted in the same letter—Deus est mortali juvare mortalem.[3] I go to read Locke on the Conduct of the Understanding: my respect for the reason as the rock of refuge to this poor exaggerated surexcited humanity increases and increases. Locke is a man who has cleared his mind of vain repetitions,[4] though without the positive and vivifying atmosphere of Spinoza about him.[5] This last, smile as you will, I have been studying lately with profit.   Your's

M. A.

here till Saturday.

MS. Yale University.

1. "That which is first of all things," and, from Goethe's vermischte Epigramme, "Courage lost—all is lost" (Honan, p. 216).

2. "What I was I still am, troubled from my childhood up with a secret unconquerable disgust with myself, a nobody; so that I, always more impoverished in hope, often can hardly suffer the thought of the thing I am; a lie among nothing but lies, a thing of dreams among dream-things, and whenever I think I am awake I am still less than that"—translated and identified by Lowry (p. 117) as Letter no. 24, Apr. 28, 1784, in *Briefswechsel zwischen Goethe und F. H. Jacobi* (1846).

3. Pliny the Elder, *Naturalis Historia* 2.5.18: "For mortal to aid mortal—this is God" (Loeb).

4. Matthew 6:7.

5. "It was Goethe who led him to Spinoza," wrote Kenneth Allott—"Matthew Arnold's Reading-Lists in Three Early Diaries," *Victorian Studies* 2 (1959):254–66—who cites (p. 256n) a "passage in *Dichtung und Wahrheit* towards the end of Bk. XIV" as "the decisive one for Arnold: 'I at last fell upon the Ethics of this philosopher. . . . Enough that I found in it a sedative for my passions, and that it seemed to open out for me a free and boundless view of both the sensible and the moral world. . . . Spinoza's reconciling calm was in striking contrast with my perturbing activity.' " Locke, as Allott also points out (p. 261), Arnold had come upon in 1845 in Victor Cousin's *Cours de l'histoire de la philosophie de xviiie siècle*, 2 (which became the subject of one of Sainte-Beuve's *Portraits littéraires* in 1847).

To Jane Martha Arnold Forster

London
My dear K   Friday, [? November 15, 1850][1]

I hope you have got the Tasso by this time: I forget if you have the Poems of Shakspeare I promised you: if not, they are still somewhere in my room.

I have just read Goethe to Lavater[2]—with more pleasure I dare say than you did. They, with the letters to Mad[am]e von Stein, belong to his impulsive youthful time, before he had quite finished building the Chinese Wall round his *inneres* which he speaks of in later life. Those to Mad[am]e von Stolberg, or many of them, belong to the same time, I believe, and I must get them.

I read his letters, Bacon, Pindar, Sophocles, Milton, Th. a Kempis &

Ecclesiasticus, & retire more and more from the modern world & modern literature, which is all only what has been before and what will be again,[3] and not bracing or edifying in the least. I have not looked at the newspapers for months, and when I hear of some new dispute or rage that has arisen, it sounds quite historical; as if it was only the smiths at Ephesus[4] being alarmed again for their trade, when the Bishops remonstrate against Cardinal Wiseman's appearance:[5] or Pompey blundering away his chances, when I hear of the King of Prussia, with such an army, getting himself & his country more shackled and deconsidéré every day.

Have you written to Tom? do you suppose him married certainly? I suppose I must gird up my loins & send him a few lines—but I hate writing in the dark.[6] Love to William. He owes me 7 gs. for the Holinshed.[7]   your's

M. A.

MS. Frederick Whitridge.

1. Dated "January 1851" by Russell (1:18), "c. February 28 or March 7, 1851" by Honan (pp. 221–22, 459), a combined authority before which the brave falter and the prudent take cover, but the date must be earlier: see note 5 below for evidence. Tom was married certainly on June 13, 1850, and letters usually required three to six months for delivery.

2. *Briefe von Goethe an Lavater: Aus den Jahren 1774 bis 1783* (1833), *Goethes Briefe an Frau von Stein*, ed. A. Schöll (1848–51), *Goethes Briefe an die Gräfin Auguste von Stolberg, verwitwete Gräfin von Bernstorff* (1839).

3. Ecclesiastes 1:9.

4. Acts 19:23–41.

5. Rome and Berlin dominated the news. In the "papal aggression crisis of 1850" Nicholas Patrick Stephen Wiseman (1802–65: *DNB*), Browning's Bishop Blougram (later), had been named cardinal on Oct. 3, just after the creation (in the Protestant view) or restoration (in the Catholic) of the Roman hierarchy in England and Wales on Sept. 30. His "appearance" in England (from Rome and Vienna) was on Nov. 11, and *The Times* on that day printed indignant diocesan communications from the bishops of Exeter, Bath and Wells, and Ripon. Others followed suit (see Wilfrid Ward, *The Life and Times of Cardinal Wiseman*, 2:548–50). See also E. R. Norman, *Anti-Catholicism in Victorian England* (1968), Walter Ralls, "The Papal Aggression of 1850: A Study in Victorian Anti-Catholicism," *Church History* 43 (Mar. 1974):242–56.

Prussia, at the same time, seemed headed for a confrontation with Austria, and a letter from the king (Nov. 5) dismissing General Radowitz, his old friend and foreign minister, was announced in *The Times* on Nov. 9 and printed on Nov. 23. The movement of Prussian troops was reported on Nov. 11, and on Nov. 13 "all subjects belonging to the reserves, Landwehr, or standing army" were summoned to active duty (p. 6).

6. Biblical but specifically (and wittily) Job 38:2–3: "Who is this that darkeneth counsel by words without knowledge? Gird up now thy loins like a man." Tom Arnold married Julia Sorell (1826–88) on Dr Arnold's birthday, a less than satisfactory marriage for both. See Bertram, pp. xlii, 163n, 184–87.

7. Holinshed's *Chronicles of Englande, Scotlande,and Ireland*, (1577) was reprinted in 1807–8 in six volumes. In 1841 Bohn's *Guinea Catalogue* (2:1479, Lot 17745) listed Holinshed's *Chronicles, with the Castrations* (4 vols, folio, 1586–87) at £7.17.6.

To Frances Lucy Wightman*

Fox How, Ambleside
Thursday Night, [? December 19, 1850][1]
We left town in pouring rain—came into light snow at Blisworth—deep snow at Tamworth—thaw at Whitmore—storm of wind at Warrington, and hard frost at Preston. This last continues. I drove over from Windermere here—6 miles—in the early morning—along the lake, and arrived like an icicle. . . . Only my mother and my youngest sister are at home. I heard family letters read—talked a little—read a Greek book—lunched—read Bacon's *Essays*—wrote.

Text. Russell, 1:15.

1. So dated only because likelier than Dec. 12.

To Frances Lucy Wightman*

Fox How
December 21, 1850
At seven came Miss Martineau[1] and Miss Brontë (Jane Eyre); talked to Miss Martineau (who blasphemes frightfully) about the prospects of the Church of England, and, wretched man that I am, promised to go and see her cow-keeping miracles to-morrow—I, who hardly know a cow from a sheep. I talked to Miss Brontë (past thirty and plain, with expressive gray eyes, though) of her curates, of French novels, and her education in a school at Brussels, and sent the lions roaring to their dens at half-past nine, and came to talk to you.

Lingen, who is Education Secretary,[2] and was once my tutor at Oxford, and a genius of good counsel to me ever since, says he means to write me a letter of advice about inspectorships, applying to Lord Lansdowne, etc. Shall I send it on to you?

Text. Russell, 1:15–16.

1. For Harriet Martineau, Ambleside neighbor and family friend since 1846, see above p. 95 n. 5; Charlotte Brontë (1816–55: *DNB*), who had published *Jane Eyre* in 1847 and *Shirley* in 1849, was visiting her. Together, they had already seen Arnold on the same

day at Edward Quillinan's, where the two ladies signed Rotha Quillinan's album—"a truly pleasant day," wrote Harriet Martineau, "no one being there in addition to the family but Mr Arnold from Fox How and ourselves." The talk "of her curates" is "our only evidence that Arnold had read *Shirley* as well as *Jane Eyre.*" (For these details and many others see Kathleen Tillotson's illuminating essay " 'Haworth Churchyard': The Making of Arnold's Elegy," *Brontë Society Transactions* 15 (1967):105–22.)The talk of "French novels" may reflect Arnold's reading of Isabelle de Charrière's novel *Caliste, ou lettres écrites de Lausanne* (1785, 1787), partially reprinted in an article in the *Revue Suisse*, 1844)—recorded in Arnold's diary, 1851, and (misrepresented) in *Note-books*, p. 1.

What Arnold fancied as gladiatorial swagger was perceived differently by Charlotte Brontë: "Striking and prepossessing in appearance, his manner displeases from its seeming foppery." But he " 'improved upon acquaintance,' " she had been told: "Ere long a real modesty appeared under his assumed conceit, and some genuine intellectual aspirations as well as high educational acquirements, displaced superficial affectations. I was given to understand that his theological opinions were very vague and unsettled, and indeed he betrayed as much in the course of conversation" (C. K. Shorter, *Charlotte Brontë and Her Circle*, p. 459, quoted by Tillotson, p. 114). Mrs. Gaskell, in her *Life of Charlotte Brontë* (ch. 23), prints part of another letter: "Your account of Mr. Arnold tallies exactly with Miss Martineau's. She, too, said that placidity and mildness (rather than originality and power) were his external characteristics. She described him as a combination of the antique Greek sage with the European modern man of science. Perhaps it was mere perversity in me to get the notion that torpid veins, and a cold, slow-beating heart, lay under his marble outside. But he is a materialist: he serenely denies us our hope of immortality, and quietly blots from man's future Heaven and the Life to come. That is why a savor of bitterness seasoned my feelings towards him." Moreover, as Kathleen Tillotson points out, Mrs Gaskell (without identifying the author) also includes a vivid description by Jane Forster of a visit to Haworth in October, a long letter to the Fox How family that Matthew Arnold would have known and perhaps drawn upon later (ch. 22).

For Arnold's elegy see Allott, p. 422, with the excellent notes, and also *Album*, pp. 3, 57, 61–62, 119–20, and below p. 313.

2. Lansdowne was Lord President of the Council, Lingen education secretary, and Arnold got the inspectorship (see below p. 203).

Jane Martha Arnold Forster to Thomas Arnold

Fox How

My dearest Tom   Monday, December 30, 1850

I should like to write one line from dear Fox How before our happy Christmas party breaks up. . . . [page omitted] It is very disagreeable to go away just before New Year's day but that is *stock-taking* day with Men of business, and William will be working extra hard at the time when most people are taking holiday.—We have had a most delightful gathering here—and have only wanted you & Julia, Willy & Fanny, and dear Walter to complete our fireside circle. If you had been here, amid one or two striking changes (such as the domestication amongst us of a perfect stranger to you, in the character of my husband—) you would see everything so much the same as when you last spent Christmas here, that you would almost imagine Time had forgotten to advance. Susy & Fan indeed are now *young women*, but they still take the same place as of old in the family group. Matt & Edward are not less boisterous in their mutual fun-making & roars of laughter over their own jokes. Mary though graver than of old, has at least recovered from the deep depression under which you last saw her.—They all tell me that I am so like my old self that they cannot imagine what right any Mr Forster can have to take me away with him—and dearest Mother! even she is as wonderfully cheerful & buoyant as ever—her dear eyes still look at her Children with the same expression of tender love, and I think you would hardly trace any fresh marks of age in her beloved face, in spite of all the anxiety she has had this year about my health, & still more about Walter's unruliness. All around too looks familiar—it is a misty, damp afternoon, and the mountains with the quiet grey clouds rolling along their sides, wear just that deep greenish purple hue which one specially associates with the winter holidays—here and there a gleam of sun steals out from one knows not where, and lights into gold & crimson the oaks on Loughrigg and the rounded ferny knolls in the Park—In the drawingroom we are a quiet party—Mother writing at her little table and I at the great one (littered over as usual with books & newspapers); close to me Master Edward reclines at ease in an arm chair (with his pocket-handkerchief over his head to defend him from the smoke—a luxury of these late degenerate days since I left home) reading Corinne.[1] Matt is stretched at full length on one sofa, reading a Christmas tale of Mrs Gaskell's which moves him to tears, & the tears to complacent admiration of his own sensibility—and on the other sofa, also exceedingly at his ease, is stretched my respected spouse reading a newspaper—till this minute, when he has marched off to the study to have a talk with the girls, who have retreated thither I suppose to read in peace—poor creatures! there is not much peace to be had generally in the drawing room.

MS. Balliol College.

1. Mme De Staël's *Corinne* (1807)—and Matthew Arnold himself, who was into her *Delphine* (1802) two days later (Honan, p. 159), was now reading Mrs Gaskell's *Moorland Cottage*, just published by Chapman and Hall for the Christmas trade.

Diary

Wednesday, January 1, 1851   Thermometer 54 at 9 a.m.

Fox How. down late. heard from F[anny]. L[ucy]. & sent my letter. read S. Augustine's letters. Spinoza. called at Greenbank with Edward & Mary.

walked to the lake with Edward—violent rain. Spinoza again, & extracted life of Epimenides. dined late. cards &c. Delphine. good day on the whole. Delphine says,

Je crois [donc] que, malgré mon goût pour la société de Paris, je retirerai ma vie et mon cœur de ce tumulte, où l'on finit toujours par recevoir quelques blessures qui vous font mal ensuite dans la retraite [Mme de Staël, *Delphine*, 1 : 23].

and

La morale et la religion du cœur ont servi d'appui à des hommes qui avaient à parcourir une carrière bien plus difficile que la mienne: ces guides ne suffiront.

Mme de Vernon says—

Il existe une manière de prendre tous les caractères du monde [*Delphine*, 1 : 39].

Thursday, January 2, 1851   down late. tremendous flood. Walter came. walked with Edward to Skelwith and Colwith. exquisite western sky as we came home. at the F. Flemings in the evening. read in D. Laertius, S. Augustine, & Delphine. indifferent day.
Delphine says.

Les qualités naturelles suffisent pour être honnête lorsque l'on est heureux: mais quand le hasard et la société vous condamnent à lutter contre votre cœur, il faut des principes réfléchis pour se defendre de soi-même [1 : 51].

Friday, January 3, 1851   weather changed to frost. brilliant day. walked without a hat to Rotha bridge to meet the letters, but they came while I was out. heard from F. L. & wrote to her. Splendid walk to Troutbeck by the Skelgill woods with Teddy, Walter & Fan. Dined at the Davys. read today in D. Laertius & Spinoza. pretty good day, but very idle & unsettled.
Spinoza says—

Nihil certo scimus bonum aut malum esse, nisi id, quod ad intelligendum reverâ conducit [vel quod impedere potest, quo minus intelligamus] [*Ethics*, Part 4, Propositio 27, p. 126: We know nothing certainly to be good or evil, except that which really conduces to understanding [or which can impede understanding] (translated by George Eliot)].

Saturday, January 4, 1851   down late. bad morning, and did little. read in
D. Laertius & Goethe's Poems. After dinner walked alone to Brathay churchyard and sate there till dark. read Spinoza. after tea, cards & chess. Spinoza
again—began letter to F. L. S. Augustine's letters & so to bed. Thorough bad
day and could never collect myself at all.
      Weather changed again to fog & rain.
      Spinoza says.

      Nihil singulare in rerum naturâ datur, quod homini sit utilius, quam
      homo qui ex ducte rationis vivit   [*Ethics*, Part IV, Propositio 35,
      Corollarium 1 (p. 130): There is no individual thing in nature more
      useful to man, than a man who lives according to reason (George
      Eliot's translation, 178)].

      and

      Quo magis unusquisque suum [utile quaerere, hoc est suum] esse con-
      servare conatur [et potest], eo magis virtute præditus est, et eo magis
      aliis utilis erit [Propositio 20 (p. 124): The more a man seeks what is
      useful to him, i.e. strives and is able to preserve his being, the more
      highly is he endowed with virtue (or power); [and on the other hand,
      so far as a man neglects to preserve what is useful to him, i.e. his being,
      so far is he weak].

Sunday, January 5, 1851   Mild dark day. read Egmont. After afternoon
church walk alone to High Close-western sky exquisite. read in D. Laertius
and Corinne. Went on with letter to Flu—better day.
      Egmont says,

      when Clarchen says she has not earned or deserved his love—In der
      liebe ist es anders. Du verdienst sie weil du dich nicht darum be-
      wirbst—und die Leute erhalten sie auch meist allein die nicht darnach
      jagen [Goethe, *Egmont*, 3: 'It is otherwise in love. You deserve it be-
      cause you have not sought it—and, for the most part, those only ob-
      tain love who seek it not.' tr. Anna Swanwick].

Monday, January 6, 1851   fine frosty morning. wrote a little to F. L. Grasmere & old bathing place with Teddy Walter & Fan. Mr. Hill in the evening.
read in Spinoza & Delphine. vile day.
      Delphine says

      Je me condamne à vous faire le récit d'un mouvement blâmable que
      j'ai à me reprocher. Il a été si passager, que je pourrais me le nier à

moi-même; mais, pour conserver son cœur dans toute sa pureté, il ne
faut pas repousser l'examen de soi; il faut triompher de la [continued
on facing page, after entry Jan. 8] répugnance qu'on éprouve à s'avouer
les mauvais sentiments qui se cachent longtemps au fond de notre
cœur avant d'en usurper l'empire [1:69].

Tuesday, January 7, 1851   Mild & dark. met the Postman in the birch
copse. sweet letter from Flu. finished my letter to her & sent it. read in Spinoza, D. Laertius, & Egmont. violent rain in the afternoon. walked to
Waterhead. After tea to Miss Martineau's lecture. better day.
     Mazzini says—(end of 1850) [1]

> For if the light of human morality becomes but a little more obscured,
> in that darkness there will arise a strife that will make those who come
> after us shudder with dread.

Wednesday, January 8, 1851   dull day with rain. read in Spinoza and
Delphine. walk with all the children to the top of Loughrigg in the evening[,] party at the Davys. tableaux, charades &c. began letter to Flu. pretty
good day.

Thursday, January 9, 1851   clearer day. read in Spinoza, D. Laertius, &
Delphine. Walk with Edward to the 1st point of Fairfield. snowy western
mountains, & exquisitely coloured foreground of rich green & brown. home
alone by Swede's Bridge. In the evening cards with Walter—his last evening.
wrote in letter to Flu.
     Spinoza says.

> quatenus tristitiæ *causas intelligimus*, eatenus ipsa desinit esse passio, hoc
> est eatenus desinit esse tristia [*Ethics*, Part 5, Propositio 18I, Scholium:
> 'So far as we understand the causes of pain, it ceases to be a passion, it
> ceases to be pain.'—George Eliot's translation, p. 228].

Friday, January 10, 1851   Wet day. Walter went. Flu's letter. wrote to her.
read in Spinoza
     —finished the Ethics & felt dreamish. called on the [?]Lutwidges. [2]
People at dinner here. read in D. Laertius. fairish day, but non possum colli-
gere me [?]sine nego engagenat—[?]
     Spinoza says—

> Qui corpus ad plurima aptum habet, is mentem habet, cujus maxima
> pars est æterna [*Ethics*, Part 5, Propositio 39: He who has a body ca-

pable of a great variety of actions has a mind the greater portion of which is eternal. George Eliot's translation, p. 239].

Saturday, January 11, 1851 rainy day—with Edward to Carlisle—slept at the Bush. read in Delphine.
Mme de Vernon says

Mon esprit! vous savez bien que je n'en ai que pour causer, et point du tout pour lire, ni pour réflechir, [. . .] je pense dans le monde; seule, je m'ennuie ou je souffre [1:213].
she says too to Delphine

avec votre caractère, vous n'entendriez raison sur rien; vous êtes trop exaltée pour qu'on puisse vous faire comprendre le réel de la vie [1:304].

Sunday, January 12, 1851 at Carlisle. fine day. heard from Flu & wrote to her. Twice at Cathedral. lunched & dined with the Taits. walk about the town with Edward. read in Delphine.

Des souffrances arides et continuelles, une liaison de toutes les heures avec un être indigne de soi, gâtent le caractère, au lieu de le perfectionner [1:217].

Monday, January 13, 1851 with Edward to the dentist. Home from Carlisle. good views across Shap Fells. read in D. Laertius & Delphine.

L'âme qui n'a jamais connu le bonheur ne peut être parfaitement bonne et douce [1:217].

Tuesday, January 14, 1851 dark, sad day. heard from Ld. L[ansdowne] & Flu. wrote to the latter. back to town by the Mall. read in D. Laertius & Delphine.

la perte de l'espérance change entièrement le caractère.

Wednesday, January 15, 1851 fine day, very tired. read an essay of Bacon's. no more. L. House. made calls. dined at club. sweet letter from Flu. wrote to her
Delphine says.

—si j'étais mourante, n'obtiendrais-je pas le droit de tout révéler après moi? Hélas! l'aurais-je même alors? *le bonheur des autres ne doit il pas nous être sacré, tant qu'il peut dépendre de notre volonté?* [1:308].

& again

vous m'avez montré mon devoir, le véritable devoir, celui qui a pour but d'épargner des souffrances aux autres: je l'ai reconnu, je m'y sou-mets— [1:314].

Thursday, January 16, 1851   blowing fine day, up late. work at L. H. put things in order at home. walked in the park. L. H. again. dined at Blackett's—young Stanley[3]—constrained & not right. read a little in S. Augustine's letters.

—Ce n'est pour notre propre avantage que tant de nobles facultés nous ont été donnés; c'est pour seconder la pensée de l'Etre suprême, en [?]épargnant du mal, en faisant du bien sur la terre à tous les êtres qu'il a crées.

Friday, January 17, 1851   fine day. no frost yet. up late. L. H. to the Strand to see Blackett, but he was out. came home. found letter from dear Flu. read in D. Laertius. dined at club. read in de Musset's Confessions. wrote to Flu. indifferent day.

Goethe says—

Nur heute, heute [nur] lass dich nicht fangen
So bist du hundertmal entgangen—   [*Notebooks*, p. 14].

Saturday, January 18, 1851   fine day. up late. L. H. Clough came. by Gordon square to Brodie's. long call there. dined at club. read French debates, & in de Musset. came home, found letter from dear Flu. read a little in S. Augustine's letters. but horribly idle, though [?]clear enough.

L'obscurité pénètre [microfilm illegible]
deuxième, ou pensée première
fin a défaut l'ordre la
le tout le
A l'égard de la première cause d'obscurité
on observera qu'il est impossible d'être clair
si l'on ne se comprend pas bien soi-même. Le ?figure ligne terme
i doit donc être s'
nt de soi-même l'idée dont [sont?] ??te.

Cette clarté dont notre esprit est
pénétré se communiquera d'elle-même, à
l'expression de la pensée.—

Sunday, January 19, 1851   fine day. Boothby⁴ & Cumin at breakfast. Grosvenor chapel. called on Ly Burgoyne, the Molesworths and Marshalls. wrote to Flu. dined at club. de Musset & a little Menander. but still very dawdling & idle.

Monday, January 20, 1851   up late. read in Goethe's poems. L. H. met dearest Flu at the Eastern Counties station. dined at club. read French debates & a little in S. Augustine. wrote to Flu. almost happy.

Tuesday, January 21, 1851   up late. read in Paradise lost. L. H. called in Eaton place—walk with the Blacketts & Mrs. Waterton.⁵ read in D. Laertius. dined at the Coleridges, walked home. wrote to Flu.

Wednesday, January 22, 1851   heard from Flu. read in Paradise Lost. L. H. lunched with Bayly at C. O. L. H. again. wrote to Flu. dined at club & read in de Musset. went to see Clough. read in Th. à Kempis.

Thursday, January 23, 1851   early to L. H. Ld. L. [?]out—breakfast & read Paradise Lost. work at L. H. called on Ly. Burgoyne—met dear Flu at Shoreditch & drove with her to [?]Belgravia. walked in Kensington Gardens. read in D. Laertius. dined at Ord's.⁶ in the evening to Ly. Molesworth's. wrote to Flu.

Friday, January 24, 1851   frost & yellow fog. Lingen & Clough at breakfast. read in Th. à Kempis & D. Laertius. work at L. H. called on Mme Bunsen & the Milmans.⁷ read again in D. Laertius. dined at the Blacketts'. with Fleming, Mr. Waterton &c. heard from Flu & wrote to her.

Saturday, January 25, 1851   Clough at breakfast. walked home with him & called on the Twinings. read in D. Laertius. wrote to Flu. read Lockhart's article on Southey. called on Mrs. Stanley. dined at club. afterwards to the Princess with Burgoynes, Hattons,⁸ &c. read a little in Delphine. heard from Flu.

1. Untraced.
2. Captain H. P. Lutwidge, R.N., a neighbor, at The Cottage, Ambleside (*Black's Picturesque Guide to the English Lakes*, p. 74; Martineau).
3. Probably, Henry Edward John Stanley (1827–1903: *DNB*), who succeeded as 3d Baron Stanley of Alderley in 1869.
4. Unidentified but perhaps one of the two old Rugbeians of that name, both under Dr Arnold and both sons of the Rev. Brooke Boothby (1784–1828)—Henry Brooke Boothby (c. 1818–93) or his brother, George William Boothby (1819–68). See Rugby and peerages. Lady Burgoyne (d. 1890), the former Mary Harriet Gore-Langton, was the wife of Sir John Montagu Burgoyne (1796–1858), older brother of Montagu George

Burgoyne (1798–1895), John Blackett's grandfather. The Rt Hon. Sir William Moles-worth (1810–55; 8th bt); his wife (m. 1844; d. 1888) was the former Andalusia Grant Carstairs. James Garth Marshall, of a prominent and wealthy family, lived at Tent Lodge (where the Tennysons honeymooned in 1850) on Coniston Water (see Tennyson 1:96n and below p. 202 n. 10).

 5. Mrs Waterton has not been identified; Arnold called on her in France in 1859 (see below p. 443).

 6. Unidentified. Perhaps, William Ord (d. July 25, 1855), of Whitfield Hall, North-umberland, formerly M.P. for Morpeth and Newcastle (*Landed*). Conceivably, Ralph Ord (c. 1771–1855), one of the three Rugby sons of Ralph Ord, of Sands, near Sedgefield, Durham.

 7. Henry Hart Milman (1791–1868: *DNB*), dean of St Paul's since 1849, was a historian, poet, dramatist, and had been Newdigate prizeman, a fellow of Brasenose, and then Professor of Poetry at Oxford.

 8. John Gibson Lockhart's review of Charles Cuthbert Southey's edition of *The Life and Correspondence of the late Robert Southey* in *Blackwood's Edinburgh Magazine*, Mar. 1851, pp. 349–67. The Princess Theatre offered a triple threat: *The Prisoner of War*, *The Loan of a Lover*, and *Alonzo the Brave and the Fair Imogene*. A. P. Stanley's mother (the former Catherine Leycester), widow of the bishop of Norwich (see above p. 160).

 Possibly, Edward Hatton Finch Hatton (1826–87), nephew of the 10th earl of Win-chilsea, of whom little is known except that he was at Eton and Brasenose College (1844–48) and a student at the Inner Temple in 1848, and a captain in the Northants Militia. But the name may be Halton or Holton.

To Jane Martha Arnold Forster*

London

My dearest K   January 25, [1851]

 Since you do not write to me, I must be the first—so long as I was at Fox How I heard your letters, but in town, unless we write to each other I shall almost lose sight of you, which must not be.

 How strong the tendency is, though, as characters take their bent, and lives their separate courses, to submit oneself gradually to the silent influence that attaches us more and more to those whose characters are like ours, and whose lives are running the same way with our own, and that detaches us from everything besides—as if we could only acquire any solidity of shape and power of acting by narrowing and narrowing our sphere, and diminish-ing the number of affections and interests which continually distract us while young, and hold us unfixed and without energy to mark our place in the world: which we thus succeed in marking only by making it a very confined and joyless one. The aimless and unsettled but also open and liberal state of our youth we *must* perhaps all leave and take refuge in our morality and character: but with most of us it is a melancholy passage from which we emerge shorn of so many beams[1] that we are almost tempted to quarrel with the law of nature which imposes it on us.

I feel this in my own case, and in no respect more strongly than in my relations to all of you. I am by nature so very different from you, the worldly element enters so much more largely into my composition, that as I become *formed* there seems to grow a gulf between us, which tends to widen till we can hardly hold any intercourse across it. But as Thomas a Kempis recommended—frequenter tibi ipsi violentiam fac[2]—and as some philosopher advised to consort with our enemies because by them we were most surely apprised of our faults,[3] so I intend not to give myself the rein in following my natural tendency, but to make war against it till it ceases to isolate me from you and leaves me with the power to discern and adopt the good which you have & I have not.

This is a general preface to saying that I mean to write about the end of every month—as I can at the time—and I hope you, my dearest K, will do the same.

I have not now left room for more than to say I was grieved to hear of you at the water cure—and that the choice had been between that & recurring to Dr Bright's medicines.[4] There are surely no symptoms of a return of the old complaint—and if there are the water cure I should think would be a dangerous remedy. I hope it is only used as a tonic against your weakness. I have a little influenza, but am else pretty well, & going on as usual.—You will be interested in hearing that the Judge still absolutely prohibits all intercourse.[5]—Kindest regards to William. Ever dearest K,   your most affectionate

M. A.

MS. Frederick Whitridge.

1. A romantic commonplace (Wordsworth, Coleridge, Shelley) but here perhaps suggesting the fallen Archangel of *Paradise Lost* 1.596.

2. Thomas à Kempis, *De imitatione Christi* 1.24.2: [Habet magnum et salubre purgatorium patiens homo . . .] qui sibi ipsi violentiam frequenter facit, [et carnem omino spiritui subjugare conatur] [(The patient man has a great and wholesome cleansing . . .) who frequently does violence to himself—i.e., denies his own will—[and who strives in every way to subjugate flesh to spirit]). Arnold transposes the Latin to the imperative mood and second person, as in his essay "Marcus Aurelius" (Super, 3:133–57, where he renders it (p. 134): "Get the habit of mastering thine inclination." See "Morality" (Allott, p. 273 and notes).

3. Benjamin Franklin (whom Arnold admired), in *Poor Richard's Almanack*: "Love your Enemies, for they tell you your Faults."

4. For hydropathy, new and fashionable in England (a girl was christened "Hydropatha"), the most famous establishment was that of Dr James Manby Gully (1808–83: *DNB*; *VF*, 8/5/76) at Great Malvern; among his clients, happily not all at the same time,

were Tennyson (see 1:222n), Bulwer (who wrote a pamphlet on it, "Confessions of a Water Patient," 1846), Carlyle, Darwin, Florence Nightingale, and many others. Jane Forster was at Great Malvern for an extended stay in Oct. 1873 (letter from Frances Arnold to Mrs Hearn, MS Rochester). Richard Bright (1759–1858: *DNB*), physician, traveler, and writer, and from 1837 physician extraordinary to Queen Victoria, first described "Bright's Disease," acute or chronic nephritis (inflammation of the kidneys), in 1827. Warm baths, diuretics, and purgatives were among the specific remedies, and it seems likely that Jane Forster suffered from it and that it may have rendered her infertile. See below p. 336 and n. 6.

     5. Judge Wightman's "counterblast" (see above p. 176n).

Diary

Sunday, January 26, 1851   breakfast with Boothby. long talk. to Hampton in the afternoon. Walk with Flu & Ly W. back to town. dined with the Blacketts. read in Lucian & Chateaubriand.

Monday, January 27, 1851   up late. read in Chateaubriand. wrote to Flu. called on Mrs Maude. C. O. talked to Lingen & Kekewich.[1] finished Egmont. dined at club. read in de Musset. coffee with Slade. accounts &c. read in S. Augustine's letters.

Tuesday, January 28, 1851   walk in the park. read in Paradise Lost. L. H. read Ford's article on the British Museum. C. O. talked with Boothby. read in D. Laertius. dined at club.[2] Marshall's. Bunsens'. Ly Burgoyne's. heard from Flu. answered her letter.

Wednesday, January 29, 1851   read in Paradise Lost at breakfast. L. H. [?]extracted &c. Edwin Portman made a long call. L. H. read a little in S. Augustine's letters—but dreadfully tired & languid. dined at Brodie's. Vaughan.[3] The Aldersons afterwards. read in Th. à Kempis & to bed.

Thursday, January 30, 1851   up late. read in Paradise Lost. wrote to Ld L. went to C. O. & talked to Lingen. read in D. Laertius & Delphine. dined at club. whist at Hunt's.[4] heard from Flu & wrote to her.

Friday, January 31, 1851   Boothby breakfasted. L. H. went to C. O. long call on Mrs. Waterton & walk in the Park. read in S. Augustine's letters. dined at club. read Stanley's Socrates.[5] walked about. read in Delphine. wrote a line to Flu.

Saturday, February 1, 1851.   Henry Bunsen breakfasted. L. H. conversation with Ld L. C. O. walk alone in the Park. L. H. dined at club. read in Ld

Holland's Reminiscences.[6] home. letter from darling Flu. began answer. read in Apocrypha & D [?]Laertius

Peut-être il est vrai que, dans la destinée la plus heureuse il y a toujours une fatigue secrète d'exister qui console d'arriver au terme, quoique court qu'ait été le voyage.

Sunday, February 2, 1851   breakfasted with the Blacketts, & to hear Wiseman. very bad. in the afternoon long call on Ly Burgoyne & Slade. long walk alone. dined with the Harrisons at the Colonnade Hotel.[7] home. finished letter to Flu. Songez que c'est dans le bonheur qu'il est aisé de fortifier la raison.

Monday February 3, 1851   up late. heard from Flu. L. H. breakfasted afterwards & read in Milton & Chateaubriand. to the Colonnade Hotel to see the Harrisons. L. H. hot bath. dined alone at Véry's.[8] wrote to Flu. ball at Blackett's. Edward came. very late to bed. Ecclesiasticus. Il faut fuir le monde, ou ne s'y montrer que triomphant.

Tuesday, February 4, 1851   up late. L. H. tiring day. through the world to the Home & Council Office: Queen opened Parliament: lunched with Boothby: L. H. dined at club, having heard from Flu & written to her. read Ld Holland's Reminiscences. Bunsens. home. read in Ecclesiasticus. La légéreté dans les principes conduirait bientôt à la légéreté dans les sentimen[t]s.

Wednesday, February 5, 1851   Coleridge & Edward at breakfast. L. H. sorted papers. C. O. called at the Blacketts. from there with Edward to the Aldersons. came back—found letter from Flu. answered it. dined at Very's with Edward. home. early to bed. read nothing all day. very tired.

Thursday, February 6, 1851   much better. Edward at breakfast. L. H. read in S. Augustine. lunch at Vérys with Edward. He went. C. O. L. H. read in Goethe's Poems. dined at club with Bayley.[9] dear letter from Flu. answered it. wretched night with toothache—read in Ecclesiasticus.

Friday, February 7, 1851   Clough at breakfast. L. H. read in Delphine. L. H. dined with Sandford. read in Delphine again. Miserable day with toothache.

Saturday, February 8, 1851   up early. went to Lintott. L. H. read in Goethe's Poems & Quarterly Review. C. O. home. letter from Flu. answered it. dined with Reeve at the Hollands. read in Las Cases.[10] Better but very idle.

La légéreté dans les principes conduirait bientôt à la légéreté dans les sentiments; l'art de la parole peut aisément tourner en dérision ce qu'il y a de plus sacré sur la terre; mais les caractères passionnés repoussent ce dédain superficiel, qui s'attaque à toutes les affections fortes et profondes.

L'enthousiasme que l'amour nous inspire est comme un nouveau principe de vie.

Sunday, February 9, 1851   up late. Boothby breakfasted. L. H. St Paul's church. called on the Blacketts. read in Delphine. dined at club with Cornewall[11] & Boothby. home. began letter to Flu. read in Delphine. still rather wretched.

Monday, February 10, 1851   walked a little before breakfast. darling letter from Flu. L. H. wrote to Flu. shopping [?]lunching, C. O. H. of Lords. dined at club. read in De Musset's Confessions. home.

Tuesday, February 11, 1851   went to dentist. L. H. lunched at club. read Edinburgh Review. C. C. L. H. dined at club—very good for nothing. Delphine.

Wednesday, February 12, 1851   Clough at breakfast. L. H. called on Blacketts. long walk across Park to Kensington] L. H. dined at club. read revue des 2 Mondes heard from Flu. wrote to her. read in Las Cases. bed.

Thursday, February 13, 1851   read in Paradise Lost. L. H. heard from Flu. wrote to her. called on Marshalls. read in S. Augustine's letters. L. H. Walrond came. dined with him at Long's.[12] walked. read in Las Cases. bed.

Friday, February 14, 1851   wretched day. L. H. read in Paradise Lost. Walrond went. quiet at home in the evening. read in S. Augustine's letters & Delphine. heard from Flu. wrote to her

Saturday, February 15, 1851   feverish & unwell. L. H. C. O. long talk with Lingen. read in Delphine, Paradise Lost & Las Cases. Dined at club.

Sunday, February 16, 1851   up late. Clough came. read in Chateaubriand. L. H. went to Hampton saw Baby[13] & Ly W. home & dined with Blacketts—young Stanley—the Burgoynes &c. wrote to Flu.

Monday, February 17, 1851   up late. copied statistics. L. H. wrote to the Judge. C. O. paid bills—walked in the park. L. H. dined at club. read in Delphine. heard from Baby—answered.

Tuesday, February 18, 1851   Clough at breakfast. L. H. read newspapers &c. at club. L. H. again. read in Paradise Lost. C. O. talk with Lingen. wrote to Flu. dined at club. Bunsens. read in Pindar & Delphine.

Wednesday, February 19, 1851   read in Chateaubriand at breakfast. L. H. heard from Flu: wrote to her. read de Falloux's article on French politics. L. H. Ly Burgoyne. read in Milton & Chateaubriand. dined at the Seniors.[14] read in Delphine—wrote to Flu. Las Cases. bed. Ld L. gone to Bowood.

Thursday, February 20, 1851   Cumin at breakfast to H. of Lords. Saw the Judge. home. read in Chateaubriand. walk with Brodie. dined with the Maudes. read in Milton. heard twice from Flu & wrote to her.

Friday, February 21, 1851   Clough at breakfast. to Laleham. back to town. dined at club. read in Byron Chateaubriand & Milton. heard from Flu & wrote to her. very anxious about Ministers.

    1. Julia Maude, daughter of Francis Hartwell, an old Laleham neighbor (see above p. 154 n. 1), married 1844, John Hartwell Maude (1812–62), a Civil Engineer (*Landed*). Trehawke Kekewich (1823–1909), of Peamore, Devon, from Christ Church (B.A. 1845); Arnold saw him years later in Edgbaston. See Foster and *Landed*.

    2. A review of various pamphlets, *Quarterly Review* 83 (Dec. 1850):136–72, by Richard Ford (1796–1858: *DNB*). For the Alfred Club see below, p. 252n.

    3. Edwin Portman (1830–1921; *VF*, 11/3/80), son of 1st Baron (later, first Viscount) Portman, attended Rugby and Balliol, was a fellow of All Souls' College 1850–57, was called to the bar in 1852, and, in 1885, was elected M.P. for North Dorset. Henry Halford Vaughan (1811–85: *DNB*), of Rugby and Christ Church, Oxford, and a fellow of Oriel 1835–42, then a barrister, and then, beating out A. P. Stanley, Regius Professor of Modern History, Oxford, 1848–58.

    4. George Ward Hunt (1825–77: *DNB*; *VF*, 3/11/71), of Eton and Christ Church, later chancellor of the exchequer and first lord of the admiralty (under Derby and Disraeli), was at this time still reading for the bar. As one of the famous reading party in Scotland in 1846, he is mentioned in Kenny and may figure in *The Bothie* as Hobbes, a healthy young animal ("brief kilted hero," "eupeptic," "those lusty legs displaying, / All from the shirt to the slipper the natural man revealing"); he aged into an unhealthy prematurely old animal. In Ape's caricature in *Vanity Fair*, Mar. 11, 1871, with the legend "The fat of the land," Hunt, age 45, looks 75, and he is described in the biographical sketch, along with several marvelous innuendos, as a "country gentleman turned politician" whose "great weight" Disraeli needed to defend "a bloated expenditure." He died of gout in Hamburg, exactly 52 years old. (On Hunt as Hobbes see Kenny, p. lvi; on Hobbes see Kathleen Tillotson, "Clough's Bothie," in *Mid-Victorian Studies*.)

    5. "Socrates," *Quarterly Review* 88 (Dec. 1850):41–69.

    6. Henry Richard Vassall Fox, 3d Lord Holland, *Foreign Reminiscences* (1850).

    7. Probably the Benson Harrisons or their son, Matthew Benson Harrison (see below p. 517 n. 1). The Colonnade Hotel was at 20–24 Charles Street, St James's (*POLD*).

    8. Verrey's Café Restaurant, 229 Regent Street, W., one of the two or three best in London.

    9. Bayley is unidentifiable among several possibilities, the most alluring of whom is F. W. N. Bayley (1808–53: *DNB*), first editor of the *Illustrated London News*, poet, and prose writer—"improvident," "constantly in difficulties"; possibly, and less interestingly, one of the two named John Arden Bayley who matriculated from Brasenose and Oriel in 1845 and 1846 (Foster).

10. Probably, Lintott and Scott, dentists, 23 Wimpole Street, Cavendish Square (*POLD*). For Las Cases see above p. 149 n. 5.

11. George Cornewall Lewis (1806–63: *DNB*), a learned man and an important figure in government circles, he became editor of the *Edinburgh Review* in Dec. 1852.

12. The famous old tavern in the Haymarket.

13. Georgina Wightman (see below p. 365 n. 1).

14. "Les Républicains et les monarchistes depuis la révolution de février," by A. De Falloux, was in *Revue des deux mondes* 9 (Feb. 1, 1851):393–422. Nassau William Senior (1790–1864: *DNB*), economist and professor of political economy at Oxford, author of many articles and books on political and economic subjects, and, later, a member of the Newcastle Commission. See below p. 439 n. 8.

To Frances Lucy Wightman*

London
February 21 [-24], 1851

Ministers have managed to get beaten by forty-eight to-night by the Radicals on a motion for enlarging the franchise. Though such a vote cannot drive them out, it makes their weakness fearfully apparent.

February 22.—I went, to Laleham and came back to town at six, and drove straight to Lansdowne House. There I found that Lord John[1] had postponed the Budget till Monday and that Lord Lansdowne was not coming back to town till to-morrow. To-morrow afternoon they will hold a Cabinet, and settle whether to resign, remodel themselves, try a little longer, or dissolve.

February 24.—I have just heard the statement in the House of Lords, and that Lord John has undertaken to reconstruct a Government. It is quite uncertain who will come in again with him of the old lot. Lord Lansdowne is very much disinclined to remain. The old set of Whigs can never come in again; but a good many of them may come in in a fresh combination, and very likely Lord Lansdowne himself. People speculate on a Clarendon Ministry. If Lord Clarendon comes in Sugden will be Chancellor—not else; he is far too much committed on the Papal Aggression question to come in with a Whig or Peelite Ministry—but why do you ask?

Text. Russell, 1:19–20.

1. Lord John Russell had resigned as prime minister the day before this letter but returned and undertook "to reconstruct a Government" on Mar. 3. Lansdowne was president of the Council. George William Frederick Villiers, earl of Clarendon, was Lord Lieutenant of Ireland but became foreign minister in 1853. Edward Burtenshaw Sugden (1781–1875: *DNB*) came in as Lord Chancellor with Derby's first cabinet two years later, in Feb. 1852, and was raised to the peerage as baron St Leonards of Slaugham (see *Album*, pp. 18, 80). The Ecclesiastical Titles Act, in response to "the Papal Aggression," was introduced by Russell on Feb. 7, reintroduced on Mar. 7, and on a third reading passed at

the end of July and, with royal assent, became law on Aug. 1. Never enforced, it was repealed in 1871. "Peelite Ministry" because Sir Robert Peel (1788–1850: *DNB*), Russell's predecessor as prime minister, had died in July.

Diary

Saturday, February 22, 1851   read in Milton at breakfast. Ministers resigned. Ld L. came back to town. heard twice from Flu & wrote twice. postponed interview with the Judge. C. O. talk with Lingen. L. H. again. Heard that Ld Stanley would not take office.[1] Dined at Blacketts'. At night read in Las Cases.

Sunday, February 23, 1851   Clough at breakfast. Quebec St Chapel with the Burgoynes. L. H. walk to Hampstead with Clough. read in Milton. Slade came. dined with Mrs Waterton. letter from Flu—answered it. read in Las Cases.

Monday, February 24, 1851   read in Paradise Lost. talk with Ld L. about appointment. C. O. L. H. again. wrote twice to Flu. dined at club. heard from Flu. read in Chateaubriand. wretched nervous day.

Tuesday, February 25, 1851   Clough came to breakfast. L. H. heard from Ld L. that they were *gone*. felt better. wrote to Flu. walk in Kensington gardens. C. O. talk with Lingen. Stanley called—walked with him. L. H. dined with Bayley at club. H. of Lords on Marriages bill. heard from Baby. wrote to her. read in Las Cases.

Wednesday, February 26, 1851   L. H. saw Lord John. heard from Flu. wrote to her. called on Ly Burgoyne. Gladstone refused to come in. C. O. they all wanted me to ask for the statistical clerk's place. No. dined at Very's with Lingen. sweet letter from Flu. answered it. but a wretched day.

Thursday, February 27, 1851   L. H. read in Goethe, & Milton. walked in the park. much better spirits. C. O. Bayley & Boothby. dined at the Burgoynes'. The Molesworths. dear letter from Flu. wrote twice to her today.

Friday, February 28, 1851   Clough at breakfast. L. H. meeting of ministers there. read in Milton & in Grote on Socrates.[2] H. of Lords. dined at club. at the Hughes's.[3] letter from Flu. wrote 3 times to her.

Saturday, March 1, 1851   very anxious still. L. H. sorted papers &c. wrote to Flu. heard twice from her. copying paper on Aggression Bill.[3] L. H. Ld L.

with the Queen. dined at club with Slade. read in Chateaubriand. uncomfortable day.

Sunday, March 2, 1851   Clough at breakfast. read in Chateaubriand. walk in Kensington Gardens. L. H. to afternoon church at St Paul's Knightsbridge. called on the Molesworths' & Ly Burgoyne. read in Milton. dined at club. wrote to Flu.

Monday, March 3, 1851   heard from Flu. L. H. C. O. wrote to Flu. read in Paradise Regained & Chateaubriand. went to H. of Lords. Ministers in again. dined at Blacketts' ball at the Marshalls.

Tuesday, March 4, 1851   L. H. to Judge's Chambers & back to Albemarle street—wrote to Flu—back to Judge's Chambers again. saw the Judge. L. H. dined at club. heard from Flu. read in Chateaubriand.

Wednesday, March 5, 1851   Clough at breakfast. L. H. heard from Flu. wrote to her. C. O. read in Milton. L. H. dined at club. read in the Initials.[4] heard again from Flu—wrote to her.

Thursday, March 6, 1851   read in Milton at breakfast. L. H. read in Pindar. left cards. went to the Strand to buy an Ossian. L. H. dined at club. read the Initials. heard from Flu. wrote to her.

Friday, March 7, 1851   read in Milton. L. H. read in Pindar. went to the Judge at Chambers. settled on engagement. wrote to Flu—heard from her. dined at club. read in Alfieri's Memoirs.

Saturday, March 8, 1851   Forster at breakfast. L. H. read in Epictetus. home. read in Pindar. L. H. went to Eaton place & saw Flu. dined tête à tête with Ld L. & went to the Princess with him.[5] home. read in Las Cases.

Sunday, March 9, 1851   Clough at breakfast. L. H. to church at Knightsbridge—afterwards walked with Flu. called on Ly Burgoyne. read in Milton. dined at L. H. Macaulay &c. read in Las Cases. wrote to Flu.

Monday, March 10, 1851   L. H. read in blue-book—and in Pindar. feverish & uneasy. walked to call on Brodie. dined at club. heard from Flu. wrote to her. read in Alfieri.

1. Edward John Stanley (1802–69: *DNB*; *VF*, 6/26/69), succeeded as 2d Baron Stanley of Alderley in 1850.

2. *History of Greece* (12 volumes, 1846–56) by George Grote (1794–1871: *DNB*), 8 (1850):551–76 (pt 2, ch. 68), the work said by Arnaldo Momigliano (*Studies in Historiography*, p. 65) to have "set new standards" and given "new impulse to the writing of Greek history." Arnold first met Grote in 1862.

3. See above pp. 178 n. 5, 194–95n.

4. Baroness Jemima Montgomery Tautphoeus, *The Initials A Novel* (1850).

5. *Love in a Maze*, with the Keans and Alfred Wigan, followed by *To Parents and Guardians* (*The Times*).

To James Peachey[1]

Berkeley Square

Sir   March 10, 1851

I am directed by the Marquis of Lansdowne to acknowledge your letter of the 8th inst; and to inform you that he will be happy to present to the House of Lords the petitions, praying for the enfranchisement of copyholds, to which it relates, as he is very favorably disposed towards such a measure.[2] I remain, Sir,   Your obedient servant,

Matthew Arnold.—

James Peachey Esqre

MS. University of Virginia.

1. James Peachey was a solicitor, with offices at 17 Salisbury Square, Fleet Street, and a home address at 3 Park Village East, Regents Park (*POLD*); he may be the author of *Treatise on the Law of Marriage and Other Family Settlements*, 1860 (Allibone).

2. That is, the conversion of copyholds into freeholds—passed (to some extent) in the Copyhold Act 1852.

Diary

Tuesday, March 11, 1851   L. H. to C. O. & called on Mrs Maude. L. H. again. read in Pindar—walked to make calls in Belgravia. read in Alfieri. heard from Flu. Ministers beaten by 1. at the Bunsens. wrote to Flu.

Wednesday, March 12, 1851   Clough at breakfast. L. H. read in Pindar. went to see Flu. read in Alfieri. dined with the Brodies. read in Las Cases. wrote to Flu.

Thursday, March 13, 1851   very restless & unsettled. L. H. read in Pindar. walked about. called on Mrs Vernon Smith.[1] read in Alfieri's Memoirs. dined at Blackett's. very bad night.

Friday, March 14, 1851   a little better. heard from Flu & wrote to her. went to C. O. & to Masterman's by water.[2] lovely day at times. read in Pindar &

Alfieri but mostly quite unsettled, roaming about. dined with Bright in Lincoln's Inn fields.[3]

Saturday, March 15, 1851   Cumin came to breakfast. after breakfast read the Times, & in Pindar. made up letters and accounts &c to Rugby with Slade, Walrond, Shairp, Arnold—read in Epictetus.

Sunday, March 16, 1851   Rugby. read in Epictetus—lunched with Bradley:[4] chapel. Goulburn preached—walked towards the Barby road. dinner at Walrond's. Shairp. read in Alfieri.

Monday, March 17, 1851   back to town. read in Alfieri. L. H. wet miserable day. read about Xenophon's life. dined at the J. Marshalls. wrote to Flu.

Tuesday, March 18, 1851   Clough at breakfast. L. H. read in Xenophon's Memorabilia. went to Kneller Hall—talk with Temple about Inspectorship. violent wet day. dined at club. letter from Flu. went nowhere.

Wednesday, March 19, 1851   wrote to Flu. L. H. read in Memorabilia & Alfieri. continual pouring rain. dined with Blackett & met Portal.[5] letter from Flu. The Education Committee met.

Thursday, March 20, 1851   L. H. walked in Kensington Gardens. wrote to Flu. long call at Blackett's and walk with him. read in Xenophon & Alfieri. dined at club. heard from Flu

Friday, March 21, 1851   Clough at breakfast. L. H. wrote to Flu. walked in Kensington Gardens. read in Xenophon and Alfieri. dined at club. heard from Flu & wrote to her.

Saturday, March 22, 1851   L. H. read in Everett's speeches.[6] went to see dear Flu. L. H. again. dined at club. began the Château des Desertes. home. feverish & unwell.

Sunday, March 23, 1851   Languid & unwell. read in Chateaubriand. L. H. all the afternoon. Ld L. appointed me Inspector. Ld L went out of town. Ld L. very ill—dined at club. read in Xenophon & the Home. very bad night.

Monday, March 24, 1851   passed the morning with Flu. walk with Slade in Kensington Gardens. dine with the G. Glyns.[7] read in Xenophon Alfieri & Chateaubriand. better day. wrote to Flu.

Tuesday, March 25, 1851   Clough in the morning. sorting papers at L. H. letter from Flu. wrote to her. C. O. walk with Stanley. dined at club. read in Alfieri & Xenophon. heard again from Flu.

Wednesday, March 26, 1851   Clough at breakfast. read in Xenophon. Great Ministerial majority on E. Titles Bills. went to Flu. read in Education pamphlet and in Alfieri. dined at club. wrote to Flu.

Thursday, March 27, 1851   wet miserable day. read in Xenophon & Chateaubriand. L. H. called on Mrs Eyre & the Vincent Thompsons.[8] dined at club. heard from Flu. wrote to her.

Friday, March 28, 1851   met Flu at St. Peter's—walked with her afterwards. read in Xenophon & Goethe's Swiss letters & Chateaubriand. walk in Kensington gardens. fine day at last. dined at Véry's & to Panorama of The Tour of Europe with Clough & Slade. wrote to dear Flu. `

Saturday, March 29, 1851   violent showery day. read in Chateaubriand & Xenophon. C. O. heard from Flu. wrote to her. did commissions for her in the afternoon. dined with Shairp at the Oxford & Cambridge Club. bad night. read in Las Cases.

Sunday, March 30, 1851   Boothby at Breakfast. to Hampton. service at Hampton Court—then at ¼ past 1 to Hampton. to church with Flu. all the afternoon with her. after dinner talked to the Judge. He consented to the engagement. talk with dear Flu. back to town.

Monday, March 31, 1851   read in Xenophon. wrote to Flu. went to Williams & Norgate's[9] showery day. dined at club. read in the Château des Désertes. heard from Flu & answered her.

Tuesday, April 1, 1851   Clough at breakfast. read in Chateaubriand. C. O. talk with Lingen. L. H. in the evening to the Bunsens. heard from Flu. wrote to her.

Wednesday, April 2, 1851   read in Goethe's Swiss letters and in Chateaubriand. called on the Twinings. L. H. wrote letters. finished Memorabilia. dined at Sir B. Brodie's. heard from Flu.

Thursday, April 3, 1851   `walk round Kensington gardens before breakfast. read in Goethe's Swiss letters. to Eaton place. sat with dear Flu. then went shopping with her. walk with Slade. dined at club. to the Monteagles.[10] wrote to Flu.

Friday, April 4, 1851   Clough at breakfast. read in Goethe's Swiss letters. to Laleham. came back at night. heard of Lady L[ansdowne]'s death. letter from Flu. answered it.

Saturday, April 5, 1851   read in Goethe's Swiss letters. dined with Brodie. shopping &c in the afternoon.

J'ignore mon avenir: y a t'il aujourd'hui un avenir clair pour personne? Nous ne sommes pas dans un temps de révolution, mais de transformation sociale: or, les transformations s'accomplissent lentement, et les générations qui se trouvent placées dans la période de la métamorphose périssent obscures et misérables. Si l'Europe (ce qui pourrait bien être) est à l'âge de la décrépitude, c'est une autre affaire: elle ne produira rien et s'éteindra dans une impuissante anarchie de passions, de moeurs, et de doctrines.— Chateaubriand[11]

Sunday, April 6, 1851   to Hampton by Twickenham. found Flu & Ly Wightman gone to church. Passed the afternoon & evening with Flu. back to town. wrote to Flu.

Monday, April 7, 1851   Poste at breakfast.[12] commissions for Flu. read in Chateaubriand. finished Goethe's Swiss letters. C. O. walk with Slade. dined at Blackett's. heard from Flu.

Tuesday, April 8, 1851   To Hampton by the ½ past 11 train. the Bensons & Mrs Wood.[13] walk with dear Flu. The Woods at dinner. slept at Hampton.

Wednesday, April 9, 1851   at Hampton. in the morning to church with Flu & sate with her. In the afternoon walked with her in Bushy Park. Back to town through Twickenham by the 20 m. past 6 train. dined at club. read Cousin's article on revolutions.[14] at the James Marshalls. wrote to Flu.

Thursday, April 10, 1851   read in Chateaubriand. sorted papers &c C. O. went to see Ly Burgoyne. read in Goethe's journals. dined at club. heard from Flu. wrote to her.

Il y a de la fatalité en nous comme hors de nous, et il ne faut pas plus se révolter contre soi que contre les autres.[15]

Friday, April 11, 1851   read in Chateaubriand at breakfast. Pindar. to the Blacketts & called with them. read in Goethe's journals. dined at club. wrote letter. heard from Flu.

Charles X was the 68th King of France.

Saturday, April 12, 1851   Clough at breakfast. heard from Ld L. that he would have me appointed at once. went to Hampton. Flu came back from Littleton with Mrs Wood. Walk with her in Bushy Park. Mrs Wood went back before dinner.

after proposing a course for the D. de Bordeaux Chateaubriand adds.—

ce que je suppose relativement au parti qu'aurait à prendre Henri n'est pas possible: en raisonnant de la sorte, je me suis placé en pensée dans un ordre de choses au-dessus de nous: ordre qui, naturel à une époque d'elevation et de magnanimité, ne paraitrait aujourd'hui qu'une exaltation de roman; c'est comme si j'opinais à l'heure qu'il est d'en revenir aux croisades; or nous sommes terre à terre dans la triste réalité d'une nature humaine amoindrie. [16]

Sunday, April 13, 1851   Hampton. twice to church. in the afternoon walked in Bushy Park with Flu. passed nearly all the day with her.

Monday, April 14, 1851   Hampton. to church in the morning. alone at lunch with Ly Wightman & Flu. walk with Flu to Teddington & back. to town by the 5 o'clock train. read in Goethe's journals. wrote to Flu. dined at Club.

Tuesday, April 15, 1851   in town. dined early at club. got the Gazette & to Hampton by the mail train. dear Flu & Ly Wightman. back from Littleton at ½ past 10.

1. Robert Vernon Smith (1800–1873: *DNB*; cr. baron Lyveden, 1859), of Eton and Christ Church, Oxford, M.P. for Northampton, had served and would serve again in various Whig ministries. In 1823 he married Emma Mary Fitzpatrick, sister of Lord Casteldown of Upper Ossory.

2. Probably, Edward Masterman, "one of H.M.'s Lieutenants for the City of London: Knott's Green, Leyton, Essex" (*Upper Ten Thousand*), on the river Lea (*Imperial Gazetteer*).

3. John Bright (1811–89: *DNB*; *VF*, 2/13/69), already a famous orator and statesman, was M.P. for Manchester.

4. George Granville Bradley (1821–1903: *DNB*; *VF*, 9/29/88) a sort of omnicompetent intellectual factotum, had been at Rugby (under Dr Arnold), University College, Oxford, where he knew all the "Clougho-Matthean circle," and then again at Rugby, where he returned as housemaster and teacher, under Tait (and, with the loss of Tait and the infliction of Goulburn, saved the school from disaster—see pp. 169 n. 4, 211). From Rugby he moved in 1858 to head Marlborough (which he *redeemed* from disaster), where Tennyson sent his son in 1866 ("I am not sending my son to Marlborough—I am sending him to Bradley"). In 1871 he became master of University College, Oxford, which he also reformed, and in 1881 succeeded A. P. Stanley as dean of Westminster and there, once more ("Stanley was no man of business"—*DNB*) exercised his genius in combining organization, administration, restoration, and even (having taken orders in 1858) salvation" (quoted from Tennyson 2:122n).

5. Melville Portal (1819–1904: *DNB*), out of Harrow and Christ Church, Oxford, was called to the bar in 1845 and was Conservative Member for the Northern division of Hampshire from 1849 till 1857. "His first speech in the House of Commons was on 25 March 1851, the seventh night of the debate on the ecclesiastical titles assumptions bill," which he voted against. "His life was spent in laborious and disinterested public service" (*DNB*). In 1855 he married the daughter of the 2d earl of Minto. The account in *WWW* lists his recreations as "shooting, fishing"; he lived at Laverstoke House, Overton, Hants, where Arnold pursued similar recreations.

6. Edward Everett (1794–1865: *DAB*), who had been a Unitarian minister, professor of Greek, editor of the *North American Review*, congressman, governor of Massachusetts, minister to England, and president of Harvard College (and was to be secretary of state and senator), "was widely admired for his florid orations" (*OCAL*). Arnold was presumably reading *Orations and Speeches on Various Occasions from 1836 to 1850*, 2d edn, 2 vols, 1850 (Allibone). George Sand's novel *Château des désertes* appeared in the *Revue des deux mondes* from Feb. 15 to Apr. 1 (Spoelberch, p. 32).

7. George Grenfell Glynn (1824–87: *DNB*), succeeded as 2d Baron Wolverton, 1873, from Rugby and University College, Oxford, banker and son of a banker, later Liberal M.P. (caricatured by Cecioni in *Vanity Fair* 2/24/72 as "The Whip") and friend of Gladstone even unto Home Rule, secretary to the treasury, paymaster-general, and postmaster-general. His wife was the former Georgiana Maria Tufnell.

8. For Mrs Eyre see above p. 32 n. 4. John Vincent Thompson, serjeant-at-law, who lived at 4 Upper Belgrave Street. His son, Vincent Thomas Thompson (1829–1910), of Rugby (1841) and Trinity College, Cambridge, barrister-at-law, married Eleanor Wade, of Leeds, in 1869 (Venn; Rugby; Foster, *Men-at-the-Bar*).

9. Booksellers, 14 Henrietta Street, W.C.

10. Thomas Spring Rice (1790–1866: *DNB*; cr. Baron Monteagle 1839), father-in-law and also brother-in-law of James Garth Marshall, had held several important government posts, including the chancellorship of the exchequer, but in 1839 had been peered, shelved, and forgotten. (In London he resided at 7 Park Street, Westminster.)

11. *Mémoires d'outre-tombe*, bk. 36, ch. 10, in a letter to Béranger (Pléiade edn 2:573).

12. Edward Poste (c. 1823–1902), barrister-at-law, of Oriel College (1840; B.A. 1844, fellow 1846), son of a scholar—the Rev. Beale Poste (1793–1871: *DNB*), archaeologist and antiquary, Tovil Hill, Maidstone, Kent—was himself a scholar. He became a student at Lincoln's Inn just a month before this date, was called to the bar in 1856, and ultimately was director of Civil Service examinations, residing at 12 Hereford Gardens, Park Lane, and, later still, 1 Park Row, Albert Gate. He wrote *The Logic of Science* (1850), edited *Philebus of Plato* (1860), translated *Aristotle on Fallacies; or, The Sophisti Elenchi* and *The Skies and Weather Forecasts of Aratus* (*Men-at-the-Bar, Annual Register*, 1902).

13. Fanny Lucy Wightman's sisters (see below pp. 290 n. 1, 268 n. 4.).

14. For Victor Cousin, whom Arnold saw much of in Paris in 1859, see below pp. 425 n. 3, 496 n. 1. His essay "Des Principes de la révolution française et du gouvernement représentatif" was in *Revue des deux mondes* 10 (Apr. 1, 1851):5–46.

15. *Mémoires d'outre-tombe*, bk. 38, ch. 1 (Pléiade edn 2:665).

16. *Mémoires d'outre-tombe*, bk. 38, ch. 14 (Pléiade edn 2: 702).

Mary Penrose Arnold to Thomas Arnold (extract)

Fox How
April 15, 1851

Matt is in London, & will probably write to you his own history, & of his happiness in the confirmation of all his hopes. Surely he must have told you of his attachment to Miss Wightman, though he so little liked to have it talked about, that even to you we have not said much—The facts are briefly these—that last spring he met with his Fanny Lucy first in the London parties to which he went—he saw that he was very much attracted—& I think I may say that there has been a mutual attachment since—but there have been great difficulties—& the Judge only gave his consent some few weeks ago. Now all goes on smoothly & happily. Dear Matt has received an appointment to an Inspectorship[1]—& now it remains to be seen when the marriage will be. I thought certainly not till this autumn, but I cannot be sure how this will be. . . . I can hardly imagine how dearest Matt will be able to stand the hard work, but the moving about will be a real good or refreshment for him, & he is not one who will make troubles of what he undertakes—& such are his powers—& his quiet effectiveness—that I doubt not he will get through his work admirably—[2]

MS. Balliol College.

1. See above p. 179. He was appointed on Apr. 15.
2. "Only think of Matt being engaged and long before this reaches you if report says true, he will be a married man—for Susy mentioned (in a letter we had from her yesterday) that Whitsuntide was the time spoken of for the great event. I hope we are likely at least before the year ends to make acquaintance with Fanny Lucy. I think it is time we should see one of our *three* new Sisters. I like what we hear of Fanny Lucy who I hope is simple and loving & unworldly though she has lived in the great London world, and must have breathed so much of an artificial atmosphere" (Frances Arnold to Tom Arnold, Apr. 28, 1851; MS Balliol).

Diary

Wednesday, April 16, 1851 Hampton. to Teddington. passed the day with Flu.

Thursday, April 17, 1851 the morning at Hampton with Flu. to lunch with her. back to town in the evening. dined at club.

Friday, April 18, 1851   in town. Clough at breakfast. read in Goethe's journals. dined with the Blacketts. heard from Flu.

Saturday, April 19, 1851   to Hampton at 8.30. fine day. The Bucklands called. out with Flu. dined & slept at Hampton.

Sunday, April 20, 1851 [Easter]   passed the day at Hampton. twice to church. dear Flu

Monday, April 21, 1851   Hampton. called on Mrs. Holberton[1] with Flu. walk with her. cows. sate in the diningroom with her. back to town. dined at club ⟨with [?]Morier⟩

Tuesday, April 22, 1851   Clough at breakfast. to Oxford. walk in Ch. Ch. meadow with Poste. dined in common room. Slept at the Mitre. wrote to Flu.

Wednesday, April 23, 1851   Oxford. Examination in the morning. exquisite day walk to the Cumnor country with Sellar. heard from Flu & wrote to her. dined in common room.

Thursday, April 24, 1851   Oxford. heard from Flu. wrote to her. dined with the Provost.[2] The election. read the Quarterly Review.

Friday, April 25, 1851   to town by the express. wrote to Flu. heard from her. dined at the club. Morier.

Saturday, April 26, 1851   in town saw Ld L for the first time since Lady L's death. back to Hampton. dear Flu looking pale. Miss Webb with her.[3] dined & slept at Hampton.

Sunday, April 27, 1851   twice at Church. passed the day with dear Flu.

Monday, April 28, 1851   The morning at Hampton. Mrs Benson & Flu went with me to the train. dined with Portal at the Alfred.

Tuesday, April 29, 1851   to Hampton by the 7 o'clock train. passed the day with Flu. dined & slept there.

Wednesday, April 30, 1851   to town. C. O. saw Ld L. dined at the Blacketts. Flu at the Spicers'.[4] wrote to her to tell her to stay next day at Hampton.

Thursday, May 1, 1851   Exhibition opened. drove to Vauxhall. to Hampton by luncheon. walk with Flu in the Park. dined quietly.

Friday, May 2, 1851   at Hampton. walk to Kingston with dear Flu across the Park. fixed the 10th of June. large party in the evening. Flu in pink & exquisite.

Saturday, May 3, 1851   to town by 11. saw Ld L. back to Hampton. Mrs Wood still there.

Sunday, May 4, 1851   at Hampton with Flu. Twice to church. wretched cold day. Mrs Wood still at Hampton.

Monday, May 5, 1851   to town by 11. Saw Ld L. drove to Hampton in a Hansom. found Flu out to meet me with Mrs Ponsonby. met her. dined & slept at Hampton. read a little in Lives of the Chancellors.[5]

Tuesday, May 6, 1851   at Hampton with dear Flu. called on Mrs Lambart with her. to town. saw Ld L. dined with Portal at club. at 10 to Eaton place & saw Flu at the window.

Wednesday, May 7, 1851   breakfast with Portal. to the Exhibition with him.[6] to lunch in E. P. dear Flu. C. O. at ½ past 3. L. H. & home writing this. dined in Eaton place.

Thursday, May 8, 1851   To the Borough Road school. then to Howell & James' to meet Flu.[7] home with her to lunch. then to Berkeley street with her and back. to L. H. dined alone with Flu & Ly W. in Eaton place.

Friday, May 9, 1851   Clough at breakfast. L. H. C. O. to see Dunn at the Borough Road schools.[8] E. P. for half an hour. dined at club. to E. P. to see Flu at the window.

Saturday, May 10, 1851   L. H. C. O. to Eaton place with Flu to the Flaxman Hall.[9] at 6 again to L. H. dined at club. read in Wordsworth's life. to E. P. to see Flu at her window.

1. Probably, the wife of Vaughan Holberton, the surgeon (see below p. 351).
  Robert Burnet David Morier (1826–93: *DNB*; knt 1882), of Balliol and, according to Geoffrey Faber (*Jowett: A Portrait with a Background*), who calls him a "genial young giant," the closest friend Jowett ever had. At this time a clerk in the Education Department, he resigned in Oct. 1852, to enter the diplomatic service (he was the nephew of a diplomat, James Justinian Morier, the author of *Hajji Baba*), soon became "*attaché* in Vienna, and spent twenty-three years in diplomatic service in Germany; later he was minister at Lisbon and Madrid, and ambassador at St Petersburg" (Tennyson, 2:48n, 175n; see also Swinburne, 3:65).
2. The provost of Oriel, Edward Hawkins.

3. Lansdowne's mother, the former Louisa Emma Fox-Strangways, wife of the 2d marquis, died Apr. 3. (For the marchioness incumbent see below p. 438 n. 4.)

Miss Webb (*Mrs* Webb in the few later references), has not been identified. She lived close by, near Eccleston Square, and is last referred to in Oct. 1871.

4. The Spicers seem the very perfection of a type. John William Gooch Spicer (1817–83), of Eton, Dragoon Guards, Surrey Militia, J.P. and D.L., United Service Club, Army and Navy, and Boodle's, married (1845) the former Juliana Hannah Webb Probyn, daughter of a Gloucestershire vicar (a younger son), and they lived nearby at Esher Place, Surrey, which had been acquired by the family in 1805. ("The present mansion stands on higher ground [than the old Esher Palace] . . . is entirely modern; and commands a rich view over the valley of the Thames"—*Imperial Gazetteer*.) In 1863 he purchased Spye Park, Wilts. Their elder son married an earl's daughter (*Landed, Upper Ten Thousand*).

5. Among several possibilities the likeliest is the wife of Spencer Cecil Brabazon Ponsonby, later Ponsonby-Fane (1824–1915), sixth son of the 4th earl of Bessborough; she was the former Louisa Anne Rose Lee Dillon (d. 1902), daughter of the 13th Viscount Dillon (*Upper Ten Thousand*).

John Campbell Campbell's *Lives of the Lord Chancellors and Keepers of the Great Seal of England, from the Earliest Times till the Reign of King George IV* was first issued in 7 vols, 1845–48.

6. Both the Great Exhibition of the Industry of All Nations in the Crystal Palace in Hyde Park and the annual Exhibition of the Royal Academy opened on May 1.

7. The Regent Street "silk mercers, glovers, hosiers, lacemen & household linen drapers, producers of novelties in ladies' dresses, mantles, lingerie, & millinery; jewellers, silversmiths, clockmakers, & travelling bag & dressing case manufacturers" (*POLD*, 1901).

8. Henry Dunn (see the letter following); about a dozen letters to him, formerly owned by Frederick L. Mulhauser, have not been traced. See Introduction, p. xxv, and below p. 325.

9. "In the hall under the cupola of the [University] College the original models are preserved of the principal plaster works, statues, bas-reliefs, etc., of John Flaxman, R.A., the greatest of our English sculptors" (Murray's *London in 1857*, p. 196).

To Jane Martha Arnold Forster

London

My dearest K   May 10, 1851

I cannot tell you how grieved I was to read that passage in your letter in which you account for your spoiled handwriting by saying that you have so often to write on the sofa: for I know my darling would not willingly be there—and it shews me that she is still far from strong. Seldom as I write to her and cold as my tone often is I never think of my K in weakness or suffering without remembering that she has been to me what no one else ever was, what no one else ever will exactly be again; unless indeed we were both to lose what we have dearest, and then we should be drawn together again, I think, as in old times.[1]

Lingen is highly indignant at Mr Forster's letter: however I think it is natural enough they should be a little jealous, and I understand from Dunn, their secretary, they do not mean mischief. I shall go and call upon him at Tottenham when I can: but it is not easy to get away for an afternoon.[2] There is a great change in Tom certainly: something a little pedantic still in his style perhaps, which comes from reading books of sentiment so much and in such pure faith—but on the whole he seems greatly cleared. What his relations with his wife are does not exactly come out in his letters I think: I dare say there is no very deep reaching sympathy between them.

Neither Flu nor my much maligned & adamantine Self could feel anything but love to you in return for loving her: and she is so loveable: I am more inclined sometimes to cry over her than anything else: it is almost impossible to be soft & kind enough with her.

I have been though the exhibition, but very hurriedly. I wish I could come and fish the Wharf[e] for a week or two.[3]—Mr Morell's[4] advice seems very good and we mean to follow it. Mamma wants to give us £50 to buy linen &c. do you think I may allow her? Kindest regards to William—ever my own K,   Your most affectionate

M. A.

MS. Frederick Whitridge.

1. With a (highly suggestive) whiff of Wordsworth's "Three years she grew" ("The memory of what has been, / And never more will be") and "Tintern Abbey."
    2. The Forsters had settled in Tottenham in 1752 (Reid, 1:6). Robert Forster (uncle of William) was "for more than half a century . . . a member of the committee of the British and Foreign School Society" (Reid, 1:298), of which Henry Dunn was secretary till 1858. Arnold corresponded with Dunn from time to time and singled him out for praise in "Schools in the Reign of Victoria" (Super, 11:222).
    3. "For sport . . . he [William Forster] entertained something like a feeling of abhorrence . . . . Nothing appeared to rouse him to more intense indignation than any persecution of the animal creation. It followed that he refrained scrupulously from all field sports. He never hunted; and though the heights of Wharfedale are crowned by great stretches of moorland, where the grouse find a congenial home, he never shot. . . . The Wharfe is one of the best trout streams in Yorkshire. But Mr. Forster never fished" (Reid, 1:283–84).
    4. John Daniel Morell (1816–91: *DNB*), an ordained minister, was a philosopher and, from 1848 till 1876, an inspector of schools, having been appointed by Lansdowne, who wanted a Dissenter and, "in looking for those who had earned distinction in literature, his attention was naturally directed to the young Dissenting minister" whose book *Historical and Critical View of the Speculative Philosophy of Europe in the Nineteenth Century* (1846) "was then attracting considerable attention." He seems to have embodied the *reverse* of everything that Arnold disliked about Dissent. He was learned (he rendered "some of Milton into Homeric Hexameters"); he had a sense of humor ("I may write a 'Treatise on Algebra in Elegiacs,' or turn Dr. Whately into iambics"); his prose was "remarkably easy, natural, and forcible; he always expressed himself with lucidity, and without any strain after rhetorical embellishment"; and, equally important, as he is said to have replied

in his youth to an old German lady who asked about his profession: "Früher war ich Theolog; jetz aber bin ich Philosoph"—"Once I was a theologian, but now I am a philosopher" (Robert M. Theobald, *Memorials of John Daniel Morell*, pp. 15, 26–8, 55). He wrote a good many other books, also, including perhaps the most successful grammars of his day. See also Connell, pp. 8, 101–3.

Diary

Sunday, May 11, 1851   breakfasted alone read in Chateaubriand. in Eaton place to church with Flu—Then to Chelsea Gardens with her. dined in Eaton place.

Monday, May 12, 1851   L. H. long afternoon in Eaton place with dear Flu. shopping with her. dined at club. [illeg.]ed from Flu.

Tuesday, May 13, 1851   L. H. to Eaton place. saw candlesticks called on Ly Burgoyne & the Blacketts. dined in Eaton place. The [?]Marsdens & Woods.[1] wrote to Flu.

Wednesday, May 14, 1851   L. H. with Mr Scott to the Wesleyan school in Westminster.[2] then to Flu. dined with the Blacketts.

Thursday, May 15, 1851   L. H. to the Blacketts & took Flu home. L. H. again then with Flu till 6. dined with the Blacketts & to the Huguenots[3] with them & Flu supper at the Blacketts & walked home with Flu. bitter cold moonshine.

Friday, May 16, 1851   Clough at breakfast. L. H. C. O. to Flu. sate a long time with her. then to the Exhibition with her. dined at the [?]Frasers'[4]— wrote to Flu at night.

Saturday, May 17, 1851   read Chateaubriand at breakfast. then to see Judge Coleridge about settlements. L. H. to meet Flu at Howell & James's. home with her. L. H. met her at dinner at the Guthries'.[5] read in Las Cases.

Sunday, May 18, 1851, to Monday, June 7, 1851:   no pages in diary

    1. For the candlesticks see below p. 210. The Marsdens cannot be confidently identified. Possibly, the Rev. John Howard Marsden (1803–91: *DNB*), rector of Great Oakley, Essex, 1840–89, whose wife was the former Caroline Moore and who was a fellow of St John's College, Cambridge, Hulsean Lecturer, and Disney Professor of Archaeology (*County Families*; Boase; *Landed*; Venn; Crockford 1883)

    2. John Scott (1792–1868: Boase), principal of the Wesleyan Training College and Normal School, Horseferry Road, Westminster (*POLD*).

3. Meyerbeer at the Royal Italian Opera, Covent Garden, with Grisi singing Valentina and Castellar as Marguerite de Valois (*The Times*).

4. Probably, John Farquhar Fraser (d. Feb. 1865), barrister, Lincoln's Inn (1817); judge of County Courts, Circuit 46 (Surrey), and author of *The Reports of Sir Edward Coke in 13 Parts*, 1826; he lived at 104 Eaton Place, Belgrave Square (Boase). Another possibility is James Fraser (1818–75: *DNB*), later bishop of Manchester, but now vicar of Cholderton, Wilts; he had been a scholar of Lincoln College, and Arnold would of course have known him as fellow and tutor of Oriel 1840–60; he married only in 1880 but his mother lived with him till her death in that year. (The "Sir Fraser" referred to below p. 244 n. 2 never married.)

5. Perhaps George James Guthrie (1785–1856: *DNB*), F.R.S., three times president of the Royal College of Surgeons, and possessor of "a considerable fortune" (he lived at 4 Berkeley Street, Berkeley Square); his first wife died in or a little before 1850. His life was scarcely an open book. Only in the *Lancet* obituary do we learn that "the fact of his second marriage was not generally known" and that he was survived by a daughter and a son by the first marriage, by his "widow, and a son between two and three years of age" by the second. In Paris in 1859 Arnold called on a Mrs Guthrie and Kate Guthrie. See below pp. 434 n. 3, 438 and the obituaries in *Annual Register, The Times*, May 2, 1856, p. 5; *Lancet*, May 10, 1856, pp. 519–20 (a long "Biographical Sketch" appeared in 1850 in *Lancet*, 1:727–36).

Mary Penrose Arnold to Thomas Arnold (extract)

Fox How
May 29, 1851

You will I hope hear from Matt, who fully intended to write to you before his marriage[1]—but I hardly think he can find time or head when the great event draws so near.—You will understand that I have not yet met Fanny Lucy—but I like extremely well all I hear of her—& as to dear Matt—the little touches in his letters to me [wd illeg.] prove how he loves & delights in her—are quite affecting—so simply, & yet I am sure so deeply true.

MS. Balliol College.

1. The marriage took place on June 10. "Old friends have to make their graceful withdrawal," Clough wrote to Tom Arnold on May 16, "so it seems to me with Matt at any rate . . . and I consider Miss Wightman as a sort of natural enemy. How can it be otherwise—shall I any longer breakfast with Matt twice a week?

"Miss Wightman, you will like to know, is small with aquiline nose, and very pleasing eyes, fair in complexion—I have only seen her, however, in her bonnet. I think she will suit well enough; she seems amiable, has seen lots of company and can't be stupid" (Mulhauser, 1:290).

"Mrs Arnold appeared to enquire after old Aunty—" Mary Wordsworth wrote in a letter on June 11, "it appears they had a Grand Kitchen or rather Garden Ball at Foxhow in honour of Matt's wedding day yesterday—our Cook and Housemaid being present" (*The Letters of Mary Wordsworth 1800–1855*, selected and edited by Mary E. Burton, pp. 332–33).

To Francis Turner Palgrave [1]

Mount Street

My dear Palgrave   Monday night, [June 9, 1851]

I must write you one line to thank you for your very pretty taper-stand, and for the kindness which made you send it. Wyndham Slade has given me an inkstand with which your taper forms a perfect match.

If you listen attentively towards 12 tomorrow you will hear heaven and earth trembling in attestation of my vows.[2] Kindest regards to Temple,[3] and believe me, my dear Palgrave,   ever yours most truly

M. Arnold

MS. British Library.

1. Francis Turner Palgrave (1824–97: *DNB*), poet, critic, influential "taste-maker," and (after Tennyson's wife and older son) "perhaps the Laureate's most faithful attendant and friend" (Tennyson, 2:27n). He was at Balliol 1842–47, a Jowett-worshiper, and afterwards a fellow of Exeter College (see above pp. 100 n. 1, 127 n. 4). He was elected Professor of Poetry at Oxford in 1885, supported by both Tennyson and Arnold; as art critic for the *Saturday Review*, "he may perhaps have had a right to claim the much-disputed rank of being the most unpopular man in London" (*The Education of Henry Adams*, ch. 14); and he was the editor of the most popular anthology of poetry in English ever issued, The Golden Treasury (1861), of which Tennyson was the éminence grise. See Gwenllian F. Palgrave, *Francis Turner Palgrave: His Journals and Memories of His Life* (1899).

2. With a (witty) echo of *Paradise Lost* 9.998-1003?

3. Frederick Temple was principal, Palgrave vice-principal, of Kneller Hall Training College, established early in 1850 under the supervision of the Committee of Council on Education. Situated on a fifty-acre estate between Twickenham and Whitton, it is well described by H. J. Roby in *Memoirs of Archbishop Temple by Seven Friends*, ed. E. G. Sandford, pp. 97–113, who points out that on "Saturday, men like Stanley, Scott, Lake, Jowett, Lingen, Sandford . . . Walrond, and many others used to come down." Macaulay came also, and Tennyson would walk over from Chapel House, Twickenham.

Diary

Tuesday, June 10, 1851   married. to Alver [1]

Saturday, June 14, 1851   I. of Wight & back to Alver

Monday, June 16, 1851   to town & settled at Hampstead

Thursday, June 19, 1851, to Saturday, July 19:   no pages in diary.]

1. "Matt is married," Clough wrote to Tom Arnold on June 14. "I, Walrond, Slade, Blackett, Edward and some Bucklands were there. Nobody cried; Matt was admirably drest, and perfectly at his ease. It rained but we did well enough—they went off before the breakfast—where old Croker sat cum Judice. She seems, as Matt calls her, a charming companion" (Mulhauser, 1:291). An old family servant remarked that "Mrs. Harnold did'nt look hearthly" (quoted from a very helpful obituary in *The Pilot*, July 6, 1901, pp. 13–14). Park Honan notes (p. 233) that they spent six days at Alverstoke—this was either in a lodging house or possibly in the Gothic villa of Croker at Alverbank, lent them for the occasion. John Wilson Croker (1780–1857: *DNB*), politician, essayist, and critic, was an old friend and near neighbor of the judge. See *Album*, pp. 47, 103.

To Thomas Arnold

London

My dearest Tom   July 2, 1851

    I must not quite lose the habit of writing to you, and I have your last letter to thank you for, and I have never written to you of your marriage, nor told you of my own, which happened on the 10th of last month. It is the worst of absence and distance that one so entirely ceases to know with any exactness how it is with those one has known and whether they continue to be the same people or are being vitally changed, that one feels to be address-ing them in the dark,[1] and is unwilling to run the risk of saying something wholly unsuitable. I can understand your desire to return home, but I cannot but think in your present position it would be very imprudent. Your wife of course knows little of England, and nothing of the difficulties attending a new start there at 8 or 9 & 20: or she would contrive to keep you at Hobart Town at all events till you had established yourself firmly in the Colonial Service. At Oxford there would be no place for you that I can see—for you know yourself that the tutors valued there are tutors for the schools which those who have continued since their degree immersed in the routine & traditions of the place are best fitted to be; the only place I can imagine you finding open would be a Rugby mastership—the most hideous and squalid of occupations: and that Goulburn, who is a very narrow-minded Evangeli-cal & advances only his own sect,[2] would not give *you*. At any rate don't come back at a venture: find out by enquiry some opening if you can, and then come, but don't come to England to look for it.

    To serve the Colonial government well, and in process of time to get moved to a better colony and a better post is the natural line for you as it seems to me.

I wonder if you would like my place. I was obliged to get something permanent when I wished to be married, and Ld Lansdowne made me an Inspector of Schools—the very appointment you held in V. Diemen's Land. It is about £700 a year here, but I suspect life is far cheaper in the colonies. I should greatly have preferred to go to the colonies myself—that is to some of the warm ones—not the American & Australian ones—as colonial secretary or some such thing: but, if it had been possible, the young lady's father would not have allowed it.

They will have told you from Fox How who she is, but hitherto only Susy has seen her. We are living at present up at Hampstead. I am still with Ld Lansdowne tho: actually appointed Inspector: but I don't receive the salary yet, till I cease acting as Private Secretary.

The convicts must certainly be a horrible nuisance: but I think there is truth in what they urge that a colony which has been made by convict labour ought not to refuse to bear its part in maintaining them: though under the pressure of the annoyance no doubt the colonists do not feel this. If there is anything you wish done or asked about with a view to your establishment in this country, tell me. My love to your wife.   Ever your affectionate-

M. A.

MS. Balliol College.

1. "I hate writing in the dark" (see above p. 178 n. 6).
2. See above p. 169 n. 4. Goulburn, elected to purge Arnoldism, was doubly anti-Thomist, opposed to both father and son as well as (in Arnold's view) the Holy Ghost. (Tom Arnold's conversion to Roman Catholicism was several years later.)

Diary

Monday, July 21, 1851   came from Hampstead to Eaton place. H. of Lords. Papal Aggression Debate.

Tuesday, July 22, 1851:   no entry

Wednesday, July 23, 1851:   no entry

Thursday, July 24, 1851, to Saturday, August 23, 1851:   no pages in diary.

Sunday, August 24, 1851, to Wednesday, August 27, 1851   [sums (division, subtraction, multiplication—no addition].

Thursday, August 28, 1851, to Saturday, August 30, 1851:   no pages in diary.

Sunday, August 31, 1851:   no entry

To William Henry Hyett[1]

38, Eaton Place

My dear Sir   July 29, 1851

Wyndham Slade sent me by your desire a copy of your son's journal
early last month, only a few days before my marriage. Since then I have been
absent from town or only occasionally there, and it is but within the last few
days that I have had an opportunity of reading the journal. I rejoice now that
I did not send you my thanks on first receiving the book, as I should then
have had to content myself with a simple acknowledgement of your kindness—whereas I am now able to express to you the extreme interest,
mingled, I may perhaps add, with a certain surprize with which I have read
it. I knew so little of your son that I by no means did justice to the enthusiasm
the information the goodness the warm interest in all things and persons most
deserving of interest which his journal proves him to have possessed: and
though perhaps it was hardly to be expected that I should have done so, with
my slight acquaintance with him, I almost feel now to have done him an
injustice in not appreciating him more highly. The book has all the freshness
which a journal not meant for publication always has: but apart from that,
and the liveliness of youth, it has a peculiar and touching interest which only
the character of the writer could have imparted to it.

It would not become me to enter into detail respecting the merits of a
book which has appeared under such circumstances: but I hope you will
allow me to say that your son's account of the voyage up the Nile, and of his
ride from Beyrout to Jerusalem, brought the places and country before me
with a freshness and vividness I have never experienced in reading any other
accounts of them.

You will excuse I hope this long letter and late acknowledgment of your
kindness, and believe me ever, my dear Sir,   most sincerely yours

M. Arnold—

W. Hyett Esqre

MS. University of Virginia.

1. William Henry Hyett (1795–1877), *né* Adams; he changed his name on succeeding to the estates of Benjamin Hyett in 1813 (*Landed;* Boase) while at Christ Church. He
lived at Painswick House, Stroud, Gloucs, and was M.P. (Stroud), D.L., and F.R.S. Wil-

liam Henry Adams Hyett (1825–50), his oldest son, was at Eton and then (1844) Balliol and (1846) the Inner Temple. His posthumous book was *Journal of a Visit to the Nile and Holy Land in 1847–48* (1851).

Diary

Monday, September 1, 1851   Left Eaton Place with dear Flu at 8 for London Bridge. crossed to Calais—close still dark, night. heaps of foreigners on board. Straight on to Paris.

Tuesday, September 2, 1851   Paris at 9 a. m. wet day—Hot bath & shopping—in the afternoon it cleared a little—to the Louvre with Flu. dined at the 3 Frères
        —took Flu home. strolled alone to the rue de [?]Bois & the river. back to bed.

Frances Lucy Wightman Arnold
to Charlotte Mary Baird Wightman

Paris, Hôtel Windsor[1]

My dearest Mama   September 2, 1851
        Here we are in dear old Paris once more: after a most prosperous journey, & for my part I do not feel in the least degree as if I had been up all night. We reached London Bridge just in time as the train started almost immediately after we got into the railway carriage, & we rattled down to Dover in fine style only stopping 4 times on the way. The turnout of people at Dover was immense, almost all being foreigners, French & German & except one other Lady besides myself all were men.
        The night was pitch dark [?]which [made] the getting all the luggage from the railway to the steamer, a work of some difficulty, particularly as the truck in which it was all placed, from being overloaded gave way & every thing was scattered on the ground; Then the noise & confusion of tongues were quite astonishing & being so dark it was difficult to rescue your own property, but finally we were all righted & got on board the steamer, & had a most capital passage. The sea as calm as a mill-pond & the night very warm. At Calais we were kept about ½ an hour while the luggage was being weighed & put in the train as it was all examined here in Paris. We had some tea & then left Calais at ½ past 2 this morning & arrived in Paris at a little after 9 & here about 10. All the hotels are crowded & we have a room au *quatrième* the only one in the house; we do not mind however as it is only for

one night. Matt is gone to Lafittes & when he returns we are going to the Louvre which is now open again, & then to dine at the "Trois Frêres" which will remind me so of last October, but every thing in Paris does that & I wish you were all here. Tell dear Papa with my best love, that the crossing last night I am sure he would have liked, it was so calm & warm. but we hope to meet you all some where or other on the Rhine on our return. Tomorrow we start at ½ past 10 for Chalons. It has poured with rain all day which is melancholy as it is our only day here but Paris is always pleasant & gay look-ing. Give my best love to dear Papa & Fanny & also to dear sister & Tiny when you see them & Georgina when you write to her, & with much love for yourself believe me as ever dearest Mama   Yr very affectionate child

F. L. Arnold

I have written in great haste. Tell dear T[in]y I was *quite* warm enough, in-deed I congratulated myself I had only my plaid. I hope to write from Lyons. Best love to Aunty when you write, also to all at Littleton & Teddington. Matt's love. He will be glad if you will forward any letter that comes for him to Eaton Place today to Chamonix where he hopes to find a nice long letter from Tiny. Tell Papa that Matt has just came back here from Lafittes and presented me with *three* beautiful bright Napoleon [?]coins.

MS. Formerly, Arnold Whitridge (text from photocopy, Patrick J. McCarthy).

   1. The Hotel Windsor was at 218, rue de Rivoli; the restaurant Trois Frères was in the Galerie Beaujolais, Palais-Royal. Charles Laffitte's bank was at 48 bis, rue Basse de Rempart, a street near the Madeleine, finally destroyed in 1902. See *Galignani's New Paris Guide for 1861*, p. 588, and Hillairet, 1:264. "Tiny" was her sister Mary Henrietta Benson.

Diary

Wednesday, September 3, 1851   from Paris to Chalons by rail at 10.30. pes-tered with toothache. Along the Yonne. grand view before Dijon. At Cha-lons great crush. H. du Parc. strolled along the Saone alone after supper.

Thursday, September 4, 1851   at 7 down the Saone to Lyons. H. de l'Un-ivers. After dinner to the observatoire. early to bed.

Friday, September 5, 1851   up late. with Flu in fiacre to the junction of the rivers. Saone not so slow. Jean Jacques' Grotto. To the banker's. H. de Ville. after dinner with Flu to the cathedral, and a little shopping. to a café by the theatre alone.

Saturday, September 6, 1851   to Grenoble. H. de 3 Da[uphins]

Sunday, September 7, 1851   Grande Chartreuse

Monday, September 8, 1851   Chambéry

Tuesday, September 9, 1851   L'Hopital Conflans

Wednesday, September 10, 1851   Chapon

Thursday, September 11, 1851   Aosta

Friday, September 12, 1851   [?] Ivrea

Saturday, September 13, 1851:   no entry

Sunday, September 14, 1851   Milan

Frances Lucy Wightman Arnold
to Caroline Elizabeth Wightman Wood

Milan, Albergo Reale
My dearest Sister   Sunday, [September 14, 1851]
      I had intended writing from Aosta, but it was so hot & I had so little
time I thought I had better postpone my letter till I got here. Yesterday was
dear little Edith's Birthday when we gave her all manner of good wishes.[1] At
present I have not heard once from home in consequence of our not going
to Chamounix, & you may imagine how anxious I am to get to Venice where
I hope to find letters. Matt wrote to Mama from Aosta but left me to tell our
adventures which have been numerous. The Grande Chartreuse[2] I was not
going to turn my back upon: as women are not admitted I was lodged in a
small house not far from the monastery where I spent rather an uncomfortable time as it was bitterly cold. Matt was allowed to have supper with me,
but at ½ past 7 he was turned out & went into the monastery where he had
a cell to sleep in. He got up at 11 & went to the Chapel & heard midnight
mass, which he said was very striking, the monks chaunting the service in a
low monotonous tone, each holding a taper: indeed every man had one and
the Chapel was lighted in that way. In the morning I went to a small chapel:
also for ladies, where I heard mass, the Père Superieur of the Chartreuse
officiating. The situation of the monastery is very fine & the size immense,
but it looked dreadfully gloomy. The weather was bad as there was a fog the
whole time we were there & it was raw cold. From the Chartreuse we went
to Chambéry & from thence to L'Hopital-Conflans [Albertville] where we
took a char à banc & went to Beaufort at which place we hoped to find mules

to take us over the mountain to Chapiù [Les Chapieux] but every mule had gone to a fair in the neighborhood, but two men who offered their services as guides assured us we should find plenty on the way, if I would not mind walking till then, which I agreed to & walked for about 3 hours & a half. We got our mule finally after waiting nearly an hour for it at a chalet & we were obliged to commence the ascent of the Col de [?]Corenez at 7 in the evening & did not get to Chapiu till past 10. Quite dark nearly all the way. I never was more alarmed, & altogether quite lost my nerve & behaved dreadfully. It was so dark & I was perched on an enormous mule, with no saddle, only a kind of pack made up with hay & my shawl, so that I felt very insecure & the guide walked about two yards in advance holding the end of a long rein. The path was very narrow & the mule crawling along the edge. Then I had my legs hanging over the edge at the most frightful height, with nothing for hundreds of feet below. I never was more glad to get to any place than Chapiu, a miserable little Auberge where we slept; & next day at 8 we started (still with the same mule & guides) to cross the Col de la Seigne & reached Courmayeur at 5 that evening. The view of Mont Blanc was very good & the day being lovely the whole scene was splendid. Matt walked the whole way, and scarcely seemed tired at all, although the heat was great, & the ascent each day very long & fatiguing. At Courmayeur we dined and afterwards went on in a char à banc to Aosta; a most beautiful drive the whole way. From Aosta we went to Milan where I began this letter to you & in vain tried to finish it, but our time there was so short & so much to be seen I could not manage it. I was quite delighted with Milan, & its cathedral is perfect. We had very fine weather there & anything more enjoyable cannot be imagined. I was very sorry to leave, as we did not seem to have half seen all that was to be seen. From Milan we went to Verona, where we spent all yesterday, but the weather unfortunately had changed & nearly all the day it rained. The Emperor of Austria was there & in the evening we went to an Equestrian entertainment held in the grand old Roman Amphitheater. It was crammed with people, & a curious scene. The Emperor we saw splendidly as he passed close to us. Also Radetsky,[3] a very ancient man. This morning we left by the train at 11 & arrived in this most interesting city about 10 minutes ago: a deplorable day & every thing looks miserable. I must finish this, Matt says, directly. Goodbye dearest Sister. Give our best love to all at St. Albans Bank, Teddington, & Aunt & Georgina when you write to them & with much for yourself & Peter & kisses to all the Chickis.[4] Believe me as ever   yr affectionate sister,

F. L. Arnold

Venice, Sept. 18th 1851

Hotel Royal Danieli

MS. *Formerly, Arnold Whitridge (text from photocopy, Patrick J. McCarthy). Printed in James H. Broderick, 'Two Notes on Arnold's "Grande Chartreuse," ' Modern Philology,* 66 (Nov. 1968):157–60.

1. Edith Caroline Wood (1849–1935), daughter of Peter Wood and Caroline Wightman Wood. She married well (see below, Arnold to his mother, Dec. 11, 1870).
2. See Arnold's poem "Stanzas from the Grande Chartreuse" (Allott, p. 301 and notes), Tinker and Lowry, pp. 248–53, and above p. 132 n. 1.
3. Joseph Venceslas Radetsky de Radetz (1766–1858), the Austrian field marshal and governor of northern Italy.
4. Of the Woods' ten children four (two surviving?) had been born by this date.

Diary

Tuesday, September 16, 1851   in malle poste betwen Milan Verona

Wednesday, September 17, 1851   Verona

Thursday, September 18, 1851   Venice

Friday, September 19, 1851   Venice

Frances Lucy Wightman Arnold to William Wightman

Venice, Hotel Royal Danieli
My dearest Papa   Friday, September 19, 1851
        I write now (in the hope that this may reach you on the 28th) to wish you very very many happy returns of that day, and to tell you how very much we should both like to give our good wishes in person. We hope to spend it at Lucerne where we were looking forward to meeting you & dear Mama & Fanny, but by a letter from Mama which I had today we find there is no chance of your coming. Our letters from Chamonix arrived today to my great joy, the first we had had since we left home. Will you tell Mama that her letter with its enclosure for Matt arrived quite safely. I also had a nice long letter from my Aunt, which was forwarded to me from Como. Our journey hitherto has been most delightful & with Italy I am quite enchanted. At Milan we had most comfortable rooms at the Albergo Reale where we stayed from Saturday night till Tuesday afternoon. The Cathedral is even more beautiful than I had imagined & I think we saw it thoroughly. The tomb of San Carlo Borromeo of course we saw. I admire it far more than that of the three kings at Cologne. We also went to the top of the Cathedral to see the view but it was not very clear. Leonardo da Vinci's fresco of the Last Supper we went to see & also to the Biblioteca Ambrosiana where we saw

the most curious old manuscripts & a letter of Lucrezia Borgia's to Cardinal Bembo. On Tuesday we left Milan at one o'clock, in the Malle poste for Verona where we arrived at 3 in the morning: we were turned out at the bureau de la poste, & walked from there to the Hotel (de due Torre) where we fortunately got a very nice room directly. We spent all Wednesday in Verona, but could not see much of it, as till late in the afternoon it rained heavily. Verona was quite gay, as the Emperor of Austria was there & in the evening we saw him very well at an Equestrian entertainment held in the Amphitheatre. It was a grand sight, as the place itself is so very fine, but I dare say you remember it well. We came here by railway on Thursday & our first view of Venice was rather miserable as it poured with rain, & yesterday it was dull & cheerless & in the afternoon rained heavily; but notwithstanding Venice more than comes up to all my expectations; and today has been lovely & we have been out since breakfast. This Hotel is in the best situation of any in Venice, being close to the Piazza San Marco, it is also now considered the best in other respects. It was formerly the Palazzo Mocenigo. We have very nice rooms looking on the Grand Canal, which we are considered very fortunate to get as the Hotel is quite full. Miss Alderson & one of her brothers have been here. They only left today. Mr Oliphant[1] is also here. We met him first at Milan & constantly since. He has been out with us the whole of today. We have been over the Doges Palace & seen every part, including the Bridge of Sighs & the dungeons. The last I was very glad to get out of. Then we went to St Mark's, which is very curious, & afterwards to several other churches. The Gondolas are quite delightful & we both like going out in them immensely. Tomorrow is our last day here, and then on Monday we must turn our steps homewards, leaving a day or two for Como and Maggiore on the way.

Sunday the 21st. I have just received a nice long letter from dear Sister for which will you thank her very much for me. It is so delightful getting letters from home. Will you give our best love to dear Mama, Aunty, Fanny & Georgina (who I suppose will be at home when this arrives for your birthday & with a great deal for yourself & wishing you very many happy returns of your birthday again & again (in all which Matt joins) believe me dearest Papa   Yr ever affectionate child

F. L. Arnold

Only the second time I have been away on your birthday.

MS. Formerly, Arnold Whitridge (text from photocopy, Patrick J. McCarthy).

1. Miss Alderson was the daughter of Sir Edward Hall Alderson. Laurence Oliphant (1819–88: *DNB*), novelist, journalist, war correspondent, M.P., traveler, and mystic, was on his way from Ceylon to England, where he settled at East Sheen (near the Wightmans)

with his mother (Margaret Oliphant, *Memoir of the Life of Laurence Oliphant*, pp. 54–59; Philip Henderson, *The Life of Laurence Oliphant*, p. 27).

Diary

Saturday, September 20, 1851	Venice
Sunday, September 21, 1851	Venice
Monday, September 22, 1851	Desenzano
Tuesday, September 23, 1851	Milan
Wednesday, September 24, 1851	Milan

Frances Lucy Wightman Arnold to [Aunty] [1]

Milan, Albergo Reale
My dearest Aunty   Wednesday, September 24, 1851
    Very many thanks for your letter, which I received at Venice where it was forwarded from Como. You may imagine how delighted I was on Friday when I had four letters, the first time I had heard since I left home, yours being of the latest date & the longest, 2 from Mama and one from Georgina. Will you thank the latter very much for me & say I hope to write to her next. I had fully intended writing to you from Venice, but could only manage one letter (to dear Papa) while we were there. We had really but one fine day (Saturday), & then Venice looked as it ought to look. It certainly is the most singular place, & I think the princely look of its grand old palaces adds so much to the interest. Matt & I delighted in the gondolas & spent most of our time in one. On Saturday we saw the Doges Palace. I thought of you so much as I went up the Grand Staircase, which is beautiful & when I looked at the fine picture that you mention of ⟨St⟩ the Doge Kneeling before Faith.[2] I am sure you would like to see the old place again very much. In the Grand Sala del Maggior Consiglio the paintings on the ceiling were taken down which was unlucky as of course they must add greatly to the whole appearance, but still the room looked magnificent. In the afternoon we went to several churches & saw the picture of Peter Martyr, but that was taken down & placed against the wall in so bad a light it was difficult to see it. Sunday morning it rained, but cleared & was very fine in the afternoon when Matt & Mr. Oliphant & I went in a gondola to the Lido. It was quite delightful there, & we spent 2 hours walking by the sea—and Matt bathed. On our

return we went into the Campanile & had a most splendid view of Venice. After the table d'hôte at five we went to the Café Florian in the Piazza San Marco to have ices & coffee. Every body in Venice seemed to be collected there; & the middle of the Square was full, as there was an Austrian band playing most exquisitely. The night was quite lovely, & the whole scene beautiful. On Monday mng at 9 we left Venice to my great regret (as I could have willingly stayed there much longer) & went by railway to Verona. The railway certainly takes away from the romance of Venice, but it is a great convenience as we were in Verona in less than 5 hours! From Mestre to Venice there is a wonderful bridge on which the railroad runs.³ It takes nearly 10 minutes to cross it. At the station there are *omnibus* Gondolas from all the different hotels to convey the new arrivals, which seem even more out of character with the place than the railway itself. We had written on to Verona to take places by the Malle poste to Brescia but on our arrival we found we could not have them, & that diligences & every conveyance were crowded in consequence of the Emperor of Austria being in these parts. We found an English family a Mr. & Mrs. [?]& [?]Miss Garner⁴ in the same case with ourselves so we made common cause and had a vetturino between us & left Verona that evening at 5 & got to Desenzano at 10 where we had great difficulty in getting rooms also on account of the Emperor but finally succeeded at the Albergo Imperiale which stands on the lake of Garda. Yesterday mng we started from Desenzano at 7 in a pouring rain & arrived at the same hour in the evening at Treviglio just in time for the last train here & got in to this hotel about 10. So we had a good day's travelling. The famille Anglaise were very civil. The Papa a fat man who drops the letter H, the Mère equally stout, & equally forgetful of that letter of the Alphabet. The daughter rather good looking & a nice girl. They went to the Hôtel de la Ville & today we called & made our adieux as our routes separate here. Tomorrow we start for Como & from there we hope to go to Maggiore, & on Monday next cross the St Gothard. We both like Milan extremely, & this second visit here we have enjoyed much. The Cathedral is so beautiful we never tire of going to it. Will you tell Sister to tell Mrs. Aleck Wood⁵ with my love that I called today at the Hôtel de la Ville on Lady Warington but she was out, so I wrote a note to ask if I could do anything for her in England, & have just had her answer saying she had nothing to send but her love. She had been out all day or would have come to see me. We have met heaps of English lately, amongst them tell Tiny, Mr. & Mrs. Guthrie, & Mr. Clack & Capt. Clack (the Whitemans friends). Matt had met the Guthries at Bowood & d[itto]. Mr. Clack at Epping. Macbean⁶ was with them & seemed highly delighted at seeing me & was most civil and attentive. She made great enquiries after Mama & Tiny, Henry, & Chickis. We met them the first time we were here

& then at Venice. I hope Fanny got all her business for Charlotte and Mary Anne finished in good time. I imagined her to be at Portsmouth seeing them off about my birthday. Will you thank Sister very much for me for her nice long letter & good wishes for that day. I received it last Sunday at Venice. I dare say dear Mama & Tiny have also written but probably directed to Lucerne. It is getting so late I must close this & say goodbye. Matt joins with me in best love to you, dear Papa, Mama, my Sister & Fanny, & believe me dearest Aunty as ever   your affectionate niece

F. L. Arnold

Love to Webber & kind regards to Richards. I hope to write to Mama in a day or two.

MS. *Formerly Arnold Whitridge (text from photocopy, Patrick J. McCarthy).*

1. "Aunty" has not been identified.

2. Ruskin, who mentions the picture several times and conceded its greatness, said: "The figure of faith is a coarse portrait of one of Titian's least graceful female models: Faith had become carnal. The eye is first caught by the flash of the Doge's armour: the heart of Venice was in her wars, not in her worship" (*The Stones of Venice*, 1:14).

3. The word *railroad*, not visible in the photocopy, is taken from the transcription, but she must have written *railway*.

4. The Garners have not been identified.

5. Charles Alexander Wood (1810–90; knt 1874), first cousin to Peter Almeric Wood (husband of Caroline Wightman), married Sophia Brownrigg (d. 1890) in 1838. Lady Warrington, the former Elizabeth Billing (d. 1854), was the wife of the 7th earl of Stamford and Warrington (1827–83).

6. The Clacks may have been William Courtenay Clack (1817–1900: *Landed*), B.A. Worcester College, 1842, rector of Moreton Hampstead, Devon ("a good residence and 62 acres of glebe . . . . The tithes were commuted in 1839 for £792 per annum"— *White's Devon*, p. 477), from 1865 till his death, and possibly his firstcousin Thomas Edward Clack (1797–?: *Landed*), "of Larkbeare Manor, Devon, and of the War Office, Pall Mall (one of H. M. Officers of Ordnance)." In London he lived at 3 Park Place, Liverpool Road (*POLD*, which lists also Henry T. Clack, 14 Argyll Place, and Samuel Clack, 31 Argyll Street, King's Cross).

John Clarmont Whiteman (married Sarah Horsley 1823), of Bryanstone Square, London, and Theydon Grove, Epping, Essex; J.P. and D.L. for Essex (high sheriff 1846) and formerly in the East India Civil Service, he died in 1866; one of his four daughters, Bessy, is mentioned by Arnold in 1885 (see below p. 411). See *POLD*, and *County*, 1871.

Probably not the Frederick Macbean (c. 1831-?), who matriculated from Magdalen College, Oxford, in May 1851, was the son of the Rector of St Peter Tavy, Devon ("who does not reside here"— *White's Devon*, p. 742), William Macbean (c. 1798–1855).

Fanny Nicholls, who appears with some frequency in these letters from now on, was not only an old friend of the Wightmans but also, in the course of time and cumulatively, baby-sitter for the Arnolds in one residence after another as well as at Eaton Place and at her own large house in Brighton. On Lady Wightman's death she received a legacy of £100 a year. In the last known reference to her, in Dec. 1882, Arnold says: "I went to see Fanny Nicholls yesterday on my way home; she was very sweet and dear; it is astonishing how she is improved by having her teeth, and by having hair not quite so brown." (She is mentioned in Harding, p. 25, as "Susy [Cropper]'s friend, Miss Nicholls.")

    Charlotte and Mary Anne, below, have not been identified; Webber and Richards were probably Wightman servants.

Diary

Thursday, September 25, 1851   Cadenabbia

Friday, September 26, 1851   Bellinzona

Saturday, September 27, 1851   Faido

Sunday, September 28, 1851   Amsteg

Frances Lucy Wightman Arnold
to Mary Henrietta Wightman Benson

Schweizer-Hof, Lucerne
My dearest Tiny   September 30, 1851
    In a letter I had from dear Mama yesterday she says you have written to me, with the hope of its reaching on my birthday, but I am sorry to say I have never received it. If you sent it to Venice or Como I shall get it, I hope, before we leave this, as we desired letters to be forwarded here, should any arrive at either of those places after we had left. Mama's letter yesterday I was enchanted to receive & hear a good account of you all. I am sorry to say I have not been able to see Miss Benson[1] as the weather has been so deplorably bad for some time & particularly so last week that we were obliged (most reluctantly) to give up going to the Lake Maggiore. We left Milan last Thursday by railway to Como, a cold dull day so that the lake looked quite dreary: at Como, we took the steamer to Cadenabbia (just opposite to Bellagio) where we found a delightful Hotel & dined & slept there & started early on Friday morning for the Lake of Lugano. On our way there we met a Mr. Steward who Matt knew a little & he joined us & has been travelling with us from that time, till we arrived here yesterday. We went all down the lake of Lugano in a boat, but the day was so cold & rainy that it was not very agreeable but still the lake itself looked grand & beautiful, but I do not admire it as much as Como. At Lugano we got a carriage & went to Bellinzona where we ar-

rived at 8 in the evening, dined & went to bed hoping that next morning it might be fine, when we had arranged all our plans for going to Intra to see Miss Benson, sleeping at Pallanza near that place, & on Sunday paying another visit to her & returning to Bellinzona in the evening. But on Saturday morning & indeed the whole day it poured with rain & was so bitterly cold that it was quite impossible to put our plans into execution & the only thing to be done was to get over the St. Gothard as fast as we could. So at one o'clock we left Bellinzona & that evening got to Faido & left next morning at 6 in a pouring rain. The drive from Faido to Airolo is as you know most lovely, but the snow in the mountains about there showed us well what the St. Gothard would be, but it was far worse than I expected. At Airolo we breakfasted & the man of the Inn there said we had better go over the Pass at the same time as the diligence, which we did. Two supplementaires to the diligence preceded our carriage & after us came the diligence itself with *8* horses. About an hour after leaving Airolo the snow began & soon was so deep that I thought we should be stuck fast, indeed the first carriage was several times. I thought much of you, wondered whereabouts you & Henry were overturned. I really thought we never should get to the Hospice at the top, as we were obliged to wait for men to come & clear the road a little for us. About half an hour from the top Matt and all the man (except Mr. Steward who had a very bad cold) had to walk & wretched work it seemed as the snow was up to their knees. At the Hospice we waited an hour while a machine came up to clear away the snow a little. So the going down was much better although much cannot be said for that; and as to the cold it was quite intense & it snowed heavily a great part of the day. We got to Amstieg [*sic*] at a little before 6 intending to dine & go on afterwards to Fluellen, but we found the inn at Amstieg so comfortable that we determined to sleep there & start early next morning; it was dear Papa's birthday when we both wished him many many happy returns of the day. I thought much of him & of you all. Of course you all dined at St. Albans Bank? Yesterday at 6 (bitter cold) we started for Fluellen hoping to find the steamer ready to bring us on here directly but when we arrived at Fluellen we heard that the time of starting was altered for that day only, & the boat would not leave till 10. So there we had to wait 2 hours, which was tiresome. However we got here at one & established ourselves at this delightful Hotel. I like Lucerne very much, & today the lake is in full beauty as it is very fine though still cold. We are now on the point of starting for the Righi, so I must finish this. I hope to write to dear Mama from the top where we hope to sleep tonight. I expect it will be awfully cold as the mountains are covered with snow. How are the Chickis. Kiss them all well for us both. I am so *very* glad to hear that Florance is so much better. Give my best love [to] Mr. & Mrs. Benson Henry & all that may be with [you] & with much from Matt as well as myself to you both, believe me dearest Ty   Yr ever affectionate

F. L. Arnold

Matt desires I will send his best regards to Mr. & Mrs. Benson. My best love to all at Hampton when you see them & Littleton also.

MS. *Formerly Arnold Whitridge (text from photocopy, Patrick J. McCarthy).*

1. The Bensons elude identification. A Miss Benson resided at 14 Chester Terrace, Eaton Square (*POLD*). Littleton, Middlesex, was a fiefdom of the Wood family. Florance John Benson (1816–53) was the halfbrother of Henry Roxby Benson (Harding, p. 40). Charles Holden Steward (1828–94), at Rugby School under Dr Arnold and at Oriel 1847–51, "held various curacies 1851–70," then became rector of Standon, Staffs, vicar of Burton-in-Winal, and finally rector of Ashchurch, Gloucs (*Rugby*; Foster)

Diary

Monday, September 29, 1851   Lucerne

Tuesday, September 30, 1851   Righi Kulm

Wednesday, October 1, 1851   diligence entre Lucerne et Bâle

Frances Lucy Wightman Arnold
to Charlotte Mary Baird Wightman

Schweizer-Hof, Lucerne
My dearest Mama   October 1, 1851
   Many many thanks for your welcome letter & good wishes on my birthday.[1] I received it on Monday on arriving here, and I need hardly say how delighted I was to hear from you, & with such a good account of all at home. I am surprised you did not get Matt's letter from Aosta sooner, as a week from there to England is an unusual time as it takes only 5 days from Venice for a letter to get home. We are now getting far on our road home & hope (D. V.) to be there about Tuesday next. May we go to Eaton Place to sleep as Matt wants to be in London for a day before he goes to Manchester which he hopes to do on Thursday the 9th. Whether I go with him is uncertain. I wrote to dear Tiny yesterday to thank her for writing to me although I have never received her letter. I told her of our proceedings since we left Milan, & our crossing the St. Gothard, which, though not so bad as when she & Henry crossed it, still was very bad & excessively so, from the

time of year. The weather we have had lately and indeed for some time has been wretched, so bitterly cold as well as wet, and the people here say it has been equally bad in Switzerland. I like Lucerne very much & this Hotel particularly. It is quite as large as Monnet's at Vevey, but I do not think quite as good. It stands close to the lake with the loveliest view imaginable. But all the mountains have a great deal of snow on them. Yesterday it was fine, but very cold. Notwithstanding we determined to go up the Righi. We left here at 2 in the steamer & went to a small village (Wagis) at the foot of the mountain where we took a horse & guide. I rode all the way up & Matt and a Swede who we had made acquaintance with (a very nice man) walked. It was a long ascent but the view magnificent the whole way. The higher we got the colder it became & when we arrived as the top I am sure Siberia could not be more bitter. The Hotel there is extremely large & good but of course from its situation very cold. We dined & had some champagne to drink dear Papa's health, as we could not on the St. Gothard. This morning we were called by the blowing of a horn at ½ past 5, and got up to see the sun rise but the morning not being clear it was not good. We breakfasted at 7 & immediately after left & got to Wagis in time for the steamer at 10, & came here. Tonight we leave Lucerne at 7 by the diligence & hope to get to Basle at 6 tomorrow morning & then go on at once by railway to Strasburg as we both want to spend a day there. Our route after that is uncertain, whether we return through France or by the Rhine. It depends upon how far the railway is open between Paris and Strasburg, which we cannot find out here. We hope to find a letter from you on our arrival in London. Matt joins with me in best love to you dear Papa, Aunty & Fanny, Georgina, all at Littleton & Teddington & believe me dearest Mama as ever   yr very affectionate child

F. L. Arnold

Love to Webber if with you. Many biens à Charlotte. Tell Fanny I thought of her on my birthday.

MS. *Formerly Arnold Whitridge (text from photocopy, Patrick J. McCarthy).*

   1. Sept. 16.

Diary

Monday, October 6, 1851   Paris

Tuesday, October 7, 1851   Paris

Wednesday, October 8, 1851   Dover

Thursday, October 9, 1851　　Eaton Place

Friday, October 10, 1851　　Hampton

Saturday, October 11, 1851　　Manchester—began inspecting with Morell.

Sunday, October 12, 1851, to Wednesday, December 24:　　no pages in diary.

To Frances Lucy Wightman Arnold*[1]

Oldham Road, Lancasterian School, Manchester
October 15, 1851

I think I shall get interested in the schools after a little time; their effects on the children are so immense, and their future effects in civilising the next generation of the lower classes, who, as things are going, will have most of the political power of the country in their hands, may be so important. It is really a fine sight in Manchester to see the anxiety felt about them, and the time and money the heads of their cotton-manufacturing population are willing to give to them. In arithmetic, geography, and history the excellence of the schools I have seen is quite wonderful, and almost all the children have an equal amount of information; it is not confined, as in schools of the richer classes, to the one or two cleverest boys. We shall certainly have a good deal of moving about; but we both like that well enough, and we can always look forward to retiring to Italy on £200 a year. I intend seriously to see what I can do in such a case in the literary way that might increase our income. But for the next three or four years I think we shall both like it well enough.

Text. Russell, 1:20.

1. So Russell, but possibly to Mary Penrose Arnold.

To Frances Lucy Wightman Arnold*

Queen's Hotel, Birmingham
December 2, 1851

I have had a hard day. Thirty pupil teachers to examine in an inconvenient room and nothing to eat except a biscuit, which a charitable lady gave me.[1] I was asked to dinner, this time at five, but excused myself on the ground of work. However, one's only difficulty will be not to know the whole of schismatical Birmingham. The schools are mostly in the hands of very intelligent Unitarians, who abound here, and belong to the class of what we call ladies and gentlemen. This is next to Liverpool the finest of the manufacturing towns: the situation high and good, the principal street capital, the shops good, cabs splendid, and the Music Hall unequalled by any Greek building in England that I have seen.

Text. Russell, 1 :21.

1. "At a school approved by an H.M.I. a boy (or girl) of thirteen might become a pupil-teacher for five years, indenturing himself to a head teacher and earning the small sum of £10 to £20 per year while he taught, and then compete for a Queen's Scholarship and matriculation at a normal school. (If the child survived the normal school, he might become a certified teacher.) Reportedly 'pale and thin,' the pupil-teachers taught all day, took 1½ hours of instruction from the master after school, prepared classes, and often worked for their parents at night. Reverend Watkins reported that five 'P. T.s' in his district died in a year. But across the nation 3,580 pupil-teachers worked in 1849 and over 15,000 in 1859—and so the system (in a era of expendable children) was perhaps a success. If a head teacher pleased Her Majesty's Inspector, he earned one pupil-teacher for every twenty-five pupils he had. Thus teachers liked the "system" (Honan, p. 260). See also H. C. Dent, *The Training of Teachers in England and Wales 1800–1975*, ch. 3, "Pupil Teachers."

To [College at Sydney]

London
December 5, 1851

I have long had the pleasure of intimately knowing Mr Clough,[1] who was for a number of years under my father at Rugby. There was certainly no one of his pupils of whom my father retained a higher—I doubt whether there was one of whom he retained so high an estimate.

Mr Clough possesses great knowledge both of ancient and modern literature. He was celebrated at Oxford for his power of imparting instruction in the former: his knowledge of the latter he has of late greatly added to. His ability is of the highest order. But it is especially in respect of his own moral qualities, and of the intimate manner in which his intellectual qualities are affected by them, that he is distinguished from the crowd of well informed and amiable men who generally offer themselves for public situations.

In patience, in self-control, in disinterestedness, in cleanness of mind and dignity of characterr, Mr Clough, even as a young man, stood above and apart from other young men. That superiority he has continued to retain.

He has always commanded the interest and respect of those about him, and on such as have approached him more closely he has never failed to exercise a very powerful influence.

At the same time that Mr Clough's friends cannot but deplore that the services of such a man should be lost here, they are deeply sensible of the signal benefit his ability and character would enable him to render to an educational institution in a new country.

M. Arnold.
late Fellow of Oriel College,
and one of H. M. Inspectors
of Schools.

MS. Bodleian Library.

1. Clough was offering himself "as a candidate for the Classical Professorship at the new [University] College at Sydney," New South Wales, the professorship was "united with that of Principal; the Principal however does not appear to have any very close connexion as such with the Students" (Mulhauser, 1:296). On the strength of the prospect of this employment (which he did not get), he had become engaged to Blanche Smith (whom he did not marry till 1854).

To [University of Edinburgh]

December 10th, 1851

I have long had the pleasure of knowing Mr Sandford,[1] and, like all his friends, can testify that his high distinctions at Oxford, and his success in private tuition, were abundantly merited by his hereditary fine scholarship, and by his solid and accurate acquaintance with ancient literature.

Since he left Oxford, Mr. Sandford's situation in the Privy Council Office has given him a practical acquaintance with Education, which the majority of men of his studious habits do not possess, but which cannot fail to prove of the highest advantage to a person placed in an educational post, however select and refined may be his audience, and however high the region of literature which he may be called upon to tread.

All Mr Sandford's friends must also feel sincere pleasure in stating their opinion, that the admirable personal qualities which have endeared him to *them*, are such as would make themselves eminently felt in the intercourse which subsists between a professor and his pupils.

M. Arnold,
Late Fellow of Oriel College,
Oxford and one of H. M.
Inspectors of Schools.

Text: Roger L. Brooks, "Matthew Arnold's Testimonial Letters for Candidates for the Greek Chair of the University of Edinburgh," Notes and Queries, Apr. 1958, pp. 161–62.

1. Francis Richard John Sandford (1824–93: *DNB*), from the University of Glasgow (where his father was Professor of Greek) and Balliol, entered the Education Office, like Ralph Lingen, several years before Arnold (succeeding him in 1870 as Secretary and therefore head) and, friend and colleague of W. E. Forster, remained there till 1884. Hon-

ors came his way—knighted in 1862, C.B. 1871, K.C B. 1879, privy councillor, 1885, Baron Sandford, 1891. The Shropshire estate in the family since the Conquest passed to him in 1892 (*Landed*).

"Sandford's name was never placed in competition for the Greek chair. He requested that his name be withdrawn from candidacy upon the meeting of the Town Council [on Mar. 2, 1852]. Four other candidates made similar requests." (Brooks, p. 162)

To [University of Edinburgh]

[? December, 1851]

I have had the pleasure of knowing Mr Price nearly all my life. He was a pupil of my father's at Laleham, and afterwards a master under him at Rugby almost the whole time he was there. My father always entertained and expressed the very highest opinion of Mr Price's ability.

I was myself Mr Price's pupil for a long time, and am, therefore, able to speak from experience of his admirable talents, his philosophical scholarship, and his remarkable gift of imparting with vivacity, clearness, and method, the knowledge he possesses. I should add that, great as is Mr Price's reputation for ability, it quite fails to do justice to the impression he produces on those persons who have been longest in intercourse with him, especially on those who have been his pupils. I consider that he possesses the very highest qualifications for a post like that of Greek Professor in the University of Edinburgh.

M. Arnold.

Text: Roger L. Brooks, "Matthew Arnold's Testimonial Letters for Candidates for the Greek Chair of the University of Edinburgh," Notes and Queries, Apr. 1958, p. 162.

Diary

Thursday, December 25, 1851

$$51—5—6$$
$$31-17—0$$
$$\overline{19—8—6}$$

$$26-17—0$$
$$\underline{5}$$
$$31-17—0 \qquad 51—5—6$$
$$\qquad\qquad\qquad 26-17—0$$
$$\qquad\qquad\qquad \overline{24—8—6}$$
$$52—5—6$$
$$17—$$

Friday, December 26, 1851

51 — 5 — 0
33 — 6 — 0
17–19 — 0

[?]wrong   4 — 6
17–15 — 0   Jany 24/52

Saturday, December 27, 1851   Private expenses 1852 (not including bills pd
by cheque)

cash in hand   £21 — 5 — 6
self by cheque   30 — 0 — 0

Sunday, December 28, 1851

In hand	21 — 5 — 6
1852. In the bank	£100
The Judge pd	25
1st quarter	109 — 4 — 5
allowances	93 – 12 — 0
	327 – 16 — 5

Monday, December 29, 1851:   no entry

To The Secretary of the Committee
of Council on Education

Fox How, Ambleside
December 29, 1851
List of Schools

Sir

   I should be much obliged if you would give directions for my being
supplied with a list of schools in my district liable to inspection, other than
those having pupil teachers or certificated Masters. I have not yet been furnished with any list of such schools.

   I have the honor to remain, Sir,   Your obedient servant,

M. Arnold.

The Secretary
Comm[itte]ee of C[ouncil] on Ed[ucation]
   [Docketed: Inspector/29 December 1851/. Arnold Esq. Applies for list
of Schools in his district liable to inspection. /AGD

1. Ack. [The list which you desire will be prepared & forwarded to you as soon as possible.

2. M: Jackson to prepare list/done/J. J. 30/12/51 [?]NZ

1. Written/30 December 1851/[?]L. J. N.
R 30 December 1851/8374

MS. Bodleian Library.

Diary

Tuesday, December 30, 1851

cheques given or drawn

Mamma	£10	
Prior	£25	
Small Oxford bills	£ 7—11	
self	£30	
Standen	11—6—3	
Standen	15	
Sheard	7—1	
	106—18—3	

Wednesday December 31, 1851:   no entry

To Arthur Hugh Clough

6. Goldsmith's Building,
Frances St. Edgbaston
My dear Clough   January 7, 1852[1]

I got your scrap today—at first I hesitated whether the *rejection* was meant of the professorship or the other matter—but it *must* be the former. On the whole, and considering all you told me (supposing you told the truth, ce qui n'arrive pas toujours en pareil cas) I can hardly bring myself to be very deeply grieved. Write me a line and tell me how it all was, and what you mean to do. If possible, *get something to do before your term at the Hall expires;*[2] living on your resources waiting for something to turn up is a bad and dispiriting business. I recommend you to make some use of the Ashburtons:[3] is it possible I could be of any service to you under any circumstances by word pen or purse? Think.

Au reste, a great career is hardly possible any longer—can hardly now be purchased even by the sacrifice of repose dignity and inward clearness—so I call no man unfortunate. I am more and more convinced that the world tends to become more comfortable for the mass, and more uncomfortable for those of any natural gift or distinction—and it is as well perhaps that it should be so—for hitherto the gifted have astonished and delighted the world, but not trained or inspired or in any real way changed it—and the world might do worse than to dismiss too high pretentions, and settle down on what it can see and handle and appreciate. I am sometimes in bad spirits, but generally in better than I used to be. I am sure however that in the air of the present times il nous manque d'aliment, and that we deteriorate in spite of our struggles—like a gifted Roman falling on the uninvigorating atmosphere of the decline of the Empire. Still nothing can absolve us from the duty of doing all we can to keep alive our courage and activity.

Written very late at night. Goodnight and keep alive, my dear Clough.   Your's cordially

M. A.

MS. Yale University.

1. Lowry (p. 122) misread "Jany" (superscript "y") as "June." The 1852 diary shows that Arnold was in Birmingham Jan. 6–8; on June 7 he was at Frampton Cotterell, Gloucs. Goldsmith's Buildings was a terrace of residential houses (*Post Office Directory of Birmingham*, 1854), one of which was a lodging house kept by Esther Smith (1851 census).

2. At the end of the month.

3. Lady Harriet Mary Montagu (c.1802–57), daughter of the 6th earl of Sandwich, in 1823 married William Bingham Baring (1799–1864: *DNB*), who succeeded in 1848 as 2d Lord Ashburton. She was one of the most famous hostesses of her day. Goldwin Smith (*Reminiscences*, ed. Haultain, p. 140) wrote that she was "perhaps the nearest counterpart that England could produce to the queen of a French *salon* before the revolution. She stalked big game, and paraded poets, peers, politicians, pedagogues, and playwrights, as well as artists, essayists, and novelists, at Bath House, Piccadilly, where she presided in London, or at The Grange, Alresford, Hants, where Clough had recently met Lansdowne, with whom she interceded for him (see Mulhauser, 1:303–6).

To Arthur Hugh Clough

Babington Hall, Derby[1]

My dear Clough   Saturday, [January 10, 1852][2]

What with Schools in the Potteries[3] starting & 2 hours to inspect, tooth ache and other incommodities I have been sore put to it lately. I return your draft, which is of Doric plainness, but perhaps is as good as any you could send.[4] Say "Mr Lingen." but you must previously mention to him that you are place-hunting and use his name to the extent you do. I am sincerely interested in this application of yours, I need not say. I think an Inspectorship would be better suited to you though than an Examinership, besides the pay being better. Hard dull work low salary stationariness, & London to be stationary in under such circumstances, do not please me. However I myself would gladly have married under any circumstances, and so, I doubt not, you feel.—I really think with L[ad]y Ashburton's help & your own character, you have an excellent prospect of getting *some* situation in the C. O. within the coming year. But be bustling about it; we are growing old, and advancing towards the deviceless darkness:[5] it would be well not to reach it till we had at least tried *some* of the things men consider desirable.—I never see the Globe, but supposed they would be glad of Ld Palmerston's going, as Blackett was the only man on the journal who liked him.[6] I shall be in town next week and shall see you without fail. Till then adieu.   Your's ever

M. A.

MS. Yale University.

1. Apparently a slip for Babington *Arms*, a tavern or public house in Babington Lane, operated by William Pass. Freebody's *Directory of the Towns of Derby* (1852) records no Babington Hall.

2. Dated by Lowry "shortly after December 19, 1851"—unaccountably, since schools would not be *starting* a week before Christmas.

3. Lowry (unhelpfully) transcribed the phrase as "schools in the Pittener"; "The Potteries" are Arnold Bennett's Five Towns, where Arnold would be on Jan. 22.

4. Clough's application for an appointment in the Education Office.

5. *OED*, 2d edn, citing this sentence, says *deviceless* derives from ἀμήχανος. Here, probably Sophoclean, as in the well-known chorus in *Antigone* 331–72 (on the ingenuity of man in devising remedies for all problems but death), but perhaps the *Homeric Hymn to Hermes* 257 ("the darkness that is ill-fated and against which there is no device").

6. Henry John Temple (1784–1865: *DNB*), 3d Viscount Palmerston and foreign minister, had indiscreetly expressed approval of Napoleon III's coup d'état of Dec. 2 to Count Walewski the French ambassador. Both the queen and the Government, having long found him an embarrassment, were ready to pounce; opportunity lay in the way and they found it. Palmerston was dismissed on Dec. 19 by Russell, who announced it to the cabinet on Dec. 22. The news was first reported in *The Times* on Wednesday, Dec. 24. The earliest possible date for this letter would therefore be Saturday, Dec. 27, but in fact, as Arnold's diary for 1852 reveals, he was in Derby on Friday, Jan. 9, and Palmerston's dismissal was much in the news. *Punch* (Jan. 10, 1852, p. 17), for instance, ran a large cartoon of a young queen receiving a very tall Palmerston and a dwarflike Russell and saying "I'm very sorry, Palmerston, that you cannot agree with your fellow servants; but as I don't feel inclined to part with John, you must go."

To Secretary of the Committee of Council on Education

9. Sion Row, Clifton
March 11, 1852

Inspection.
Change of date of Indentures

Sir,

I have the honor to acknowledge the receipt of your letter of yesterdays date, relating to the above subject.

I had intended to propose a change of the date of Indentures in those Schools only, which were named in the second list which accompanied the enclosed one.

I fully perceive the inconvenience there would be in making any change in the cases you refer to. The arrangement which you have had the goodness to propose to meet those cases, will entirely obviate all difficulty.

I should be much obliged if the Forms of instruction for the Ibstock, Bardon Park, & Leicester Schools could be issued to me as soon as possible.

I have the honor to be Sir,   Your obedient servant
M. Arnold.—

MS. Bodleian Library.

To Mary Carpenter[1]

3. Imperial Square, Cheltenham
Dear Miss Carpenter   April 4, 1852

I find there would be difficulty in apprenticing Pupil Teachers, even if adequate candidates could be found, in schools such as that in St James's Back. I still think it will not always be necessary to exclude such schools from this advantage. At present however, and especially till it is seen what effect Memorials such as that you shewed me may produce, it will be better to let the matter stand over. I shall still hope if I am in Bristol in May to pay my visit to your Ragged school in which I am greatly interested. I should like to see what sort of examination the best boys could pass, though abandoning for the present the idea of admitting them as apprentices.

Will you send me *here*

1 The copy of your Memorial you were kind enough to promise me

2 The Form of Report on your school I gave you to fill up, taking care

to complete your part of it before sending it to me.   I remain, dear Miss Carpenter,   ever yours faithfully

M. Arnold.—

MS. *Manchester College, Oxford.*

1. Mary Carpenter (1807–77: *DNB*), philanthropist, social worker, writer, a Unitarian Mother Teresa—daughter of Lant Carpenter (1780–1840: *DNB)* and strongly influenced by him. She had founded a Ragged School at Bristol in 1846. See *Life and Works* by her nephew J. Estlin Carpenter (esp. pp. 87–93) and below p. 334–35.

To Arthur Hugh Clough

3 Imperial Square, Cheltenham
My dear Clough   Good Friday, [April 9, 1852]
I have this morning received your note—to my great joy. I did not know what had become of you. Did they tell you I called at Doubting Castle[1] the very day you escaped from it. I took it very ill you did not come & dine that day in Eaton Place—the ____ye have always with you,[2] but me ye have not always. However all will be forgiven if you obey me now. From Rugby you will come and see me at Derby, at my expense. You will come early on a Saturday morning and go back late on a Monday night. Now this must absolutely be, therefore resign yourself. I go to Derby on Tuesday, and shall be there some fortnight or three weeks.

I submit myself to the order of events and revolve with the solar system in general. Particulars when we meet.

O fool, port. means portable or pocket edition—and a beast of a book it must be. Capell's text is *painfully* faulty—so much so that a very moderately read Shakespearian detects something wrong every page. "Their currents turn *away* instead of *awry*[3]—and heaps more. But I stick to Homer.

Adieu & love me. Write by return of post to me *here.* I go on Tuesday morning. Kindest regards to Shairp.[4] Flu sends her kind regards to you. I have a real craving to see you again. Tell me if you are likely to have anything to do.—How life rushes away, and youth. One has dawdled and scrupled and fiddle faddled—and it is all over. Adieu again my dear Clough.   Your ever affectionate

M. A.

MS. *Yale University.*

1. In Bunyan's *Pilgrim's Progress,* the castle of Giant Despair. Arnold called at University Hall, where Clough (his appointment terminated) remained till Feb. 29. (Arnold made no entries in his diary Feb. 28-Mar. 2 or—see below—Apr. 7–20.)
    2. Matthew 26:11, John 12:8.

3. *Hamlet* 3.1.87: "turn awry And lose the name of action." Edward Capell's 18th
c. editions of Shakespeare were censured in their own day.
4. In Rugby—and the envelope was postmarked Rugby on the next day.

To James Toovey[1]

Derby
Dear Sir   April 21, 1852
I shall be much obliged if you will now have the books of mine which
are at 101 Mount Street packed for removal, and lists made of the contents
of each box. I spoke to you about them, if you remember, in January. If
volumes are missing in one or two sets it is that I have the missing volumes
with me. I am, dear Sir,   faithfully your's
M. Arnold.—

Jas Toovey Esqre

MS. Yale University.

1. James Toovey (1813/1814–1893), was a bookseller at 42 Piccadilly, who "had a
splendid collection of rare books" (Boase).

To Arthur Hugh Clough

Ibstock British School
My dear Clough   April 22, 1852[1]
I was sincerely disappointed not to see you: however I suppose it was
inevitable. Let me know what you are doing, and what your prospects are.
With respect to literary employment much may be said—I will mention one or two things.
1. An edition of the Greek lyric poets before Sophocles, that should be
readable. It should be in English & drenched in flesh & blood—each poet's
remains should be ⟨prefixed⟩ preceded by his life, and instead of ⟨useless⟩
repulsive references to Ath. Stob. &c. it should be simply narrated under
what circumstances we get each fragment, what ⟨are⟩ is the character of
Athenaeus and Stobaeus's collections, in what context the fragment comes
&c. All this in English, as if you were writing a book for educated persons
interested in poetry, & knowing Greek, to read. I could go on for ever with
this scheme—a delicious book might thus be made. Every fragment should
be followed by its literal prose English translation.
⟨a⟩ 2. The same for Theocritus and his contemporaries—preceded by a
history of the state of literature and the world at that time[.]

3. A judicious translation of Diog. Laertius, leaving out the trash, and taking away the dry compilatory character of the lives—making them living biographies so far as they go.

4. Lives of the English Poets from where Johnson ends—and in his method: biographical but above this, *critical*: presupposing detailed lives of each poet, and contracting the whole.

I am going to lunch with a farmer. Adieu.   Ever your's affectionately

M. A.

MS. Yale University.

1. Postmarked DERBY/Ap 23/1852. Addressed to Clough at Oxford & Cambridge Club, Pall Mall, London.

To The Secretary of the Committe of Council on Education

[May 22, 1852]

County	Name of School	Month proposed for inspection
Gloucester	Gloucester B. S.	April
	Cheltenham Bethesda Westm	April
Leicester	Hathenage Westm	December
Stafford	Etruria B. S.	September
Nottingham	Neward Westm	December

(There are P. Ts apprenticed already in the Newark Wes. S—and in the Cheltenham Bethesda Wes. S. candidates have been lately examined and recommended for apprenticeship.)

May 22/52
Matthew Arnold.

MS. Bodleian Library.

To Wyndham Slade*

38 Eaton Place
My dear Wyndham   [? July 17, 1852][1]

I called at your lodgings last Saturday, and found that Walrond would not be up, but that the trio at breakfast would be myself, you, and Captain

"Apollyon" Slade.[2] I then resolved to absent myself, as I do not like the taste of brimstone in my tea.

With respect to the Salisbury election it may be as you say, but it is reported here that on the polling day Baring Wall,[3] looking very nice, was closeted for some hours with your brother's committee, and that afterwards all Slade's men voted for Wall.

I have been in North Lincolnshire, where there is a sharp contest, and been much amused by talking to the farmers, and seeing how absolutely necessary all the electioneering humbug of shaking hands, clapping on the back, kissing wives and children, etc., still is with these people. I think Lord Derby[4] will have a gain of from ten to twenty votes in the new Parliament, but what that will do for him remains to be seen.

The baby (he is now squalling upstairs) is my first & last, remember.[5] The alarm they give one for their mother's sake, & then the plague of their nursing & rearing is more than the pleasure of their society can ever repay one for.

Your brother is now willing to go to Stockholm, he told me. Will this change your plans? Let me have a line when you can. Shall you not return to town at all?   Ever yours from the heart,

M. A.

Text. Russell, 1:21–22 (corrected from MS by Kenneth Allott).

1. In this month Arnold was in London only on weekends; the Salisbury elections were held on July 10.

2. General Sir John Slade (1762–1859) was the father of fifteen children by two wives. "Apollyon" (Revelation 9:11, 17–18) was Herbert Dawson Slade (1824–1900), Wyndham's older brother, in the first Dragoon Guards, retired as honorary major general in 1881 (Whitaker). Frederick William Slade (1801–63), a halfbrother, succeeded as second baronet on the death of Sir John on Aug. 13, 1859, and was defeated for Parliament for the third time on Aug. 18 (Boase).

3. Charles Baring Wall (1775 or 1776–1853), of Norman Court, Hants, Eton, Christ Church, Member for Salisbury, J.P. and D.L. of Hampshire. "He had been for many years a Director of the British Institution, and his aid was usually sought in Committees of the House of Commons on matters relative to art. Among his immediate friends and dependents he was much esteemed for his kindliness of disposition and unaffected simplicity of manners" (*Annual Register;* Boase; *Who's Who of British Members of Parliament*).

4. Edward George Geoffrey Smith Stanley (1799–1869: *DNB; VF,* 5/29/69), 14th earl of Derby, three times prime minister, formed his first cabinet in Feb. 1852, and remained in office till December.

5. Thomas Arnold, the first child and, as will be seen over and over in these letters, sickly (with the Arnold heart) all his life, was born on Tuesday, July 6, 1852 (while Arnold was certifying pupil teachers in Boston), died Nov. 23, 1868. Arnold, who was in New Leake, Wainfleet, and again in Boston, on Wednesday and Thursday, first saw his firstborn on July 9.

To Samuel W. Wayte[1]

Boston

Dear Wayte   July 19, 1852

Your letter has only just reached me here. I am sure my mother will be most happy to see Miss Wayte if she will call upon her when she is in the neighbourhood of Fox How. I have written to my mother to tell her of Miss Wayte's wishes. Believe me   ever yours truly

M. Arnold.—

MS. John Rylands Library, University of Manchester.

1. Samuel William Wayte (1819–98), from Bristol and Bristol College, then at Trinity College, Oxford, from 1838, where he was a fellow from 1842 to 1866 (lecturer, tutor, dean, senior bursar) and then president 1866–78. He was unassertively High Church and at the same time, at least in his younger days, "strongly liberal" and a supporter of Stanley's appointment as Select Preacher (*The Times*, Sept. 13, 1898, p. 5; Foster; Boase). He never married; "Miss Wayte" was probably his sister.

To Mary Penrose Arnold*

Hampton[1]

My dearest Mother   August 19, 1852

It is just 11 o'clock at night, and I have been here about an hour. When I left town for Wales about a fortnight or more ago[2] Fanny Lucy was intending to write to you in a day or two: I find her daily letter to me took up so much of her strength that she has only been able to write to you within the last day or two. Had I known this I should certainly have sent you a second hand account of her: but I kept expecting to hear from you, for I never got an answer to a letter I wrote you just before I left town in which I announced Flu's coming letter—nor, by the way, have I had any answer to a long letter I wrote to K at the same time.

After more than a fortnight's absence in Wales you will believe what it is to me to have my dear Flu again, and to have her looking so much better too, though still delicate. The baby I have been taken to see—and though he was not very gracious, as he had been kept awake to receive his papa, I can see how flourishing he looks, and feel what a weight he is. Believe me my dearest Mother it is now a great satisfaction to me to think the dear child should be called after his grandfather, though the name was I confess rather a pill at first to me who am sensitive on such matters: but I would not for the world now that it had been settled otherwise. I think he will be a dear little boy—sweet and patient I fancy his little countenance is already.

Clough has been with me for the last few days in Wales: he is likely to go to America in the autumn[3] to try his fortune there as a tutor. If he, with several powerful friends, and, as far as he is personally concerned, Tom's superior in all respects, cannot find a settlement in England, how should Tom find one.—But I am not at all sure that Tom might not find it answer to settle in the U. States in the same business as Clough. But of this hereafter.

You will receive this my dearest Mother on the morning of your birthday. Accept every loving and grateful wish from a son to whom you have for nearly thirty years been such a mother as few sons have. The more I see of the world the more I feel thankful for the bringing up we had: so unworldly, so sound, and so pure.

God bless you, my dear Mother, and believe me ever your truly affectionate child

M. Arnold.—

Flu's love & best wishes—and baby's.

MS. Balliol College.

1. Where the Wightmans lived.

2. He inspected in Bangor on Monday, July 26. No record in diary after Tuesday, July 27, till Thursday, Aug. 5 (when Arnold was in Shrewsbury), except that he lent Clough £10 on Aug. 3 (Guthrie 2:25; see below p. 246 n. 1). No record for Saturday-Sunday, Aug. 7–8, or the next weekend. ("We" in Clough's letter to Blanche Smith, July 30, 1852 [Mulhauser, 1:319], refers not to Arnold but to Oliver Farrar, as the transcript in the Honnold Library reveals.) On Aug. 19 Arnold had not seen his wife for more than two weeks, and Clough's letter to Blanche Smith dated "[2? August 1852]" perhaps dates from Aug. 20, when Arnold was at Hampton. Arnold and Clough were together on Aug. 3 and also (as here) "for the last few days in Wales"; Clough wrote to Emerson from [Hampton] on Aug. 6. They dined together on [? Aug. 2] (Mulhauser, 1:319).

3. Clough sailed on Oct. 30.

To Frances Lucy Wightman Arnold *

Rugby
August 27, 1852

I have just come back from dining at the School-House to write this to you. I found Shairp had engaged me there, and as Goulburn had often asked me, and I had never gone, I went to-night; but I was in a great fidget for fear of being prevented from writing my letter. I cannot tell you how strange the feeling was of dining in the old house, in the very room where I used to sit after every one was gone to bed composing my themes, because it was such a pretty room, it was a pleasure to sit up in it. Mrs. Goulburn[1] is a very nice person, one of the Northamptonshire Cartwrights. I sat next her at dinner.

It would be such a pleasure to go over with you the places I knew from the time I was eight till I was twenty. Then all the people who remember me and my family would be *so* pleased to see you. You would like to see where I used to play with my brothers and sisters, and walk with the governess, and bathe, and learn dancing and many other things. We must certainly come here from Birmingham.

Text. Russell, 1:23.

1. Julia Cartwright (d. 1903), who had married Goulburn in 1851, was the daughter of Lt Col. William Ralph Cartwright of Aynhoe, Northants (*Landed*).

To Wyndham Slade*

Strands, near Wastwater
My dear Wyndham   September 15, 1852

I only received your letter *this morning*. Eaton Place is a howling wilderness[1] at present, and letters may lie there for months before they are forwarded. I should not have got yours now, only my wife had a dress sent to her, and the old woman who takes care of the house in Eaton Place crammed everything with my name on it that she could lay her hands upon into the box.

With respect to your questions, the Committee of Council insist on *boarded floors*; but, worse still, they insist on seeing and approving beforehand the building plans for all schools they aid: therefore, if Lady Slade[2] wants a grant to help her build her school, she must apply before she begins it, for she will get none afterwards. However, if she is only anxious to get her school inspected, or to have pupil teachers in it, or to have a certificated master or mistress, any or all of these luxuries she may obtain though she builds her school herself, and in her own fashion. But for the Committee to give any assistance towards *building or fittings*, they must first approve the building plans.

There—I hope I have been intelligible.

I owed you a letter, which I was intending to pay. Do you remember sleeping at this little inn at the end of Wastwater two years ago, and going to Crummock and Buttermere next day? I am making the very same promenade now with my wife; I have just been looking at your name and mine written in the fremdenbuch in my hand. How pleasant it was having you here—couldn't you come now if you are at home—the partridges must be getting wild, and we should be *so* glad to see you. You are one of the few young gentlemen, my dear love, of whom I have never got tired. Fanny Lucy and I are here till the 10th of October; we shall be at Fox Ow again at the end of this week. Write me a line, then, and tell me whether you can manage to be good and come. We will go and see Edinburgh together; it is only 4½ hours from Fox How. Write at once.   Ever yours affectionately,

M. Arnold.

Text. Russell, 1 : 24—25 (corrected from MS by Kenneth Allott).

1. Deuteronomy 32:10.

2. Slade's mother, the former Matilda Ellen Dawson, the general's second wife (m. 1822, d. 1868).

To The Secretary of the Committee of Council on Education

The Secretary   Fox How, Ambleside
&c. &c. &c.   September 29, 1852

Inspection
Delay in transmission
of Reports.

Sir

I have the honor to inform you, in reply to your letter of the 28th inst, that the last of my Reports on the schools in my district requiring to be visited in the months of July and August, was transmitted by me to the Office yesterday.

The delay in the transmission of these Reports has arisen from the delay, on the part of the managers of one or two Welsh schools, in filling up and forwarding to me the Forms of Report on their schools, which, from the absence of the Secretary or Treasurer or from some other cause, had not been filled up when I visited the schools. The last of these missing Forms of Report, (that on the Marian Glas B. S.) only reached me on Sunday last. I regret however that I did not forward the Reports on other schools to the office as I concluded them, since inconvenience appears to have been caused by the delay in their transmission. Many of them have been lying by me, finished, for the last month: and I regret to have unnessarily kept them back until I could transmit the other Reports belonging to the same period which I had brought with me to this place, along with them. I remain, Sir,   your obedient servant

M. Arnold.—

MS. Bodleian Library.

To Wyndham Slade*

Mr. Sansom's, Derby[1]

My dear Wyndham October 22, 1852

An infernal steel pen which I must change. So—now I can get on. I presume you are no longer enjoying the equivocal hospitality of Sir Fraser; & are blazing away in your ancestral fields.[2] Need I say that I am passionately fond of the Colchic bird, and that your rifle is, I know, unerring? As for me, I shall never look along the deadly tube again, I expect; however, this will be no great blessing for the brute creation, as I never used to hit them.

I wish you could have been with us in Westmorland, as we had splendid weather, and many days of wandering perfectly successful. Do you remember our week, and the fearful way in which you used to blaspheme, as the daily saturation of your raiment commenced on some lonely mountain or other? Next year I am going abroad, I think. The child of my declining years,[3] without brother or sister, unique of his kind, will have apartments at the Château de Lisbon,[4] while his mother and I seek September fevers in South Italy. Such, at least, is our present intention.

Unless Cannon gets out of quad [*for* quod?]I intend coming to the metropolis in a month's time, and then I hope we shall meet; I should so like to sit and talk for an evening with you on passing events. I have published some poems,[5] which, out of friendship, I forbear to send you; you shall, however, if you are weak enough to desire it, have them when we meet. Can you get from Hyman the address of one William Rossetti for me?—an ingenuous youth who used to write articles in a defunct review, the name of which I forget.[6] I write this very late at night, with Smith, a young Derby banker, *très sport*, completing an orgy in the next room. When that good young man is calm these lodgings are pleasant enough. You are to come and see me fighting the battle of life as an Inspector of Schools some day; this next year I mean to make you fulfil the promise. We can always receive you & not in the Pickwickian sense of the Member for Barnstaple.

Smith is in a state of collapse. He will be very miserable to-morrow. Good-night. Let me have a line here, and believe me, ever yours sincerely

M. Arnold.

Text. Russell, 1:25–26 (corrected from MS by Kenneth Allott).

1. Thomas Sansom, a clerk, New Uttoxeter Road, Derby, is the only Sansom listed in *Freebody's Directory of the Towns of Derby* (1852).

2. Identified by Slade as Sir William Augustus Fraser (1826–98: *DNB*; 4th bt), of Eton and Christ Church, Oxford, elected in July Conservative Member for Barnstaple. He was a young, rich bachelor, even in old age, and was caricatured by Ape in *Vanity Fair*,

1/9/75: "Well acquainted, well liked, picturesque in appearance, remarkable for readiness of converse and store of anecdote, he is received with equal pleasure and satisfaction by all the ladies and yet is on the best terms with all the men of the town. . . . Tracing his genealogy as far back as the tenth century . . . and being an archæologist of some pretensions, he is yet quite unaffected and thoroughly accessible; and he has the most complete collection of caricatures in England."

The "Colchic bird" is *Phasianus Colchicus*, the golden pheasant.

3. Thomas.

4. Unidentified, unclear, un-French ("Lisbonne").

5. *Empedocles on Etna, and Other Poems*, by A, published by Fellowes.

6. Adolf *Heimann* (1809–74), professor of German at University College, and his family were close friends of the Rossettis; in the 1840s he tutored the children in German in exchange for Italian lessons from the father (William Michael Rossetti, *Dante Gabriel Rossetti: His Family-Letters with a Memoir*, 1:87; *Selected Letters of William Michael Rossetti*, ed. Roger W. Peattie, p. 2). William Michael Rossetti (1829–1919: *DNB*), brother of Dante and Christina Rossetti (later, editor of their poetry and memorialist), had edited *The Germ* (the "defunct review"), literary organ of the Pre-Raphaelite Brotherhood, of which he was the scribe and factotum, for its four numbers, all in 1850. He reviewed *The Strayed Reveller, and Other Poems* in the second.

To Arthur Hugh Clough

Milford B[oys] S[chool]

My dear Clough   October 28, 1852

I have got your note: Shairp I hope will come to me for a day, and then he can bring the money.[1]

As to that article:[2] I am anxious to say that so long as I am prosperous, nothing would please me more than for you to make use of me, at any time, as if I were your brother.

And now what shall I say? First as to the poems. Write me from America concerning them, but do not read them in the hurry of this week. Keep them, as the Solitary did his Bible, for the silent deep.[3]

More and more I feel that the difference between a mature and a youthful age of the world compels the poetry of the former to use great plainness of speech as compared with that of the latter: and that Keats and Shelley were on a false track when they set themselves to reproduce the exuberance of expression, the charm, the richness of images, and the felicity, of the Elizabethan poets. Yet critics cannot get to learn this, because the Elizabethan poets are our greatest, and our canons of poetry are founded on their works. They still think that the object of poetry is to produce exquisite bits and images—such as Shelley's *clouds shepherded by the slow unwilling wind*,[4] and Keats passim: whereas modern poetry can only subsist by *its contents*; by be-

coming a complete magister vitae as the poetry of the ancients did: by including, as theirs did, religion with poetry,[5] instead of existing as poetry only,
and leaving religious wants to be supplied by the Christian religion, as a
power existing independent of the poetical power. But the language, style,
and general proceedings of a poetry which has such an immense task to perform, must be very plain direct and severe: and it must not lose itself in parts
and episodes and ornamental work, but must press forwards to the whole.[6]

A new sheet will cut short my discourse: however, let us, as far as we
can, continue to exchange our thoughts, as with all our differences we agree
more with one another than with the rest of the world, I think. What do you
say to a bi-monthly mail?

It was perhaps as well that the Rugby meeting was a Bacchic rout, for
after all on those occasions there is nothing to be said.—God bless you wherever you go—with all my scepticism I can still say that. I shall go over and
see Miss Smith from Hampton in December, and perhaps take Fanny Lucy
with me. I am not very well or in very good spirits, but I subsist:—what a
difference there is between reading in poetry & morals of the loss of youth,
and experiencing it! And after all there is so much to be done, if one could
but do it.—Goodbye again and again, my dear Clough—   your ever
affectionate

M. Arnold.—

MS. Yale University.

1. The £10 borrowed on Aug. 3 (see above p. 241 n. 2).
2. "Article," meaning matter or subject—misunderstood (unaccountably) by
Lowry as Clough's "Recent English Poetry," published in *North American Review*, July
1853 (reprinted as "Review of Some Poems by Alexander Smith and Matthew Arnold,"
in *The Poems and Prose Remains of Arthur Hugh Clough*, 1869, 1:357–83). On Apr. 6, 1853,
Clough wrote to Blanche Smith: "I am going to write an article in the 'North American
Review,' on recent English poetry. I have been interrupted in my regular quiet Plutarchan
work, which suits me much better than reviewing Alexander Smith & Co. M. Arnold's
'Tristram' has been giving me pleasure" (*Poems and Prose Remains*, 1:204; see also Mulhauser, 2:424).
3. Wordsworth, *The Excursion* 3.846, 861–64.
4. Shelley, *Prometheus Unbound* 2.1.147.
5. David DeLaura has pointed out to the editor the similarity of this to Goethe's "I
was best pleased with the most ancient men and schools, because poetry, religion, and
philosophy were completely combined into one" (*Poetry and Truth from My Own Life*, tr.
R. O. Moon, p. 189; 9.231–2, Hamburg edn, ed. Truz).
6. Lowry notes the foreshadowing here of some of the ideas of "Preface to First
Edition of *Poems* (1853)" and "The Study of Poetry" (Super, 1:1–15, 9:161–88).

To Herbert Hill

Derby

My dear Mr. Hill,   November 5, 1852

Your criticisms always give me pleasure—they are both kind and just. Scarcely anyone seems to me to speak on poetical matters with such delicacy and judgement: probably because you have such a genuine interest in them, and are thoroughly what the French call a conscientious reader of the productions you criticise.

I am still much too near my own poems to decide impartially on the justice of the particular exceptions you take to them: with regard to the conclusion of Tristram and Iseult,[1] the story of Merlin, of which I am particularly fond, was brought in on purpose to relieve the poem which would else I thought have ended too sadly: but perhaps the new element introduced is too much. I read the story of Tristram and Iseult some years ago at Thun in a French Review on the romance literature: I had never met with it before, and it fastened upon me: when I got back to England I looked at the Morte d'Arthur and took what I could, but the poem was in the main formed, and I could not well disturb it. If I had read the story first in the Morte d'Arthur I should have managed it differently. I am by no means satisfied with Tristram in the second part myself.

With regard to the unrhymed metres some like them, but more would agree with you in disliking them: they come natural to me however when I attempt certain subjects in a certain vein. The strain of thought generally is no doubt much too doleful and monotonous. I had no notion *how* monotonous till I had the volume printed before me. I thought too when the poems were in manuscript they would possess a more general attraction than their predecessors: I now see they will not—and on this head I am sure you are quite right—and it is a great fault—no one will more readily allow this than I. But I hope still to do better some day—one can only take one's natural course, and try to get rid of some faults at every new trial. You need not doubt that my productions will always find you out as soon as they appear, and I am sure I shall always feel cleared and aided by your judgement upon them.

With kindest regards to Mrs Hill believe me dear Mr Hill   ever gratefully and sincerely yours

M. Arnold.

Text: R. E. C. Houghton, 'Letter of Matthew Arnold,' TLS, 31 (May 19, 1932), 368.

1. See Allott, p. 206, especially headnote, and below, pp. 264, 280.

To Mary Penrose Arnold*

Derby

My dearest Mother   November 25, 1852

Here I am again to find dearest Baby much better—only coughing occasionally and then loosely—and in high spirits and with what colour belongs to him restored to his cheeks. Dearest Flu is a little bilious and knocked up with nursing him and she had a very troublesome time at Mr Sansom's after I left her as other lodgers entered into possession, and she was driven from pillar to post—but we are now settled at the Midland, the best of all possible hotels where the people know us and shew the greatest possible kindness to baby. I go back to Newark tomorrow morning, but shall reach town late in the evening: and baby is so much better that he and his Mamma will probably meet me there, going direct from this place. But Mr Evans[1] who will see him tonight will decide this.

I had my own doubts about his dear little heart having constantly remarked its singular agitations at times. But I should not be the least surprised if Brodie[2] or whoever sees him pronounces it only to be an infantine irregularity, and that there is no structural defect.

I have been since Monday at Lincoln, hard worked but *subsisting* on the Cathedral. Every evening as it grew dark I mounted the hill to it and remained through the evening service in the nave or transepts, more soothed and refreshed than I could have been by anything else. I came down the valley of the Trent today—you have no idea what majestic floods![3] I asked a great deal about them: the new bank near Fledborough has given way and that place and Ragnall and Durham are all floating. I astonished the country people by knowing the names of the remote villages by there: I looked affectionately in the bright morning towards Fledborough: my recollections of it are the only approach I have to a memory of a golden age: I thought how I should like once more to see it with you, dearest Mother, and to look with you on the grey church and the immense meadow and the sparkling Trent.[4]—We will talk of it again for it might be managed from Coleby. Love to dear Mary & thanks for her letter.   Ever your affectionate son

M. Arnold.

I got your letter just as I left Lincoln this morning.

MS. Balliol College.

1. Samuel H. Evans, surgeon, in Full Street, Derby (*History, Gazetteer and Directory of the County of Derby*, by Francis White & Co. 1857).

2. Sir Benjamin Collins Brodie, the elder (1783–1862: *DNB*), surgeon, profes-

sor of comparative anatomy and physiology, Royal College of Surgeons, and, early on, something of a heart specialist who attended three reigning monarchs (the Queen and her two predecessors), and was rewarded with a baronetcy by William IV, who valued his conversation along with his professional skills. See below pp. 347, 425. His son (see above p. 52 n. 9), was a contemporary of Jowett at Balliol and very much part of the Old Boy network.

3. "The heavy rains which have continued for more than two months have produced wide-spread destruction and loss of life. . . . The land-waters meeting the high tides of the Thames, have flooded those parts of the metropolis which lie upon its banks. . . . In the Midland Counties a wide expanse of country was covered by the waters; the people dwelt in the upper stories of their houses. . . . At Shrewsbury more than 700 houses were flooded. . . . The whole vale of Gloucester was one wide-spreading sea. . . . A terrible disaster occurred at Hereford. . . . Market Harborough and Leicester were inundated. . . . The lower parts of Birmingham were inundated. . . . Northamptonshire and Cambridgeshire suffered severely . . . Leicester was flooded a second time (*Annual Register*, pp. 198–89, Nov. 1852).

4. The diction and landscape of this sentence suggest "The Scholar-Gipsy" (Allott, p. 355) writ small and early.

To Arthur Hugh Clough

Battersea

My dear Clough   December 14, 1852

—I write to you from an evening sitting of the candidates for certificates at the Training School here. It is a Church of England place but such is my respectability that I am admitted to their mysteries.

I have no doubt that you will do well *socially* in the U[nited] States: you are English, you are well introduced—and you have personal merit—the object for you is to do well *commercially*. Value the first only so far as it helps the second. It would be a poor consolation for having not established oneself at the end of a year and a half to be able to say—I have got into the best American Society. If you are to succeed there, you will begin at once, and will be the fashion as a tutor.

What sort of beings are the Yankees really? Better or worse in masses than they are individually? They me font l'effet of a nation not having on a wedding garment. It is true that the well born, the well mannered, the highly cultivated—are called no longer, because they have shown such incapacity for administering the world: but it is too bad that when our Heavenly Father has whipped in these long ugly yellow rascallions from the highways & hedges they should not clean and polish themselves a little before taking the places of honour.[1]

As for my poems they have weight, I think, but little or no charm

What Poets feel not, when they make,
A pleasure in creating,
The world, in *its* turn, will not take
Pleasure in contemplating.[2]

There is an oracular quatrain for you, terribly true. I feel now where my poems (this set) are all wrong, which I did not a year ago: but I doubt whether I shall ever have heat & radiance enough to pierce the clouds that are massed round me.[3] Not in my little social sphere indeed, with you & Walrond: there I could crackle to my grave—but vis à vis of the world.— This volume[4] is going off though: a nice notice of it was in the Guardian— and Froude will review it in the April Westminster, calling me by my name. He is much pleased.—You must tell me what Emerson says. Make him look at it. *You* in your heart are saying *mollis et expes* over again.[5] But woe was upon me if I analysed not my situation: & Werter Réné and such like[6] none of them analyse the modern situation in its true *blankness* and *barrenness*, and un*poetrylessness*.

Now my dear Clough you were a good boy to write when you did, but you are not to write me scraps across the ὑγρὰ κέλευθα[7] of the Atlantic, or I shall dry up as a correspondent. But write me a nice long letter as if I was an ἀνάλογον[8] (at least) of Miss Blanche Smith—& then we will establish a regular bimonthly mail. God bless you.

Flu & I shall go & see Miss Smith from Hampton.   Ever your's affectionately

M.A.—

MS. Yale University.

1. Matthew 22:11–14, Luke 14:23.
2. "A Caution to Poets" (Allott, p. 300), published in *New Poems*, 1867.
3. Echoing "In Utrumque Paratus" (Allott, p. 44, ll. 29–35).
4. *Empedocles on Etna* (see above p. 245 n. 5), by "A," was reviewed in the *Guardian*, Dec. 8, anonymously, (Allott-Super, p. 567) and by Froude (also anonymously) in the *Westminster Review*, Jan. 1854. "Vis à vis of" is neither French nor English.
5. "Weak and hopeless," Horace, *Epodes* 16.37.
6. The introspective heroes of Goethe's *Sorrows of Young Werther* and Chateaubriand's *René*—"such like" would include Childe Harold, Obermann, etc.
7. "The watery ways" (*Odyssey* 3.71, 9.252)—i.e., the sea.
8. "Analogue" or "equivalent"—familiar in English since Coleridge introduced it in 1810.

To Frances Lucy Wightman Arnold*

Battersea, Friday, [? December 17, 1852]
This certainly has been one of the most uncomfortable weeks I ever spent. Battersea is so far off, the roads so execrable, and the rain so incessant. I cannot bear to take my cab from London over Battersea Bridge, as it seems so absurd to pay eightpence for the sake of the half-mile on this side; but that half-mile is one continued slough, as there is not a yard of flagging, I believe, in all Battersea. Did I tell you that I have papers sent me to look over which will give me to the 20th of January in London without moving, then for a week to Huntingdonshire schools, then another week in London for the Inspector's meeting and other matters, and then Birmingham for a month, and then London?

Text. Russell, 1:27–28.

To Charles De La Pryme [1]

The Alfred [2]
Dear Sir   January 18, 1853,
Pray accept my best thanks for your poem and for the kind note which accompanied it. I see the latter is dated the 14th but they only reached me this morning. With regard to the wish which you express that I should add Latin Poems to my English ones—in the first place I fear my Latin Poetry would be sadly incorrect—in the second those who now complain of the want of modern interest in my Poems, would then complain ten times louder. But I am a sincere admirer of the accomplishment of Latin Verse, notwithstanding.   I remain, dear Sir,   Yours faithfully
Matthew Arnold.—

MS. Mark Samuels Lasner

1. Charles De La Pryme (1818 [or -15?]-99), a Christian gourmet dilettante, was the son of George Pryme (d. 1868), a Cambridge barrister-at-law and M.P., of a Protestant family from Ypres that settled in The Levels in the seventeenth century and anglicized the name. Charles, re-gallicizing it, attended Trinity College, Cambridge (B.A. 1839, M.A. 1842), was a student at Lincoln's Inn, married Sophia Cubitt, of Fritton House, Suffolk, in 1869, by whom he had three sons, was J.P., Hunts, and (appropriately, since his mother was a Thackeray and since he was fond of the pleasures of the table) a member of the Reform Club and one of the founders of the Devonshire Club. He published *Ænigma* in the 1860s; *Ars cænandi, novem Canticis depicta* (23 pages privately printed, on one side only), 1868; *Ad Reginam* ("a Latin elegiac ode on the Jubilee of Queen Victoria"), 1887; *The Roman Embassy; a Letter to Viscount Palmerston,* and *The Life of Christ: an*

Eclectic Gospel from the Old and New Testament, 1865 (Boase; Kelly; *Landed*, 1840.) (He was nominated as "probably" the recipient of this letter in John Wilson's catalogue.)

    2. "Alfred Club, No. 23 Albemarle Street. Established 1808; limited to 600 members; entrance fee, 8 guineas; annual subscription, 8 guineas [Arnold paid up in Jan. 1853 and 1854, as his diaries show]. Formerly known by its cockney appellation of *Half-read*" (Peter Cunningham, *Hand-book of London. Past and Present*, New Edn: 1850), it was a minor-league Athenæum, with quite as many bishops: "I stood the Alfred as long as I could, but when the seventeenth Bishop was proposed I gave in; I really could not enter the place without being put in mind of my Catechism," a member declared. "The Bishops, it is said, resigned the club when a billiard-table was introduced" (Ralph Nevill, *London Clubs: Their History and Treasures*, p. 283). In 1855 it formed "a sort of coalition" with the Oriental Club, to which Arnold migrated (and paid £10 in Jan. 1855). Byron, who had been a member, mentions it several times—see especially his *Letters and Journals*, ed. Prothero, 1:86, 5:424.

To Arthur Hugh Clough

Edgbaston

My dear Clough   February 12, 1853

    I received your letter ten days since—just as I was leaving London— but I have since that time had too much to do to attempt answering it, or indeed to attempt anything else that needed any thing of "recueillement." I do not like to put off writing any longer, but to say the truth I do not feel in the vein to write even now, nor do I feel certain that I can write as I should wish. I am past thirty, and three parts iced over—and my pen, it seems to me is even stiffer and more cramped than my feeling.

    But I will write historically, as I can write naturally in no other way. I did not really think you had been hurt at anything I did or left undone while we were together in town: that is, I did not think any impression of hurt you might have had for a moment, had lasted. I remember your being annoyed once or twice, and that I was vexed with myself: but at that time I was absorbed in my speculations and plans and agitations respecting Fanny Lucy, and was as egoistic and anti-social as possible. People in the condition in which I then was always are. I thought I had said this and explained one or two pieces of apparent carelessness in this way: and that you had quite understood it. So entirely indeed am I convinced that being in love generally unfits a man for the society of his friends, that I remember often smiling to myself at my own selfishness in half compelling you several times to meet me in the last few months before you left England, and thinking that it was only I who could make such unreasonable demands or find pleasure in meeting and being with a person, for the mere sake of meeting and being with them, without regarding whether they would be absent and preoccupied or not. I never, while we were both in London, had any feeling towards you but one of attachment and affection: if I did not enter into much explanation when you expressed annoyance, it was really because I thought the mention of my circumstances accounted for all and more than all that had annoyed you. I remember Walrond telling me you were vexed one day that on a return to town after a longish absence I let him stop in Gordon Square without me: I was then expecting to find a letter—or something of that sort—it all seems trivial now, but it was enough at the time to be the cause of heedlessnesses selfishnesses and heartlessnesses—in all directions but one—without number. It ought not to have been so perhaps—but it was so—and I quite thought you had understood that it was so.

There was one time indeed—shortly after you had published the Bothie[1]—that I felt a strong disposition to intellectual seclusion, and to the barring out all influences that I felt troubled without advancing me: but I soon found that it was needless to secure myself against a danger from which my own weakness even more than my strength—my coldness and want of intellectual robustness—sufficiently exempted me—and besides your company and mode of being always had a charm and a salutary effect for me, and I could not have foregone these on a mere theory of intellectual dietetics.

In short, my dear Clough, I cannot say more than that I really have clung to you in spirit more than to any other man—and have never been seriously estranged from you at any time—for the estrangement I have just spoken of was merely a contemplated one and it never took place: I remember saying something about it to you at the time—and your answer, which struck me for the genuineness and faith it exhibited as compared with my own—not want of faith exactly—but invincible languor of spirit, and fickleness and insincerity even in the gravest matters. All this is dreary work—and I cannot go on with it now: but tomorrow night I will try again—for I have one or two things more to say. Goodnight now.—

Sunday. 6 P. M.

I will not look at what I wrote last night—one endeavours to write deliberately out what is in one's mind, without any veils of flippancy levity metaphor or demi-mot, and one succeeds only in putting upon the paper a string of dreary dead sentences that correspond to nothing in one's inmost heart or mind, and only represent themselves. It was your own fault partly for forcing me to it. I will not go on with it: only remember, *pray* remember that I am and always shall be, whatever I do or say, powerfully attracted towards you, and vitally connected with you: this I am sure of: the period of my developement (God forgive me the d—d expression!) coincides with that of my friendship with you so exactly that I am for ever linked with you by intellectual bonds—the strongest of all: more than you are with me: for your developement was really over before you knew me, and you had properly speaking come to your *assiette* for life. You ask me in what I think or have thought you going wrong: in this: that you would never take your assiette as something determined final and unchangeable for you and proceed to work away on the basis of that: but were always poking and patching and cobbling at the assiette itself—could never finally, as it seemed—"resolve to be thyself"[2]—but were looking for this and that experience, and doubting whether you ought not to adopt this or that mode of being of persons qui ne vous valaient pas because it might possibly be nearer the truth than your own: you had no reason for thinking it *was,* but it *might* be—and so you would try to adapt yourself to it. You have I am convinced lost infinite time in this way: it is what I call your morbid conscientiousness—you are the most conscientious man I ever knew: but on some lines morbidly so, and it spoils your action.

There—but now we will have done with this: we are each very near to the other—write and tell me that you feel this: as to my behaviour in London I have told you the simple truth: it is I fear too simple than that (excuse the idiom) you with your raffinements should believe and appreciate it.

There is a power of truth in your letter and in what you say about America and this country: yes—*congestion of the brain* is what we suffer from—I always feel it and say it—and cry for air like my own Empedocles.[3] But this letter shall be what it is. I have a number of things I want to talk to you about—they shall wait till I have heard again from you. Pardon me, but we *will* exchange intellectual aperçus—we shall both be the better for it. Only let us pray all the time—God keep us both from aridity! *Arid*—that is what the times are.—Write soon and tell me you are well—I was sure you were not well. God bless you. Flu sends her kindest remembrances.

   ever yours

        M. A.

We called the other day at Combe Hurst but found vacuas sedes et inania arcana.[4] But we shall meet in town. What does Emerson say to my poems— or is he gone crazy as Miss Martineau says. But this is probably one of her d____d lies.[5] Once more fare*well*, in every sense.

MS. Yale University.

  1. See the letter to Clough above, p. 127 n. 5.
  2. "Self-Dependence," l. 3 (Allott, p. 148).
  3. *Empedocles on Etna* 2.217.
  4. ["The first Roman to subdue the Jews and set foot in their temple by right of conquest was Gnaeus Pompey; thereafter, it was common knowledge that there were no representations of the gods within, but that] the place was empty and the secret shrine

contained nothing" (Tacitus, *Histories* 5.9.1: Loeb). Combe Hurst was Blanche Smith's countryhouse, near Kingston, Surrey.

5. See above p. 250, below p. 258.

To Frances Lucy Wightman Arnold*

The Bull, Cambridge
February 28, 1853

I have had a long tiring day, and it certainly will be a relief when I get these Eastern Counties over. The worst of it is that invitations to go and see schools are *rained* upon me; and managers who have held out till now against the Government plan ask me on my father's account to come and inspect them, and to refuse is hard.

I have seen nothing of this place. I see there is a long collegiate-looking building opposite.[1] It seems so strange to be in a place of colleges that is not Oxford. You never knew such a scrape as I had of it this morning; it was one minute *past* the time when I drove up to Shoreditch, but they let me in. To-day there was a stoppage in Smithfield, and we had to go round by the Bank and Austin Friars; all down Bishopsgate Street we tore. What a filthy line is the Eastern Counties, and what bad carriages! But how unjust the world is to Essex!

I thought the valley of the Lea we came up this morning delightful, and the whole country very nice till about Chesterford. At the station here I had just time to eat a bun and book for St. Ives. We arrived at the latter place at half-past two, and I walked the two miles to Fenstanton, as it would have been a long business waiting for a fly to get ready. The school is a smallish affair, and at a quarter to five I went to Mr. Coote's.[2] He is the principal man of the place, being a brewer and coal merchant, and is a rich, clever dissenter. He has a nice old house, standing in grounds a little out of the town. I met at dinner there another Dissenter, who wanted to take me home to sleep, and offered to send me to all my schools if I would spend the week with him. He lives near Erith. I refused, however, but next year I shall go to him and Coote instead of coming to the inn here. It—the Inn—is a pretty good one apparently. I have very good front rooms; it is a newer affair altogether than the Angel.[3] I am off early to-morrow for Erith. I thought of you to-night as I drove through St. Ives, and of that bitter cold uncomfortable journey this time last year.

Text. Russell, 1 : 28–29.

1. The Bull was on Trumpington Street and the "building opposite" was Corpus Christi College!

2. Arnold had met Thomas Coote, Esq., at Fen-Stanton a year earlier (Guthrie 2:8).

3. Of the many dozens of inns and hotels with this name, the most famous, because of Pickwickian associations, is at Bury St Edmonds, but Arnold here may refer to the one in the Hampton-Teddington area frequented by Judge Wightman and his friends (see *Album*, pp. 40, 103).

To Frances Lucy Wightman Arnold *

Cambridge
March 2, 1853

At ten I went to my school here, a very large one, which kept me till past one; then I came back here, and at two went out to look at the places. At Trinity I found every one was absent whom I knew, but at Christ's I luckily found Mr. Gell,[1] who is a fellow and tutor there, who was very glad to see me; he was an old pupil of my father's, and my father's picture was hanging in his room. He took me all over Cambridge, and I have since dined with him, and a Mr. Clark, the Proctor,[2] has asked me to dinner to-morrow, but I shall not go, as I think of going to Ely to see the Cathedral.

The two things I wanted to see in Cambridge were, the statue of Newton and King's College Chapel;[3] the former is hardly as effective as I expected, because the chapel, or rather ante-chapel, where it stands, is so poor; yet it is noble for all that. King's College Chapel deserves all that can be said of it. Yet I feel that the Middle Ages and all their poetry and impressiveness are in Oxford and not here. I want you sadly to go about with me; everything would be just doubly as interesting.

Text. Russell, 1:29–30.

1. Frederick Gell (1820–1902), brother of John Philip (see above p. 165 n. 8) of Rugby and (like his father and two brothers) Trinity College, Cambridge, was elected fellow of Christ's College in 1843 (later lecturer, dean, assistant tutor). In 1859 he became domestic chaplain to the bishop of London, was bishop of Madras 1861–99 and died in India (*WWW; Upper Ten Thousand*).

2. William George Clark (1821–78: *DNB*) became a fellow of Trinity College in 1844 and then tutor and vice-master and was later Public Orator; he was a Shakespearean scholar and editor, a classicist, poet, and traveler and travel writer. A man of great charm, he was "the delight of every private company which was capable of relishing finely turned, but not over-studied, conversation" (Edward Graham, *The Harrow Life of Henry Montagu Butler*, p. xxxiii), he was a friend, and sometimes the guest, of the Tennysons, and he endowed the Clark lectures in English literature at Trinity.

3. With Wordsworth's *Prelude* 3.60–64, in mind.

To Frances Lucy Wightman Arnold*

Sudbury
March 8, 1853

This is positively the first moment I have had. I am obliged to remain here to-night, having found an immense school and a great number of pupil teachers; however, I shall get on to Ipswich to-morrow morning. I have fallen on my legs here, being most hospitably entertained by a Quaker who has a large house here.¹ It is a curious place, and I am writing in the hall of it, at which all the pupil teachers are gathered together at their work. The hall is completely covered over as to its walls with a vast collection of stuffed birds, which gives it a ghastly effect enough.

I did not arrive here till just two, as the train was late; went to the school, and found there were three of them. About four o'clock I found myself so exhausted, having eaten nothing since breakfast, that I sent out for a bun, and ate it before the astonished school. Since then I have had a very good extempore dinner on mutton chops and bread pudding, all the Quaker household having dined early, and now I am in for the pupil teachers till ten o'clock.

Text. Russell, 1:31.

1. Apparently, Henry Sparrow Pratt, at no 17 (now no. 38) Friar Street (where "later there was a bird-stuffing shop"), "a large house," with "a large garden behind . . . and a large very fine studio-type room—almost a hall" and "adjacent to the old Quaker Burial Ground" (personal letter from Edith Freeman, Sudbury, "with a special interest in the history of Sudbury").

To Frances Lucy Wightman Arnold*

Ipswich Western School
Wednesday, 5 P. M., March 10 [? *for* 9], 1853

I am too utterly tired out to write. It certainly was nicer when you came with me, though so dreadfully expensive; but it was the only thing that could make this life anything but positive purgatory. I was well taken care of by my Quaker last night; his collection of stuffed birds is really splendid. I could have passed days looking at it; every British bird you could name he has, and the eggs of all which is almost as curious. He has stuffed all the birds himself, being an enthusiastic amateur; the collection of sea-fowl, and of all varieties of the hawk and falcon, was beautiful. I get here at twelve, and in half an hour am going on to Norwich, and thence to Lowestoft, which I shall not reach before eleven to-night.

Text. Russell, 1:32.

To Arthur Hugh Clough

23, Grosvenor St West, Grosvenor Place[1]

My dear Clough   March 21, 1853

I got your letter at Halstead in Essex on Friday evening last. This is the thinnest paper I can lay my hand upon: would that I could but write upon it. We will not discuss what is past any more: as to the Italian poem,[2] if I forbore to comment it was that I had nothing special to say—what is to be said when a thing does not suit you—suiting and not suiting is a subjective affair and only time determines, by the colour a thing takes with years, whether it *ought* to have suited or no.

I am glad to hear a good account of Emerson's health—I thought his insanity was one of Miss Martineau's terrific lies;[3] sane he certainly is, though somewhat incolore as the French say—very thin and ineffectual, and self-defensive only. Tell me when you can something about his life and manner of going on—and his standing in the Boston world.

Margaret Fuller—what do you think of her?[4] I have given, after some hesitation, half a guinea for the three volumes concerning her—partly moved by the low price partly by interest about that pretty[5] brazen female. I incline to think that the meeting with her would have made me return all the contents of my spiritual stomach but through the screen of a book I willingly look at her and allow her her exquisite intelligence and fineness of aperçus. But my G-d what rot did she and the other females dogs of Boston talk about the Greek mythology! The absence of men of any culture in America, where everybody knows that the Earth is an oblate sp[h]eroid[6] and nobody knows anything worth knowing, must have made her run riot so wildly, and for many years made her insufferable.

Miss Bronte[7] has written a hideous undelightful convulsed constricted novel—what does Thackeray say to it.[8] It is one of the most utterly disagreeable books I ever read—and having seen her makes it more so. She is so entirely—what Margaret Fuller was partially—a fire without aliment—one of the most distressing barren sights one can witness. Religion or devotion or whatever it is to be called may be impossible for such people now: but they have at any rate not found a substitute for it and it was better for the world when they comforted themselves with it.

Thackeray's Esmond you know everyone here calls a failure—but I do not think so—it is one of the most readable books I ever met—and Thackeray is certainly a first rate journeyman though not a great artist:—It gives you an insight into the *heaven born* character of Waverley and Indiana and such like when you read the undeniably powerful but most un-heaven-born productions of the present people—Thackeray—the woman Stowe[9]

&c. The woman Stowe by her picture must be a Gorgon—I can quite believe all you tell me of her—a strong Dissenter-religious middle-class person—she will never go far, I think.

Look at Alexander Smith's poems[10] which some people speak of and let me know what you think of them. The article on Wordsworth, I hear, is Lockhart's,[11] very just though cold. Perhaps it does not sufficiently praise his *diction*: his *manner* was often bad, but his diction scarcely ever—and Byron's[12] Moore's &c.—constantly.

Goodnight—no more paper.

Read some articles of Ampère's in the Revue des 2 Mondes on America:[13] what he says is so cool clear désabusé and true that it will do you good in the atmosphere of inflation exaggeration and intoxication in which you live.

We will yet see the young lady—though not soon, I fear. I am frightfully worked at present. I read Homer and toujours Homer.   ever your's
                    M. A.—

Susy is going to be married to John Cropper—second son of the principal Liverpool Cropper.[14]

MS. Yale University.

1. The Arnolds' London home—see below p. 308. The letter may have been written on Sunday, Mar. 20; on Monday, Arnold inspected in Hitchin, Herts.

2. Clough's *Amours de Voyage*, published serially in *Atlantic Monthly* in 1858 and then in *Poems* (1862).

3. Presumably, in conversation at Fox How. See above pp. 95–96 n. 5, 180 n. 1.

4. Margaret Fuller (1810–50), the American protofeminist intellectual and prolific author and (triumphing over the sex barrier) Transcendentalist, whom Clough had met in Rome in 1849. *Memoirs of Margaret Fuller Ossoli*, by Emerson, W. H. Channing, and J. F. Clarke, included letters from a European trip in 1846–47, which revealed her to be an admirer of George Sand and Rachel as ardent as Arnold himself. See below p. 267. Her "rot" about mythology was collected in *Margaret and Her Friends; or Ten Conversations with Margaret Fuller upon the Mythology of the Greeks and Its Expression in Art* reported by Catherine W. Healey, Boston, Roberts Brothers, 1895.

5. Transcribed hitherto as "partly," but both ascenders are decidedly crossed as is the doubled *t* in *letter, utterly,* and *better* also in this letter.

6. *OED* cites Brewster's *Newton* (1855).

7. See above p. 179. *Villette* was published in January. In Dec. 1847 Charlotte Bronte tactlessly (because of similarities in the marital situations of Rochester and Thackeray) but innocently had dedicated the second edition of *Jane Eyre* to Thackeray and scandalous rumors spread.

8. William Makepeace Thackeray (1811–63: *DNB*) had met Clough in Oxford in Oct. 1848, and, like Clough, had sailed on the *Canada* in Nov. 1852, just after the publication of *Henry Esmond* in October. His opinions of *Villette* are in his *Letters*, ed. Ray, 3:233, 248, 252.

9. Harriet Beecher Stowe (1811–96) published *Uncle Tom's Cabin* in Mar. 1852; it

appeared in England (and elsewhere) soon after, and Arnold read it in November (*Note-books*, p. 552).

    10. See above p. 246 n. 2.

    11. Actually, Whitwell Elwin (not J. G. Lockhart), "Memoirs of Wordsworth, *Quarterly Review*, 92 (Dec. 1852):182–236 (one paragraph by Lockhart, according to *Wellesley*, 1:736).

    12. Super's correction of Lowry's "beyond" (Allott-Super, p. 291).

    13. Jean Jacques Ampère's "Promenades en Amérique"—New York, Boston, Cambridge (and Harvard), Montreal, Quebec, Niagara, Buffalo, Detroit, Chicago, Cincinnati, Cleveland, West Point, Albany, Philadelphia, Washington, Charleston, New Orleans—appeared in nine articles in *Revue des deux mondes*, Jan.-June, 1853. (Four further articles describe Cuba and Mexico.) Arnold's adjectives seem fair enough, though his *right* to use the fourth is not obvious.

    14. Susanna Elizabeth Lydia Arnold (1830–1911) married John Wakefield Cropper (1830–92) on Aug. 23, at Rydal Chapel. Her husband, grandson of James Cropper (1784–1840: *DNB*), famous philanthropist and Quaker, founder of the mercantile house of Cropper, Benson and Co., second son of John Cropper (1797–1874), and brother of James Cropper (1823–1900), William E. Forster's friend and fellow politician, lived at Dingle Bank, Liverpool. See *Landed*; *Upper Ten Thousand*; Kelly; Arnold-Forster.

To Frances Lucy Wightman Arnold*

Aspley Guise

Tuesday, March 21 [*for* 22], 1853

I am staying with Mr. How,[1] a venerable Quaker, and his wife in the prettiest little cottage imaginable, with lawn and conservatory, and all that a cottage ought to have. He has the land all around, and his family have had it for generations; but his grand-uncle, an old bachelor, who built this to live quietly in, and who let the family house, being bothered by the tenant about repairs, etc., sold the house; at the same time he retained all the land, so that what was once their own house overshadows the Hows in their cottage. However, the house is now unoccupied, having fallen into great decay; and as the present Mr. How, who has no family, will not buy it back, it will probably tumble down. The same grand-uncle redeemed his sins by collecting a really splendid library—you know I am particular,—which the present people have built a room for, and had catalogued, and the catalogue will be a great resource to me this evening. I go to Ampthill by a most circuitous route to-morrow, and return here quite late to have tea and to sleep, which will be far pleasanter than sleeping at the Ampthill inn.

    How charming it will be to be stationary for three days again without a journey!

Text. Russell, 1:32–33.

1. William Fitzwilliam How, a Quaker from Aspley Guise, who, the bastard son of William Briggins How (1768–1804), was born Dec. 1785 and died at age 78 on Mar. 30, 1864. The "grand-uncle" was in fact an *uncle*, Richard Thomas How (1765–1835); the "splendid library" was created by Richard How (1727–1801), grandfather of Arnold's host, and by Richard Thomas How. Twenty years earlier, in 1833, a cousin, Rachel Howard, wrote in a letter that complements Arnold's admirably: "We proceeded directly to Aspley where we found Richard Thomas How prepared to receive us, and a truly hospitable welcome. He is an old Bachelor and lives in as antiquated a place as one often sees. The approach is overarched, at a great height, by interlocking branches of noble pines, the stems of which remind one of the aisle of some ruined abbey. Then the neat white paling and tall lime trees before the house, the latticed porch entwined with roses, the low ceilings and casement windows, furniture of fine old walnut or other English wood of a more ancient date than mahogany, the white dimity curtains, black painted window seats, corner cupboard with old china etc were all in strict keeping; and scarcely anything within doors or without reminded us of modern luxuries. . . . After tea we inspected the library. I sigh'd over the heap of books as I reflected how very little of real truth could be gleaned from the laboured compositions of men, who were far too learned to be wise. There are however, a number of what are called valuable books. . . . There was a copy of the celebrated Answer of Henry the Eight[h] to Luther, which gained him the title of Defender of the Faith; a latin Bible most beautifully written on thin vellum, and exquisitely illuminated; another MS of much later date, in which a thick layer of gold forming the first letter of the chapter was strangely bestowed on parchment actually sewed together in various places where the skins had been torn in the dressing" (*The Story of Aspley Guise; The Success of an English Village*, Woburn Sands and District Society, 1980, pp. 16–17; Catalogue of the How Papers, County Record Office, Bedford; *Annual Monitor for 1865, or Obituary of the Members of the Society of Friends in Great Britain and Ireland for the Year 1864*, London, 1864, p. 162).

To Jane Martha Arnold Forster*

London

My dearest K   April 14, 1853

I have kept putting off my answer to your last letter, that I might not be obliged to write in a hurry, and I must not wait any longer, though it is now time to go to bed.

What William has said to Chapman is amply sufficient: all I wished him to convey to him was that he, one of his contributors, was interested in the appearance of Froude's article: and that he has fully done.[1] But I have a letter from Froude by which it appears that he thinks of getting the article into the Quarterly instead of the Westminster. This no doubt would be much to be preferred if it were possible, but will Lockhart consent? I doubt it. However I think Froudes's article will ultimately appear somewhere.

There is an article by Forster on A. Smith—a most elaborate one—in last week's Examiner—which is worth reading.[2] It can do me no good, meanwhile, to be irritated with that young man who has certainly an extraordinary faculty, although I think he is a phenomenon of a very dubious character: but—il fait son métier—faisons le nôtre. I am now occupied with a thing[3] that gives me more pleasure than anything I have ever done yet—which is a good sign—but whether I shall not ultimately spoil it by being obliged to strike it off in fragments, instead of at one heat, I cannot quite say. I think of publishing it, with the narrative poems of my first volume, Tristram & Iseult of my second, and one or two more, February next, with my name and a preface. Fellowes is very willing to do this—or indeed anything else which I propose: I, too, have felt the objection of his obscurity and inactivity—but I do not think that can ultimately affect the book much: it is a poor sale which is surprized by advertisements:—and his doing everything at his own risk is a great thing.

Why is Villette disagreeable? Because the writer's mind contains nothing but hunger rebellion and rage—and therefore that is all she can in fact put into her book. No fine writing can hide this thoroughly—and it will be fatal to her in the long run.—My Novel[4] I have just finished—I have read it with great pleasure though Bulwer's nature is by no means a perfect one either, which makes itself felt in his book: but his *gush*, his better humour, his abundant materials, and his mellowed constructive skill—all these are great things.

My love and thanks to William. I shall get the Westminster from Mudie next month, and read his Jamaica article.[5] I heard from Fox How with *delight* of your improved case and walking powers. God bless you, my darling—
your ever truly affectionate

M. A.—

Flu's best love: baby is doing well, and looking beautiful.[6]

MS. Frederick Whitridge.

1. John Chapman (1822–94: *DNB*), physician, author, publisher, and from 1851 nominal editor (for George Eliot—still Marian Evans) of the *Westminster Review.* He was also an irresistible philanderer, as George Eliot had already discovered. Chapman had got Forster, an important contributor, by promising a journal "thoroughly unshackled and free" (see Gordon Haight, *George Eliot and John Chapman,* p. 156; Reid, 1:286–93). James Anthony Froude's article "Arnold's Poems" appeared in the *Westminster Review* 5 (Jan. 1854):146–59. See below p. 283. John Gibson Lockhart (1794–1854: *DNB*) was editor of the *Quarterly Review.*

2. John Forster (1812–76: *DNB*), biographer (notably of his friends Landor and Dickens), historian, critic, essayist, friend of Leigh Hunt, Lamb, Tennyson, Swinburne, and others, was editor of the *Examiner* 1847–55, where his essay—long, with many extracts, and unsigned—appeared on Apr. 9, pp. 227–9. See below p. 264. The first book of Alexander Smith (1830–67: *DNB*), a Scottish "spasmodic" poet, was his *Poems* (1853), of which his most famous work, "A Life-Drama," occupied the first 156 (of 190) pages.

3. "Sohrab and Rustum" (Allott, p. 319) first appeared in *Poems* (1853), with the famous Preface (Super, 1:1–15; Allott pp. 654–71).
4. Published Feb. 4.
5. "British Philanthropy and Jamaica Distress," *Westminster Review* 59 (Apr. 1853): 327–62.
6. Tommy Arnold.

To Arthur Hugh Clough

London

My dear Clough   May 1 [and 3], 1853

I do not know that the tone of your letters exactly facilitates correspondence—however, let it be as you will. I for my part think that what Curran said of the constitution of the state holds true of individual moral constitutions: it does not do to lay bare their foundations too constantly.[1] It is very true I am not myself in writing—but it is of no use reproaching me with it, since so it must be.

I do not think we did each other harm at Oxford. I look back to that time with pleasure. All activity to which the conscience does not give its consent is mere *philisterey*,[2] and it is always a good thing to have been preserved from this. I catch myself desiring now at times political life, and this and that; and I say to myself—you do not desire these things because you are really adapted to them, and therefore the desire for them is merely contemptible—and it is so. I am nothing and very probably never shall be anything—but there are characters which are truest to themselves by never being anything, when circumstances do not suit. If you had never met me, I do not think you would have been the happier or the wiser on that account: though I do not think I have increased your stock of happiness.

You have, however, on the whole, added to mine. You do not tell me what you are doing: Mrs Lingen[3] told me last night you had six pupils: she is a great friend you know of *your* friend's: we talked a great deal about you—not that I like her (Mrs Lingen) much. Your friend has been to see Fanny Lucy—but I was from home: I shall manage to see her some day. You will come all right, I think, when you are once married.

If you have been looking over North's Plutarch lately you are probably right about it—but I cannot help thinking (I am going on with this Tuesday night May 3rd) that there is a freshness in his style and language which is like a new world to one—it produces the same effect on me as Cotton's Montaigne does:—if North could be read *safely*, without one's continually suspecting an error, and in a handy volume, I think he would be delightful reading. You are quite right to incorporate Long.[4] I should much like to see what you have done. Stick to literature—it is the great comforter after all. I should like to read an article of your's on me—I should read it with a curious feeling—my version of Tristram and Iseult comes from an article in the Revue de Paris, on Fauriel, I think:[5] the story of Merlin is imported from the Morte d'Arthur. If I republish that poem I shall try to make it more intelligible: I wish I had you with me to put marks against the places where something is wanted. The whole affair is by no means thoroughly successful.

I have just got through a thing which pleases me better than anything I have yet done[6]—but it is pain and grief composing with such interruptions as I have: however in this case the material was a thoroughly good one, and what a thing is this! and how little do young writers feel what a thing it is— how it is *everything*.

I feel immensely—more and more clearly—what I *want*—what I have (I believe) lost and choked by my treatment of myself and the studies to which I have addicted myself. But what ought I to have done in preference to what I have done? there is the question.[7]

As to Alexander Smith I have not read him[8]—I shrink from what is so intensely immature—but I think the extracts I have seen most remarkable— and I think at the same time that he will not go far. I have not room or time for my reasons—but I think so. This kind does not go far: it dies like Keats or loses itself like Browning.

You know (or you do not know) that Froude, who is one of the very few people who much liked my last vein, or [thought me] to be other than the black villain my Maker made me [, will review my Poems for the Westminster].[9] Tell me about yourself—and above all do not dream of my using you as food for speculation: that is simply a morbid suspicion: I like to hear all about you because I am fond of you.

Good bye again—   your incorrigible and affectionate

                                                              M. A.

My father's journals are out—they are a mere bookseller's catchpenny, in my judgment: but they are a convenient size—but there is nothing new in them.[10]

MS. Yale University.

1. John Philpot Curran (1750–1817: *DNB*), Irish barrister and judge, said this in his defense of Archibald Hamilton Rowan: "This is the kind of subject which I feel myself overawed when I approach. There are certain fundamental principles which nothing but necessity should expose to a public examination; they are pillars, the depth of whose foundation you cannot explore without endangering their strength" (quoted by Lowry, p. 137, from *Speeches of John Philpot Curran*, New York, 1911, pp. 68–69.) See also Super 5:467.

2. *Philisterey* (for *philisterei*), David DeLaura's correction of Lowry's reading *philistercy*, meaning philistinism, narrow-mindedness, pedantry.

3. The former Emma Hutton (daughter of Robert Hutton, Putney Park, Surrey), who married Lingen in 1852, a "great friend" of Blanche Smith (later, Mrs Clough).

4. Charles Cotton's translation of Montaigne's *Essays* (1685). Clough, having rejected North's translation (from the French) of Plutarch and incorporated George Long's, used the so-called Dryden Plutarch: "The present translation is a revision of that published at the end of the seventeenth century, with a life of Plutarch written by Dryden, whose name it was presumed, would throw some reflected lustre on the humbler workmen who performed, better or worse, the more serious labour" (Katherine Chorley, *Arthur Hugh Clough*, p. 279n). Clough had asked Blanche Smith to send a sample sheet of the translation to "Matt Arnold to be criticized by him" (Mulhauser, 2:413).

5. Théodore de La Villemarqué's articles in the *Revue de Paris* on "Les Poèmes Gallois et les romans de la Table Ronde," which "treat of Fauriel's work and give the story of Tristram and Iseult, principally in the first article." (See *Revue de Paris*, 3d ser. 34 [1841]: 262–82, 335–58.) "Arnold says his account of Merlin and Vivien came from Malory, but there are two articles which may have helped him"—La Villemarqué's "Visite au tombeau de Merlin," *Revue de Paris*, 2d ser., 41 (1837):45–62, and Louandre's "L'Enchanteur Merlin," *Revue de Paris*, 3d ser., 16 (1840):109–42 (Lowry, p. 137). For Fauriel see below Appendix B.

6. "Sohrab and Rustum"; "pain and grief" is from Psalm 39:3, *Book of Common Prayer*.

7. Arnold combines the *Book of Common Prayer* and Shakespeare—"Morning Prayer, A General Confession" ("We have left undone those things which we ought to have done; And we have done those things which we ought not to have done") and *Hamlet* 3.1.56.

8. He had read the extracts in Forster's review (see above p. 261).

9. Super's emendations of Arnold's syntactical oversight "as he turned his sheet of paper" (Allott-Super, p. 570).

10. *Thomas Arnold's Travelling Journals*, ed. A. P. Stanley (1852).

To Mary Penrose Arnold*

Hampton
My dearest Mother   Monday, [May 9, 1853]

You have not heard from me for a very long time—but Flu has told you of dear Baby's attacks.[1] He has had no more of them, and is now down here for a week and doing very well though looking delicate. He can now sit by himself on the floor and will I think walk at a year old, though we doubt whether his ancles are not a little weak. He has left off his knitted jackets in which he looked like a little skinned ape and wears braided brown holland pinafores with long sleeves over his frock, in which he looks very pretty, though they are still too large for him. He has also begun to wear shoes and stockings—the prettiest little black shoes in the world with immense bows, and his legs now look smaller than ever.

Poor Flu has been in misery from tooth ache for some time past: all yesterday she was in bed and at this present writing (12 ½ p. m.) is still there, but is soon to get up, being better. I think she will have to lose the tooth, though: under chloroform, because she dreads the operation so much, and in her state I dread it too for her: and her head being very good and her nerves not irritable I do not think her a bad subject for chloroform.

I for my part am very well, and from tooth ache, my old enemy, have been for some time past remarkably free. All my spare time has been spent on a poem which I have just finished,[2] and which I think by far the best thing I have yet done—and that it will be generally liked—though one can never be sure of this. I have had the greatest pleasure in composing it—a rare thing with me, and, as I think, a good test of the pleasure what you write is likely to afford to others: but then the story is a very noble and excellent one. Fan I am sure will be delighted with it and K.

I have settled with Fellowes to publish this and one or two more new ones with the most popular of the old ones, next winter or spring, with a preface and my name.[3] I never felt so sure of myself, or so *really* & *truly* at ease as to criticism, as I have done lately.—There is an article on me in the last N. British which I will send you.[4]—Can it be by Blackie? I think Froude's review will come sooner or later, but at *present* even about this I feel indifferent. Miss Blackett[5] told Flu that Ld John Russell said "in his opinion Matthew Arnold was the one rising young poet of the present day." This pleased me greatly from Lord John—if it is true.[6]

You ask about Alexander Smith. There are beautiful passages in him—but I think it doubtful how he will turn.

Here is a long letter and all about myself. However you will like that. Flu and [?]Trot[7] send their love.   Ever your most affectionate

M. A.

Love to Willy's family.[8] She will not have twins, you will see. People with bad figures always [?]will [?]seem [?]immense [?]in size. How does the pupil succeed? Write to me in *London.*

MS. Balliol College.

1. Tommy's.
2. "Sohrab and Rustum."
3. *Poems: A New Edition* (Nov. 1853).
4. "Glimpses of Poetry," *North British Review* 19 (May 1853):209–18, was not by John Stuart Blackie (1809–95: *DNB*), the Scottish professor, translator, and writer, to whom there are letters later, but by George David Boyle (*Wellesley,* 1:1193).
5. John Blackett's sister, Frances Mary (later, Fanny du Quaire), whose name occurs often in Arnold's letters and diaries (see above p. 75 n. 1).
6. Lord John Russell became foreign secretary in the earl of Aberdeen's cabinet in

Dec. 1852, but, though remaining in the cabinet "without office," was replaced in Feb. by the earl of Clarendon. In June 1854 he became Lord President of Council and in Jan. 1855 resigned.

    7. "Trot": Tommy?

    8. William Delafield Arnold married Frances Anne Hodgson (1824/1825–58) in India in Apr. 1850. They had four children, all of whom were adopted by the Forsters after William's death in Apr. 1859 and later assumed the name Arnold-Forster: Edward Penrose (b. Aug. 1851); Florence Mary (1854–1936); Hugh Oakeley (1855–1909); and Frances Egerton (1857–1921). He returned to England for three years on sick leave in Jan. 1853. This letter suggests that his wife miscarried before October. (See Woodward, pp. 180–228; Arnold-Forster, pp. 531–32.) Lady Lawrence, wife of Sir Henry Lawrence, the Lahore Resident, wrote to Mrs Arnold (whom she had visited at Fox How in 1847) in Feb. 1850, to assure (or reassure) her that William, only 21, had chosen an acceptable bride: "Your son might have searched India through and not found another girl of Miss Hodgson's stamp, and this I say after months of almost daily intercourse with her" (*The Right Honourable Hugh Oakeley Arnold-Forster: A Memoir*, by His Wife, p. 7; Maud Diver, *Honoria Lawrence: A Fragment of Indian History*, 1936, p. 328; Woodward, p. 195; and below pp. 333–34 n. 8).

To Mary Penrose Arnold*

Louth

My dearest Mother   Tuesday night, [July 12, 1853][1]

    I got back to London on Saturday, and got your letter yesterday, it having been forwarded to me from Boston. This morning I again left London, and having been busy all the afternoon at Boston, have come on here tonight, as I have a large school here tomorrow. I like this place—it is so entirely an old country town; and it is in nearly the best part of Lincolnshire: I have been shaking off the burden of the day by a walk tonight along the Market Rasen road, over the skirts of the wolds, between hedges full of elder blossom and white roses. And the spire of Louth church comes everywhere into the view so beautifully.

    I have been reading Margaret Fuller again, and been greatly struck with her sincere striving to be good and helpful. Her address to the poor women in the Penitentiary is really beautiful. "Cultivate the spirit of prayer. I do not mean agitation and excitement, but a deep desire for truth, purity, and goodness, and you will daily learn how near He is to every one of us."[2] Nothing can be better than that.

    This is only a line to thank you for your letter, and to give a sign of life. Your money matters are better than I expected. It is affecting what you say about Walter,[3] but perhaps he can hardly feel too much and too bitterly. It will be good for him in the long run.

    Is Edward still at Florence?[4] I want to write to him. There is a *chance* of his getting the curacy of Littleton.—Dear little Tom is very well, but, owing to his being [supposed] not to cry, rather spoiled. He has no notion at present that he is not to have whatever he wants instantly. But he has a sweet little face.—I think K looking better. I long to be at Fox How with you. God bless you, my dearest mother.   Ever your most affectionate son,

M. A.—

I return to town on Friday. I have directed the Times to be sent straight to you for the present. I am afraid you have had it irregularly lately owing to my erratic life.

MS. Balliol College.

1. The 1853 diary confirms the peregrinations and dates (Guthrie 2:44); elder blossoms in early summer and Tennyson's Lady Godiva (obviously in warm weather) saw "The white-flowered elder thicket."
2. See above p. 258.
3. See below p. 277.
4. Edward had been ordained by the bishop of Oxford in 1852 (he became a school inspector in Apr. 1854). Fanny Lucy Arnold's sister Caroline Wightman in 1845 married Peter A. L. Wood (1816–97), curate of Littleton, Middlesex (where his father was rector), from 1843, who moved to Devizes in 1853, leaving a possible opening for Edward Arnold (Hopkinson, pp. 41–42; *Annual Register*, 1856; and Harding, pp. 30–31.)

To Arthur Hugh Clough

Penrhyn Arms, Bangor
My dear Clough   Wednesday night, [July 27, 1853]
    I sincerely wish you were here. To be amongst Tals and Pens and Llans makes my thoughts turn to you at once—and you would so like being here, I know.—I wonder if a house I observed at Colwyn today was your Aunt's.[1]
    I read with great pleasure last night in bed your article on Social Theories.[2] Much of it was truly noble, and well written. But you have yet to learn a sort of literary economy, which forbids to *gaspiller* your treasures. Choose, as far as you can, *adequate subjects*, and put your mark upon them. But I have more and more respect for your literary ability, and wholesome abundance, so unlike the strangled poverty stricken driblets of some of us.
    Now you are again in London, cultivate all sorts of acquaintances, your Lewises and all.[3] It is one of your best circumstances that you get on with these men and that they like you. And their acquaintance is almost indispensable for a practical acquaintance with these times.
    I said nothing while we were together about the subject of your letters—or many of them—because I thought there was no need so to do. We will leave the past to itself—for the present I can sincerely say that I never felt

more strongly than now—or so strongly—how close I am to you—and, in my own feeling, to you alone.

Let me know how you start. I am inclined to think you will toss off the work very easily.[4] £300 a year, got without grimacing or false pretences, is something certainly which deserves respect, and attention before one rejects it.

You will laugh if I tell you I am deplorably ennuyé. I seem to myself to have lost all ressort—

> For whom each year we see
> Breeds new beginnings, disappointments new—[5]

One gets tired at last of one's own elasticity.

Write to me at the Beaumaris Post office.   Ever your's affectionately
                                                                                                    M. A.

MS. Yale University.

1. Clough had four aunts: Ann Jemima, Catherine, Martha Matilda, Anna Maria (*Landed*).

2. On Charles Eliot Norton's book "Considerations on Some Recent Social Theories," *North American Review* 77 (July 1853): 106–17—the issue that included Clough's "Recent English Poetry" (see above p. 246 n. 2)—reprinted partially in Clough's *Poems and Prose Remains* (1869), 1:409–17, and *Prose Remains* (1888), 405–12, and complete in Buckner B. Trawick's *Selected Prose Works of Arthur Hugh Clough* (1964), pp. 258–69.

3. George Cornewall Lewis, editor of *Edinburgh Review*.

4. Clough reached England about July 10 and (as he wrote to Emerson) had accepted an "Examinership in the Education department of the Council Office, Salary 300£ a year, work 6 hours a day" (Mulhauser, 2:457).

5. "The Scholar-Gipsy," ll. 176–77 (Allott, p. 355).

To Arthur Hugh Clough

Barmouth
August 3, [1853]

Well my dear Clough you should have been with me tonight to see the sunset of our first fine day over the great Carnarvonshire promontory. What an outline is that! The most accurate lurid[1] Mediterranean thing in these islands, eh?

If you knew the refreshment it was to me to think of you in London again. Froude expressed himself warmly on this head yesterday. He dined with us at Beddgelert (Flu & me) as we passed through yesterday. I stay with him for two days a fortnight hence—perhaps ascend Snowdon by night with him. He is *softened* more than I can tell you, but I think in baddish spirits. Kingsley has been staying with him. His poem is in hexameters, and on *Per-*

*seus & Andromeda.*² Eh? Froude says much of it is very good. Now I think, a priori, the man is too *coarse a workman* for poetry.

I have written out my Sohrab & Rustum, and like it less. —Composition, in the painter's sense—that is the devil. And, when one thinks of it, our painters cannot *compose* though they can show great genius—so too in poetry is it not to be expected that in this same article of *composition* the awkward incorrect Northern nature should shew itself? though we may have feeling—fire—eloquence—as much as our betters.

I am trying to re-read Valentine—but stick—except in the scenery bits.³ I am beginning the Tempest. How ill he often writes! but how often too how incomparably!

Write to me at Beaumaris my dear. Perhaps you have: I have been away these three days.

See that the Minutes for last year are sent to the *Holyhead & Dyffryn* schools.⁴ Tell me about your work.   Your affectionate

M. A.

Read the details about poor Keats at the end of Haydon's first and the beginning of his second vol. Haydon himself is a false *butcher*—revolting.⁵

MS. Yale University.

1. The word could be read as "lucid" (which has been suggested) or, equally, "livid," but "lurid" was Arnold's sunset epithet: "the sun / Went lurid down o'er flooded plains" ("Resignation," ll. 10–11); "the sun went lurid down" ("Balder Dead," l. 194).

2. *Andromeda and Other Poems* was published in 1858.

3. George Sand's novel (1832), recalled nostalgically in the essay "George Sand" (1877; Super, 8:216–36, esp. pp. 220, 224).

4. Where Arnold was to be on Aug. 8 and 10.

5. Benjamin Robert Haydon (1786–1846: *DNB*), historical painter and friend of Keats, died a suicide. *The Life of Benjamin Robert Haydon, from His Autobiography and Journals*, ed. Tom Taylor (1853), recorded of Keats that "for six weeks he was scarcely sober and . . . he once covered his tongue with Cayenne pepper, in order to appreciate the 'delicious coldness of claret in all its glory,' " a passage that Arnold cited in his essay "John Keats" in 1880 (Super, 9:205–16) and that outraged others as well as Arnold. Charles Cowden Clarke, for instance, called the passage "mean-spirited and trumpery twaddle" (*The Keats Circle*, ed. Hyder Edward Rollins, 1:264; see also 1:xcii).

To Arthur Hugh Clough

Fox How

My dear Clough   August 25, [1853]

Here I am at last nearly stupefied by 8 months inspecting. However I am in better health than usual thanks to knocking about in open cars in

Wales. Several of the Welsh Managers are complaining that they have not got the last volumes of Minutes—will you just ask how this is.

I should like you to see Froude—quantum mutatus! He goes to church, has family prayers—says the Nemesis ought never to have been published &c. &c.—his friends say that he is altogether changed and re-entered within the giron de l'Eglise—at any rate within the giron de la religion chrétienne: but I do not see the matter in this light and think that he conforms in the same sense in which Spinoza advised his mother to conform—and having purified his moral being, all that was mere fume and vanity and love of notoriety and opposition in his proceedings he has abandoned and regrets. This is my view. He is getting more and more literary, and vise au solide instead of beating the air.[1] May we all follow his example!

Did I tell you he dislikes all Hexameters. I repeated to him some I thought my best—he said he thought they were as good as any, but not the thing.[2]

William Forster who has been very ill is here. They think here that your article on me is obscure and peu favorable—but I do not myself think either of these things. I told you Froude says he can certainly review me in January.[3]

He recommends prefacing Tristram & Iseult with an extract from Dunlop's Hist. of fiction to tell the story, in preference to telling it in my own words: thus also to preface Mycerinus with a literal translation of the passage of Herodotus which concerns him. I think this is good advice. He rather discounsels from a preface, but I shall try my hand at it, at any rate, I think. I thought of a division of the poems according to their character and subjects, into Antiquity—Middle Age—& Temps Moderne—but this also he dissuades from.[4] What do you think?

Write me a good long letter and not a scrubby scrap. Tell me how you get on.   ever your's

M. A.

MS. Yale University.

1. For James Anthony Froude and *The Nemesis of Faith* see above p. 145 n. 2. "Quantum mutatus [ab illo . . .]," how changed [from that Hector], *Aeneid* 2.274; "giron de l'église," bosom of the church; "vise au solide," aiming at something substantial; "beating the air," 1 Corinthians 9:26.

2. Arnold's only hexameters appear to be "Translations from Homer" (Allott, pp. 504–7), of which the date of composition is unknown, published in *On Translating Homer* (1860).

3. For Clough's article see above p. 246 n. 2; for Froude's, above p. 262 n. 1.

4. Arnold followed Froude's counsel but, happily disregarding his "discounsel," wrote the famous Preface (Super, 1:2–15). See above p. 266.

To Thomas Longman[1]

T. Longman Esqre   Fox How, Ambleside
Dear Sir   August 27, 1853
I had the pleasure of meeting you once or twice at Mr Price's during
last spring, and I hope you will allow me to avail myself of that introduction
in now addressing you.

I published anonymously in 1849 a volume of poems with the title of
"The Strayed Reveller and other Poems." I published another volume—
"Empedocles on Etna and other Poems"—in the winter of last year. Both
were undertaken by Mr Fellowes of Ludgate Street at his own risk.

The first of these volumes has now paid its expenses—the second has
not yet done so. As however the sale of both volumes appears to be injured
by their being anonymous, and as they both contain several poems not likely
to be popular, I wish now to publish a new volume, bearing my name, to
consist of those poems of the previous volumes which have been the most
liked, together with a new poem which I think more likely to be popular
than any of those which I have hitherto published.

I should be extremely glad, on every account, if you would consent to
undertake this new volume. As Mr Fellowes objected that it would render
unsaleable the volume last published, I have offered to pay him the outlay
incurred by him on that volume, and to cancel what copies remain of it, and
of the previous volume.

I really think that such a volume as I now propose to form would sell, if
brought out by you and published with my name. I may mention perhaps
that Mr Froude whose name you probably know proposes to review it, when
it appears, in the Westminster. And he and many others with whom I have
spoken on the subject agree in thinking that my name would be of considerable advantage to the sale of the new volume, independently of its own
merits, from the interest attaching to my father.

As I know that a volume of poems is a hasardous undertaking, I shall
not be the least surprized if you decline to undertake mine at your own risk:
but as I am very desirous to give the present volume the advantage of being
brought out by your house, I hope that in that case you would still consent
to publish it for me at my own expense.

A letter will find me at this place for the next week, and I remain, dear
Sir,   your's faithfully

M. Arnold.—

MS. University of Reading.

1. Thomas Longman (1804–79: *DNB*) had succeeded as head of the famous and
venerable firm in 1842, which lost no luster under him. The manuscript is docketed:

"only on Com[missio]n." Arnold was of course small beer, and he is not mentioned in Harold Cox and John E. Chandler, *The House of Longman* (1925). They came to terms and Longman published *Poems*, 1853—see below p. 274.

To Arthur Hugh Clough

Fox How
My dear Clough   September 6 [1853]
   When more than one Candidate is examined you shall have all the papers; but it continually happens that for one vacancy only one Candidate is examined, and it would not do to insist upon having a spare candidate to fall back upon *in case* the successful one afterwards miscarried, as a boy who is examined is always disapppointed if he is not taken.
   Blackett is here, and goes on Thursday. I have sent him this evening to a ball with my sisters—it is a great pleasure having him here. Conington and Goldwin Smith are reading at Grasmere and dine with us tomorrow. Goldwin Smith has the funereal solemnity of an undertaker: I suppose he caught it from Conington. They are working hard at an edition of Virgil.
   If you have opportunity look at an article on India in *August's* Fraser. It is by my brother Willy, but do not mention this. It is poor in ideas, but see if you do not think the style very vigorous[1].
   London must be getting awful, and I suppose you have no chance of leaving it. Sandford's return will be a godsend—he is a far better fellow than Lingen and has real geniality—remember me to him particularly.[2] Lingen I think a bore.
   As to conformity I only recommend it in so far as it frees us from the unnatural and unhealthy attitude of contradiction and opposition—the *Qual der Negation* as Goethe calls it.[3] Only positive convictions and feelings are worth anything—and the glow of these one can never feel so long as one is pugnacious and out of temper. This is my firm belief.
   I do not believe that the Reformation caused the Elizabethan literature—but that both sprang out of the active animated condition of the human spirit in Europe at that time. After the fall of the Roman Empire the barbarians powerfully turned up the soil of Europe—and after a little time when the violent ploughing was over and things had settled a little, a vigorous crop of new ideas was the result. Italy bore the first crop—but the soil having been before much exhausted soon left bearing. The virgin soils of Germany and England went on longer—but they too are I think beginning to fail. I think there never yet has been a perfect literature or a perfect art because the energetic nations spoil them by their illusions and their want of taste—and the nations who lose their illusions lose also their energy and creative power.

Certainly Goethe had all the *negative* recommendations for a perfect artist but he wanted the *positive*—Shakspeare had the positive and wanted the negative. The Iliad and what I know of Raphael's works seem to me to be in a juster measure and a happier vein than anything else.

If one loved what was beautiful and interesting in itself *passionately* enough, one would produce what was excellent without troubling oneself with religious dogmas at all. As it is, we are *warm* only when dealing with these last—and what is frigid is always bad. I would have others—most others stick to the old religious dogmas because I sincerely feel that this *warmth* is the great blessing, and this frigidity the great curse—and on the old religious road they have still the best chance of getting the one and avoiding the other.   ever your's

M. A.

Republish at Boston by all means.

MS. Yale University.

    1. "What Is the Indian Question?" *Fraser's Magazine* 48 (1853):234–48, by William Delafield Arnold (Lowry), who had returned to England, on sick leave, a few months earlier, who lectured at Kendal and Ambleside on India (and other subjects), and who "wrote a series of articles about [the Indian Mutiny] which appeared anonymously in *Fraser's Magazine* from December 1857 to December 1858" (Woodward, pp. 200, 215).

    2. For Lingen see above p. 118, for Sandford above p. 229. Both submerged themselves in their careers, so remarkably parallel, far more than Arnold ever thought of doing (and both were rewarded), but Arnold was much closer to Sandford than to Lingen, whose impersonality seems by comparison almost Kafkaesque. Lowry's note (p. 143) is off the mark.

    3. Untraced.

To Thomas Longman

Fox How, Ambleside
My dear Sir   September 29, 1853
    I am much obliged to you for your letter of yesterday's date.[1] The type of the specimen page (which I return) will I think do very well.

    I have written to Mr Froude to say that I could publish in October if in that case his article could appear in January's Westminster: if it cannot at any rate appear till April, I have told him that I shall wait till November to publish. As soon as I hear from him I will write to you, but I suppose there is no reason why we should not begin to print at once. I remain, my dear Sir,   your's truly

M. Arnold.—

I think 750 copies will be enough to print—I am glad you think I may publish the book at 5s/—I think the price of the last (6s/ for a volume of 240 pages) was an obstacle to its sale.

MS. *University of Reading.*

1. See above p. 272.

To Rosella Pitman [1]

Miss Pitman   Fox How, Ambleside
Dear Madam   October 1,1853
    The Examination in your school will in future take place in May or June. I am afraid you must wait till that time for another Pupil Teacher—unless indeed (which I do not recollect) you had a candidate at my last visit who was examined, but rejected at the Council Office on the ground of numbers: such a candidate might now be admitted in place of the one you have lost, on application at the Council Office, as they have probably kept her Examination paper.   I am, dear Madam,   faithfully yours
M. Arnold.—

MS. *I. J. Pitman.*

    1. Sister of Isaac Pitman (1813–97: *DNB*; knt 1894), inventor of phonography (a highly successful system of shorthand), she was mistress of Bethnal Green Abbey Street School from Mar. 1849, and was certified in Apr. 1851, by the Privy Council on Education. Arnold's inspection reports are inscribed on the official "Schoolmistresses Certificate" (photocopy, U.Va.) in 1854–58, 1860, 1864–71. His last report reads: "This school ranks with the one or two very best girls' schools I have ever known, and I take leave of it with great regret. *Matthew Arnold.—*"

To Arthur Hugh Clough

                                     Derby
My dear Clough   October 10, [1853]
    I am greatly a debtor both to you and to Poste [1] for your trouble, although you have not found my passage. But never mind—I have boldly quoted it from memory—it consists only of a single line.
    Forgive my scold the other day—when one is trying to emerge to hard land it is irritating to find your friend not only persisting in "weltering to the parching wind" [2] himself, but doing his best to pull you back into the Sea also.
    The Preface is done—there is a certain *Geist* in it I think, but it is far

less *precise* than I had intended. How difficult it is to write prose: and why? because of the *articulations of the discourse*: one leaps these over in Poetry—places one thought cheek by jowl with another without introducing them and leaves them—but in prose this will not do. It is of course not right in poetry either—but we all do it: you meant something of this in your expression about *sequence* in that article, which struck me as a lovely aperçu when I read it.[3]

I am here for 6 weeks, busy enough—I really think the new volume will do—but time will shew.

Imagine a claim from Oriel for £30 caution money. What on earth is to be done.   ever your's affectionately

M. Arnold.—

Pray thank Poste again for me.

MS. Yale University.

1. Edward Poste (see above p. 202 n. 12), whom Arnold and Clough would have known at Oriel College when all three were fellows in the forties. The unidentified passage, in the 1853 Preface, could be the one almost attributed to Aristotle ("All depends upon the subject"—Super, 1:7).
2. Milton, "Lycidas," l. 13,
3. "It may be the fault of our point of view; but certainly we do not find even here that happy, unimpeded sequence which is the charm of really good writers" (Clough on Alexander Smith's "A Life-Drama," in *North America Review* rpt in *Selected Prose Works*, ed. Trawick, p. 167); but he had earlier (p. 156) mentioned Arnold's "passing without notice from Tristram's dramatic musings and talkings, to his own not more coherent narrative."

To Jane Arnold Forster

Burslem

My darling K   October 31, 1853

Excuse this scrap—I write from a school. Mary[1] told you it was impossible for me to come on Saturday—I was in London. I am very busy for this next month, but I earnestly desire to see you. I am grieved at what you say of the bad prospects of trade for the winter in your letter to Mary—how the *cares* of life deepen about one: after 30 one understands why the ancients, with their strong practical sense, talk so perpetually about *Cura*—it is a better word than sorrows and miseries and all the modern more sentimental expressions—*Cares* is just what it is.—My very kindest love to William.

[illeg. wd][2] I am quite vexed that [?]Mary Burbury[3] (entirely without my knowledge) should have proposed William's asking Ludlow to review me. I would never ask any man to review me (Froude proposed it) and to ask Ludlow who I believe is the author of a precious piece of ⟨K⟩cant in the N. British which I have attacked in the preface, would be preposterous. You— Froude—Shairp—I believe the list of those whose reading of me I anticipate with any pleasure stops there or thereabouts. There is only one *esoteric* poem in this collection:[4] only one, that is, calculated to interest none but the writer and a few esprits maladifs: you, who are not an esprit maladif, will nevertheless discover it and read it for my sake.—The preface, I think, will stand. I am anxious for William to read that.

All doing very well at Derby. I think of having Walter there, and putting him to a tutor.   ever your most affectionate brother

M. A.—

MS. Frederick Whitridge.

1. Mary Twining, their sister.
2. The word (which looks like "Paget") has been lined through, as have "Mary" in the next line and both instances of "Ludlow." John Malcolm Forbes Ludlow (1821–1911: *DNB*), social reformer, Christian Socialist, and writer, friend of Charles Kingsley, Tom Hughes, and F. D. Maurice, was *not* the perpetrator of the "precious piece of ⟨K⟩cant," "Theories of Poetry and a New Poet [Alexander Smith]" in *North British Review* Aug. 1853; the author was in fact David Masson (1822–1907: *DNB*), professor of English literature, University College, London, 1853–65, and then at Edinburgh University, biographer, editor of *Macmillan's Magazine*, 1859–67 (see Super, 1:221–23, 11:518). His prescient claim that poetry was "sublimated biography," "a true allegory of the state of one's mind," fell afoul of Arnold's most cherished critical principles in the 1853 Preface, a last-ditch stand against history (and his own practice), just as the real Ludlow's attack on Victor Hugo fell afoul of Swinburne's in 1859–60 (Swinburne, 1:32–33).
3. Unidentified.
4. The new poems are "Sohrab and Rustum," "Philomela," "Thekla's Answer," "The Church of Brou," and "The Neckan," not one of which can be ruled out. Arnold does not use the words *esoteric* or *esprits maladifs* elsewhere in these letters.

To Mary Penrose Arnold

London
My dearest Mother   November 9, 1853

You will have received six copies of my new volume. Will you give one to Mrs Wordsworth from me, telling her that I send it her for the sake of the Memorial verses, imperfect tribute as they are: one to Mrs Fletcher—and send one, as soon as you have an opportunity, to dear Tom. You see the first series was evidently *not* sent to him. You will have three copies left for yourself and for Fox-How. I have sent the book to Uncle Trevenen and to the Bucklands.

I think the book will hold me, in public repute, pretty much at the point where the last left me—not advance me and not pull me down from it. If so it was worth publishing, for I shall probably make something by the poems in their present shape, whereas if I had left them as they were, I should have continued to make nothing. The war and the great length of time that has passed since most of the poems in this collection were written makes me myself regard it with less interest than I should have thought possible.

I am not very well lately—have had one or two things to bother me—and more and more have the feeling that I do not do my inspecting work really well and satisfactorily—but I have also lately had a stronger wish than usual not to vacillate and be helpless, but to do my duty, whatever that may be: and out of that wish one may always hope to make something.

God bless you my dearest Mother. The children[1] are both quite well. The old nurse leaves us on Monday. Deane[2] is not satisfactory, perhaps, but I think this—every month we keep her she becomes less necessary to Toddy—and by the time she ought to go he will be able to spare her.   Your most affectionate son,

M. A.

MS. Frederick Whitridge.

1. Trevenen William ("Budge") was born on Oct. 15.
2. Payments to Deane (always a mononym) are noted in the diaries till Dec. 19, 1856. "Toddy" is Tom, the older son.

To Elizabeth Cleghorn Gaskell[1]

Mrs Gaskell   Derby
Dear Madam   November 18, 1853
It is always agreeable to try to repay, in however slight a degree, the pleasure one has received; and I was so much gratified to hear from my Mother, that you, whose books had given me such sincere delight, had found pleasure in reading some of my Poems, that I have ventured, although personally unacquainted with you, to send you a volume in which they are for the first time collected with my name.

I hope you will not be repelled from the first poem of the collection by its Eastern names;[2] for I think you will find the story a very human one.   Believe me, dear Madam, with sincere gratitude and respect, ever faithfully yours,

M. Arnold.—

MS. John Rylands University Library of Manchester.

1. Elizabeth Cleghorn Gaskell (1810–65: *DNB*), the novelist and friend and biographer of Charlotte Brontë, knew the Fox How family if not Arnold himself (see above p. 180).

2. "Sohrab and Rustum."

To John Duke Coleridge

Derby

My dear Coleridge   November 22, 1853

I am just starting on a journey, but I must write one line to say how much pleasure your letter has given me.

Send anything for me to the Council office; it will be forwarded.

I have not time to defend Sohrab and Rustum—but Homer sows his [?]similes very thick at times: look at the 2nd book of the Iliad, line 455, and on from there. Virgil does not, but his manner is different altogether.

I think it is certainly true about the Miltonic air of parts of it—but Milton is a sufficiently great master to imitate—the cranes are not taken direct from him,[1] as far as I can remember, but the passage is no doubt an imitation of his Manner—so with many others. Tennyson is another thing—but one has him so in one's head one cannot help imitating him sometimes: but except in the last 2 lines I thought I had kept him out of Sohrab and Rustum.[2] Mark any other places you notice—for I should wish to alter such.

frore is (I believe) *frozen*—the German participle *gefrorenes*.

The motto is a fragment by Choerilus of Samos.[3] I think you will end by liking Sohrab & Rustum best—not from any merit of mine in it, but from the incomparable beauty and nobleness of the story. I wish you would get your father to look at it in some spare half hour.

I have just heard that *Goldwin Smith* wrote that notice of Poems by A which no doubt you saw in the Times.[4]   In great haste your's,

M. Arnold.—

So you don't agree with the preface?
Excuse the official envelope—I have no other at hand.

MS. Baron Coleridge.

1. "Sohrab and Rustum," ll. 111–16, *Paradise Lost* 7.425–31.

2. Lowry (p. 145n) compares "Morte D'Arthur," ll. 192–93, but the conclusion (ll. 265–72) seems a nearer likeness. See next letter.

3. The motto to *The Strayed Reveller, and Other Poems*, printed (with E. H. Coleridge's translation) in Allott, p. 680. J. D. Coleridge reviewed this volume in the *Christian Remembrancer*, Apr. 1854 (rpt Dawson, pp. 96–113).

4. *The Times*, Nov. 4, 1853, p. 5, two and a half columns of mingled praise and

censure, including the statement that Arnold "is a good deal influenced by Tennyson, and he is in danger of inheriting some of that poet's faults."

To Arthur Hugh Clough

Derby

My dear Clough   November 25, [18]53

Just read through Tennyson's Morte d'Arthur and Sohrab & Rustum one after the other, and you will see the difference in the *tissue* of the style of the two poems, and in its *movement*. I think the likeness, where there is likeness, (except in the two last lines which I own are a regular slip) [1] proceeds from our both having imitated Homer. But never mind—you are a dear soul. I am in great hopes you will one day like the poem—really like it. There is no one to whose aperçus I attach the value I do to yours—but I think you are sometimes—with regard to *me* especially—a little cross and wilful.

I send you two letters [2]—not that you may see the praise of me in them (and I can sincerely say that praise of *myself*—talking about imagination—genius and so on—does not give me, at heart, the slightest flutter of pleasure—seeing people interested in what I have made, does—) but that you may see how heartily two very different people seem to have taken to Sohrab and Rustum. This is something, at any rate. Hill's criticism is always delicate and good—and his style in prose has something of the beauty of his father in law's. [3] How well all the third page is written.

Return me the letters—write a line to P. O. Lincoln. I am worked to death. God bless you.   ever your's

M. A.

MS. Yale University.

1. See the preceding letter.
2. Probably, from Froude and Blackett (see below).
3. Herbert Hill, Jr, and Robert Southey.

To John Fenwick Burgoyne Blackett*

Lincoln

My dear Blackett   November 26, 1853

You knew, I am sure, what pleasure your letter would give me. I certainly was very anxious that you should like Sohrab and Rustum—Clough, as usual, remained in suspense whether he liked it or no: Lingen wrote me four sheets on behalf of sticking to modern subjects: but your letter, and one from Froude, (which I must send you, in spite of the praise) came to reassure me.

I still however think it very doubtful whether the book will succeed: the Leader and the Spectator are certain to disparage it; the Examiner *may* praise it, but will very likely take no notice at all: the great hope is that the Times may trumpet it once more.[1] Just imagine the effect of the last notice in that paper: it has brought Empedocles to the railway bookstall at Derby.

What you say about the similes looks very just upon paper: I can only say that I took a great deal of trouble to orientalize them, (the Bahrein diver[2] was originally an ordinary fisher) because I thought they looked strange, and jarred, if Western. But it is very possible you may be right.

I am worked to death just now, and have a horrid cold and cough: but at the end of next week I hope to get to town. We are not going to the sea after all—but are coming to Eaton Place (don't start, to No. 38)[3] for, I hope, two months.

I appreciated your sister's rancour. But mis-spelling (of *English* words— mis-spelling of French words, like your's sometimes, is mere ignorance, and demands compassion, not blame) is such an odious affectation that I always check it. But remember me affectionately to her.

So Parliament is at all events dumb till January.—Thank God. Ever, my dear Blackett, affectionately your's,

M. Arnold.—

Thank you again & again for your letter.—I don't know the [?]Pyrethra[4] man's address—no more does Flu, who sends her kindest remembrances.

MS. Balliol College.

1. See above p. 279.
2. "Sohrab and Rustum," ll. 284–90.
3. Where the Wightmans lived.
4. No such word—perhaps Arnold's mistake for *Pyrethrum*, the name of several plants, a medicine and an insecticide (*OED*).

To Arthur Hugh Clough

Coleby
My dear Clough   November 30, [1853]
I think "if indeed this one desire rules all"[1]—*is* rather Tennysonian— at any rate it is not good.

The resemblance in the other passage I cannot for the life of me see.

I think the poem has, if not the *rapidity*, at least the *fluidity* of Homer: and that it is in this respect that it is un Tennysonian: and that it is a sense of this which makes Froude and Blackett say it is a step in advance of Tennyson in this strain.

A thousand things make one compose or not compose: composition seems to keep alive in me a *cheerfulness*—a sort of Tuchtigheit, or natural soundness and valiancy, which I think the present age is fast losing—this is why I like it.

I am glad you like the Gipsy Scholar—but what does it *do* for you? Homer *animates*—Shakespeare *animates*—in its poor way I think Sohrab & Rustum *animates*—the Gipsy Scholar at best awakens a pleasing melancholy. But this is not what we want.

> The complaining millions of men
> Darken in labour and pain— [2]

what they want is something to *animate* and *ennoble* them—not merely to add zest to their melancholy or grace to their dreams.—I believe a feeling of this kind is the basis of my nature—and of my poetics.

You certainly do not seem to me sufficiently to desire and earnestly strive towards—assured knowledge—activity—happiness.

You are too content to *fluctuate*—to be ever learning, never coming to the knowledge of the truth. This is why, with you, I feel it necessary to stiffen myself—and hold fast my rudder.

My poems, however, viewed *absolutely*, are certainly little or nothing.

I shall be in town on Friday night I hope. I will then speak to you about Caroline Hall, the Derby P[upil]. T[eacher].[3]   Ever your's affectionately

M. Arnold.—

MS. Yale University.

1. "Sohrab and Rustum," l. 74, altered to "But, if this one desire indeed rules all."
2. "The Youth of Nature," ll. 51–52 (Allott, p. 258).
3. Not listed in White's *History, Gazetteer and Directory of the County of Derby* (1857).

To Jane Martha Arnold Forster

38, Eaton Place

My darling K   Sunday, [?December 4, 1853]

I seem to want to see *you* and be with *you* more than anyone when my Poems are making their way, or beginning to make it—you were my first hearer—you dear K—and such a sympathising—dear—animating hearer, too.

I should like, now, to go abroad—above all—to Rome—to live for some months quite quietly there—to see no English, and to hear nothing more about my Poems. It does me no good hearing the discussion of them— yet of course I cannot help being occupied by it. I intend soon to try and make some strong resolution in this respect—and *keep it.*

The Spectator elaborately and rather méchamment attacks—Rintoul himself was the "apparently intelligent critic." [1] Most of what he says is precisely what I do *not* believe. The Leader to my surprise behaves with extraordinary civility—one may say friendliness, though not committing itself too far. [2] The Press is very praising too—I am surprised at that also—but very glad. [3] The Examiner will probably come next week. I am very anxious to see that, as Ld Lansdowne and such as he, go mainly, I think, by what Forster says. [4]

I heard last night from Froude that Chapman had just written to him "begging for the article on me which he had twice refused." So it will appear in January. Whose doing is this? Greg's or William's? [5]

Love to William, who I hope is better. I shall send the newspapers containing notices home, so you can get from Mamma any you want to see.   Ever your own affectionate

M. A.

Eckermann [6] is I think certainly genuine, and most interesting. But read him in German—such beautiful easy German.

We are here for 2 months.

MS. Frederick Whitridge.

1. *Spectator,* Dec. 3, 1853, Supplement, pp. 5–6, to which Arnold replied in his brief "Preface to Second Edition of Poems (1854)" (Super 1:16–17, 224). Robert Stephen Rintoul (1787–1858: *DNB*) was the founder and editor of the *Spectator,* which reviewed Arnold Apr. 4, 1854.

2. *Leader,* Nov. 26 (and Dec. 3), 1853, by G. H. Lewes (rpt in Dawson, pp. 77–84).

3. Dec. 3, 1853, p. 736.

4. No review has been traced in the *Examiner,* of which John Forster was the editor (see above p. 262 n. 2) and which noticed William Arnold's novel *Oakfield* on Apr. 1, 1854 (p. 196).

5. Froude's article in the *Westminster Review,* Jan. 1854 (see above p. 262 n. 1).

6. *Conversations with Eckermann* had been published in 1850 in John Oxenford's translation.

William E. Forster to Ellis Yarnall

January 1, 1854
To-day is the break-up of a large family party. We have been ten brothers and sisters this last week under our mother Mrs. Arnold's roof; and most pleasant and refreshing it is to me to find myself—only son as I am—the member of so large and united a family, every member of which it is most pleasant for me to be with.

Text: Reid, 1:301.

To Charles Augustin Sainte-Beuve[1]

Privy Council Office, Londres.
Monsieur,   6 janvier 1854.
J'ai osé vous envoyer un recueil de mes poèmes, qui ont attiré dernièrement quelque attention ici, et dont on vient de parler dans la revue de Westminster et dans le Times.[2] En vous les envoyant je ne fais que vous restituer ce que je vous ai pris; puisque c'est dans une de vos charmantes Causeries que j'ai trouvé des renseignements sur l'épisode de la mort de Sohrab, qui m'ont donné le courage de commencer enfin mon poème.[3] J'en avais lu une notice très courte dans une note de l'histoire de Perse de Sir John Malcolm[4]; et je conçus alors le dessein de le mettre en vers; mais je me vis aussitôt forcé de renoncer, faute des détails nécessaires que je ne réussis à apprendre que plus tard, et en lisant votre article. Mon poème principal, donc, Monsieur, vous appartient en grande partie; mais si vous daignez le lire vous vous direz sans doute que, là aussi on voit trop clairement "de quelle hauteur la poésie épique, chez les modernes, est déchue"[5]—et vous vous soucierez peu d'y trouver quelque chose qui vous appartient. Et cependant, Monsieur, je vous l'envoie; non pas avec l'absurde prétention de vous charmer, mais tout simplement afin de vous dire avec quel plaisir je lis et relis continuellement, depuis bientôt cinq ans,[6] vos ouvrages de critique littéraire. Depuis la mort de Goethe vous êtes resté, selon moi, le seul guide et la seule espérance de ceux qui aiment surtout la vérité dans les arts et dans la littérature, et qui pourtant désirent trouver une critique vraie, naturelle et sérieuse—une critique possédant à fond la connaissance des choses littéraires et imbue d'un esprit essentiellement philosophique et européen. Pour moi, Monsieur, toutes les fois que le chagrin me prend en regardant la littérature de nos jours—avec ses productions hâtives et à peine ébauchées, avec son peu de savoir, avec son manque total de convenance et de mesure, avec son esprit de secte

étroit et inintelligent—je me rejette plus que jamais vers vous; et bien que vous ne parliez en général que de la littérature française, cependant, comme vous regardez toute chose d'un point de vue universel, tout le monde peut toujours trouver de l'instruction en vous lisant.

Il m'est impossible, Monsieur, en me servant d'une langue étrangère, de vous exprimer ma reconnaissance d'une manière assez vive et assez sincère—et j'aurais beaucoup préféré, en vous remettant mes poèmes, de vous écrire en anglais:[7] mais je me suis dit qu'enfin ce serait trop que de vous envoyer de la prose et de la poésie anglaise à la fois.

Si par hasard, Monsieur, après avoir jété les yeux sur ces vers, vous daigniez m'honorer de quelques mots de réponse,[8] vous pourriez me les adresser ici:—j'ai un emploi sous le Comité de l'Instruction Publique.   Agréez, Monsieur, mes hommages sincères et respectueux.

Matthew Arnold.—

MS. L'Institut de France.

1. Charles Augustin Sainte-Beuve (1804–69), a nasty, little, ugly, malicious, sexually deformed, half-man, half-toady, and whole scandal-monger, was France's greatest literary critic-historian and easily one of the most interesting of Arnold's acquaintances. Although they met personally only once (see below pp. 491, 495,) or possibly twice (Arnold had apparently called on Mar. 30, according to his diary), they were very much aware of each other, and their correspondence is gathered in these volumes. "I have learnt a great deal from him, and the news of his death struck me as if it had been that of some one very near to me," Arnold wrote (Oct. 16, 1869), and Arnold named him, with Goethe, Wordsworth, and Newman, as one of the "four people from whom I am conscious of having *learnt.*" Arnold paid his tuition charges in two excellent essays on Sainte-Beuve (Super, 8:304–9, 11:106–19), the former in the *Academy* in 1869, the latter in the *Encyclopædia Britannica* in 1886, and in both he particularizes his debt: Sainte-Beuve was "born a *naturalist,*" a searcher for the "real data," showing "Man as he is and as his history and the productions of his spirit show him"; he was a "great critic" because of his love of "truth and measure."

The relationship was first documented by Bonnerot, in an appendix, "Lettres inédites d'Arnold à Sainte-Beuve," which does him no honor. Details of its inadequacies can be found in R. H. Super's article "Documents in the Matthew Arnold—Sainte-Beuve Relationship," *Modern Philology* 60 (1963):206–10, and, with additional evidence, in *Album*, 23–24, 85.

2. See above pp. 250 n. 4, 279.

3. Sainte-Beuve's essay, "Le Livre des Rois, par le poète persan Firdousi, publié et traduit par M. Jules Mohl," was reprinted in *Causeries du lundi* (Dec. 1850) from the *Constitutionnel*, Feb. 1850 (Bonnerot, p. 518, and Allott, p. 320).

4. *History of Persia* (1815)—see Tinker and Lowry, pp. 75–77, and Allott, pp. 319–22.

5. From Sainte-Beuve's essay (Bonnerot, p. 518n).

6. See above p. 89 n. 4.

7. Unidiomatic—"préféré . . . vous écrire."

8. Sainte-Beuve's reply has not been traced, but Arnold refers to it below p. 295n.
(The extra accent, jêté, is Arnold's.)

To Jane Martha Arnold Forster*

London
My dearest K   February 27, 1854
So Mr. Forster is dead.[1] I do not know when I have been more affected
than in reading your letter. The lives and deaths of the "pure in heart" have,
perhaps, the privilege of touching us more deeply than those of others—
partly, no doubt, because with them the disproportion of suffering to desert
seems so unusually great. However, with them one feels—even I feel—that
for their purity's sake, if for that alone, whatever delusions they may have
wandered in, and whatever impossibilities they may have dreamed of, they
shall undoubtedly, in some sense or other, see God.
    My love to William; he knows how truly, by this time, he has made
relations of us all.   Ever your most affectionate
                                                        M. A.

Text. Russell, 1:38.

    1. On Jan. 27: "At the home of Samuel Law, in Knox county, East Tennessee,
North America [on an antislavery mission], in his 70th year, William Forster, of Norwich,
a wealthy and benevolent member of the Society of Friends, the contemporary and intimate associate of Elizabeth Fry, Sir Fowell Buxton, and Joseph John Gurney" (*Annual
Register*, 1854, p. 265). "Pure in heart": Matthew 5:8.

To Frances Lucy Wightman Arnold*

Sudbury
Tuesday, 6 P.M. [? March 14, 1854]
I got here a little before two, had a sandwich, and then went to the school.
I don't know why, but I certainly find inspecting peculiarly oppressive just
now; but I must tackle to, as it would not do to let this feeling get too strong.
All this afternoon I have been haunted by a vision of living with you at Berne,
on a diplomatic appointment, and how different that would be from this incessant grind in schools; but I could laugh at myself, too, for the way in which
I went on drawing out our life in my mind. After five I took a short walk, got
back to dinner at a quarter to six, dined, and started the pupil teachers, and am
just writing this to catch the post. Direct to me, P.O., Ipswich.

Text. Russell, 1:30–31.

To William Cox Bennett[1]

W. T.[*sic*] Bennett Esq: London
Dear Sir   July 15, 1854
    Pray accept my thanks for your Poems which have just reached me here, having been forwarded from Fox How—and for your letter which accompanied them and the kind expressions of interest which it contains. Believe me, dear Sir,   faithfully your's

                                      M. Arnold.—

MS. Munson-Williams-Proctor Institute.

    1. William Cox Bennett (1820–95: *DNB*), writer and poet, who later became a strong supporter of Gladstone and (probably not coincidentally) a member of the London Council of the Education League. (See Tennyson, 2:129, 531.) Bennett's *Poems* was published in 1850.

To Susanna Elizabeth Lydia Arnold Cropper

                                6, Esplanade, Dover
My dearest Susy   July 28, [1854]
    When are you and John likely to be starting for the Continent? or shall you not go at all this year? I am divided in wishing. I wish you to go because then we may see you here. Not to go—because then we may go together next year. Flu and I have just been across to Antwerp & Brussels for four days and a half, which was all we could afford—that cost us just £15. But, short as the excursion was, it was delightful—and we have firmly resolved to save our money from this time forth and to go abroad next year for six or seven weeks at least, if we live. Next year we shall be better off than this. And we have both agreed that there are no two people we should so much like to go with as you and John—we should all suit one another so well. So at any rate you must go again with us next year.
    Why should you not instead of going abroad this year come to this place, which is really charming, for three or four weeks. You have no notion, after your filthy Rampsides and Redcars, what a south of England watering place like this is. And the weather is charming, too. You might run over for a week or ten days to the Continent after we left Dover and then come to the North and we would have a delightful time together. I am sure you would like to see the two boys here and how they thrive and enjoy their little

lives.—Do come, you dear soul. Give our love to John. I am sure he would like best a foreign journey we all four made together.

I send you some letters you may like to see. Send them to Fan when you have read them. Have you got the cholera? I see it is at Liverpool. You are an idle girl and never write, even to   your affectionate eldest brother,

M. A.—

Now *do* come here.

MS. Frederick Whitridge.

To Wyndham Slade *

6 Esplanade, Dover
My dear Wyndham   July 28, 1854
The blue sky and the calm sea were too tempting when I came down here last week; so on Saturday we bolted, and returned yesterday, having been grilled alive, enjoyed ourselves immensely, spent £15, eaten one good dinner, and seen Brussels, Ghent, and Antwerp. Antwerp I had never seen, so we made that our object. I have so little money this year that I really could not have afforded to spend more than what I have spent on travelling, so I am glad that I went at once, when my work compelled me to be back in a few days, and did not wait till my holidays began, when I should certainly have gone farther, spent more money, and been more embarrassed than ever on my return.[1]

But we have both recorded a solemn vow, if we live, to spend at least seven weeks abroad next year, and to make all our arrangements, from this time forth,[2] in conformity with this resolution.

Antwerp is well worth seeing, though I hate poking about in the North. But Rubens's great pictures are there; and hardly Raphael himself is better worth seeing than Rubens at his best. If you have not yet seen the Descent from the Cross and the Crucifixion, go and see them.

Brussels I had often seen. It is a white, sparkling, cheerful, wicked little place, which, however, one finds rather good for one's spirits.

I must say the *ennui* of having to return is somewhat lessened by returning to this place, which is charming. You must come here. We are here for three weeks from next Monday.

Why has Frank Lawley given up his seat to go to Australia? Has he had a *malheur* upon the turf, or is it that he wants to learn politics in earnest?[3]   Write to me, you good soul, and believe me,   ever yours,

M. Arnold.

Flu's kindest remembrances to you—also Tom's—also Trevenen's. I have read the Vicomte de Launay.[4] The letters appeared first in the Constitution-nel or somewhere first. They are very readable.

Text. Russell, 1:38–39 (corected from MS by Kenneth Allott).

1. The 1854 diary has no entries from Thursday, July 20, through Tuesday, July 25.
2. "From this time forth for evermore," Psalms 113, 115, 121, also used in the letter preceding.
3. See above p. 167 n. 2.
4. *Lettres parisiennes* (1843), by Mme Emile de Girardin, first appeared as "a highly successful . . . weekly gossip column" in *La Presse*, 1836–39, under the pseudonym "Charles de Launay" (*OCFL*).

To Wyndham Slade*

6 Esplanade, Dover
My dear Wyndham   August 3, 1854
An agreeable letter of mine, relating all my recent doings, has probably by this time reached you. It was sent to Montys.[1] I shall not write it over again, but content myself with entreating you to beware of cholera.[2] Both the Wilts Yeomanry and the Somersetshire Militia are, I should think, very unfit to die.

I am very anxious to hear what it all is about young Lawley, but prob-ably being, like me, in the provinces, you are in the same benighted state as myself.

Tempests blow daily, and the boats come in in a filthy state from the habits of the passengers. It is a real pleasure to see the landings, day after day. In fact, it is so pleasant here that come you must; only give me a line to say when. All but a bed we can give you.   Ever yours,

M. A.

My love to J. D. Coleridge, and tell him that the limited circulation of the *Christian Remembrancer* makes the unquestionable viciousness of his article of little importance.[3] I am sure he will be gratified to think that it is so. This must go, for I am off to Canterbury.

Text. Russell, 1:39–40 (corrected from MS by Kenneth Allott).

1. Montys Court, Taunton, Somerset.
2. "This dreadful pestilence . . . raged with considerable violence in the summer quarter of this year, producing, in England and Wales, an excess of deaths above the av-erage of 21,607" (*Annual Register*, 1854, p. 159). See above p. 141.
3. See above p. 141.

To Frances Lucy Wightman Arnold*

Cavalry Barracks, Brighton
August 16, 1854.

I mean to sleep here to-night, instead of at Hastings, as it is very pleasant, and I think Henry likes my being here.[1] I have the rooms of a Sir Geo. Leith,[2] who is away at present, and am very comfortable. We dined last night at eight, only Henry, myself, and one other officer, Watson by name,[3] but it was extremely pleasant. We had a capital dinner, champagne and claret, and after dinner Henry and I played picquet, 6d. a game, the *parti* ending in my being winner of one sixpence. We did not go to bed till one o'clock. This morning I breakfasted alone in the messroom very comfortably, and was off to my school before any of them were up, getting back here about twelve, when I went to the stables and riding school with Henry, and was introduced to several officers. Captain Holden[4] came and lunched with us, and I found him very pleasant. The Colonel in command here,[5] Mr. Clayton,[6] and, I think, Watson again, dine to-night.

Text. Russell, 1:40–41.

1. Henry Roxby Benson (1818–92), Arnold's brother-in-law (see next letter), at this time captain in the 17th Light Dragoons or Lancers, had married Mary Henrietta Wightman in 1845. He had a meritorious career in the Crimea, beginning soon after the date of this letter, and later in India, went on half-pay in 1862, was promoted general in 1881, the year of his retirement. He was also a talented watercolorist. In Jan. 1874 (see below), Arnold introduced him by letter to G. M. Marsh, the American minister to Italy. See also Harding, pp. 50–55.

2. Sir George Hector Leith, from 1877 Leith-Buchanan (1833–1903; 4th bt), in the 17th Lancers, 1852–59, promoted captain in 1855. He owned about 2,000 acres in Dumbarton (*WWW*; Kelly; *Upper Ten Thousand*).

3. Perhaps John Watson, later General Sir John (1828/1829–1919; K.C.B. 1886), who saw service in India during three decades, was A.D.C to the queen 1870–81 (*Upper Ten Thousand*; Kelly; *WWW*).

4. Henry Holden (1824–98), of Holden Hall, or Palace House, Lancashire, captain, 13th Light Dragoons, later colonel, 13th Hussars (*Upper Ten Thousand*; *County Families*, 1904). In June 1854 he had married Eleanor Eliza White (daughter of Henry White, later 1st Baron Annaly) at St George's, Hanover Square (*Annual Register*).

5. James M'Queen (1798–1883), promoted major in the 15th Light Dragoons in 1841, placed on half-pay in 1842, promoted general in 1877 (Boase; *Upper Ten Thousand*). See the next letter.

6. (Sir) Fitz-Roy Augustus Talbot Clayton (1834–1913), of Fyfield House, Maidenhead, Berks, was the only son of the Rev. Augustus Clayton, Combe Bank, Kent (whose wife was the daughter of the dean of Salisbury). He seems to have had shaky *beginnings*: he attended Eton, as all the sources indicate, but only in 1850, and in the "Upper School—Remove." He was in the Grenadier Guards (Crimea, 1854–55, medal and clasps, Turkish medal), rising to the rank of lieutenantcolonel, retired in 1871, and

next year married a daughter of the 3d marquis of Headfort, settled down in affluent mediocrity, and fathered three sons; K.C.V.O. (1909); J.P. Berks; deputy chairman, Royal National Lifeboat Institution (*WWW*; *Upper Ten Thousand*; *County Families*; Kelly; *Whitaker*, obituary in *The Times*, Aug. 2, 1913, p. 9). But see the next letter.

To Wyndham Slade*

Dover

My dear Wyndham   August 21, 1854

I should greatly have liked seeing you here, but I almost feared you would hardly think it worth while to come right across England when you found that our foreign excursion had been already made. Certainly I *was* rather perfidious, but after five months of London no one could have resisted the first sight of the French coast staring one in the face, and the boats perpetually steaming off under one's nose, in the loveliest weather that ever was in the world. You would have liked this place too, if you had come; however, you did *not* come, and there is an end of the matter for this year.

I have been in Brighton this last week, living in barracks with my brother-in-law, Henry Benson, who commands the depôt of the 17th there. I saw several men of the 13th, and also of the gallant 4th, though not the Brown who I see by to-day's paper has been distinguishing himself.[1] There were, however, but few officers there; the old Colonel (M'Queen) who commands the whole of them I liked, and dining at mess I liked—so far as the dinners are concerned, very much. The young officers, the cornets, are certainly the drawbacks—such precious young *nincompoops*; I don't mean anything serious to be blamed in them, but the sort of faults boys coming straight from school to a messroom would naturally have: they *behave so badly*. This is an instance of what I mean. A precious young simpleton called Clayton,[2] inoffensive enough *du reste*, when the cloth is removed pulls off three heavy rings from his fingers and goes on spinning them on the table before him for about a quarter of an hour—this with the Colonel and different people dining, and talking going on. I think every one before he gets a commission should be compelled to pass at least a year at one of the Universities and to pass the first examination, whatever it is. After all, college does civilise a boy wonderfully.

We are going to London by sea to-morrow if it is fine; it is much cheaper, and I want to see the Downs, the Nore, Pegwell Bay, etc., which I have never seen. We go straight on to Fox How on Wednesday or Thursday. Is it quite impossible for you to come and look at us there in the next six weeks? It is likely to be fine now, I do really think, even there. Poor Lawley's case is made so deplorable by the Times returning to it—& by his being classed with O'Flaherty.[3]

Flu's kindest remembrances. Write to me at Fox How.   ever yours
affectionately,

M. Arnold.

Text. Russell, 1 : 41–43 (corrected from MS by Kenneth Allott).

1. "At the end of July, Gen. Sir George Brown [1790–1865, commander of the Light Division] had quitted Varna on board the *Fury*, to reconnoitre Sebastopol. The vessel crept into the mouth of the harbour during the night, close under the huge batteries, and remained there till discovered at daybreak, when a hot fire of shot and shell was opened upon her. The *Fury*, however, escaped without the slightest damage, and Sir George Brown returned to head-quarters at Varna" (*Annual Register*, p. 287). See Dod's *Peerage. Baronetage, and Knightage* (1858); Boase; and obituary in *Annual Register*, 1865.

2. See the letter preceding.

3. "Why is Mr Gladstone like Diogenes? Because he can't find a good man" (*The Times*, Aug. 21, p. 6). For Lawley see above p. 167 n. 2. His case was discussed in a long leader in *The Times*, Aug. 4, 1854, p. 9, and his dismissal as Gladstone's private secretary confirmed on Aug. 22, p. 8. Edmund O'Flaherty, Irish commissioner of income tax, was indicted on three counts of forgery and had fled to the United States (*The Times*, Aug. 17, p. 6). Lawley was "classed with O'Flaherty" by Arnold, not by *The Times*; both had been appointed by Gladstone.

To Charles Augustin Sainte-Beuve

Fox How. près d'Ambleside. le 29 Septembre 1854

Monsieur,

L'article de la Revue des Deux-Mondes[1] a été un véritable bonheur pour moi, en tant qu'il est devenu l'occasion de m'attirer une lettre de vous. Vous parlez de faire un examen des principes poétiques exposés dans ma préface: cela serait, assurément, un très grand honneur pour moi, et me ferait beaucoup de plaisir; cependant, ce qui me fait plus de plaisir encore, c'est d'avoir su intéresser à mes tâtonnemen[t]s critiques et poétiques celui de tous les écrivains vivants dont l'enseignement littéraire m'a le plus éclairé.

Dans quelques jours, Monsieur, vous recevrez, je l'espère, ce poème d'Empédocle que vous me demandez. J'ai prié mon éditeur de vous remettre, en même temps, un exemplaire de la seconde édition de mon dernier recueil. A la tête de celle-ci vous trouverez quelques mots de réponse aux objections et aux réfutations qu'avait attirées ma préface.

En ce qui regarde la valeur absolue et la portée des vues littéraires qu'-exprime l'auteur de l'article de la Revue, vous-même, Monsieur, vous savez mieux que personne à quoi vous en tenir: seulement, que ma compatriote, dans sa qualité d'Anglaise,[2] ne vous abuse pas ni sur l'influence qu'exercent les poèmes de Shelley chez nous, ni sur son véritable rang parmi les poètes

Anglais. M. Arthur Dudley a commencé , je crois, par Shelley, et, apparemment, il compte aussi finir par lui. Cela se voit assez souvent: en attendant, il voit tout dans lui et dans ses œuvres, et veut y rattacher toute la littérature actuelle de son pays. Mais tout cela est fort arbitraire. Shelley était, sans doute, un homme très remarquable: mais c'était plutôt un *homme*, un *être*, extrêmement intéressant, qu'un grand artiste: et jamais il n'a commandé ni l'attention ni la sympathie du grand nombre des lecteurs. D'ailleurs il est mort très jeune, et sans être atteint à la pleine maturité de son talent. Parler de lui comme d'un *maître* et le préférer hautement à Byron (que M. Arthur Dudley, du reste, traite un peu sans façon, en le qualifiant du titre d'"*esprit léger*') c'est simplement ridicule. C'est à peu près comme si l'on rapporterait à Jean Paul ou à Novale, plutôt qu'à Goethe et à Schiller, tout le mouvement littéraire de l'Allemagne depuis cinquante ans.

J'ai réfléchi avec la plus grande attention sur ce que vous me dites relativement au choix des sujets, et à l'intérêt supérieur que possèdent les choses modernes: ces choses, vous avez raison, sans doute, Monsieur,—vous et Homère aussi,—à les préférer,—toutes choses égales d'ailleurs—comme matière poétique, à celles du passé: seulement, j'oserai vous demander, n'existe-t-il pas des époques *trop claires* où les événements présents deviennent, pour le poète, presque intraitables? Virgile ou Apollone de Rhodes, par exemple, ont-ils mal fait, à l'époque où ils vécurent, de laisser à côté les evénements [*sic*] contemporains pour s'occuper des faits d'Enée et de Jason? ces œuvres *de cabinet et d'étude* ne sont-elles pas, quelquefois, les seules possibles?—et n'ont-elles pas bien, elles aussi, leur valeur? Mais, me direz-vous, il faut de la nouveauté dans la manière de présenter les choses passées, et les *approprier au temps*. Oui, sans doute, cela est vrai, je le sens: peut-être même que toute la *question est* là!

Je vous écris cette lettre d'une petite campagne dans le *Westmorland*, tout près du lac d'*Ullswater* et de *Patterdale*, d'où est datée une belle lettre de Benjamin Constant à Madame de Charrière—voilà encore deux connaissances littéraires que je dois surtout à vous, Monsieur.   Agréez, je vous prie, les expressions de ma reconnaissance et de ma considération la plus distinguée,

Matthew Arnold.—

MS. *L'Institut de France.*

1. "Poèmes de Matthew Arnold et d'Alexandre Smith," *Revue des deux mondes*, Sept. 15, 1854, by "Arthur Dudley," pseudonym of Mme Marie Pauline Rose Blaze de Bury, *née* Stuart (1814–94), the second of three articles "Du Mouvement poétique en Angleterre depuis Shelley." (Her husband, Henri Blaze de Bury, was brother to the wife of François Buloz, editor of the *Revue des deux mondes*.) Arnold of course knew her identity—"ma compatriote, dans sa qualité d'Anglaise"—but it was never really concealed and was printed (for example) in *La Grande Encyclopédie* in 1886. See Boase; obituary in

The Times, Jan. 29, 1894, p. 6; Marie-Louise Pailleron, *François Buloz et ses amis* (1923), pp. 192–204, with a portrait; Iris Esther Sells, *Matthew Arnold and France* (1935), who first published Arnold's letters to Mme Blaze de Bury (pp. 268–71); and Bonnerot, pp. 520–21. For Sainte-Beuve's reply to this letter see below pp. 299–300.

2. Idiom requires "*en* sa qualité," "sans *avoir* atteint," "rapportait," "attention *à* ce que vous me dites," "de laisser *de* côté," and at the end "l'expression."

To Jane Martha Arnold Forster

Fox How

My dearest K   October 10, 1854

I would not let Flu write, because I wished to write myself and say how very sorry we both are not to be able to pay you and William the visit we so much wished and hoped to pay this autumn. But I must at once begin inspecting—and as I begin in Shropshire and Liverpool is on our road there, I take Flu and the children to the Dingle[1] on Monday—going away myself for a week the day after, and leaving them there. I shall be for a week at Oxford inspecting schools in that neighbourhood—and on Tuesday the 24th I hope we shall all meet at Crewe, and proceed to Derby together. If Mamma comes to Edward, you and William must come to us for a Saturday and Sunday at least at Derby—or, if she does not come, you must still come to us, or we must go to you, for that time.

I have so much to say to you, you dear soul. It was odd—as your letter about the country you went through on the Italian side of the Alps was being read it brought to my mind delightfully just what had been present to it when many of the poems of mine which are nearest to me were composed—and then came your sentence saying that what you had seen had brought these Poems to your mind. That was a *correspondence* to give one real pleasure—but there is no one and never will be any one who enters into what I have done as you have entered into it, dearest K,—and to whom I so want to communicate what I do. I have finished a poem which I think is better than Sohrab and Rustum, though here I do not think they consider it so—but I am nearly sure you will think so—and William too I think will like it. You will see it in November, I hope. You can hardly tell what pleasure Sainte Beuve's letter gave me, because you do not know how highly I estimate him as a critic. His intention of reviewing me, though, I know very well, arises more from his interest in the questions raised in the preface, than from his caring much about the poems.[2] The article in the Revue des deux Mondes is a confused affair—a piece of theorising—the author having a mania for finding everything in *Shelley* whether it is there or no.

I should like to know what William thinks of this very pretty Westminster quarrel. Miss Martineau and her brother James, and their hatreds, remind one of the family of Pelops.³ She proposed to me to take part in the Review (from Chapman) but for that I have not time.

Write to me my darling K, when you have time, and with love to William believe me   ever your faithless but most affectionate brother

M. A.

I do so *long* for you to see the children. Louisa Twining⁴ has made a beautiful sketch of Tom.

MS. Frederick Whitridge.

1. The Liverpool suburb where his sister Susanna Cropper lived and where Arnold died. See above p. 266 n. 14.

2. "On January 14, 1856, Sainte-Beuve published in the *Moniteur* the third of the lectures on Virgil he had prepared for the Collège de France. In discussing the proper subject of poetry, he summarized Arnold's 1853 Preface in the most complimentary terms, and alluded also (by paraphrase) to Arnold's letter to himself of September 29, 1854. . . . The lectures were collected as *Etude sur Virgile*, published Mar. 7, 1857" (R. H. Super, "Documents in the Matthew Arnold—Sainte-Beuve Relationship," *Modern Philology* 60 (1963):207.

3. Harriet Martineau's book *Letters on the Laws of Man's Nature and Development* (1851)—letters between herself, besotted, and Henry George Atkinson, the mesmerist— had been devastated by her brother James Martineau in an article, "Mesmeric Atheism," in *Prospective Review* (of which he was one of the editors), 7 (June 1851):224–62. Her book *The Positive Philosophy of Auguste Comte* (1853) was noticed in *Westminster Review* 6 (July 1854):173–94, though not by her brother (who was turned down by the editor) but (probably) by Richard Congreve (*Wellesley*, 3:621). See R. K. Webb, *Harriet Martineau: A Radical Victorian*, pp. 19–20, 299–301.

4. Louisa Twining, sister of William Aldred Twining, deceased husband of Arnold's sister Mary, was (like her own sister Elizabeth, 1805–89: *DNB*), a philanthropist, social worker, and author (see Allibone).

To Frances Lucy Wightman Arnold*

Madely Wood
Wednesday,¹ October 17 [*for* 18?], 1854

This must be a scrap, for I must get off as soon as I can in order to get to Lilleshall, nine miles of cross country road, in time to dress for dinner; and, while I *am* here, the managers do not like not to be able to talk to me. I have had a cold, wet journey, and only a bun for luncheon. I got to Wellington at one o'clock, and came on here—six miles—on the top of an omnibus—a dawdling conveyance, and a cold, wet drive. I felt rather disconsolate between Liverpool and Shrewsbury. . . . We have had such a happy time at Fox

How. Then, too, I have had time for employment that I like, and now I am going back to an employment which I certainly do *not* like, and which leaves me little time for anything else. I read about fifty pages of *Hypatia*, which is certainly very vigorous and interesting; however, that did not comfort me much, and I betook myself to Hesiod, a Greek friend I had with me, with excellent effect; we will talk about *Hypatia* when we meet.[2]

Text. Russell, 1:43.

> 1. The 1854 diary shows that he was in Madeley Wood on Tuesday, Oct. 17.
> 2. Kingsley's novel, published in May 1853.

To Frances Lucy Wightman Arnold*

Oxford

October 21 [*for* 19], 1854[1]

I am afraid it is quite impossible for me to get back to Liverpool. I shall be detained so long by a large double school at Banbury to-morrow that it will be impossible for me to get to Liverpool till three or four on Saturday morning, and then to begin on Monday morning at Charlbury, thirteen miles from here. I am afraid it is out of the question. I am just back from Witney; as cold and uncomfortable a life I have had since I left you as one could desire. My bedroom here is fust and frowsiness itself, and last night I could not get to sleep. I have seen no one but Lake for a minute after my arrival last night. I was off for Witney at eight this morning. I shall be hurried in writing at Banbury to-morrow. I dine in Oriel to-night—in Common Room at six.

Text. Russell, 1:43-44.

> 1. He was in Oxford on the weekend, and the diary shows that he was in Witney on Thursday, Oct. 19, Banbury on Friday, Charlbury on Monday, Oct. 23.

To Mary Penrose Arnold*

Oxford

My dearest Mother   Sunday, [October 22, 1854]

If you enjoyed having us I am sure it is also true that never have I so much enjoyed being at Fox-How as this last time. In the discomforts of the present I find myself perpetually looking forward to being there again, and to the best and pleasantest peace I ever obtain.

This place is certainly not healthy at present, though the cholera (which has been very bad indeed here—worse than in London)—is dying out. But I have caught a cold on my chest, which affects my breathing and spoils my sleep. And altogether I am not very well—but the first going to work again—being a sudden change from shelter and rest to exposure and toil—always knocks one about a little. It will wear off in a few days, I dare say.

I am writing from Walrond's rooms in Balliol. This time *thirteen* years ago I was wandering about this quadrangle a freshman, as I see other freshmen doing now. The time seems prodigious—I do not certainly feel thirteen years older than when I came up to Oxford. My stay here is rather spoilt by this horrid cold, and also by the intense dirt and frowsiness of the Star where I am staying: but I am going with Walrond today to explore the Cumner country—and on Thursday I got up alone into one of the little coombs that Papa was so fond of and which I had in my mind in the Gipsy Scholar—and felt the peculiar *sentiment* of this country and neighbourhood as deeply as ever. But I am much struck with the apathy and *poorness* of the people here, as they now strike me and their petty pottering habits compared with the students of Paris or Germany—or even of London. Animation, and interest, and the power of work seem so sadly wanting in them. And I think this is so: and the place in losing Newman and his followers has lost its religious movement which after all kept it from stagnating—and has not yet, so far as I see, got anything better. However we must hope that the coming changes, and perhaps the infusion of Dissenters—sons of that muscular hard-working, un-blasé middle class;—for it is this, in spite of its abominable disagreeableness—may brace the flaccid sinews of Oxford a little.

Was it not a terrible over-turn at the Dingle? You should have seen poor Budge's white astonished face when I met him—and heard him begin to roar when the danger was well over and he had sufficiently recovered from his astonishment to be able to indulge his feelings. You can imagine what a delight it will be to rejoin them at Derby, if we all live, on Tuesday. I hear that sweet soul Toddy often asks for his *de* Papa.

Arthur Stanley comes tomorrow, and I meet him at dinner here. I have seen scarcely anyone as yet, except Walrond. Fan's parcel has been duly delivered.   My love to all, and believe me, my dearest Mother,   ever your most affectionate son—

M. A.

No Independance [*sic*] has come today. If the Leader comes to Fox How, please forward it to me at Derby. It will not come after this.

MS. Balliol College.

To Wyndham Slade*

Derby

My dear Wyndham   November 6, 1854

I am writing this from a British school, where I am holding an examination of pupil teacher apprentices, surrounded by an innumerable company
of youths and—you dog—maidens. I shall not be in London till the very
end of this month, but then, I hope, for two months.

It was very odd that on the day when I got your letter I returned from
a visit, in Staffordshire, to un nommé Philips, who married a Miss Buller,
sister to young Buller your fellow-lodger.[1] This Reginald Buller was there &
we talked a great deal about you. I like him very much, though, as I told his
sister, his appearance does not certainly give one the impression of his belonging to the wealth-producing classes. But he seems a very good fellow.

The news from the East seems a little improved to-day, at least the Varna
despatch seems to establish that it was *Turkish* redoubts, and, consequently,
Turkish cannon, that were captured.

As for the light cavalry loss, those gentlemen, I imagine, will be more
missed at reviews than in the field.[2]

The English cavalry never seem to do much good, and, I imagine, are a
great deal too costly and too beautifully dressed and mounted for real service.
I heard the other day from a man to whom Sir William Napier[3] had said it,
that while the British infantry was the best in the world, the cavalry of several
other nations was better, even in equal numbers; he instanced the French and
the Austrian.

The siege is awfully interesting; one thinks they *must* take the place,
though, after all; the loss of prestige will be so great if they do not.

The plague of babies is for the present stayed. The matter to which you
refer is one of considerable mystery: it looks easy, indeed, as you say: but
these things are not precisely as they seem.[4]

Edward is coming to-night; from him I shall hear what your brother did
at All Souls.[5] How I wish you were here for a week!

I have got another volume coming out in December; all the short things
have appeared before, but there is one long thing at the beginning I think
you will like.

Fanny Lucy desires to be most kindly remembered, at least she did this
morning when I told her I should write to you. The big baby pulls his elder
brother over and over.—   Ever yours,

M. A.

Text. Russell, 1:46–47 (corrected from MS by Kenneth Allott).

1. Adelaide Louisa Buller (d. 1860), daughter of Edward (later, Sir Edward Manningham-) Buller (1800–1892; cr. bt 1866), of Dilhorn Hall, co. Stafford, married Jan. 21, 1852, John William Philips, of Heybridge, co. Stafford. Her brother was Reginald John Buller (1832–88), who rose to a colonelcy in the Grenadier Guards, married in July 1888, and died two weeks later.

2. The famous charge of the Light Brigade took place on Oct. 25. (Tennyson's poem was written and published in December.)

3. Lt-Gen. Sir William Francis Patrick Napier (1785–1860: *DNB*), historian of the Peninsular War, now retired and writing.

4. This cryptic paragraph was omitted in Russell. Trevenen was born Oct. 15, 1853, Richard Nov. 14, 1855. One of the *Sonnets from the Portuguese* may be relevant: "Where I, who thought to sink,/ Was caught up into love, and taught the whole / Of a new rhythm."

5. George FitzClarence Slade (1831–1904), with a degree of B.A. (Balliol) was elected a fellow of All Souls' College in 1854 (Foster).

Charles Augustin Sainte-Beuve to Matthew Arnold

Paris

Monsieur,—   6 9bre 1854 [November 6, 1854]

Je ne veux point pourtant paraître tout-à-fait ingrat. J'ai reçu votre agréable lettre et, assez longtemps après Empédocle avec les Poèmes qui l'accompagnent. J'y ai lu avec un plaisir tout particulier les Stances à notre ami Obermann. Vous ne savez peut-être pas que l'auteur, M. de Senancour, est mort il y a quelques années à Sèvres près Paris où on l'avait transporté. Il n'a eu à son enterrement que deux personnes, et on a gravé sur sa tombe ces mots qu'il avait indiqués: 'Eternité, deviens mon asyle.' Je traduirai ces Stances que vous lui avez consacrées et je vous les enverrai pour être sûr de l'exactitude.

Je crois bien que nous ne sommes pas loin d'être d'accord sur ce qui est du choix des meilleurs sujets en poésie. Il est bien vrai que les sujets modernes sont trop clairs et ne prètent guère qu'à l'histoire. On ne fait pas un véritable poème épique avec Pharsale ni avec nos guerres de l'Empire, mais d'un autre côté, en acceptant vos deux exemples de Virgile et d'Apollonius de Rhodes, je m'en empare en les divisant. L'Enéide a vécu et vit par l'appropriation d'un sujet antique à un temps présent et par l'infusion d'un souffle et d'un esprit tout romain refluant jusqu'aux origines. L'âme des Scipions y respire par endroits, et on pleure au: 'tu Marcellus eris.'—Apollonius, au contraire, malgré son admirable chant sur Médée dont Virgile s'est tout servi n'a fait dans l'ensemble qu'un poème savant et mort, et pas un coeur Alexandrin n'a palpité au moment de sa naissance comme faisait le jeune Romain pour l'Enéide.

Je me serais peut-être déjà amusé à déduire par écrit toutes ces raisons si vous ne m'annonciez que dans la Préface d'un seconde édition, vous avez répondu aux critiques. Je n'ai point encore reçu cette seconde édition à laquelle j'attache du prix. Vous voyez, Monsieur, à quel point je m'accoutume à être votre débiteur. Vous qui voyagez, vous reviendrez certainement un de ces jours à Paris, dès que vous y serez, soyez assez bon pour m'en avertir par une petite lettre jetée à la poste (car autrement on se manque souvent) et j'aurai alors grand plaisir à apprendre de vous bien des choses littéraires et poétiques dont je n'ai eu que le gout vif et le bégaiement.   Agréez, je vous prie, l'assurance de mes sentiments les plus distingués et obligés,

Sainte-Beuve.

No. 11, rue Mont-Parnasse.

Text. Arnold Whitridge, *Unpublished Letters of Matthew Arnold*, pp. 68–70.

1. This letter first appeared in *Unpublished Letters of Matthew Arnold* (1923), ed. Arnold Whitridge, pp. 68–70—not in 1921 in the *French Quarterly*, as Bonnerot claims— and was reprinted in Jean Bonnerot's edition of Sainte-Beuve's *Correspondance*, 9:473–74. Whitridge (with both Bonnerots following his lead) misconstrued Sainte-Beuve's date (written as indicated above) to be *September 6*, as R. H. Super pointed out in correcting it in "Documents in the Matthew Arnold—Sainte-Beuve Relationship," *Modern Philology* 60 (1963):206–7.

To Mary Penrose Arnold*

London

My dearest Mother   December 9, 1854

You will have received six copies of my new volume[1]—will you give one to Mrs Wordsworth from me, telling her that I send it her for the sake of the Memorial Verses, imperfect tribute as they are: one to Mrs Fletcher— and send one, as soon as you have an opportunity, to dear Tom. You see the first series was evidently *not* sent to him. You will have three copies left for yourself and for Fox-How. I have sent the book to Uncle Trevenen and to the Bucklands.

I think this book will hold me, in public repute, pretty much at the point where the last left me—not advance me and not pull me down from it. If so it was worth publishing—for I shall probably make something by the poems in their present shape, whereas if I had left them as they were, I should have continued to make nothing. The war and the great length of time that has passed since most of the poems in this collection were written makes me myself regard it with less interest than I should have thought possible.

I am not very well lately—have had one or two things to bother me— and more and more have the feeling that I do not do my inspecting work really well and satisfactorily—but I have also lately had a stronger wish than usual not to vacillate and be helpless, but to do my duty, whatever that may be: and out of that wish one may always hope to make something.

God bless you my dearest Mother. The children are both quite well. The old nurse leaves us on Monday.[2] Deane is not satisfactory—perhaps— but I think this: every month we keep her she becomes less necessary to Toddy—and by the time she ought to go he will be able to spare her. Your most affectionate son

M. A.

MS. Frederick Whitridge.

    1. *Poems*, Second Series, dated 1855.

    2. Unidentified. Mrs Bottle? Mrs Pears? Mrs Bousfield?—all mentioned in diary in 1854 but not later.

To Jane Martha Arnold Forster*

London

My darling K   December 12, 1854

No one ever writes to me so pleasantly about my poems as you do, and there is no one whom I so much like to think of as reading them.

I think Balder will consolidate the peculiar sort of reputation that I got by Sohrab and Rustum—and many will complain that I am settling myself permanently in that field of antiquity, as if there was no other. But I have in fact done with this field in completing Balder—and what I do next will be, if I can do it, wholly different.[1]

I have had a letter from Arthur Stanley who remarks on the similes much as you do—so I dare say what you both say is true—he likes Balder as a whole better than Sohrab—but thinks it too short—and this is true, too, I think—and I must some day add a first book with an account of the circumstances of the death of Balder itself.

I felt sure William would be interested from what I knew of his Scandinavian interests—Mallet however, tell him, and his version of the Edda is all the poem is based upon—there are several things in the Westminster article I could have used, if I had had it in time.[2]

It is hard to think of any volume like that of mine having a sale in England just now, with the war going on and the one cry being for newspapers—but I daresay the book will dribble away in a year's time or so.

If you could but see Toddy—When I went out and kissed him and wished him Goodbye yesterday morning he kissed me and said—"God bless you, Matt."—He had heard his Mamma say it, and he now repeats everything. He said to me today "Where is Fanny Lucy, Papa?" He is the most *bewitching boy* certainly, as he calls himself, at present. Trevenen is getting a dear old boy too, and is very handsome. Old nurse left us yesterday, and Deane now has both children. Love to William, and to dear Mary with thanks for her letter which gave me great pleasure.   Ever your most truly affectionate

M. A.

MS. Frederick Whitridge.

    1. "Balder Dead" (Allott, p. 376).

    2. Translations of P. H. Mallet's *Introduction à l'histoire de Dannemarc* and *Monumens de la mythologie et de la poésie des Celtes et particulièrement des anciens Scandinaves* by I. A. Blackwell and, especially, Bishop Percy (Allott, p. 376). "The Odin-Religion," *Westminster Review,* American edn, 122 (Oct. 1854):165–83 (Balder, pp. 171–72).

To Charles Augustin Sainte-Beuve

Londres

19 Decembre 1854

Vous direz, Monsieur, que je compte trop sur votre patience: je viens de publier un dernier recueil de mes poésies, et j'ai prié l'éditeur de vous en envoyer un exemplaire. Il n'y a là rien de nouveau hors le poème de *Balder,* imprimé en tête du volume:—tout le reste a déjà paru—ou dans ce volume d'*Empédocle* que vous avez, ou dans un autre recueil plus ancien encore.

Envoyez-moi, je vous en prie, Monsieur, cette traduction que vous m'avez fait l'honneur de faire des Stances à *Obermann.*[1] Je la lirai avec le plus vif intérêt. Tout ce que vous me dites—tout ce que vous pourrez encore me dire—sur ce grand esprit inconnu, et qui a passé comme une ombre, me sera fort précieux.

Votre obligeante invitation me tente singulièrement—malheureusement, depuis trois ans je ne voyage plus. Soyez sûr cependant, Monsieur, que, la première fois que je me trouverai à Paris, je m'empresserai à venir[2] vous voir et vous remercier.   Agréez, je vous prie, l'assurance de mes hommages les plus respectueux.

M. Arnold.—

P. S Vous avez enfin reçu, j'espère, l'exemplaire de la seconde édition de mon premier recueil qui vous était destiné.

MS. L'Institut de France.

1. Published in *Chateaubriand et son group littéraire* (1860), rendered in French prose by Sainte-Beuve and his private secretary and poet-friend, Auguste Lacaussade. See below p. 306.

2. Arnold ought to have written "je m'empresserai *de* venir."

To Rosella Pitman

Education Department, Council Office, Downing Street, London:
January 17, 1855
Private

Dear Madam

On enquiry here I find that your Managers were informed that if they undertook to begin removing the asphalt floor in *one* of the schools before my next visit, two of the candidates might be at once admitted in your school. One, I think, was to be Wise—and the other was left to the choice of the Managers.

To that communication on the part of this office no answer appears to have been returned. I have forwarded therefore your letter to the Secretary, and the Managers will be again applied to for their decision, which, from what Mr Buxton[1] said to me when I was last in Abbey Street, will, I have no doubt, be such as to enable the C. of C. to consent to the immediate admission of two of your candidates. If admitted they will be paid from June last.

If you can find a suitable assistant Teacher let me know, and I will see what can be done. The aid of these assistant Teachers is, in my opinion, most useful—but there is a difficulty in procuring them. Believe me,   truly yours

M. Arnold.—

MS. I. J. Pitman.

1. Perhaps Charles Buxton (1822/1823–71), son of Sir Thomas Fowell Buxton (and cousin of W. E. Forster), J.P. Norfolk and Surrey, and liberal M.P. from 1857 till his death (*Annual Register,* Allibone).

Charles Augustin Sainte-Beuve to Matthew Arnold

Mon cher Monsieur   le 11 février 1855

J'ai reçu le 2d édition que vous m'annonciez. Je suis bien reconnaissant de tant d'aimables attentions. Il vient d'arriver un grand changement dans ma vie: j'ai été nommé Professeur de Poésie Latine au Collège de France, et je renonce (au moins pour un long temps) à la critique des oeuvres du jour. Me voilà classique bon gré mal gré, et par cela, d'autant plus des vôtres. Cependant j'ai fait comme vous et j'ai jeté un de mes regards en arrière vers notre ami Obermann. Voici un Essai de traduction que je vous envoie de vos stances si senties. Il y a des points qui restent douteux pour moi et pour les amis que j'ai consultés ici: ainsi les deux derniers vers de la première stance 'drive the rack,' éclairez-moi. Veuillez aussi porter votre attention sur la stance 7e et les glaciers qui épargnent l'âme? Ai-je saisi le sens juste? aussi pour le reste veuillez me donner votre note juste. Cela sera imprimé dans un volume qui paraîtra à la fin de l'année et où je reparle d'Obermann.

Text. Arnold Whitridge, 'Matthew Arnold and Sainte-Beuve,' PMLA, 53 (Mar. 1938):303–13.

To Mary Penrose Arnold*

Birmingham
My dearest Mother   February 27, 1855
    I ought before this to have thanked you for sending the letter, which is ennobling and refreshing as everything which proceeds from him always is— besides the pathetic interest of the circumstances of its writing and finding[1]. I think he was 35 when that letter was written—and how he had forecast and resolved, even then, the serious interests and welfare of his children—at a time when to many men their children are still little more than playthings. He might well hope to bring up children, when he made that bringing up so distinctly his thought beforehand—and we who treat the matter so carelessly and lazily—we can hardly expect ours to do more than *grow up* at hazard— not be *brought* up at all. But this is just what makes him great—that he was not only a good man saving his own soul by righteousness[2]—but that he carried so many others with him in his hand, and saved them, if they would let him, along with himself.
    Dear Mary was invaluable to us, and we have missed her terribly these last two evenings. I so liked hearing her and Flu talk in the evening as they sate at work while I read—now all is silence, unless when I sometimes read out a sentence or two. Tell her I find Etty's Life a great improvement on Montgomery's—in fact decidedly interesting—of all dull stagnant unedifying *entourages* that of middle-class Dissent, which environed Montgomery, seems to me the stupidest.[3]
    I should like to have Mary staying with us one six months of the year, and Fan the other. There is a letter from Fan to Mary lying about somewhere, which I would forward but cannot lay my hand upon it—Edward would say I have kept it to read; but I have not.

It is no use telling you of little Tom's fascinations by letter when you have Mary with you upon whom they have been exercised. His cod liver oil seems to suit him wonderfully, and his appetite is better than I have ever known it. After he had been some time in bed tonight, and had had his usual course of biscuit, jujube, and supper, the maid appeared with a request for "another biscuit for Master Arnold." Trev. is very cross with some teeth.

I hope by the end of this week we shall be settled in London—My dearest Mother how I should like to have you quietly with us there. Ever your most affectionate

M. A.

Tell Rowland that I think her glass one of the most elegant and pretty that I have ever seen—and that it is to stand on our dressing room mantel piece in London.

MS. Frederick Whitridge.

1. A letter from Dr Thomas Arnold.
2. Ezekiel 14:14, 20—the germ of "Rugby Chapel," ll. 124 ff.
3. William Etty (1787–1849: *DNB*), R.A., enormously popular (and wealthy) painter, especially of female figures. Arnold borrowed Alexander Gilchrist's *Life* of Etty, recently published in two volumes, as well as Montgomery's *Memoirs*, from Mudie's (*Notebooks*, p. 557).

James Montgomery (1771–1854: *DNB*), poetaster, reviewer, newspaper editor and owner of *Sheffield Iris*, and hymnist. "On the whole he may be characterised as something less than a genius and something more than a mediocrity. . . . The life of Montgomery has been written with the most formidable prolixity by his friends, Dr John Holland and the Rev. James Everett, in seven volumes, London, 1854–6" (*DNB*).

To Jean Baptiste François Ernest de Chatelain[1]

Monsieur le Chevalier de Chatelain   23. Grosvenor Street West
My dear Sir   March 6, 1855

Many thanks for the copy of your translation of my "Memorial Verses" which you have been good enough to send me. I do not presume to consider myself an adequate judge of its merits: but the second part especially, that which relates to Goethe, seems to me very happily turned. Believe me, very faithfully your's

M. Arnold.—

MS. Yale University.

1. Jean Baptiste François Ernest Chevalier de Chatelain (1801–81: *DNB*), journalist, translator, and republican, naturalized a British subject in 1848, produced "upwards of fifty works" in his English years (his wife, equally prolific, "became insane from over-

work," according to Allibone). Tennyson, some of whose poems he also translated, snubbed him with equal finesse (Tennyson 2:128, 195). "Memorial Verses" ("Souvenirs. Aux Mânes de Goethe, de Byron, et de Wordsworth. 1850") was included in *Beautés de la poësie anglaise* (1862).

To Charles Augustin Sainte-Beuve

London
Mon cher Monsieur   8 mars 1855
    Il m'est impossible de vous dire jusqu'à quel point votre traduction me semble admirable d'exactitude et de sentiment.[1] Le livre d' "Obermann" étant écrit en français, et l'idée de lui se liant toujours, dans ma pensée, avec celle de la Suisse Française, les Stances que j'ai dédiées à sa mémoire me semblent gagner beaucoup, en fait de couleur locale et de vérité, à être revêtues d'une forme française. Je vous assure qu'à présent je lis mon poème avec plus de plaisir dans votre traduction que dans l'original.
    Il n'y a que très peu à changer. "*Rack*" est un mot de la vieille langue anglaise pour signifier les *bords*, la *frange* d'un nuage qui passe. Shakespeare s'en sert dans la "Tempête"—

> "Le monde," dit-il, "se dissoudra,"
> and, like this unsubstantial pageant faded,
> Leave not a *rack* behind—[2]

    Mais ce mot s'écrit de plus d'une manière. Ce que j'ai voulu dire dans les deux derniers vers de la 1ère Stance, le voici-"les nuages, chassés devant les vents d'automne, balayent le sentier à leur passage." Dans la Stance 7ème le sens sera exactement rendu en omettant ces deux petits mots "*ne*" "*que*"— et en laissant subsister tout le reste—"bien que les glaciers versent de loin sur ces feuillets" &c.—Les glaciers *prêtent, donnent quelque chose* de l'âme de leurs neiges au livre d'Obermann.[3]
    J'ai fait çà et là, quelques légères corrections sur la copie de la traduction, lesquelles vous garderez ou non comme il vous plaira.
    J'avais bien lu dans un journal belge que vous étiez acquis au Collège de France comme Professeur de Poésie Latine.[4] En vous, mon cher Monsieur, on aura enfin un Professeur qui sache traiter la littérature *classique* comme littérature *vivante*, et non comme matière seulement de sèche érudition et d'étymologie.[5]   Agréez, mon cher Monsieur mes hommages et mes remercimen[t]s réitérés.

                                                        Matthew Arnold.—

MS. L'Institut de France.

1. See above p. 302. Sainte-Beuve quoted the remainder of this paragraph in the second edition (1860) of *Chateaubriand et son groupe littéraire sous l'empire* (Bonnerot, p. 525n).

2. *The Tempest* 4.1.155–56.

3. An amusing misunderstanding by Sainte-Beuve—and also Bonnerot. Arnold's 7th stanza reads:

> "Yes, though the virgin mountain-air
> Fresh through these pages blows;
> Though to these leaves the glaciers spare
> The soul of their white snows;"

which Sainte-Beuve rendered finally as: "Oui! bien que l'air vierge de la montagne souffle frais à travers ces pages; bien que les glaciers versent de loin sur ces feuillets l'âme de leurs neiges muettes."

Earlier, however, misconstruing "spare" as "save" ("Woodman, spare that tree!") and puzzled, Sainte-Beuve in his letter of Feb. 11 drew Arnold's attention to the line "et les glaciers qui épargnent l'âme," and Arnold explained as seen above. Bonnerot (p. 526n), in turn, finding no place for "*ne*" "*que*" in the seventh stanza, failed to reflect that the version of the translation seen by Arnold, obviously accommodating the restrictive adverb, was different from the version printed by Sainte-Beuve; and he erred also in calling *muettes* "un enjolivement à la place de *white* qui a dû paraître une épithète plate," for l. 28 (as Sainte-Beuve saw it) read "The soul of their mute snows" (Allott, p. 137n).

4. Sainte-Beuve was appointed in Nov.-Dec. 1854. In his letter to Arnold on Feb. 11 Sainte-Beuve had written: "Il vient d'arriver un grand changement dans ma vie: j'ai été nommé Professeur de Poésie Latine au Collège de France." The "journal belge" may have been *Le Courier belge* (see above p. 110 n. 5); Arnold could scarcely have learned of the appointment "lors de son bref séjour en Belgique" (Bonnerot, p. 526n)—in July 1854!

5. This sentence (seriously misquoted in Sainte-Beuve's *Correspondance*, 10.66) was off the mark, for the début at the Collège de France, on Mar. 9, was a disaster, and after Mar. 14 the appointment was effectively (though not legally) terminated: he retained the title till his death. See *Correspondance*, 10:66–181.)

To John William Parker, Jr[1]

J. W. Parker Esqre junr

Education Department, Council Office, Downing Street, London:

My dear Sir   March 20, 1855

I think in the first stanza the comma will not do—for *mild* refers to *flowering*—not to *garden*—and to put in a comma would make it at least doubtful to which of the two it was meant to refer.[2]

In the second case I think the comma will be an improvement. I had left it out because *last* agrees with *us* in the following line & is governed by *leave*. Still I think the comma is wanted.

If it is not giving you too much trouble, will you substitute *boiling* for *black-worn* as an epithet for the cauldrons of the Guiers Mort, in the last line of the second stanza of the Poem. If it is now too late to make this change it does not matter. Believe me,   your's very truly

M. Arnold.—

MS. *Yale University.*

1. John William Parker, Jr (1820–60: *DNB*), son of John William Parker (1792–1870: *DNB*), the publisher, who had been printer to Cambridge University Press till 1854. They had taken over *Fraser's Magazine*, as proprietors and editor, in 1848, and Froude succeeded the son as editor in 1860. He was, as Arnold points out later, an "intimate friend" of William Delafield Arnold.

2. "Stanzas from the Grande Chartreuse" (Allott p. 301), published in *Fraser's Magazine*, Apr. 1855. The "first stanza" probably means the first of the two stanzas (the tenth) mentioned by Parker, though unrecorded revisions have been made in it. Parker's comma was retained in l. 110, and *boiling* was adopted in l. 12.

To Thomas Arnold

Education Department, Council Office, Downing Street, London:
My dearest Tom   March 28, 1855
      In spite of this terrible looking date I write to you from Grosvenor Street West—the same house we have now had for three years when in London. I got your letter two or three nights ago—when I came in, as we have just come in tonight, from dining in Eaton Place close by with the Wightmans. The Judge is on the circuit, at Norwich: and our party has been, besides ourselves, Lady Wightman, a Miss Nicholls who is an old friend of the Wightmans and generally lives with them, and Mrs Benson, Flu's sister, whose husband is now commanding the 17th Lancers in the Crimea. Quite a world of people of whom I now see so much, and of whom you know nothing. I was speaking of you to them tonight—and Flu told them, what I had told her, how I had disfigured your nose when we were boys: Edward, who is now an assistant Inspector, and who will be up tomorrow from Lincolnshire for the Inspectors' conference, will come and dine with them, I hope, along with us tomorrow.
      My day has been one of those that exemplify the difference between the old country and the colonies. My school for today was at Waddesdon— a village on the Bicester road, six miles from Aylesbury: I got up, in a yellow foggy morning, at ¼ past 7, leaving Flu in bed—breakfasted alone at 8, and was off, having seen the two children in their beds, in a cab for Euston Square at ¼ to 9: started by the Express at ¼ past 9, and was at Aylesbury (43 miles)

at ¼ before eleven—turning off the old Birmingham line which you remember so well at Tring: at Aylesbury I got into a fly and drove to Waddesdon—got there about 12—went to lunch with an old Wesleyan farmer and his wife at their farmhouse among the fields—this part might have suited Australia as well as England, except that your farm buildings are not so hoary and old—then to the school, a very small one, at 1: recommended the managers to come to terms with the clergyman, get their children into the National School, and shut up their dissenting one—and at 2 got into my fly and was at Euston Square again by ¼ to 5. Having had no walking, I walked from there to the Cumberland Gate end of Oxford Street carrying my plaid and portfolio in my hand—then got into a Hansom and drove here. We are in a street at the bottom of Grosvenor Place—leading from that to Eaton Square—I wonder if you remember it. When I got home I went & sate in the nursery, both the children having bad colds, till it was time to dress for dinner—and then took Tom down with me, who ran about the room and put my things in order while I dressed.—There is a history![1]

I hope you have got my book by this time—what you will like best, I think, will be the Gipsy Scholar—I am sure that old Cumner and Oxford country will strike a chord in you. For the preface I doubt if you will care not having much before your eyes the sins and offences at which it is directed: the fact being that we have numbers of young gentlemen with really wonderful powers of perception and expression, but to whom there is wholly wanting a "bedeutendes Individuum"[2]—so that their productions are most unedifying and unsatisfactory. But this is a long story.

As to church matters—I think people in general concern themselves less with them than they did when you left England—but certainly religion is not, to all appearances at least, losing ground here: but since the great people of Newman's party went over, the disputes among the comparatively unimportant remains of these do not excite much interest. I am going to hear Manning at the Spanish Chapel next Sunday. Newman gives himself up almost entirely to organizing and educating the Roman Catholics—and is gone off greatly, they say, as a preacher.[3]

God bless you, my dearest Tom: I cannot tell you the almost painful longing I sometimes have to see you once more.—My love to your wife and kisses to your children. Flu's love to both of you— ever your most truly affectionate brother

M. A.—

MS. Balliol College.

1. En voilà une histoire!
2. Literally, a significant individual personality or identity—Goethe's phrase in a

letter to Karl Friedrich von Reinhard, May 8, 1811 (*Goethes Briefe in Drei Banden*, Berlin and Weimar, 1984, 2:209). Arnold renders it as "noble or powerful nature" in *On Translating Homer* (Super, 1:189).

3. Tom Arnold, formally received into the Roman Catholic Church on Jan. 12, 1856, wrote to Newman from Hobart Town for counsel in Apr./May 1855 (see *Letters of Thomas Arnold the Younger*, ed. Bertram, pp. 60–61). Henry Edward Manning (1808–92: *DNB*) attended Harrow (where he became something of a Byronist) and Balliol (thirteen years before Arnold), was received into the Roman Catholic Church in 1851, consecrated bishop in 1865, enthroned as cardinal in 1875. Arnold got to know him personally at the Athenæum, to which he was elected by committee thirteen years after Arnold (see *Album*, pp. 104–5, 114–5). The Spanish Chapel was in Spanish Place, Manchester Square.

To John William Parker, Jr

J. W. Parker Esqre   23, Grosvenor St. West
My dear Sir   April 6, 1855
    Many thanks for your note and cheque.—I assure you I consider the latter liberal payment for the short poem I sent you. Believe me,   your's very faithfully

                                                                M. Arnold.—

MS. Haverford College.

To John Murray[1]

J. Murray Esqre   23, Grosvenor Street West, Eaton Square.
My dear Sir   April 11, 1855.
    Mr Arthur Stanley has written to me requesting me to call upon you with reference to his proposal for transferring my father's works into your hands. If it is convenient to you I will call upon you in Albemarle Street at 12 o'clock on Friday: and perhaps you will have the kindness not to take any steps for advertising the works until I have had the pleasure of seeing you.
    I must beg of you to excuse an official envelope, which is the only one I have by me at this moment. I remain, my dear Sir,   your's faithfully,
                                                            Matthew Arnold.—

MS. John Murray.

    1. John Murray (1808–92: *DNB*), the publisher (and son, father, grandfather, and great-grandfather of a publisher) on Albemarle Street. Benjamin Fellowes, the publisher, died Mar. 10, 1855 (*Gentleman's Magazine*). See the next letter and below pp. 312–13.

To John William Parker, Jr

J. W. Parker, Esqre junr
      Education Department, Council Office, Downing Street, London:
                   Private
My dear Sir   April 11, 1855
    You will think I flood Fraser with my verses—but I am about a thing
in memory of poor Charlotte Brontë which I think may suit you when it is
done, and which I should like to appear at no great distance of time from her
death.[1] Will you tell me whether you still have room for it in the next number. I shall not be able to send it to you until the 23rd or 24th—and it will
be in an irregular metre (like that of two Poems in my last volume—"The
Youth of Nature" & "The Youth of Man"—if ever you happened to see
them) which many people consider objectionable. It will not be so long as
the Chartreuse poem.
    Excuse this official paper and envelope which is all I have at hand—and
please direct to me in Grosvenor Street West (23) as usual.
    I think there will be the same difficulty on young Fellowes's part in
giving up those of the works which are in his hands or in any way in his
power as there was on his father's—so after all it may be some years before
anything can be done. Believe me, my dear Sir,   Your's very truly
                                   Matthew Arnold.—

MS. Yale University.

    1. "Haworth Churchyard" (Allott, p. 422) appeared in *Fraser's Magazine* in May.
See below pp. 315, 317.

To Frances Lucy Wightman Arnold*

                                         Ampthill
                     Wednesday, [April 18, 1855]
    I shall have no dinner at all today except so far as the mutton chop I had
at one o'clock with one of the Committee may count for one. But that will
do me no harm. I mean to walk from here to Aspley, six miles, the road
running really through beautiful country. I passed Millbrook, the Carrs'
place,[1] on my way here. Their house and grounds are really charming, but I
hadn't time to stop and go in, which I was really sorry for. The newspaper
makes one melancholy. It appears Louis Napoleon is certainly going to the
Crimea after all; and when once he is there the English Army will have the

character of nothing but a contingent, and France will more and more take the position of head of the Alliance, disposing of England as suits her best. And it seems the renewed bombardment has not, in fact, done anything. How I should like to live quietly in Switzerland with you and the boys!

Text. Russell, 1:45.

    1. Unidentified.

To Mary Penrose Arnold*

⟨Education Department, Council Office, Downing Street, London:⟩
                                         Evesham

My dearest Mother   April 25, 1855
    I write to you from the girls' British school here, while the Pupil Teachers are at work—I wish you could look out of the window with me and see our dear old friend the Avon here a large river—and the Cotswolds bounding the plain, and the plain itself one garden for this is one of the richest and most beautiful parts of England. I was here this time three years ago, coming from Cheltenham and returning there—and I should like very well to be going to Cheltenham now, to find Flu and our old lodgings there, and to stay a fortnight in that very cheerful place—for it is not now the season and one is not overwhelmed with people—and Cheltenham itself and the country about it as as [*sic*] pleasant as anything in England.
    I left Flu at Oxford this morning—she returns to London in the middle of the day, and I follow her tonight. We have had a very pleasant four days at Oriel with the Hawkinses: the girls are improved and the Provost is always, I think, agreeable and pleasant: Mrs Hawkins and her silly girlish shyness and her incredible feebleness it is hard not to be impatient with.[1] We slept in the rooms which you must remember very well, looking out into Oriel Lane: and met a great many Heads of Houses and dignitaries, the inferiority of all of them to the Provost being quite remarkable. I was not at all prepared for his being so pleasant—I think one's being removed from academic Life and its usages makes him treat one altogether in a simpler more natural way. I found him, not tolerable only, but actually very agreeable, and enjoyed being with him. Imagine his having quoted from a Poem of mine in a note to a sermon which he has just published! He seems to me very worn and thin.
    I saw Justice Coleridge on Friday: he is going to ascertain all details about our relations with Fellowes: he wanted me to edit the works—but, if the Roman History is to be edited with reference to more recent works on the subject, I do not consider myself competent, and proposed Arthur Stan-

ley. The Judge however was anxious that at any rate I should edit jointly with him—and anything that I can do I will, although editing is a business I have no acquaintance with. Justice Coleridge proposed of himself that the works should be given to young Parker when we get them into our own hands: and young Parker would certainly be the best man, I think; I don't know why uncle Trevenen objects to him—However I suppose we are now almost pledged to Murray.

It was such a pleasure to see that dear K on her passage—and looking more like her old self than I have seen her look for many years. There is a charm about her which nothing can wear out.—Tell Mary that we are in ecstasies at the thought of her visit to London, which came upon us quite unexpectedly: let me know exactly when she comes that I may make no country engagements for that time. I did not forget her 23rd birthday tell her—and have ordered for her a book she will, I think, like: poor Professor Reed's Lectures on English Literature which have been published by his brother in law since his death: there is a very good picture of him at the beginning of the book.[2]—There will be some lines of mine in the next Fraser (without name) on poor Charlotte Bronte: Harriet Martineau is alluded to in them, and if she is well enough, you must forward the copy of the magazine which I will send you, to her, after you have read the lines. I am glad to have the opportunity to speak of her with respect at this time—and for merits which she undoubtedly has.   With love to all, ever, my dearest Mother,
Your most affectionate son,

M. A.—

You see how William's Edinburgh article is spoken of in the Times.[3]—Let me know as soon as it is settled when you go to Scotland and when you return.—Flu told you the abominable news about herself, I think. She is very properly sorry and ashamed.[4]

MS. Balliol College.

1. Edward Hawkins (see above p. 47) was provost of Oriel 1828–74, long before and after Arnold's fellowship. His wife, Mary Anne (*née* Buckle) died in 1892; their two surviving daughters were Margaret (d. 1870) and Mary Frances (d. 1908), both (like their older brother) unmarried. He published *Psalms, Lessons, and Prayers for Every Morning and Evening in the Week*, 2d edn, 1855.

2. Henry Hope Reed (1808–54: *DAB*) had been professor of rhetoric and English literature at the University of Pennsylvania. In 1845 he published *Thomas Arnold's Lectures on Modern History*; his own *Lectures on the British Poets* were edited by his brother William B. Reed.

3. William Forster's article "The Autocracy of the Czars," *Edinburgh Review* 101 (1855):500–32 (the *Times* reference has not been found).

4. This remains a mystery. (It is probably not relevant that she was two months pregnant.)

To Jane Martha Arnold Forster

⟨Education Department, Council Office, Downing Street, London:⟩

23, Grosvenor St, West

My dearest K　　　　　　　　　　　　　　　　　　　May 7, 1855

That dear old Edward was quite right in defending me against your strictures—I have never seen so much as the outside (to my knowledge) either of the physiological or philosophical treatises of Harriet Martineau—but I think her character a fine one, and her independence and efforts to be sincere with herself worthy of admiration. I was glad of an opportunity of expressing my admiration at this time, when she has much to suffer—the more so as speculations like those to which she had given herself are so utterly antipathetic to me that I never could return her friendliness to myself by even a decent amount of interest and sympathy for her labours.[1]

You must not return the Fraser (which is the copy Parker sent to me) as I never keep my own works for fear of being tempted to read them. If the Poem displeases you however you have my free permission to make away with the magazine containing it in any manner you please—and I say this, my darling K, without a tinge of vice or bitterness—for there are many things which those I was very fond of might write which I myself should not wish to keep. I am very glad William likes the Poem.

Tell Edward he has behaved basely in not coming *here*; and that he is to write at once and state definitively when he *is* coming: has he forgotten that I owe him £5.

I have come in here to write this—but we are all at Teddington with the Wightmans for 3 or 4 (or, as little Tom counts, 4 or 3) days—and I am going back there directly having inspected a school in London this morning. Now this sort of bliss will I know move Edward's envious bile. My love to that dear old boy.

Of course you saw the notice in the Times' leader of William's article. I could not get the Review at the Provost's (that worthy has ceased to take any periodical literature whatever except the Illustrated News—so like him)—but the Wightmans have got it at Teddington, and I shall now be able to read it. My love to William. You are both of you most truly kind about the children: there is no one with whom I would so soon have little Tom as you; it is not quite certain yet, however, that the Judge will get the N. Wales circuit.

I am not going to write any more for the magazines. I have not time.

ever your most affectionate brother—my own dear K,

M. A.—

MS. Frederick Whitridge.

1. Arnold's mother was equally bemused (see the next letter).

To Mary Penrose Arnold*

London
My dearest Mother   Wednesday, [? May 16, 1855]
   I have waited and waited in hopes of writing to you at leisure: but I have
been so perpetually changing my place that I have hardly been able to keep
up with the merest business correspondence.
   As to the poem in Fraser I hope K sent you a letter I wrote to her on
that subject—in which I told her that I knew absolutely nothing of Harriet
Martineau's works on debated matters—had not even seen them, that I knew
of: nor do I ever mention her creed with the slightest applause, but only her
boldness in avowing it.
   The want of independence of mind, the shutting their eyes and professing to believe what they do not, the running blindly together in herds for
fear of some obscure danger and horror if they go alone—is so eminently a
vice of the English, I think, of the last 100 years—has led them and is leading
them into such scrapes and bewilderment, that I cannot but praise a person
whose one effort seems to have been to deal perfectly honestly and sincerely
with herself—although for the speculations into which this effort has led her
I have not the slightest sympathy.
   I shall never be found to identify myself with her and her people—but
neither shall I join, nor have I the least community of feeling with, her at-
tackers. And I think a perfectly impartial person may say all in her praise that
I have said.
   This has been written while Flu was getting ready to go out, and here
she is—Goodbye then, my dearest Mother. The children are still at Teddington, but return tomorrow. We dine tomorrow at L[ansdown]e House,
which for Flu's sake, who has never dined there, I am very glad of. We dined
last night at the Coleridges'! Dear Mary I have not seen since Saturday. I will
write again as soon as ever I can.   Your most affectionate
                                                                M. A.—

MS. Balliol College.

Elizabeth Cleghorn Gaskell to Matthew Arnold[1]

Plymouth Grove, Manchester
My dear Mr Arnold   May 25, [1855]
   I have just read 'Haworth Churchyard'.—(I knew it must be yours from
the advertisement, but I have only had the oppy of seeing Fraser this morning.) I do thank you for it—the poetry of it seems above my praise, so I am

not speaking of that,—but for the beautiful & touching honour you render her; & that mention of Emily Bronte which would have made her heart leap up with joy, could she have read it. Those were sacred to her who appreciated Emily's wonderful powers; she was hungry & craving for every word that seemed to do justice to Emily.

I hardly know whether to tell you,—but they lie all buried under heavy stones just close before the altar in Haworth *Church*.—one longs for her & Emily to have had their burial-places where the breeze from their own moors might have stirred the grass growing over them. I wish I could express my honour & deep love for her as a woman—one of the noblest

MS. Frederick Whitridge (incomplete).

1. The surviving portion of this amusing letter was first printed in *Album*, p. 3.

Jane Martha Arnold Forster to Thomas Arnold

Wharfeside

May 30, [1855]

I spent a morning with dear old Matt & Fanny Lucy. I cannot say that I think life in London & the constant intercourse with Judge Wightman (who though clever & kind-hearted is I should think as thoroughly worthy a man as ever lived) are very good for dearest Matt—for I think both he & Fanny Lucy are quite enough inclined to value the externals & proprieties of life—but the dear boy's great affectionateness is always both touching & refreshing to me—and I believe he never sees me without going back in thought to the old times when we were "the three elder ones" & after all the artificial London life can never win a great hold upon him, while the fount of his love for his "little Tom" wells up so fresh & deep. I can hardly describe to you how he is bound up in that child—and seeing this, the darling's frailty makes one tremble for looking at that delicate nervous little form, & the face so sensitive & thoughtful, one cannot but feel that it is a most uncertain treasure. Still, he was even more delicate as a baby. Little Trevenen is a sturdy handsome child—a great contrast to his brother— striking if you attempt to touch him, & not causing a moment's anxiety to anyone.

MS. Balliol College.

To Elizabeth Cleghorn Gaskell

23, Grosvenor St. West

My dear Mrs Gaskell   June 1, 1855

I must find time to send you at least one word of thanks for your most kind letter. Few people's satisfaction could have given me so much pleasure as yours.

I am afraid the metre in which the poem was composed must have interfered with many people's enjoyment of it—but I could not manage to say what I wished as I wished in any other metre: and I was greatly desirous to say something, at such a time, in honour and respect of both those who are the chief personages of the poem. How good is poor Harriet Martineau's sketch in the Daily News! you will have smiled to yourself, I am sure, in reading my lines, in spite of all that was sad in that subject, to think of our conversation at dinner, and how I was pumping you.

I am almost sorry you told me about the place of their burial. It really seems to put the finishing touch to the strange cross-grained character of the fortunes of that ill-fated family that they should even be placed after death in the wrong, uncongenial spot.[1]

Farewell, my dear Mrs Gaskell, with renewed thanks. May *you*, at any rate, long continue living and working, and delighting us all.   Ever most sincerely your's

M. Arnold.—

MS. John Rylands University Library Manchester.

1. Arnold's second "mis-burial": in "Stanzas in Memory of the Author of 'Obermann,' " he had buried Senancour in Switzerland rather than near Paris, as Sainte-Beuve pointed out (see above p. 299); and in this poem he misplaced all *three* Brontë sisters ("the grass blows from their graves to thy own")—Emily and Charlotte were, as Mrs Gaskell points out, in a vault in the church, not the churchyard, and Anne was buried miles away in Scarborough, where she died.

To Mary Penrose Arnold

⟨Education Department, Council Office, Downing Street, London:⟩

Grosvenor St. West

My dearest Mother   June 3, 1855

All three of the enclosed you will like to see. I make a present of them all to my dear Fan, when you have read them. Dear Tom's letter is a great pleasure to me.[1]

I am writing in the drawing-room before breakfast with Tom standing perfectly quiet in one window and Trev. in the other watching a band play. "Papa dear, is it going?—it *is* going"—

Toddy has just awakened—and now he is coming up to me to be followed shortly by his fat brother. They are two dear little men, and really now no trouble at all—and with them and one little girl I should have all the family I wish for. Trev. does not talk at all, but understands everything, and is a good boy.

We are not going the Welsh circuit, as the Judge cannot get it this year, one of the chiefs having taken it: to lose the journey in Wales & £75 is a bore but to keep the children with us and go to the sea with them is a considerable pleasure on the other side. K, you know, was to have taken them. I think I shall ask her to take them in November instead, as Ly Wightman has offered to take Flu for her confinement—and (besides the saving of expense) it is a great thing for her at such a time to be in a perfectly comfortable house where she has none of the anxieties of servants and housekeeping. I shall keep the children with me at Derby till the beginning of December, and Fan must come and keep house for me there: then, if K will take them, I shall send them to her for three weeks or so, till their Mamma is quite her dear self again. I wish you could see the boys—Tom playing the Marseillaise on a paper-knife and Budge dragging the litter-basket round & round the room to the tune of Cheer Boys Cheer. God bless you my dearest Mother—our united warmest love to you all—   Ever your most affectionate

M. A.

I cannot find Gladstone's speech anywhere.[2] I thought you had had the paper containing it. *Pray* don't let our coming bring you back a day sooner from Scotland. Why not come and join us at *Folkestone* and *Boulogne* instead of going to Scotland at all. It would be cheaper and far pleasanter and then we would all go north together.

Flu says you are with Susy. My love to that unnatural girl, and to John.[3]

MS: Balliol College.

1. Fan's autograph album (referred to occasionally in these letters) is not known.
2. On Thursday, May 24, Gladstone addressed the House urging negotiations with Russia about peace in the Crimea on the grounds that the goals had been achieved: "If the war was continued in order to obtain military glory, we should tempt the justice of Him in whose hands was the fate of armies, to launch upon us His wrath" (*Annual Register*, 113–14).
3. John Cropper.

To Jane Martha Arnold Forster*

⟨Education Department, Council Office, Downing Street, London:⟩
Teddington
My dearest K   June 18, 1855
    I have not been able to write to you since the death of William's mother[1]—and now comes the death of poor Holberton also to remind one of one's mortality. How the days slip away and how little one does in them—that is more and more my thought in hearing of every fresh death among those whom I have known—and it becomes sadder and more serious as one advances in life. I hear today that Sir Edward Buxton is dangerously ill: I hope this is not true.

    The Judge has not got the North Wales circuit—one of the Chiefs took it: so the two dear little boys remain with us and we all go to Dover together on the 16th of next month, I hope. The not losing them consoles me for losing the £75 which the circuit would have been worth. I daresay if you are at home in November you will take them for two or three weeks and perhaps me with them for part of that time while their Mamma is confined: Lady Wightman has offered to take her in in Eaton Place for that business[2]—and the relief to her of having a perfectly comfortable house and no housekeeping troubles at such a time is so great that I would not have her refuse the offer for the world: besides that I wish her to have the best London advice this time, as the poor dear little thing is rather low about herself, although I hope and believe without any cause.

    The two boys can hardly be at an age, I think, when they will be pleasanter company than they are now. They are perfectly well, and consequently in the best humour and spirits. This large house and garden suit them exactly: we have been here nearly a fortnight and shall stay a week longer. I wish you could have seen Tom stop as he walked in the garden with me yesterday while the birds were singing with great vigour—put his little finger to his mouth as a sign to listen, and say—"Papa["]—

"Do you hear the mavis singing?"

which is the first line of a song called "Mary of Argyle"[3] which is one of his songs, and which he applied of his own thought in this pretty way. Every one notices and pets the child—he is so singularly winning and *unexpected* in all he says and does.

    Go to Auvergne by all means—you say in N. Italy you seemed to perceive where I had got my poetry—but, if you have fine weather, you will perceive it yet more in Auvergne—The country has such beautiful forms and such a southern air. The point is the Baths of the Mont D'Or: the inns or boarding houses there are very good: and from there you must go up the Mont D'Or: and do not miss two things—the old bourg of La Tour D'Auvergne: and a Nemi-like lake at the Cantal side of Mont D'Or. Clermont and the Puy de Dôme (where Pascal made the experiments which resulted in perfecting the barometer) you are sure to see: for they are on the great road of Auvergne. The country on the side of Thiers and Issoire is said to be very beautiful: it is far less known than the rest of Auvergne: I have not seen it. All that country is the very heart and nucleus of old France: there are very few English—and at the baths of the Mont D'Or many French of the best kind. Travelling and living accommodations are very good. Tell me again when you have settled to go.

Willy has got a newspaper appointment and some chance of an Examinership under the new Civil-service-reform plan.[4] He comes back from Dowlish tomorrow.

It is very late and I must go to bed. Flu's sincerest love with mine to William and you both.   Ever your most affectionate

M. A.—

MS. Frederick Whitridge.

1. Sister of Sir Thomas Fowell Buxton, she died at age 70 on June 5 (*Annual Monitor*, 1856, p. 77). Sir Edward North Buxton (1812–58; 2d bt), was her brother. Thomas Henry Holberton, Esq., of Hampton, Middlesex, died at age 83 on June 15 "at Anglesea, near Gosport, after an illness of ten days" (*The Times*, June 19, p. 1). See the next letter.

2. The birth of Richard Penrose Arnold on Nov. 14.

3. Words by Charles Jefferys, music by Sidney Nelson, published by Harry May (London, n.d.): "I have heard the mavis singing / His love-song to the moon; I have seen the dew-drop clinging / To the rose just barely born: But a sweeter song has cheered me, / At the Evening's gentle close; And I've seen an eye still brighter / than the dew drop on the rose; 'Twas thy voice my gentle Mary / And thine artless winning smile that made the world an Eden, Bonny Mary of Argyle!"

4. "He worked for a time on the staff of *The Economist*, and was thinking of applying for the editorship of that paper, when, in the late summer of 1855, a letter came from John Lawrence, Chief Commissioner of the Punjab, asking him to accept the new post of Director of Public Instruction in that territory. . . . He did not refuse the bidding" (Woodward, p. 201).

To Mary Penrose Arnold

Teddington

My dearest Mother   June 20, [1855]

Fan says you meant to write to us: so, while Flu is going to bed I will forestall you, taking the first piece of paper I can find. We have been here now for nearly a fortnight: every morning I go up to town at 9 o'clock with the Judge and return with him at 5 while Tom and Trev. run about here the whole day, and are in such flourishing case as they never yet, the former especially, have known. The good character they get wherever they go for manners and behaviour is due in the first instance perhaps to the pains Flu takes with them—but Deane also deserves some credit for it, and has lately been going on much better.

At this season of the year this regal and cheerful region of the Thames is perfectly superb: and these old villas with their huge walled gardens have an air of settled civilisation unknown in Yorkshire and Lancashire. I wish you could be here for a day or two. While we are here we have sent Willy to sleep in Grosvenor St. West, which for one week at least will save him house-rent. If he can get one of these examinerships along with his Economist appointment, he may, I think, do well enough: that is, until he is 40 and begins to feel the difference between being something and nothing. I am up in London daily, and in Grosvenor St. West for an hour or two, and generally see Willy who is in capital spirits, and as all my brothers, I must say, always are, very amiable to me.

The Bp of Oxford[1] whom I met today made me a long speech about my poems, both volumes of which he said he had just read through for the second time—and preferred Balder to everything. I send you a stupidish criticism which was sent to me. Mr Truman's poems have some good bits— one on Professor Wilson very good.[2] Did [you] read his poem on Fox How? It is not good, but in an excellent spirit. Poor Holberton is buried tomorrow. It is affecting to see how everybody liked him and respects him.

It is said that the French, after three bloody attacks, gained the Malak-hoff tower and were then driven out of it by the fire of the Russian ships. My paper is at an end—so with love to all I must stop.   Ever your most affectionate

M. A.—

MS. Balliol College.

1. Samuel Wilberforce (1805–73: *DNB*; *VF*, 7/24/69), "Soapy Sam," bishop of Oxford 1845–69, then of Winchester for the rest of his life. (The epithet, though well and truly earned over a number of years, dates only from 1864.) For Arnold's measured appraisal of him see letter Feb. 2, 1864.

2. Joseph Truman (dates unknown) published *Poems* (Nottingham, 1855), referred to here, *Poems* (1859), *Effie Campbell and Other Poems* (1864), *Afterthoughts* (privately printed, 1889), in the brief preface to which he quoted from two letters from Arnold to himself: " 'I have not often,' he wrote once, 'read anything more true and more happily expressed, I wish all who knew Wilson could see it. It is a pity you did not send the lines to *Blackwood*.' And at another time, 'Your "Elleray" is still in my memory, and will always remain there.' " His last recorded book was *Later Poems*, 1910.

John Wilson (1785–1854: *DNB*), "Christopher North," author, critic, reviewer, and professor of moral philosophy at Edinburgh. In the Lake Country he lived at Elleray, overlooking Lake Windermere, less than a dozen miles from Fox How.

To J. H. Beale[1]

July 4, 1855

Many thanks for your statistics, which will be both useful and interesting to me. I have read with pleasure the article of yours in the Banbury paper on the three education bills. [Arnold goes on to express regrets at having to miss a meeting, and tells Beale that he looks forward to seeing him in October. On Education Department stationery]

Text. Occasional List, No. 73 . . . Ximenes and Jarndyce, Lot 789 [1986]

1. J. H. (or A. J.?) Beale was a teacher at the Banbury Boys School, which Arnold inspected regularly from Oct. 1854. See below pp. 328, 345.

To Arthur Hugh Clough

⟨Education Department, Council Office, Downing Street, London:⟩
Brighton
My dear Clough   August 2, 1855

This day I send in *Deal Wes[leya]n* (an August case)—will you kindly take it promptly as Harris the master has received one of the appointments to New S. Wales and will sail very shortly?[1]

Will you also see why Annie Hinchley, Mistress of the Dunmow B. S.—has not had her certificate sent to her?

I wish you would write me a long letter. From the extracts I have seen from Maud, he seems in his old age to be coming to your manner in the Bothie and the Roman poem. That manner, as you know, I do not like: but certainly, if it is to be used, you use it with far more freedom vigour and abundance than he does—Altogether I think this volume a lamentable production, and like so much of our literature thoroughly and intensely *provincial*, not European.[2]

With the usual prayer that no fine spirits may be so drenched in the daily cares of life as finally to become imbruted,[3] I remain,   Your friend to command

M. A.—

MS. Yale University.

1. Arnold had inspected Harris's Deal Wesleyan School, Kent, on July 17, Annie Hinchley's Dunmow School, Essex, on May 1 (diary).

2. Tennyson's *Maud and Other Poems*, published on July 28, included the Wellington ode, "To the Rev. F. D. Maurice," "The Charge of the Light Brigade," and four other poems, all (for better or worse) guilty as charged—only "The Daisy" is truly exempt.

3. Clough married Blanche Smith on June 12, 1854, a child was born and died in April and, as he wrote to a friend on July 27: "I am overwhelmed with schools and school-papers" (Mulhauser, 2:504). His "Roman poem" was "Amours de Voyage," sometimes known as *Roman Elegies and Roman Hexameters*, first printed in the *Atlantic Monthly* in 1858 and then in *Poems*, 1862 (London, Boston).

To Frances Lucy Wightman Arnold*

Council Office
Thursday, [August 16 or 23, 1855] [1]
I am having rather hard work at the Boro' Road—hard work compared with common inspecting, for I have the afternoon till five as well as the mornings; but I am rather interested in seeing the Training School for the first time. I am much struck with the utter unfitness of women for teachers or lecturers. No doubt, it is no natural incapacity, but the fault of their bring-ing-up. They are quick learners enough, and there is nothing to complain of in the *students* on the female side; but when one goes from hearing one of the lecturers on the male side to hear a lecturer on the female side there is a vast difference. However, the men lecturers at the Boro' Road are certainly above the average, one from his great experience, the other from his great ability. You should have heard the rubbish the female Principal, a really clever young woman, talked to her class of girls of seventeen to eighteen about a lesson in Milton.

Text. Russell, 1:53–54.

1. A vexatious problem. Russell, supplying the year-date, merged two (or three?) letters. A. K. Davis (*Checklist*, p. 21) compounded the felony by giving the date as Aug. 23, whereas the diary (Guthrie 2:98) shows that Arnold inspected the Boro' Road school, in southeast London, "for the first time" in the week beginning Sunday, Aug. 12, and remained there till Thursday, Aug. 16. He may have returned on Friday, Aug. 24 (2:99). Russell's third paragraph clearly should be dated Sept. 20 (q.v.). His second was written after Sept. 10, and *faute de mieux* has been merged here with the third.

To [?]Frances Lucy Wightman Arnold*

[Thursday, September 20, 1855]
I have got the *Allgemeine Zeitung* (did I tell you?) containing the mention of my poems. It is very uninteresting, however. And some one has sent me *The Sun*, containing a flaming account of the first series. [1] I surely told you this, however?

There is no news to-day, except that 4000 cannon have been found in Sebastobol.[2] Things being as they are, I do not see anything to object to in the Emperor's message. But the situation is altogether disagreeable until the English fleet or army perform some brilliant exploit.

Text: Russell, 1 :54.

   1. Arnold must have been weary of the recurrent comparisons in the former; and *The Sun*, though it flamed for *Poems* (1854), sputtered out for *Poems*, Second Series: "Shelley's Einfluss.—Matthew Arnold und A. Smith," *Allgemeine Zeitung*, May 8, 1855, Special Supplement, p. 2 (unsigned); *The Sun*, Sept. 10, 1855, p. [3], cols. 6, 7, also unsigned, reviewed both *Poems* (1854) and *Poems*, Second Series (1855): "It is something quite refreshing to meet once in a way—as in the instance of Mr. Arnold—with a poet who can write both musically and coherently." The reviewer devastates "that miserable *Maud*," as well as Browning, "the croakings of Elizabeth Barrett Browning," and the Spasmodics. He singles out "The Church of Brou" for special praise and calls Arnold a "young poet gifted with rare powers alike of judgment, of taste, and of imagination," refers to "The Strayed Reveller" as a "stray driveller," dismisses "Mycerinus," "Philomela," "Cadmus and Harmonia," praises "The Forsaken Merman." *Poems* Second Series is "a volume as unworthy of his powers as could well be. Everything in the book from first to last . . . is calculated, we fear, rather to retard than to advance the poetic reputation of which we have here, in our comments upon the volume of 1854, notified the brilliant and auspicious commencement." The reviews may have been the work of Charles Kent, the editor and proprietor of the *Sun*. See Arnold's letter to his mother Feb. 4, 1872, and note.
   2. The capture of Sebastopol on Sept. 9 was announced in *The Times* two days later; the report about the "4,000 cannon" appeared on Sept. 20 (p. 7), along with the order of the day in which Emperor Alexander expressed his "warm gratitude" to the defeated Russian army: "But," he said, "there are impossibilities even for heroes." These "will give new proof of their warlike virtues . . . and will . . . always fight the enemies that attempt to touch our sacred arch, the honour and territorial integrity of our country."

To Henry Dunn[1]

My dear Mr Dunn   [? October, 1855][2]
   You remember the Van Diemen's Land Mastership about which I spoke to you? Can you help me to a man whom you feel you can really recommend. Those whom I knew and have applied to, I find too firmly established in this country to be willing to leave it: and I do not care to make a nomination at all, unless of a really good man. So, unless you can recommend some one to me (and I am sure you will not recommend a merely *passable* Teacher for such an appointment) I shall leave the nomination to the committee of council—and they will probably send out a student from Kneller Hall.
   I am extremely busy with Examination papers. I must say I have been

remarkably struck by the excellent *handwriting* of your Female *students*. It is by far the best I have yet come to.

I hope your cold is quite gone by this time. Believe me,   Ever most truly yours

M. Arnold.—

P. S. Mr Saunders knows the details respecting the salary—&c &c—of the appointment in case you should wish to have them. Pray let me hear not later than Monday.

MS. *British and Foreign School Society Archives Centre.*

1. Henry Dunn (1800–1878: Boase), secretary of the British and Foreign School Society (see above p. 207n). Of the eleven letters to Dunn on record, only three have been traced. Among his thirty-odd books and pamphlets one is worth special mention here, *Facts, Not Fairy-Tales: Brief Notes on Matthew Arnold's "Literature and Dogma"* (1873), to which Arnold alluded "with esteem" in *God and the Bible* (see Super, 7:191, 455, and 11: 222). The British and Foreign School Society (founded in 1808), a nonsectarian institution for the education of the laboring and manufacturing classes, in "1854 placed their institutions at the Borough Road and Stockwell on a collegiate footing" (*Encyclopædia Britannica*, 11th edn, 8:982). See also Thomas Adkins, *The History of St. John's College, Battersea* (1906).

2. The date is a guess. We know little, or (for the most part) less than little, about Arnold in Sept.-Oct. The diary is blank from Sept. 5 to Oct. 17. He went to Liverpool on Oct. 18 or 19, probably for the weekend, and the diary resumes on Monday, Oct. 22. The handwriting seems exactly like that of the letter to Dunn, below, on Dec. 10. Kneller Hall (see above p. 210) became the Royal Military School of Music in 1856.

To Henry Dunn

⟨Education Department, Council Office, Downing Street, London:⟩
                                                    38, Eaton Place
My dear Mr Dunn   December 10, 1855
    Mr Marjoribanks,[1] whom you know, wants to come and see me about the Bushey school, and I told him I should be at home on the *morning* of today: I have now a note from him in which, interpreting *morning* rather widely, he says that he shall be here between 1 and 2 o'clock. Considering his age and that he is coming from Bushey, I do not like to put him off—but I am afraid his visit will make me a little late at the Boro. road, and of this you will perhaps kindly let the students who are to teach before me be informed. I hope at any rate to be with you by a ¼ before 3.   Ever very truly your's

M. Arnold.—

MS. *British and Foreign School Society Archive Centre.*

1. Unidentified.

To William Forster

⟨Education Department, Council Office, Downing Street, London:⟩
38, Eaton Place
My dear William   December 19, 1855
    I want you, if you don't object to write and ask Milnes for his interest in getting me admitted a member of the Athenæum as a literary adventurer without ballot.[1] He is a member of the Committee and has no doubt great influence with the other members—and he has always so far as I have heard expressed himself kindly about me. I hear that people are admitted as literary and scientific men on the very smallest grounds, if the Committee choose: even for a single pamphlet, or Essay:—so there is, I think, no presumption in my trying to get thus admitted: if there was I would not ask you, of course, to apply for me.

(Sgd) Matt. Arnold

MS. *Trinity College, Cambridge (transcript).*

    1. Arnold was elected promptly—see below p. 330.

To James Hepworth[1]

Mr Hepworth—
                Education Department, Council Office, Downing Street, London:
Dear Sir   December 27, 1855
    Was any one of your Pupil Teachers up for a Queen's Scholarship the other day. I did not see him at the Boro Road, if he was. I write to ask, because, if you had no one up I may as well send in my Report on your school at once: for there will then be no longer any reason for delaying it.
    With all the good wishes of the season to you, believe me,   truly your's

M. Arnold.

MS. *Bodleian Library.*

    1. James Hepworth was a schoolmaster at the Great Meeting Schools, in East Bond St, Leicester, which Arnold had inspected on Nov. 27; he lived at 16 Guthlaxton St (White's *History, Gazetteer, and Directory of the Counties of Leicestershire and Rutland*, 1863, pp. 192, 245, 278). Ten letters from Arnold to Hepworth are known, from this one to 1872—most of them after Leicester was no longer one of his districts—but Arnold deliberately remained stiffly formal.

To Wyndham Slade*

38 Eaton Place
My dear Wyndham   December 29, 1855
I am quite provoked about the godfathership, the more so as if I had really thought you would have liked to be godfather there is nobody in the world, now that I have knocked off my dear Waller[1] with Master Trevenen, whom I myself should more have liked for the office. But the truth is that the night you dined in Eaton Place, and we were talking about names, you said, after Waller had said that the boy ought to be called by the sweet name which I myself bear, that you too thought family names ought to be kept to, and that if you were me you would not give the child a name like Wyndham. It occurred to me afterwards that you had perhaps said this thinking that it would be rather a bore, and also *un peu ridicule*, for you to fill the office of godfather; and as I remembered that I, when unmarried, had precisely the same feeling, and, in fact, always declined to fill the office, I determined to say no more about the matter to you, and to ask other people. Accordingly, we have now got two ecclesiastics—the old Archbishop of Dublin for one, and Peter Wood for the other.[2] This is a long story, but it is precisely the story of how the matter happened, and of what passed in my mind, and I know you will readily forgive me if I made a mistake as to what your real feeling was. I could not bear the notion, that was the fact, of boring you with such an office, which you might, I thought, have accepted because you did not know how to refuse.

This cursed long story has spoilt my letter. You know Waller has accepted the post offered & given up all thought of japanning himself for good. He comes up on Monday. Come, you too, as soon as you can. I am full of a tragedy of the time of the end of the Roman Republic[3]—one of the most colossal times of the world, I think. You and Nina will both appear in it. It won't see the light, however, before 1857. I have only read about a hundred pages of Macaulay. I thought my chariot wheels went heavier than when I was reading the first two volumes. Read Prescott's *Philip the Second*. I think it is just the book you would like. You ought also to read Lewes's *Life of Goethe*. The time is short.   Ever yours most sincerely,

M. Arnold.

Text. Russell, 1 : 55–57.

1. Glossed by Slade: "Waller is Theodore Walrond C. B."
2. Richard Penrose Arnold, born on Nov. 14, was named for the "old Archbishop," Richard Whately; Peter Wood (see above p. 268), now from Devizes, Wilts, was his wife's brother-in-law.

3. The tragedy on Lucretius never materialized except for a few fragments printed in Tinker and Lowry, pp. 345–47. The sentence "You and Nina will both appear in it" was supplied by Tinker and Lowry "from the original manuscript of the letter which we have seen" (p. 342n). Macaulay's *History of England*, vols 3, 4, William H. Prescott's *History of Philip II, King of Spain*, vols 1, 2, and G. H. Lewes's *Life of Goethe* all appear in the "Lists of Reading" from Dec. through March (*Note-books*, pp. 558–59).

To A. J. Beale[1]

Mr Beale   ⟨Education Department, Council Office, Downing Street,⟩
38, Eaton Place, London
Dear Sir   January 8, 1856
I have just received your letter of yesterday's date. I have already, a week ago, both written an official letter, and myself spoken to Mr Sandford about your case and that of the Miss Fulchers. You need not fear but that the lost paper will be allowed for: to make the matter quite sure I will go myself to the Council Office tomorrow and speak about it again.

I quite appreciate the difficulty of the position in which a teacher, successful as you are, stands, when he finds himself compelled to undergo an examination for the special necessities of which his previous training may not have have qualified him: but I have good hope that this may be your last time of trial.

Remember me kindly to Mr Cadbury,[2] when you see him, and to any other friends at Banbury, and believe me,   your's faithfully
Matthew Arnold.—

MS. Yale University.

1. A. J. (or J. H.?) Beale see above p. 322.
2. James Cadbury (c. 1803–88), a minister from Grimsbury, Banbury, listed in the *Annual Monitor*, 1888 (*British and Irish Biography* 1:047), is no doubt the same as the author of *A New History of Banbury, before and after a Maine Liquor Law*, 1855 (Allibone).

To James Hepworth

Mr Hepworth   Council Office
Dear Sir   January 30, 1856
Read over the enclosed papers carefully, and let me know at your earliest convenience whether the appointment to which they relate is one which would suit you.

I wish them to be kept to yourself, and this to be considered as a strictly private communication. I remain, Dear Sir,   faithfully your's
                                                        Matthew Arnold.—

MS. Bodleian Library.

To James Hepworth

⟨Education Department, Council Office, Downing Street, London:⟩
                                                17 George St, Edgbaston
Dear Sir   February 6, 1856
     I have received your letter of the 2nd at this place.

     No information whatever can be obtained at the Council Office respecting the appointment in question, other than such as is contained in the papers I sent you. I think this is stated in one of the papers forwarded. The appointment does not rest with the Committee of Council, nor have they anything whatever to do with arranging the terms of it: they have merely been requested to *recommend* a Teacher for a certain described situation.

     I cannot therefore undertake to be the medium of any negotiations or questions respecting the conditions of the appointment: indeed were I willing to be so, it would be in vain, for all the answer I should receive at the Council Office would be that they had nothing whatever to do with determining those conditions.

     I advise you therefore to make up your mind with respect to the appointment purely and simply on the conditions stated.

     I think so highly of your powers of *organizing* and *working a school, that I will gladly recommend you if you desire it.* At the same time I will by no means take upon myself the responsibility of *advising* you or any man to accept an appointment such as that now in question. There are great drawbacks, no doubt, to the advantages of Indian appointments: these have, as was certain to be the case, and as is right, presented themselves to you: in such a case every man must decide for himself. I have a brother holding a high appointment in India who so suffers from the climate that he would abandon his appointment for one of a fourth of its value in this country. Others again bear the climate without suffering and enjoy their Indian life more than they enjoyed life in England. Every man, as I say, must judge for himself: you must consider your health, your constitutional tendencies, your domestic circumstances: I do not the least *press*

you to take the appointment: only I thought it right to propose it to you.
Believe me   faithfully your's

M. Arnold.—

MS. Bodleian Library.

To Jane Martha Arnold Forster*

⟨Education Department, Council Office, Downing Street, London:⟩
Edgbaston
My dearest K   February 17, 1856

I shall send you tomorrow by post a volume of Montalembert's about England,[1] which, if you have not read it already will interest both you and William I think. Read particularly the chapter on the Liberté de tester and on English Public Schools and Universities. What he says about the Public Schools and Universities comes curiously from a foreigner, and just now:— but I think there is much truth in it—and that if the aristocratical institutions of England could be saved by anything, they would be saved by these. But as George Sand says in the end of her Memoirs (which you should read)— L'humanité tend à se niveler: elle le veut, elle le doit, elle le fera:[2] and though it does not particularly rejoice me to think so, I believe that this is true, and that the English aristocratic system, splendid fruits as it has undoubtedly borne, must go. I say it does not rejoice me to think this, because what a middle class and people we have in England! of whom Saint Simon says truly—"Sur tous les chantiers de l'Angleterre il n'existe pas une seule grande idée."—[3]

I write this—pamphlet, it is getting like—today because I shall have not a minute to write it tomorrow. They will have told you from Fox How that there has been a negocation [*sic*] about my going to the Mauritius, and that I am not going. I hope they have sent you all the *pièces*. They think at Fox How that I have these offers from my merits, and that I am getting on: but it is not so—this offer came by an accident, and on account of no supposed merit or fitness of mine whatever.

I am elected at the Athenæum, tell William—and look forward with rapture to the use of that library in London. It is really as good as having the books of one's own—one can use them at a club in such perfect quiet and comfort. My love to William—how I wish you both would meet Mamma here next week. ever, my dearest K,   your most affectionate brother

M. A.—

Flu's love to you both. We have got a lovely picture (daguerretype) of little Tom. I am writing in the dark. God bless you.

MS. Frederick Whitridge.

1. Charles Forbes René comte de Montalembert (1810–70), London-born (French father, Scots mother) journalist, historian, orator, Catholic educator, Anglophile—*De l'Avenir politique de l'Angleterre* (1855), translated from the French (1856). (The two chapters are nos. 7, "On the Law of Entails," and 10, "The Schools and the Universities.") With Lacordaire and Lamennais, Montalembert was a leader of liberal Catholic thought in France, though some considered him "a bigot and an Ultramontane" (see Senior, 1: 318, 315). In May 1858 Arnold met him at breakfast at Gladstone's (see below p. 301), and in *A French Eton* drew on his book on Lacordaire (Super, 2:374). In London in 1855 "il s'entretient avec les hommes principaux d'Etat, lord Aberdeen, lord Canning, gouverneur général des Indes, lord Brougham, lord Lyndhurst, Gladstone surtout qu'il visite à plusieurs reprises: 'Je trouve en lui, dit-il, un coeur ouvert, une âme droite, une intelligence singulièrement élevée' " (R. P. Lecanuet, *Montalembert*, 3:143: "L'Eglise et le second empire," Paris, 1902). He heard Gladstone in the House and commented p. 146): "Il parle avec éloquence, noblesse, sincérité. . . . Enfin, c'est l'homme supérieur, a mon avis, de l'Angleterre actuelle." See the long obituary in the *Annual Register*, pp. 159–61.

2. George Sand, *Histoire de ma vie*, pt 5, ch. 13 (Pléiade edn, 2:456).

3. Untraced.

To William Delafield Arnold

11 Lower Belgrave Street, London

My dearest Willy   March 31, 1856

The above is a false date, for I am writing from the Athenæum—but the above is my address, if you write to me, for the next two or three months.

I was elected here in February (at the Athenæum) and could not have got to a place more perfectly to my mind. I am sitting now, at ½ past 12 in the day, writing at a window in the great Drawing Room with only two other people in the room—every side of this magnificent room covered with books and the room opening into others also full of books—it is a cloudless day and the wind has this very morning changed from the east which has been cursing us for the last month to a delicious south: I look out upon the façade of the Senior United and the open place in front between that club and ours, and on the roofs and colonnade of the old Italian opera—and the Park below the Duke of York's column is full of people waiting for the guns to fire—for the peace was signed yesterday—Sunday—the guns fired last night from 10 to ½ past—but they are going to begin again this morning.[1] We got back from Birmingham some three weeks ago, and are settled in a charming little house belonging to the Miss Rickettses, aunts of Mrs Charles Buckland,[2] close to Eaton Square—we dine in our old fashion every night in Eaton Place—but can hardly yet be said to have begun to enjoy ourselves, so utterly impossible was it to be happy during the prevalence of the late savage east wind.

I have been extremely interested by your letters—by none more than by those in which you speak of your new employment—I too have felt the absurdity and disadvantage of our hereditary connexion in the minds of all people with Education, and am always tempted to say to people, "My good friends, this is a matter for which my father certainly had a specialité, but for which I have none whatever." You however will throw yourself thoroughly into the work, and will do it well—you have more to do of an important kind than I have, certainly—but whatever you had had to do, you would have thrown yourself heartily into and would have done it well—in this way you cease to feel the burden of the work—I on the contrary half cannot half will not throw myself into it, and feel the weight of it doubly in consequence—I am inclined to think it would have been the same with any active line of life on which I had found myself engaged—even with politics—so I am glad my sphere is a humble one and must try more and more to do something worth doing in my own way, since I cannot bring myself to do more than a halting sort of half-work in other people's way.

I am so amused by your having already written an article stirring up some one.[3] How I pity your unfortunate superior if he is not a man who really puts his shoulder to the wheel. His subordinate will be a thorn in his side, poor soul—and quite right too that it should be so—for no man should accept a chief place without meaning to give himself to it. Tell me however in what sense it is that that man—I forget his name—the man who is going to lend you his house for a time up at the hills—is your chief. I thought you were yourself a head of a Department.

Since you went it has been proposed to me to go to the Mauritius with a salary of £1500 a year as Colonial Secretary—but my income here is above £900 a year now and in seven years time will be above £1000—not to speak of my having London for my district and being likely to get rid of all my outlying counties—of all my district, that is, except Middlesex and Kent—and Sir James Stephen to whom Lingen referred the matter for advice for me wrote a long letter so strongly counselling me to stay as I was that I at once determined to stay.[4] The climate of the Mauritius is heavenly and we could have taken the children—I should have sate all day on a coral rock, bathing my legs in the Southern ocean.

There is nothing here in literature worth speaking of—except that the National Review[5] is doing well—that Ruskin has published a new volume of Modern Painters even fuller than the others of true aperçus, even more than the others deprived of the *ordo concatenatioque veri* which is the one thing needful.[6] However to have good and faithful aperçus is a great thing. It may also interest you to know that your literary successor in the Economist is in my opinion a stick.[7]

We have not seen Eddy since our return, for Mr Ford is afraid to let him come to us, there being measles in Eaton Place, with which we are in constant communication. Our own children are quite well however and I hope we shall have dear little Eddy in a week or two. My love to Fanny[8]—Flu will write to her, she *says*, but I doubt. *You* write to *me*.   Ever your most affectionate

M. A.

I have seen Sir Laurence Peel once or twice, and like him very much.[9]

MS. Balliol College.

1. At 10 o'clock in front of the Mansion House the Lord Mayor of London read a brief dispatch from the home secretary: "I have the honour to acquaint your Lordship that a despatch has been this morning received from the Earl of Clarendon, Her Majesty's Principal Secretary of State for Foreign Affairs, dated Paris, the 30th, announcing that a definitive treaty for the restoration of peace, and for the maintenance of the integrity and independence of the Ottoman Empire by the Plenipotentiaries of Her Majesty, of the Emperor of the French, of the King of Sardinia, and of the Sultan, and also of the Emperor of Austria and of the King of Prussia, on the one part, and of the Emperor of all the Russias on the other" (*Annual Register*, p. 70).

2. Charles Thomas Buckland, Indian civil servant and author, in 1845 married Caroline A. Ricketts, one of the three daughters of Sir Henry Ricketts (1802–86: *DNB*), also an Indian civil servant. Her two sisters were Elizabeth and Marianne Ricketts (Buckland's obituary in *Annual Register*, 1894; *Landed*, 1849); as the diary shows (Guthrie 2: 134), the Arnolds took the house from Mar. 3.

3. "Protestantism: Zwingli and His Times," *Fraser's Magazine* 53 (Mar. 1856): 326–41.

4. Sir James Stephen (1789–1859), formerly colonial under-secretary, then professor of modern history, Cambridge, and (1855–7) at East India College, Haileybury.

5. The new monthly, founded in 1855, jointly edited by R. H. Hutton and Walter Bagehot, lasted a decade. See H. McLachlan, *The Unitarian Movement in the Religious Life of England*, pp. 195–97, the excellent description in *Wellesley*, 3:135–46, and below p. 344.

6. Ruskin's *Modern Painters*, III, was issued Jan. 15, 1856. "Ordo concatenatioque veri," "order and connectedness of truth,"—used again below p. 336. "One thing needful" (Luke 10:42)—later used in Latin, "Porro Unum Est Necessarium," as the title of ch. 5 of *Culture and Anarchy* (the Nonconformists' "favorite text," as Arnold wrote to George Smith in June 1868) and of an article in 1878.

7. Unidentified. See above p. 320 n. 4.

8. Eddy was William's eldest child, Edward Penrose Arnold, later, Arnold-Forster, born in India. Later, he joined his parents in India (see Woodward, pp. 214–15). Fanny

was his mother, Frances Anne Hodgson Arnold (see above p. 267), daughter of Maj. Gen. John Anthony Hodgson (d. 1848), of Sheraton, Durham.

Mr Ford is not securely identifiable in the Chinese (or Indian) boxes of possibilities, but he was probably the Rev. Charles Ford (1797–1863), who attended Balliol College 1815–19 (B.A.; M.A. 1821), formerly rector of Billingford and now of Postwick, Norfolk (1843–63).

He was the eldest son of Sir Francis Ford (1717–1801; 1st bt), of St Marylebone, Westminster, and the uncle of William Ford (1821–1905, son of the 2d bt), of the Bengal Civil Service, who in 1845 married Catherine Margaret Hodgson, eldest daughter of General Hodgson. General Hodgson's only son, Hon. Maj. Gen. Hugh Norris Hodgson (1827-?), of the Bengal Staff Corps, was a brigadier in the Punjab under Lord Dalhousie in 1854 (William Lee-Warner, _Life of the Marquis of Dalhousie_, 1904, 2:290). Frances Anne Hodgson Arnold was therefore the younger sister of Mrs William Ford and niece-by-marriage of the Rev. Charles Ford (who had five children, mostly born in the 1840s) with whom Eddy may have been staying, measles-free, in Norfolk. In 1875 Eddy married Edith Mary Ford, second daughter of William Ford, "managed his adopted father's Greenholme Mills at Burley-in-Wharfdale, living at Cathedine (now The Court), a house about a mile from the Forster home, Wharfeside," was J.P. and D.L., fathered four children, and translated Schiller (Arnold-Forster, pp. 531–32; _WWW_). For the Fords see Kelly; _WWW_; _Upper Ten Thousand_; Baldwin, p. 5; for the General Hodgsons see Kelly, _Upper Ten Thousand_; and Whitaker.

9. Sir Lawrence Peel (1799–1884: _DNB_), first cousin of Sir Robert Peel, the statesman, attended Rugby (but long before Arnold's day) and then St John's College, Cambridge. He became chief justice of the Supreme Court of Calcutta (and was knighted) in 1842, from which he retired in Nov. 1855, and returned to the appropriate, prescriptive honors in England.

To Mary Carpenter

11, Lower Belgrave Street, London

My dear Madam   March 31, 1856

Your letter of Feb[ruar]y 2nd has just reached me, but the annual which you speak of in it has not been forwarded, although I have no doubt it is at Fox: How, and that I shall receive it in due time—so I offer you my thanks for it in advance. My mother is at present staying in Devonshire, and the house at Fox: How is shut up—from time to time parcels of letters are sent from thence to my mother and in such a parcel was your letter to me which was forwarded to me by my mother from Torquay—But books and periodicals they do not forward to her from Fox How—and this accounts for my not yet having received the "Liberty Bell." [1]

My time is so much occupied with business—I work so slowly both in prose and verse—and, above all, I have so little personal experience of the working of Slavery, and so little acquaintance with the details of the Slave-Question, that I dare not promise you a contribution. Still the cause is one of those which have sides that may be seized even by the inexperienced and ignorant—and if I find after looking over your Annual that I can do anything which would be suitable for its pages, I will gladly try to do it and will send it to you as soon as it is done.

Owing to my mother's absence from Westmorland I have heard nothing for some time respecting Harriet Martineau's state: but when I was in Birmingham a month ago I heard from her relations there that there was little change. [2]

With many thanks to you for your kind recollection of me, and hoping that I may one day have the pleasure of again meeting you, I remain, my dear Madam,   Yours very truly,

M. Arnold.—

MS. Harvard University.

1. *The Liberty Bell,* "By Friends of Freedom," an annual, was published in Boston 1839–58.

2. More here than meets the eye. "From 1855 she was expecting death at any moment. She survived for another twenty-one years. . . . But she managed to keep going with, at one time or another, oysters, game, champagne, turtle, brandy, and laudanum—and she got a fantastic amount of work done."

Mary Carpenter's compassion was characteristically otherworldly, for in January she had trodden on a viper. She "wrote lamenting that Miss Martineau did not have the comforts that she derived from her religion, Miss Martineau sent back a sizzling reply that led Miss Carpenter's brother to intercede and ask that she not be proud with a humble Christian like Mary. The fury redoubled. It was always the Christians who were humble, she sneered; when they stood up for what they believed, it was called zeal for the Gospel; when she stood up for what she believed in, it was called pride and haughtiness. There was too much truckling to the Christians, and now that Mary had insulted her by pitying her, it would be treachery to the truth and cruelty to mankind not to defend the loftiness and breadth of the principles of her faith" (R. K. Webb, *Harriet Martineau,* pp. 310–11, 302).

To Jane Martha Arnold Forster*

The Athenæum
My dearest K   March 31, 1856

Laurie, the British Inspector,[1] is coming your way soon, and I want you to be kind to him. He is rather odd, but has sterling qualities—he has quite made his own way in the world—having been brought up, the son of a poor Scotch Minister, to some trade which he forsook from a desire to educate himself—having carried into effect this desire at Edinborough and Berlin, and been nearly starved in the process—and finally having attracted the notice of the Combes in Edinburgh,[2] and been by them recommended as Tutor to Ld John Russell's children—from which situation he passed to others of the same kind in great families, and finally was made an Inspector.

He has a genius, in my opinion for estimating the character of boys— of *little* boys, certainly,—and for dealing with them.

And how are you, my dear, dear, soul? I read William's speech the other day with great interest. I see Baines has poured himself out in today's Times. Ld John's measure is said to be of Shuttleworth's concoction—and if so, I think it will succeed—for Shuttleworth knows better than most people what will go down in the way of education.[3]

Have you seen Ruskin's new volume of "Modern Painters?" I ask you because I saw William alluded to him in his speech. Full of excellent aperçus, as usual—but the man's character too febrile irritable and weak to allow him to possess the ordo concatenatioque veri.[4] You see I treat you as if you were Lady Jane Grey.[5]

When are you coming to London, for coming you are.—I am glad peace is made, as it has to be—it is all a stupid affair together. Write to me soon at 11, Lower Belgrave Street. Do you see anything of Bright at Ben Rhydding?[6] This Athenæum is a place at which I enjoy something resembling beatitude.   Ever your most affectionate

M. A.

My love to William. Trevenen can say "Cuckoo, Cherry Tree"—that is the latest domestic news.—God bless you.

MS. Frederick Whitridge.

1. James Stuart Laurie (1831 or 1832–1904: *DNB*) later a barrister-at-law and author, director of public instruction, Ceylon, was always concerned with education, even after resigning his inspectorship in protest in 1863. He was obviously a man of immense charm (his own "children's favourite," Arnold said, inviting him to Dickie's birthday party, "mad but excellent with children"), and Arnold remained in touch with him at least till 1883. (See also *WWW*; *Men-at-the-Bar*; Super, 7:400.)

2. George Combe (1788–1858: *DNB*), a well-known, well-traveled, and highly successful phrenologist; he figures prominently in George Eliot's life (see Gordon S. Haight, *George Eliot*, esp. pp. 100–101). But, more to the point, he was also a very important supporter of state influence in education (Connell, pp. 48–49).

3. On Mar. 6 Russell, who, though now secretary for the colonies in Palmerston's cabinet, had been Lord President of the Council and was still a leading member of the Committee, introduced to the House twelve Resolutions on national education proposing sweeping revisions. Edward Baines (1800–1890: *DNB*; knt. 1880), journalist, economist, editor of the *Leeds Mercury*, and M.P. for Leeds 1859–74, and his older brother, Matthew Talbot Baines (1799–1860: *DNB*), Member for Leeds 1852–59, now in Palmerston's cabinet as chancellor of the Duchy of Lancaster, whose identities are sometimes confused, were both in the thick of the discussion, an extended account of which (includ-

ing the twelve Resolutions) is printed in the *Annual Register*, pp. 155–80. The latter weighed in in the House debates; Arnold's references, both in his letters and *Prose Works*, are always to the former. Edward Baines's long letter, against "Lord J. Russell's Plan of Education," was in *The Times*, p. 12.

    4. "Order and connectedness of truth" (see above p. 333 n. 5).

    5. Arnold apparently means that his sister was as learned as Lady Jane Grey. See below p. 374. Forster's speech has not been traced.

    6. A "hydropathic establishment" in Wharfdale, Yorkshire. For Richard Bright see above pp. 189–90 n. 4.

To Jane Martha Arnold Forster*

London
Tuesday Morning, [April 29 or May 6, 1856]

Many thanks, my dearest K, for your extracts—my poems are making their way, I think, though slowly, and perhaps never to make way very far. There must always be some people however to whom the literalness and sincerity of them has a charm—after all that American Review[1] which hit upon this last—their sincerity—as their most interesting quality was not far wrong. It seems to me strange sometimes to hear of people taking pleasure in this or that poem which was written years ago—which then nobody took pleasure in but you—which I then perhaps wondered that nobody took pleasure in—but since had made up my mind that nobody was likely to. The fact is however that the state of mind expressed in many of the poems is one that is becoming more common—and you see that even the Obermann stanzas are taken up with interest by some.

I think I shall be able to do something more in time, but am sadly bothered and hindered at present—and that puts one in *deprimirter Stimmung*,[2] which is a fatal thing. To make a habitual war on depression and low spirits which in one's early youth one is apt to indulge and be somewhat interested in, is one of the things one learns as one gets older—they are noxious alike to body and mind, and already partake of the nature of death.

Poor John Blackett is dead[3]—I send you a short note I had from his sister yesterday to tell me of it. This is indeed "one's own generation falling also." I had more *rapports* with him than with almost any one that I have known—there was a radical good intelligence between us which was based on a natural affinity. I had lived so much with him that I felt mixed up with his career—and his being cut short in it seems a sort of intimation to *me*.

Let me know as soon as it is settled when you come up here on your way abroad—and pray don't shoot through like an arrow.—What a good course Willy seems starting to run. My love to William.   Ever most affectionately yours,

M. A.—

MS. Frederick Whitridge.

    1. Unidentified.

    2. A mood of dejection—and much closer to Coleridge than to Keats.

    3. On Apr. 25 (see above p. 75).

To Bessie Rayner Parkes [1]

Miss Parkes—

11, Lower Belgrave Street

Dear Madam   Saturday morning, [? June 7, 1856] [2]

I received your note yesterday—I am sorry to say I had formed before I received it an engagement which will prevent my having the pleasure of hearing Mrs Jameson's lecture this afternoon, and I shall be much obliged to you if you will kindly express to her my sincere regret at being thus prevented. [3]

I am glad to have had the pleasure of making your acquaintance although I certainly did not know, when I saw you at Halstead, whose acquaintance I was making—and think I was ill-used by our mutual acquaintance in not being introduced to you. Believe me, dear Madam,   very truly yours

M. Arnold.—

MS. Girton College.

    1. Bessie Rayner Parkes (1829–1925), poet and protofeminist: *Poems* (1852), *Summer Sketches and Other Poems* (1853), *Gabriel* (1856), *History of Our Cat Aspasia* (2d edn 1856), *Remarks on the Education of Girls* (1856), etc. She (like her father) figures significantly in George Eliot's life and letters. In 1868 she married Louis Swanton Belloc and became the mother of Hilaire Belloc (1870–1953). See Allibone and Gordon Haight, *George Eliot: A Biography.*

    2. The stationery is watermarked 1855. Arnold was in Halstead on May 23 and 29.

    3. Anna Brownell Jameson (1794–1860: *DNB*), also an author, feminist, traveler, friend of Bessie Parkes, Lady Byron, Ottilie von Goethe, and many others, and well known for her *Companion to the Most Celebrated Private Galleries of Art in London* (1844), including a catalogue of "The Collection of the Marquess of Lansdowne at Lansdowne House and at Bowood." "During her latter years Anna was much engaged in public service work. In 1855 she lectured on 'Sisters of Charity Abroad and at Home'; in 1856 on 'Communion of Labour' " (*Anne Jameson Letters and Friendships (1812–1860)*, ed. Mrs Steuart Erskine, p. 285); published in the first half of Sept. 1856 (*Publishers' Circular*); both are listed in Allibone.

To Mary Penrose Arnold

38, Eaton Place
My dearest Mother   Sunday, [? August 2, 1856]
    I meant to have sent you this half sheet in return for your's yesterday, but I have two Reports on hand just now, and am sorely pressed. I have had an offer to go as secretary to a Commission to enquire into Foreign Military Education: we should go to Paris, Berlin, Vienna, Turin—and be away 4 months or so—I should get three guineas a day & my travelling expenses, keeping my Inspectorship & its salary all the time:—pleasant enough, you will say: yes—but the Commissioners are our dear Lake and two Engineer Colonels—the offer came to me from Lake with a sort of intimation that it was I who was to do the work of the Commission. I thought I did not know my men quite well enough (except Lake) to be safe—so I have declined to go as Secretary—but offered to go as 4th Commissioner without a Secretary—I should then stand on firm ground with them: however this I don't think they will care to effect. I will send you in a day or two a copy of my letter to Lake.
    I take for granted you have heard what Matt Buckland tells me, having heard it in a letter from his brother Charles—that Willy has had to sell out, but has nevertheless accepted the Education Appointment: that he grumbles greatly: that he has started for the Punjab: that Ld Dalhousie[1] and another Member of Council made great interest for him, but that the Military authorities (the natural fruit of Oakfield, this) were dead against him—finally that the Education appointment is a good deal better than Willy thought— nearly £2000 a year. "W. hates the ⟨climate⟩ country," says Charles Buckland, and in return the ⟨climate⟩ country spites him."
    I think Edward will be here tomorrow. You know there is a hitch about his [?]business. I cannot say I shall be sorry if the marriage goes off. The longer I live the more I see that marriage with a narrow income and precarious future is a sort of gambling state which can only be supported by those of firm nerves and strong ready wits: the feeble sink under the anxiety of it. You have known the strong and therefore have no notion of prudence. But I sincerely think such a marriage as he now contemplates will not be for Edward's happiness.
    Love to all my dear girls, and to Walter, if he is still with you. Always your most affectionate son.

                                                                    M. A.

I am fast getting entirely free from debt—for the first time these I don't know how many years. Tell Fan Trev. grows such a fat old darling.
    Uncle Trevenen's is rather a black account certainly.

MS. Balliol College.

1. James Andrew Broun Ramsay (1812–60: *DNB*), 10th earl and first marquis of Dalhousie, governor-general of India from 1848 till Feb. 1856, had been in England since mid-May.

To Jane Martha Arnold Forster

Brighton
Sunday, August 10, [1856]

August the 10th, my dearest K, and your birthday was the 1st and I meant you to have had a letter on that day. I was going to have sent it to Kissingen when a suspicion arose in my mind that you might no longer be there—and I wrote and asked Mamma how this was, and learnt that you were on the point of returning to Wharfeside[1]. Since I heard this I have been perpetually moving about, and owe this quiet morning to a violent bilious attack, which has kept me from going to hear Sortain, the only minister, so far as I know, whom I care to hear, throughout the churches and chapels of England.[2]

I have often thought of you, my dearest K—I can truly say, seldom as I write, that you are one of those oftenest in my mind and who first occur to me in connexion with what interests me deeply.

I have just been, as you know, the Oxford circuit with the Judge—the earlier places in it Oxford Worcester Stafford and Shrewsbury I knew well enough—but from Shrewsbury to Gloucester all was new to me, and the border country between England and South Wales—the primitive Silurian country, where Arthur reigned—is one of the most beautiful and interesting countries in the world. From Shrewsbury to Ludlow, between the hills of Caradoc and the Long Mynd, are many places where I could willingly live. I went one day to fish at Downton Castle, which is a great place in the gorge of the Teme about 5 miles from Ludlow: I left the railway at a small station a mile or two from Ludlow and walked as I could get directed across the fields to Downton-Castle: fields they were not so much as a park-like fern-covered country on the fringes of a forest with perpetual dips and dingles—rabbits stirring in the fern all about one, the thyme scenting the air and the murmur of the Teme in the forest valley beneath—and far away in the beautiful sunlight the soft ranges of the Welsh hills fading away one behind the other in the distance—I was quite alone and as I rested on the stiles I thought of you because what it all brought most vividly to my mind was the story of Emma and her Nurse[3] which we used to read when we were children, and the description of the pleasant hills of that Montgomeryshire country—the first description of a country which I remember to have taken powerful hold upon me. Why this country is so interesting is because it is not *terminated*—it goes off from the beautiful border country of Hereford and Shropshire into

Wales, and from Wales to the sea without meeting with any region worse than itself to shut it in. Ludlow Castle is very fine—Ross is over-praised, to my mind—but the Wye, "*the sylvan Wye*,"[4] which we went down in a boat all the way from Goodrich to Shepstow is not overpraised and cannot be. It is like a dream—and—what is so rare in England—you descend for some thirty miles between the most exquisite hills with no road on either hand to break the seclusion—nothing but a foot-track on one side of the river. Tintern we saw in heavenly weather—but this I have no time for.

My finances are this year for the first time since my marriage getting, I hope, into a healthy state—so I mean to keep quiet in order to let them get thoroughly round—but next year I shall make an urgent appeal to my family and friends to adopt my dear little boys for six weeks, and disappear for that time—which I long to do—taking Flu with me, who is the best travelling companion in the world. Write to me at 6, Esplanade, Dover, there's a dear soul, in the course of the week. The children stay here with Fanny Nicholls till Friday, when they join us at Dover. They are very brisk and well—dear Baby getting quite fat, and the best and sweetest tempered little boy in the world. The two others are amusingly glad to have me back—I feel something nibbling my hand sometimes like a little soft mouse: and when I look down it is Tom kissing it. Budge is getting on with his talking, but it is rather the unknown tongue[5] which he speaks at present. I must end as I should have begun with my love and good wishes for your birthday, my dearest K, and with love to William I am always   your most affectionate brother

M. A.—

MS. Frederick Whitridge.

1. Kissingen was the most-frequented wateringplace in Bavaria; some of the springs were thought to be specifically beneficial for nephritis. See above pp. 189–90 n. 4, 337 n. 6.

2. Joseph Sortain, a graduate of Trinity College, Dublin, was for many years minister at the North Street Chapel, Brighton, and author of several books and pamphlets. He died in 1860 at the age of 50 (Allibone; *Annual Register*).

3. *Memoirs of Emma and Her Nurse*, by Lucy Lyttelton Cameron (1781–1858: *DNB*), very popular author of religious stories for children. The "description" must have been that on pp. 105–6 in the 1820 edition: "The pleasantest time Jane spent was in walking out with her little mistress [Emma]. Sometimes she was allowed to go beyond the park, accompanied by an old footman, who had very little else to do, than to assist in carrying his young lady. Then Jane would take her little mistress to the castle hill, and shew her the distant mountains, the towers and villages, rising midst sweet woodland scenery: and here the little ones would play among the ruins in the beds of thyme. Sometimes Jane would shew her the little church where her mother's remains were at rest. Jane seldom gathered any sweet flowers for her, or shewed her any fine views, but she would try to lead her mind to contemplate her first Creator, who had made all these lovely objects to lead us to himself." See Introduction, p. xxxi.

DNB points out that Dr Arnold, a "warm admirer," said in one of his sermons:

"The knowledge and the love of Christ can nowhere be more readily gained by young children than from some of the short stories of Mrs Cameron." Her sister, Mary Martha Sherwood (1775–1851: *DNB*), was even more popular and prolific. Of her "most notable production, *The History of the Fairchild Family; or The Child's Manual, Being a Collection of Stories Calculated To Show the Importance and Effects of a Religious Education, DNB* writes: "Most children in the English middle-class born in the first quarter of the nineteenth century may be said to have been brought up on the 'Fairchild Family.' " Its most notable effect is Christina Rossetti's poem "Goblin Market."

    4. Wordsworth's "Tintern Abbey," l. 56.

    5. I Corinthians 14:2 (etc.).

To Wyndham Slade *

Brighton

My dear Wyndham   August 10, 1856

    I look across the sea to you, and imagine your agreeable countenance looking out from a window on the other side. I don't wonder you migrated, for after your some years' experience of Dieppe, you must have sighed for it again when you found yourselves at Boulogne. That place I consider we exhausted in our two days last year, and I never wish to pass another whole day there.

    The whole Alderson family are now at Dieppe—Packy you know: I consider him rather a young ass—but the youngest, Cecil, I have been seeing a good deal of on the Oxford circuit, where he went marshal to his father—and like him very much. He is a mere boy—but I am sure you will like him, & hope you will find him out, if you have not already done so, & be kind to him.[1]

    The circuit was better than I expected, because more of a tour. All the country from Shrewsbury to Gloucester was new to me, and Ludlow and Herefordshire are well worth seeing; and we went down the Wye by boat from Goodrich Castle to Chepstow, one of the most beautiful water passages in the world. I tried fishing once or twice, and in very renowned waters, but with the heat and the sunshine and the thunderyness it was of no use. I find that we must have made an exchange of rods on our return from the Laverstoke expedition; at least, I think it is yours that I have, and I hope you have got mine. Yours is much the newest, and would pass for by far the best rod, but mine, though old and a little strained, is a great favourite of mine, and the best balanced rod I have ever known, so pray take care of it. I don't know whether you are fishing at Dieppe, but I should certainly try the chalk country inland there. I met an old gentleman the other day who assured me it abounded in trout streams, and the more I see of other trout streams the more I am convinced of the ineffable superiority of those in the chalk.

I have been here for a few days. I like the place, but have been laid up by a thundering bilious attack, the result of the heat, bad cookery, and port wine of the circuit. The living on circuit is very bad, of the worst tavern kind, everything greasy and ill served. The one comfort is the perpetual haunch of venison, which even a bad cook cannot well spoil. Fanny Lucy and I go on to Folkestone to-morrow. We go to Dover, to our old quarters on the Esplanade (No. 6), on Thursday, and shall be there till the 27th. Charmed to see you if you can come. About the 29th we go up to Westmorland. I have determined, as my affairs are doing better, to lie by and get thoroughly sound this year, and then next year I hope I may get abroad for a good six weeks or two months without borrowing or forestalling. I am glad you don't re-propose the Pyrenees, as it would be dreadfully tempting, and it is better I should stay at home. Write to me and tell me of your movements and doings, and whether we shall see you at Dover. My compliments to your mother and sister,[2] and believe me, ever yours,

M. A.

Text. Russell, 1 : 60 – 62.

1. See above p. 105n. Frederick Cecil Alderson (1836 – 1907: *WWW*), the fifth son of Lord Alderson, attended Eton and Trinity College, Cambridge, was ordained, held various curacies and rectorates, was chaplain-in-ordinary to the queen 1899 – 1901, canon of Peterborough from 1891, rector of Lutterworth from 1893, and a member of the Athenæum.

2. Lady Slade (*née* Dawson) died in 1868; she had *two* daughters, Sophia Louise (b. 1837) and Gertrude Matilda (1841 – 1919).

To Mrs Godlee[1]

⟨Education Department, Council Office, Downing Street, London:⟩
Fox How, Ambleside
My dear Mrs Godlee   September 19, 1856
I write this one line to let you know that I keep you waiting for an answer to your letter of the 15th only because I have written to the Council Office on the subject, and have not yet received an answer. As soon as I receive it you shall hear from me.   Very truly your's

M. Arnold.—

MS. University of Virginia.

1. Unidentified, but perhaps a schoolmistress. Arnold sent her a copy of *A French Eton* in July 1864.

To Richard Holt Hutton[1]

R. H. Hutton Esq.

⟨Education Department, Council Office, Downing Street, London:⟩

Wharfeside, Otley, Yorkshire

My dear Sir   October 27, 1856

I have just received at this place your letter dated the 25th inst: the former letter to which you refer, enclosing a note from Mr Herbert New,[2] I have never received. I have been moving about from place to place lately, and I fear that I have thus missed it.

I beg to thank you most sincerely for your flattering proposal: I assure you the subject tempts me so much that the rate of your remuneration would weigh very little with me in deciding whether to try it or not: but the real truth is I am so much occupied that I feel I could not do justice either to your Review or to myself by any article which I could produce for you under my present circumstances. I am therefore compelled gratefully to decline this offer from you as I have declined similar offers from others: but perhaps you will allow me to say that I have been so much interested by your Review that it is with unusual reluctance that I forego the opportunity which you kindly extend to me of contributing to it.[3] It was only a day or two ago that I read the article on Shelley in the last number:[4] that article and one or two others (in which I imagine that I trace the same hand) seem to me to be of the very first quality: shewing not talent only but a concern for the *simple truth* which is rare in English literature as it is in English politics and English religion— whatever zeal variety and ability may be exhibited by the performers in each of these three spheres.

Believe me, my dear Sir, in much haste,   Your faithful and obliged servant

M. Arnold

MS. *New York Public Library (Montague Collection).*

1. Richard Holt Hutton (1826–97: *DNB*), critic, theologian (he started out a Unitarian from Leeds and ended up an Anglican from London), and journalist (joint-editor, with Walter Bagehot, of the *National Review* and, from 1861, joint-editor and part-proprietor of the *Spectator*, which involved him (moral earnestness) in an amusing passage-at-arms with Swinburne (amoral irreverence). See Swinburne, 2:72n.

2. Herbert New (1821–93: Boase) was a solicitor at Evesham from 1843 till his death, partner in a law firm that failed spectacularly a few months after his death, alderman, registrar, mayor several times, and the author of *Simon de Montfort and the Battle of Evesham*, another book, and two or three articles with a religious tendency.

3. Arnold came round eight years later and sent two essays to the *National Re-*

view, "Joubert; or, a French Coleridge" and "The Function of Criticism at the Present Time."

4. Bagehot's "Percy Bysshe Shelley," *National Review* 3 (1856):342–79, but he had had an article in every preceding issue, most recently on Gibbon, Macaulay, and Sir Robert Peel.

To A. J. Beale

⟨Education Department, Council Office, Downing Street, London:⟩
Wharfeside, nr. Otley, Yorkshire
My dear Sir   October 28, 1856
Your letter of the 23rd has been forwarded to me here. I think 6 Pupil Teachers for an average yearly attendance of 180 is as much as is likely to be granted—and I think it might create disapppointment if any hope was held out that a larger proportion would be admitted. This is in fact giving two extra apprentices in consideration of Collett's Queen Scholarship.

I, too, am sincerely anxious that you should be successful this time, and I have little doubt you will be if you keep yourself free from over-strain and over-excitement as the time approaches. Drawing is now very useful: I hope you will not devote too much time or trouble to qualifying yourself for the Music papers.

Will you be good enough to tell Mr Cadbury, who will perhaps kindly acquaint the other members of the Committees, that I have fixed the 17th and 18th of Nov[em]ber for the Banbury schools. I will take the two Infant Schools in the *afternoon* of Monday the 17th, and the Pupil Teachers in the afternoon and evening of that same day—and I will take the Boys' and Girls' British Schools the next day, Tuesday. I shall come from London on Monday Morning, and shall hope to be at the Central Infant School between 1 and 2 o'clock.

Believe me,   faithfully your's

M. Arnold.—

P. S. I will beg of you also to be kind enough to enquire at the Red Lion Inn, and at the Post-office, whether there are any letters for me: and, if there are, to desire that they may be forwarded to me at the Council Office.

MS. University of Texas.

To Mary Penrose Arnold

38, Eaton Place

My dearest Mother   November 2, [1856]

Let me first say, while I remember it, that Flu wishes you to be told that we have one baby's-petticoat which does not belong to us, and that baby has left two of his petticoats behind him.

Will you, as soon as you have Fell's *little bill*,[1] send me the account of what I owe you, and I will send you a cheque for the amount.

I was very glad to have your letter. Poor dear little Tom seems certainly better, and is restored to his usual looks. I think we shall take him to Brodie, whose opinion I have more respect for than that of most of the faculty: for Latham, who is the usual man to consult in heart cases, I have none at all.[2] Little Tom has this afternoon had an unlucky accident, his forehead having come in contact as he was running with a tray which one of the servants was bringing into the room for luncheon: he was a good deal hurt and there is a huge swelling and will be a very black bruise, but what we dislike is the upsetting him and making him sob. He has got over it now however and made a good dinner—his first consolation was that he thought the *red jelly* he saw on the table would do his forehead a great deal of good. The little darling says if he hears me say we will do so and so if we live—"Yes, Please God we all live" and Budge, having seen me kiss him for this, has taken to exclaiming on all occasions "Ple Go we all lib" à propos of nothing at all.

Baby is doing very well, having got rid of the wheezing sound in his breathing—but he still breathes short, and now and then coughs at night—but Dr Hutton has given him some medicine which suits him very well and he no longer occasions us the slightest uneasiness. He is a dear little boy but I do not see so much of him as I should like, because we keep him as much in one air as possible. He is going down in the carriage tomorrow to Teddington that nurse may see her baby who is reported to be doing very well and to be grown a remarkably pretty child, though small.

Flu and I dine with the Stanleys tonight, Arthur being in town.[3] We stay here till the 19th or 20th of next month—then we go to Hampton. Tell Fan that the Secretary to the Manchester Mechanics' Institute, whom I met the other day, told me that my Poems were greatly read from their library: and that a short time ago he had read Sohrab & Rustum aloud to between two or three hundred working men, and that they had all been melted by it. The American edition of my poems has been sent me, and I mean to make you a present of it: I will send it in a day or two. You may also tell Fan that Tennyson said to a Mr Sellar[4] the other day who told Charles Arnold, who told me, that if anything happened to him I ought to be his successor. A thousand thanks for all your care of dear baby. With love to Fan, and all at Fox How.   Always your most affectionate son

M. A.—

I hope Banks is better. Tell us when you have news of Willy, and keep us informed about poor dear Tom.

MS. Balliol College.

1. William Fell was a surgeon in Ambleside (Martineau).
2. For Brodie see above p. 248 n. 2. The allusion to Peter Mere Latham (1789–1875: *DNB*) is portentous. A distinguished man, he was appointed physician extraordinary to the Queen in 1837. His chief work was *Lectures on Clinical Medicine, Comprising Diseases of the Heart* (1845): "His discussion of the symptoms and post-mortem appearances of angina pectoris in relation to the case of Dr Thomas Arnold of Rugby School is a model of the best kind of clinical dissertation" (*DNB*).
Charles Hutton, M.D., below, the family physician for several decades, who lived nearby at 26 Lowndes Street, Belgrave Square, is mentioned frequently in these letters (though never with a first name or address, which come from the *POLD*). The last reference to him ("dear little Dr Hutton") is on Apr. 20, 1887, on his death.
3. A. P. Stanley (who married in 1863), his mother, and his sister Mary (1812–79).
4. William Young Sellar (see above p. 127 n. 4) and Arnold clearly did not take to each other and in fact did not see each other again for nearly a quarter-century—see the letter to Sellar on May 21, 1880. Hardly the "good friend" of Lowry's note, Sellar was struck by Arnold's "'grand manner' . . . which—though it savoured of affectation—was really natural to him, and . . . was neither repellent nor did it put you off your ease" (E. M. Sellar, *Recollections and Impressions*, pp. 151–52), whereas Arnold—unless his particle was part and parcel of this particular "grand manner"—forgot all about Sellar for more than three decades.

To James Hepworth

Mr Hepworth—
        Education Department, Council Office, Downing Street, London:
Dear Sir   December 2, 1856
        The first revision of certificates will not take place till the expiration of a term of seven years after the date of the Minute prescribing it: not, therefore, till after the expiration of several years from this time. The entries on your certificate will go towards raising the value of your certificate: but you will raise its value yet more, if, being re-examined, you give proofs of having made progress since your last Examination.

I, too, shall be sincerely sorry not to see my friends at Leicester again: but my district was too wide for me, and the limiting it to the metropolitan counties will enable me to have a home—so I have something to be glad of also. Remember me kindly to your Pupil Teachers: if I find that the delay in the appointment of the new Inspectors is likely seriously to delay the payment of your stipends, I must try and manage to visit you once more myself. Truly yours

M. Arnold.—

MS. Bodleian Library.

To Jane Martha Arnold Forster*

⟨Education Department, Council Office, Downing Street, London:⟩

101 Mount Street

My dearest K   December 6, 1856

I am writing to you from my old rooms in Mount Street, which are now occupied by Wyndham Slade, of whom you have heard me speak: he is a barrister, and out daily, following his avocations, from 11 to 5—during this space of time he puts his rooms at my disposal—and I fly and hide myself here from the everlasting going in and coming out of Eaton Place, in the profoundest secrecy, no one but Wyndham Slade knowing where I am. "Hide thy life"—said Epicurus[1]—and the exquisite zest there is in doing so can only be appreciated by those who, desiring to introduce some method into their lives, have suffered from the malicious pleasure the world takes in trying to distract them till they are as shatter-brained as the world itself.

The air is like balm today, and little Tom will go out, I think, in Eaton Square—for the first time since we have been in London. We had, indeed, an alarm about him, and I think it nearly developed in me the complaint he is said to have—at least that alarm added to large dinners and a hot bed-room have produced in me a fuller beating of the heart than I like—but I get better as Tom gets better, and he really seems getting better every day. His spirits and appetite are now very good again—yet he has not lost the extraordinary goodness which he has shown ever since his attack here in London: yesterday he scratched Budge as appeared by the scores on the fat old thing's neck—but that is really the only outrage he has committed. Budge on the other hand has acquired in Eaton Place rather a bad character for furious passion: and he does sometimes seem to take all of a sudden an extraordinary twist: but I do not think he is always well managed when I am out and I have great faith in his dear old heart. Every day when I come in about half past 5, Budge, who never sits down at any other time, announces that he is very tired and must lie down with Papa on the bed, and there he reposes for about a quarter of an hour with his head on my shoulder, asking me from time to time if I love him, and assuring me "ur do love Papa"—and "Tiddy Tom *may* have my *Gee*"—"Diddy *may* have my whip"—and all the other concessions which the fat old duck thinks will give me pleasure.

Ly Wightman is going to have Tom's picture taken by a young artist who has been recommended to her. Tell William that Fanny Blackett has brought me a Horace, which poor Johnny Blackett desired her just before his death to get for me, which would make his mouth water. We were both much interested in the Bradford paper, and in Mary's account of the proceedings.[2] About Tom I say nothing.[3] I thought of him on his birth-day last Sunday. I don't hear of your going to Fox How—and indeed the quieter the house is just then, I suppose, the better. How I wish we were to pass Xmas together! Flu and I look out for houses, but find none—you have no notion of the frightful rents asked in the country round London. We go to Hampton on the 20th. Love to William—I am always, my dearest K,   your most affectionate—

M. A.

Compliments to the Raven and cat. Has William taken any more victims through the Denham glen at nightfall?

MS. Frederick Whitridge.

1. Λάθε βιώσας, Epicurus, Fragment 86 (Cyril Bailey, *Epicurus the Extant Remains*, p. 139)—famous because discussed at length in Plutarch's essay in *Moralia*, "Is 'Live Unknown' a Wise Precept," and by Erasmus, and others.

2. Untraced, but probably candidates feinting and maneuvering for the general election coming up in June 1857 (see Reid, 1 : 306–9).

3. Tom Arnold, nine years absent, had his troubles and must have been feeling despised and rejected of men. Having been formally received into the Roman Catholic Church in January, he reached London from Hobart Town in October, met aboard ship by the Forsters (his first sight of William), visited his mother—"I saw Matt at Fox How; putting out of sight the whiskers (which considering their bushiness it is difficult to do) I consider the old boy very little changed"—and proceeded forthwith to the Catholic University, Dublin, where Newman, himself shunted off there as rector, had got him an appointment. Whately, the Anglican archbishop of Dublin, oldest and closest of family friends, cold-shouldered him. His brother William, in his most self-righteous *Oakfield* mood, sent a bigoted letter. His pregnant wife, with whom relations were strained, wrote to him from England about wearing a hat and flannel drawers. See *Letters of Thomas Arnold the Younger 1850–1900*, ed. Bertram, pp. 77–86.)

To Herbert Fry[1]

Herbert Fry Esqre

38, Eaton Place

Sir   December 18, 1856

The Messrs Longman have forwarded to me within the last few days only your letter of the 28th ult. in which you express a wish to include my portrait in a collection which you are forming of the portraits of eminent living persons.

I sincerely assure you that I feel much flattered by your request, which, however, I must beg you to excuse me from complying with, as I cannot consider myself sufficiently celebrated to merit a place in such a collection.   I have the honour to be, Sir,   Your obedient servant,

Matthew Arnold.—

MS. National Portrait Gallery, London.

1. Herbert Fry (1830–85: Boase) was a compiler of useful books and guides—e.g., *National Gallery of Photographic Portraits* (1858), for which he is soliciting Arnold's here, *The Shilling [*later, *Royal] Guide to the London Charities* (1863–85, annually), *London Illustrated by Eighteen Bird's-eye Views of the Principal Streets* (1885), *Our Schools and Colleges* (1867), as well as some travel guides. He was not a photographer and had nothing to do with the firm (founded 1864) of Elliott and Fry.

To Mary Penrose Arnold

Hampton

My dearest Mother—   January 16, [1857]

We half hoped to hear from some of you today—but at any rate I write tonight to say that dearest Diddy continues to go on well—he has had no convulsions since Sunday and has today been particularly lively and well, having reaped much benefit from his favourite stimulant, calomel, which Mr Holberton is greatly afraid of, but which Dr Hutton strongly urged us to give. I have just been up and seen him asleep on his nurse's arm with a tinge of colour on his sweet round pale cheeks—she, I am sorry to say, breathing very uneasily, being bilious and unwell from want of exercise—she is to go out tomorrow, and might have gone out today, for Diddy sate more than half an hour alone with me in the drawing-room, as good as gold, amusing himself with the Leader while I read the Times. His brothers have had colds and have been rather fractious and unamiable for the last day or two—two of the little Oliver Lambarts came to dine with them yesterday and Tom got into one of his tantrums, and did not shew to advantage. Little Rodulph Augustus Arnold (!) my godson is five months younger than Tom and a tiny little under-sized shrimp, but with the pluck of all the Lambarts—think of his saying to Tom, who had cried at being shut up in a room by himself, in a most contemptuous tone when he came out—"You great goose!" Ly Cavan is in small lodgings close by the Palace, and we are going to call on her tomorrow.[1] Did I tell you of Tom's describing to me Diddy's illness when I came back from town—"He is in the nursery—he's very ill—he's had a fit— he's dead—where shall we put him?"—all in the most perfectly uncon- cerned tone. I have just seen dear old Budge fast asleep, with a new boat which his Grandmamma Wightman has given him on the pillow beside him, with one of his fat hands resting upon it.—I am aghast sometimes when I think of bringing them up—but then I think of Papa, and the mountains that he managed to move so easily.[2] I am sorry to say Nurse and Emma quarrel,[3] and indeed Nurse's temper is her weak point. Her child was christened to- day—the most pretty lively little fellow you ever saw—Flu & I godfather and godmother. Don't forget to tell me Tom's Dublin address—and do some of you write me from time to time. Louisa Twining called here today, and said, I am sorry to say, in effect that old Mr Twining was breaking.[4] Tell Mary that she may pay her £5.15s. to me here (Hampton, Middlesex) as the Hampton P. O. is now a money order office. My affairs are fast coming into good order, you will be glad to hear. God bless you my dearest Mother—with love to all   ever your most affectionate

M. A.—

MS. Balliol College.

1. Vaughan Holberton, a surgeon from Hampton (*POLD*, 1860), was perhaps a son of Thomas Henry Holberton (above, p. 320 n. 1).
[For the Lambarts see above p. 80.] Rodulph Augustus Arnold Lambart (1852– 1923) and probably his brother Percy Francis Lambart (1851–1933). Lady Cavan could be the Countess Dowager (why not "Aunt Lydia?"), widowed since 1837, or Caroline Au- gusta Littleton Lambart (d. 1892, daughter of Lord Hatherton), wife of the 8th earl of Cavan ("small lodgings" near the Palace?), neither of whom is alluded to by name else- where in these letters.
2. I Corinthians 13:2.
3. Nurse's name (Norman) is revealed below p. 379.
4. Richard Twining (1772–1857: *DNB*), Mary Arnold Twining's father-in-law and Louisa's father (see above p. 295 n. 4), died on Oct. 14.

To Susanna Elizabeth Lydia Arnold Cropper

The Athenæum
London
My dearest Susy   January 28, [1857]
        You will have been astonished, I hope, before this, by the arrival of the long-promised Shakespeare—not the identical one promised, indeed, for

when I proposed to remove it there was an outcry as to the gap that would be left in the shelf, and I yielded: but as I saw no prospect, if my books continued at Hampton, of your getting your Shakespeare for many years I ordered you an edition (far better than the old Capell) in a great many volumes, and told the bookseller to send it you by railway. The Valpy edition, which I chose, is in a most readable form, and the prettiest printed, as I think, of all the modern editions of Shakespeare.

I wish you could see my books, or rather those of them which are in the book-cases at Hampton. They are nearly what I designed to make them—a collection of the chefs d'œuvre in all the languages which I can read—excluding, therefore, even in English, a great many writers whose works are considered indispensable in an English library, but yet have no claim to rank (in my opinion) among the chefs d'œuvre of the literature of the *world*. This does not make exactly an entertaining library—but I think it makes the most solid, useful, and satisfactory library possible, and a library the mere contemplation of which improves one: amusing books one can always get for the little term for which one wants them at libraries and such places.

Baby is better again today, but had a very bad day the day before yesterday—fortunately, however, no convulsion. Tom and Trev. are beautifully well, and dear old Budge would comfort you to see, he has such cherry cheeks pretty brown curls and irrepressible jolliness. How is your little kangaroo?[1] How is my dear John? has he invented a new stove lately, bless him? Don't forget to bring my umbrella case when you come to town—and when will that be? We shall very likely stay at Hampton till the middle of May—if so, and you come to town we can take you in most likely: that will be a true pleasure. With my love to John,   ever your most affectionate,

M. A.

MS. Frederick Whitridge.

1. Presumably, the daughter, Lucy Ada Cropper.

Frances Lucy Wightman Arnold
to Mary Penrose Arnold

[? late January or early February, 1857]
Conversation I have just overheard between Tom & Trev. Tom (who wants something that Budge has possession of) 'Budge *do* let me have it'
(Budge gruffly). 'No'
(Tom) Oh but Budgy dear I have got a chilblain you know'

(Budge rather softened by the fact of the chilblain but still not quite subdued)
No, Can't Tiddy Tom'
(Tom in a very amiable tone) 'Oh but Budge dear, I thought you always *liked* to lend things to Tiddy Tom'!!!!
(Budge completely softened) [wd illeg] I do Tiddy Tom [wd illeg]
So Tom gets the wished for article.
Tom's wheedling tone & Budge's dear old innocence were as good as a play. I can't help inclosing this though I have finished my letter.

MS. Balliol College.

To James Hepworth

Mr Hepworth.

Education Department, Council Office, Downing Street, London:
My dear Sir   March 28, 1857
I have requested that your desire may, if possible, be complied with, and the case will be gone into again—this is all that I have it in my power to do for you: I am not at all sanguine that they will grant the extra Pupil Teacher.
You will be glad to hear that I thought Mr Beattie[1] far more successful than any artist to whom I have ever sate. Believe me,   Your's truly,
M. Arnold.—

MS. Bodleian Library.

1. Apparently, William Beattie, a sculptor, *fl.* 1829–64, when he exhibited at the Royal Academy and the British Institution; he was also employed by the firm of Wedgwood (Rupert Gunnis, *Dictionary of British Sculptors, 1660–1851*).

To George Henry Sumner[1]

The Athenæum
My dear Sumner   April 11, 1857
I should be extremely glad if I could prevail upon you to go down to Oxford to give me a vote, as to an old acquaintance and Balliol man, for the Poetry Professorship. The election is on the 5th of May. I am half ashamed to ask you or any one else to take so much trouble on my account: but the Christ Church people are making a very active whip for their candidate, Bode, and their numbers will overpower me unless I can persuade a good many of the non-resident members of Convocation to go down and support

me.   Pray do what you can for me, and believe me, my dear Sumner, ever sincerely your's

M. Arnold.—

My address is—
St Albans Bank / Hampton / Middlesex—

MS. Boston Public Library.

1. George Henry Summer (1824–1909), son of a bishop, nephew of an archbishop, and, inevitably, himself a bishop—of Guildford, from 1888—came out of Eton and then Balliol a year behind Arnold (B.A. 1845, M.A. 1848), had been since 1850 rector of Old Alresford, Hants, and became in due course (1881) a member of the Athenæum Club (*WWW*). Of John Ernest Bode (1816–74: *DNB*), author of *Ballads from Herodotus*, Allott (below) wrote: "There is nothing in his verses to suggest that the electors made a mistake in electing Matthew Arnold."

To William Henry Lucas[1]

St. Albans Bank, Hampton, Middlesex

My dear Lucas   April 16, 1857

Remember when we played whist together and listen favourably while I entreat you to come to Oxford on the 5th of May and give me your vote for the Poetry Professorship. You know the strength of Christ Church—and they are making a desperate whip to secure Bode's election—so that their numbers will sweep me away unless I can prevail on a number of my old friends and acquaintances to come and give me their help. I wish I could transport the knightly Bowen from Corcyra for the day of the election.[2]

Pray come if you possibly can—forgive my troubling you with the request—and believe me, my dear Lucas,   ever sincerely yours

M. Arnold.

Text. Kenneth Allott, 'Matthew Arnold: Two Unpublished Letters,' Notes and Queries, New Series, 2 (Aug. 1955):356.

1. Lucas (see above p. 70), whose obscurity makes Bode (above) seem a star of the first magnitude, perfectly exemplifies Epicurus' admonition "Hide thy life." He lived next door to no great man, edited no forgotten classical text, composed no little volume of verses on nature or death, published no commemorative sermons, he merely lived 98 years with four chronicled accomplishments: he attended Oxford, was ordained and held curacies and a vicariate, voted for Arnold instead of a nonentity, and played whist.

2. George Ferguson Bowen (1821–99: *DNB*) had been at Trinity College, Oxford, and then, a year after Lucas, became a fellow of Brasenose in 1845, while Arnold was at Oriel. In 1847 he went to Corfu (Corcyra) as president of the university. In 1854 he became chief secretary to the governor of the Ionian Islands, was knighted next year, and in 1857 married him an Ionian wife. He became governor of Queensland in 1859 and, old boyism rallying, his influence was sought in 1865 in favor of an appointment for the

hapless Tom Arnold, now (temporarily) back in his Anglican mode. (Matthew Arnold wrote Bowen an eight-page letter in March!) Bowen became governor of New Zealand in 1867, ten years later of Victoria (where he stretched out a hand to the hapless Richard Penrose Arnold), was sent to Mauritius in 1879, and to Hong Kong in 1882—and home to England, in ill health, in 1885.

To George Henry Sumner

Hampton

My dear Sumner   April 25, 1857

Very many thanks for your hint—but I had written to your cousin the day before I heard from you.[1] Some of the Balliol Fellows had undertaken to canvass the Balliol men for me—all but four or five of my own contemporaries, like you, to whom I wished to write myself: but when I saw that your cousin's name was not on the list which Lake sent me of those Balliol men who had promised to go and vote, I wrote to him myself, as I am tolerably well acquainted with him.

It would be a real pleasure to me to see you again, but as decorum forbids my being at Oxford on the 5th of May, I shall lose, I am sorry to say, that opportunity of seeing both you and many other old friends. I am ever, my dear Sumner, most sincerely your's

M. Arnold.—

P. S. Pray do not neglect any occasion of securing a vote which may present itself to you—for Ch. Ch. is horribly strong and the Censors are appealing to their non-residents "in the name of the College" to come up.

MS. Boston Public Library.

1. Probably Robert George Moncrieff Sumner (c. 1825–85), at Balliol 1843–46, later a barrister, possibly his older brother John Henry Robertson Sumner (c. 1822–1910), at Balliol in 1839, sons of John Bird Sumner (1780–1862: *DNB*), archbishop of Canterbury, and first cousins of George Henry Sumner.

To Jane Martha Arnold Forster*

Hampton

My dearest K   Sunday, May 2, 1857

On no account send me your Keller: I never borrow maps, and I wish I could say I never lent them.[1] I have lent my Keller to somebody or other—and I shall never see it again. My one consolation is that Williams and Norgate tell me the map is quite obsolete, and that there are three new ones on the same scale, all better.

We talk of going abroad for three weeks—but I sometimes have doubts whether we shall manage it—What to do with the three children is too embarrassing. Else I have a positive thirst to see the Alps again, and two or three things I have in hand which I cannot finish till I have again breathed and smelt Swiss air. I shall be baffled, I dare say, as one continually is in so much—but I remember Goethe—"Homer and Polygnotus daily teach me more and more that our life is a Hell, through which one must struggle as one best can." [2]

This is gloomy—but your letter, my dearest K, made me a little gloomy. I am sure you are more alone than is good for you—how I wish that while William is necessarily much engaged and away from home you could come to us for one little fortnight or three weeks. Is it quite impossible—now that we have ample room in this house on the beautiful Thames bank, the only riant part of England—we could and would but too gladly take in William too if he could come with you—but he is a restless creature and would not stay if he came. It would be such a deep pleasure to Flu as well as to me if you would come—such a boon too if you could come now, for I shall be away from her for two or three days in the week after next and the week after that. We have this house till the 1st of June certain—do think of it.

The day I read your letter I said to Budge as I was dressing for dinner— "Budge, you must go and see your Aunt Forster"—"No," says Budge, "*do* let me 'top with Papa." So I turn to Tom, and when I remind him of the Noah's ark Tom says he will go and stop with you "for two days." Upon which Budge begins to howl, and running up to Tom who is sitting on the camp bed in my dressing room entreats him not to go away from him. "Why not, Budge?" says Tom. "Because I do love you so, Tiddy Tom," says Budge. "Oh," says Tom, waving his hand with a melancholy air—"this is *false*, Budge—this is all *false!*" You should have seen the sweet little melancholy face of the rogue as he said this.

I ought to have been writing to Mamma [3] to send her the enclosed—but I could not forbear writing to you, so I send them to you, and you must forward them to Mamma. I think I elude his thrust with grace and dignity. The letters need not to be kept: they were only preserved for you and Mamma.

The weaning goes on well, on the whole—Diddy gets very pretty, but he is fretful. *Do* come and see him, and love always   your most affectionate brother,

M. A.

Love to William. Tell him to think of me between 12 and 5 on Tuesday, when the voting for the Poetry Chair will be going on. It is impossible to be sure how it will go.

MS. Frederick Whitridge.

1. But see above pp. 121, 134. Williams and Norgate were booksellers at 14 Henrietta Street, W.C., where Arnold kept an account and where, in 1854, he sent two copies of *Poems* (Guthrie, 2:93) and, in 1857, one of *Merope* (2:200).

2. Arnold quotes this in *On Translating Homer* and gives his source as *Briefwechsel zwischen Schiller und Goethe*, 6:230 (Super 1:102n).

3. See the next letter.

To Mary Penrose Arnold[1]

Hampton
My dearest Mother   Sunday Evening, [May 10, 1857]

It seems an age since I wrote you more than a few lines—and indeed I have never had such a surfeit of letter-writing as in the last six weeks. But you have been much in my thoughts, and I believe that not Fanny Lucy herself felt my success more deeply than you my own dearest Mother. In the first place a son is his mother's own flesh and blood which makes her feel his well-doing like her own—and then, in my well doing, you may truly feel that the memory of Papa helps so much as to give you a yet closer and dearer connection with it than most mothers, even, have with their sons' well-doing. I am never tired of thinking how he would have rejoiced in his son's thus obtaining a share in the permanence and grandeur of that *august* place which he loved so much and to which he so gladly attached himself—how there could hardly perhaps have been conferred on me a distinction, of those conferred by men, which he would have so much prized. This doubles the worth of the distinction in my eyes—although it is in itself very pleasant to me, from the way in which it has been bestowed, and from its finding me in a profession which admits of no rise and no distinction.

Flu and I came up to London on the 5th and went together to the telegraph station at Charing Cross. About 4 we got a message from Walrond—nothing certain is known, but it is rumoured that you are ahead. We went to get some toys for the children in the Lowther Arcade, and could scarcely have found a more genuine distraction than in selecting waggons for Tom and Trev—with horses of precisely the same colour, not one of which should have a hair more in his tail than the other—and a musical cart for Diddy. A little after 5 we went back to the Telegraph office and got the following message—"Nothing declared, but you are said to be quite safe: Go to Eaton Place." To Eaton Place we went, as if sent by Budge, and there a little after 6 o'clock we were joined by the Judge in the highest state of joyful excitement with the news of my majority of 85 which had been telegraphed to him from Oxford after he had started and had been given to him at the Paddington Station.

The income is £130 a year, or thereabouts: the duties consist as far as I can learn in assisting to[2] look over the prize compositions—in delivering a Latin oration in praise of Founders at every alternate Commemoration—and in preparing and giving three Latin lectures on ancient poetry in the course of the year. These lectures I hope to give in English.[3]—I go to Oxford on Tuesday, and shall be there for a day or two, and shall hear more. Keble voted for me after all—he told the Coleridges he was so much pleased with my letter that he could not refrain. Send me that letter with his if you have still got them—I said they might be destroyed—but Stanley wants to see them. Archdeacon Randall voted for me, and Noel Ellison who said he "*must* come and vote for a son of dear Tom Arnold." Write him a line, if you know him at all, and thank him for yourself and me. I have written to thank Archdeacon Randall. I had support from all sides: Canon Miller went and voted for me ("that son of a great & good man"—he called me) and Archdeacon Denison. Also Sir John Yarde Buller and Henley, of the high Tory party.[4] It was an immense victory—some 200 more voted than have ever, it is said, voted in a Professorship election before. It is a great lesson to Ch. Ch. which was rather disposed to imagine it could carry anything by its great numbers.

Good bye, my dearest Mother—kiss my darling Fan for me—I have been up to see the three dear little brown heads on their pillows—all asleep. We talk and think so often of coming to see you this autumn. I think your Borrowdale plan a very good one.   Ever with Flu's love   your most affectionate

M.A.—

My affectionate thanks to Mrs Wordsworth and Mrs Fletcher for their kind interest in my success.[5] My very kind regards also to Miss Martineau, who I rejoice to think is better.

MS. Balliol College.

1. Parts of this letter were printed, with editorial adjustments, in Ward 1 : 74–75,76.
2. A Gallicism (and witticism)—he had to be there but do nothing.
3. See below pp. 360–61.
4. All of course in Foster: James Randall (1790–1882), archdeacon of Berks (*Annual Register*); Noel Thomas Ellison (c. 1791–1858), tutor, fellow, bursar of Balliol and rector of Nettlecombe, Somerset; John Cale Miller (1814–88: *DNB*), hon. canon of Worcester at this time; George Anthony Denison (1805–96: *DNB*), archdeacon of Taunton (Arnold is unmentioned in his *Notes of My Life*); John Buller Yarde-Buller (1799–1871; 3d bt, cr. Baron Churston, 1858), of Oriel College and 39 Belgrave Square, Conservative Member for Devon 1832–57; and Joseph Warner Henley (1793–1884: *DNB*), also also Conservative M.P. (Oxon).
5. Mrs Wordsworth died in 1859, age 89.

To George Henry Sumner

Hampton

My dear Sumner   May 11, 1857

A thousand thanks for your support before the victory and for your congratulations after it. As one seems destined never to see one's old acquaintances it is the more pleasant to find on such occasions as this that they have not forgotten one. I consider that I am indebted for the splendid triumph I had above all to the faithful support of the Balliol men. I am told I had nearly 70 votes from the dear old College.

Remember me kindly to Charles Conybeare[1] when you meet him, who will not I am sure be sorry for my success so far as I personally am concerned, though of course he did not wish his college to be defeated. I hear they fully expected to win.   Ever most truly your's

M. Arnold.—

MS. Boston Public Library.

1. Charles Ranken Conybeare (c. 1821–85), at Christ Church during Arnold's Balliol years, was vicar of Pyrton, Oxon, 1852–57, and then of Itchin Stoke, Hants (Foster).

To Thomas Arnold

⟨Education Department, Council Office, Downing Street, London:⟩

Hampton

My dear Tom   May 15th, 1857

My thoughts have often turned to you during my canvass for the Professorship—and they have turned to you more than ever during the last few days which I have been spending at Oxford. You alone of my brothers are associated with that life at Oxford, the *freest* and most delightful part, perhaps of my life—when with you and Clough and Walrond I shook off all the bonds and formalities of the place, and enjoyed the spring of life and that unforgotten Oxfordshire and Berkshire country. Did you ever read a poem of mine called "the scholar Gipsy"[1]—it was meant to fix the remembrances of those delightful wanderings of ours in the Cumner hills before they were quite effaced—and as such Clough and Walrond accepted it—and it has had much success at Oxford, I am told, as was perhaps likely from its couleur locale.[2] I am hardly ever at Oxford now, but the sentiment of the place is overpowering to me when I have leisure to feel it and can shake off the interruptions which it is not so easy to shake off now as it was when we were young. But on Tuesday afternoon I smuggled myself away, and got up into one of our old coombs among the Cumner hills, and into a field waving deep with cowslips and grasses and gathered such a bunch as you and I and K used to gather in the cowslip field on the Lutterworth road long years ago.

You dear old boy I love your congratulations although I see and hear so little of you—and, alas! *can* see and hear but so little of you. I was supported by people of all opinions—the great bond of union being, I believe, the affectionate interest felt in papa's memory. I think it probable that I shall lecture in English: there is no direction whatever in the Statute as to the language in which the lectures shall be: and the Latin has so died out, even among scholars, that it seems idle to entomb in that dead language a lecture which, in English, might be stimulating and interesting.

Now for some good news for you. I dined in University the other night—(and how I thought of you! and what a noble portrait of an English Gentleman is that of Windham!)[3] and Hedley told me that there were owing to you some arrears on account of your scholarship amounting to between £30 and £50: and that you could have the money by writing to him or to the bursar, begging that any money due to you might be paid to your bankers, whoever they are.

We are living in a house of the Judge's here, with a lawn running down to the Thames: beautiful in this weather. Love to Julia and the children from Flu—   ever your most affectionate

M. A.—

MS. National Library of Scotland.

1. See above pp. 249, 269.
2. Known in English (for a century) as "local color."
3. William Windham (1750–1810: *DNB*), statesman, whose portrait, by Sir Thomas Lawrence, is in University College, Oxford, where William Hedley (c. 1819–84) was a fellow and, at various times, bursar, tutor, and dean (Foster).

To Robert Scott[1]

The Revd the Master
of Balliol

St Albans Bank, Hampton
My dear Master   May 18, 1857

I am very much obliged to you for so soon mentioning my wish respecting the Lectures. After I had met you the other day I saw the Master of Pembroke, who suggested that I should write to the Vice Chancellor to ask for his sanction to my proposal to lecture in English:[2] I have not yet done so, however, and now I shall not do so, as the vote in the Hebdomadal Council has settled the matter. I imagine that no opposition to the proposal will be made in Convocation, and that the proposal will be brought before Convocation by the Hebdomadal Council. If there are any further steps which in your opinion I ought to take in the matter, perhaps you will have the kindness to let me hear from you.

As there can be no doubt that learned men have generally ceased to make use of the Latin [language] to write on learned subjects, it seems unreasonable to compel the Poetry Professor to be more learned than the learned. I have heard that the objection to lectures in English is that they might distract undergraduates from their graver studies: but three lectures in a year could not do this: and I have no intention to multiply them, so that I shall make no very formidable demand on the time and attention of members of the University.   With renewed thanks, I remain, dear Mr Master, sincerely yours

Matthew Arnold.—

MS. Pusey House.

1. Robert Scott (1811–87: *DNB*), master of Balliol 1854–70. "Posterity has not been kind to Scott. Of the great *Greek-English Lexicon* a contemporary quatrain said:

> Two men wrote a lexicon, Liddell and Scott;
> One half was clever, one half was not.
> Give me the answer, boys, quick, to this riddle:
> Which was by Scott, and which was by Liddell?

and it is clear that he was elected Master of Balliol in a raw power play to block Jowett, who then had to wait sixteen years until, in another political maneuver, just as raw but far more subtle, Scott was shunted off to Rochester in order to make room for Jowett. See Geoffrey Faber, *Jowett, A Portrait with a Background*, pp. 109–10, 349–51" (quoted from Tennyson, 2:112n).

2. The master of Pembroke was Francis Jeune (1806–68: *DNB*) from 1843 till 1864, when he became bishop of Peterborough. From 1850 he served as the most active member of the commission of inquiry that dragged Oxford University (to some extent) into the nineteenth century. For his wife, who survived him by many years, see Mar. 21, 1887. (For the vice-chancellor see the next letter.)

To Richard Lynch Cotton[1]

London[2]

Dear Mr Vice Chancellor   May 22, 1857

The Master of Balliol kindly undertook to bring to the knowledge of the Hebdomadal Council my desire to lecture, as Poetry Professor, in English, but I am anxious also to state to yourself as the interpreter of the Statutes, the reasons which have led me to entertain this desire.

—Those Members of the University, who have spoken to me on the subject, have almost without a single exception, expressed their strong wish & hope that I should lecture in English; and I find that the Statute respecting the duties of the Poetry Professor contains no direction whatever as to the language in which the lectures shall be delivered.

The Statute appears to enjoin, indeed, that the Professor shall treat of the *Ancient* Poets, & that his lectures shall be of a learned & serious cast: this seems to be the spirit, at least, of the injunctions of the Statute; & this spirit I fully hope to follow, to the best of my power, whether I lecture in Latin or in English.—At the time when this Professorship was founded Latin was the universal language of learned men in treating subjects relating to Classical Antiquity, and indeed in treating many other subjects: and it was natural that lectures on the Ancient Poets should be delivered in the Latin language. But, it can hardly be denied, that of late years learned men have more & more abandoned the use of the Latin language even in treating subjects of pure learning, while the indisposition on the part of students to receive instruction conveyed by a modern Teacher in a dead language, has become even greater, perhaps, than the indisposition of the learned to convey it.

I think, therefore, that the Poetry lecture would be far more widely interesting at the present time if delivered in English: I think that it would reach a great number of members of the University whom it would not reach if delivered in Latin, and would thus have a chance of being far more generally useful. At the same time the lectures should, in my opinion, be of such a character, as to promote & animate the study of the Poetical literature of classical Antiquity. The greater the number of hearers they attract the more effectually they will do this.

The Lectures are so few in number that it is impossible to conceive that they should create any interruption in the regular course of study of the Under-Graduates, however fully attended by them; although, indeed, Lectures which tended to encourage the serious study of the Classical Poets, could hardly be deemed an interruption of the regular course of study at Oxford.

I trust therefore that you will believe me, when I assure you that it is from no desire to save myself trouble but from a sincere wish to make the Poetry Chair serve, to the utmost extent of my power, the purposes for which it was instituted, that I am anxious to obtain your sanction to my proposal to lecture in English.

xxxx/signed/ M. Arnold

MS. Pusey House (transcript by Frances Lucy Wightman Arnold).

1. Richard Lynch Cotton (1794–1880: *DNB*), provost of Worcester College 1839–80 and vice-chancellor 1852–57 (1852–56 in *DNB*, corrected in *Concise DNB*). He was an amiable nonentity ("his kindness was unfailing and his piety sincere" is the highest praise meted him, an ordained Anglican priest, by the *DNB*, understandably eager to shorten his term of office). His sole distinctions appear to be that he did not not try to block the reforms that Jeune's commission advocated and that he did not require Arnold to lecture in Latin.

2. "London" and the date are in Arnold's hand; all the rest, with the signature, in his wife's.

To Robert Scott

The Revd the Master of Balliol—

Hampton

My dear Master   May 22, 1857

I send you a copy of a letter which I have this day addressed to the Vice Chancellor. I found that as the interpreter of the Statutes he has the power to hold me to whatever interpretation he chooses to put upon the Statutes— so, for fear he should rule that *sollemnis oratio* is equivalent to *Latina oratio*, I thought it best to write him the enclosed letter, which I hope will succeed in convincing him.

I think that the sense of the preposterousness of an Englishman lecturing to Englishmen in a dead language is at the present day so strong, that even Copleston or Keble would now fail to obtain the audience which they ob-tained twenty years ago.[1] Only the most intelligent and cultivated of the members of the University attended the Latin Lectures then—but I doubt whether even these would attend the same lectures now.

You have been so kind in assisting me in my endeavours to obtain the sanction of the authorities of the University to my proposal to lecture in English that I am unwilling to leave you uninformed of any steps which I take in the matter, although I should be most reluctant to trouble you un-necessarily. Pray do not think it necessary to return the enclosed, and believe me, my dear Master,   ever very truly your's

M. Arnold.—

MS. Pusey House.

1. Edward Copleston (1776–1849: *DNB*), bishop of Llandaff and provost of Oriel when Dr Arnold was fellow, was Professor of Poetry 1802–12.

To Jane Martha Arnold Forster*

⟨Education Department, Council Office, Downing Street, London:⟩

21. Waterloo Crescent, Dover

My dearest K　　　　　　　　　　　　　　　　　　July 25, 1857

We calculated your movements and came to the conclusion that you would be at the Grange when Flu's letter reached Mamma proposing to send the children direct from London to Fox How. You were most kind, my dearest K, in your willingness to receive them—and so, I am sure, was William: and it is a real grief to me that you should not have the opportunity of cementing your intimacy with Tom and Trev. as few things could be so good for them, dear little fellows—but Flu wished them & so did I to have a full month here, as this place suits Tom so well—they will therefore be here until Monday the 10th of August—then they will be a day or two in London—so that they would only just have reached Wharfeside as you were leaving it. Flu also dreaded the double journey for Tom. He is getting better, but is so fragile that one cannot take too much care of him. I will not write about him but I should like to talk to you of him and to shew him to you. Budge is getting splendid and is really a boy for whom one entertains a respect. He makes friends in all directions and when I go out with him he receives salutes from mustachioed gentlemen on all sides and turning round to me with a sparkling blush he says—*I know 'im!* Diddy is a dear little pretty soul, but a Turk.

We are expecting the Judge Lady Wightman & Georgina today to stay till Monday.[1]—How delightful this place is it is vain to say to the barbarous inhabitants of the north. Flu & I hope to start on Tuesday week, the 4th of August—we go by Paris and Basle to Lucerne—then by the Titlis (for Obermann's sake) and Grimsel to Zermatt, where we meet Wyndham Slade & some of his family—then in company with them to Vevey & Geneva & home by France. What are *you* going to do—tell me soon and exactly—how long you mean to be out and how much money to spend. What are the Croppers, that unwriting couple, going to do. Do tell me this. I am well in the middle of my Merope, and please myself pretty well—though between indolence and nervousness I am a bad worker:—what I learn in studying Sophocles for my present purpose is, or seems to me, wonderful: so far exceeding all that one would learn in years' reading of him without such a purpose. And what a man! What works! I must read Merope to you. I think and hope it will have what Buddha called—the "character of *Fixity*—that true sign of the Law."[2]—I send you a rough draft of a testimonial I mean to give to Temple for Rugby[3]—return it to me telling me how you like it—I have not yet sent it. He is the *one* man who *may* do something of the same work Papa did. God bless you—our united affectionate love to you prospectively for your birthday. Love to William,   your ever affectionate

M. A.—

Flu thinks *Anglo Bengalee* in the Times is Willy[4]—but it surely is not? How good is Sir C. Napier![5]

MS. Frederick Whitridge.

1. Charlotte Georgina Eleanor Wightman (1835–83), of whom precious little is known: "Very much younger than her sisters [and called "Baby"], she never married, devoting herself to her ageing parents and, indeed, to the various other members of her family" (Harding, pp. 27–28, pictured following p. 18).
2. Perhaps a paraphrase of vv. 101–2 of Burnouf's translation of the *Saddharmapundarika sutra*, ch. 2: "La règle de la loi est perpétuellement stable, et la nature de ses conditions est toujours lumineuse; les Buddhas, qui sont les Meilleurs des hommes, après l'avoir reconnue, enseigneront l'unique véhicule qui est le mien, / Ainsi que la stabilité de la loi, et sa perfection qui subsiste perpétuellement dans le monde sans être ébranlée; et les Buddhas enseigneront l'état de Bôdhi, jusqu'au centre de la terre, en vertu de leur habilité dans l'emploi des moyens [dont ils disposent]" (E. Burnouf, *Le Lotus de La Bonne Loi* [Paris, 1925], 1:34).
3. See the next letter.
4. A long letter called "Bengal Mutinies" in *The Times*, July 22, p. 10.
5. *Life and Opinions of General Sir Charles James Napier G. C. B.* (4 vols, 1857), which the journals were reviewing.

To The Trustees of Rugby School

[?August, 1857]

In the most important qualities of a schoolmaster, in the union of piety, energy, and cheerfulness, in the faculty of governing the young, in the power of commanding at once the respect and the affection of those under his charge, Mr Temple, more than any other man whom I have ever known, resembles, to the best of my observation and judgment, my late father.

Text. Memoirs of Archbishop Temple by Seven Friends, ed. Ernest Grey Sandford, 1:153.

To Alexander Macmillan[1]

A. Macmillan Esqre
          Education Department, Council Office, Downing Street, London:
My dear Sir   October 12, 1857
     My father's life is not in the hands of his family but in those of Mr Stanley, to whom I will communicate your enquiry. I do not myself think that Fellowes, the present publisher, will consent, so long as he has any-

thing to do with the book, to publish a materially cheaper edition of it.— How very successful, and deservedly, Tom Brown has been! Believe me,   faithfully your's,

M. Arnold.—

MS. Berg Collection.

1. Alexander Macmillan (1818–96)—whose older and better known brother Daniel (1813–57) had died on June 27—were Cambridge booksellers and publishers (the firm opened a branch office in London in 1858). Thomas Hughes's *Tom Brown's School Days*, published in April, went to five editions in its first year.

To A. J. Beale

Mr Beale—
      ⟨Education Department, Council Office, Downing Street, London:⟩
                                                   Burley, nr Otley
Dear Sir   October 18, 1857
      Thank you for your letter of the 12th with its enclosures. If you will send me word for how many scholars you desire to claim good conduct certificates I will either send the requisite number of certificates or bring them with me when I come. Believe me,   truly your's,

M. Arnold.—

MS. Historical Society of Pennsylvania.

To A. J. Beale

Mr Beale   Borough Road Training School
My Dear Sir   December 8, 1857
      Will you be good enough to let me have one line *here* by return of post to say whether you wish your assistant to be an assistant *under the A[ssistant]. T[eachers]. Minute*, receiving £25 from the Committee of Council yearly, or an assistant *master*, holding a certificate.[1] If you remember we discussed the question as to which of these assistants would be most beneficial—but neither you nor Mr Cadbury mention on what you have decided.   Ever truly your's

M. Arnold.—

MS. University of Virginia.

1. Both Minutes are in Arnold's *Reports on Elementary Schools 1852–82* (1910), pp. 296–99. "Even the general public by this time knows pretty well what a certificate

of merit is," Arnold wrote a few years later. "It is a document, issued by a department of State, attesting that the holder has passed a satisfactory examination in the subjects of elementary instruction" ("Mr. Walter and the Schoolmasters' Certificates," in Super, 2:257–61.)

To William Martin Leake[1]

Colonel Leake—
&c. &c. &c.   9, Wilton Place[2]
Sir   December 23, 1857
    I have taken the liberty of desiring my publisher to send you a copy of a tragedy of mine which has just appeared.

    Should you cast your eye over it, you will perceive but too clearly that I have never been in Greece: but, with the warmest interest in all that relates to the geography and natural features of that country, I have found no author except Pausanias himself from whose works on this subject I have derived so much instruction and pleasure, as from yours. I am anxious, therefore, to lose no opportunity, however slight, of testifying to you my gratitude for your invaluable topographical labours; a gratitude, let me add, which was always most strongly expressed by my father, Dr Arnold.   I have the honour to remain, Sir,   Your obedient humble servant,

                        Matthew Arnold.—

MS. Hertfordshire County Council.

    1. William Martin Leake (1777–1860: *DNB*), classical topographer and numismatist, whose book *Travels in the Morea* (partly derived from Pausanias, *Description of Greece*) Arnold alludes to. See below p. 372 n. 2.

    2. Temporary shelter, no doubt. *POLD*, 1857, records no no. 9 Wilton Place, S.W. No. 11 was a lodging house in the name of James Rowsell. (A Mrs Thompson was at no. 8, Hon George Chapple Norton at no. 10.)

To William Hepworth Thompson[1]

The Revd Professor Thompson
&c. &c. &c.   9, Wilton Place S. W.
My dear Sir   December 23, 1857
    It gave me great pleasure to hear from Arthur Stanley some time ago that you had expressed approval of one or two of my poems, and I hope you will allow me to trouble you with a copy of a tragedy which I have just published. There are so few people who will know or care anything about such an attempt, that you must pardon an author's zeal for his offspring which

leads him to obtrude it upon the notice of one of the very few qualified to judge it perfectly. Believe me, my dear Sir,   Yours very truly

M. Arnold.—

MS. Gordon Ray.

1. William Hepworth Thompson (1810–86: *DNB*) was the Regius Professor of Greek at Cambridge, where he was Master of Trinity College from 1866 to 1886. As an undergraduate, he belonged to the Apostles (unless, in all his stateliness, they belonged to him) in the Tennyson-Hallam days of glory. (See Tennyson, 1 : 347.)

To A. J. Beale

Mr Beale—   London
My Dear Sir   December 28, 1857
    I am in the midst of the revision of more papers than I can well get through and have only time for one line to tell you that *Stanley Reeves*, the young man who will, I hope, come to you was an old Pupil teacher of mine at Birmingham, and far exceeds the ordinary run of Pupil teachers in manners and accomplishment. He was however brought up in a school in some respects singular—in the school attached to Mr George Dawson's chapel—and of the congregation of the chapel I believe he was a member. It is well that you should know this: but I have great hopes, on the whole, that you will find him a thoroughly serviceable agreeable coadjutor—as I feel sure, on the other hand, that I am sending him (if he goes) to a school in which he may learn a great deal that will be most valuable to him.   With the best wishes of the season to you, I am, dear Sir,   truly your's

M. Arnold.—

MS. University of Virginia.

To Thomas Arnold

9, Wilton Place
My dear Tom   December 28, [1857]
    I was delighted to hear from you—you would have heard from me, at any rate, in a day or two, as I have desired that a copy of Merope may be sent to you as soon as she makes her appearance. There has been a delay in getting the binding done, owing to the Xmas holidays, or she would have appeared sooner.
    How refreshing it is to meet with anyone who knows anything about any literary matter! There are so few people in England who have ever read

Alfieri or heard of Maffei that I must ask you, at the risk of insulting you, how you came to know that each had composed a *Merope*. Your savoir I knew, but not that it extended to such matters, on which even the most cultivated English are generally so ignorant. You do not now mention Voltaire, whose Merope is more famous than either of the other two, and is well worth reading—though I think Maffei's poetically the best tragedy of the three, as you will see by my Preface which I think you will find interesting.[1]

A great transformation in the intellectual nature of the English, and, consequently, in their estimate of their own writers, is, I have long felt, inevitable. When this transformation comes the popularity of Wordsworth, Shelley, Coleridge, and others, remarkable men as they were, will not be the better for it. I am very much interested in what you say about Pope. I will read the Essay on Criticism again—certainly poetry was a power in England in his time, which it is not now—now it is almost exclusively "virginibus puerisque"[2] and not for the sanest and most promising of these—then it was for *men* at large. You ask why is this—I think it is because Pope's poetry was *adequate* (to use a term I am always using), to Pope's age—that is, it reflected completely the best general culture and intelligence of that age: therefore the cultivated and intelligent men of that time all found something of themselves in it. But it was a poor time, after all—so the poetry is not and cannot be a first-class one. On the other hand our *time* is a first class one—an infinitely fuller richer age than Pope's; but our poetry is not *adequate* to it: it interests therefore only a small body of sectaries; hundreds of cultivated & intelligent men find nothing that speaks to them in it. But it is a hard thing to make poetry adequate to a first-class epoch. The eternal greatness of the literature of the Greece of Pericles is that it is the *adequate* expression of a first-class epoch. Shakspeare again, is the infinitely *more than adequate* expression of a *second class* epoch. It is the immense distinction of Voltaire & Goethe, with all their shortcomings, that they approach *near* to being adequate exponents of first-class epochs. And so on—till more paper was covered than I have to cover. It is singular—but all this is the very matter debated in my inaugural lecture,[3] & the debating of which will be continued in the two next. I have a vow against sending MSS to anyone: the disadvantage to a work in being read in MSS is so incredibly great, according to my own feeling—but you shall have the three lectures printed, if we all live, in June or July next.[4] Write and tell me what you think of Merope: in literary matters we may still have strong sympathy. Là, vous ne vous êtes pas cramponné à une légende morte.[5]—Admire my politeness in having recourse to French to say an uncivil thing, and with our united love and good wishes for Xmas and the new year to you all—believe me always,   your most affectionate

M. A.—

Carlyle is part man—of genius—part fanatic—and part tom-fool.

MS. Morgan Library.

1. As Arnold points out in the Preface to Merope (Super, 1: 38–64), Scipio Maffei's *Merope* appeared in 1713, Voltaire's in 1736, Vittorio Alfieri's in 1783,

2. Horace, *Odes* 3.1.4, is usually cited for this common locution.

3. "On the Modern Element in Literature," delivered Nov. 14, 1857 (Super, 1:18–37).

4. R. H. Super's note: "None of the titles of the individual lectures in this first series has survived. . . . Of that delivered on May 8, 1858, we know nothing except that his wife was not pleased with it; the third, on May 29, she liked better. The fourth, on December 4, was mainly on the feudal state of society and the scholastic philosophy, and at that time at least he intended to devote the fifth, on March 12, 1859, to 'Dante, the troubadours, and the early Drama,' and to 'examine the origin of what is called the "romantic" sentiment about women, which the Germans quite falsely are fond of giving themselves the credit of originating' " (Super, 1:225). See below pp. 391, 415 n. 5.

5. There, at any rate, you haven't "clung to a dead time's exploded dream." Arnold alludes to this sentence below p. 380 n. 2.

To Mary Penrose Arnold*

London

My dearest Mother   Sunday, [January 3, 1858]

You wished to see everything about Merope, so I send you these—they have lost no time in opening cry. The Athenæum is a choice specimen of style and the Spectator of argumentation—the Saturday Review is not otherwise to be complained of than so far as it is deadly prosy. I have yet had very few letters, as to get through a tragedy & Preface takes more time than to turn the leaves of a volume of short poems. I have had a kind note from old Colonel Leake & a very flattering one from Harriet Martineau. Perhaps it would be kind if you sent the Saturday Review on to her, as she is a good deal mentioned in a notice of an absurd pamphlet of Congreve's on India.[1]

I am very anxious to see what Lewes says about Merope, as I have a very high opinion of his literary judgment—but the Leader is silent this week. A long article is coming in the Daily News, but not by Harriet Martineau. It is singular what irritation the dispute between classicism and romanticism seems always to call forth—but I remember Voltaire's lamentation that the "literae humanae" *humane* letters, should be so desperately *inhuman*, and am determined in print to be always scrupulously polite. The bane of English reviewing and newspaper-writing is and has always been its grossièreté.

I am very glad you were interested in Merope. I want to know what dearest K thinks of it—and William—and my dear Fan must write to me. Tell Mary we have a charming locket for her with the little boys' hair in three distinct curls.—I hope there has been no mistake about K's copy of Merope. I am afraid I told Longman to send it to Fox How.   Ever your affectionate

M. A.

MS. Balliol College.

1. *Merope* was reviewed in the *Athenæum*, Jan. 2, p. 13 ("Mr Arnold's theory upon poesy is much better than his practice"); in the *Saturday Review*, Jan. 2, pp. 19–20; in the *Spectator*, Jan. 2, p. 25 ("'Wilful man must have his way,' much more wilful poet"); and by G. H. Lewes in the *Leader*, on Jan. 30, pp. 112–13 (mostly reprinted in Dawson). Richard Congreve's pamphlet "Positive Philosophy on the Indian Question" and Harriet Martineau's *British Rule in India* were reviewed together in the *Saturday Review* on pp. 15–16 ("So here we have the two principal representatives of Positivism in England directly at issue, historically, morally, socially, and politically").

To Herbert Hill

Education Department, Council Office, Downing Street, London:
My dear Mr Hill   January 7, 1858
   I am up to my eyes in Grammar papers worked by the schoolmasters & students at their Xmas examination for certificates—the revision of these is the most tedious part of my year's business—to look over for days one after the other long passages of English parsing and paraphrasing—and *such* paraphrasing!—You remember in Milton

> "though all the giant brood
> "Of Phlegra with the heroic race &c."—[1]

one of my hopeful subjects paraphrases this—

> though all those extraordinary
> "specimens of humanity who fought
> "at Phlegra—" &c.

   This is a long Preface to say that I can write but a short letter—I must find time, however, to tell you what sincere pleasure your liking for Merope gives me. No doubt you are right about the rhythms—if ever I try another of these tragedies I shall attempt to keep as much as I possibly can to received rhythms, as in the first Stasimon. I am glad you select that one for mention, as I am very fond of it myself. I am glad you suggest Deianeira, too: she is just in point and I had not thought of her—the critics have been saying that Merope's tender heartedness is *un*Greek. What you say about "race" & "his" is true—and must be attended to if the poem ever comes to a second edition. I agree also that the passage

"the rushing thundering" &c.

is doubtful—the Orestes bit is a favourite of mine—although perhaps it does not come in quite right there.

I must tell you that in Gell's Itinerary[2] he mentions the hedges of wild roses in the Atœan villages:[3] and generally, what with Leake Gell & Pausanias, I think I have got the local matters pretty faithful.

I am truly sorry to hear a bad account of the health of your family—we are all pretty well, except that I myself am headachy and influenza-ish. May the frost brave us all up again! Do not forget our address if you come to town—I should greatly like to shew you my little boys.   With kindest remembrances to Mrs Hill, believe me,   ever affectionately your's

M. Arnold.—

I am reading Dante in *Italian* for the first time. O what force!

MS. *Fitzwilliam Museum.*

1. *Paradise Lost* 1.576–77.
2. Sir William Gell's *Itinerary of the Morea* (1810) or one of his other books; on the reading list for Sept. 1857 was "Gell's Argolis*" (for Gell's *Attica*, 1817?). Gell is not mentioned in the commentaries on *Merope*. See above p. 367.
3. *Merope* l. 1821.

Friedrich Max Mueller to Matthew Arnold[1]

53 St John Street, Oxford
My dear Arnold   January 8, 1858

This time I plead guilty. I did not like to write to you and thank you for your book, before having read it. Then I began to read it, but did not take very kindly to it at first. Then other work had to be done, of a Philindic rather than Philellenic character; and so I had not yet finished Merope, when your letter arrived. I have done so now, and I mean to read it again. A poet no doubt has the right of choosing his own path, and if he wishes to imitate rather, than to create new forms of poetry, he has a very good excuse at this time of the world's history. But may not a poet be classical, and yet modern and English? I am afraid I shall join John Bull in his clamour for once—I think he has a right to say, talis eum sis utinam noster esses! John Bull cannot enjoy Merope. He may enjoy the description of the death of Æpytus—he may fill [*for* feel] a thrill at the words "Thy son," as even at Voltaire's "Vous

alliez l'immoler"—and the pleading of Merope for peace will go to the heart of many an English mother. But to enjoy the whole tragedy, to value every line and the choice of every epithet will always be the privilege of a few carefully educated men whose taste for Greek classical beauty has not been drowned by Greek & Latin scholarship. Their sympathy is not strong or warm enough to keep a poet alive. A man like you should say, Soyons ancêtres, let us be Classics—Sophocles wrote for his Athenian fig-eaters, Voltaire for his Rhinoceros nosed gamins—Is the London cockney worse than these? I do not believe it, if you lay hold of him well, drag him out of himself, and make himself see what a noble fellow, what a fair specimen of a divine image he really is. He would admire Merope if he dared. But he is a shy fellow, afraid of false quantities and all that. Bernays will rejoice in your poem; so would Geibel, the poet, who has just published a tragedy Brunhild—he has spent many years in-Greece, and has some fine descriptions of Greek scenery in his earlier poems—As to myself I have to thank you for a breeze of fresh pure Greek air—and yet I would wish you some English clouds—ay some London smoke—on the blue sky of your classical soul.   Ever yours
MMüller.

MS. Frederick Whitridge.

1. Printed and annotated in *Album,* pp. 20, 81–82. The Latin quotation is from Xenophon's *Hellenica,* 4.1.38 (Super 9.359).

Charles Augustin Sainte-Beuve to Matthew Arnold

ce 8 Janvier 1858
"Celui qui fait gracieusement les Grâces, celui-là est très doux parmi les humains: ceux qui les font, mais qui ne les font qu'après bien du temps, sont peu nobles de nature."

Voilà, Monsieur, tout ce que je savais de l'antique Mérope. Vous êtes de ceux qui font très gracieusement les Grâces, et je ne veux pas mettre trop de temps à vous en remercier. Je serai un bien mauvais juge de votre poésie, mais j'apprécie la tentative et toutes les ingénieuses et délicates raisons dont vous l'appuyez. Vous êtes du petit nombre des esprits restés fidèles au culte du grand art: et votre épigraphe attique[1] n'est pas un vain mot. Je vous demeure bien reconnaissant du souvenir que vous voulez bien m'accorder, et que je vous paie de loin par toute l'estime et l'appréciation dont je suis capable. Agréez en, Monsieur, l'expression bien sincère,

Ste Beuve

MS. Balliol College.

1. Θιλοκαλοῦμεν μετ᾽ εὐτελείας—"For we are lovers of beauty yet with no extravagance" (Thucydides, *History* 2.40 (1), quoted in Allott p. 681).

To Jane Martha Arnold Forster

My dearest K   [c. January 8, 1858]

I never think a performance of mine fairly launched until I have your opinion on it. I am truly rejoiced that you and William like Merope. The poem is a tragedy according to the celebrated definition which has not yet, so far as I know, given place to a better—"Tragedy is the imitation of some action that is serious and entire, & of proper magnitude, effecting through pity and fear the purification of those feelings of the soul." [1]

The more you look at that famous definition (Aristotle's) the better you will like it.

You generally lay your finger on points where at any rate I can understand what you mean, which one cannot always do apropos of one's critics' objections. It is true that Polyphontes is the most interesting personage, I think: though I suppose Merope ought to be. It is doubtful whether in the first stasimon the chorus do not philosophize too much for their age and sex—I felt the difficulty and shewed I felt it at the point you have observed. It is to be said that the characters in tragedy of this sort are in the highest degree idealized—so that each may be at the very summit of what it is naturally possible for them to attain to—maidens brought up in company with such a personage as Merope, and such solemn events, may well be allowed to have risen to the best feeling & thinking of their sex—but they must not transcend that. Whether my Messeniannes [*sic*] do or not I cannot quite determine. Think at any rate of Lady Jane Grey and such as her.[2]

I think you will come to like the choruses—although this part of ancient tragedy is for modern readers, I well know, the doubtful part. You will see what Stanley says: his letter I enclose.

You must remember that this form of drama is above all calculated for the stage—a sort of *opera-stage*: and that as much as the Elizabethan drama *loses* by being acted the Greek drama gains.

All this I have written with Diddy alone in the room with me—I have had him down because his brothers are passing the day in Eaton Place, and he was alone in his nursery—The little darling is mad for me to wind up a moving squirrel he has—and he has been so good that I must do it.

A happy new year to you and William—Diddy says "um" when I ask if he sends his love. When shall we see you in town?   ever your most affectionate,

M. A.—

I must ask you to send me back some day my *Bouddhisme* to make a reference for my next lecture[3]—the book is now unprocurable. You shall have it again.

MS. Frederick Whitridge.

1. Aristotle, *Poetics* 6.49b20 (condensed).
2. See above p. 336.
3. On May 8, 1858; little is known about its subject (see above p. 370 n. 4 and below pp. 388 n. 1, 391). See also above p. 364 n. 2.

James Anthony Froude to Matthew Arnold[1]

Northdown
My dear Arnold   January 10, [1858]
 You must excuse the meagre letter of thanks which I am for the present able to send you for Merope. I am stifled with Proof sheet & MS. and can scarcely rally a thought for more than my immediate work.

On first reading however, (I have not been able to manage more) my impression is that it is the best reproduction of Greek Tragedy I have ever seen. And at the same time I cannot as yet satisfy myself that the result is adequate to your powers. You have caught the echo of Sophocles, but the voice itself was something different.—In Sophocles you have the *whole* of his insight into human things—you have a man speaking his complete convictions got with a sense of the limitations of mystery which was round him, into which he would have looked further if he could.

No one will say that our position now is exactly the same as his. Submit modern emotion & modern speculation to what process you will, steep it in nitric acid: throw out every particle of spasm, false sentiment unreality and there will remain more than Sophocles had. The Problem of life presents itself far differently. And if you intend, as you must intend in a Drama to open out the springs which have led to action; modes of reasoning and modes of feeling must & will suggest themselves. The Poet will feel them, the reader will expect them; truth demands them—beyond what fresh habits of thought can supply.

We are conscious of something in ourselves more subtle & more complicated of emotions to which the reproduction, at least of Greek poetry can give no rest and to which we feel that the Poet capable of so high an effort of imitative art could have given rest, had he ventured to be original.

It is true that if you choose a Greek story, you must represent the Actors as feeling like Greeks. Yet that is an objection to the subject. The interest is therefore to us necessarily imperfect.—But in fact to exhibit Greek poetry exhaustively you ought to have been a Greek and to have been without experiences of two thousand years.

Will you understand what I mean if I say that the overwhelming powers with which Sophocles takes possession of us is due not so much to what he says as to what he does not say, to a certain aweful sense of Infinity which you see in this expression of all great men modern or antient when they are shewing us their whole hearts.—

I am very stupid. I cannot explain myself better. I wouldn't have written at all till I could have given more time to the Poem, but for fear you should suspect me of carelessness—You shall have the best which I have to give in a few weeks.   Ever faithfully yours

J. A. Froude

MS. Frederick Whitridge.

1. Printed with commentary in *Album,* pp. 8–9, 64–65.

To William Edward Forster

Education Department, Council Office, Downing Street, London:
My dear William   January 11, 1858
I was very glad to hear from you—and believe me that there is no subject on which I should not hear your opinion with interest—and that those who are cumbered about much Greek and Latin *scholarship* are by no means the best judges of Greek and Latin *literature.*

As to the choice of the subject—I think people are *frightened* from these subjects somewhat, and would enjoy them more if they got more familiar with them. Stanley whose first letter I sent to Jane says in a second in answer to one in which I had mentioned 4 or 5 other subjects which I *must* treat sooner or later before leaving Greece—"In spite of all my protestations I have so much *secret delight* in these classical revivals that I cannot find it in my heart to object to one of your projects:" and Max Müller says in a very clever letter—"John Bull would admire Merope if he dared—but he is a shy fellow afraid of making false quantities and of exposing himself—and so he looks askance at it." [1]

For the rest, one has oneself to consider as well as the public, and one *cannot* always give them what they ask for. I remember even Goethe says that only once—with his Hermann & Dorothea—did he give the German public what they were demanding of him.

Now I will take your remarks in order, but very briefly it must be, for I am overdone with grammar papers to look over. "used up" some one else has objected to—the two words being separated, the phrase does not offend me—but I never keep a phrase, if I can help it, that has an equivocal sound for anybody—so we will in future read "wore-out."[2] The Aroanian trout had a musical note according to the tradition:[3] Pausanias says that when he came to Cleitor in his tour through Arcadia he passed a summer evening on the river-bank waiting to hear them begin: I need not say he was disappointed. Generally speaking, the history topography & natural history of Merope are faithful—that is so far as anything about Greece from one who has not seen it can be faithful.

As to Merope not exciting you—on the stage (for which these things are meant) I think the chief situations *would* excite you: and it is easy to *overwrite* a situation for acting. For an unconscious testimony to this truth see that masterpiece of bad criticism, the Times's remarks on Rachel's acting.[4] But we must beware of taking our notions of *excitement* from the modern *drame* or from the modern novel—from Adrienne Lecouvreur or from Night & Morning. Certainly the Greek tragic drama does not excite & harrow us to the extent that these do: I *think*, neither does Shakspeare. Not one hundredth part of the *excitement* have I ever felt at seeing Lear or Othello on the stage that I have felt at the Corsican brothers or Adrienne Lecouvreur.[5] And, perhaps, this is necessary. For in good tragedy the poet must *controul* his matter—and in the drame & novel the matter is uncontrollable. There is a kind of pity & fear (Kotzebue is a great master of it)[6] which *cannot* be purified: it is the most agitating and overwhelming, certainly, but, for the sake of a higher result, we must renounce this. Pity & fear of a certain kind—say *commiseration & awe* and you will perhaps better feel what I mean—I think Merope *does* excite: as does Greek tragedy in general.—

I allow however that the problem for the poet is, or should be, to unite the highest degree of agitatingness on the part of his subject-matter, with the highest degree of controul and assuagement on the part of his own exhibition of it:—Shakspeare, under immense difficulties, goes further in this respect than the Greeks, and so far he is an advance upon them.

I think in the plot you sketch the interest *must* have dropped as it drops in Voltaire's tragedy. Such a marriage-tie as Merope's would have not been one to inspire the smallest simple or tragic reluctance to cut it violently. But I am sure you are wrong in your notion that the Greek poets tolerated what we call "repulsive" situations a bit more than we do. There are some excellent remarks in Grote on the liberties Sophocles took with the horrible old legends in order to adapt them to his own poetical feeling & to the refined modern feeling of his time, which are worth your looking at.[7] I feel *sure* Sophocles would not have treated the subject in the way you suggest, though it might have been very effectively treated in that way: but Walter Scott would have been far more likely to treat it so than Sophocles.

Michelet has well shown that Christianity has had credit given to it with regard to the extinction of slavery which it does not deserve: and I cannot but think that the same may be said with respect to the treatment of women. The influence of women in Greece was immense.

The *conflict of feelings in Merope's nature* is what, I think, the tragedy turns upon: I think this would come out upon the stage: and this makes Merope the principal person. The most *attractive*, however, I certainly agree with you, is Polyphontes.—I have a thousand things to say to you about other matters, but have neither time nor room. It is a great pleasure to me to interest you by what I do. What a noble letter is dear Willy's![8] There is a tremendous eulogy in the Daily News:[9] very effective—slashing, clever, self-confident, and tant soit peu grossière—but that is the English taste. I am only afraid the public will say with Dalgetty—"To say so much good of the Marquis you must be the Marquis himself."[10] Love to dearest K.   ever your's affectionately

M. A.—

MS. Frederick Whitridge.

    1. For Max Müller's letter see above.
    2. *Merope* ll. 216–17 (altered in the first reprinting, 1885).
    3. *Merope* ll. 1611–12, from Pausanias, *Description of Greece* bk. 8, "Arcadia," 21.2.
    4. "Death of Mademoiselle Rachel," *The Times*, Jan. 7, p. 6. Arnold has a point. *The Times* said that Racine and Corneille, made tolerable to "John Bull" only by the "transcendent genius" of Rachel, now will be "consigned to their shelves, never to redescend, till some new histrionic genius calls them once more from their hiding place."
    5. "Adrienne Lecouvreur," the drama (1849) by Eugène Scribe and G.J.B.E.W. Legouvé (one of Rachel's great roles); *Night and Morning*, the novel (1841) by Bulwer Lytton; "The Corsican Brothers," a drama (1852) translated from the French by Dion Boucicault.
    6. August von Kotzebue (1761–1819), German dramatist and novelist.
    7. Grote's *History of Greece*, 1 (1846), 511–12 (pt 1, ch., 16).
    8. Unidentified—a personal letter?
    9. Untraced.
    10. Arnold's recollection (and improvement) of Scott's *A Legend of Montrose*, ch. 13.

To Mary Penrose Arnold*

The Athenæum
My dearest Mother   January 18, 1858
    I send you today two or three newspapers, none of them exactly favourable, but which you will perhaps like to see. In spite of the aversion of people to the unfamiliar stranger introduced to them, her appearance evidently makes them think and turn themselves about it—and this will do

them good: while their disinclination will do me no harm, as their curiosity will make them buy Merope, and I have no intention of producing, like Euripides, 70 dramas in this style, but shall now turn to something wholly different. The Leader, for which I look with some interest, has not yet spoken.[1]

If Susy is still with you will you thank her for me for her note conveying Miss Martineau's approval of Merope—and tell her that if I did not write myself it was because I have really more on my hands than I can well manage—especially with my bad dawdling habits. But I was and always am very glad to hear from dear Susy—and was delighted to find Merope had interested her.

I sent Merope to Tom but have not yet heard from him. In a letter I wrote to him I touched in one sentence on his change of religious profession—which it is possible he may not have liked.[2]

We have made efforts to go tomorrow night to one of the grand representations at the opera—but prices are too high. It is just possible that William Delafield, with whom we dined last Friday, may do something for us—but I don't think it is probable.[3] Flu will be more disappointed than I—for to see the royal party I do not care one straw—I only wanted to see Helen Faucit in Lady Macbeth—as she has retired from the stage, and is not easily to be seen now.[4]

Norman leaves us tonight—but we have got Mrs Tuffin, of whom you have heard, in her place. Norman was often very disagreeable—but she was also in many respects an excellent nurse—above all she had an authority over the children which servants seldom have—and we shall miss her, I am sure.[5] As for the children, baby will fret a little, but the two boys will not care a bit—and have already told Norman that "they want Mrs Tuffin to come because she will tell them about soldiers"—her husband having been a dragoon.

There is an article in the Edinburgh which has many vicious remarks on Papa.[6] I do not think it would by any means delight you to read it, so I advise you to abstain. It is the article on Tom Brown. It is by no means very ably done, and will excite no sympathy, I feel sure, and do no harm. No doubt blots existed in his character and administration as in those of all mortal men but this article does not hit them, and invents for him a physiognomy which no one who had ever seen him would recognize for his. Love to all— let me hear how Walter is going on—   Ever your most affectionate son—

M. A.—

MS. Balliol College.

1. See above p. 378–79.

2. See above p. 370 n. 5.

3. A significant allusion. William Delafield (1797/1798–1870), Matthew Arnold's first cousin once removed, was one of the sons of Joseph Delafield (b. 1749), brother of Arnold's paternal grandmother, Martha Delafield Arnold. Joseph Delafield seems a Samuel Smiles subject. He acquired money as a brewer and social status as the husband (m. 1790) of Frances Combe (1761–1803) of Cobham Park, Surrey. Her brother, Harvey Christian Combe (1752–1818), had "inherited a landed property" on his father's death in 1797, and with him Delafield apparently joined to form the brewery firm of Combe, Delafield, and Co. (*Landed*, 1849, 1871, 1939; *Imperial Gazetteer*).

William Delafield had long been affluent. In the 1840s he lived at 4 Stanhope Place, Hyde Park. He moved then to 64 Upper Seymour Street, Portman Square, and then again, in 1857 or 1858, to 40 Lowndes Square, an address just vacated by the earl of Bandon. Some time later (before 1870) Combe, Delafield and Co. became merely Combe and Co. He is mentioned several times later in these letters—nearly dead of spinal neuralgia in Nov. 1862, for example, and actually dead on Jan. 8, 1870—when (commerce genuflecting to culture) he left a legacy of £2,000 to Arnold (see Arnold to his mother Jan. 16, 1870). His sister Charlotte, married to a Captain Philips (probably Capt. Nathaniel George Philips, 23 Belgrave Road, S.W.), is also mentioned from time to time. His older brother John emigrated to the United States and prospered mightily (see below Arnold's letter to Fan, July 4, 1886). Little else is on record about the Delafields apart from occasional allusions in these letters, references in Wymer, and the death notice in *The Times*, Jan. 11, p. 1. (After the Arnolds settled at Cobham in 1873 Charles Combe [1836–1920] and his family and the Arnolds saw a great deal of each other.)

4. For opera his choices were Balfe's new opera "The Rose of Castille" or Bellini's "La Sonnambula," with Piccolomini, both at Her Majesty's Theatre. Helen Faucit was playing there in *Lady Macbeth* (see below p. 386).

5. See above p. 379. Mrs Tuffin, yet another mononym and constantly mentioned in the letters, remained with the Arnolds more than thirteen years, leaving finally in 1871 when her husband, who had served in the Crimea with the 17th Lancers, was discharged from military service (see especially below Arnold's letters to his mother Apr. 16 and Oct. 8, 1871.

6. Fitzjames Stephen, "Tom Brown's Schooldays," *Edinburgh Review* 107 (1858): 172–93. See below pp. 389 and n. 5, 487.

To Charles Thomas Saunders[1]

Education Department, Council Office, Downing Street, London:
Dear Charles Saunders   January 23, 1858
Your name is on the list of candidates for appointments in the Excise not for the *next vacancy*, but for the next nomination that it *falls to my turn* to make.—Before my turn comes, some time may still elapse, as *all* the Inspectors have a certain number of nominations.   Faithfully your's

M. Arnold.—

MS. Huntington Library.

1. Unidentified—but he got the appointment in 1866 to the Inland Revenue Department, Stamping Department, where he remained at least till 1901 ("Official Directory," *POLD*).

To [?William Finch] Edwards[1]

Mr Edwards
          Education Department, Council Office, Downing Street, London:
Dear Sir   January 30, 1858
     Will you be kind enough to forward the enclosed to C. Saunders. I
addressed it to him at Bromley, according to the address which he himself
gave me in his letter, to which it is an answer: but it has been returned to me
through the Dead Letter Office.   Faithfully your's
                                                         M. Arnold.—

MS. University of Virginia.

     1. Perhaps William Finch Edwards (1826–?), M.A., Trinity College, Cambridge,
1852, called to the bar 1853, who was an examiner in the Education Office from some
time in the early sixties (*Men-at-the-Bar, POLD*, 1865).

To Frances Bunsen Trevenen Whately Arnold*

                                                        The Athenæum
My dearest Fan   February 3, 1858
     If you knew what a pleasure it was to me to hear from you you would
write oftener. I have but little time this evening, for I have been at work all
day on my General Report[1] and it is now just post time. With respect to your
question—There is a *Rhyming Dictionary* and there is a book called a "Guide
to English Verse Composition" published, I *believe,* by Smith & Elder—but
all this is sad lumber—and the young lady had much better content herself
with imitating the metres she finds most attract her in the poetry she reads.
Nobody, I imagine, ever began to good purpose in any other way. But what
a prospect for a girl to cultivate a poetical gift now!
     I never saw either of the books I have mentioned, nor I [*for* do] I know
anybody who have [*sic*] used them except Faber—so I cannot speak to their
merits as to the performance of what they profess.[2]
     The Leader was very gratifying.[3] A great many letters I have not sent
you and indeed it rather goes against the grain with me to send you newspapers—I am so dead sick of criticism. Had it been one of my earlier volumes, I should have sent you a multitude of letters—but with this I soon got

tired, seeing it was not going to take as I wished. Instead of reading it for what it is worth everybody begins to consider whether it does not betray a design to substitute tragedies à la Grecque for every other kind of poetical composition in England—and falls into an attitude of violent resistance to such an imaginary design. What I meant them was to see in it [*sic*] a specimen of the world created by the Greek imagination: this imagination was different from our own, and it is hard for us to appreciate, even to understand it: but it had a peculiar power, grandeur, and dignity—and these are worth trying to get an apprehension of. But the British public prefer like all obstinate multitudes to "die in their sins,"[4] and I have no intention to keep preaching in the wilderness.

The book sells well, but it must be remembered that a good many people read it from curiosity. Temple writes me word that "he has read it with astonishment at its goodness."

What a delightful letter from dear old Mary, and how happily she seems to be settled! I liked so much her words "the red glow over the Forest hills." I know them so well, and that glow too—and admire them and it so much.

Poor Mrs Over![5] My love to my dearest Mother—tell me about Mrs Fletcher—   Your ever affectionate

M. A.—

Tom is better—but it seems impossible to be quite sure whether he has the whooping cough or no.

MS. *Frederick Whitridge.*

1. Reprinted in Arnold's *Reports on Elementary Schools 1852–82*, pp. 58–70.

2. John Walker's *Rhyming Dictionary*, first published in 1775 and endlessly reprinted. "Guide to English Verse Composition" has not been identified. Frederick William Faber since 1849 had been superior of the London Oratory, first at King William Street, then at Brompton.

3. See above p. 371 n. 1.

4. John 8:21, 24.

5. Unidentified (not Owen, but perhaps Ovens).

To James Hepworth

Mr Hepworth—
          Education Department, Council Office, Downing Street, London:
My dear Sir   February 4, 1858
          The report on your school is by no means to be considered an unfavourable one, and will not the least tend to counterbalance the other favourable ones, when those reports entered on the certificates are weighed for the

purpose of a revision of the certificates. You must remember that you are new to Mr Alderson and that he is new to you:[1] I feel sure that a second visit will remove your unfavourable impression: I myself have thought his manner to children, when I once saw him in a school, both gentle and agreeable.   I am always glad to hear of you, and remain   truly your's
M. Arnold.—

MS. Bodleian Library.

1. Charles H. Alderson (1831–1913), out of Eton and Trinity College, Oxford, and a fellow of All Souls', was the second son of Sir Edward Alderson and younger brother of Packy, the "young ass" (see above p. 342). He was a school inspector 1857–82, chief inspector 1882–85, second charity commissioner 1885–1900, chief charity commissioner for England and Wales 1900–1903; C.B. 1899, K.C.B. 1903; Athenæum (*WWW*; *County Families*; Kelly). Alderson's second visit, a year later, made the same impression (see below p. 416).

To Frances Mary Blackett du Quaire*[1]

The Athenæum
My dear Fanny   February 9, 1858
I hope by this time you have *Merope*. I got Drummond Wolff to undertake the transmission of her. I am anxious to explain to you that you are not the least bound to like her, as she is calculated rather to inaugurate my Professorship with dignity than to move deeply the present race of *humans*. No one is more sensible of this than I am, only I have such a real love for this form and this old Greek world that perhaps I infuse a little soul into my dealings with them which saves me from being entirely *ennuyeux*, professorial, and pedantic; still you will not find in *Merope* what you wish to find, and I excuse you beforehand for wishing to find something different, and being a little dissatisfied with me; and I promise you, too, to give you a better satisfaction some day, if I live.

I often think of poor dear Johnny and the pleasure that he would have taken in *Merope*, he having much the same special fondness for this sort of thing that I have. Make Browning look at it, if he is at Florence; one of the very best antique fragments I know is a fragment of a Hippolytus by him.[2] As to his wife, I regard her as hopelessly confirmed in her aberration from health, nature, beauty, and truth.[3]

The poem is a great deal reviewed here, very civilly, but very expostulatingly.

I dined at Lord Granville's on Sunday, and found all the Ministerial people saying, "What a stormy time we shall have!"

The Duke of Argyll said with a sublime virtue that we were not to shrink from doing what was right because other people did and said what was wrong. There is no doubt that between India and the "French Colonels' Bill," as their enemies call it, the Government are in a critical situation. It is said that Lord Derby is both willing and eager to come in. Bright has appeared with a strong manifesto about Reform, written with great spirit; but, in the first place, no one cares as yet about the Reform question; in the second place, every one agrees that Bright could not be active in the House for a week without breaking down again.[4]

When shall we all meet? We have taken a house in Chester Square. It is a very small one, but it will be something to unpack one's portmanteau for the first time since I was married, now nearly seven years ago. Write still to the Privy Council Office, and believe me   always affectionately yours,

M. A.

Text. Russell, 1:69–71.

1. Frances Mary Blackett du Quaire (c. 1822?-95), sister of John and Montagu Blackett. She seems to have been already well established in Paris in 1851, when Nassau William Senior saw her several times (*Journals Kept in France and Italy from 1848 to 1852*, ed. M. C. M. Simpson, 2:285). She married the mysterious Count Henri du Quaire between Dec. 6, 1856 (when Arnold referred to her as Fanny Blackett), and Mar. 28, 1859 (when he called her du Quaire). In Apr. 1860 Mérimée, who saw her at the splendid (and famous) costume "Bal de l'Hotel d'Albe," given by the empress, commented to his old friend the empress's mother: "Il y avait aussi quelques Anglaises en nymphes, en grecques et en marquises Louis XV, qui ressemblaient à des chien savants. Je suis fâché que Miss Blackett, dont j'oublie le nom actuel, fût du nombre des plus cocasses" (*Correspondance*, 9:461). Her husband must have died in 1866—on May 10 Arnold dined with her in Paris at the Café Anglais: "she expresses great concern for appearances just now, was dressed in black, very well, but very quietly." In any case, she did not go down for the count but rallied and stayed the course for three more decades—till her own death in 1895. She is mentioned frequently in the diaries, and Arnold's last reference to her in a letter to Lucy in Dec. 1887: he is going to see "poor Fanny du Quaire, who has been quite ill with bronchitis, and whose affairs, besides, are in a bad state."

2. "Artemis Prologizes," *Men and Women* (1855).

3. An implied criticism of *Aurora Leigh* (1857)?

4. A "stormy time" indeed. Parliament resumed on Feb. 4, coping with the repercussions of the Indian Mutiny and of the attempt to assassinate the French emperor ("the colonels" having more or less officially protested "an improper degree of shelter and countenance" to foreign refugees in England, where the plot was allegedly hatched). Palmerston's government resigned and the two Houses adjourned on Feb. 22. Granville George Leveson-Gower (1815–91: *DNB*; *VF*, 3/13/69), 2d Earl Granville, who lived at 16 Bruton Street, foreign secretary under Lord John Russell and again later under Gladstone, was the leader of the House of Lords and (more to the point here), as Lord President of the Privy Council, Arnold's superior in the Education Office. George Douglas Campbell (1823–1900: *DNB*; *VF*, 4/17/69), 8th duke of Argyll, was postmaster-general. Ed-

ward George Geoffrey Smith Stanley, earl of Derby, headed the new Conservative government, his second cabinet. John Bright, now M.P. for Birmingham (elected in Aug. 1857), after a six-month interval for recruiting his health had just "returned to the House of Commons amid general applause on 9 Feb. 1858" (*DNB*). See *Annual Register; Album;* Swinburne, 1:239, 2:53.

To Thomas Arnold

Council Office

My dear Tom   February 11, 1858

I hear from home that you have expressed some anxiety lest I should have taken amiss your letter to me about Merope. There was not a word in it which anybody could take amiss—and if there had been, I do not think I should have been apt to take it so. I have been a good deal criticized, and am now, I think, with respect to criticism, more curious than sensitive. I mean I listen to it more with reference to the testimony it gives me of the state of public feeling and public taste about literature, and of what can and cannot be done to influence or change that taste and feeling, than with reference to its praise or blame of me myself; though of course I am not without the natural liking for praise and dislike of blame. But the personal matter grows less and less important for me, and the general matter more and more.

I think you are right that Merope as an isolated work will not produce any powerful effect—but then a work like Merope is nothing without the stage. I think Merope is weak from her isolation, and not through her affinity with what you call the pagan world, from which world I do not think as you do that the present world is more and more moving away.

But as I have neither the time nor the means nor probably the talent to produce a series of works, I do not say like Merope, but belonging to the same sphere of imagination, to establish a school of actors for them, and to provide a stage for them—to do in fact in England in my own way what the great classical school did in France in their way—I shall not persevere in producing works like Merope, although there are one or two other old Greek stories on which I *must* try my hand some day!

We have at last taken a house,—in Chester Square,—and the Judge is going to enable us to furnish [it]. We shall have this year been married 7 years, and never had a house for more than 4 months at a time. I write this during the Inspectors' Conference, with talking going on all round me.

Love to all your party—and write to me soon.   Your ever affectionate

M. A.

MS. Balliol College.

To Helena Faucit[1]

Madam   March 6, 1858
I take the liberty of sending you a copy of a tragedy which I have lately
published, with a view to ascertain whether it would be possible to induce
you, were it brought upon the stage, to undertake the principal character.
In a tragedy of this kind, depending little for its success upon the com-
plication of its stage-business, everything turns upon the nobleness, serious-
ness, and powers of feeling of the actor; and I would certainly make no attempt to get *Merope* represented unless I had a prospect of obtaining the help
of the artist who alone, in the present state of the English stage, seems to me
to display these qualities in an eminent degree. . . .
It is very possible, madam, that you may find yourself unable to give me
the benefit of your assistance for my tragedy, but I am glad, at any rate, to
have the opportunity of expressing the admiration with which your delightful talent has often inspired me, and the respect with which I am,
Madam,   your obedient humble servant,

Matthew Arnold .

Text. Theodore Martin, Helena Faucit (Lady Martin), p. 256.

1. Helena Savile Faucit (1817–98: *DNB*) was the reigning queen of the British
stage, "the greatest interpreter of the poetical drama that living memory can recall" (*DNB*,
which quotes from this letter). When her husband, Theodore Martin (1816–1909: *DNB*;
VF, 7/7/77), was knighted in 1880, she became Lady Martin. Arnold aimed high, but,
though she had appeared in at least three dramas by Browning, she flinched at *Merope*,
which, her husband explained, "was carefully read, and Miss Faucit wrote in reply, pointing out some of the difficulties which she saw would stand in the way of its success on the
stage." See below p. 387. On Martin see below p. 450 and n. 6 and *Album*, pp. 106–7.

To Council of Marlborough College

Education Department, Council Office, Downing Street, London:
March 15th, 1858
I have been acquainted with Mr. Bradley[1] for many years, and have the
highest opinion of his talents and acquirements, which procured for him the
most honorable distinction at Rugby, and at the University.
I have also had peculiar opportunities of judging of Mr. Bradley's success
as a Master at Rugby. While there was no Master who succeeded better in
animating and fixing the attention of his pupils during their school lessons,
there was none, perhaps, who succeeded so well in inspiring parents with
confidence in his judicious kindness and watchful care towards his pupils

out of School.   I have the honour to remain,   Your obedient
humble servant,

MATTHEW ARNOLD

Text. Mr. Bradley's Testimonials (Rugby: Crossley and Billington, 1858), p. 10.

1. See above pp. 201–2.

To Helena Faucit

[c. April 1, 1858]
[Mr. Arnold, with whom we had many friends in common, wrote in
reply requesting that he might be allowed] to call and make his acknowledgments in person for her kindness. If I derive [he added] no other result from
the attempt to get *Merope* acted, I shall then, at least, have derived from it the
great pleasure of making your acquaintance.[1]

Text. Theodore Martin, Helena Faucit (Lady Martin), pp. 256–7.

1. "They accordingly met, when, I believe, her reasons satisfied him that, while she
might personally have pleasure in acting the part of Merope, it would not be advisable to
put his drama to the more than doubtful test of a public representation. At all events she
heard no more of his wish, and Mr Arnold became, and continued till his death, a personal
friend" (*Helena Faucit*, p. 257).

To Mary Penrose Arnold

Stanley Cottage, Richmond Hill, Surrey
My dearest Mother   Good Friday, [April 2,] 1858
    Pray take good note of the above address, and let us soon hear from you.
We came down yesterday, having decided to come here rather than to Brighton because it is so much easier to run up and look at the progress of our
house. And at this time of the year the air of Richmond was thought to be
equally favourable for Tom. His spirits are better and his appetite is again
pretty good, but he still makes us both very uneasy—his thinness has so
much increased, and his weakness and indisposition to play about, with it.
His breathing also is again very short and there is a loud creaking sound with
it which we have not observed till lately. We hope this comes from phlegm
on the chest which he cannot get rid of and which has occasioned the perpetual cough which has so harassed him—and that as the warm weather
comes on he will lose his cough and this difficulty of breathing along with it.
The cough seems subsiding—but this morning he had a fit which lasted

without a cessation of more than 3 seconds at a time from 6½ to 8. So we do not often have him out of our minds as you may suppose—or indeed out of our sight—for he passes most of the day with his Mamma. The air here is beautiful, and his appetite and spirits seem the better for it today: but since dinner he has not seemed so well, as the operation of eating fatigues him. Budge and the Baby are quite well, and the latter in the most splendid spirits. We have a charming little house, on the very top of the hill looking right over the grand view. Today it is cold and windy, but as April advances it will be charming. I have a day or two's holiday at Easter & hope to make great progress in my lecture.[1] The Wightmans have taken a larger house near (not half so good a view as ours, though) and come down next week. The new house gets on fast, and at last looks clean having been stripped of all paper from top to bottom and washed with lime water before painting. I send you Helen Faucit's note with one from Gladstone—Fan need not return either. There is a very interesting article on Merope in the new number of the National—I do not know who wrote it. I will send it soon. Tell me if you have seen the Dublin University?[2] It is clever & I will send it if you have not. Tell me all about Mary and Woodhouse,[3] and how Walter gets on. I have great hopes Tommy will come all right—it is Willy's birthday on Thursday.[4]   Ever your most affectionate son

M. A.—

MS. Balliol College.

1. Of his second lecture as Professor of Poetry, delivered on May 8, we know next to nothing except that apparently it continued the subject of the "adequacy" of ancient poetry to its age, that it mentioned Buddhism, and that his wife liked it less than the first and third lectures (see above pp. 370 n. 4, 375, and below p. 391).

2. W. C. Roscoe, "*Merope*: a Tragedy," *National Review* 3 (1858):259–79; *Dublin University Review* Mar. 1858, pp. 331–44—on three volumes by Arnold (and two by Denis Florence MacCarthy): "Mr. Arnold's first volume contains much that is exceedingly beautiful, a little that is poor, somewhat that is execrably bad. But, on the whole, a volume of such promise has scarcely appeared in the present generation. His second volume contains some fine things, and a good deal of rubbish. His third volume [*Merope*] is a piece of clever, systematic rubbish." (The latter was by the Rev. William Alexander, later archbishop of Armagh and primate of all Ireland—see the letter to him below, when Arnold learned he was the author [? March 1869].)

3. On Jan. 8 Mary Arnold Twining had married the Rev. John Simeon Hiley (1811–65), of Woodhouse, near Loughborough, Leics, in Burley-in Wharfedale. Hiley (of Trinity College, Dublin, and then St John's College, Cambridge, B.A. and M.A., 1844), was "a large owner in the township" with "a handsome residence near the church," of which he was perpetual curate (White, *History, Gazetteer, and Directory of the Counties of Leicester and Rutland*, pp. 464–65; *Annual Register*, Venn).

4. His birthday was in fact on Wednesday—Apr. 7!

To Mary Penrose Arnold

2. Chester Square

My dearest Mother   May 16, 1858

Flu has written to Fox How lately, and I have been so hard pressed that I have been willing to leave it to her to say what we both felt at the news of poor dear Fanny.[1] I think of her often, and see her as distinctly as if she stood before me. It is very sad to remember how often I thought her listless manners apathy, and how she sometimes seemed to me one of those who are less to be pitied if they have much to endure because they feel little— when after all her languor must have so often come from her weakness— and she was gradually being shaken and undermined by what she appeared to feel so slightly. I suppose the children will certainly come home, poor little things.

You must tell K if she is still with you that I missed her dreadfully at Oxford, though I was glad to have William. But she is my original audience and my best. I had a good many people, but not so many as the first time— hardly any undergraduates—and the theatre was, to me, depressingly too big for us. Besides the attempt to form general ideas is one which the Englishman naturally sets himself against: and the one grand'-idée of these introductory lectures is to establish a formula which shall *suit* all literature: an attempt which so far as I know has not yet even been made in England.

If you can find me a little bit of Papa's handwriting now, I shall be very glad.

Flu and I go down to Laleham to dine & sleep on Tuesday. I am to be god-father to Matt Buckland's little boy.[2] On Saturday we go to Devizes for two or three days thence to Oxford for two or three more—but shall be settled here again, I hope, about the end of next week.[3]

I cannot tell you how perpetual a pleasure our house is to us—or how unalterably bent we are on having you and Fan here next month. I met Remusat at dinner the other day—the Frenchman who wrote that article on Papa which we so liked—he is very pleasant and I think I shall try and get him to dinner.[4] Oddly enough I met at the same party young Stephen: him who wrote the disagreeable article in the Edinbro—He is not a bad fellow either, in spite of his bad article.[5] My love to all at Fox How and believe me always   your most affectionate son—

M. A.

Write to us *here*.

MS. Balliol College.

1. Apparently, Fanny Buckland, daughter of John and Frances Arnold Buckland.

2. Unidentified but obviously the third son—probably Charles Arnold Buckland, later lieutenant, R.N., Coast Guard, out of Bantry, who served aboard the *Amethyst* in Peru in 1877 and was promoted lieutenant in 1882 (Whitaker, p. 80). Buckland's first, second, and fourth sons (born in 1854, 1856, 1864), Oxonians all, are listed in Foster.

3. The Peter Woods lived at Devizes; Arnold's third lecture at Oxford was on May 29.

4. Charles François Marie comte de Rémusat (1797–1875), politician and miscellaneous writer, especially on philosophical and English politics and history. The article is identified in Super, 3:454: "Des Controverses religieuses en Angleterre, II. Coleridge— [Thomas] Arnold," *Revue des deux mondes* 5 (Oct. 1, 1856):492–529. (Arnold cites Rémusat in Super, 2:227.)

5. James Fitzjames Stephen (1829–94: *DNB*), journalist (especially *Saturday Review* and *Pall Mall Gazette*), jurist (especially noted for works on the law of evidence and on criminal law, in India as well as at home), and judge of the Queen's Bench. He was massive not only intellectually but also physically, as the Spy cartoon in *Vanity Fair* 3/7/85 makes evident. At Trinity College, Cambridge, he was an "Apostle," made K.C.S.I. in 1877, created a baronet in 1891. "He is also a D.C.L. of Oxford, and an LL.B. of London. He is a very able man indeed, very learned and very sound, and one of the great lights of the Bench. . . . He has also published in the *Nineteenth Century* his opinion that we could live very well without religion. In the trial of causes, he looks tremendous when his moral indignation rises" (*Vanity Fair*). On his later (adversarial) relations with Arnold see James A. Colaiaco, *James Fitzjames Stephen and the Crisis of Victorian Thought*, pp. 18–23—and p. 128: "While Arnold's weapon was the rapier, Stephen's was the bludgeon." See below p. 413.

To Mary Penrose Arnold

Abingdon[1]
Oxford
My dearest Mother   May 30, [1858]
    I have just been writing to Edward, and that reminds me that I have not written to you *myself*, although Flu has, to tell you how unalterably purposed we are not to let you pass on to him before you have paid a fortnight's visit to us. There is really so much to do and see in London which is particularly brilliant this spring that it would be a pity on Fan's account to hurry through, and I am sure you will enjoy it when you are once there. You shall be as quiet as ever you like and not dine out at all if you had rather not, but have your friends to see you in Chester Square.

    Flu told you that the Bishop of Salisbury begged me the other day to let him know if you came, as he must come up from Salisbury to see you.[2]

    We have had a long week away from the three dear little boys—but Tom is at Brighton so we shall not see him when we return tomorrow—but to see Budge and Diddy will be a great pleasure—and to hear Master Dids say in his pretty voice when I call out—Where's the Baby?—*Here he is.* I don't think that jolly old Budge misses us much, as he takes life as he finds it, sensible boy, and makes himself happy with anybody he is with. But Baby will be very glad to see us again.

Lately Tom had a return of cough, and a slight pain in the side, which made us consent to Fanny's taking him to Brighton[3]—but I hope to fetch him back at the end of this week, as it is better for him to be under his Mamma's training and with his brothers, if possible.

I gave my third lecture yesterday. Flu liked it better than the second— and I always find that she thinks as a great many people think—but I believe the second lecture will stand well enough when it is printed. I should like nothing better than for you to hear the lectures—but to read in MSS they would be detestable. I will read you one at Fox How.[4]

Is Fanny's letter to K, asking her to take the children, to be seen.

There is an article on Merope in this Fraser, and one in the New Quarterly Review, which I will send you.[5] Flu has been terribly plagued with tooth-ache this week, but is better. She expects her confinement (has she told you?) in December.[6]

With love to Fan   your ever most affectionate

M. A.—

I breakfasted with Gladstone the other day, and was interested in seeing him. I met Montalembert.[7]

MS. Balliol College.

1. The stationery is embossed "Abingdon," a village then half a dozen miles from Oxford and very much Arnold's "Cumner country" (see Francis Wylie, "The Scholar-Gipsy Country," in Tinker and Lowry, pp. 351–73), where, as the diary shows, the Arnolds stopped May 20–30, except for a visit to Devizes (see above p. 390) and school inspections in London or Wantage.

2. Walter Kerr Hamilton (1808–69: *DNB*), bishop of Salisbury since 1854, had been Dr Arnold's pupil at Laleham.

3. Fanny Nicholls.

4. See above p. 370 n. 4.

5. *Fraser's Magazine* 57 (1858):691–701, by John Connington (?), reprinted in Dawson; *New Quarterly Review* no. 21 (May 1858):123–35 (unsigned).

6. Lucy Charlotte Arnold, born on Dec. 25.

7. See above p. 331. Gladstone's *Diaries*, 5:295, on May 4: "Count Montalembert."

To Mary Penrose Arnold

My dearest Mother—   [? June 6, 1858]

six days is better than three but will not quite do. We will make a compromise: we will give up the fortnight and you shall agree to stay a full seven days—so as to be *over* the week with us, at least: that is if you come on a Monday, you are not to be allowed to go before the *Tuesday week* following. Let it be settled so: indeed nothing is so tiring as to be in London only for a day or two. We are keeping for your coming the Crystal Palace where we have not been for years.

Let us know as soon as possible when we may have the great pleasure of seeing you my dearest Mother. We talk of it constantly—Any time between the 16th of this month and the 12th of July on which day I start for the circuit will suit us equally well. On Saturday Flu I and Budge go down to Brighton to fetch Tom—return on Monday: then on Tuesday Flu & I go to Oxford, and return on Wednesday after Commemoration to dine with the Taits. I write this in my little library before breakfast. Dear old Budge has just joined me and I hear the Baby's chirp upstairs. Budge breakfasts with us every morning now Tom is away, and is getting [to be] a famous companion. He has had a fall off a chair this morning—and the treatment for his accident is to be that he is to have an egg for breakfast and to begin with toast instead of bread and butter.

Budge says—"Papa de', I want my breakfast to[o]"—he and I always fall to at a quarter to ⟨eight⟩ nine without waiting for his Mamma. Flu has had two teeth out (under chloroform) and is now all right again. I was with her at the second operation; and the chloroform-taking is a most unpleasant sight—far worse than the extraction.

We go to Dover early in August and shall be actually engaged there till the 25th. Saturday the 28th would be the earliest day we should come north if we came then—but tell us exactly what suits you best this year.[1]

What do you think of the New Quarterly?[2] It is cleverly done. My love to all at home. Does not Fan like the thoughts of London?   Ever your's

M. A.

MS. Balliol College.

1. In fact, as the diary shows, he inspected in Kent (Dover, Deal, Margate, Folkestone, Tenterden, Ashford, Elham, Tunbridge Wells) Aug. 3–24, then crossed from Dover to Calais, spent one night in Paris, and went on Thursday, Aug. 26, to Geneva (see below p. 403). Judge Wightman was "staying" with them in Dover (see below p. 403). He veered sharply from this schedule and in fact (after his Swiss vacation with Walrond) went to Fox How on Sept. 16 (diary).

2. The review of *Merope*.

Mary Penrose Arnold to Thomas Arnold

2 Chester Square, [London]

June 28, [1858]

We found Matt in a very pretty & comfortable house here—with everything in such good proportions that nothing seems cramped or confined. They have furnished it with very good taste, & are repaid for their patience in waiting houseless so long by being better able now to meet the expenses. They are very near the Wightmans, & it is amusing to see what pleasure the Judge takes in all their arrangements & in seeing the House admired.

They gave one of their first dinner parties to day inviting Judge Coleridge & the Taits here to meet me—and it was a very pleasant evening. The three little boys presence [*for* present] all their characteristic differences— Tom a refined delicate looking little creature—as if he had not much stability about him—Trevenen much the reverse with a sensible truthful face which it does one good to look at. Little Richard—being fair but a sturdy stout little man who seems to have a good hold on life.

MS. Balliol College.

To A. J. Beale

Mr Beale

Education Department, Council Office, Downing Street, London:

My dear Sir   July 10, 1858

I am sincerely glad to find that your school continues to have the success which your exertions so well merit. You do not mention your own health, but that, I hope, is now quite reestablished. I have read the Banbury Guardian with much interest.

I will see about your Certificate. It certainly ought to have been sent to you before this.   Ever faithfully yours

M. Arnold.

MS. Public Library, Dunedin, N. Z.

To Frances Lucy Wightman Arnold *

Vevey

My darling   Saturday, August 28, 1858

I shall go back to where I left off in my last letter. We were just going to dine at Philippe's—we walked there—it is too far—in the Rue Montorgueil.[1] When you are there the rooms are low and small—the dinner very good certainly, but not perceptibly better than the dinners you get at the Trois Frères, Maison Dorée, &c: I should say it was a better place to give a party in than to come into and have a chance dinner. We then strolled on the Boulevard—had ice at one café and coffee at another—then back to our hotel where young Grenfell left us—charmed with his day, poor fellow, as he is tied for some weeks to a French tutor whom he detests, and never sees a compatriote.[2] Next morning we were up not quite so early as we should have been, and only just caught the train at a ¼ to 8: you remember you and I nearly missed on our first tour the 11 o'clock train at the same station, that for Lyons, which is a long way off. We were just in time however, getting into the salle d'attente just as the doors were opened to let the people out. We manage very well, Walrond settling with the drivers while I get the tickets. I thought of you as we passed out into the open valley of the Seine and shot away towards Fontainebleau—how new that line and country were to both of us, and how we looked out of the window for every place to be seen on both sides of the road! Seen a second time, the Lyons line is a dull one: I am glad to have seen it once more, however, and now, I think, if ever I pass by again, it shall be at night. We had for companions a shaky old Englishman with a peevish wife, and a Genevese and his wife, very pleasant people with whom we talked a great deal. It came out at the very end of the day that she was a granddaughter of old Mrs. Marcet and connected with all the Romilly set.[3] At Tonnerre we had a very good breakfast, which was lucky, as the train was a little behind time, and the stoppages at all the other places came to little or nothing. At Dijon we just found time to telegraph to the Ecu at Geneva for beds. The day was bright but cold, with occasional showers and as there had been much rain the night before, we had no dust. The train was by no means crowded, and better travelling I have never known. At Macon at 5 p.m. we unhooked from the Lyons train (in 1851 you and I passed Macon by steamboat, the line being then only finished to Chalon) and started on the new line to Geneva. We got a mouthful to eat at Macon, but as I have told you, the stopping-time was taken away. From Macon leaving the Saone, you go along the valley of the Veyle through a dead flat, richly green, and wooded country to Bourg: behind us the sun was setting beautifully over the Charolais mountains, the outliers of the Cevennes: but in front storm-cloud and rain and a rain-bow were over the Jura. We dropped our Genevese friends at Bourg, the capital of the department of the Ain, and went on alone with our two English to the passage of the Ain and Amberieux, where the line enters the Jura: it was now past 7, at which time it is nearly dark here, and the rain began. This was provoking, so I went to sleep. I woke up occasionally to hear the rain pattering, and to see black obscure ridges close to the carriage window—these were the defiles of the Jura—but the immediate sides of the defiles we went through did not seem high. Finally it cleared, and as we approached Geneva at 11 the moon came out, and we saw the tall white houses, with their lights, scattered about the valley of the Rhone, and the high line of the Jura in the distance, beautifully soft and clear. We drove straight to the Ecu, found they had kept very good rooms for us, looking

right over the Rhone.[4] We had tea, I sate for a while by my open window—
and then went to bed. Next morning we were up at 7—a beautiful morning—and there was the exquisite lake before us, with the Rhone issuing out
of it, and the sun on the rocky summits of the Jura—all that one thinks of so
often when one cannot see them with one's eyes. After breakfast we strolled
about the town and by the lake. I bought a map of Savoy, and we went to see
the model of Mont Blanc. Then we took a calèche about 12 and drove to
Ferney. We did not drive by the great public road to Gex, but kept along a
little winding cross road shaded over with trees, all among the country houses
of the Genevese. We stopped at a campagne, where the driver told us the
gardener had permission to sell the fruit, and bought all the peaches and figs
we could carry for a fabulously small price, then drove on up a little hill to
the Petit Saconnex, a small village: and there, on looking back, was Mont
Blanc in all his glory with a few clouds playing about the middle of him, but
his head and all his long line of Aiguilles cutting the blue sky sharp and
bright, without a speck of mist. Then on to Ferney, where the terrace has
the most beautiful view possible— [5]

Sunday morning—more is left of Voltaire than I expected, but I cannot
describe Ferney here. We drove slowly back to Geneva, with Mont Blanc
before us all the way—went and bathed in the lake—delightful—then back
to the 5 o'clock table d'hôte. After dinner we drove again to the Petit Saconnex to see the sunset over Mont Blanc: we were a little too late, but what we
saw was very impressive: then we drove to the junction of the Rhone and
the Arve, which we reached to see just by twilight—then back to Geneva to
have our coffee at the Café du Nord, and to walk about the quays till bed-
time. Yesterday morning we left Geneva by the 9 a.m. boat: we could not
leave this lake so soon, so we put in here for Sunday. One of the things I
most long for is to come here with you. It seems absurd to tell you, now I
have come without you, how I long for you, but so it is: I have not yet once,
for a moment, felt as I generally feel abroad, as I felt last year with you: for
the first time in my life I feel willing to go back at any moment, and do not
mind what happens to shorten the journey. Walrond is the best and most
faithful of companions, too: but as a Frenchman settled in England and married to an Englishwoman said to me this morning—there is nothing in the
world so agreeable as travelling with one's wife. But then his poor wife said
to me that it was but a half pleasure away from one's children: and "how
many reasons for unhappiness," she asked me, "have you left at home? I have
left two." But I will never come to Switzerland again without you. The
Italian was right who said that unless you were accompanied by *une dame* you
were best perfectly alone.—I must just finish my journal—we got here about
½ past 1 yesterday: got rooms high up, but looking over the lake—had

luncheon, and started immediately for Meillerie. As we neared the opposite side we undressed, jumped out of the boat and swam to the famous rocks. It blew uncomfortably as we came back. Walrond rowed all the way there & back to quicken the boat. We dined at the 8 o'clock table d'hote: pretty good but this hotel is too crowded. We are now going to walk about Clarens Montreux &c: then to dine at the 5 o'clock table d'hôte, and after dinner to Bex. Tomorrow, I hope, over the Diablerets. I shall find a letter from my darling girl at Zermatt, I hope & trust. Write your next to me at the *Hotel de la Couronne*, not the Ecu, at Geneva. A thousand loves for your dear letter to Geneva written from London. I thought of you yesterday on your journey to Fox How.—Love to all there, and kisses to my 3 darling birdies. I dreamed last night you had a little girl: but she was very ugly.[6] God bless you—I am again and again and always your fondly and tenderly attached & devoted—

Cangrande.[7]

That sweet little Tom! Give him a dozen kisses for his Papa. I perpetually think of you all: even of Diddy.

MS. Frederick Whitridge.

1. Near Les Halles and St Eustache. He also went to Père Lachaise Cemetery, La Sainte Chapelle, and Sainte Clothilde (diary).

2. One of the three sons of Algernon Grenfell (see above pp. 10 n. 1, 67), probably the youngest, Edward Frederick Grenfell, c. 1841–70 (Rugby; Foster).

3. Jane Marcet (1758–1858: *DNB*), born in Switzerland, sister of William Haldimand (see below p. 477 n. 2), was "well known for her 'Conversations on Chemistry,' 'Conversations on Political Economy,' and other elementary works on scientific subjects, as well as for her 'Stories for very little Children,' 'Mary's Grammar,' &c" (*Annual Register*, Allibone). She died on June 28 in Stratton Street, at the home of her son-in-law Edward Romilly (1804–70), formerly M.P. for Ludlow, son of Sir Samuel Romilly and husband of her daughter Sophia (m. 1830, d. 1877). As "old Mrs Marcet" had no granddaughter, the train companion was no doubt a grandniece. See below p. 401 n. 2.

4. Hotel de l'Ecu de Genève, Place du Rhone 2: "beaucoups d'Américains" (Baedeker's *La Suisse*, 1859).

5. Diary (Guthrie 2:216), Thursday, Aug. 26: "To Geneva. Fine day with showers. Night & rain at Amberieux & through the Jura. Eau [*for* Ecu] de Genève." Friday, 27: "To Ferney. terrace & berceau. The seamed & spotted summits of the Jura at morning. bathed in the lake. After dinner to Petit Sacconex & junction of the Arve & Rhone." Saturday, 28: "to Vevey by 9 a. m. boat. Jura. Day of gleams & half lights. From Vevey to [over "Fox How"] Meillerie; bathed at Meillerie: dine & slept at 3 Couronnes": "tout près du lac, l'un des plus grands hôtels de la Suisse (4 étages), fort bien situé, monté et organisé; beaucoup d'Anglais" (Baedeker's *La Suisse*).

6. Lucy was born Dec. 15.

7. Big Dog, in the honored bestiary tradition of nicknames.

To Frances Lucy Wightman Arnold*

Hotel du Mont Cervin, [Zermatt]
September 1, 1858

Here I am at last, but without you, alas! I have got your letter, and am more vexed than I can say at your having had no letter from me last Thursday. By this time you will have found that I wrote it and posted it on Wednesday, as I promised. Now I shall continue my account of myself. After writing to you on Sunday, Walrond and I set off to walk to the Chateau de Blonay, an old castellated house standing among those exquisite hills of park and lawn which are interposed between the high mountains and Vevey, and which make Vevey so soft and beautiful. The family were at dinner, so we could not go in, but we walked about the terraces and into the village church, with beautiful views of the Lake of Geneva, and got back to Vevey just in time for the five o'clock *table d'hôte*. The dinner was very good, but at six Walrond and I had to leave it to get to the steamboat, which departed, as at Villeneuve, just as it got dark. The evening was rather heavy and overcast, but Clarens and Montreux still looked beautiful as we passed them. I walked up and down on the pier at Villeneuve till the train started for Bex—ten miles. The railroad is just open. We got to the Hotel de l'Union at Bex about half-past nine; it is a dirty place, though Murray calls it good. We engaged a guide to take us over the Diablerets next day, had some tea, and went to bed. Walrond complained of insects, but I saw none. However, I was on a different storey from him. I slept badly, the bed being uncomfortably short for me; but at six o'clock I was up, and at half-past seven we had started with our guide, the Dent de Morcles glittering in front of us, and Bex and its trees in shade. The pass of the Diablerets is not much travelled. It cuts off a great corner from Bex to Sion, but it is long—the ascent easy enough, but the descent on the Sion side steep in parts and very stony. The Diablerets and his glaciers are very fine, and the long descent towards the Vallais,[1] along the valley of the Liserne, with hundreds of feet of precipice above and below for two or three miles, is very fine too. At a little chapel, dedicated to St. Bernard, you make a sudden turn, and the Vallais lies all before you, and in the middle of it Sion, with its hills and castles. We stopped at one or two little places for bread, milk, and country wine, but we made the day's journey in less time than Murray allots to it, even with good walking. Walrond walks fast—too fast for my taste, for I like to look about me more—and stops very little.

We got to Sion about a quarter past five, and went to the Lion d'Or, an immense stony old house in the somewhat gloomy but picturesque old town, the capital of the Vallais. We ought to have gone to the Poste which Murray recommended, not to the Lion d'Or; however, there we went.[2] We went and had a bath at the hospital, and dined about seven. At half-past eight arrived the diligence from Bex, which ought to have brought our bags. . . . Walrond went to the diligence office, and there were no bags come. We had walked all day, and had nothing but the things we wore; however, there was no help for it. [At] Eleven we went to bed, having adjoining rooms. I slept for an hour or two, when I woke feeling myself attacked; I had taken the precaution to get some matches from the waiter, not liking the aspect of the bedrooms. I found my enemy and despatched him, but kept the candle lighted. I slept pretty well for the rest of the night, but the Lion d'Or is a filthy hole; it makes me feel sick to think of it. The next morning Walrond was out at seven, and bought a comb, soap, and toothbrushes, so we made a decent toilette; and at eight, as we finished breakfast, the right diligence arrived from Bex with our things. With this diligence we went on, up the Vallais, to Viss [*for* Visp]. There we arrived about two in the afternoon, and went into the inn, the Solect [*for* Soleil] for luncheon. I took up the strangers' book, and there was Edward's name.

Text. *Russell, 1 :79–82.*

1. "The spelling 'Vallais' prevailed till the end of the 18th century, and was officially superseded in the early 19th century by 'Valais,' a form that is very rarely found previously" (*Encyclopædia Britannica*, 11th edn, 17:839).
2. Baedeker preferred the Lion d'or, adding "on y trouve de bon vin de Valais" (Baedeker's *La Suisse*, 1859, p. 208).

To Frances Lucy Wightman Arnold*

Hotel [*or* Hospice] du Grand St Bernard
September 4, 1858

I wrote to you from Zermatt. When I had finished my letter Walrond and I started for the Riffel. It is a long climb of more than two hours, and after our four hours' walk from St. Nicholas in the morning I felt the climb a good pull. We rested at the hotel on the Riffel, which we both thought an uninviting, dreary place;[1] ate some bread and drank some Swiss wine there, and talked to the travellers who were preparing to go up Monte Rosa next morning, and then climbed up the ridge of the mountain on whose slopes the hotel is perched to the Gorner Grat, by which time we had both of us, I think, had climbing enough for one day. We got up just as the sun set, and saw lying magnificently close before us, separated only by a broad river of glacier, Monte Rosa, the Lyskamm, the Jumeaux, the Breithorn, and the St. Théodule, while to the right of them the extraordinary peak of the Matterhorn, too steep for much snow to rest upon, ran up all by itself into the sky. We came down slowly, for it was difficult to leave the mountains while there was any light upon them. We got back to Zermatt about a quarter past seven, got tubs of warm water, as we nearly always manage to do, washed and dressed, and dined in great comfort, the Lingens sitting by us. There were a good many people in the inn, several of them great Alpine climbers, such as Hinchcliff, who has written about the high passes. Davies was there, too, the clergyman with a beard, who has been up the Finster Aarhorn. He came and talked to me a long time, reminding me that he had met you and me at the Cromptons'; he made himself very agreeable. We made acquaintance also with Sergeant Deasy, the member for Cork, who was there, and William Cowper, too, who was there with his wife, came and talked to me.[2] We had thought of going up the Cima de Jazzi, but as to do this it would be necessary to go up the Riffel again, and to sleep at the very unpromising inn there, we decided to go straight over the St. Théodule. The Lingens were going too, and they started with Sergeant Deasy at five the next morning. We were rather tired, and had, besides, all our arrangements to make about guides and porters, and did not get off till twenty minutes past seven. It was a fine morning, but the clouds were low; we had two capital guides. We all went fast, and got on the snow in about three hours after leaving Zermatt, I having first passed round my pot of cold cream, which I must tell you is becoming celebrated in Switzerland for the good it has done. We all had veils, too, and as the sun was a good deal clouded, we did not feel the glare of the snow much. It is a curious and interesting thing to go once over a great snow pass; the St. Théodule is a very easy one, and I cannot tell you how I wished for you. It ·is a walk of two or three hours over not very steeply inclined plains of snow; you go in Indian file, in a track of steps made by your predecessors in the snow. Very occasionally you come to a small crevasse, across which you generally find a plank laid, where the guides make a good deal of fuss, and you have to go carefully; but there is really not the least danger. The view down into the crevasses is sometimes very fine, with no bottom to be reached by the eye, and beautiful green lights playing about the broken walls of ice. There is a hut on the top of the pass (11,185 feet above the sea—the greatest height I have ever been), where two women live in the summer, and sell wine, bread, *kirschwasser*, etc., to the passers. We caught the Lingens up at the hut, and, climbing to a little peak just above, tried to see what we could through the driving mist. High up in the sky it cleared occasionally, and we had glimpses of the top of the Matterhorn, the top of Monte Rosa, the top of the Breithorn, but their trunks were all in mist. We had some hot wine, and set off down the pass on the Italian side. The snow stretches much less way on this side than on that of Switzerland, but all the way down to Breuil, a little hamlet at the immediate foot of the mountain, there is nothing Italian in the vegetation or the mountain forms. Walrond and I got down at a great pace, and reached the new inn at Breuil at a quarter past two.[3] The Lingens

came about half an hour after, and found us drinking beer. One of the effects
of Alpine walking is to produce an insatiable thirst. Mrs. Lingen crossed in a
chaise à porteur. Lingen rode up to where the snow began. We were obliged
to stop at Breuil, as the next sleeping-place, Chatillon (you and I passed it
together that night from Aosta to Ivrea), was six hours off. So after settling
with the Lingens to dine at seven, Walrond and I started to look for some
lakes marked in my map as being on a mountain near [by]. We had a long
business looking for them. When we at last found them they were mere
snow-water lakes, dirty, and not worth looking at, but in scrambling about
we had found a number of perfectly bright little streams worthy of Westmorland—water such as my eye so often longs in vain for in this country,—and
their banks covered with the giant gentian and the Alpine rhododendron,
the latter with a few red blossoms still here and there upon him. We got back
just before seven, after a hard day. The dinner was bad, but the evening was
pleasant enough—ourselves, the Lingens, Sergeant Deasy, and a young Irish
barrister, a friend of his. Next morning Walrond and I were off before seven
to descend the Val Tournanche to Chatillon. At the village of Val Tournanche, two hours down the valley, is the Sardinian Passport station,[4] and as the
rising made a delay, we struck up to a little lake of clear water we heard of a
little way off among the hills, and had a charming bathe. When we got back
to the village the Lingens caught us up, and we went on together to Chatillon. There we got into the Val d'Aosta, and, as you may remember, that is
Italy indeed. We had some fruit and wine at Chatillon, and there we parted
with Sergeant Deasy and the Lingens, and we went on together in a carriage
to the Aosta, three hours off. We got to Aosta just at sunset—a fine evening,
but not such weather as you and I had. We passed the dirty Couronne, where
you were alarmed by the great spider,[5] and drove through the town to a new
hotel outside it, on the Courmayeur side, kept by an old Chamouni guide,
the Hotel du Mont Blanc. There at half-past seven we dined. We fell in with
old Mr. Campbell, who has the church in Westbourne Terrace, and his
daughters.[6] We had a capital dinner, and the hotel excellent. Here I must
stop for the present and post this. I will go on from Chamouni, where we
are going over the Col de Balme tomorrow.

    My face is now set steadily homewards, Chamouni, Geneva, Dijon,
Paris, London, Fox How. Kiss my darling little boys for me.

M. A.

Text. Russell, 1:82—86.

    1. "Zermatt n'est cependant plus le terme du pèlerinage depuis qu'on a bâti en
1854, sur le Riffelberg, 2500' au-dessus de Zermatt, une petite auberge, très bien tenue
par les frères Seiler" (Baedeker's *La Suisse*).
    2. Thomas Woodbine *Hinchliff* (1825—82: *DNB*), author of *Summer Months among*

the Alps, with the Ascent of Monte Rosa (1857), "took an active part in the foundation of the Alpine Club [in 1857], of which he was the first honorary secretary, and president from 1874 to 1877." At some (recent) time a terminal *e* had been dropped from his last name but never a medial *c* (*DNB*; Allibone; Venn). Arnold was elected to membership in the Alpine Club in 1859 (see below. p. 475).

John Llewellyn Davies (1826–1916: *DNB*), like Hinchliff (and at the same time), of Trinity College, Cambridge, and like Leslie Stephen (whom he had coached for Trinity Hall) an Alpinist, and associated ideologically and theologically with F. D. Maurice, Charles Kingsley, John Malcolm Forbes Ludlow, was rector of Christ Church, Marylebone.

Sir Charles Crompton (1797–1865: *DNB*), justice of the Queen's Bench, and pretty clearly a Wightman acquaintance, lived, in London, at 22 Hyde Park Square (Kelly). His daughter, Mary Crompton (d. 1895), married John Llewellyn Davies in 1859; his son Henry Crompton (1836–1904) married Lucy Romilly (daughter of first Lord Romilly and niece of Sophia Marcet) in 1870 (*Upper Ten Thousand*; Kelly; *County Families*; and above p. 394 and n).

Rickard Deasy (1812–83: *DNB*), "Bayard of the Irish bench," was M.P. for co. Cork and had recently been named third serjeant-at-law in Ireland; in 1859 he was appointed solicitor general, in 1860 attorney general, in 1861, a banner year, baron of the Court of Exchequer in February (and he married in April), and finally, in 1878, Lord Justice of Appeal.

William Francis Cowper (1811–88: *DNB*) was the nephew of one prime minister (Melbourne) and the stepson of another (Palmerston, from whom he inherited estates on his mother's death in 1869 and whose name he then added to his own, becoming Cowper-Temple) and served in liberal governments below cabinet rank, having been vice-president of the Committee of Council under Palmerston in 1857–58, until Derby's cabinet was formed in February. He was created Baron Mount Temple under Gladstone in 1880. (His wife was the former Georgiana Tollemache.)

3. "Une nouvelle auberge ("*Hotel du Mont-Cervin à Valtornanche, montagne du Giommein*"), assez bonne" (Baedeker's *La Suisse*).

4. "On vise ici le passeport gratis" (Baedeker).

5. On the honeymoon, Sept. 11, 1851—but neither the spider nor the hotel was reported in her letter to her sister.

6. The Rev. Archibald Montgomery Campbell (c. 1790–1859), of St John's College, Cambridge (B.A. 1811, M.A. 1816), was rector of Little Steeping, Lincs, perpetual curate of St James, Paddington, Sussex Gardens, Hyde Park, and canon, not residentiary, of St Paul's Cathedral. He lived at 13 Sussex Gardens, a few streets from Westbourne Terrace, where no church, no Campbell is listed in the Street Directory in 1857 or 1858 (*POLD*). His son (c. 1821–71), of the same name, entered Rugby, age 13, in 1834, under Dr Arnold but several years before Matthew Arnold (Venn; Rugby)

To Jane Martha Arnold Forster*

Hotel Clerc, Martigny

My dearest K   August [*for* September] 6, 1858

Here is a pouring wet day, to give me an opportunity of paying my long-standing debt to you. I have never thanked you for sending me Kings-

ley's remarks on my poems, which you rightly judged I should like to hear.[1]
They reached me when I was worried with an accumulation of all sorts of
business, and I kept putting off and putting off writing to thank you for
them—at last, when I had fairly made up my mind to write, I heard you
were gone to Holland. What on earth did you go to do there?

Kingsley's remarks were very *handsome*, especially coming from a
brother in the craft. I should like to send you a letter which I had from
Froude about Merope, just at the same time that your record of Kingsley's
criticisms reached me.[2] If I can find it when I return to England I will send it
to you. It was to beg me to discontinue the Merope line, but entered into
very interesting developments, as the French say,[3] in doing so. Indeed if the
opinion of the general public about my poems were the same as that of the
leading literary men, I should—make more money by them than I do. But,
more than this, I should gain the stimulus necessary to enable me to produce
my best—all that I have in me, whatever that may be—to produce which is
no light matter with an existence so hampered as mine is. People do not
understand what a temptation there is, if you cannot bear anything not *very
good*, to transfer your operations to a region where form is everything: perfection of a certain kind may there be attained or at least approached without
knocking yourself to pieces: but to attain or approach perfection in the region of thought & feeling and to unite this with perfection of form, demands
not merely an effort and a labour, but an actual tearing of oneself to pieces,
which one does not readily consent to (although one is sometimes forced to
it) unless one can devote one's whole life to poetry. Wordsworth could give
his whole life to it—Shelley and Byron both could, and were besides driven
by their demon to do so: Tennyson, a far inferior natural power to either
of the three, can: but of the moderns Goethe is the only one, I think, of
those who have had an *existence assujetie*,[4] who has thrown himself with a
great result into poetry. And even he felt what I say: for he could no doubt
have done more, *poetically*, had he been freer: but it is not so light a matter, when you have other grave claims on your powers, to submit volun-
tarily to the exhaustion of the best poetical production in a time like this:
Goethe speaks somewhere of the endless matters on which he had employed
himself, and says that with the labour he had given to them he might have
produced half a dozen more good tragedies: but to produce these he says, I
must have been *sehr zerrissen*.[5] It is only in the best poetical epochs (such as
the Elizabethan) that you can descend into yourself and produce the best
of your thought & feeling naturally, and without an overwhelming and in
some degree morbid effort: for then all the people around you are more or
less doing the same thing: it is natural, it is the bent of the time to do it:
its being the bent of the time, indeed, is what makes the time a *poetical* one.

But enough of this,—to use such a transition as dear old Tom would think proper.

It is nearly a fortnight since Walrond and I started and in ten days I hope to be at home again. They will have kept you more or less informed, from Fox How, I dare say, of our travelling proceedings: we have hitherto done just what we intended: Geneva, Bex & the Diablerets, Zermatt, and the Grand St Bernard: the fates are against us today for the first time (Tom again) for at this moment we ought to be on the Col de Balme, and we are here kept to the house by good heavy Westmorland rain. It will be curious if I again miss Chamouni, which I have missed so often: but we are resolutely staying over the day here, not to miss it if the weather will give us a chance. If it rains tomorrow, however, we shall go on to Geneva. I am glad to have been here again, and Walrond has admirable qualities for a travelling companion: but I have found two things: one, that I am not sure but I have begun to feel with Papa about the time lost of mere mountain and lake hunting (though everyone should see the Alps once to know what they are) and to desire to bestow my travelling solely on eventful countries and cities: the other that I miss Flu as a travelling companion more than I could have believed possible, and will certainly never travel again for *mere pleasure* without her. To go to Rome or Greece would not be travelling for mere pleasure, I consider, but to Rome I would not easily go without her. I shall conclude with one anecdote of dear old Budge. Just before we left Dover, the Judge, who was staying with us, took us all in a carriage to St Radigund's Abbey, a beautiful ruin near Dover. We entered the precinct, and there were the beautiful ruins, and capitals and fragments of arches lying about on the grass as you see them at such places: we all said, how beautiful &c. &c.: but Budge, surveying the litter with the greatest contempt, exclaimed at last these words—"What a nasty, *beastly* place this is!" You have no idea what a comic effect the child and his speech produced.

God bless you my dear old K: suppose you write me a line to reach me at the *Hotel Windsor, Paris*, on or before this day week: if not that, write to me soon at Fox How. My love to William—   Your ever affectionate

M. A.—

MS. Balliol College.

1. Untraced. Charles Kingsley had discussed *The Strayed Reveller, and Other Poems* in a review in 1849 in *Fraser's*, and Arnold had sent him *Poems: A New Edition* (1853) and also *Poems* Second Series (1854). Arnold had read (or at least started) *Hypatia* but did not send (or at least did not record sending) *Merope*. They never knew each other well and (perhaps for that reason) remained on good terms. See *Album*, pp. 25, 87, and below the letter to Rose Kingsley, Jan. 20, 1875.

2. Apparently *not* the letter from Froude about *Merope* printed above.

3. "Entrer dans des développements intéressants" (to go into interesting details).
4. Cf. "all / Whom labours, self-ordained, enthrall," "Resignation," ll. 13–14.
5. As in "knocking yourself to pieces" or "tearing of oneself to pieces," above. See Introduction pp. xxxi, xliv–xlv.

To Mary Penrose Arnold

Woodhouse[1]

My dearest Mother   Saturday, October 23, [1858]

On this day week we left you, after one of those pleasant times at Fox How which cannot be repeated for ever, but which still seem so natural a part of the year that there would be a great blank in it without them. If Flu had been stronger the enjoyment would have been more complete: but I never remember to have myself felt so well there since I was a boy—and the dear little boys are getting to enjoy Fox How as much as their Papa, which makes it pleasanter to me every year. I should like to pass a week alone with Fan and you there to see what it is like—sometimes towards six in the evening the little boys must be not altogether a bad miss.

We had at Crewe as you know, the disaster of missing our train: but I would go the same way again, only taking the precaution to write the day before to the Station-Master at Crewe to tell him to keep the Derby train: he told me they kept it if they received notice. Flu seems to have managed very well on the whole—and Tom and Trev. are such good travellers, being always too much amused and interested to be fretful even at night & when tired and sleepy, that I pity no one on their account though Diddy seems to have been a bargain! I travelled through the night and reached Chester Square between 5 and 6 the next morning—went to bed and slept till 10, and in the evening dined with Walrond at his Club. When we came back from Switzerland he was as brown as I—but the month of London and hard work has quite blanched him. Next day I went to Witney and in the evening to Oxford—at Oxford I found that Riddell[2] had engaged very clean good lodgings for me in Beaumont Street, at the house of a Balliol scout: I have been very comfortable there and find it very convenient as Beaumont Street is near the station: I found the benefit of the plan of going to lodgings instead of an inn when I came to pay yesterday: for I paid £1.10 for five days, including tea & breakfast daily, wax light, gas fires etc. with two excellent rooms: while for one bedroom and the same extras at the Star I should have paid nearly £5, and been smothered in fust besides. It is always pleasant to me to be in Oxford, I know the place and people so well and they seem so glad to see me. I dined twice in Oriel, once in Balliol, and once with the Bunsens, meeting at the latter place Froude and Max Muller. Froude has been reinstated in his privileges as a M. A. and member of Common Room at Exeter, which he had forfeited at the time of the row about his Nemesis.[3] The Rector called upon him and begged him to come back, asking him only for some general expression of assent to, or non-dissent from, the 39 Articles—which Froude had no difficulty in giving. I found him reading in the Bodleian—and as pleased as a child with his restored cap & gown. Banbury is a place where I am well liked among schools & managers—and I had presents of grapes & Banbury cakes there which made me long for the children. The grapes were the best open-air-upland grapes I have ever seen in England—quite amber-coloured, and as sweet as the Vevey grapes. I heard from a man at Banbury that Caird, the Scotch minister[4] who preached before the Queen, was greatly taken with Merope, which I thought singular. I am very likely going to dine in the Birmingham Town Hall next Friday, to hear Bright:[5] it will be a good opportunity to hear one of his great efforts: is Wm Forster going. I have made arrangements as to schools which will enable me to go if I like, and my place is secured, if I want it. In that case we shall stay here till this day week. I came here yesterday from Banbury, passing an hour at Rugby to see the Temples. Charles Arnold's house is now *quite full*. I called there but they were out. I saw Sam,[6] fatter than ever. Temple looked pale, I thought but unworn and in famous spirits. They seem really thriving. He & his sister[7] spoke very kindly [paper cut: ?& ?warmly] of Walter. I got here about 8, and was very pleasantly [paper cut: ?welcomed ?received. ?It] is a real comfort to Mary to have Flu here, and Mr Hiley takes wonderfully to the boys, and goes about holding Tom by the hand, and with Budge hanging to his coat—they are great favourites with the servants. We woke up this morning to a foggy drizzly morning but it has cleared and is now (½ past 12) very fine. So after dinner the fishing expedition is to take place. Think of that. Thank Fan for her note & for reading the office packet. Let us hear as often as you can. I hope your finger is well again. Did you keep it covered with gold beater's skin? With the united love of all here to you & Fan, I am always, my dearest Mother,   your most affectionate son

M. A.—

Mary seems very strong but not very comfortable.

MS. Balliol College.

1. Where the Hileys lived (see above p. 388 n. 3).

2. James Riddell (1823–66: *DNB*), a classical scholar, was at Balliol with Arnold and (fellow, tutor, lecturer) remained there all his short life. He won first place in the Open Scholarship at Balliol in Nov. 1840; "second place was won by Matthew Arnold after an unusually fierce contest with two other candidates" (J. P. Curgenven, "Matthew Arnold in Two Scholarship Examinations," *R.E.S.* 22, no. 85 (1946):54–56).

3. See above p. 145 n. 2. The rector was John Prideaux Lightfoot (c. 1803–87), successor to Joseph Loscombe Richards (died 1854). See Foster and *Annual Register*.

4. John Caird (1820–98: *DNB*), later principal of Glasgow University, was minister

at Park Church, Glasgow in 1858. "In 1857 he preached before the Queen at Balmoral a sermon from Romans 12.11 ['Not slothful in business; fervent in spirit; serving the Lord'], which on her majesty's command, he soon afterwards published under the title 'Religion in Common Life.' It sold in enormous quantities, and Dean Stanley considered it the 'greatest sermon of the century' " (*DNB*). The "man at Banbury" might have been A. J. Beale or James Cadbury (see above p. 328).

    5. See above p. 385n. Bright was probably the greatest English orator of the nineteenth century, and this Birmingham speech, his second there in two days, was special, even for him: "a speech in defence of his views on foreign affairs, containing an epigram of which the consequences were afterwards disclosed. English foreign policy, he declared, was 'neither more nor less than a gigantic system of outdoor relief for the aristocracy' " (*DNB*).

    6. Unidentified.

    7. Temple became headmaster of Rugby School in Nov. 1857, and his sister, Jennetta Octavia Temple (1819–90), was the head of his household (he married only in 1876). "Miss Temple was no ordinary woman. It was necessary to know her well before she could be appreciated, but she was worth knowing. . . . She had all, and more than all, of his outspoken speech and directness of action" (*Memoirs of Archbishop Temple*, ed. E. G. Sandford, 1 : 514). (In the second omission below no descender shows and "surprised" is therefore ruled out.)

To Frances Bunsen Trevenen Whately Arnold*

London,

My dearest Fan   November 4, 1858

    I have thought a good deal of Fox How today. I have not yet got over the profound disgust which the first loss of the country creates in me at my return to London, and with the prospect of tramping on stone pavements for nine months to come. I was at Hammersmith today, and even there the fog was less, and the blue sky visible in breaks, and the trees had still some leaves upon them, and the enclosures showed a sort of tendency to become fields, though of a blackish and miserable kind. I inspected a little school at Hammersmith, lunched at a hideous square red-brick barrack, which a great auctioneer has just built and furnished at an immense expense in a brickfield, to serve him for a country retreat, and came back to London through Shepherd's Bush and Bayswater, in bright sunshine, which duly dwindled away as I approached the Marble Arch, and disappeared in impenetrable fog as I reached Belgravia. There I found little Tom, much better, preparing to go with Flu in the carriage to Howell and James; and Budge and Baby I despatched to Hyde Park with the nurses, to breathe a somewhat lighter atmosphere than that of Chester Square. The rogues are both wonderfully well, however, and Baby looking so splendid that a lady stopped her carriage in Lowndes Square yesterday, got out of it, and accosted Charlotte[1] to know who he was. Our house is delightful inside, and very pleasant to return to, though at present I cannot quite forgive it for not being twenty miles out of London. My books will come about the 14th of this month. I have a great bookcase put up for them in the study; I have also hung there what pictures I have—a little gallery you have not yet seen. At Colnaghi's yesterday I got a print of papa (as Jane declares I gave her mine, which I doubt), which Colnaghi is to frame; it will hang by itself in the dining-room over the mantelpiece.[2] Do look if you can find at Fox How two volumes of Michelet's *Histoire de France* of mine (8vo in paper), and one volume of Warton's *History of Poetry*, also a parcel of about 100 or 150 leaves of Rousseau's *Nouvelle Heloise*. They have not turned up at the unpacking, and I hope and trust they are at Fox How. Pray relieve my mind about them soon.

Flu will have told you that I heard Bright to perfection. The company was dismally obscure, the dinner abominably bad, the speaking, all but his, unutterably wearisome; but his speech made amends. He is an orator of almost the highest rank—voice and manner excellent; perhaps not quite flow enough—not that he halts or stammers, but I like to have sometimes more of a *rush* than he ever gives you. He is a far better speaker than Gladstone. . . . If you have not read Montalembert's article on India and the Indian Debate of this last spring in the House of Commons, you should try and get it. It is in a French periodical, *Le Correspondant*. The periodical has been suppressed in France, and I know not what vengeance taken on author and editor. I am sorry mamma's finger is not yet well. One should be a baby to heal fast. My love to her, and believe me   always your affectionate brother,

M. A.

Text. Russell, 1 : 86–88.

1. "Charlotte," apparently a nursemaid with only one name, first mentioned here, appears in later letters in connection with the children.

2. An engraving of the oil portrait by Thomas Phillips. See Richard Ormond, *Early Victorian Portraits*, 1 : 17.

Constance de Rothschild's Journal

Wednesday, November 17th, [1858]: was the examination day and with a little heart beating I accompanied Mlle to the school. Mr Arnold had just arrived and was talking to Mamma in Miss Devenham's little parlor. He is a tall pleasant faced man and looks very amiable. He questioned the children well but little, poor Isabella Gambell was so frightened that she burst into tears and was obliged to go into the garden. Mr Arnold pronounced the school to be in charming order, the appearance of the girls he found very nice, their writing neat, their reading good, their arithmetic passable. We just looked in on Mrs Phibey when we returned, so as to give Mr Arnold an idea of the plaiting schools.[1]

Text. Lucy Cohen, Lady de Rothschild and Her Daughters, 1821–1932, pp. 103–4.

1. "During those years straw-plaiting was the staple and main feature of the county. Schools for teaching children to plait were held by a few old women in the village. One of these schools at Aston Clinton was presided over by a little cripple. . . . The atmosphere was asphyxiating." This marked the beginning of Arnold's long and close friendship with Lady de Rothschild—see below p. 499.

To Mary Penrose Arnold

⟨Education Department, Council Office, Downing Street,⟩ London:
My dearest Mother   December 1, 1858

I hope by this time the finger which seems to have been horribly troublesome has not even a trace left of its miseries. I ought to have written to you before—and tell Fan I have not forgotten her stamps—but I have been put to it with my lecture and school-business.[1] My lecture is now close at hand—I have not finished yet, but shall do so with ease. Perhaps Fan will be able to come & hear the next, in March or April, which will be on Dante, the troubadours, and the early Drama. The present [one] is mainly on the feudal state of society and the scholastic philosophy: I am myself not badly satisfied with it, and it is necessary to my course: but I dare say it will not be found interesting. When the course is finished and published it will form a body of doctrine true, as I of course think, but very novel and strange in England.

Tell Fan that I had a letter from the Editor of the Dublin University Magazine the other day,[2] asking me if I would become a contributor of poetry to his Magazine, which I civilly declined. Did I tell you that another man wrote to me to say that he composed on principles which he believed were also mine, and asking me to read his MSS tragedy of Judas Maccabeus for him? Did I tell you also, as I am on the chapter of myself, that a French Dictionnaire des Contemporains has just been published, which the Saturday Review says is excellent, and which contains a biography of me, correct in its facts, and flattering in its judgments: in revenge the biography of Papa which follows is meagre in the extreme, and the writer seems to be ignorant that he is dead. But the Dictionary on the whole seems excellent—and is a most useful & much wanted reference book: our only English book of the kind "Men of the Time" is a trumpery affair, compiled by a clique who have seen nothing and who know nobody.

We have had another very serious alarm with darling little Tom. He was much better—and last Friday went out in the carriage, and on Saturday was taken across to Lady Mayne's[3] to see Punch & Judy. His cough came on again in the night, all Sunday he was ill: and on Monday we thought he would not live through the day. When I first saw him on Monday morning he was more changed than I have ever seen him in any of his attacks: perfectly livid, and his breathing a husky rattle. Dr Hutton thought him sinking and revived him with port wine and water: the heart was finally relieved by hot fomentations to the chest and by putting the feet in mustard and water. Towards evening when I was sitting with him the darling fell into a doze with his arm round my neck twiddling my hair: when he woke he was better and asked for [a] cool drink: soon after he took a little toast, later still a little partridge; and revived wonderfully. He does not revive as usual, though, and his cough was again troublesome last night. The anxiety in which he keeps us you may imagine. Budge & Baby have colds, but common childrens' colds: they are packed off to Eaton Place with Charlotte in the morning and do not return till bed-time. Flu keeps wonderfully well. I leave her today to go to Chelmsford with the Judge: I had rather stop in London, but with her confinement in prospect the £75 of the Western Circuit Marshalship is a boon not to be refused: I shall be again in Chester Square on Friday night: in Oxford on Saturday: again in London all Sunday: then at Maidstone on Monday. The circuit ends, so far as I am concerned, at the end of next week: so it is easy work. The police have orders from the Maynes (this is private) to go for doctor or nurse at any hour of the day or night that we desire them. As I shall be more or less away, and the nurse is at Hampton Court, this is a comfort. Tell dear old Tom I did not forget his birthday, but write yesterday I could not. Love to all—   Your ever most affectionate

M. A.—

Willy's extracts[4] were very gratifying: just what I should have expected. I have got my books from Hampton: & they are up, looking charming.
Please bring this here with you. M. A. / Williams best thanks for sending him the papers it prints [?]better

MS. Balliol College.

1. His fourth lecture as Professor of Poetry, on Dec. 4; the fifth was on Mar. 12, 1859. See Super, 1:225, and below p. 414 and n.
2. Cheyne Brady (*New CBEL*, col. 1845).

3. Sir Richard Mayne (1796–1868: *DNB*), police commissioner, and Lady Mayne (*née* Carvick) were neighbors, at 80, Chester Square.
4. Unidentified.

To Zoe Skene Thomson[1]

Education Department, Council Office, Downing Street, London:
My dear Mrs Thomson   December 3, 1858
It is possible I may not be able to finish the writing out of my lecture in time to come and lunch with you tomorrow, so pray do not expect me until I actually arrive. If I cannot come to luncheon I hope at any rate to give myself the pleasure of coming to see you after my lecture. I have been travelling from Chelmsford with the Judge today, when I ought to have been writing out my lecture, and that has thrown me back.   Believe me, with very kind regards to the Provost,   ever most truly yours
M. Arnold.—

MS. Bryn Mawr College.

1. Zoë Skene Thomson, wife of William Thomson (1819–90: *DNB*), at this time provost of Queen's College, Oxford, and archbishop of York in 1862. A Scotsman her father, Rhalou Rizo-Rangabe her mother, "a Greek beauty of aristocratic descent," she was noble, pursued, and antique, and he, sixteen years older, fathered nine children, each of whom, "as it arrived, marked a step higher in the Church for him" (H. Kirk-Smith, *William Thomson Archbishop of York*, pp. 9, 169). Ape caricatured him as the "Archbishop of Society" in *Vanity Fair* 6/24/71. Whether *she* was present at Monckton Milnes's Yorkshire home, Fryston, in 1863 when the fledgling Swinburne recited some of his shockers to an astonished audience that included the archbishop as well as Thackeray and his daughters, has not been revealed (Edmund Gosse, *Life of Algernon Charles Swinburne*, ch. 3). See Tuckwell, pp. 265–68; Arnold's letter to his mother, Nov. 9, 1862.

To Jane Martha Arnold Forster *

The Athenæum
My dearest K   January 21, [1859]
This must be short, for instead of beginning it as I intended long ago I have been reading on and on at Dasent's Introduction to his Tales from the Norse[1] (which read) and now it is time to go home and dress for dinner to receive the Judge who dines with us. But for days I have been wishing to write to you, my dearest, to say to you that Flu and I have from the first wished you to be godmother to our little girl: it was monstrous that you were not godmother to one of our children: and here comes a dear little girl to

receive your care instead of another "great troublesome boy," as little Tom says. Mrs Benson[2] who was with Flu at the baby's birth, will be the other godmother: and Wyndham Slade has proposed himself for godpapa: perhaps he will have Mr Whiteman for associate. You *must manage* to come up for the christening, if it is only for that day, or a day or two: but we can settle this after I hear from you.

Tell my dearest Mother I have written so little of late because I am overwhelmed with grammar papers to be looked over—and not choosing as I grow older and my time shortens, to give up my own work entirely for any routine business, I have a hard time of it just at present. When I have finished these papers I have a General Report and a Training School Report to get out of hand: the inspection of schools going on alongside of this all the while: so at the beginning of next month, when my office work is again reduced to inspecting, I shall feel myself quite a free man.

I was deeply grieved when I saw poor Dicky Harrison's death. Mrs Wordsworth's was to have been expected—but it is touching when it happens. Harriet Martineau's notice,[3] transferred from the Daily News to today's Times, has some excellent and affecting points: but it is marred by a certain *denigrement* in parts, and by a patronising tone almost throughout. I thought Bright's speech[4] read as well as any but his Birmingham speeches: what a good speaker he is! I am so glad they heard him. I was glad to have the fuller report of William's speech: I should like to have been at Bradford with you that evening. You see the Times, after hanging poised for a day or two, at last rolls its waves decidedly against Bright's scheme.[5] You hear everybody saying that it is unfair to the Counties: but I don't think there is much in that. The real cause for alarm is in the prospect of the people the great towns would return. Imagine eight Coxes for Finsbury. I don't know whether William has ever seen that awful being, the one Cox.[6]

I must stop: you can't think how nicely the two boys go on with Mrs Querini,[7] their governess. From my little study I can hear all that passes. She said to Budge this morning—Who do you love best of anybody in the world?—Nobody at all, says Budge.—Yes, says Mrs Querini, you love your Papa and Mamma.—Well, says Budge.—But, goes on Mrs Querini, you are to love God more than anyone, more even than your Papa and Mamma.— No I sha'nt, says Budge. Jolly little heathen. My love to all—I am ever— your most affectionate

M. A.—

Do you know that the one inch ordnance sheet with Burley, Otley, Ilkley &c in it, is published at last. So is the Malham sheet.

MS. Frederick Whitridge.

1. George Webbe Dasent (1817–96: *DNB*, knt 1876) translated *Popular Tales from the Norse* (1859). He had been assistant editor of *The Times* since 1845.

2. Arnold's sister-in-law, the former Mary Henrietta Wightman, now Mrs Henry Roxby Benson.

3. Richard Harrison (b. 1832), the son of Wordsworth Harrison, of the Westmorland family, died on Jan. 3 *(Landed)*. See below p. 516 and n.

Mary Hutchinson Wordsworth died on Jan. 17. The obituary (p. 4) could be viewed differently: "Making allowances for prejudices, neither few nor small, but easily displaced when reason and kindliness had opportunity to work, she was a truly wise woman, equal to all occasions of action and supplying other persons' needs and deficiencies. . . . Not one is left now of the eminent persons who rendered that cluster of valleys so eminent as it has been. Dr. Arnold went first in the vigour of his years . . . Southey . . . Hartley Coleridge . . . the Quillinans . . . Professor Wilson . . . Mrs Fletcher . . . and the three venerable Wordsworths."

4. At a Conference of Reformers on Jan. 17, St. George's Hall, Bradford, on Bright's proposed Reform Bill (William Robertson, *Life and Times of John Bright*, pp. 361–62).

5. Echoing "like swimmers in the sea, / Poised on the top of a huge wave of fate, / Which hangs uncertain to which side to fall," on which Harriet Martineau commented, "There never was such a wave seen at Brighton, or elsewhere" (Allott, p. 337).

6. William Cox (1817–89), the Member for Finsbury 1857 till Apr. 1859, and then 1861–65 (Boase).

7. The first of several references to her in these letters (another mononym—even in *POLD*, which in 1862 lists her address as 12 Coulson Street, Chelsea). Her daughter, Catherine, became Lucy's governess in Feb. 1866.

To Mary Penrose Arnold*[1]

2, Chester Square

My dearest Mother   January 28, [1859]

If I had written to you yesterday it could only have been one line: today I hope to do a little better. In addition to my other engagements I have had to spend a good deal of time with a dentist lately, and to undergo a good deal of discomfort: however I hope I shall derive benefit from it in my old age. I was attacked with tooth-ache after a bad cold I caught about three weeks ago, and have had it more or less ever since—sometimes changing into general face and ear ache. There is an extraordinary good dentist called Rahn[2] to whom I go and I hope he will be able in the end to do something for me without my losing any more teeth—but we have had some unpleasant sawing and drilling work to go through.

I cannot make out all Ro[w]land's letter: but the plan for changing the site of the retreat to the ash place seems to be excellent. It will then be approached by a shrubbery path, and present itself to no one who does not go to seek for it. I quite agree with you that the plan recommended in Bonney's printed paper[3] is not a desirable one. The ordinary plan is the best: and it ought to be kept in order with perfect ease, being so near the house. To keep the damp out of such a place is the great thing. I think it is quite worth spending £12 over it: the old retreat was really a nuisance.

It is odd that you should have mentioned when you did what Coleridge and Lake had told you. The night before I got your letter I heard from [Fitzjames] Stephen the Secretary to the Education Commission asking me to call upon him—and I saw him yesterday. He proposed to me to go as the Foreign Assistant Commissioner of the Commission to France and the French speaking countries—Belgium Switzerland and Piedmont—to report on the systems of elementary education there.[4] Lingen makes no difficulty, as Stephen, who had been to see him on the subject, says: but I shall see Lingen myself today. There are to be two Foreign A. Cs—one for France, one for Germany. I cannot tell you how much I like the errand—and, above all, to have the French district. I am to have £50 a month, besides travelling expenses and 5 guineas a week for expenses of living &c. And my Inspector-ship will go on all the time. I shall be 4 or 5 months, probably, abroad: so we think of letting this house for the season, as we shall get nearly £200 for it: sending the three youngest children to Brighton, and establishing ourselves in Paris with little Tom. I have not had the official appointment yet, so say nothing about it to strangers till you hear again. No doubt I owe this, also, to Lake. I am very much pleased, and so is Flu. Lake talked to me mysteriously about it two months ago: Sir C. Trevelyan[5] promised them the funds: but then came a hitch, for Disraeli said they should not have them. Then the Duke of Newcastle wrote to Ld Derby, and finally, Ld Derby has just decided that the Commission shall have their two Foreign Agents. But I had quite dismissed the matter from my thoughts & had made up my mind to go the Home Circuit with the Judge. I shall probably go at the end of February or beginning of March. The monthly nurse is gone, and Mrs Tuffin manages the little baby excellently. Flu has an inflamed eye, but is all right otherwise: so are the three little boys: Diddy a greater beauty than ever. Love to dearest K and thanks for her letter. You hear hardly any talk about Reform here now: it is all about war in Italy. Love to all.   Your affectionate,

M. A.

MS. Frederick Whitridge.

1. Russell (1:89) prints an extract from this letter, says it was addressed to Frances Arnold, and misdates it Jan. 18 (the latter error noted in Super, 2:328 and in *Checklist*).

2. Charles Rahn, at 29 Brook Street (*POLD*, 1859). The Arnolds continued with him till June 1868 and then we hear no more. See below p. 498.

3. Richard Bonney, Ambleside plumber (Martineau).

4. The Newcastle Commission, a turning point in Arnold's life—see below p. 418.
5. Charles Edward Trevelyan (1807–1886; K.C.B. 1848), who had done and would do distinguished work in India, was now assistant secretary to the Treasury.

To Mary Penrose Arnold*

London
My dearest Mother   February 16, 1859

At last I have come to an end of my Reports, which seemed interminable—but I finished writing out the last at 12 o'clock last night. And now I must thank you for more letters than one—and above all for that extract from dear Papa's letter. I had seen it before, though—or, what is more probable, he said much the same thing in a letter to Coleridge or some other of his friends, about the same time. But I was not the less glad to see it again.

The baby is to be christened on Sunday. I wish you would try and get K to come up with a return ticket on the Saturday. I so seldom see her and the journey is so easy—and I should always think with more pleasure of her godmothership to little Lucy Charlotte if she stood in person.[1] Besides every one ought to see Diddy before he loses his beauty—K especially. Perhaps he will come back from France with his hair darkened and his skin browned. But at present he is a perfect picture.

I think now we shall certainly go: for the Commission have made a formal application to Ld Salisbury for the loan of me, and the Duke of Newcastle has also written a private letter to him.[2] Lingen also wishes me to go. We, or I, shall start, I think, next Monday fortnight:[3] at one time I thought of starting next Monday week, but I shall hardly be ready by that time. Besides I think of being presented at the *levée* on March 2nd, in order to be capable of going to Courts abroad, if necessary.[4] I like the thoughts of the Mission more and more. You know that I have no special interest in the subject of public education—but a mission like this appeals even to the general interest which every educated man cannot help feeling in such a subject. I shall for five months get free from the routine work of it, of which I sometimes get very sick, and be dealing with its history and principles. Then foreign life is still to me perfectly delightful, and *liberating* in the highest degree: although I get more and more satisfied to live generally in England, and convinced that I shall work best, in the long run, by living in the country which is my own. But when I think of the borders of the Lake of Geneva in May, and the Narcissuses, and the lilies, I can hardly sit still.

I shall try and give one lecture at Oxford before I go, on the troubadours:[5] I know pretty much what I want to say, but am doubtful whether I can put it together in time. But I can work harder than I did of old, though still very far from hard, as great workers count hardness. I think we shall be back in England early in August—spend that month at Dover—and then, I hope and trust, come north in September.[6]

How delighted we should be, my dearest Mother, if you and Fan would come to us now and stay with us till we go. Is it quite impossible. London is really pleasanter than any other place in February and March and Flu would so like to shew you her little girl. She gets on capitally. I only hope the change to Paris will not upset her or Flu. The others are quite well. Tom wonderfully so for him. I have had one or two things lately about my poems which I will communicate to you and Fan some day.   Ever your most affectionate—

M. A.—

I think we have heard of a very good tenant for our house, if we go. What are the accounts of Uncle Penrose? I saw Frank the other night at the Athenæum; and his account was bad.[7]

MS. National Archives of Canada.

1. "Did you hear of my flight up to London last week to attend the christening of my little goddaughter Lucy Charlotte? I should hardly have honoured the little lady by taking such a long journey on her sole behalf but as Matt was going abroad, I did not know when I might see them all again. Matt is a lucky Mortal! I think of his getting the pay for his Commissionership—*keeping* his other salary all the time and letting his house for some £200 or more just for the season! and the unfortunate country pays for all!" (Jane Arnold to Tom Arnold, Mar. 3, 1859, MS Balliol).

2. James Brownlow William Gascoyne-Cecil (1791–1868), 2d marquis of Salisbury, was Lord President of the Council in Derby's second cabinet, Feb. 1858—June, 1859; Henry Pelham Fiennes Pelham Clinton (1811–64), 5th duke of Newcastle, who had been secretary for war and also for the colonies (and in June was to be the latter again), in the interim was appointed chairman of the parliamentary commission of inquiry in June 1858.

3. In the event, as his diary shows, the date was Tuesday, Mar. 15: "left London by 8.30 p.m. train moonshiny but blowing night" (Guthrie 2:234).

4. "The following presentations to the Queen took place, the names having been previously left at the Lord Chamberlains's office, and submitted to the Queen for approval. . . . Mr. Matthew Arnold (Foreign Assistant Commissioner to the Education Commission), on going abroad, by the Marquis of Lansdowne" (*The Times*, Mar. 3, p. 5).

5. See above pp. 370 n. 4, 391. He delivered the lecture on the troubadours at Oxford on Saturday, Mar. 12 (Super, 1:125). Heretofore nothing has been known about it, but it must have been based on Claude Fauriel's *Histoire de la poésie provençal* (3 vols, Paris, 1846), of which Arnold's copy is in the library of Balliol College. See below, Appendix B. Arnold had drawn upon an article by Fauriel for his poem "Tristram and Iseult" (see above p. 265 n. 5).

6. He returned to England on Aug. 1, inspected for a couple of weeks, and on Aug. 14 returned to France, where he remained till Aug. 24 (Guthrie 2:240–42, which is blank for Aug. 25–Nov. 9).

7. Her brother John Penrose (1778–1859), vicar of Bracebridge, and his son Francis Cranmer Penrose (1817–1903), an architect. (See above p. 36 n. 2, and below p. 489.)

To James Hepworth

Mr Hepworth

Education Department, Council Office, Downing Street, London:

My dear Sir   February 26, 1859

Pray convey my thanks to Mr Dare for his volume of poetry which I shall read with interest.[1] I don't know whether he is any relation to a pupil teacher of that name who was formerly in my district.

I am glad your schools are at last to be enlarged: not before they needed it. If my sister stays in the neighbourhood at Loughborough I shall pay my old friends in the Leicester Schools a visit some day. I think you need be under no apprehension with respect to the revision of your certificate. Mr Alderson spoke to me very favourably of your school, and I think you will like him better as you know him more. Believe me,   truly yours

M. Arnold.—

MS. Bodleian Library.

1. Probably, Joseph Dare, author of *The Garland of Gratitude* (1849), identified in White, *History, Gazetteer, and Directory of the Counties of Leicester and Rutland* as a missionary living at 122 Church Gates, Leicester.

To The Marquis of Salisbury

The Marquis of Salisbury K. G.   2, Chester Square

My Lord   March 2, 1859

I trust you will allow me to express, not merely in my official letter to Mr Lingen, but directly to your Lordship, my grateful thanks to you for permitting me to accept the very interesting foreign employment which has been offered to me by the Duke of Newcastle's Commission.[1]

I proceed to Paris on the 15th of this month; and, should your Lordship think fit to see me before my departure, I shall gladly do myself the honour of waiting upon you at any time and place that you may appoint. I have the honour to be, My Lord,   Your Lordship's faithful and obliged servant

M. Arnold

MS. Hatfield House (transcript by Donald Mason).

1. See pp. 413, 416–19. For a detailed account of the commission see *Reminiscences of William Rogers*, compiled by R. H. Hadden (1888), ch. 5, "Royal Commission on Education."

Henry Petty Fitzmaurice Marquis of Lansdowne to Matthew Arnold

Dear Arnold   Saturday, [March 5, 1859]

Here is the letter for Lord Cowley you wished to have.[1] I hear he has been [?]absent [?]for the Government & may arrive to-day or tomorrow but will probably not remain longer than a few days.

With best wishes for your journey proving as agreeable as I have no doubt it will be successfull. believe me   Yours sincerely

Lansdowne

MS. British Library.

1. Henry Richard Charles Wellesley (1804–84), 1st Earl Cowley (cr. 1857), ambassador at Paris, 1852–67.

To Ralph Robert Wheeler Lingen

⟨Education Department, Council Office, Downing Street, London:⟩

2, Chester Square

My dear Lingen   March 6, 1859

Alderson was here yesterday and I went carefully through his spring cases with him. The enclosed Memorandum shews the result; and shews, I think, that he can perfectly well get though my cases without help beyond the very slight help which Laurie will give him.[1]

As I have myself the papers for all my March and April cases, the only direction to be given at the Council Office, if you sanction Alderson's acting for me, will be To send my May & June cases to Alderson, instead of to me.

I shall certainly come and see you before I go, but the necessary preparations for my journey drive me rather hard. Thanks for the Report, which I see is for Belgium, not for Holland as I thought. I will take care *not* to return it.   Ever sincerely yours

M. Arnold.

I will send back the Education Commission Portfolio tomorrow. [Memoranda attached]

MS. Public Record Office, London.

1. For Laurie see above p. 335. A memorandum attached lists the "March and April cases of Mr. Alderson now disposed of" and adds:

"Mr. Alderson has now (March 5th) *15* March & April cases undisposed of.—Mr. Arnold proposes to transfer to Mr. Alderson *20* March & April cases, making a total of 35 cases for Mr. Alderson to dispose of between March 5th and May 1st. Of these Mr. Alderson can perfectly well dispose in the time.

"Mr. Arnold's six remaining March and April cases will be disposed of by Mr. Laurie, who has but 16 March and April cases of his own. [signed] *M.A.*

"All Mr. Arnold's May and June cases are to be referred, if Mr. Lingen approves, to Mr. Alderson, who can perfectly undertake them, having in those months but 3 cases of his own. [signed] *M. A.*"

Granville George Leveson-Gower Earl Granville to Matthew Arnold

16. Bruton Street, London. W.

My dear Mr Arnold   March 9, 1859

I send you ⟨three⟩ four letters which may be of use to you. Lord Lansdowne's Minute letter to Cowley will open all official doors to you.

Yrs sin[cerel]y

Granville

I shall be very happy to see you on my return from the Country any morning.

MS. British Library.

Newcastle Commission

[March 15, 1859]

"Early in the session of 1858, during the late Lord Derby's second Government, the House of Commons voted an address to Her Majesty praying for the appointment of a Royal Commission to inquire into the subject of popular education, and on the 30th of June the Commission was issued. It consisted of the Duke of Newcastle, Sir John Coleridge, the Rev. W. C. Lake, Mr. Goldwin Smith, Mr. Nassau Senior, Mr. Edward Miall, and myself. We were 'to enquire into the present state of popular education in England, and to consider and report what measures, if any, are required for the extension of sound and cheap elementary instruction to all classes of the people'" (*Reminiscences of William Rogers*, ed. Hadden, pp. 129–30).

"The Commission resolved to appoint assistant commissioners to investigate various aspects of popular education in England, and two more to go to the Continent on similar missions. On January 25, 1859, Fitzjames Stephen, secretary to the Education Commission, wrote to Arnold privately to inquire whether he would accept one of the latter posts. 'The salary would be £50 a month, 15/- a day allowance & expenses of locomotion.' The Committee of Council had already given its consent. Arnold called on Stephen two days later. At first his mission was to include France and the French-speaking countries, Belgium, Switzerland, and Piedmont. . . . Mark Pattison was appointed to visit the German-speaking countries. After some alterations in the plan, Arnold reported upon France, the French cantons of Switzerland, and Holland, and Pattison reported upon Germany alone" (Super 2.327–38).

Arnold left for Paris on Tuesday, March 15, in the evening, went to a hotel for one night, and then took an apartment and began his duties ('left letters') on the day after his arrival.

Paris in 1859, with a population of over a million, was between two worlds, what with the eviscerating modernization going on under Emperor Napoleon III and his Préfet de la Seine, Baron Haussmann (so well described in David H. Pinkney's *Napoleon III and the Rebuilding of Paris*), and it had altered even more when Arnold went back again six years later. But Arnold, thirty-six years old, moved in a small and very distinguished and Anglophile official, intellectual, and social circle (among whom he must have seemed a young pup) of which the Tuileries Gardens could be seen as the physical center. The officials that he met in the ministries and offices were of course Imperialists. Most of the luminaries that he mingled with in the *salons* were *ancien régime*—that is, either Legitimists (supporters of the Bourbons) or Orleanists (supporters of Louis Philippe), liberals, more or less and of various stripe, at least by comparison with the Imperialists, from before the 1848 revolution. (See below p. 471. As Arnold wrote in *England and the Italian Question* (Super 1.76): "The English in France, if they see anything at all of French society, see almost exclusively that of Paris, and, in Paris, that of members of the Orleanist or Legitimist parties. These parties undoubtedly contain nearly all which in France is most distinguished by birth, manners and education. Undoubtedly they regard Louis Napoleon with aversion. Undoubtedly, for them, he is a self-imposed despot, not an elected chief. But they are not the French nation. They are an almost imperceptible minority of the French nation, and their influence is every day becoming less."

Beginning on March 29 he kept a special Newcastle Commission Journal (not included in Guthrie's transcriptions of the diaries), still an *aide-mémoire* but necessarily much more detailed than the other diaries and here transcribed for the first time. But Arnold, a government representative on an official commission, never indulged himself, in journal or letter, in even a hint of an indiscretion or even a personal remark. Madame de Circourt, badly burned four years earlier, was partially paralysed; Sainte-Beuve, radiant center and attractive target of a force-field of malice, assuredly did not stint himself of gossip; his own friends did not like him and there was much (very much) for them to be indiscreet about—physical (hypospadias), political (toadyism), social (scandal-mongering with a forked tongue), domestic (living with his mother, servant-mistresses); his references to Henri du Quaire are strangely infrequent and noncommittal; Baroness de Rothschild, of the English branch of the family and married to a chauvinist Proustian *roué* of the French branch, mothered four children and yearned for England.

Arnold, being an Arnold, was a natural educator but by no means a natural school inspector, and the Newcastle Commission *experience*, something like a *rite de passage* even for a sophisticate like him, must have made all those grubby little children in the provincial schoolrooms more depressing than ever.

Diary (Yale): Guthrie 2:234–35.

15 [March] Tuesday.   left London by 8.30 p.m. train moonshiny but blowing night.

16 [March] Wednesday.   Paris. Hôtel Windsor

17 [March] Thursday.   left letters &c dined with the du Quaires

18 [March] Friday.   took an apartment at 14 rue de Caumartin. dined at Meurice's,[1] and to the Ambigu to see F. Lemaitre in the Maitre d'Ecole.

19 [March] Saturday.   left letters—dined at Meurice's. to station at night to meet Flu & children. Frosty night. Tom coughing.

20 [March] Sunday.   Tom ill—rooms cold and sunless. Flue & I dined rue Caumartin. called in Dr. Shrimpton to Tom. all the children with colds.

21 [March] Monday.   driving out with Flu to leave letters. dined with her at ⟨Meurice's⟩ Trois Frères. children ill.

22 [March] Tuesday.   called on Guizot. settled to move to Meurice's. Tom very ill. called in Trousseau. Letters from Embassy came late at night. dined in rue Caumartin.

23 [March] Wednesday.   Trousseau saw Tom. Move to Meurice's in afternoon. All the children but Tom better. Dined at Trois Frères. after calling on Mme Mohl.

24 [March] Thursday.   Trousseau away & Shrimpton came back to Tom. Wrote letters to Ministers & Préfet & took them with Ld Cowley's called on Mme de Circourt.[2] dined at Table d'hôte.

25 [March] Friday.   M. de Circourt called. Went to see the Ministers of the Intérieur. Then to the Embassy, and saw two of the attachées. dined at Table d'hôte.

26 [March] Saturday.   lunched at the Alphonse de Rothschilds. walked with Flu in the afternoon. dined at the Mohls'. Met Cousin, Villemain, Mignet, Barth. St Hilaire, & Victor Laprade. Very pleasant.

1. Mar. 18: "Here," said Thackeray, in the first chapter of *The Paris Sketch Book* (1840), "you will find apartments at any price; a very neat room, for instance, for three

francs daily; an English breakfast of eternal boiled eggs, or grilled ham; a nondescript dinner, profuse but cold; and a society which will rejoice your heart. Here are young gentlemen from the universities; young merchants on a lark; large families of nine daughters, with fat father and mother; officers of dragoons, and lawyers' clerks." Dickens mentions it in the beginning of *Pictures from Italy* (1846) and also stayed there again, with Wilkie Collins, in 1855. Ruskin often put up there. Longfellow spent a month there in 1836, Melville a night in 1849, Henry James a fortnight in 1899, and in *The Ambassadors* (8.3) Mrs Pocock receives Strether Lambert in her *salon* there: "The glazed and gilded room, all red damask, ormolu, mirrors, clocks, looked south, and the shutters were bowed upon the summer morning; but the Tuileries garden and what was beyond it . . . were things visible through gaps. . . ." (See Brian N. Morton, *Americans in Paris,* "Rue de Rivoli, No. 28," and Catherine Reynolds, "Paris Journal, Hôtel Meurice," *Gourmet: The Magazine of Good Living,* July 1992, pp. 42–44, 104–5.)

2. Mar. 24: La Comtesse de Circourt (1808–63, before her marriage, in 1830, Anastasie de Klustine, of a well-connected Russian family) presided over a "salon plein d'éclectisme français et de cosmopolitisme," the "rendez-vous de l'élite intellectuelle," including Cavour, whose friend and confidante she had been since 1835, and Monckton Milnes, whom the Circourts traveled with in Italy and visited in Yorkshire. Sainte-Beuve wrote a memorial article on her in the *Constitutionnel,* quoted in Huber-Saladin, pp. 127–28. Her husband, whom Arnold saw often in this visit (and again in 1865), Adolphe Marie Pierre comte de Circourt (1801–79), politically a Legitimist, had been in the Ministry of the Interior and later of Foreign Affairs (and also, as Lamartine's friend and emissary, had been in Berlin). "'Circourt,' said Tocqueville, 'is my dictionary. When I wish to know what has been done or what has been said on any occasion, I go to Circourt. He draws out one of the drawers in his capacious head, and finds there all that I want arranged and ticketed.'" Tocqueville and Senior are a little patronising about both of them, especially Madame—if, as the context strongly suggests, she is "Mrs. T" in the lines following those just quoted (*Correspondence & Conversations of Alexis de Tocqueville with Nassau William Senior,* ed. M. C. M. Simpson, 2d edn, 2:170–71). Arnold called on the Circourts not only in Paris but also in La Celle-Saint-Cloud, and one cannot help thinking that he was Arnold's "dictionary" as well as Tocqueville's. See Le Colonel Huber-Saladin, *Le Comte de Circourt, son temps, ses écrits. Madame de Circourt, son salon, ses correspondances;* Circourt, *Fragments d'une vie inédite de Camoëns* (1891); *Comte Cavour et la Comtesse de Circourt, lettres inédites,* ed. Count Nigra (Rome, 1894; tr. A. J. Butler, London, 1894); Jean Bonnerot, *Sainte-Beuve Correspondance Générale,* 11:438n; and Bessie Rayner Belloc, *In a Walled Garden.*

For Guizot, Trousseau, the Rothschilds, the Mohls, and the others, see below pp. 422–26, 430.

To Henry Drummond Charles Wolff

Hôtel Meurice, Paris

My dear Wolff   March 26, 1859

You cruelly let me leave London without your promised letters for Madame Gould,[1] and some senator you mentioned, a descendant, I think, of Barrabbas [*sic*].[2] Pray let me have them—that for Madame Gould may be of great use to me as the regular presentations at the Tuileries are at an end for the year, and to get presented needs some influence like that of Madame Gould which is said to be excellent. They say here that

MS. Hertfordshire County Council (incomplete).

1. She was "the wife of a Portuguese merchant but an Englishwoman. She had been, in early life, a friend of Madame Montijo, and had chaperoned the Empress about Paris before her marriage. It was said that it had been by her advice that Napoleon III. was persuaded to propose to the Empress. The result was that Madame Gould became one of the most influential persons about the Court. She was a very kind and amiable woman, the mother of two or three sons, one of whom entered diplomacy and ended by being Minister, I think, in Servia" (Wolff's *Rambling Recollections*, 1:231). In truth, she was the "wife of an *Irish* merchant who had made a fortune importing port wine from Portugal into Britain"—and was the great-great-grandmother of Mrs Yehudi Menuhin (Jasper Ridley, *Napoleon III and Eugénie*, pp. 383, 387n). Arnold called on her on Wednesday, Apr. 13 (Guthrie 2:237).

2. "Who for a certain sedition made in the city, and for murder, was cast into prison" (Luke 23:19) or "Now Barabbas was a robber" (John 18:40).

François Guizot to ?[1]

Paris
27 Mars 1859

Permettez moi, Monsieur,[2] de vous adresser et de recommander *parti-culièrement* à votre bienveillance le porteur de cette lettre, Mr Arnold, inspecteur des écoles primaires de Londres, et envoyé en France par le gouvernement anglais pour étudier l'état de l'instruction primaire chez nous, et en faire l'objet d'un Rapport. Les écoles de votre Institut sont au nombre de celles qu'il lui importe le plus de bien connaître, et elles sont excellentes à montrer aux étrangers. Je vous prie de bien accueillir Mr Arnold, et de lui donner tous les renseignements, tous les moyens, d'observation qui sont en votre pouvoir. Il mérite toute votre confiance, et je serai très reconnaissant de l'obligeance que vous voudrez bien lui témoigner.   Recevez, Monsieur, l'assurance de ma considération la plus distinguée

Guizot
ancien Ministre

[Added in corner in another hand: Ce Mr est celui dont le cher f Baudime Assissane a entretenu le ch. f Jean L'aumonier

MS. Frederick Whitridge.

1. Guizot was the perfect man for Arnold, introduced by Lord Granville, to seek out, and he is mentioned frequently in *The Popular Education of France*, in which ch. 7 deals

with the "Law of 1833" (printed as an appendix with the original report). His name occurs often in these letters, and in 1865, in Paris again for the Middle Class School Commission, Arnold saw him once more. (The letter is printed in *Album*, pp. 55–56, 117–18.) He was of course well known in England, where he had spent a year in exile, and his name was a handy rhyme, even in 1881, in *Patience*: "Tupper and Tennyson, Daniel Defoe, Anthony Trollope and Mister Guizot."

2. Probably Frère Philippe (Matthieu Bransiet), superior of the Institut des Frères Chrétiennes (see Super, 2:40–41, 71, 77, 418, and Guthrie 2:236, Apr. 1: "opening of the Frères Schools"), but possibly Léon de Laborde, Garde Générale des Archives (Jean Bonnerot, 10:393n), whom Arnold saw on Mar. 29 and again ("M. Laborde at the Institut [des Inscriptions et Belles-Lettres]") on Apr. 1 (Guthrie 2:236).

Diary (Yale): Guthrie, 2:235

27 [March] Sunday.   Tom very ill and sinking. walked a little alone, & with Budge. Waddington[1] & M. Rendu called. Trousseau came back. dined at table d'hôte. To Crémerie Imperiale with Flu. writing letters at night.

28 [March] Monday.   Tom better. Trousseau sanguine about him. Lovely day—our first. called on Mme de Staël with M. de Circourt. the Baroness Alphonse sent us her father in law's box at the opera, dined at table d'hôte. to the opera with the du Quaires. Herculanum. home early.

1. Mar. 27: William Henry Waddington (1826–94; *VF*, 9/28/78), "son of a wealthy English protestant industrialist naturalized as a French citizen, was born in France and educated in England, entering Rugby in 1841 (under Dr Arnold) and Trinity College, Cambridge, in 1845. Always a scholar, he was an archaeologist of distinction and also a politician. He was minister of public instruction in 1873 and again in 1876, and in Dec. 1877, he became minister of foreign affairs and represented France at the Berlin Congress in 1878. Next year he served as prime minister for a few months, and from 1883 to 1893 was the French Ambassador in London" (*Album*, p. 79). Eugène Rendu (1824–1903), head of the bureau of "Personnel de l'instruction primaire," in the ministry of public instruction, "had published interesting reports on popular education in German and England" (*Almanach impérial*, 1859, p. 178; Bonnerot, *Correspondance Générale de Sainte-Beuve*, 9:267n; Arnold, "The Popular Education of France," Super, 2:43n). For Mme de Staël and Baroness Alphonse see pp. 425–26.

To Mary Penrose Arnold

Hôtel Meurice, Paris
My dearest Mother   March 28, 1859
It is long since I have written to you. I have had little heart for writing or for anything else, while my poor little Tom has been so ill. Today for the first time things look a little brighter: in the first place it is a lovely day with

a soft wind and a cloudless sky—the first day we have had in which the climate can be said in any degree to differ from the English climate at this time of year. Then dear little Tom, after a terrible day yesterday, seems in the night to have taken a decided turn for the better—and Trousseau,[1] who has seen him this morning, says that this time, also, he will recover—"cette fois ci il se remettra."—Friday and Saturday he seemed better and had better nights—but there was no diminution of the inflammation on the lungs which has been complicating his disease of the heart—Trousseau had been obliged to go to the country for some days, and we were in the hands of an English doctor of no great value. The darling was wasted to a shadow, and would take nothing solid or liquid except water: at first he took eau de riz, a sort of barley water, but he got tired of that and used to beg us piteously not to tease him with anything but water. Yesterday the fever and weakness were so great and the breathing so very difficult that I thought the end must be coming at last: however Trousseau came back, and saw him about 5 in the afternoon and gave him digitalis: the weakness did not abate but towards 9 he began to doze, and Trousseau had luckily told us to try him with milk, which we found he took readily whenever he woke.—Flu and I made an expedition to the Crémerie Imperiale which is supplied with milk from the Emperor's farm in the country, and there we got the most delicious milk for him. As the night wore on the sleep got easier and easier, and this morning he woke, for the first time since his illness, without a cry of distress and a cough. Trousseau says the fever is decidedly arrested: he is still to have nothing but milk, and bread or bun sopped in it: he will not touch more than a few morsels of the solid food, but the milk he takes to more and more. It is now ½ past 10 at night, and he is sleeping in the room where I write this, breathing short & moaning at times, but certainly better. Flu is at the opera: she has been a perfect prisoner to his bedside since his illness; but today the Rothschilds[2] gave us their box at the opera, to see a magnificent new opera they are giving here representing the destruction of Herculaneum: we asked Mme du Quaire, her husband, and Montagu Blackett her brother, as the box, one of the best in the house, in the centre of the Grand Tier, holds six: I took Flu there at 8 o'clock and came away myself at ½ past 9 making the du Quaires promise to keep Flu if possible to the end, and then to bring her back here. Tom does not like being left by his Mamma and me both at once—"*one* of you may go"—he always says: however when fairly left with Mrs Tuffin he is always perfectly good and happy: but he frets much at the prospect of our leaving him. He particularly likes having me to sleep with him—but he Flu and I in a French bed is rather warm work—and I, you know, am a bad sleeper: so generally between 3 and 4 when the neck of the night is broken, I slip away to my own room and get two or three hours' good sleep. We are extremely struck with Trousseau: he is one of the most celebrated doctors in Europe, and reminds me of Brodie in his brusquerie and sternness: but he is kind to children, in treating whom lies his special talent. He is very tall, about 60, with one of the most remarkable countenances I ever saw. He keeps saying as he watches Tom—"Pauvre chat! Pauvre chat!" He is extremely struck with our two nurses—and indeed the English nurses enjoy a great reputation here. Trousseau says that when Tom's bronchitis is subdued, he shall commence a treatment to get the disease of the heart under [control], if possible: this is the point in which we are so anxious to see how he proceeds.

I have told you little about Paris—of that I will write hereafter: I should enjoy myself here immensely if it were not for Tom's illness: I have an opportunity of seeing a set of personages who in ten years will have disappeared and will not be replaced. At dinner on Saturday I met Villemain, Cousin, Barthélemy St Hilaire, and Mignet. Tomorrow I dine at Mme de Stael's to meet the Duke of Broglie. I hope to see Thiers on Wednesday, and I am going to Guizot's reception on Thursday evening.[3] This society is still the first in the world, sorely tried as it is. Our rooms here are delightful: au troisième, in the pure good air, and looking full south, right over the Tuileries gardens and the Seine. From the first I had a presentiment it would go all right with Willy: how I shall like to see the dear old boy here, with Walter. Baby has still a cough—but is the best and sweetest of little girls, never crying or giving any trouble: Budge and Diddy are quite well again. My love to dear Fan, Ro[w]land, and Banks. I am here for a month to come, at least.   Ever your most affectionate son, my dearest mother,

M. A.—

MS. Balliol College.

1. For Armand Trousseau see below p. 430.

2. Baron Alphonse de Rothschild (1827–1905; *VF*, 9/20/94), son of James de Rothschild (1792–1868), married (1857) to his cousin Leonora de Rothschild (1837–1911), daughter of Baron Lionel Nathan de Rothschild (*DNB*; *VF*, 9/22/77), of the English branch (Cohen). The opera was Félicien David's *Herculanum*, and the house was not the familiar Palais Garnier (which opened in 1875) but the Académie Impériale de Musique, rue Le Peletier.

3. Mary Mohl (1793–1883: *DNB*) and her husband Jules, or Julius (1800–1876: *DNB*), a famous orientalist (see above p. 285 n. 3), "whose receptions in the Rue du Bac for nearly forty years attracted a galaxy of talent," provided a stellar cast of characters for the preparation of *The Popular Education of France*: two professors at the Sorbonne, François Villemain (1790–1870, for thirty-seven years permanent secretary of the Académie Française) and Victor Cousin (1792–1867), intimate friend of Lord Brougham, a famous book collector (see A. B. N. Peat, *Gossip from Paris during the Second Empire*, p. 229), and very much the Don Juan in his younger days, had both been minister of public instruction

1839–44, Cousin for only an interval in 1840 (Super, 4:361), and together were the subject of one of Sainte-Beuve's *Causeries du lundi* (1849); Jules Barthélemy-Saint-Hilaire (1805–95), was a savant (translator of Aristotle, etc.), politician and private secretary to Thiers; Auguste Mignet (1796–1884), a noted historian; Victor Richard de Laprade (1812–83), a poet and like Villemain, Cousin, and Mignet, a member of the Académie Française.

Mme de Staël (Adélaïde de Staël, *née* Vernet), widow (d. 1876) of Baron Auguste de Staël-Holstein (1790–1827), son of the famous author; his sister, Albertine (d. 1833), was married in 1814 to Achille Léonce Charles Victor duc de Broglie (1785–1870), diplomat and former minister of public instruction (under Louis Philippe), now retired from public life (Ghislain de Diesbach, *Madame de Staël*, Paris, 1983, p. 545; Arnaud Chaffanjon, *Mme de Staël et sa descendance*, p. 179); Adolphe Thiers (1797–1877), statesman and historian, was later first president of the Third Republic; and François Guizot (see letter preceding) were all three in the Académie Française.

Diary (Yale): Guthrie, 2:236

29 [March] Tuesday.   (see journal from hence.) call on M. Franck from 10 to 11.* M. Mérimée at 12*. on M. Laborde from 12 to 3.[1]

Newcastle Commission Journal (Yale)

March 29. Tuesday   Tom very poorly. Slept but taking milk regularly. Gloomy day. To the Archive in the Mairie to see M. de Laborde. He took me over the Archives, and the Hôtel de Soubise. Shopping with Flu. Then to dinner at Mme de Stael's Salon by the duc de Broglie. Villemain and others there. Very interesting. Slept with Tom. bad night.

March 30. Wednesday   Tom certainly better. Trousseau very kind. Out with Budge to Laffitte's.[2] then alone to see Mérimée. Cousin at the Sorbonne. then to Sainte Beuve. Cousin well worth seeing. Walked a little later with Flu. then called on M. de Circourt. Wet day—cleared toward afternoon. dined at 7 with Flu at the 3 Frères. Tom playing in the [?Tuileries] and wonderfully better Heard at last from M. Rouland. [Diary, Guthrie, 2:236, adds: 'call on Mme Mohl'.]

March 31. Thursday.   Fine but cold day. Tom still mending wonderfully. In the afternoon to the rue de l'Ouest, to see the opening of the Frères' new school. Heard the Curé of St. Sulpice & the Père Felix. To M. Guizot's in the evening. Villemain there—but all very formal & dull. [Diary, Guthrie, 2:236, adds: '10. M. Franck* Embassy 2 Gustave Rouland*.'][3]

April 1. Friday.   Cold wet day. Called on M. de Laborde at the Institut. introduced to Count Beugnot, M. Laboulaye, M. Ravaisson, Ernest Rénan[4]

&c. Saw Guizot, Villemain and Mérimée there. Then to the Ministry of Public Instruction. Saw M. Gustave Rouland, &c, after waiting a long time, the Minister was very bavard, and of no mark. Late for the table d'hôte—so dined in the coffee-room with Flu. In the evening to Madame de Staël's—talked a good deal with Guizot & the duc de Broglie. Then to the Mohls. Few people there. [Diary, Guthrie, 2:236, adds: '10 M. Franck* Thiers.']

April 2nd, Saturday.   Tom still going on very well. in afternoon left Guizot's letters; after at the Hôtel de Ville, & saw M. Landois. dined at the Lutteroths. Sate by Mohl—very pleasant. M. de Circourt took me to the Duchess de Rauzan's. introduced to M. de Kergorlay and Mme de [?]Blaen—the latter charming.⁵ [Diary, Guthrie, 2:236, adds: '10 M. Franck . . . M. Villemain 1½']

April 3rd. Sunday.   Very fine warm day. Flu & I drove with Tom in the afternoon to the Bois de Boulogne and the Cascade. Tom tired. Dined at the Louvre splendid room—tolerable dinner.⁶

April 4th. Monday.   took Tom out a drive—dined at the table d'hôte and to the Français.⁷ Madeleine Brohan and Regnier very good.

April 5th Tuesday.   Still very hot. Called on Lady Augusta Bruce and saw Lady Elgin.⁸ Called on Mérimée and sate with him a long time. dined at the Trois Frères.

1. Mar. 29: Léon marquis de Laborde (1807–69), archaeologist, art critic, and politician, had been Garde Générale des Archives since Mar. 1857 (*Petit Robert; Sainte-Beuve Correspondance,* 10:393n)

2. Mar. 30: Bank, Charles Laffitte, 48*bis,* rue Basse du Rempart.

3. Mar. 31: The Frères de l'Ecoles Chrétiennes, of which the mother house was in the Rue Oudinot, "supported 10 establishments and 80 classes" in Paris (*Galignani's New Paris Guide for 1861,* p. 120). See Arnold's discussion in Super, 2:39–44. The curé of Saint-Sulpice was M. Hamon, honorary canon (*Almanach impérial,* 1859, p. 1003).

Adolphe Franck (1809–93), professor at the Collège de France, director of and contributor to the *Dictionnaire des sciences philosophiques,* author of a learned treatise on the religious philosophy of the Hebrews, and a member of the Conseil supérieur de l'instruction publique, he was remarkable for his talented *vulgarisation* of esoteric subjects" (Super, 4:359; *Grande Encyclopédie*).

4. Apr. 1: Ernest Renan (1823–92; *VF,* 2/22/79; 10/5 1910), already known as an Oriental scholar (elected in 1856 to the Académie des Inscriptions et Belles Lettres), won more fame later as a historian, critic, philosopher, and autobiographer. This meeting is one of the very few on record of the two men, of nearly the same age and of backgrounds (familial, spiritual), interests, and attitudes startlingly similar in crucial ways. Arnold's recognition a few months later (see below pp. 515–16) of their common ground brought forth a cottage industry on the subject admirably discussed in S. M. B. Coulling's article "Renan's Influence on Arnold's Literary and Social Criticism," *Florida State University Studies,* no. 5 (1952):95–112. Many references and two new letters to Renan are in these volumes, Dec. 16, 1871, May 12, 1873.

Arnold distinguishes Monsieur [Gustave] Rouland (1806–78, Grand Officier de la Légion d'Honneur), minister of public instruction from 1856 to 1863 (see "The Popular Education of France," Super, 2:30), from his son of the same name (Chevalier de la Légion d'Honneur), and in the same ministry, "directeur du personnel et du secrétariat générale, chef du cabinet" (*Almanach impérial*, 1859, pp. 176–77, and Bonnerot, *Correspondance de Sainte-Beuve*, 10:439n). The relations of Rouland *père* and Sainte-Beuve were icy.

Jean Gaspard Félix Ravaisson-Mollien (1813–1900), philosopher and archaeologist, held numerous posts under the minister of public instruction; from 1853 he was inspector general of higher education (*Grande Encyclopédie*).

Edouard René Lefebvre de Laboulaye (1811–83), professor of comparative law in the Collège de France and a member of the Académie des Inscriptions et Belles-Lettres (Super, 4:134, 366; *Almanach national*, 1850, p. 766).

Comte Auguste Arthur Beugnot (1797–1865), elected deputy from Haute-Marne in 1848, was a member of the Académie des Inscriptions (*Grande Encyclopédie*).

5. Apr. 2: Apparently, Narcisse Landois (born 1800), "inspecteur pour les écoles primaires publiques ou libres" and a member of the Academic Council of the Académie de Paris (*Almanach impérial*, 1859).

Henri Lutteroth (1802–89), writer on theology: "L'un des hommes les plus savants de l'Eglise protestante et qui lui ont rendu le plus de service" (*Dictionnaire universel illustreé de la France contemporaine*). His book *De la Réformation en France, pendant sa première période* (Paris, 1858) and eleven other titles are listed in the catalogue of the Bibliothèque Nationale; another, *Russia and the Jesuits, from 1772 to 1829* appeared in London in 1858.

Claire (daughter of the duchesse de Duras), duchesse de Rauzan (1799–1863), a very old friend of Chateaubriand ("La charmante Clara") and Sainte-Beuve, married in 1819 comte Henri Louis Chastellux, who became then duc de Rauzan (Chateaubriand's *Mémoires d'Outre-Tombe*, bk 23, ch. 5; Mérimée's *Correspondance*, 8:179, 12:63; Sainte-Beuve's "Madame de Duras," *Portraits de Femmes*).

Jean Florian Hervé (1803–73), comte de Kergorlay, politician and author (1861) of *Etude littéraire sur Alexis Tocqueville* (*Grande Encyclopédie*). "His Legitimist principles have prevented his taking any part in public life, but Tocqueville rated him very highly. 'Not one of us,' he said, 'has the intelligence or the cultivation of Kergorlay. If he had come forward he would have been the first in the very first rank' " (Senior, 2:363).

Mme de [?]Blaen remains unidentified. (*Blanc* would be a possible reading, but not with the nobiliary particle.)

6. Apr. 3: The Grand Hôtel du Louvre, at 166, 168 Rue de Rivoli, "opened in 1857, said to be the largest and most magnificent establishment of its kind in Europe" (Bohn's *Paris and Its Environs*, 1859, ed. Thomas Forester, p. 46).

7. Apr 4: The drama was Jules Lecomte's comedy *Le Luxe* (*Moniteur universel*, Apr. 4, p. 387). Madeleine Brohan (1833–1900), from a well-known acting family, praised by Gautier and Paul de Saint-Victor, had made her début at the Comédie française in 1851. François Joseph Pierre Tousez Regnier de la Brière (1807–85), known as Regnier, son of an actress and himself a famous actor, and sociétaire of the Comédie française since 1834, was by this time director of studies of the National Academy of Music (Lyonnet; *Grande Encyclopédie*). Regnier was an old friend of Macready, Dickens, and Wilkie Collins (who dedicated *The Law and the Lady* to him (see Dickens's *Letters*, Pilgrim Edn, 5:8n).

8. Apr. 5: Lady Augusta Bruce (1822–76), who married A. P. Stanley in 1863, was the daughter of the countess of Elgin (wife of the 7th earl), who died in Paris in Apr. 1860. See *Album*, p. 90.

Prosper Mérimée to Matthew Arnold

[c. April 5, 1859]

M. Mérimée présente ses compts empressés à Monsieur Arnold. Il est chargé par le Nonce du Pape de dire à M. A. que S. E. sera enchantée de le voir, & qu'elle est tous les jours à ses ordres vers midi, excepté *les samedi[s]*.

MS. Peter Thwaites.

1. Prosper Mérimée (1803–70), short-story writer, as well as archaeologist, historian, and an old friend of the Empress Eugénie (see below p. 490). Arnold saw Mérimée on Apr. 5 at no. 52 rue de Lille, and the Papal nuncio on Apr. 11 (Guthrie 2:236–37). The nuncio was Son Excellence Monsignor Sacconi, archevêque de Nicée (*Almanach impérial*, 1859), to whom Arnold "had been introduced through . . . [the] kindness" of George Bowyer (1811–83: *DNB*), M.P., a prominent Catholic convert and author, and, from 1860, 7th baronet (see Super, 2:273).

Newcastle Commission Journal (Yale)

April 6th Wednesday. Called on Thiers, and at Madame de Circourt's (where Amédée Thierry was) and talked with her a long while. Dined at the table d'hôte—afterwards to the Duchesse de Rauzan's—very few people & dull—introduced to M. Viennet—Saw M. Montcalm, the sole survivor of his family.[1] Called on Ld Cowley in the morning.

April 7, Thursday. Called early on M. Rapet. In the afternoon to the Hôtel de Ville with him, and again saw M. Landois. Very hot indeed. Dined at 3 Frères with Flu. Dressed and to M. Drouyn de Lhuy's to meet M. de Circourt, but missed him.[2] Home much disgusted.

April 8th Friday. M. Rapet called early and took me to a school in the rue du Faubourg Montmartre. In the afternoon to the rue Oudinot with Mrs. Tuffin & the children. Found the Frère Philippe gone. Drove round the Institut & home. dined at table d'hôte. afterwards with Flu to Mme Lutteroth's—met Lady Ducie[3] there and others—on to the Mohls, nobody there, but Mohl very pleasant. weather changed, and raining.

1. Apr. 6: Amédée Thierry (1797–1873), historian and administrator (conseiller d'état en service ordinaire), who lived at 122 rue de Grenelle (*Almanach impérial*, 1859, p. 89; Hillairet, 1:611); his more famous brother, Augustin Thierry, also a historian, died in 1856.

Jean Pons Guillaume Viennet (1777–1868), "an indefatigable writer of fables, epistles, and satires, epic poetry . . . , and epic dramas, all keeping lifelessly to classical models and now seldom mentioned" (*OCFL*).

Montcalm was a descendant of Louis Joseph marquis de Montcalm de Saint-Véran, the French adversary of General Wolfe at Quebec in 1759.

2. Apr. 7: Jean Jacques Rapet (1805–82) was inspector of primary schools in Paris and, in 1861, inspector general, and as Arnold makes clear in these letters he was indispensable. He lacked the glitter of the académiciens and did not frequent the *salons*—he was in fact exactly what Arnold affectionately called him, "an old functionary of primary instruction"—but he did the work, as Arnold knew, and as he acknowledged in his memorial notice, "A French Worthy" (Super, 10:89–93, and notes, pp. 476–79) as well as in *The Popular Education of France* (Super, 2:1–165, and notes).

Edouard Drouyn de Lhuys (1805–81), politician and diplomat, had been ambassador to Great Britain and Ireland and, later, twice minister of foreign affairs under the emperor (*Almanach national pour 1848-1849-1850*, p. 34; *Petit Robert*).

3. Apr. 8: Lady Ducie was either the countess dowager of Ducie (1807–1865), widow of the 2d earl (d. 1853) or possibly the wife (d. 1895) of the third.

Armand Trousseau to Matthew Arnold

[Paris]

Monsieur   [April 8, 1859]

J'avais hier pris plusieurs rendez-vous qui m'ont empêché de me rendre à votre appel.

Je viens d'examiner Master Tom et je serais d'avis de lui faire prendre le soir avant qu'il ne s'endorme un petit granule d'atropine. Vous en trouverez chez tous les pharmaciens du quartier.   Veuillez agréer l'expression de mes sentiments les plus distingués.

A. Trousseau

Je trouve d'ailleurs Tom beaucoup mieux.

MS. *Frederick Whitridge.*

1. Armand Trousseau (1801–67), No. 52, rue Basse-du-Rempart, "a French physician so eminent that he is noticed in practically all French biographical dictionaries, even small ones, was the author of several books, especially *Cliniques médicales de l'Hôtel Dieu* in three volumes. His speciality was children's diseases. . . . 'Je prie M. le Pharmacien d'envoyer, chez M. Arnold (50) Hotel Meurice—10 granules d'atropine de 1 Milligramme chaque—Paris le 8 avril 59 A Trousseau' " (*Album*, pp. 9, 67–68). The prescription is written on the back of Mérimée's letter to Arnold, above.

To T. J. Blachford

Paris

The Secretary to the Education Commission

Sir   April 9, 1859

In reply to your letter of the 7th instant, I beg to inform you that I most willingly accede to the proposal of the Commissioners that I should include the German cantons of Switzerland in the countries which I am to visit, and that Holland should be visited by Mr Pattison.[1] Both time and expense will be saved by such an arrangement. I have the honour to be, Sir,   your obedient servant,

M. Arnold.—

MS. Public Record Office, London.

1. Mark Pattison (1813–34: *DNB*), formerly fellow and tutor of Lincoln College, Oxford, but more recently (1858) Berlin correspondent for *The Times*. In 1861 he was elected rector of Lincoln College. For other official letters to Blachford (who remains a functionary without an identity, unlisted even in the *Post Office London Directories*) see below p. 440 and vol. 2.

Newcastle Commission Journal (Yale)

April 9th. [Saturday]   To the Embassy, but could not see Lord Cowley. Again to the rue Oudinot with Flu and the children. Saw the Père Supe-rior—very civil. dined at the table d'hôte, having first called on the Baroness Alphonse. After dinner with Flu to Madame [?]Nassau's[1]—rather dull.

April 10th. Sunday.   Wet, stormy day. In the afternoon with Flu to the rue Vaugirard to see the Confirmation of the Boys at the Institution S. Nicolas. dined at Véry's with Flu.

April 11th Monday.   Saw Lord Cowley—then to the Nuncio's and talked with him a long time. He gives me a letter to Lacordaire. Thence to see Villemain—talked a long time to him. dined at table d'hôte and with Flu to the Variétés. The first piece a clever quiz on Michelet's L'Amour. Poor Dejazet.[2] In afternoon to Luxembourg Gardens.

1. Apr. 9: Madame [?]Nassau (or ?Napon ?Nasson) remains beyond reach.
2. Apr. 11: At the Théâtre des Variétés, after Michelet's "L'Amour," they saw the famous actress Virginie Déjazet (1798–1875) in *Chérubin, ou le page de Napoléon*, in two acts, by Charles Desnoyer and Adrien, which had opened there two days before.

To Jules Michelet

Hôtel Meurice

Monsieur   10 avril 1859

Permettez moi de vous rappeler qu'en 1847 j'eue l'honneur de vous être présenté par M. Philarète Chasles.[1] Vous m'avez reçu alors avec une grande bonté, et vous m'avez parlé avec intérêt des travaux de mon père, dont l'histoire de Rome vous était connu. Je suis à Paris maintenant en mission de mon Gouvernement, pour étudier l'état de l'instruction primaire en France, et en faire l'objet d'un Rapport. Me permettez vous, Monsieur, de venir vous voir, et de vous demander quelques renseignemen[t]s sur la condition actuelle de vos populations, urbaines et rurales, dont on m'a recommandé dans le but de ma mission de m'informer avec soin, et sur laquelle personne autant que vous, Monsieur, ne serait en état de me donner des informations utiles.   Veuillez agréer, Monsieur, l'expression de mes hommages empressés,

Matthew Arnold.

MS. Bibliothèque Historique de la Ville de Paris.

1. See above pp. 93n, 99. Arnold saw Michelet on Apr. 14 and 15 (Guthrie 2:237), presumably at no. 10 rue des Postes (now, Lhomond), near the Panthéon (Hillairet, 2:42).

To Mary Penrose Arnold

Paris

My dearest Mother   April 12, 1859

The telegraphic message about poor dear Willy is certainly formidable[1]—if I had had it on Friday last I should have been much tempted to go off myself. What a chapter of mischances—first his leaving Egypt just as Walter reached it—then his not stopping at Malta where Walter was going to call—then his being laid up at Gibraltar, almost within reach of home. The climate of Gibraltar just now must be perfect—that is one thing in his favour. Here we have all the changeableness of the north—a few days ago almost intolerable sunshine—on Sunday April showers—and today the gloom, biting wind, and harsh dust of March. I have at last a cold, which it takes a good deal to give me and which when I have it takes the form of bronchitis—but I soon shake it off. Little Tom is coughing more today, but in spite of that is gaining ground steadily, and has today eaten famously— bread and butter and chicken for his breakfast—bread and butter and cold tongue for his second breakfast—and he has just made an excellent dinner. He drinks tumbler after tumbler of milk in the day—and it is in prescribing milk for him that Trousseau seems to me to have rendered him such a service. It is a wonder no one thought of it before. He takes a pill of atropine every night, which seems to suit him famously.

Meantime I am being ruined, as our bill here averages 500 fr. (£20) a *week*, exclusive of all incidental expenses—carriage hire—dress—dining at restaurants—theatre &c. My total receipts from the Commission amount to only £18 a week—so I am at present an actual loser by my employment.

However it is very interesting and I hope to bring round the balance when I diminish my party. The worst of it is that owing to this abominable deputation our house in Chester Square does not let. So about Easter Tuesday, when Walrond and the Sandfords, who are coming over here for Easter, return I hope to pack off along with them all the party but Flu. They will go to Chester Square and we hope to make arrangements for Miss Nicholls to be with them there for a few weeks till the weather gets decidedly warmer, and then to take little Tom to Brighton. The others will stay on in Chester Square under the protection of Eaton Place. Then, at the end of July they will all, I hope, meet us at Dover. I hope to get Flu to do this, as she requires rest and change—Tom's illness and the nursing of the baby having rather overfatigued her. We should then start for a month's tour in the departments—and after that go to Switzerland. Things look very warlike, but Lord Cowley told me yesterday that he hoped they should pull through. I think Count Cavour has succeeded at last in rendering the English a little more just to the Italian cause, of which I am glad.[2] I have told you nothing of what I am doing here. I shall be able some day to tell you my history from my Journal. God bless you, my dearest Mother—send me the earliest news of Willy. I still cannot help hoping it may be favourable.   Your ever affectionate

M. A.—

I want to hear of William's election proceedings. The Rothschilds say the best informed people think the new Parliament will be much the same as the last, Ld Derby gaining a few votes. I should think this would be the case.[3] But no one was for English politics here just now—or for anything beyond the war question.

MS. Balliol College.

1. See below p. 434. The four children left India for England at the end of January. William Delafield Arnold, suffering from "intermittent dysentery" sailed in February. "But when he had embarked his health . . . became alarmingly worse. He was kept prisoner at Cairo by fever, ague, and excruciating pain in the chest and side. The doctors were still sanguine, but he did not put much trust in the doctors; and now there was only a French one available, and 'I wish I knew the French for Bowels.' After this rueful jest he sounded a sudden note of appeal. 'If any Brother or Brother in law has spare Cash or Leisure to come and help me it would be a Charity.' This letter, written on 5 March, reached Fox How by the middle of the month, and on the 18th Walter, the youngest brother, left England for Alexandria," where William Arnold now rested and where a doctor "had diagnosed congestion of the liver and advised him to sail for Liverpool next day . . . on the *Laconia*. On the way out of the harbour she passed the ship that was bringing Walter to meet him.

"Diarrhoea attacked him again and made him very weak and, in consequence, occasionally light-headed. . . . they landed [at Gibraltar] on 7 April 1859: his thirty-first birthday. . . . Between two and three o'clock on . . . [April 8th] he fell into a coma from which he never roused" (Woodward, pp. 223–6).

    2. Camillo Bensi conte di Cavour (1810–61), premier of Sardinia (of which Victor Emmanuel II was king), supplied the intellect with which the king was not burdened and maneuvered the French emperor (at a price) into a war, on Apr. 27, to eject the Austrians from the Piedmont.

    3. The Rothschilds were not quite wrong but certainly not right. The election was close, and Derby's Conservative party did in fact gain some seats but could not govern: Palmerston's second cabinet took over in June and lasted six years. In Leeds William Forster came in third, losing out to Edward Baines, his old adversary (see above p. 336n) (*Annual Register*, 1859, p. 503; E. L. Woodward, *The Age of Reform*, p. 641).

Newcastle Commission Journal (Yale)

April 12th. Tuesday.   Heard that poor Willy had stopped at Gibraltar, "dangereusement malade." Went to ⟨Luxembourg gardens⟩ the Faubourg St. Antoine with Flu, Tom, and [?]Budge. Trees and flowers beautiful. dined at the table d'hôte, then to the Louvre with Flu to hear Jasmin.[1] His patois hardly intelligible.

April 13th.   M. Rapet came for me—as I was going out with him received Susy's letter—'Dear Willy died at San Roque"!—Saw School and establishment of Soeurs. Dined at Mrs. Gould's. Sate by Mme. Batthyany. She charming. Very cold.[2]

April 14th Thursday.   Called on M. Franck. afterwards on Count Beugnot—very long conversation with him, and very interesting. Wrote to my Mother, and went out with Budge—very cold and raw. dined at table d'hôte and to Mrs Guthrie's in the evening.[3] Very stupid. Violent rain, and wind. [Diary, Guthrie, 2:237, adds: 'M. Rapet* M. Michelet* heard of Willy']

    1. Apr. 12: Jacques Boé (1798–1864), known as Jasmin, Gascon poet who wrote in the langue d'oc (and apparently spoke in it too). Six years earlier Nassau Senior, hearing "one or two pages" of a poem by Jasmin, remarked, "I could make out a word or two but not the general sense." He was told that Jasmin's auditors at a *salon* "had translations in their hands. Besides, he is a great actor; his delivery doubles the effect of his verses" (Senior, 1:189).

    2. Apr. 13: Presumably the "school in the rue de la Sourdière [off rue St Honoré, near St Roch], kept by the Sisters" (Super 2:110).

    Probably the widow of Lajos Batthyány (1806–48) comte de Németujvar, the Hungarian nationalist who was shot by the Austrians (*Petit Robert*) or, to avoid hanging, "stabbed himself . . . and bled to death in the night of the 5th of October 1849" (*Encyclopædia Britannica*, 11th edn).

    3. Apr. 14: Mrs Guthrie remains unidentified but was perhaps the widow of George James Guthrie (1785–1856: *DNB*), the famous and wealthy surgeon (see above p. 209 n. 5).

To Mary Penrose Arnold*

Paris

April 14, 1859

What can one do, my dearest Mother, except bow one's head, and be silent? My poor, dear Willy! If he had but known of my being here, and had telegraphed to me from Malta, I might have reached him from Gibraltar in time. And no one else could. I like to imagine, even now that it is so entirely vain, the arriving at Gibraltar—the standing by his bedside—the taking his poor hand—I whom he would hardly perhaps have expected to see there—I of whom he thought so far more than I deserved—and who shewed him, poor boy, so far less tenderness than *he* deserved.

How strange it seems that he should have overlived his first terrible illness when his wife was alive to nurse him and he had but one child to suffer by his loss, to die now alone with only a chance acquaintance to attend him, and leaving those four poor little orphans to whom no tenderness can ever quite replace a father and a mother.—And then that he should have overlived the misery of his poor wife's death, to struggle through a year's loneliness, and then to die, too. Poor Fanny[1]—she at Dharmsala, and he by the Rock of Gibraltar.—God bless you—what I *can* be to you and to all of them, I will be— Your's ever,

M. A.—

MS. Balliol College.

1. See above p. 207 n. 8.

Frances Lucy Wightman Arnold
to Mary Penrose Arnold

Dear Mother   Friday, [April 15, 1859]

I was so sorry that Matt's letter went to you yesterday without my sending a few lines with it. I do indeed grieve for you dear dear Mother. I am sure you know I grieve with you for I did truly love your darling Willy: for besides his having ever been to me a most kind & loving brother, I so admired all his great noble qualities. It must be such a heavy trial to lose a child, and to you who have been such a tender sweet loving Mother, connecting yourself with and entering into every interest of your children so warmly & keenly, always feeling for & with them so entirely—What must it be! The first gone among your nine darlings. God grant you help & comfort dear Mother.

I feel very much being so far from you just now & wish dear Matt could get home that you might have the comfort of having all your remaining dear ones with you. All I write seems so cold & unmeaning & so little to express all I so sincerely feel. At first I could hardly realize the truth & indeed now it seems very very difficult; dear dear Willy! God bless you dear Mother. I do so love you & grieve for you in this great sorrow. You have ever been to me more than I can say or thank you for. I am so glad I knew dear Willy so well, it makes me feel so much more to *belong* to you having known & loved him as I did.　　　Ever your very loving daughter

FL Arnold

MS. Balliol College.

Newcastle Commission Journal (Yale)

April 15th. Friday.　　　M. Rapet called—blasting wet day, with hailstorms. called on Guizot and sate with him some time: then to the Frères in the rue de Fleurus, and saw their establishments. Then to Michelet—saw his wife, and talked with him a long time.[1] Heard from Fan of the second telegraph— "Arnold est mort, le neuf!" Dined at Véfour's with Flu. to bed early.

April 16th. Saturday.　　　Cold, windy day, bright sunshine and hailstorms alternately. Walked before breakfast to the rue de Clichy to see Rendu—he was out. After breakfast sate at home with Tom and brought up this journal. with Flu to the Louvre, & saw the Napoleon relics. Then alone to get mourning hat-band, & home by rue Vivienne & the Boulevard. Dined at table d'hôte, and then with Flu to Fanny du Quaire's. Found her alone, and sate a long time. Home and to bed.

April 17th. Sunday.　　　Bitter cold day, with little sun. Sate at home all morning writing to [Fitzjames] Stephen. In the afternoon walked with Flu. Dined with the du Quaires—Mrs. Procter.[2]

April 18th Monday.　　　M. Rapet called and took me to the Faubourg St. Antoine. Flu went to the Exposition in the afternoon with Fanny du Quaire, while I went to the rue Bleue and saw M. Cohen [*for* Cohn]. Dined at table d'hôte, and afterwards alone to the Palais Royal. Arnal very amusing.[3] Home early. [Diary, Guthrie, 2:237, adds: 'M. Guizot']

April 19th Tuesday.　　　Still cold day irritating weather. Trousseau saw Tom and was greatly pleased with him. Flu & I took Tom & Trev to dine at Véry's: then she & I drove to call on Mme Lutteroth, Lady Slade, and Mme Batthyany. Found them all at home. In the afternoon the weather changed to cold rain. I dined at Ld Cowley's—M. de Flahault, Résigny, Ld Ward, [Lt] Col. Claremont &c.[4] [Diary, Guthrie, 2:237 adds: 'the duc de Broglie . . . Mme de Circourt']

April 20th Wednesday.　　Still wet, a dry wind less cold. M. Rapet took me in the morning to the Faubourg St. Marceau [*for* Martin?] and to Mme Pape. In the afternoon met Wyndham Slade & Cumin. Flu and I and Budge walked about a little. afterwards Flu & I dined at the Café Vachette with Wyndham & Cumin.[5] Dinner not first rate. Very wet evening.

April 21. Thursday.　　Gloomy damp morning. Early to the rue de Clichy to call on M. Rendu. He fuller of Italy than of public education. Back to Meurice's to breakfast—then to call on M. de Laboulaye. he very interesting indeed. Home & Madame Lutteroth called. Wrote journal, and out. Walked to the Slades' with Flu, and dined there. She to Church afterward with Lady Slade. Wyndham Cumin & I to the Bouffes Parisiens to see Orphée aux Enfers. Then to Tortoni for ice, and home.[6]

April 22nd, Good Friday.　　Bright day, but cold. Wrote to my mother, and took Tom & Budge out in the Tuileries Gardens. After their dinner Flu Cumin Tom and I in a carriage to the Bois de Boulogne. Beautiful—walked down the hill towards St. Cloud. Tom in great force and gathering daisies. Home, & Cumin dined at the table d'hôte with us: then Flu & I to the Service at the Madeleine. Stupid sermon.

April 23rd, Saturday.　　Still bright cold weather. Flu and I after breakfast to call on Lady Augusta Bruce—saw Lady Elgin. Home to the children's dinner, and then with Flu to the Sainte Chapelle. Tom with a cold, & very feverish & unwell. Better as the afternoon went on. Fanny Blackett came, & dined with us at the table d'hôte. I took her home afterwards.

April 24th, Easter Sunday.　　Rather milder. Tom much better. At 12 with Flu to the Mess at the Tuileries—saw the Emperor & Empress admirably. E[illeg. ?Elysee] full of the war news. Took Budge & Diddy in the Champs Elysées, and gave them a ride on the wooden horses. Home and took out Tom to call on Fanny du Quaire—coming home met Flu, & a short drive with her and Tom in the Champs Elysées, & called on the Slades. To Philippe's to dine with Cumin: found it full: then to Véry's. Dined very well—a wet evening. home.

April 25th.　　Decided change to warm weather, but windy. Went to M. Rapet—with him to M. Magin's. a long & interesting visit. Settled departmental tour: then to Meurice's—from there to the banker's, and on the way back lunched at the Maison Dorée.[7] Tom wonderfully better. Fanny du

Quaire called and took out him & Diddy. Flu & I walked a little, & drove to Kate Guthrie's. I very seedy. M. Rendu called. Dined at the table d'hôte. Afterwards Flu & I called on the Spanish family au premier. Then to Fanny du Quaire's to say goodbye. Then bill paying, packing, &c.

April 26th. Tuesday. Beautiful morning, and calm. Up at 6—with Flu & children to 8 o'clock train. Saw them off—Tom well, and Flu in fair force. Walked back to Meurice's & breakfasted. Then wrote letters and this journal. Walked to make calls on the other side the Seine. no one at home. Then to call on the Seniors at the Hotel de Westminster—Talked a long time with Minnie. Then to Mme. de Circourt's. Home & dressed—and then to the Slades—After dinner to the Porte St. Martin to see the Closerie des Genêts—the Princess Clothilde there.[8] Beautiful night—walked home— ices at Tortoni's.

1. Apr. 15: Michelet lived at no. 44 rue de l'Ouest, not far from the Cimetière du Montparnasse (*Almanach impérial*, 1859, p. 1086). His (second) wife was the former Adèle Malairet, "a lady of some literary capacity, and of republican belongings," according to George Saintsbury (*Encyclopædia Britannica*, 11th edn).

2. Apr. 17: Anne B. Procter (1799–1888), *née* Skepper, wife of Bryan Waller Procter (1787–1874), "Barry Cornwall," friend of Leigh Hunt, Dickens, and Charles Lamb, of whom he wrote a biography (1864). See below her charming letter to Arnold twenty years later, Feb. 9, 1879, after they had met again at Fanny du Quaire's.

3. Apr. 18: Faubourg St Antoine, no. 254 L'Orphélinat Eugène-Napoléon, which had opened in Dec. 1856 (Hillairet, 1:499).

The Exposition Universelle (1855), in the Palais de l'Industrie (demolished in 1900), on the site now occupied by parts of the Grand Palais, Petit Palais, Place Georges Clémenceau, and the Avenue Alexandre III (Hillairet, 1:299).

In "the excellent Jewish schools of Paris, to which M. Albert Cohn, the President of the Jewish Benefit Society, kindly conducted me, the boys answered my questions on geography, and, still more, on history, as well as the best instructed scholars whom I have ever found in an English school" (Super, 2:107).

Etienne Arnal (1794–1872), a comedian, who, having established his considerable reputation at the Théâtre du Vaudeville, had moved to the Palais Royal in 1856 (Lyonnet, 1:44–47). The offerings were *Dada de Paimboeuf, Une Tempête, Elle était à l'Ambigu,* and *Une Giroflée* (*Gazette de France*, Apr. 18).

4. Apr. 19: The very sublime of discretion. Auguste comte de Flahault [*or* Flahaut] de la Billarderie (1785–1870), the putative natural son of the novelist Mme de Souza (one of Sainte-Beuve's *Portraits de Femmes*) and Talleyrand and himself the former lover of Hortense de Beauharnais (1783–1837), step-daughter and sister-in-law of Napoleon Bonaparte, queen of Holland, and mother of Napoleon III (whose father was not certainly her husband), by whom he had a son (later, duc de Morny), who was thus the "frère utérin" of the Emperor. He was a general and a senator and had been ambassador to the Court of St James. He was married to Baroness Keith of Dunheath, co. Dumbarton, and in 1843 their daughter married the 5th earl of Kerry (later 4th marquis of Lansdowne) and Arnold would have seen him at Lansdowne House. (See *Petit Robert; Almanach*

impérial; Jasper Ridley, *Napoleon III and Eugénie*, pp. 24–25; Swinburne, 1:29n; and several of Victor Hugo's poems.)

Marie Louis Jules d'Y de Résigny (b. 1789) was also a general and, less intimately no doubt than Flahaut, former Bonapartist (Vapereau, *Dictionnaire universel des contemporains*).

William Ward (1817–85; *VF*, 6/18/70), 10th Baron Ward, later (1860) 1st earl of Dudley.

Lieut. Colonel Claremont was the military attaché at the Embassy (*Almanach impérial*, 1859, p. 184).

5. Apr. 20: Marie Pape-Carpantier (1815–78), director of the Ecole normale maternelle since 1848 and then of "inspection générale des 'salles d'asiles,' " and author of several pedagogical works, most recently *Histoire et leçons de choses pour les enfants* (1858) (*Petit Robert*).

Café Vachette, no. 32 boulevard Poissonnière—later, at no. 27 boulevard St Michel (*Galignani's New Paris Guide*, p. 589; Hillairet, 2:472).

6. Apr. 21: Théâtre des Bouffes-Parisiens (salle d'hiver), at no. 4 rue Monsigny (as now), a few blocks off what is now the avenue de l'Opéra, of which Offenbach himself had been the director for four years and where his *Orphée aux Enfers* had opened in 1858 (Hillairet, 2:138). The Café Tortoni was at no. 22 boulevard des Italiens.

7. Apr. 25: Alfred Joseph Auguste Marrens-Magin (b. 1806): "M. Magin, now Inspector General of primary instruction, and formerly Rector of the Academy of Nancy . . . has peculiar qualifications, in his wide experience, his thorough mastery of the whole system of French education, his perfect disinterestedness, and his singular clearness of judgment, for guiding an inquirer charged with such an errand as mine. If I have not wholly failed in finding my way through the complicated general question which in France I had to study, it is M. Magin whom I have had, almost always, to thank for my clue" (Super, 2:30–31). He was also the author of several books on pedagogy (Vapereau, *Dictionnaire universel des contemporains*).

Maison Dorée, at no. 1 rue Laffitte, corner of boulevard des Italiens (*Galignani's New Paris Guide*, pp. 226, 589).

8. Apr. 26: For Nassau Senior see above p. 194 n. 14. His friends included Alexis de Tocqueville (died Apr. 16, to whose widow Senior wrote a letter of condolence from the Hôtel de Westminster on Apr. 25) and Cavour, and he knew (and recorded his conversations with) all the prominent figures in France in the Second Empire, including Guizot and Thiers. His wife (d. 1877) was the former Mary Charlotte Mair, which was also the name of his only daughter, "Minnie," later M. C. M. Simpson, editor of her father's journals and "conversations" with many of those whom Arnold met socially in Paris on this visit. Goldwin Smith's summary sketch of him in *Reminiscences*, pp. 117–18, is worth reading.

Closerie des Genêts, a play by Frédéric de Soulié at the Théâtre de l'Ambigu, boulevard Saint Martin—with perhaps a symbolic and certainly a dramatic public appearance of the bartered bride. In Jan. 1859, a little before her sixteenth birthday, Princess Clotilde, daughter of Victor Emmanuel II, had married Prince (Jerome) Napoleon (1822–91), "Plon-Plon," a well-known (or ill-known) libertine more than twice her age, nephew of Napoleon Bonaparte, having been swapped (along with Nice and Savoy) by her father and Cavour for a declaration of war by France against Austria—which (the emperor paid cash) came the next day, Apr. 27. See above p. 433 n. 4.

To T. J. Blachford

T. J. Blachford Esqre   Paris
Sir   April 26, 1859
    I have the honour to return, signed, the enclosed Treasury Receipt
which you forwarded to me.
    I should be glad if the sum of one hundred pounds might again be paid,
in the middle of *next* month, to my account with Messrs Twinings. I will
keep you informed of my address in order that the Treasury Receipt may be
duly sent to me for signature. I have the honour to be, Sir,   your obedient
servant,

                                                        M. Arnold.—

MS. Public Record Office, London.

Newcastle Commission Journal (Yale)

April 27, Wednesday.   Out after breakfast to make calls the other side the
Seine. Walked through the Luxembourg picture gallery. Saw M. Charles
Jourdain at the Ministère de l'Instruction publique Saw M. Rendu. Called
on Mme Mohl, & sate with her a long time. Beautiful day and very warm—
but a strong breeze. Home and found Flu's letter announcing their arrival at
Folkestone. Wrote to her, and wrote this. Then strolled on the Boulevard
with Wyndham Slade—home & dressed for Lady Elgin's. At dinner Lady
Augusta Bruce Mr. & Lady Frances Baillie, Miss Farquhar &c. M. Mohl in
the evening.[1] Walked back with Mr. Baillie—sate a long time with Fanny
Du Quaire. then home to bed.

April 28, Thursday.   Out after breakfast to the Palais Royal—then to the
banker's. Drove thence to Guizot's—found him with his son & Dumont. He
very animated. told me that Austria had accepted the mediation & France
refused it. Then to the Ministère de l'Instruction publique. Saw M. Charles
Jourdain, M. Barraudot, and M. Rendu. Got the promise of having my
letters for the Préfets tomorrow. Then to the rue de Sèvres and had a long
conversation with the Père Etienne. A charming countenance, and a most
interesting man. Then to the duc de Broglie's—but found him out. back
to Meurice's and wrote to Flu—no letter from her. Called at Mme. de
Staël's—she was out. Back to Meurice's: Wyndham came & we walked
to Véfour's—very bad dinner: then to Palais Royal theatre, for a wonder,
stupid.[2] Home & to bed. Warm, showery & sunshiny, April day.

1. Apr. 27: Jourdain has not been identified. Lady Frances Baillie (1831–94), daughter of Lady Elgin, had married Evan P. Montagu Baillie (d. 1874) in 1855. Miss Farquhar was probably Maria Farquhar (daughter of Sir Thomas Harvie Farquhar) married in 1860 to William Halliday Cosway. Her widowed mother lived at Dale Cottage, Grasmere, in 1855 (Martineau). See below p. 442.

2. Apr. 28: Pierre Sylvain *Dumon* (b. 1797), politician and former minister of public works under Guizot (Vapereau, *Dictionnaire universel des contemporains*).

Père Etienne was "The Superior-General of the Female Religious Orders in France," the Lazaristes (Congrégation des Prêtres de la Mission), at no. 95 rue de Sèvres (see next letter, Super 2: 71, 77, and Hillairet, 1 : 501, 2 : 521). Arnold recalls this interview in a letter to Cowie, below, Nov. 21, 1868.

Dada le Paimboeuf, La Clé, Fanian, Elle était à l'Ambigu, and *Le Punch* were on the bill at the Palais Royal (*Gazette de France*).

To Frances Lucy Wightman Arnold*

Paris

April 28, 1859

I quite counted on another line from you today to tell me of your safe arrival in London. The post has only just come in, eveything on the line of railway being disorganised by the passage of the troops, but there is nothing for me. Now I cannot hear tomorrow, for you will think I am gone away from here, and not know where to write to me. But I do not go to Brittany till Saturday morning, as my letter for the Préfets will not be ready till the middle of the day tomorrow.

I have seen Guizot, Dumont, a number of the officials at the Ministère de l'Instruction Publique, and the Pere Etienne, the Superior General of the Female Religious Orders in France. This last is a most interesting man, one of the most striking persons I have seen here, but more of him hereafter. I finished my round by calling on the Duc de Broglie, but he was out. Now I am going to call on Madame de Stael, and then coming back to meet Wyndham Slade, that we may dine together.

Guizot told me the great news, which I suppose you all know today in England, but which has been kept out of the papers here—that Austria had accepted the English mediation and that France had refused it; so in a few days the cannon will begin to roar. The moment is certainly most interesting and agitating.

There is not much enthusiasm here, but a great deal of excitement at the perpetual sight of troops marching past. All this grand military spectacle so animates and interests the French. Miles of infantry have just gone past to the Lyons station, all in heavy marching order, with their drinking cups round their necks, their round loaves of brown bread fastened to their knapsacks, and their tent-poles stuck through a strap on their backs. How I wish for you all and my darling boys!

I had a pleasant dinner at Lady Elgin's last night. I sat between Lady Frances Baillie and Miss Farquhar. She had an enthusiasm about Fox How and my father. I walked home with Baillie—he and his wife charming people. You shall see them when you come back here. The Nuncio's letters to the bishops and archbishops have come, and I am now only waiting for Mr. Roulards' [*for* Rouland's].

Text. Russell, 1:92–94.

Jules Michelet to George Sand

Paris
29 avril [18]59

M. Michelet présent ses hommages affectueuses à Madame Georges Sand. Il prend la liberté de lui présenter un très honorable gentilhomme, M. Arnold, envoyé par son gouvernement pour faire une enquête sur l'état de notre enseignement primaire que nos voisins ont la bonté de croire très avancé.[1]

MS. Frederick Whitridge.

1. "In 1859 M. Michelet gave me a letter to her, which would have enabled me to present myself in more regular fashion. Madame Sand was then in Paris. But a day or two passed before I could call, and when I called, Madame Sand had left Paris and had gone back to Nohant. The impression of 1846 has remained my sole impression of her" (Super, 8:218). George Sand left Paris on May 4, in the morning (*Correspondance*, ed. Georges Lubin, 15:405).

Newcastle Commission Journal (Yale)

April 29, Friday. Rather colder—but still soft air and April weather. after breakfast to call on M. de Kergorlay then to get maps. Mitchell[1] called and I wrote this. Heard, beyond all expectation from dear Flu. Got my letters from the Minister. Mitchell dined at table d'hôte with me. Strolled on boulevard, packed and to bed.

April 30. Saturday. Off by Morning Express to Nantes. Fine day. Hôtel de France.

May 1. Sunday. At Nantes—Wet day, holding up occasionally. Saw the town and called at the Bishop's Palace.

May 2, Monday. Off at 7 to Quimper in the Malle Poste. Fine day. after 9 a.m. Got to Quimper at 1½ next morning. The Hôtel de l'Epée.

May 3. Tuesday.   Called on the Bishop. found the Préfet absent. Saw the town. fished a little in the evening.

May 4. Wednesday.   Fished. Called on M. de Carré and talked a long time.

May 5. Thursday.   Called on M. de Leguinquis.—With him to see a school for farmers' sons. Fished. In the evening M. Leguinquis came. Long conversation with him.[2]

May 6. Friday.   Off at 5½ in diligence for Auray. Reached Auray about 4 p.m. drove straight to Carnac. Back to Auray & slept at the Pavillon d'En Haut.

May 7, Saturday.   Off at 2 a. m. in diligence by Vannes to Rennes. At night from Rennes to Paris.

May 8, Sunday.   in Paris. Saw the du Quaires, Mrs Waterton,[3] Burgoynes &c.

1. Apr. 29: Probably Alexander Mitchell (1831–73), in the Fifth Form at Eton in 1847 and then at Christ Church, Oxford. He entered the army in 1850 and was in the Grenadier Guards for six years, rising to a captaincy, and, as an "Independent Liberal," M.P. for Berwick-upon-Tweed 1865–68. He married Fanny Georgiana Jane Hasler, to whom Arnold addressed several letters after Mitchell's death, whom he visited, and who, in 1877, married Baron Reay. As this Journal shows below, Arnold saw much of him in Paris in August. (Peerage, s.v. Reay; *Who's Who of British Members of Parliament*).

2. May 1–5: The bishop of Nantes, whom Arnold apparently did not see, was Monsignor (Antoine Matthias Alexandre) Jacqueret (b. 1803). The bishop of Quimper was Monsignor (René Nicolas) Sergent (b. 1802). (See below p. 447 and Super, 2:120.) The préfet of the Département de Finistère, at Quimper, was Charles Richard (*Almanach impérial*, 1859). Carré is unidentified. Leguinquis was the inspecteur de l'académie at Quimper, under the Académie de Rennes (*Almanach impérial*, p. 579).

3. May 8: Mrs Waterton has not been identified. Lady Burgoyne (see above p. 187 n. 1) was now the *widow* of Sir John Montagu Burgoyne. Her son, the 10th baronet, of the same name, and her daughter, Mary Caroline, were both married. In London, Lady Burgoyne lived at 7 Lowndes Square, but later moved to 5 South Eaton Place, S. W.

To Frances Lucy Wightman Arnold*

Hôtel Meurice, Paris
Sunday, May 8, 1859

Now I must tell you something of my history. If I allowed myself, I should fill the letter with talk of your joining me. I had a misgiving that you would not get my Quimper letter in a hurry, but it was only on Thursday, the day I wrote, that your letter reached me, and I have a particular dislike to writing in the dark when I know a letter is on its road to me. I am glad to be out of Brittany, as the dirt and the badness of the food had begun to make me feverish and unwell. I am rejoiced you were not with me there, though I am glad to have seen the country. Nearly all Thursday I passed with the Quimper Inspector, and on Friday morning at half-past five I started by diligence for Auray, in the Morbihan. My bill at the Hotel de l'Epée for three days and nights was 17 francs 50 centimes. Think of that! and all my expenditure in Brittany was in the same proportion.

Brittany is a country of low hills, *landes* covered with furze and broom, and small orchards and meadows with high banks dividing them, on which banks grow pollard oaks. The whole effect is of a densely enclosed, wooded country, though the extent of *landes* is very considerable.

I left the diligence at Auray at half-past four in the afternoon, after a sitting of eleven hours, and immediately ordered a conveyance for Carnac, about ten miles off on the sea-shore.[1] The great Druidical monument is there, and I stopped at Auray on purpose to see it. It is a very wild country—broom and furze, broom and furze everywhere—and a few patches of pine forest. The sea runs into the land everywhere, and beautiful church towers rise on all sides of you, for this is a land of churches. The stones of Carnac are very singular, but the chapel of St. Michel, on a hill between the stones and the village of Carnac, I liked better still; the view over the stones and the strange country of Morbihan (the little sea), on the spur of Carnac by the sea, and beyond the bay and peninsula of Quiberon, where the emigrants landed, and beyond that the Atlantic. All this at between six and seven on a perfectly still, cloudless evening in May, with the sea like glass, and the solitude all round entire. I got back to Auray at eight. It was to Auray that the emigrants after their surrender were taken and shot in the market place, on which my inn, the Pavillon d'en Haut, looks out. My dinner was soup, Carnac oysters, shrimps, *fricandeau* of veal, breast of veal, asparagus, etc.; cider was the drink. This looks well, but everything was so detestable that my dinner was, in fact, made on bread and cheese. To get to my room I had to tread a labyrinth of dirty passages, and my room smelt like a stable. However, I did not try the room long, for at half-past one I was called, and at half-past two blundered in the dark through the passages and the courtyard to the Diligence Office, and took my place for Rennes. Again I got the *coupé*, and again a corner; but I am very sick of diligences, the distances seem so long in them. By this journey to Rennes I have pretty well seen Brittany, all except the northern line of St. Malo, Dinan, and Brest. We passed through Meyerbeer's Ploër-mel,[2] and there I got an interesting companion, in a *chef de bataillon* of the 7th Infantry, whose regiment had been in garrison at Brest, and was on its way to Paris for Italy. His *bataillon* was at Ploërmel, but he got leave to go to Rennes to see his old mother, who is eighty-five. He was a C. B., and wore the decoration, and one of the best possible specimens, I imagine, of a French officer. His regiment was in the Crimea, and nearly every man has the Victoria medal. The country was covered with men on "congé renouvelable" coming in to join the regiment. My acquaintance's *bataillon* was one thousand strong, and the entire regiment was four *bataillons*. This shows you what a French regiment on its war footing is. He was full of the war, and we talked of it incessantly. He said the army would be as much as any one against a war of conquest such as the first Napoleon's wars, and if Napoleon III. attempts such a thing, he said, "on le renversera." But he had a great enthusiasm for the Italian cause, and this is certainly gaining ground in France. The reading he had with him was a new book on the *Art of War*, and his spirit and enthusiasm were really interesting, his appearance and manner very good, but I tell you I imagine he was a favourable specimen. When we got to Rennes at four o'clock he was received in the arms of three women and a boy—aunts, cousins, etc.—in the costume of the country, and of the regular peasant class, and embraced all his relations before me without the slightest awkwardness.

The enthusiasm of the French people for the army is remarkable; almost every peasant we passed in the diligence took off his hat to this officer, though you never see them salute a gentleman, as such; but they feel that the army is the proud point of the nation, and that it is made out of themselves. At Rennes I shaved, washed, saw the cathedral and the old Parliament House of Brittany, dined at an infamous *table d'hôte* at the Hotel de France, where I met a pleasant Spaniard, and at seven in the evening was at the station starting for Paris. I was tired and slept well, having just had a good deal of conversation with a French naval officer on his way from Rennes to Cherbourg. The military and naval movement here is immense, but I am convinced that the *nation* in France at present means fairly. What the Emperor means it is harder to tell. But his proclamation was excellent.[3]

I am going to write a few lines to my mother. Let me have one line here on Tuesday. I will write to you also on that day. God bless you. Love to all at Teddington.

M. A.

Text. Russell, 1:94–97.

1. See Arnold's poem "Stanzas from Carnac" and notes in Allott, p. 492.
2. Meyerbeer's opera, "Le Pardon de Ploërmel" (or "Dinorah"), opened at the Opéra Comique on Apr. 4, 1859, the "great event of the season" (*Galignani's Messenger*, Apr. 10, p. 2).
3. "On the 3d of May the French Emperor directed a communication to be made to the Corps Législatif, which amounted to a manifesto of war"—quoted in *Annual Register*, pp. 231–32.

To Mary Penrose Arnold*

Paris

My dearest Mother   Sunday, May 8, 1859

It is only this morning, on my return from Brittany, that I receive your letter. I had fully hoped to write to you from Quimper or Auray, but had hardly time even to write to Flu. I do not think you can do better than put up dear Willy's name, age, &c with simply a text added—that proposed has great appositeness—I myself prefer texts that are rather an ejaculation of mourning over the dead—but this is not the usual feeling—on the whole, I think it is decisive in favour of the text proposed that Willy put another text from the same Sermon over his poor wife. I thought of him the other day at Carnac while I looked over the perfectly still & bright Atlantic by Quiberon Bay and saw the sails passing in the distance where he would have passed had he lived to come home. One has a baffled painful feeling in his having died so perfectly without a sign—but how often this seems to happen!—Flu has sent me dear Fan's letter with the last details—which are very interesting. I want to see little Eddy.[1]

I could not but think of you in Brittany, with Cranics and Trevenecs all about me—and the peasantry with their expressive rather mournful faces— long noses and dark eyes—reminding me perpetually of dear Tom & Uncle Trevenen—and utterly unlike the French. And I had the climate of England—grey skies and cool air—and the grey rock of the north, too, and the clear rushing water. One is haunted by the name *Plantagenet* there—the moment one enters Anjou, from which the family came, the broom begins—and Brittany seems all in flower with it, with furze mixed. I had no notion the waste stretches of landes, where there is nothing but these plants, heath, & rock, were still so considerable: the enclosed county is very like England, small bright green pastures, separated by high banks as in Devonshire and Cornwall, full of pollard oaks just coming into leaf. The country from a height looks like a mixture of landes and oak forest. But even the field banks are covered with broom. I went to Carnac to see the Druidical stones, which are very solemn and imposing. The sea is close by, with the sickle-shaped peninsula of Quiberon, where the emigrants landed and were beaten by Hoche, sweeping out into it. The Breton peasant has still a great deal of his old religious feeling—May is the Mois de Marie, and the sailors in whom Brittany abounds pay their thanks particularly in this month—every evening there is service in the Cathedrals and sermon—at Quimper (where the cathedral is beautiful) I went in one evening—the service lasts from 7½ to 9—it is in the nave which is nearly full—the bishop & clergy in a reserved place in front near the pulpit, then a mixed audience of gentry peasantry soldiers and sailors. There is one great lamp hung in the middle of the nave—no other light except that the image of Marie, which stands on the screen between the choir and the nave, looking towards the people with really a beautiful expression and attitude, has a branchwork of lights all round it during the services of this month—and below it a perfect conservatory of flowers, all *white*—lilies, white rhododendrons, white azaleas, arums, &c.—The preacher was a jesuit from Paris, and I soon had enough of him. But the Bishop of Quimper, Monseigneur Sergent, to whom I paid a long visit, is a very remarkable person—he is celebrated for his tolerance, and the sagacity and knowledge with which he spoke about the people and their education struck me exceedingly. I pick up a good deal that is very interesting and instructive—and the French ecclesiastics I must say are not the least interesting objects among those which I see. In the south I am going to see Lacordaire, and Cardinal Miolan[d], the Archbishop of Toulouse.[2] The latter the Papal Nuncio said was so bigoted a catholic that he would not give a Protestant a letter to him: but the Superior of the Soeurs has given me one: I am anxious to see him as Guizot says he is an excellent man, though austere. Of one thing I am convinced more & more—of the profoundly democratic spirit which exists among the lower orders, even among the Breton peasants. Not a spirit which will necessarily be turbulent or overthrow the present government—but a spirit which has irrevocably broken with the past, and which makes the revival of an aristocratic society *impossible*. The Orleanists &c. you see and hear plenty of in Paris, especially if you are English: but they go only skin deep into the nation: the legitimists, not so much as that; they are utterly insignificant. The clergy is very strong, and, on the whole favourable to the present régime.—I must stop—Flu will keep you informed of me: but will you some of you write to me, not later than by Wednesday's or Thursday's post, at the Poste Restante, Toulouse, Haute Garonne, France. Direct *Monsieur* Arnold. I am sorry, sorrier than I can well say, at William's ill success at Leeds.[3] Flu mentions it in a letter, but I have seen no particulars—indeed of the English elections I at present know next to nothing as the French papers which alone are acceptable in Brittany, hardly mention them. I see today, however, that the Tories have carried South Lancashire. I hope that the Liberals in the house will go to work at once and shew no quarter to this detestable government. Could you send to me at Toulouse some local papers with full accounts of the Leeds election & speeches. Love to my darling K, and to all.   Your ever affectionate son,

M. A.—

MS. *Frederick Whitridge.*

1. Edward Penrose Arnold, William Arnold's oldest child.
2. The nuncio gave him a letter to Lacordaire, Père Etienne to Monsignor

(Jean Marie) Mioland *archbishop* (*not* cardinal) of Toulouse and Narbonne (see above pp. 429, 447–48, and below pp. 453–54). Arnold's confusion arose not because he didn't know a cardinal from a canary but probably because the circumstances virtually provoked gossip. Archbishops and bishops were named by the head of state. Mioland's predecessor at Toulouse was *Cardinal* D'Astros (his successor, Monsignor Deprez, coming from Limoges, became a cardinal in 1879), but Mioland had been coadjutor archbishop since 1849, and, though D'Astros died in 1851, Mioland remained coadjutor till 1857. Arnold apparently did not see Mioland, who died on July 16 (*Almanach impérial*, 1859, p. 401; Gulik, *Hierarchia catholica medii aevi*, 7:70, 367, 8:501, 551).

    3. See above p. 434 n. 3.

Newcastle Commission Journal (Yale)

May 9. Monday.   called on M. Magin—dined with the Slades, with them to the Français. La Camaraderie[1] very good. Walked home. [Diary, Guthrie, 2:238, adds: 'hair cut take stalls at Français call on G. Sand, Cousin, Embassy, Rapet, Magin, Protestant Agent—']

May 10, Tuesday.   breakfasted with the Seniors. To get money &c. The Emperor went to Italy. Off in the evening to Bordeaux—fine evening. [Diary, Guthrie, 2:236, adds: 'Jews Schools? write to Flu call on Mad[am]e de Lutteroth & Mad[am]e de Circourt']

    1. May 9: Eugène Scribe's "La Camaraderie ou la courte échelle." For "Protestant Agent" see the next letter.

To Frances Lucy Wightman Arnold*

Paris

My darling Flu   Tuesday, May 10, [1859], 3 p.m.

    No letter from you, which is a grievous disappointment, but there is nothing of which I am surer than that it is not my darling's own fault. But all through yesterday I had been looking forward to hearing today—and I went out to breakfast this morning comforting myself with the thought that when I came back I should see your dear handwriting: I think it must be that you are still at Teddington—and that your letters posted there did not reach London in time for the mail train. I start tonight for Bordeaux and I am afraid it is too much to expect a letter from you there tomorrow but I have told the people here to forward your letter to me there, as soon as it comes.—After I wrote to you on Sunday I wrote a long letter to my mother—I never thanked you for sending me that most interesting letter of Fan's: then I went and had a hot bath which took the ache of the diligence out of my bones:

then I dined at the table d'hôte, sitting by a Captain Tomms, a brother of the Crimean general,[1] whom I see a good deal of here: then I strolled a little on the boulevard and finally went to Fanny du Quaire's. There I found Lady Burgoyne, her daughter & Col. Bruce, Henrietta Hampden,[2] a young Austrian, Mrs Waterton & her daughter Fanny, who is a great beauty, but not to my thinking so pretty as poor Maud. Col. Bruce is a grand gauche blond Anglais—I agree with Fanny in thinking him rather stupid: he cannot tell what to do with himself here, and lies in bed most of the day. Toddy is improved by her marriage and looks very well—but she never had much talk. I was tired and went home to bed about 11. Yesterday I went across the river before breakfast to see Magin the Inspector General, (whom I like extremely) and Rapet: came back here and breakfasted—then made calls on the Seniors, Mrs. Waterton and Lady Burgoyne, came back here and dressed and drove to Lady Slade's to dinner. Their cook has got his hand in, and the dinner was excellent: at 20 min. past 7 the two girls and I started in the carriage for the Français. We had Stalls de Balcon just where you and I were: the piece was La Camaraderie a 5 act comedy by Scribe and the whole strength of the company played—Regnier, whom you remember, capital— and besides him Madl. Plessy, their best actress and a splendidly handsome woman, and Samson the father of the Company,[3] whom you did not see. It was one of the best comedies, and one of the best acted that I ever saw, and if it is given while you are here you must go: you cannot imagine how the girls enjoyed themselves. It was followed by a modern comedy in two acts in verse—these are always dull, and we did not stay for it—but walked home together by the desire of the two girls. I have a note today from Lady Slade to say how much they enjoyed it. We got home about 11—just enough of the theatre, in my opinion. This morning I went early to the Oratoire to see the head of the Protestant School Agency:[4] then at 11 to breakfast with the Seniors—Miss Minnie makes herself very pleasant: they had the Polish General who commanded the Sardinian Army in the Novara Campaign and the talk was all about battles: the Pole gives the Sardinian Army a bad name but to look at him I should say their defeats must have been more owing to the general than the men. It appears certain that Francis Joseph, who is the most obstinate young fool on earth, keeps Hess at Vienna because he is jealous of him & has quarrelled with him; and Gyiulay is a mere general d'antichambre. If this is so, and it looks likely, the Austrians will be well beaten and well they will deserve it. But it is said here that the French do not at present expect to do more than drive them back upon Verona: Verona, Mantua, &c are too strong to take. Duvergier d'Hausanne, who was a deputy & minister under Louis Philippe, was also at Senior's, & another Orleanist ex-deputy, Lanjuinais.[5] After breakfast I went to the bank for money, went in and talked to the girls at the shop at the corner about the children, and came back here to have my great disappointment about the letter: then Monsieur Magin came to bring me letters of introduction for the South: and then came Theodore Martin, who brought down his wife, (Helen Faucit) and introduced me to her. She is an intellectual looking person[6]—but, as a woman, dowdy and untidy. She gave a reading unexpectedly at a house where she was dining the other night, of which the papers say wonders. Now I must pack up: and then I shall go and pay Gallois' bill, dine at the table d'hôte and set off for the Orleans station. How I miss you all, my darlings. Have all my sweet boys up to you separately and kiss them for Papa and tell them how he thinks of them & love[s] them: and kiss my sweet little Lu [?]Luee for me too. Tell Mrs Tuffin it makes me quite happy to think that you have got her to take care of you. I looked yesterday at what Budge says is her likeness. Write by Thursday's post to me at Toulouse, Haute Garonne. If you write tomorrow, to Bordeaux. I will write again on Thursday—and again on Sunday. God bless you, my own love—   Your own, always,

Cangrande.[7]

MS. Frederick Whitridge.

1. Unidentified.

2. Lt Col. Robert Bruce (1825—99), later colonel, 23d Fusiliers, son of Sir James Robertson, 2d baronet, had won several military medals. He married Mary Caroline ("Toddy") Burgoyne (d. 1893) in Feb. 1859.

Henrietta Hampden, the daughter of Renn Dickson Hampden (1793—1868: *DNB*), bishop of Hereford, one of the "Oxford Noetics," and intimate of Whately, Thomas Arnold, Keble, Hawkins, and the others. (Hampden was the storm center of one of the most notorious, prolonged, and bitter ecclesiastical controversies of the whole century; she published *Some Memorials* of her father in 1871.)

3. Jeanne Sylvanie Sophie Arnould-Plessy (1819—97), "Toujours belle, élégante, femme savante et charmante," noted later as *l'actrice de Marivaux*; Joseph Isidore Samson (1793—1871), "doyen de la Comédie" (Lyonnet).

4. "The Oratoire, in the rue Saint Honoré [at no. 145], belonging to the Protestants of the Confession of Geneva, [is] the most spacious church possessed by any Protestant sect in Paris" (*Paris and Its Environs*, ed. Thomas Forester, Bohn's Illustrated Library, 1859, p. 375; see also Hillairet, 2:424—25).

5. "*Tuesday, May 10th.*—Duvergier, Lanjuinais, and Chrzanowski breakfasted with us. We begged Chrzanowski to tell us what is to happen"—and the conversation is reported for five pages, though Arnold's name is unmentioned (Senior, 2:265—70). Gen. Albert Chrzanowski (1788—1861), Prosper Duvergier de Hauranne (1798—1881), Victor Ambroise, Vicomte Lanjuinais (1802—69), Heinrich Hermann Josef, freiherr von Hess (1788—1870), and Ferencz Gyulai (misread by Russell as "Gieslay"), comte de Maros-Németh Nádaska (1798—1868), are all noticed in *Encyclopædia Britannica*, 11th edn.

6. Theodore Martin, known for the *Bon Gaultier Ballads* (1845, with W. E. Aytoun) and, for Arnold certainly, as the husband of Helena Faucit (see above pp. 386—87), be-

came later the biographer of the Prince Consort and was a poet, translator, and parliamentary agent. See *Album*, pp. 51, 106–7.

7. See above, p. 396 n. 7. Russell's text signs off with "Ever yours, M. A."

Newcastle Commission Journal (Yale)

May 11, Wednesday.   Dull cold morning at Bordeaux. Hot bath. then saw the Archbishop & Secrétaire General. At Hôtel de France.

May 12, Thursday.   The Inspecteur de l'Académie called. With him and the Rector to the training school. Wrote letters in the afternoon. Walked about & to reading room.

May 13, Friday.   Hot day. Walked about seeing streets & churches. At 12½ with the Inspecteur Primaire to Blanquefort to see schools.[1] Walked to the Castle. Back to Bordeaux in the evening.

1. May 11–13: The archbishop was in fact Son Eminence M. le *Cardinal* (Ferdinand François Auguste) Donnet, the secrétaire-général M. Ferrand, the rector M. C. Dutrey, the inspecteur de l'académie M. Dauzet and the inspecteur primaire M. Benoît (both praised by Arnold in some interesting pages, Super, 2:123–30, and all listed in *Almanach impérial*, 1859, pp. 379, 554, 632).

To Frances Lucy Wightman Arnold*

Bordeaux
Saturday Morning, May 14, 1859

After I wrote to you the day before yesterday, I wrote a long letter to Lord Lansdowne, and that took me till six o'clock—the *table d'hôte* time. I sat by a Frenchman of Martinique, who was very pleasant. After dinner I strolled along the Quai des Chations [*for* Chartrons], which extends down the river a long way. The nuisance is one cannot go *on* the river to see the town and environs from it, as steamers are almost wholly wanting. There are two a day, morning and evening, to the mouth of the river, but the Ferry steamers which one has in such abundance at Liverpool are wholly wanting. The stream and tide are so powerful that little row boats are no use. It was a gloomy evening, blowing up with dust for a storm, which broke in rain just as I got into the reading room, under the Great Theatre. I have not been to the theatre—it is too hot. Yesterday morning I was up at seven—a day without a cloud. I was out at eight, wandering about the town, looking at old streets, churches, and market people. After breakfast I strolled to the post, going to the Prefecture on the way to read the Emperor's address to the army.[1] Very poor and empty, I think; not to be compared with his Manifesto, which was excellent. I got your letter and the *Galignani*, came back and read them under the porch of the hotel. By this time came a light open carriage I had ordered to take me to Blanquefort, and at the same time came the inspector, whom the authorities have given me—the head one of the Department, a Monsieur Benoit, a man of sixty or more, an old officer of the First Empire, who was at Vimeira [*for* Vimieiro][2] and in the capitulation of Cintra, and afterwards made the campaigns of Germany and the final campaign of France. He was what we call a jolly old fellow. We had a beautiful drive through a country of villas, gardens, and vines to Blanquefort, a little bourg about seven miles from here. I saw four schools there, and was much interested. The best was the girls' school, kept by the Soeurs of the Immaculate Conception. Afterwards we made the schoolmaster guide us to the ruined castle, which is in a green hollow on a little river at the foot of hills covered with vines at about a mile from Blanquefort. It is like every other ruined feudal castle, but the stone beautifully fresh, and the vegetation luxuriant. I scrambled to the top of the principal tower, and had a splendid view over the country. Not a soul, from M. Benoit to the *paysanne* who lives in a hut in the ruin, knew anything about the Black Prince's connexion with the castle; and M. Benoit told me there is no talk or tradition of him whatever in the country. The lions of England are clean gone from the gate, if they ever existed there. The Revolution has cleared out the feudal ages from the minds of the country people to an extent incredible with us. We got back here at six. After dinner another storm, from which I took refuge in the great reading-room, which has the *Times*. I read *Daniella*[3] to an end and went to bed. I write this before breakfast, then I shall pack up, and start at half-past eleven for Toulouse. I must tell you one or two good things here. One is a triple medallion picture of Marshal Randon, Prince Napoleon, and Marshal Vaillant,[4] with the Prince in the middle, and the names underneath, so as to run Randon (rendons) Napoleon Vaillant. Kiss my darlings for me. I shall write again from Toulouse tomorrow.

Text. Russell, 1 : 101–3.

1. At Genoa, on May 12, quoted in *Annual Register*, pp. 236–37.
2. Where Wellington defeated the French in Aug. 1808.
3. *La Daniella* (1857), George Sand's novel.
4. With a wit lost in the underbrush of explanation. Marshal Count Randon (1795–1871), minister of war briefly in 1851, was reappointed to that post May 9, 1859, replacing Marshal Vaillant (1790–1892), minister since 1854, who, summarily dismissed for incompetence, became now commander of the army of the Alpes: "J'ai toléré votre négligence pendant la paix; je ne dois pas la tolérer en guerre. J'ai nommé le Maréchale Randon votre successeur" (Senior, 2 : 268–69). See *Grande Encyclopédie*; *Almanach impérial*; 1859, *Encyclopædia Britannica*, 11th edn, *s.v.* "Italy," "Italian Wars."

Newcastle Commission Journal (Yale)

May 14th.   To Toulouse at 11 a.m. Fine morning, but changed at Agen and very wet & miserable. At Toulouse Hôtel de l'Europe.

May 15th. Sunday.   Fine morning after the rain but windy & cold. to the Column. After breakfast to make calls &c. Found the premier Président at home—long conversation with him. dined at table d'hôte.

May 16th, Monday.   Saw the town, and to the Cemetery. Still so so weather. In the evening the two Inspecteurs primaires called. Strolled about.

May 17. Tuesday.   In the morning with an Inspecteur primaire to the schools of the banlieue of Toulouse. In the afternoon at statistics with the Inspecteur de l'Académie, and seeing the Lycée. After dinner to call on the Rector.[1]

May 18, Wednesday.   To Musée & Town Hall—then off to Castelnaudary. Thence to Sorèze. Saw the Père Lacordaire[2] & his school—slept at village inn—better weather.

May 19 Thursday.   off about 5 for Castelnaudary: Thence by train to Carcassone. The weather at last hot. Saw the Cité de Carcassone. off about 4 by rail through Narbonne & Cette to Montpellier.[3]

May 20 Friday.   splendid southern weather. To the promenade of Montpellier—breakfasted—and to the Musée—very interesting Greuzes. In the afternoon to Nismes. Dined alone & strolled about.

May 21, Saturday.   To M. Deloche. With him to training schools & primary schools: then to the Maison Carrée and to call on the chief Protestant Pasteur. After dinner he came again—strolled about with him, and saw the Roman baths. Town poorly illuminated for the news of Montebello.[4]

May 22nd, Sunday.   To the Tourmagne. Arid singular country, with all its richness. To Arles—very hot, but storm showers. Saw the Amphitheatre, theatre, Cemetery, Cloisters, &c. Dined at the Hôtel du Nord, and back to Nismes. Plagued by Mosquitoes.

1. May 15–17: M. O. Piou was "premier président de la cour impériale de Toulouse" (*Almanach impérial*, 1859, p. 584). Only M. Cun is named as an inspecteur de l'instruction primaire at Toulouse; the inspecteur de l'académie was M. Peyrot; the Rector was M. C. Rocher (*Almanach impérial*, 1859, p. 584; Super 2:266).

2. May 18: Jean Baptiste Henri Lacordaire (1802–61), a liberal Catholic who reestablished the Dominicans in France, "the most renowned preacher in Europe," and founder of "one of the most successful private schools in France" (Arnold) in an old abbey

in the village of Sorèze. Arnold's wonderful essay *A French Eton* (Super, 2:262–325), surely the most beautiful by-product of a government report in existence, recounts his visit with Lacordaire with something of the tonality and passionate cadences of his near-poems in prose on Newman, George Sand, and Emerson.

"At nine I took my leave of Lacordaire and returned to the village inn, clean, because it is frequented by the relations of pupils. There I supped with my fellow travellers, the old scholars; charming companions they proved themselves. Late we sat, much *vin de Cahors* we drank, and great friends we became. Before we parted, one of them, the Bézier youth studying at Paris, with the amiability of his race assured me (God forgive him!) that he was well acquainted with my poems" (Super, 2:278).

3. May 19: See Super, 2:278–79 (at Carcassonne, "You rub your eyes and think that you are looking at a vignette in *Ivanhoe*") and Arnold's poem "A Southern Night" ("Cette, with its glistening houses white, Curves with the curving beach away") and notes in Allott, p. 495.

4. May 21: M. Deloche, at Nîmes, was the inspecteur de l'académie, Montpellier. The "chief Protestant Pasteur" was apparently M. Tachard, but interestingly the second name listed is that of [Ernest] Fontanès, to whom Arnold wrote about two dozen letters beginning Sept. 20, 1872, though there is no evidence that they met at Nîmes (*Almanach impérial*, 1859, pp. 569, 409).

The Austrian retreat from Montebello was announced on May 21.

To Jane Martha Arnold Forster

Hôtel du Luxembourg, Nismes

My dearest K   Sunday, May 22, 1859

I have to thank you for a letter and I cannot be here without thinking of you and dear Papa whom this south of France continually brings to my mind. You were most likely at this very hôtel it is improved and enlarged since that time but there is still left the old façade and name "Hotel du Luxembourg" which I imagine saluted your eyes as you drove up—and today I have been to Arles, where you were, and tomorrow I shall be at Avignon where you were also. I cannot express to you the effect which this Roman south of France has upon me[1]—the astonishing greatness of the ancient world, of which the provincial corners were so noble—its immense superiority to the Teutonic middle age—its gradual return, as civilisation advances, to the command of the world—all this, which its literature made me believe in beforehand, impresses itself upon my senses when I see these Gallo Roman towns. I like to trace a certain affinity in the spirit of these buildings between the Romans and the English: "you and the Romans," Guizot said to me the other day, "are the only two governing nations of the world": and ludicrously as we fail in the practice of architecture there is a gravity composure and strength about the Roman buildings which reminds me of the English character more than of anything else in the world. The French build beautifully, a thousand times better than we do—but in all they do, and they are doing a wonderful deal, there is something "coquet" in the grace and beauty which is utterly beneath the Roman dignity—which is quite Gaulish, in the spirit of that very clever people for whom two centuries ago Cæsar who beat them so soundly had evidently with all his appreciation of their cleverness so deep-rooted a contempt. But they have improved since that time with all the mixture of race they have had, and are certainly now a very wonderful people, though not the least Roman. Their prosperity and improvement is wonderful—the state of cultivation of this south of France, the exquisite order and perfection of its vast olive and vine crops, strike eyes even as ignorant as mine—and the one thing the people desire is to carry on this material improvement without anarchy and at the same time without any restoration of feudalism. You ask me whether they are attached to the present government: they are sincerely grateful to it for having restored order—I saw today at Arles on the Roman obelisk an inscription to Louis Napoleon with the simple words—"il nous a sauvés de l'Anarchie"—which you may depend upon it expresses the sincere feeling of the industrious classes. But above all the French peasant (who feeds the army and is the real power of France) sticks to this man and is disposed to maintain him because he is the symbol, after all, of that final breach with the past and with a feudal aristocracy by means of which the peasant has become a person[n]age and which he is firmly resolved shall never be filled up. In his mind, both branches of the Bourbons are connected with the old pre-revolution system, and that is why they are both antipathic to him. And there is a good deal of truth in the French peasant's view: Louis Napoleon is as little connected with the past as the French peasant—he has the ideas of the modern world in which he was long knocked about in a way in which the members of the old royal races—our queen or the Emperors of Russia and Austria cannot have them—in a way in which even the old aristocracies cannot have them. His uncle had them, too, and was a man of genius which this man is not—but he went off his centre with success and dashed himself to pieces. But you may depend upon it that it is a "mot" of the first Napoleon's which is now inspiring this second Napoleon—that the sovereign who put himself at the head of the cause of the peoples of Europe would be the master of the future.—And I firmly believe that his desire in invading Italy is to obtain the preeminence which he believes will accrue to him and to France by executing this idea of his uncle—not to get some perilous and useless kingdom of Etruria established again. In this sense he is, what the Italians call him, L'uomo del secolo:[2] and our worst chance is that our politicians and diplomatists are so bound up in routine and the traditions of the past, as I can perceive very well even by hearing Lord Cowley talk, that they cannot even conceive such a course as that of the French Emperor, and will be entirely unprepared for everything that happens. But this is the worst of aristocracies, with all their merits: they are *inaccessible to ideas*; and when civilisation comes to that point that ideas, and not mere tenacity, are wanted for the government of the world, they break down. So it was at Rome—so, I fear, it will be with us, unless our aristocracy, always so prudent, can get from others, and use, the lights which it has not itself. But our people's strong point is not intellectual coup d'œil, any more than our aristocracy's: & this is our worst chance.

There—I have filled my letter with all this dissertation—but it is every word true, and I like to write to you what I think. I wrote to Lord Lansdowne the other day, and told him as much as I could. There is a man with an open intelligence, if he had youth, faith, and commanding energy! But the true type of the British political nobleman is Lord Derby— with eloquence, high feeling, and good intentions—but the ideas of a school-boy.

I thought nothing could have been better than William's appearance at Leeds—but I was too provoked when I found how narrowly he had missed success. My love to him—I should like to wring his hand for poor dear Willy's sake.[3] Write me a line to Paris within the next week—you shall then have a more proper journalizing letter in answer. It is very hot, but I drink chocolate and get as brown and stout as Queen Pomone. Think of me at Vaucluse on Wednesday. My dearest K, you know how truly I am always   your affectionate brother,

M. A.—

Kiss the poor little darlings for me if they are with you when this reaches you. I shall be at Meurice's in Paris.

MS. *Frederick Whitridge.*

1. Part of the effect of this epiphany was pretty clearly *Culture and Anarchy!*
2. Arnold uses the phrase again below p. 479 and also in *England and the Italian Question* (Super, 1:91).
3. The Forsters, rich and childless, had taken in William Arnold's four children (whom they later adopted).

Newcastle Commission Journal (Yale)

May 23rd, Monday.   In a carriage to the Pont du Gard—bathed a little above it, a thunderstorm in the distance. On to Avignon, with a fine view back on the Cevennes. At Avignon at 7 p.m.

May 24th, Tuesday. To Vaucluse—a fine day. The water very high, with dashing breaks—lunched at the Hôtel de Pétrarque et de Laure. Strolled up to the Grande Place after dinner with two French picture dealers.

May 25th Wednesday. Very hot. Early to Orange to see the theatre—back to Avignon. breakfasted at station, and then a long séance with the Abbé Bonafous.[1] Thunder-storm came on. To the Popes' Palace, terrace &c view under storm-sky very fine. The Brights & Sir John & Lady Duckworth came from Italy—passed the evening with them.

May 26, Thursday. To Lyons. Rhone very high, and storms of rain from Valence onwards. Mrs. Longueville Clarke and her daughter.[2] Dined with them—afterwards strolled about Lyons.

May 27, Friday. Fine day. to Paris. Showers after Dijon. dined alone at Meurice's—then to see the du Quaires.

May 28, Saturday. To see Ary Scheffer's pictures.[3] Saw Mme de Circourt. dined alone at Véry's.

May 29, Sunday. After breakfast to M. de Circourt, and with him to see the antiques at the Louvre. After dining at table d'hôte went to see the du Quaires.

May 30, Monday. Called on Monckton Milnes,[4] afterwards M. de Circourt came with letters from Switzerland. Dined at table d'hôte. afterwards to M. Rapet's, and with him to see evening schools.

May 31, Tuesday. Wrote letters and drove about to make calls. Every one out but Fanny du Quaire. Dined alone at the Maison Dorée. Strolled in the Champs Elysées.

June 1, Wednesday. Saw Lord Brougham.[5] Called on M. Magin and had a long conversation with him. Heard from Lord Lansdowne, Lord Cowley and M. de Montalembert. Went to see M. Albert Cohen [*for* Cohn], and talked with him a long time. Dined at table d'hôte—then off by the [?]mail train to Amiens. Dull weather in Paris this time.

June 2, Thursday. Warm, very showery day. Went to see the Cathedral— then wrote letters—then called at the Prefecture, the Bishop's Palace and M. Allou's[6] all out. Came back & wrote journal. M. Allou called. Walked to the Citadel—then back to dine at the table d'hôte at the hôtel du Rhin. After dinner to M. Allou's and had a long business conversation. Home by the cathedral. Coffee in the Salle à Manger. I notice the feeling getting up against England.

June 3, Friday.   To Calais to meet dearest Flu. Her steamer grounded twice, but at last got in. Damp raw weather. Slept at Dessin's [7]—abandoned & melancholy. Saw the Beaumont Holbein.

June 4, Saturday.   Off at 7.45 a.m. for Brussels. Breakfasted at Lille. Warm fine day. At Brussels after dinner. drove round by Laeken & about the town. Dined & slept at the Bellevue.

June 5, Sunday.   Up late, to St. Gudule, the Post Office & the Hôtel de Ville. In afternoon to Antwerp. It came on wet. Dined & slept at the St. Antoine. To the Cathedral to see the pictures, and after dinner in the wet to the banks of the Scheldt [*for* Schelde].

June 6, Monday.   Fine morning. Off early by Moerdyk & Rotterdam to the Hague. At Rotterdam saw the statue of Erasmus, the Park, and the church. To the Bellevue at the Hague.

June 7th, Thursday.   Very hot—trying climate. Called at the British Legation—Mr. Ward [8] absent. Walked in the Bois. At 2 again to the Legation, and with Mr. Ward to the Affaires Etrangères. In the evening with Flu to Scheveningen. It came on wet, but fine sunset.

June 8, Wednesday.   ⟨To the Home Office, and saw the Réferendaire.[9] Long conversation with him⟩ With Flu to the Museum. Saw the shirts &c worn by William the Third the last day or two of his life and the whole dress of William the Silent when assassinated—the pistols &c. After dinner drove in the Bois and heard the music. Very hot weather,

June 9, Thursday.   To the Home Office, and saw the Réferendaire. Long conversation with him. Then with Flu to the Baron Steengracht's Collection. Then with M. Van Citters to large poor school.[10] Afterwards to dine at Scheveningen, and pleasant walk on the sands. Met Mr. Ward there.

June 10, Friday.   Off in the morning to Leyden. Damp cloudy oppressive day. Called on M. Leemans, and afterwards saw the Botanic Gardens, University, Library, Museum of Natural History, Burg and Town Hall. Back to the Hague to dine and sleep.

June 11, Saturday.   In morning to Amsterdam. Still warm. to call on M. Beeloo—found him out. Dined at table d'hôte—then to M. Beeloo, and long conversation.[11]

1. May 25: Abbé Bonafous, inspecteur d'académie d'Aix, at Avignon. Sir John Thomas Buller Duckworth (1809–87, succeeded as second and last baronet in 1817), out

of Eton and Oriel College, Oxford (B.A. 1829), M.P. for Exeter 1845–57; his wife, the former Mary Buller, survived him.

2. May 26: Mrs Longueville Clarke was perhaps the wife of Loftus Longueville Tottenham Clarke (d. Apr. 24, 1863), admitted to Trinity Hall, Cambridge, in 1811, and later barrister-at-law of the Supreme Court of Calcutta (Venn).

3. May 28: Ary Scheffer (1795–1858), well-known and fashionable painter, whose niece (and adopted daughter), Cornélie Scheffer, Renan had married in 1856.

4. May 30: Mérimée, who saw also Milnes, was less discreet and wrote to an English friend on May 31: "Monckton Milnes, qui est ici depuis quelques jours, est très affirmatif. Il annonce que le 10 du mois prochain, à deux heures après minuit, vous, Messieurs les whigs, mangerez lord Derby et compagnie" (*Correspondance*, 9:128). Milnes predicted the menu exactly. See below p. 461.

5. June 1: Henry Peter Brougham (1778–1868: *DNB*), Baron Brougham and Vaux, one of the founders and mainstays of the *Edinburgh Review*, had been Lord Chancellor twice, and is important in the history of reform (legal, social, educational) in early nineteenth-century England. His obituary in the *Annual Register* summed him up as "almost everything in turn—a mathematician, an historian, a biographer, an essayist and reviewer, a physical philosopher, a moral and political philosopher, an educator of the people, a lawyer, an orator, a statesman, a philanthropist." But a contemporary said: "If the lord chancellor only knew a little law, he would know a little of every thing." Brougham had long owned a house in Cannes, where he died and was buried. See *Album*, p. 81. For Albert *Cohn* see above p. 438 n. 3.

6. June 2: Allou was the inspecteur de l'académie de Douai, at Amiens (*Almanach impérial*, p. 563).

7. June 3: Dessin's (or Dessein's), the old established inn known to Sterne (see the opening pages of *A Sentimental Journey*), Turner, and Ruskin, who mentions it several times (*Works*, ed. Cook and Wedderburn, 2:398, 12:381, 35:416). See below, p. 460.

8. June 7: John Ward, identified by Arnold as "the British Secretary of the Legation in Holland" and "the British Chargé d'Affaires at the Hague" (Super, 2: 200n, 204).

9. June 8: "M. [Hendrik] Vollenhoven, the Referendary charged with the department of primary instruction. . . . M. Vollenhoven not only furnished me with all the official documents which I wished to consult on the subject of primary instruction in Holland, but obligingly placed me in communication with the school-inspectors of the localities which I proposed to visit" (Super 2:204,421).

10. June 9: "My guide at the Hague was M. van Citters, a member of one of the best families in Holland, of good fortune, and a man of letters, but, with the public spirit of which I have before spoken as distinguishing his countrymen, giving his services gratuitously as a school-inspector" (Super, 2:204).

11. June 10–11: As William the Silent evoked Dr Arnold, so the old universities recalled Oxford. "It was impossible for me to enter without emotion the halls and lecture-rooms of Leyden and Utrecht, illustrious by the memory of a host of great names, and recalling by their academic costume, their academic language, or their classical predilections, the venerable Universities of our own country" (Super, 2:188). Beeloo has not been identified.

To Mary Penrose Arnold*

Amsterdam

My dearest Mother   Sunday, June 12, 1859

I wrote to you about 10 days ago from Amiens—I don't think I told
you where to write—at all events I have not heard since, and am very anxious to have some news of you all. I went on from Amiens to Calais the day
after I wrote to you—there I met dear Flu, and we slept at Dessin's which
has fallen into a melancholy state of damp and desertion: the old master is
still there however. Next day we went on to Brussels—and on Sunday evening on from Brussels to Antwerp. On Monday morning from Antwerp to
Rotterdam and thence to the Hague: we stayed at the Hague nearly all the
week having only left it yesterday. A small taste of Holland is sufficient, one
place is so exactly like another: it is like England more than any other part of
the continent is—that is it is like the slightly old-fashioned red-brick England of parts of London and the towns of the southern counties—like the
new characterless towns of the midland counties & the north it is not in the
least. The people occupy separate houses, as in England instead of living in
flats—this makes the houses smaller and more varying in size than in the
continental towns in general. The language sounds much more like English
than the German does—and better than the German, less pedantic—but it
has none of the distinction & command which the Latin element so happily
gives to the English language. The climate is detestable—when the sun
shines the exhalations from the canals make an atmosphere which is the closest and the most unwholesome I ever breathed—and when the sun does not
shine the weather is raw grey and cold. The general impression Holland,
curious as it is, makes on me, is one of mortal *Ennui*: I know no country &
people where that word seems to me to apply with such force. You have the
feeling which oppresses you so in Suffolk & Norfolk that it all leads nowhere,
that you are not even on the way to any beautiful or interesting country. The
Hague is a town of 70,000 people, with a number of streets of excellent
houses, bordered with fine trees—I never saw a city where the well to do
classes seemed to have given the whole place so much their own air of wealth
finished cleanliness & comfort—but I never saw one, either, in which my
heart would have so sunk at the thought of living. This place is far better—
for it has great animation and movement—and it has one of the two interesting things I have seen in Holland—the Palace or old Hôtel de Ville—an
immense Renaissance building all stone & marble within & without. Its size
and its stone amidst the pettiness and brick of Holland produces on me the
effect of a mountain—and is a wonderful refreshment. The other interesting

object in Holland is the face of William the Silent, the founder of the House of Orange, which meets one everywhere in statues or pictures. You remember how great a reverence Papa had for him and he is one of the finest characters in history—his face is thoughtful & melancholy—quite a history in it—and is interesting in the highest degree. Pictures we have seen without end, it is a great pleasure to me to find I get fonder & fonder of seeing them—can pass, without having or wishing to have the least of a connoisseur's spirit about them, more and more hours in looking at them with untired interest. We are now just going to see a private collection here—then we are going to Saardam [Zaandam] to see the hut where Peter the Great lived while working as a ship's carpenter—one of the best incidents in history, and one of the spots I would on no account leave Holland without seeing. I am not much taken with their people, but not speaking their language is a great disadvantage. I doubt however whether they have not a good deal fallen off from the élan which made them so great in the 16th & 17th century. It is the Norman element in England which has kept her from getting stupid & humdrum too, as the pure Germanic nations tend to become for want of a little effervescing salt with their magnesia. Tomorrow we shall go to Haarlem—I to see a training school—Flu to hear the organ: the next day to Utrecht—the day after, I hope to Paris. We had accounts of the children today, dated Thursday: all going well. I think not a day passes without my thinking 5 or 6 times of you, dear Fan, & Fox How—I never so much longed to be there, and certainly get fonder of it every year—and how this day brings it and all of you present to me! Write to me at Meurice's at Paris—we hope to be there in a few days and shall stay there till Monday or Tuesday week next—but before that time I will write again. I see the Emperor's address to the Italians confirms all I think as to the line he is taking. I see too by a telegraphic despatch that our Government is beaten— which I am heartily glad of so far as they, & above all Lord Malmesbury & Lord Derby, are concerned[1]—but I am not very sanguine as to the esprit de conduite & lumières[2] of their successors. Flu's love—she will be glad to be out of Holland. I am always, my dearest Mother, CC—Your most affectionate son

M. A.—

I have heard & seen nothing of Edward. How is my dear old Susy. Will she & John meet us in Switzerland?

MS. Balliol College.

1. James Howard Harris (1807–89: *DNB*; *VF*, 7/25/74), 3d earl of Malmesbury, Derby's foreign secretary, was a strong supporter (and old friend) of Napoleon III.

2. Close to Burke's "The men of England, the men, I mean of light and leading in England" etc. (*Reflections on the Revolution in France*, p. 111, World's Classics edn).

Newcastle Commission Journal (Yale)

June 12, Sunday.   Rainy morning. to church. Afterwards with Bolander to the Palace, and went to the top. then to the Museum. Christ bearing the Cross—a small picture by Rubens. Portrait of William the Third holding a candle. Dined at the Hôtel des Pays Bas with the Dents.[1] then drove with them to the synagogue of the Portuguese Jews, and all round the town. To Café.

June 13. Monday.   Much colder. First to see Jews' schools—then to Saardam [Zaandam]. Great crowd, and dull raw day, but Peter's hut very interesting. Saw M. Six's collection. Gerard Dous wonderful.[2] After dinner to Café.

June 14, Tuesday.   Cold, fresh day. Off at 10½ a.m. to Haarlem, with the Dents. Breakfasted there. then to the organ in the noble church. Then I went to the Training School—saw an elementary school for children of the richer classes, and two for poor children. Then to station, and walked a little in the Bois d'Haarlem. Back to a late dinner here, passing a great fire at the entrance to Amsterdam. Dined & to the Café. Wrote this & to bed.

June 15th, Wednesday.   To Utrecht in the middle of the day. Called on M. Hoijtema[3] and with him to see two great elementary schools and the University. Dined at table d'hôte. The inn, Pays Bas, a desert. After dinner drove with Flu to Zeist. Perpetual country houses and better country. Beautiful church at Utrecht, but interior spoiled. I strolled about in the evening, and had coffee.

June 16, Thursday.   Off at 8½ by train to Rotterdam—thence by steamer back to Moerdyk, Antwerp, & Brussels. At dinner at the Bellevue found the Dents. After dinner I strolled about & had coffee with Mr. Dent. Flu went out with his wife and sister. fine but cold.

June 17, Friday.   Off at 8¼ to Paris. Flu with a hay-cold After dining alone at Meurice's we strolled about a little: found the Du Quaires out. Good accounts from Broughtons.[4]

June 18, Saturday.   Dear Flu not the thing. Went with her to Ary Scheffer's pictures, after having made a long call on M. Lorrain.[5] Dined at the table d'hôte and then drove in the Bois de Boulogne.

June 19, Sunday.   Flu not well, and the weather bad. M. Lorrain called and sate some time. In the afternoon with Flu to Archer Gurney's chapel⁶— and afterwards to dine at Véry's.

1. June 12: Bolander has not been identified. John Dent Dent (1826–94), of Stanhope Place, London, and Ribston Hall, Wetherby, Yorks, was educated at Eton and Trinity College, Cambridge, was M.P. for Knaresborough 1852–57, for Scarborough 1857–59, 1860–74; later a director and then chairman of the North Eastern Railway. His wife (d. 1917) was the former Mary Hebden Woodall (*Landed*; Boase; *Who's Who of British Members of Parliament*, 1:108).

2. June 13: Dou's paintings at Zaandam are now in the Rijksmuseum, Amsterdam: The Dentist, A Girl at the Window, A Candle-light Effect (*Bryan's Dictionary of Painters and Engravers*, s.v. Dou).

3. June 15: "M. van Hoijtema . . . he is a Government official . . . a man of great intelligence, experience, and weight. At the same time that he is a school-inspector of Utrecht, he is also first judge of the Military court of the province" (Super, 2:197)

4. June 17: *Hay-cold* is not in *OED*. The Rev. Delves Broughton (1812–63), brother of the 10th Baronet Broughton, with his family. His wife (the former Jane Bennett) died in 1860; they had four children, of whom the youngest was the novelist Rhoda Broughton (1840–1920: *DNB*), whom Arnold knew well in later years (see *Album*, pp. 77–78).

5. June 18: Paul Lorain, "distinguished in the service of public instruction in France, was one of the agents employed by M. Guizot in the inspection of 1833; his most interesting book [*Tableau de l'instruction primaire en France*, Paris, 1837] is a summary of the results of the whole inspection" (Super, 2:65–66).

6. June 19: Archer Thompson Gurney (1820–87: *DNB*) was called to the bar in 1842 but abandoned it for the church, and after various curacies was appointed chaplain to the Embassy in Paris, at the Court Chapel, no. 3, rue d'Aguesseau (where he remained till 1871). See Hailleret, 1:68, *Galignani's New Paris Guide*, 1861, pp. 122, 588, and Tennyson 2:119, 560.

To Frances Bunsen Trevenen Whately Arnold*

Paris
Sunday, June 19, 1859

We have a dull suite of rooms here in the inner court, but charmingly furnished and plenty of them—an ante-room, a dressing-room, a sitting-room, and a bedroom. I care very little for the look-out at this time of year; one is out so much, and when indoors, occupied. I am delighted to be out of Holland and back here, where the soil is dry and one can communicate with the natives. What wounds one's feelings in Holland is the perpetual consciousness that the country has no business there at all. You see it all below the level of the water, soppy, hideous, and artificial; and because it exists against nature, nobody can exist there except at a frightful expense, which is very well for the natives, who may be thankful to live on any terms, but disagreeable for foreigners, who do not like to pay twice as much as elsewhere for being half as comfortable. How I thought of the abundance and prodigality of the truly "boon" nature [1] of Guienne and Languedoc, from which I had just come. In Holland what is most disagreeable is the climate; you live in a constant smell of ooze, at least in summer,—hot ooze when in the sun, cold ooze when you go under the trees. The pleasant moment is when you get on the open beach, at Schevening, for instance, with the waves tumbling and the wind whistling; but even then you cannot help feeling that the sea ought, if it had its rights, to be *over* the beach and rolling across the country for miles inland. Last Wednesday morning we left Amsterdam, and I went to Utrecht. At Utrecht you begin to have a sniff of dry, wholesome air, and the trees look as if they stood in real ground, and the grass as if it was not growing in the water. In the evening we drove out six miles on the prettiest side to Zeist, a Moravian village—one succession of country houses, gardens, and small parks, the best we had seen in Holland, but even there *quel ennui*! The next day by rail to Rotterdam, where we embarked on the Maas. The sweep of Rotterdam seen from the river, wrapt in smoke, with its towers and spires, and brick houses, breaking through, with masts of ships everywhere, reminds one very much of London; in fact, the great towns of Holland remind one constantly of one side of England—its commercial side; but never does one feel more the splendid variety of England, that it has so much more than its mere commercial side; and even its commercial side it has on a scale so prodigious that this has a grandiosity of its own which in Holland is nowhere to be found. It was a dull, cold, blustering day—unluckily, we have too many of them in England,—and when we finally landed and looked back across the broad Maas at the cloudy plains and trees of Holland, I felt that we had got into the real world again, though I dislike Belgium, and think the Belgians, on the whole, the most contemptible people in Europe. We went right through Antwerp to Brussels, which is a desert just now; slept there, and on by the express on Friday morning here, arriving about six o'clock. The fashionable world has left Paris, and there are fewer carriages than in the spring, but Paris, like London, has always immense life and movement in its streets. I did not tell you of two things I was very much interested in seeing in the museum at the Hague: one, the shirt and undershirt worn by our William III. the last two days of his life, while he kept his bed after his fatal fall from his horse; the other, the entire dress which William the Silent wore when he was assassinated, with the pistol and ball which did the deed.

Now we are going to church. We hope on Wednesday night to go to Strasbourg. Suppose you write to me there at the Hôtel de Ville de Paris. We shall be two days there. I am seeing a great deal, but you at Fox How are never long out of my mind. I am glad you saw Blackie.[2] I believe he is an animated, pleasant man, with a liking for all sorts of things that are excellent. *Au reste*, an *esprit* as confused and hoity toity as possible, and as capable of translating Homer as of making the Apollo Belvedere.

My love to my dearest mamma, and to Edward, who is a rogue for giving me no news of himself, from Flu and myself both, and I am always your affectionate brother,

M. A.

Text. Russell, 1 : 106–9.

1. "But Nature boon / Poured forth profuse" (*Paradise Lost* 4. 242–43).
2. John Stuart Blackie (see above p. 266 n. 4 and Super, 1 : 207).

Newcastle Commission Journal (Yale)

June 20, Monday. Flu still far from well. I called on Lord Cowley and had a long and interesting conversation. Dined at the table d'hôte. M. Du Quaire called late.

June 21, Tuesday. Flu no better. Called on M. Magin, and sate with him a long time. Dined at table d'hôte—Hudson there, and very kind to Flu. Fanny Du Quaire called in the evening. In afternoon with M. Cohen [*for* Cohn] to all the Jew schools.

June 22, Wednesday. Dear Flu a little better—called on Rapet, & with him to British school. Dined at the table d'hôte and to the Français to see Figaro.[1] Flu liked it & was not tired. Walked home.

June 23, Thursday. Flu on the whole better. Drove out with her in the morning—packing in the afternoon. Off at 8 p.m. to Nancy. Flu not comfortable in the train.

June 24, Friday. At Nancy at 4 a.m. Hôtel de France dirty. Up at 8 and out to see M. Millot.[2] Then back to dear Flu & about the town with her a little: but her attack returned, and a very bad day with her. With M. Millot to schools: then dined and off at 6 to Strasbourg. Dearest Flu very ill and suffering in the train. Got ⟨here⟩ to Strasbourg, and in splendid quarters there by about 11 at night.

1. June 22: Beaumarchais, "Le Mariage de Figaro."
2. June 24: Millot was the secrétaire de l'académie de Nancy (*Almanach impérial*, 1859, p. 571).

To Mary Penrose Arnold*

Strasbourg
My dearest Mother   June 25, 1859
    I have Fan's letter this morning with a delightfully good account of you all—and a real summer day without a cloud in the sky has come at last to make travelling pleasant, and to light up this charming old town with its high roofs and great houses, the old ones of white plaster, and the new ones of the most beautiful pink stone in the world. The whole country round, the plain of Alsace, is to me one of the pleasantest anywhere: so genially productive, so well cultivated and so cheerful—yet with the Vosges and the Black Forest and the Alps to hinder its being prosaic. And one is getting near Switzerland, and I shall see the lake of Geneva, I hope and trust, before the month of June quite ends. I had promised myself to see it in May, with the spring flowers out in the fields—but that could not be managed. And the news of another great French victory[1] has just come—and every house has the tricolor waving out of its windows—and tonight, this beautiful night that it is going to be, every window will be lighted up, and the spire of the Cathedral will be illuminated, which is a sight. I shall go down towards the Rhine & Desaix's Monument to see the effect from there. All this is very well, but there is a dark side as there always is—poor Flu is not at all well. She arrived in Paris with a violent intermittent cold and slight diarrhœa: the cold which was like hay fever, yielded to quinine, but the diarrhœa was very obstinate, and she had a wretched time in Paris, as weak and miserable as possible, no remedies producing much effect, and she having to pass most of her day in bed, without companion or maid, and I obliged to be a good deal out. The rooms we had at Meurice's did not suit her—and on Thursday night we started for Nancy, where we arrived at 4 in the morning and got to bed—but she would get up at about 10 when I went out, and the diarrhœa again became very troublesome with terrible pain. At 6 in the evening I put her into the train to come here—but once or twice I thought she would have had to stop at some wretched little place on the line, she suffered so much and was so exhausted. I got her on however and was rewarded for the effort by getting charming rooms here au premier, in the front of the house with all the sun—a large bed-room & sitting-room. She got to sleep after taking some arrow-root, and had a good night on one of those French beds which make all other beds seem instruments of torture, and has had no more diarrhœa since. But she is very weak and in great pain so this morning I got a doctor, the best here, who has prescribed for her, and keeps her in bed which is the great thing. Quiet and rest and a good air are what she wants, he says, and Switzerland

will do her a great deal of good, I hope and believe. But having such splendid quarters I shall stay on here till over Monday. Then to Berne—then, I hope, to Geneva for a week. So pray write to me at the *Hôtel de la Couronne*, Geneva—10 p. m. Dearest Flu is decidedly better—the doctor's preparation of gum orange flower water & opium seems to have quieted her and done her good—this evening she has crept to the balcony to see what she could of the illuminations.

The doctor forbade brandy & water and ordered her to take bordeaux & water—another instance of the extraordinary value which the French, I notice attach to bordeaux wine as a stomachic, quite contrary to our notions: to be sure our claret is so doctored & adulterated with brandy & messes that it is no longer a pure bordeaux, which the French assert to be the best and wholesomest of tonic astringents. From what I have seen I am beginning to think they are right and certainly it has suited Flu admirably besides being so much more palatable than brandy. She has not lost much in not seeing the illuminations they are so formal—long invariable lines of light following the lines of the house architecture: the spire of the Minster is curious to see lighted up, but I confess not so beautiful as I expected. But one ought to see it from the hills twenty miles off. You know the people here are among the Frenchest of the French, in spite of their German race & language: it strikes one as something unnatural to see this German town and German speaking people all mad for joy at a victory gained by the French over other Germans: the fact speaks much for the French power of managing & attaching its conquests, but little for the German character. The Rhine provinces in 1815 after having belonged to France for only 10 years objected exceedingly to being given back to Germany. The truth is that though French occupation is very detestable French administration since the revolution is, it must be said, equitable & enlightened and promotes the comfort of the populations administered. They are getting very angry here with Prussia—and, if Prussia goes to war, there will be a cry in this country to compel the Emperor to take the limit of the Rhine, whether he wishes it or no. That the French will beat the Prussians all to pieces—even far more completely and rapidly than they are beating the Austrians, there cannot be a moment's doubt: and they know it themselves. I had a long and very interesting conversation with Lord Cowley, tête à tête for about three quarters of an hour the other day: he seemed to like hearing what I had to say, and told me a great deal about the French Emperor and about the Court of Vienna, and their inconceivable infatuation as to their own military superiority to the French. He entirely shared my conviction as to the French always beating any number of Germans who come into the field against them: they will never be beaten by any nation but the English, for to every other nation they are, in efficiency & intelligence, decidedly superior. I shall put together either for a pamphlet or for Fraser, a sort of résumé of the present question, as the result of what I have thought, read, and observed here, about it.[2] I am very well and only wish I was not so lazy, but hope & believe one is less so from 40 to 50, if one lives, than at any other time of life. The loss of youth ought to operate as a spur to one, to live more by the head when one can live less by the body. Have you seen Mill's book on Liberty?[3] It is worth reading attentively, being one of the few books that inculcate tolerance in an unalarming and inoffensive way. I must stop— but don't forget to tell dear Susy what real pleasure it gives us both to hear that she is herself again, dear old soul. My next must be to K—but let her see this, as a sign of life from me, bless her. Edward is an impostor; I have long known it. My term is lengthened a month—but I shall be back in England about the 1st August, if all goes well: & the children will meet us at Dover where we shall stop. Tell me how Caroline (my love to her) goes on: Flu & I often talk of her little boy, and how much we should like to see him. My love to Rowland—Fan does not say whether she did my commission to dear old Bankes. Your ever affectionate

M. A.—

The children's address is Atlingworth House, Marine Parade, Brighton.

MS. Balliol College.

1. The Battle of Solferino (see *Annual Register*, pp. 93–94).
2. *England and the Italian Question* (Super, 1:65–96, and notes, pp. 234–38).
3. John Stuart Mill's *On Liberty*, published in the first half of Feb. 1859 (*Publishers' Circular*).

Newcastle Commission Journal (Yale)

June 25, Saturday.   Flu slept well—but still far from right. Sent for a doctor, who was very encouraging, but said she must keep quiet. She all day in bed. I to call on M. Mædon and with him to the Protestant [?]Female Training School. Found Flu better. Dined alone at the table d'hôte. Illumination for news of Solferino.

June 26, Sunday.   Dearest Flu better. With M. Mædon to see the Bishop, the Rector, M. [?]Fritry, the Inspecteur d'Académie, &c.[1] Flu up in the afternoon, but I still alone at the table d'hôte. Beautiful weather.

June 27, Monday.   Flu decidedly better. In the morning to the Inspector's Bureau. At 1½ p.m. with Flu M. Mædon & the Inspecteur primaire first to the Orangerie, where Flu was left—then to the Robertson schools. Brought

Flu back, and out again to see the garden &c of the Ecole Normale. Excellent Director. Dined alone at table d'hôte—but afterwards dear Flu drove with me to the Kehl bridge, & walked over it with me. She really better—and weather lovely.

June 28, Tuesday.   Flu still going on well. I out to get money, and to the Cathedral. Then wrote this. Off to Bale in middle of the day. Slept at Trois Rois.

June 29, Wednesday.   Wet day. Off in middle of day, by [new] route rail,[2] to Berne. At the Faucon.

June 30, Thursday.   At Berne. To Embassy, and with Secretary of Legation to the Minister of the Interior. Bathed. Weather clearing. Drove in the evening.

July 1, Friday.   Fine day. To Geneva by rail to Bienne, thence steamer to Yverdon, thence rail to Geneva. Day magnificent in the afternoon and evening. In Geneva at the Couronne. [?]Sailed in the evening.

July 2, Saturday.   At Geneva; bathed; drove in the evening. Called on M. Cardolle[3]

1. June 25–26: [?]Mædon and [?]Fritry, unidentified, are not named in the *Almanach impérial*, 1859; the bishop was Monsignor (André) Roess (p. 403); the recteur de l'académie was M. O. Delcosso (p. 582); the inspecteur de l'instruction primaire, M. Payen (p. 582).

2. June 29: "Down to the year 1855 the only railway in Switzerland was a short line from Zürich to Baden. . . . The reason of this was not, as generally supposed, the extreme natural difficulties of the country. . . . the real difficulty consisted in the extraordinary and incredible jealousies between not only the different cantons, but the different communes or parishes, and the legal difficulties in obtaining the land. . . . *The Central Swiss Railway*, from Basle . . . to Berne . . . open" (Murray's *Handbook for Travellers in Switzerland and the Alps of Savoy and Piedmont*, 1861, pp. xxiii–xxiv).

3. July 2: The words transcribed as "Called on M. de Cardolle" are heavily blotted, and the reading is a guess. See below p. 475.

To Jane Martha Arnold Forster

Hôtel de la Couronne, Geneva
My dearest K   Saturday, July 2, 1859

I suppose I shall not have another of your dear long letters until I write to you again—though I begged Mamma to keep you informed of my existence by sending you my letter to her. Dear Flu has been very well—diarrhœa setting in, upon a state of health enfeebled by nursing and anxiety, reduced her very much, and though I have great confidence in her tenacity, I was rather alarmed about her on the journey from Paris to Strasbourg. At Strasbourg however perfect rest excellent quarters and the sedatives of a curious little doctor brought her round—and though for some days she continued very weak and shaky, I think she has now got quite round and is better than she has been since little Lucy was born. We have unmixedly good accounts of her and her brothers—little Lucy, Miss Nicholls says, gets prettier and prettier every day—if I get back and see her at the beginning of August I shall scarcely know her, she will be so much grown. Dicky gets fatter and fatter—Tom has got over his last cough and seems setting in for his summer spell of good health—poor Budge seems the least flourishing, as the state of his mesenteric glands is said to be wrong, and he is losing flesh and firmness. There is no one of them I miss more than that darling old rogue, and as each of the others is a special favourite with other people I always fancy Budge particularly appreciates my fondness for him and purrs up against me like a dear fat kitten. It is Tom's birthday on Wednesday—he expects nothing on it from Flu and me as he knows we are too far off to send him a toy—but we have been today to have our photographs taken and are going to send them to him in a letter for a surprize: if they are good I shall have copies struck off for a birthday present to you also: but I don't much expect they will be.— There is hardly a soul here though the weather is beautiful: I have never known so few English travelling. We have a great room au second here, both windows looking right down the lake of Geneva: it is to this inn that Papa used to come—I still like it the best though the English go more to the Ecu and the Bergues. But, though in full seasons one complains of the rush and crowding, all the inns are certainly made a little dull just now by the great absence of travellers, organized as they are for the reception of such numbers: the great staircases and passages look deserted, and the tables d'hôte have some three or four guests lost at one end of one of their long tables. But Geneva itself I retain all my fondness for and it is certainly one of the places in the world where I could most willingly live. The purity of the water all about is to me a great charm—and it is one that so many of the Swiss places—even Zermatt & Chamounix—are without. We came to Basle on Tuesday evening from Strasbourg—there the weather was bad and we came on to Berne by the new line through the Jura (which is beautiful) in cloud and rain—and at Berne we had dull weather, which made that dull town duller still. We came here on Friday by the new route rail from Berne to Bienne, steamer from Bienne to Yverdon, & rail again thence to Geneva. It was a dull morning, but the day gradually cleared, and by the time we got into the lake of Neuchâtel the weather was perfect—the rich wooded sides of the Jura all burnished with the sunshine, and that cheerful lake bluer and cheerfuller than ever. When we came on the first view of the lake of Geneva just before Lausanne the whole region had its glorious fine weather look, and presently through the great Savoy gap came the chain of Mont Blanc, snowed and frosted and sparkling down to a lower level than you ever saw him—so severe has been the weather here and so long continued the rains. All today has been another of these perfect summer days, though there is a haze which prevented the rosy effect on Mont Blanc at sunset tonight which I drove up to Saconnex on purpose that Flu might see: but it is much rarer than people think. I never shall forget that my first sight of the high Alps—the Oberland, in 1848—was with this rosy glow upon them in perfection. It is a great temptation to go up to Chamounix—but it lies out of the line of my business too decidedly. I have to go to Sion to see the Cantonal authorities there—and I dare say, if this fine weather continues, we shall be tempted up to Zermatt for a Saturday and Sunday. Write to me here at the *Ecu*, as we shall go to that inn, by Flu's wish, on our return here in a week or so. I have not said a word about politics: you ask if the literary class in France do not form an important opposition to the Government: a few of them, such as Villemain, make determined opposition and have a certain importance: but generally speaking a strong government like the Emperor's has a tendency to rally the literary men to it, though it does not improve them: and the young literary men come out for the most part as journalists and pamphleteers on the Government side, and look upon Villemain and his set as belonging to an extinct world. The Emperor's great force is that he is so carrying the present generation of Frenchmen along with him, and making every other party in France look obsolete and cliquish. All this by virtue of his fibre populaire, which is his great endowment.[1] I think of writing a sort of resumé of the present condition of things in Europe in relation to the Italian question, if I get time or rather resolution. You should read Mill on Liberty: has William?—What Cobden, I see, says of the growing good feelings of the Americans towards England is quite confirmed by all one sees of their travellers here abroad.[2] What a blessing the growth of such a feeling may prove. My love to William and kiss all your dear little things for Flu & me—tell Eddy Tom and Trev. will be so glad to see him again. I am always, my dearest K,   your most affectionate brother

M. A.—

MS. Frederick Whitridge.

    1. "It is that he possesses, largely and deeply interwoven in his constitution, the popular fibre" (*England and the Italian Question* [Super, 1 : 81]). See above pp. 467–68.
    2. Cobden's return home on June 29 after four months in the United States was reported briefly in *The Times* (July 1, p. 10, reprinting from the *Manchester Examiner*) but lengthily in *Galignani's Messenger* on July 2 (p. 4): "We have made strong and fast friends,"

he said on arriving in Liverpool, "and bound them in ties of interest which will ever make them the portion of peace between America and England. . . . I come back in the belief that there is a more cordial feeling of attachment between the old and new country than the ordinary channels of public opinion enable us to appreciate."

To Thomas Arnold [son]

Vevey

My darling old boy   July 4, 1859

Many happy returns of your birthday, and I hope it will be a long time before you spend another one away from dear Mamma and me. I want you here very much, it is such a pretty place and such beautiful weather. The inn looks out on a pretty garden with trees, and you just cross the garden and go down some steps, and there you are at the lake, an immense lake, bigger than any you ever saw in your life, more than ten times as big as Windermere. At the bottom of the steps are very pretty boats, with flags of different nations, so that all the visitors here may go out in boats with flags of their own nation: some little American boys here go out in a boat with the American flag, and Mamma and I are going out tonight with the English flag. But first I am going out by myself to bathe and a fine splash there will be when I go in; but no dear little boys in blue poplin to splash, only the boatman. This water would not hurt blue poplin, it is fresh. Yesterday when we were going off from a pier where our steamer had stopped to take in passengers, a man comes running down, just too late for the boat: what does he do but jump from the pier thinking to jump on board, but he fell short and went souse into the water, far out of his depth: then there was a fine calling out the women on the pier running to the edge to look at him, then throwing up their hands, screaming, and running back: the man went bobbing up and down, and was just going to sink when a man took a great boat-hook and hooked it into his clothes then a number of men took hold and they hauled him up like a great big fish, all dripping and nearly drowned. Mamma did not scream. The day after tomorrow she will have a long ride on a mule. I hope she will not get very stiff. How I wish Budge was here to ride on a mule: my next letter must be to him. My love to all and tell dear Miss Nicholls how happy it makes me to think of you all with her. God bless my darling boy: I am your own loving,

Papa.

P. S. I send you a picture of my old place.

MS. Frederick Whitridge.

Newcastle Commission Journal (Yale)

July 3, Sunday. to see the English Consul. In the afternoon to Vevey. Few people at Monnet's.[1]

July 4th, Monday. Very hot. Bathed. After dinner in boat on lake with Flu. Americans letting off bad fireworks for their Anniversary.

July 5th, Tuesday. Bathed & to Martigny. Very hot day. Thunder-storm at Martigny. Hot at Hôtel Clerc, and bad dinner. Strolled about with Flu in evening.

July 6th, Wednesday. Over Tête Noire to Chamouni: very hot. Flu got on wonderfully. Dear little Tom's birthday.

July 7th, Thursday. Quiet at Chamouni—to Glacier des Bossons in a carriage. Splendid weather.

July 8th, Friday. to the Chalets of Plan-Pras. Flu on mule. Lunched there. Then I went on alone nearly to the top [of Brévent]. After dinner drove to the Mer de Glace. The Source of the Arve gone to nothing.

July 9th, Saturday. In Coupé of diligence to Geneva. Tremendous dust and heat. Bathed. This time at the Ecu, which is excellent. Drove in the evening.

1. July 3: Monnet was "the excellent landlord" of the Trois Couronnes, "one of the best Inns in Switzerland" (Murray's *Handbook for Travellers in Switzerland and the Alps of Savoy and Piedmont*, p. 179).

To Jane Martha Arnold Forster*

Geneva

My dearest K July 9, 1859

Your letter reached me at Chamounix, and I knew I should answer it quicker by waiting till I got down to this place. It would be very pleasant to meet William, but I am afraid he will be arriving on the stage as we are going off it. We stay here till Thursday the 14th—then go to Lausanne till Monday the 18th —then to Fribourg, and back here, I hope, by the 20th or 21st. On the 23rd we shall be at Lyons—on the 25th at Chateauroux or thereabouts as I have a visit to pay to George Sand (Michelet has given me a letter to her): on the 27th or 28th in Paris. It may be regarded as certain that Friday Saturday & Sunday, the 29th 30th & 31st, we shall be at Meurice's in Paris: the rest is not quite so certain, but highly probable. At Lyons we shall be at the Grand Hôtel de Lyon, the new inn. On your birthday, if all is well, we certainly return to England, meeting the children at Dover. I do so wish dear mamma and Fan would come to us there for their sea excursion, instead of going to the Grange or Llandidno [*sic*]. We could perfectly take them in, and Dover in August is certainly the pleasantest sea-place in the world. Few things I should like better than going along the path under the cliffs towards the Foreland with Fan: with all the movement of the world passing through the narrow channel on our right. Budge will be big enough this year to go with us—I hear from Miss Nicholls he has been very good lately at his lessons, being very anxious to have a letter from me, which was to be the reward of his continued industry: but what the dear old boy would like, says Miss Nicholls, would be to be all day and every day riding about the downs on a donkey. I cannot much afflict myself yet at his and Tom's resolute indifference to learning: Diddy monopolizes all the studious advice of his family, and really gets on very fast. I wish you would encourage Mamma & Fan to come to Dover to us: I am going to write to her about it. Flu says she will take your children for you next year to let you go abroad with William if you will time your absence to correspond with our stay at Dover—as she would prefer to have them at that temple of health the seashore. One sentence of Miss Nicholls's gives us, who know the child, the best news in the world about little Tom: "he goes whistling all the day long," she says. You know he is too weak to sing, so he solaces his musical taste by perpetual whistling while he is well, like a little bullfinch, poor little darling: but directly he is ill, his pipe stops. How interesting are public affairs—I really think I shall finish & bring out my pamphlet—what pains the English aristocracy seem to be taking to justify all I have said about their want of ideas. I hope the Emperor does not mean to stop before the Austrians are out of Venice as well as Lombardy: if he does it will be out of apprehension at the attitude of England (Prussia, I have told you, they do not care for a rush) but it would be a mistake on his part and on England's. Write to me within a post or two of getting this at the Hôtel Gibbon, Lausanne. Dearest Flu is all right again, and the best of travellers. She was nearly at the top of the Brevent yesterday, at the chalets of Plan-Pras. Being at Martigny we took two days' holiday to Chamounix, the weather was so splendid. But I do not care to come to Switzerland again, unless it is to bring Budge & Dicky a few years hence: meanwhile I believe I am elected a member of the Alpine Club,[1] though entirely undeserving of such an honour. My love to dear old Walter, and tell him how cordially happy his success at Durham makes me. God bless you, my dear old soul—I am   your always affectionate

M. A.—

I am getting very much to want to be back in England. Partly the children, but partly also affection for that foolish old country.

MS. Frederick Whitridge.

1. A rare reference to the Alpine Club, founded in 1857. See above p. 401 n. 2.

Newcastle Commission Journal (Yale)

July 10th, Sunday.   At Geneva.

July 11th, Monday.   Called on the Consul and M. De Cardolle. Drove to the Salève in the evening. I walked to the top of the gap. Still splendid weather.

To Mary Penrose Arnold

                                                               Geneva
My dearest Mother   July 11, 1859
By this time you will have had Flu's letter from Vevay [*sic*], and have heard that she has got over her attack. Since she wrote to you she has ridden on a mule over the Tete Noire from Martigny to Chamounix, and at Chamounix she has ridden nearly up to the top of the Brevent, and is getting quite sunburnt and strong. I was frightened about her at Nancy, but even then clung to the belief, which has turned out true, that her journey would in the end do her good: so much does every one's state of health turn upon the force and vivacity of their spirits, and so powerfully does foreign travel act, in the young at least, towards stimulating and strengthening these. The beauty of this place in the present incomparable weather is something past belief: one looks from the Jura to the lake and from the lake to Mont Blanc and is never tired. I have letters, besides my official introductions, to the best people here and could pass a month here very pleasantly. We are this time at the Ecu by Flu's desire, and perhaps it is a better inn for ladies than the Couronne: our sitting room and bed-room are en suite, all three windows looking full on the Rhone and across the Rhone to the Jura: the aspect is north, so we never have the sun on the windows, and the blessing of that in this climate and weather (the thermometer has been at 120) you may imagine. It is almost impossible to go out in the day time: about 4 I go out in a boat & bathe: after dinner we drive out in a carriage: tonight we drove to the Salève, the limestone mountain which stands so finely over Geneva: Flu lingered about near

the carriage and I took off my coat and climbed up the Pas de l'Echelle between the Grand and Petit Salève so as to get to the crown of the ridge just at sunset, and catch the rosy light on Mont Blanc, and the sun sinking behind the Jura.

We have been to you so regularly in the autumn since our marriage that I will not deny it is a disappointment not to come this year, and I think it is inconsiderate in Edward to have taken no account of our usual September visit; but perhaps we were getting too large a party for *you*, my dear Mother. I should be much inclined to come to you with Flu if we could establish the children comfortably in the neighbourhood: the year would not be like itself without a visit to Fox How. Will you see, before you go to K, if you can secure rooms at the white house between Spring Cottage and Violet Bank, for six weeks from the 1st September. That has always seemed to me such a cheerful house, with a warm aspect. I dare say you would not mind, if Flu and I came to you, our keeping little Tom with us: he could sleep in our room, and he is so often a prisoner to the house that I do not like separating him from his Mamma unless he has Miss Nicholls. Then there would be Mrs Tuffin, Charlotte, & the three other children. They would want a sitting room and two bed-rooms, one of which, if the other was a good one, might be a small room for Charlotte only: in arranging for them I give you carte blanche as to terms. We should like Rydal better for them than Ambleside, as they would be much easier to get at. Little darlings, it is nearly three months since I have seen them. I send you a letter I have just received from little Tom: but take care of it for me. Fanny Nicholls says she cannot see the fat he speaks of, but that he is certainly in great force.

In writing to K a day or two ago I asked her to try and help us persuade you to come to us at Dover for August, with Fan. We shall be there on the 1st. I see you now speak of giving up Llandidno [*sic*], for which I wanted you to substitute Dover, but are you wise to give up the sea entirely, for a whole year, after being so long used to it as a yearly change? We shall have ample room, and you will never do justice to the merits of that most charming of sea places till you have seen it in our company, and with Budge bathing on the shore. I am extremely pleased about Walter: what is he going to do now? I saw here today a Mrs Fielden, late Miss Yates, who said she knew me (Susy's old subject of vanity) by my likeness to Susy: but what she pleased me by was the warmth of admiration with which she spoke of the tact and sweetness with which that dear old girl managed her position in the Cropper family, and of the delight of old Mrs Cropper in her. She (Mrs Fielden) is clever and lively but rather too overpowering: her husband has a northern accent, but I liked him very much[1]—write to me at the Hôtel Gibbon, Lausanne—and

believe me, my dearest Mother, with love to all at Fox How,   your most
affectionate son,

M. A.—

MS. Balliol College.

1. Samuel Fielden (1816–89), J.P., of Centre Vale, Todmorden, Lancs, and W. R.
Yorks, married to Sarah Jane Yates (d. 1910), of Liverpool. They were a cotton-manufacturing family, and a statue to John Fielden, father of Samuel, was set up in Todmorden in
1861 (*Landed*; *Imperial Gazetteer*).

Newcastle Commission Journal (Yale)

July 12, Tuesday.   I saw M. Piguet[1]—called again on M. De Cardolle. Off
to S. Cergues. SN[Diary, Guthrie, 2:239, adds: 'Neuchatel*]

July 13, Wednesday.   to top of the Dole. Flu wonderful. back to Geneva
by 1 o'clock

July 14, Thursday.   to Lausanne by railway, after bathing. Bad room at the
Hotel Gibbon.

July 15, Friday.   Changed to a good room. Called at the Château and saw
the Président. Down to Mr. Haldemann's and bathed.[2] Magnificent weather.
Drove to the Signal in the evening.

July 16, Saturday.   At Normal School with Education Minister. Bathed as
before—with Flu to M. Haldemann's in the evening.

July 17, Sunday.   Called on M. Vuillemin. With Flu to church in the
evening. Strolled about.

1. July 12: "At Geneva, M. Piguet, the Councillor of State charged with the Department of Public Instruction, not only gave me oral information of the greatest value,
but had the kindness to procure for me the whole body of printed documents relating to
public education in the French Cantons" (Super, 2:167).
2. July 15: "At Lausanne I had the pleasure of conversing with the President of the
Council of State, with the Councillor at the head of the Department of Public Instruction,
and with the Director of the Normal School [Vuillemin, as below?] . . . on the state of
popular education in the important Canton of Vaud" (Super, 2:167).
William Haldimann *or* Haldimand (1784–1862: *DNB*), former M.P. and director
of the Bank of England, an English philanthropist of Swiss descent, one of the founders
of the Blind Asylum in Lausanne and a large contributor toward the erection of an Anglican church at Ouchy, had lived since 1828 at his villa, Denantou, near Lausanne, where
Arnold bathed and visited (Murray's *Handbook for Travellers in Switzerland*, p. 178). He was
a prominent part of the resident English colony in Lausanne, where everyone called on

him, including Charles Dickens, who became a friend and named a son for him, and he was the brother of Jane Marcet (see above p. 396 n. 3; Edgar Johnson, *Charles Dickens*, 2: 599–600, 614).

To Jane Martha Arnold Forster*

Lausanne

My dearest K   Sunday night, July 17, 1859

I forget now what I told you in my last letter, but I write in great haste having just received yours to tell you that finding the holidays begun in all the Swiss schools and the schools closed, and having seen the chief authorities and got the necessary papers, I am not going on to Fribourg and Neufchâtel, but am going tomorrow to Geneva and Lyons.[1] At Lyons we shall stay Tuesday and Wednesday and go on Wednesday night to Paris. So on Thursday morning, the 21st, we shall be at the Hôtel Meurice, at Paris.[2] If I knew where to write to William I would write and tell him this, as he will surely stay and meet us in Paris. I am terribly afraid this will reach you too late for you to communicate with him except by that detestable engine the telegraph. Our inn at Lyons will be the Grand Hôtel de Lyon. I shall leave Paris again on Friday the 22nd in order to see one or two more of the departments of the Centre. I have arranged to leave Flu there in order not to expose her to the bad and dirty inns of the French provinces in these terrible heats. I shall rejoin her Sunday or Monday and about the end of that week we hope to be at Dover.

I have not been in such spirits for a long time as those which the news of this peace has thrown me into.[3] Louis Napoleon's preponderance was really beginning to haunt me—he had possessed himself of an incomparable position, our English government entirely misunderstood the situation and were holding language that could only damage themselves, not affect him, everything was going smoothly for him, and he was going to have obtained the unwilling recognition of the liberal party through Europe as the necessary man of his time—when suddenly he stumbles, falls flat on his face, and loses his chance for this time. I am sorry for the Italians—but it is incomparably better for Europe that they should wait a little longer for their independence, than that the first power in Europe morally and materially should be the French Empire. Morally after this blunder it loses its advantage, however strong it may yet be materially. I said to Ld Cowley the other day that I was convinced Louis Napoleon's one great and dangerous error was that he exaggerated the power of the clergy, and bid for their support far higher than it was worth. I little thought how soon he would give a far more signal proof of this error of his than I ever expected. There can be no doubt that what made him nervous and resolved him suddenly to pull up was the growing and threatening discontent of the French clergy (which is nearly all ultramontane) at the Pope's position in these Italian complications. Accordingly the French clergy are enchanted at the peace: but they are the only people really pleased with it—and their applause is not exactly that which a prudent man would wish to have. Their great organ, Louis Veuillot,[4] thanks God that the war ends by one Emperor *giving* and the other *receiving* Lombardy: and that the hateful and anarchical doctrine of a people having itself any voice in its own assignment receives no countenance. There is a creditable and agreeable ally for l'uomo del Secolo![5]

We are off early tomorrow morning, and I must pack up. I am getting on, and think I shall make an interesting pamphlet—but Heaven knows how the thing will look when altogether. If it looks not as I mean it, I shall not publish it. Little Lucy has got a tooth, and Budge is learning to spell. Kiss your dear children for us: the porter here has something which reminds both Flu and me of poor dear Willy—remember to notice him when you next come here. I was rather horrified the other day by finding that Edward and Caroline wanted to stay on at Fox How and that our autumn visit at Fox How which we have made so many years, was knocked on the head: but I think anyway we were getting rather a large party for Mamma, and I have asked her to get lodgings for the nurses & children, which will remove all difficulties: Flu and I could not have gone to Westmorland leaving them to a London September. Mind you come as you intended. God bless you—write to me at Meurice's—I am always   your most affectionate

M. A.—

Flu's love.

MS. Frederick Whitridge.

1. "I arrived in Switzerland at the end of June, and found the primary schools just closed for the holidays. Holidays are long in Switzerland, and I could not wait there until they should be over. The Normal School at Lausanne—the only normal school in French Switzerland—was also closed. To see the Swiss schools in actual operation, therefore, I found impossible" (Super, 2:166).

2. Guthrie's transcription of the diary shows that beginning on July 17 Arnold lined through the visits projected: Gion, Fribourg and S. Nicholas (18–19), Geneva (20), Chateauroux and Lyons (22), La Châtre (23), Paris (24), Chateauroux (25), Nohant (26), Paris (27).

3. *Annual Register*, July 12 (p. 99): "The conditions of Peace are the following:— [i] 'An Italian Confederation under the honorary presidency of the Pope. [ii] The Emperor of Austria gives up his rights over Lombardy to the Emperor of the French, who remits them to the King of Sardinia. [iii] The Emperor of Austria keeps Venetia, but it is to form a part of the Italian Confederation. [iv] A general amnesty.' "

4. Louis Veuillot (1813–83), ultramontane editor of the ultraconservative daily *L'Univers*, "probably the most militant and virulent Roman Catholic writer of the 19th century" (*OCFL*, with incorrect date of death)—whom Swinburne, many years and viruses later, described as "that son of a bitch run mad with the itch" (Swinburne, 4:41). See the pamphlet *England and the Italian Question* (Super, 1:89–91) for the very language of Arnold's letter.

    5. See above p. 455 and n. 2.

Newcastle Commission Journal (Yale)

July 18, Monday.   to Geneva in the morning. Bathed in the Rhone baths. Then in afternoon to Lyons. Hot tiring journey. Tremendous heat at Lyons.

July 19, Tuesday.   Called on the Rector and M. Vivien.[1] In the evening strolled about with Flu.

July 20, Wednesday.   With the Inspecteur Primaire to see schools. Then a little about with Flu. Dined and off to Paris. Very hot journey.

July 21st, Thursday.   Working at pamphlet. William Forster came. He dined with us at table d'hôte—then to S. Cloud.[2]

July 22nd. Friday.[3]   Still at pamphlet.

July 23rd. Saturday.   do.

July 24th. Sunday.   do. to church with Flu—dined at Trois Frères.

July 25th, Monday.   Saw Lord Cowley. Sent off pamphlet.

July 26th. Tuesday.   to Pré Catelan at night.[4]

July 27th. Wednesday.   to Versailles—Dined there—back to Paris in the evening.

July 28th.   At night to Calais.

July 29 to August 14th   at Dover.

    1. July 19: M. de La Saussaye was the rector of the académie de Lyon, M. Vivien the inspecteur de l'academie; the inspecteur primaire, below, was M. Mazeran (*Almanach impérial*, p. 567). "S. Nicholas" (lined through) presumably refers to the Collegiate Church of St. Nicholas at Fribourg, which Arnold did *not* visit from Lausanne, because of his revised schedule.

    2. July 21: To see the Circourts at La Celle-St-Cloud.

    3. July 22: Châteauroux lined through (like La Châtre and Nohant, below), meaning that he was not going to call on George Sand because of an altered itinerary.

    4. July 26: The public garden, Bois de Boulogne.

To Richard Monckton Milnes*

1 Wellesley Terrace, Dover

My dear Mr. Milnes   August 3, 1859

I have desired the publisher to send you a copy of a pamphlet of mine on the Italian question, which embodies some of the French experiences I inflicted on you in Paris.[1] You know, you entirely belong to the "Aristocratie Anglaise," in the broad (and just) French acceptance of the term. But then you differ from them by having what Sainte Beuve calls an "intelligence ouverte et traversée,"[2] and they in general have every good quality except that. I am only here for a few days on business, and return to France next week. No one knows my address, and I see no newspapers. I have so much on my hands just now. But still I have a natural solicitude to hear how "the judicious" take my *résumé* of the Italian question, which I cannot help thinking is true; and if you would let me have one line to tell me whether you have read it, and whether you agree with it, you would do me a great kindness.— Believe me, dear Mr. Milnes,   very truly yours,

M. Arnold.

Text: Russell, 1:116–17.

1. *England and the Italian Question*, published by Longman, Green (of which "*L'aristocratie anglaise*" are the opening words [Super, 1:65]).
2. See above p. 91 n. 4.

To Mary Penrose Arnold

⟨Education Department, Council Office, Downing Street, London:⟩

1, Wellesley Terrace, Dover

My dearest Mother   August 4, 1859

No one writes me such pleasant letters about anything I do, or likes them just as I wish them to be liked, so much as my own family. I am delighted with your letter and dearest K's. I felt almost sure the pamphlet would please you. I am living here as in the wilderness, seeing no newspapers and no one knowing my address—so I am not likely to hear anything about the reception of the pamphlet—but I have sent it about very freely to people who I wished should read it, and we shall see. I have heard only from Lingen, who "decidedly likes it." And there are very few productions which he "decidedly likes."

I am sick of the pedantry and trimming of Prussia, but I wish her stronger with all my heart, no Prussian can wish it more—the sooner she absorbs all the little German kingdoms round her the better I shall be pleased. But the sooner she sees that if she wants to be a *great* German power she must do this, the better for her—and many Prussians would themselves echo almost every word I have said in the pamphlet. As long as Prussia remains only her present size and population, she is in a false position—she *must* temporise, and can *do* nothing. I wish you would send a copy to Bunsen, telling him at the same time of my sincere wishes for the aggrandisement of his country.

K forgot to tell me Tom's address: I wanted to send him the pamphlet. The news that Ld Carlisle[1] has promised to do something for him is the best I have heard this many a long day. I shall send Ld C. my pamphlet to keep the family in his mind—I knew him, very slightly, some years ago.

I wish you could see Dicky and Lucy—they are two such very pretty children. Yesterday Flu, I, Tom, Trev., Dick, Lucy, Mrs Tuffin, Charlotte, and Thomas, little Tom's chairman, proceeded to Shakespeare's Cliff, and there, by the piles on which the railway runs, we undressed Budge and Dick, and let them bathe. They take to the water like ducks—and you should have seen that lovely little figure of Dick's laid down flat on the bright shingle with his sweet face upwards and his golden hair all floating about him waiting for the wave to come up and wash over him. Mrs Tuffin gets more and more invaluable—she has two days' holiday to go and see her sister at Canterbury and has begged as a favour to be allowed to take Dicky with her, not to be separated from all her children. Dick graciously says he *tinks* he will go.—I expect to be here till Saturday week—then to Paris for ten days—then in Chester Square till the end of the month; then on the 1st of September to dear old Fox How. Neither Lord Villiers[2] nor the Commission pay their debts to me at present, which is awkward—but all will come right in time—

Your ever affectionate son—

M. A.—

MS. Balliol College.

1. George William Frederick Howard (1802–64: *DNB*), seventh earl of Carlisle, had been chief secretary for Ireland and was now Lord-Lieutenant. Tom Arnold saw him there in 1857 at a St. Patrick's ball: "The exertions of the good-natured Lord Carlisle, as with red and glowing face—the George round his neck and the Garter binding his knee—he laboured through the crowded country-dance, 'hands across, down the middle,' &c., &c., were exceedingly praiseworthy, and also slightly comic. As he passed us he said, with a laugh, 'Hot work, Mrs. Arnold! was it as bad as this in Tasmania?' 'Miss Martineau,' he adds, 'had given me a note of introduction to Lord Carlisle' (*Passages in a Wandering Life*, p. 165 and note). See the letter to him Aug. 26, 1860.

2. Charles Pelham Villiers (1802–98: *DNB*; *VF*, 8/31/72), nephew of the 3d earl of Clarendon and brother of the 4th (with the title and precedency of an earl's son), privy councillor since 1853, had just taken office, with cabinet rank, as president of the Poor Law Board.

To William Ewart Gladstone

The Rt Honble W. E. Gladstone—

&c. &c. &c.—   1, Wellesley Terrace, Dover

My dear Sir   August 5, 1859

I am here only for a few days before I return to France where I am engaged for the Education Commission in enquiring into the working of the French law of public instruction—for these few days my friends do not know my address and I see no newspapers:—you must allow me to tell you what sincere pleasure, being thus cut off from general communication, I have received from your most kind note which the Longmans forwarded to me this morning. It is an honour to be read by you—a still greater honour to be read by you with sympathy—the greatest honour of all to be read by you with sympathy when one writes of Italy, for which you yourself, by what you have written, have done so much.[1]

In the last few months I have visited nearly every part of France and seen all classes of society from archbishops and Prefects to village schoolmasters and peasants—indeed it was this alone which gave me any right to trouble the public on the Italian question. With respect to public opinion and the course of events in France I think what is said in the pamphlet is based on solid experience and may be relied on: the rest of the pamphlet must stand on its own merits. Lord Cowley told me the other day, after my pamphlet was finished, that the Emperor had said to him—"Every man has his idea which haunts him all his life long: mine is to do something for Italy—and I shall probably go to my grave without doing it."   Believe me, my dear Sir, with renewed thanks and with the most sincere respect, Your faithful & obliged servant,

Matthew Arnold.—

MS. British Library.

1. The celebrated pamphlets of 1851 and 1852: *Two Letters to the Earl of Aberdeen on the State Prosecutions of the Neapolitan Government* and *An Examination of the Official Reply of the Neapolitan Government.* F. T. Palgrave (knowing only the Fitzjames Stephen review of Arnold's pamphlet—see below p. 487) called it "degrading twaddle—neither new nor true. . . . What trash too about 'prestige' and 'aggression' and the 'English Aristocracy' and the 'popular fibre'!" (Mulhauser, 2:70). *The Gladstone Diaries*, ed. H. C. G. Matthew (5:414) note only (Aug. 2) "Arnold on It. question" and next day "Wrote to M. Arnold."

To A. J. Beale

Mr Beale
⟨Education Department, Council Office, Downing Street, London:⟩
                                                            Dover
Dear Sir   August 6, 1859
I have been for the last five months on the Continent upon a mission from the Government to enquire into the working of the laws of public instruction in France and elsewhere, for the information of the Education Commission. I have only just returned and received only yesterday your letter of the 25th ult. with a copy of the Guardian.[1] I am heartily glad you are still doing so well. I am here but for a few days, and then return to Paris again. When I come home I shall be occupied with my Report for every moment of time that I can spare, and I am afraid, therefore, there is no chance whatever of my being able to take part in your Prize Scheme Examination this year. Still I hope to pay you my usual visit of inspection, but certainly not before the 1st November. I have just published a pamphlet on the Italian question, founded very much on what I have myself seen and heard abroad. I think it would interest you, and I would send you a copy if I had one, but I have not, and have now no time to send for any—I will bring you one in November, if you will remind me of it at the time.   Ever truly yours
                                                    M. Arnold.—

MS. Morgan Library.

1. Probably "New Education Minute" followed by "Instructions to her Majesty's Inspectors on the Foregoing Matter" signed by Lingen (*Guardian*, July 20, 1859, pp. 637– 38).

To Arthur Hugh Clough

                                        1, Wellesley Terrace, Dover
My dear old soul.   August 11, 1859
I find that, au fond, when I compose anything, I care more, still, for your opinion than that of any one else about it—so you may imagine what pleasure your note, received this morning, gave me. It had been lying in Chester Square, and was forwarded by a chance opportunity. I had supposed that you thought me still abroad.

Indeed I am only here for a few days, to get some Kent schools done, and few know my address.

I use *reason* from a way of thinking I have about the ancient and modern or ante Christian and post Christian worlds, which I am not sure that you sympathise in, which I am developing in my lectures, and which it would be tedious to talk about here.[1]

The correction about the Prussian army is most important. I have no knowledge of Prussia from personal experience—I was astonished at what I heard from French officers about their army—finding myself one day at dinner, in Paris, by a Prussian diplomate,[2] I questioned him closely on the subject—not making any distinction, certainly, between officers & men, but talking of l'armée Prussienne. I could hardly believe that they had not even picked troops, Guards, or a household brigade, who served for longer than 3 years. He assured me they had not, however, and himself thought it a cause of weakness for the Prussian army, though not to the same extent that the French do. The French lay the most astonishing stress on *old soldiers* and having *seen service*: it would astonish you to find how they value the Crimean training for their men, and they say it is worth our while to have a perpetual Indian Mutiny for the good it does our troops. If you assure me that you *know* that the *officers* of the Prussian army serve for longer than the 3 years, I will change *man* to *private*.[3] If it is as you say the Prussians have a more instructed body of officers than I imagined, but the fact remains as to the "gros" of their army. And I imagine raw troops only fight well on quite exceptional occasions, such as the national uprising of 1813. Lord Cowley, who has been much in Germany, and was inclined to overrate the Austrians, told me I was quite right about the Prussians: "The French," he said, "would walk over and over and over them in a fortnight"—and Pellissier[4] told the Emperor that with 80,000 men at Nancy he would undertake to dispose of any army the Prussians would bring into France.

I do not wish to depreciate Prussia—I sincerely wish she was stronger (and a little *depedantified* at the same time) but people here all overrate her force, and she can only become strong by being helped and encouraged to absorb the wretched little German states.

The strong point of the pamphlet is, I firmly believe, that it is in the main true—being convinced of the truth of it and having carried it all in my head some weeks, I wrote it with great zest and pleasure. I don't know how it is going on, but I imagine well. I am to hear from the Longmans tomorrow. I had a very warm note from Gladstone about it just before he made his speech.[5] How my great Whig friends take it, I know not—I wrote in the earnest desire to influence them, and to approach them on an acceptable side—but they are *very* hard to get at. I should like it to be read by the middle classes who I am told are savagely & blindly anti-Louis-Napoleon-ist—tell Walrond he ought to make Dasent get it reviewed in the Times—without that it will never reach below intelligent London society. They certainly misconceive Louis Napoleon in this country and may end by *misdriving* him—not that he will come to any good if left to himself and treated with all fairness. Still, with fairness let us treat him, and all men & things.

I sent Lowe a copy[6]—has he said anything about it? A horrid thought strikes me that it was *he* who said, at Calne, "the most unjustifiable war &c."—but if he *did* say it, he shouldn't have. I saw it in some French newspaper. I am so glad you are with him as his secretary. Let me have a line *here*. I return to Paris for a week or so on Sunday. Kindest regards from us both to your wife—   your ever affectionate

M. A.

MS. Yale University.

1. Arnold's phrase "use reason" is not clear—possibly he refers to the opening of Part 2 of *England and the Italian Question* (Super, 1:70) but more likely to an allusion in his note to Clough accompanying the presentation copy of the pamphlet. For the "lectures" Lowry cites (p. 150n) "The Modern Element in Literature" and (oddly) "Pagan and Medieval Religious Sentiment" (Super 1:18–37; 3:212–31). Arnold quotes Clough's approval in the next letter.

2. Unidentifiable, but the *Almanach impérial* (p. 35) lists four at the Prussian Ministry, 78 rue de Lille: M. le comte de Pourtalès, minister; M. le prince Henri VII de Reuss, secretary of the Legation; MM. le baron de Thile, and le comte de Hatzfeldt, *Attachés.*

3. The pamphlet was not reprinted by Arnold.

4. Aimable Jean Jacques Pélissier (1794–1864), commander of the Crimean army and, after the capture of Sebastopol in 1855, marshal and duc de Malakoff, in 1858 had been ambassador at London and was now vice-president of the Senate and a member of the Privy Council (*Petit Robert; Almanach impérial*).

5. As chancellor of the Exchequer on July 28 (*The Times*, July 29, pp. 7–8).

6. Arnold's first reference to Robert Lowe (1811–92: *DNB; VF,* 2/27/69), politician, at this time M.P. for Calne and, more to the point, vice-president of the Committee of Council on Education and (in that capacity) Arnold's bête noire and, to some extent, nemesis later, in the battle over "The Twice-Revised Code" and its repercussions (see Super, 2:212–51, and the notes pp. 347–64). "I am become private secretary to our Vice-President, viz. Lowe, and am a little more hurried about in consequence," Clough wrote to a friend on July 29 (Mulhauser, 2:570).

To Jane Martha Arnold Forster*

⟨Education Office, Council Office, Downing Street, London:⟩
Dover

My dearest K   August 13, 1859

I never thanked you for your letter, because I meant my note to Mamma to thank you both: but I was very glad to have it and to know that you read the pamphlet with pleasure.

We want very much, both Flu and I, to have the full true and particular account of William's ascent of Mt Blanc. There is nothing I should more like to have done, and I sincerely congratulate him. Besides Hudson's letter in the Times, I met an Oxford man here yesterday who had been at Chamouni[x] with his wife when the party returned, and had had them all named to him. I think William was so right in taking the grand route, as he had never been up before—you are hardly considered to have been up Mt Blanc at all unless you have been up the orthodox way, which every one knows so well from Albert Smith.[1] A second time I should not care what way I went. I want to hear some particulars—the best accounts seem to shew that there is no *difficulty* now the guides are so used to the ascent, but that it is a mere question of being able to endure the fatigue. I want to know also about the weather— and if there was really a good and *enjoyable* view from the top. Also whether William's face was skinned.

I could talk to you a great deal about the pamphlet (I want to know how William likes *that*—he will find a passage at p. 39—line 1—softened and left more *open* in consequence of some conversation we had) but I have not time to go beyond this sheet. You and Clough are I believe the two people I in my heart care most to please by what I write—Clough (for a wonder) is this time satisfied—even delighted "with one or two insignificant exceptions," he says, "I believe all you say is probably right, and if right most important for English people to consider." Harriet Martineau in the Daily News I have not seen[2]—Edward says it is disapproving. I have seen no English papers abroad, but I fancied the D. News had been much the same way as the pamphlet—but Harriet herself is a little incalculable. I want to see the Morning Post which has an article, because of its connection with Lord Palmerston. There is a very clever and long answer to the pamphlet in today's Saturday Review, by Fitzjames Stephen, the man who ill-treated Papa in reviewing Tom Brown. He is exceedingly civil, this time, and no one can complain of his tone. Like you, he does not seem convinced by the *nationalities* section. As it first stood it was longer, exhausting the cases more: I had pointed out that isolated spots like Malta & Gibraltar could be, and in fact nearly were, *de*nationalised and Anglicised: as to the Ionian Islands, I said, what I believe to be true, that if Greece ever becomes a really great nation it will be impossible for us to keep them, being the size they are, on the Greek frontier as they are, and the Greek race being what it is. All this I left out because I thought this about Corfu might give offence and I wished to be as much swallowed as possible. But the worst of the English is that in foreign politics they search so very much more for what they like and wish to be true than for what *is* true. In Paris there is certainly a larger body of people than in London who treat foreign politics as a science, as a matter to *know* upon before *feeling* upon.

I must stop—but write to me at the Hotel Meurice in Paris—I go there tomorrow night. I send you Gladstone's note, and also one from the Judge— the latter to shew you his *firm sound touch*, both physically and intellectually, at the age of very nearly 75. Tell William I should be very glad if he could find out how either Bright or Cobden liked my pamphlet. I sent it to both of them—and do not feel at all to know what view they would be likely to take of it. They are both well worth convincing. Send Gladstone's note on to Fox How—and with love to William & kisses to the dear children, believe me, my dearest K,   your ever affectionate

M. A.—

MS. Frederick Whitridge.

1. "Another Ascent of Mont Blanc," *The Times*, Aug. 11, p. 10, on the ascent from Chamounix of the Revs. E. Headland, G. Hodgkinson, C. Hudson, George Joad and William Forster with their six guides. Albert Richard Smith (1816–60: *DNB*), author, playwright, novelist, and lecturer. In 1851 "he made an ascent of Mont Blanc and . . . [in 1852] produced at the Egyptian Hall in Piccadilly an entertainment descriptive of the ascent and of Anglo-continental life, which became the most popular exhibition of the kind ever known. . . . He also wrote: 'Handbook of Mr. Albert Smith's Ascent of Mont Blanc,' four editions, and edited the 'Mont Blanc Gazette,' 1858" (*DNB*).

2. Reviewed somewhat "unfavourably" (unsigned) in the *Daily News*, Aug. 8, 1859, p. 2 (noted in R. K. Webb, *Harriet Martineau*, p. 322 and n). Stephen's article, in the *Saturday Review* on Aug. 13, was published together with Arnold's by Merle M. Bevington.

Newcastle Commission Journal (Yale)

August 14th. Sunday.   At night to Paris. Rough passage but not ill.

August 15th. Monday.   Fêtes. Saw the Stanleys, ⟨Magin⟩ Mitchell, the Prices. Dined with the Stanleys at the Poissonerie Anglaise. Then to see illuminations. Showery. Home early with Mrs Stanley, and to bed.

August 16th, Tuesday.   Early to see Magin. Then to Merimée. He took a copy of my pamphlet for M. Fould. Then to Sorbonne, but Cousin out. Then to office of Siècle,[1] to banker's, and to Guizot's, all on foot. Dined at table d'hôte with Mitchell & Mr. Baker. Had coffee with them on the Boulevard, to bed early.

1. Aug. 16: Achille Fould (1800–1867), banker (Fould, Oppenheim et Cie) and politician (député de la Seine), and, though an Orleanist and a Jew, he was after all Louis Napoleon's banker, had been his ministre des finances since 1849, and was now (1852–60) ministre d'état et de la maison de l'empereur (Jasper Ridley, *Napoleon III and Eugénie*, pp. 245–46, 262, 341, *Almanach national pour 1848-1849-1850*, pp. 69, 192, *Almanach impérial*, p. 98).

Le Siècle, "founded in 1836, one of the first cheap daily papers, had a circulation, unprecedented at the time, of 38,000, largely among small traders and the working classes. It supplied news, opinions ready-made, and a *roman-feuilleton*. It was pro-Revolutionary in politics when founded and, in so far as politics were allowed, succeeded in remaining democratic during the Second Empire" (*OCFL*). "The *Siècle* writes in fetters," wrote Arnold at this time, in a witty passage (Super, 1:89) surpassed nowhere in his work. (Baker has not been identified.)

To Mary Penrose Arnold*

Paris
My dearest Mother   August 16, 1859

I must write on what I can lay my hands on, for if I go out to buy more paper I shall miss the post—I saw in the Times the death of Uncle Penrose[1]—I have often thought of him since I read your account of your last meeting with him—it was very affecting. Though not a successful man—at least not successful in proportion to his powers and, I suppose, not successful in proportion to his wishes, he never seemed an unhappy man—and for that, whether it was self-command or real content, I always admired him. But I believe he was on the whole a happy man—and, if he was that, what does his more or less of success matter now?

This is my last appearance abroad as "Monsieur le Professeur Docteur Arnold, Directeur Général de toutes les Ecoles de la Grande Bretagne"—as my French friends will have it that I am. I go down to Berri on Sunday to see George Sand,[2] and return here to meet the Wightmans on Monday, and Wednesday or Thursday I hope to be in London again—and on the 1st September, according to my original intention, to come with Flu and little Tom to Fox How. I am very glad we have Mrs Askew's[3] [rooms] and very glad *indeed* that we can have them on the 6th without waiting till the 7th. I am anxious you should see Diddy again before his beautiful infantine roundness leaves him which it may do any day—Budge is now a regular bony boy, with angles and square chest, when stripped—but Diddy is still the exquisitely rounded child he was at two years old, and when he is naked neither chairmen nor soldiers nor any one else on the beach near him, can take their eyes off him. It has made me very happy to see the darlings again, and to find them growing up such dear manageable children—at least to me—and I think not unmanageable in the nursery, though Mrs Tuffin certainly spoils them. After the first day or two, when they found that I took the quarrelling and fighting very seriously, they got much better, and the last week was all peace. They imitate all I do and say in the most absurd manner. Tom has now hours in which he says he is "writing his poems." Poor little Lucy's neck is very sore but as it seems to enable her to cut her teeth without illness or suffering such as her brothers had, one cannot complain: it is not in sight luckily, and she has the prettiest face in the world.

I am very curious to see Harriet Martineau's article of which I have heard a good deal.[4] As far as I see the newspapers will not let themselves be convinced but they will take *something* of the undoubted truth, for so it is, which I have told them about France & the Emperor. Cumin tells me H. Martineau praised me full as much as the Editor of the D. News, who admired the pamphlet but was against its doctrines, would stand—more than he would have stood, probably, in the case of any other contributor. The Saturday Review you will have seen—one cannot complain of it. The Italians have behaved so well that every one now tries to make out he was in some sense or other for them: but two things are certain—one—that the highest classes call them aristocracy or what you will, were at the breaking out of the war, and I believe still are, far more Austrian than the middle and lower classes—the other that it was the language of these highest classes which was taken by foreign nations as the exponent of the English feeling with respect to Italy and the war. And we have certainly suffered from it on the Continent.

I saw Prosper Mérimée this morning, a well-known author here & member of the French Academy: he is private Secretary to the Empress and a great favourite at court—he asked me for a copy of my pamphlet to send to M. Fould, the minister who is gone with the Emperor to Tarbes,[5] that he might read it himself and give it to the Emperor to read if he thought fit. Mérimée said, as many of the intimate Imperialists say, that the one thing which induced the Emperor to make peace, was the sight of the field of Solferino after the battle: that he was shocked greatly, and that he is a humane and kind-hearted man, there is no doubt: but that he made the peace of Villafranca solely because he was shocked, it is absurd to say. If true it would show that he is a much weaker man than either his friends or his enemies at present suppose. I saw the Prices yesterday & today: they are going to Switzerland. He looking extremely well, and stouter: talking just as usual, but a little slower & graver: she looking much worn, but still herself. The fêtes, what I saw of them, were like all fêtes, very stupid. Love to all and believe me always, my dearest Mother,   your most affectionate son—

M. A.—

Wish Walter joy of his birthday, if he is with you, when this reaches you, with my love.

MS. Balliol College.

1. John Penrose (see above p. 415).
2. He changed his mind—see below p. 495.

3. The name may be "Asher" or "Asker." If Askew, it must refer to the Rev. and Mrs. Henry W. Askew, at Glenridding House, about ten miles distant from Fox How (Martineau, *Black's Picturesque Guide to the English Lakes*, p. 191; *Imperial Gazetteer, Landed*; Harrow; Venn).

4. See above p. 487 and n. 2. The editor of the *Daily News* was Thomas Walker (1822–98: *DNB*), "distinguished for his support of the cause of Italian liberty."

5. Tarbes is near Lourdes, which was the scene of Fould's humiliation a year earlier, when ("a Jew hated by the Catholic Ultramontanists") he had been required by the emperor to reopen the famous grotto (to which access had been forbidden by the government) where "the fourteen-year-old Bernadette Soubirous saw a vision of her 'lady'. . . . the British press, with *The Times* in the lead, launched a violent attack on 'the White Lady of Lourdes' as a blasphemous lie propagated by Veuillot. . . . Bernadette unconsciously played her part in presenting the Second Empire to the British public as a dark realm of Papist ignorance, superstition and tyranny" (Jasper Ridley, *Napoleon III and Eugénie*, pp. 440–41).

Newcastle Commission Journal (Yale)

August 17. Wednesday.   Early to Magin. Worked with him at the Ministère de l'I. P. Saw Rendu there. Then home—wrote letters and this. Out to take letters to Embassy. Back and dressed, and to dine at Philippe's with Mitchell & his friend. Met Bowyer & his wife there. Very good dinner. Strolled about and home to bed.

August 18, Thursday.   At 8 to Magin's, worked & breakfasted with him, then at 12 with him to the Ministère and worked till 3. Home and wrote letters—then to dine at the [Grand Hôtel du] Louvre—missed Mitchell, but good dinner. To the Cirque de l'Impératrice][1]—utterly assommant. Strolled about and had coffee—then home to bed.

August 19, Friday.   breakfasted & to Magin's—then with him to the Ministère. Home and wrote letters—then walked about a little, dressed and to Sainte Beuve. Dined with him at the Restaurant du quartier. Then home with him & looked over letters from G Sand, Alf. de Musset, Planche &c &c.[2] Very interesting. Walked home.

1. Aug. 18: Formerly, Cirque Nationale, on the Champs-Elysées at the avenue Marigny, an easy walk from the Meurice: "un cirque monumentale, en meulière, digne de l'avenue des Champs-Elysées; Pradier, Bosio et Duret le décorèrent" (Hillairet, 1:99, illustrated).

2. Aug. 19: The "restaurant Edon, 18 de la rue de l'Ancienne-Comédie. . . . ce restaurant était tenu par un gros homme, nommé Pinson, en habit noir et cravat blanche, dès le matin, qui avait su attirer chez lui une clientèle d'élite" (André Billy, *Sainte-Beuve, sa vie et son temps*, 1:247).

Alfred de Musset (1810–57), the poet, playwright, and novelist, was also famous for his loveaffair(s) in 1833–35 with George Sand and his use of it or them in several works.

(She made use of it herself in *Elle et lui*, 1859—see below p. 495 n. 2.) Gustave Planche (1808–57) was the literary and art critic for the *Revue des deux mondes*, a "critic of the very first order," as Arnold wrote later (Super, 3:254), *fade* though he may seem compared with the "amour insensé" of Musset and George Sand.

To Frances Lucy Wightman Arnold*

Paris

August 19, 1859

I sent you the *Galignani*, as probably you have not seen the *Globe*, and you may imagine the sensation the extract with my name produced among my acquaintances at this hotel, where every one spells the *Galignani* through from beginning to end. I want you to give Dr. Hutton a copy of the pamphlet, and ask him to present it with my compliments to Mr. Seymour Fitzgerald,[1] who voted for me at Oxford. He is all the other way, but that is no reason he should not read what may do him good. You see how well this man is going on—first his amnesty,[2] and then his removal of the newspaper pains and penalties. I am going to-morrow to pass an hour with the Circourts; he writes me word that they are delighted with the pamphlet. The first day they got it, he and his wife read it aloud together, and then he translated it, extempore, from beginning to end, for the benefit of a friend staying with them, "who knows not your tongue." Lord Cowley is at Chantilly, so I have no means of knowing how he likes it.

I dine tonight with Sainte Beuve, who is gazetted today Commander of the Legion of Honour. I have almost made up my mind not to go into Berri. I think I shall gain more by getting another day's work with Magin here. I like him more and more, and shall make, I think, with his help, a very interesting report. You may rely on my leaving Paris, Wednesday night, unless there is a wonderfully good tidal train on Thursday, which I don't think. If I am in Paris on Sunday I shall go to St. Germain, which I have never seen. The English seem coming at last, as they are to be seen everywhere. I am nearly the whole day with Magin, and never dine at the *table d'hôte*.—

Ever yours.

I had a very pleasant letter from Wm. Forster about my pamphlet, and about his ascent of Mont Blanc.

Text: Russell, 1:120–1.

1. William Robert Seymour Vesey Fitzgerald (1818–85: *DNB*; knt 1866), M.P. for Horsham, had been under-secretary for foreign affairs in Derby's second cabinet and was later governor of Bombay. (He was caricatured by Ape in *Vanity Fair* 5/2/74.)

2. On Aug. 15 the emperor granted "an amnesty to all political prisoners and de-

tainees in Algeria and Cayenne, thus releasing all those who had been detained after the June Days of 1848, after the coup d'état, and after the round-up that followed Orsini's bombs" (Ridley, *Napoleon III and Eugénie*, p. 456). "Pains and penalties" was a hoary phrase (Pope's *Dunciad* 4.341; Junius), but it occurs in Mill's *On Liberty*, which Arnold had read recently.

To Mary Penrose Arnold

Paris

My dearest Mother   August 19, 1859

Though I wrote so lately I must write a line today to carry to you my love on your birthday, and earnest hopes that you may long be what you are now and have been for so many years—the dearest possible and best possible and most affectionate possible point of union for all your children.

I have almost given up my intention of going into Berri to see George Sand. In the first place, as I have already once seen her, it is not worth going merely to see her—and, though I should much like to hear what she could tell me about the Berri peasants, she is so [?]⟨French⟩ [?]unfrench and so taciturn that it is quite possible I might not get much out of her, while out of M. Magin, the Inspector General with whom I am working here, I get a great deal. So I think I shall stay here till the Wightmans come on Tuesday evening—pass one day with them, and return on Wednesday night to England. All I much care for in Paris (beyond work) is to go about the streets— it is too hot to go about on foot and without Flu I never go about in a carriage—so I don't care to stay on here at present. My pamphlet is extremely liked by those of my French acquaintances who have read it: the best of them, M. de Circourt, writes me word that the same afternoon that he got it he not only read it aloud to his wife, but translated it from beginning to end into French for the benefit of a friend who was staying with them. The first article in today's Galignani[1] is an article from the Globe with a long extract from the pamphlet, mentioning my name. I sincerely hope it will circulate in England—for all in it about France & the Emperor himself is undoubtedly, and to all intelligent persons here with any means of judging, strikingly true—and against such a man as the Emperor it is not enough that England should abstain from committing gross faults of policy, it is necessary, unless France is to take the lead from her completely, that she should pursue an actively good and intelligent line of policy. But an intelligent policy there cannot be, where people cannot and will not learn the *facts*. [about 5 lines torn off here, p. 3, for autograph bottom of p. 4] Villafranca peace is passing away here, and the Emperor has produced an excellent effect by his amnesty and annulment of the press penalties.

I am getting together a good deal of interesting information about the subject for which I came abroad, and hope to make a report which may be useful. On the whole I am struck with the justness and exactness of the French administration in *little things*—and as little things are the immense majority, this goes far to explain the force and success of their administration in general.

God bless you, my dearest Mother—I [3 words cut off except upper part of ascenders: shall drink your] health on Sunday [about 5 lines torn off here for autograph]

MS. Balliol College.

1. *The Globe* recommended *England and the Italian Question* on Aug. 1, p. 1, concluding: "Mr Arnold's views are candid and generous toward all parties; and if they are some times a little those of a poet, there are poetical as well as prosaic elements in all human affairs and actions." *Galignani's Messenger* printed excerpts on Aug. 19, p. 4.

Newcastle Commission Journal (Yale)

August 20th. Saturday.   Breakfasted and to Magin—with him to the Ministère—then to call on Villemain, who very agreeaable and gracious. Then to La Celle S. Cloud by Rueil and Bougival. Pleasant visit—M. de Circourt walked down the butte with me. Back to Paris to a very bad dinner alone, at the Maison Dorée.

August 21, Sunday.   My mother's birthday. Breakfasted and to the [Grand Hôtel du] Louvre, where I called on Lady Mayne, having met Sir Richard in the street. Back and wrote this, and to dear Flu. Then to call on Mohl, but found him gone to England. dined at the Louvre with Mitchell. drove afterwards with him in the Bois de Boulogne. Coffee on boulevard. Home to bed.

To Frances Lucy Wightman Arnold*

Paris
August 21, 1859

I shall not leave Paris till Thursday evening, because I find the annual Public Séance of the Académie Française is fixed for Thursday, and as Guizot is to speak, though I really would rather get home now, I should afterwards be sorry if I had missed it. The meeting is at two in the afternoon, and I shall start by the mail train at 7.30. Everybody said I *must* stop, but I think it was Sainte Beuve who finally persuaded me. Villemain speaks first, and then Guizot speaks and crowns the Laureate for the year, a young lady; and all the Institut will be there. M. de Circourt is coming into Paris to be present.

Now I will go back a little. After writing to you on Friday, I strolled out a little, came back and dressed, and drove to Sainte Beuve's, which is an immense way off, close to the Brittany railway. He had determined to take me to dine *chez le Restaurant du Quartier*, the only good one, he says, and we dined in the cabinet where G. Sand, when she is in Paris, comes and dines every day. Sainte Beuve gave me an excellent dinner, and was in full vein of conversation, which, as his conversation is about the best to be heard in France, was charming. After dinner he took me back to his own house, where we had tea; and he showed me a number of letters he had had from G. Sand and Alf. de Musset at the time of their love affair, and then again at the time of their rupture. You may imagine how interesting this was after *Elle et Lui*. I will tell you about them when we meet.[1] Sainte Beuve says I must read *Lui et Elle*, to finish the history, and then to complete it all, a few pages in the *Memoirs* of Mogador[2] about Musset. As for G. Sand and him, Sainte Beuve says, "tout le mal qu'ils ont dit l'un de l'autre est vrai." But De Musset's letters were, I must say, those of a *gentleman* of the very first water. Sainte Beuve rather advised me to go and see George Sand, but I am still disinclined "to take so long a journey to see such a fat old Muse," as M. de Circourt says in his funny English. All Sainte Beuve told me of her present proceedings made me less care about seeing her; however, if Berri was nearer, the weather less hot, and French travelling less of a bore, I should go—as it is I shall not. After all, by staying I shall get another visit to Cousin, which is some compensation. I stayed with Sainte Beuve till midnight, and would not have missed my evening for all the world. I think he likes me, and likes my caring so much about his criticisms and appreciating his extraordinary delicacy of tact and judgment in literature. I walked home, and had a wakeful night. Yesterday I worked with Magin in the morning, and then went to see Villemain. He gave me a ticket for Thursday (they are very hard to have), and I *hope* to get two more through the Minister of Public Instruction, so as to be able to take two of your party. Villemain brought out *Merope*, which he likes, naturally, more than the English do. He was extremely gracious, and presented me to an old grandee who came in as *un Anglais qui nous juge parfaitement*. He expresses great interest about my pamphlet, and said he should certainly speak of it in the periodical press, which is excellent, as he can do what he likes in the *Débats* and the *Revue des Deux Mondes*. I left him to go to the St. Germain railway, and partly by rail, partly by omnibus, and partly by walking, got to Les Bruyères soon after four. Mme. de Circourt looked dreadfully ill, and I thought would have fainted with the effort of coming into the drawing-room and crawling to the sofa; however, her salts revived her, and without the least allusion to her health, she began to talk about my pamphlet. I think they both heartily like it, and they say that I have *appreciéd les choses avec une justesse extraordinaire.* They have already sent off their own copy to M. de Cavour, so you were wrong. They want others to distribute. For once M. de Circourt talked French, and we three and a very pleasant Comte de Beauwysse, who was staying with them, a Frenchman of the old school, who knows nothing but French and a little Latin, had a very pleasant hour. I had refused to dine when he wrote to me here to ask me, thinking I should put them out, but was sorry afterwards, as I found they had a party, and amongst the party Mlle. Von Arnim, the daughter of Bettina, Goethe's friend, who is said to be as charming as her mother. I got a glimpse of her on a balcony as I came away, and thought her very handsome and striking-looking. She was to sit down to dinner with four gentlemen she had refused, two French and two German. Les Bruyères is a very pretty place of several acres, on a beautiful range of heathy forest hill commanding the valley of the Seine, with views of Marly, St. Germain, etc. God bless you. Tell the boys I love them, and love to hear of them being such good, dear boys while I am away.　　　—Ever yours.

Text: Russell, 1:122–25.

1. While London earnestly pondered *On Liberty, Adam Bede,* and *The Origin of Species,* Paris was sniggering delightedly over that special blend of clinical lubricity and elegant prose—ce délire de la volupté où le plaisir s'épure par son excès—that so endears French culture to us all. After Musset's several accounts of that *liaison (fameuse),* George Sand returned the compliment in *Elle et Lui* in 1859, and Musset's brother Paul blustered back with *Lui et Elle* (1859), a "bitter attack on George Sand" (*OCFL*), and then (as Henry James has it) Louise Colet, who had been at various times the mistress of Cousin (who fathered her daughter Henriette), Villemain, and (notoriously) Flaubert, as well as of Musset, "cried like Correggio '*Anch'io son pittore!*' and put forth a tale entitled *Lui,* the purpose of which was to prove . . . that she used to roam in the Bois de Boulogne in the small hours of the night in a low-necked dress, while 'He,' roaming hand in hand with her, showered kisses upon her shoulders. 'Orpheus and the Bacchantes' these contributions to erotic history were happily called" (Letter 11, *Parisian Sketches*).

2. *Adieux au monde, mémoires de Céleste Mogador* (5 vols, 1853–54, of the eight projected, suppressed as scandal-mongering but reissued in 1859)—by Céleste Venard, comtesse de Chabrillan, called "Mogador."

Newcastle Commission Journal (Yale)

August 22, Monday.　　　Breakfasted in coffee-room with Col. Hamilton[1]— then to Magin. worked with him till 3. Back to Meurice's and read, and wrote this. dined at table d'hôte—strolled about with Col. Hamilton— home to bed.

August 23rd. Tuesday.   Breakfasted and worked in my own room. Out to call on Cousin, but found him gone into the country. Back and wrote to Flu, & worked; then to the Nord station to meet the Wightmans: walked home with the Judge—dined with them in their rooms; afterwards with Fanny & Georgina to the boulevard, and had coffee.

August 24th, Wednesday.   Breakfasted with the Wightmans. They changed to the Windsor. Drove about with Georgina, leaving copies of my pamphlet. Came back and worked at analysing Rectors's reports. Dined at Café Riche[2] with the Maynes and the Judge Georgina and Fanny. They went to the Opera, I drove in the Bois de Boulogne with Lady Wightman. Sate with her afterwards at the Windsor and had coffee. Home, wrote this, worked at reports and to bed.

August 25th, Thursday.   Worked at reports before breakfast. breakfasted at the Windsor with the Wightmans—then drove with the Judge to return papers. Home & packed up—at 2 with Georgina to Institut, to the Séance Annuelle. Guizot very striking. dined with the Wightmans at the Windsor, then to the Nord station—there met Mary & Mr. Hiley—very hot night to Calais—got over in dead calm, with occasional thunder and rain. Home in Chester Square about 9 a.m. on Friday, August 26th.

1. Aug. 22: Perhaps, Christian Monteith Hamilton (c. 1825-?), "son of J. G. Hamilton, Esq., Glasgow," lieutenant-colonel, 92 Highlanders (Rugby); possibly described below as an "old pupil of my father's and friend of our family" (Sept. 1878).

2. Aug. 24: The Café Riche was at no. 16 boulevard des Italiens. Arnold had perhaps had his fill of Meyerbeer's "Les Huguenots" (see above p. 209 n. 3).

To Mary Penrose Arnold*

Education Department, Council Office, Downing Street, London:
My dearest Mother   August 29 [and 30], 1859
        I arrived on Friday, but would not write till I could with some certainty announce our coming northward. You will have heard that in Paris at the railway station I fell in with Mary & Mr Hiley, and that we travelled together to London—with Mary I talked a great deal but Mr Hiley was so drowsy that I had but little talk with him—Mary looked very thin, I thought, but seemed to have enjoyed her journey. On hearing that Budge and Dicky were looking pale the dear old soul wanted us to send them to her with Charlotte, to stay at Woodhouse till Mary herself proceeds to Westmorland a fortnight hence: but this morning there is a note from her telling us of the alarming illness of Mr Hiley's brother, and that both she and her husband are going to

Yorkshire—and though she still offers Woodhouse to the children in the kindest manner, of course we shall not send them there in her absence. I am the easier consoled as I find that though pale, their appetite and spirits are good, and besides the weather here has become much cooler. So they will do very well till Friday week, when I hope Mrs Askew will be able to receive them. I find a heavy school left for my inspection here—but I shall get over it tomorrow and next day, and on Thursday the 1st September fully hope, as I first intended, to make the delightful start for Fox How. I found Flu with a troublesome toothache and looking very good for nothing—she has had no freedom from it since I came home—but this morning she went to Mr Rahn, my wonderful American, and he told her that she would have no rest till two or three back teeth, which were broken off down to the gum, were out—so this afternoon she drove to Rahn's in the carriage with Dr Hutton, and had three out under chloroform administered by Dr Hutton.

Athenæum, Tuesday—

I was interrupted yesterday, and now can thank you for your note, and Edward for his. Tell Edward that I will try to get the Examiners here as I should much like to read his articles—but surely he has himself the numbers in which they appeared.[1] Tell him also that there is no French guide for Algeria—the French have not yet taken to regarding Algiers as a health and pleasure place—but the best book of information for invalids respecting Algiers is said to be a book by an English clergyman called Davies, which was reviewed in the Saturday Review.[2] I have one or two notes or newspaper articles to shew you—an excellent one of the latter in this week's Economist,[3] I imagine by Mr Greg. But I thought Harriet Martineau very good indeed, and exceedingly civil—nay, flattering.—Flu is very shaky today, having been in fact very drunk yesterday—for that is what *being under chloroform* really amounts to. But the detestable festering stumps are gone. I am rheumatic and full of pains coming back after five months of dry air into this variable one—but I have not more to complain of than a day on the hills will set right.—I have often thought, since I published this on the Italian question, about dear Papa's pamphlets: whatever talent I have in this direction I certainly inherit from him—for his pamphleteering talent was one of his very strongest and most pronounced literary sides, if he had been in the way of developing it. It is the one literary side on which I feel myself in close contact with him—and that is a great pleasure. Even the *positive* style of statement I inherit.   Ever your most affectionate

M. A.—

MS. Balliol College.

1. Two letters, both signed "E.P.A." appeared in the *Examiner*, "The Peace and the Alarm of Invasion," July 23, pp. 467–68, and "Acknowledgement of Actual Governments," on Sept. 3, p. 564. It seems probable that Edward Arnold was to some extent a staff writer and contributed unsigned "article*s*" in several "number*s*." David Hopkinson (p. 66) writes that "He was continuously on sick leave from March 1859 until the spring of the following year. There is no doubt that he was seriously ill (probably with the chest or throat complaint which had troubled him since undergraduate days.)" He published five articles on National Education in the *Examiner*, Oct. 8, 15, pp. 649, 660–61; Nov. 5, 19, 26, pp. 707–8, 739–40, 755–56.

2. The Rev. Edward William Lewis Davies, *Algiers in 1857: Its Accessibility, Climate, and Resources Described, with Especial Reference to English Invalids*, 1858, reviewed in the *Saturday Review*, Mar. 6, 1858, pp. 247–48.

3. "The Quarrelsome French Press," *Economist* 17 (Aug. 13, 1859), p. 897. (A review of *England and the Italian Question* appeared there Aug. 27, p. 956.)

To Louisa Lady de Rothschild[1]

Fox How, Ambleside

Dear Lady Rothschild   September 21, 1859

Your note has followed me to the north of England where I shall be staying till the end of next month, so that it is impossible for me to have the pleasure of accepting your very kind invitation. I am sorry not to be able to come and see your beautiful hills in this autumn weather—though, if that were all, the beauty of the hills and lakes I am now living amongst might console me for not seeing any other country, however beautiful—but by not coming to Buckinghamshire I also lose the pleasure of seeing *you*, and that loss makes me sincerely regret the distance of the North. I hope, however, to find you still at Aston Clinton when I come to inspect your school in the winter.[2] I have had a long and interesting stay abroad, about which I shall be glad to tell you.   With my compliments to Sir Anthony, believe me, dear Lady Rothschild,   very truly yours

M. Arnold.—

MS. British Library.

1. Anthony de Rothschild (1810–76: *DNB*; cr. bt, 1847), of the *London* branch of the legendary family (as distinguished from the Frankfort, Vienna, Paris, and Naples branches), son of Nathan Mayer Rothschild (1777–1836: *DNB*) and brother of Lionel Nathan de Rothschild, in 1840 married Louisa Montefiore (1821–1910), herself the daughter of a Rothschild. (For the *Paris* Rothschilds—his uncle James, first cousin Alphonse, and niece Leonora—see above p. 425 n. 2.)

    The Anthony de Rothschilds in 1853 "settled in a country house, Aston Clinton, in Buckinghamshire [20 or 25 miles east and slightly north of Oxford]. At first it was quite small, but Sir Anthony gradually enlarged it, furnishing it in the French style, with his unerring taste." Their two daughters, Constance (later, Lady Battersea) and Annie (later,

Mrs Eliot Yorke) founded there first a girls' school and then an infants' school, and it was there, on Nov. 17, 1858, that Arnold, inspector of schools, first met Lady de Rothschild, to whom over a hundred letters are printed here. See Cohen, pp. 72, 102–4, and above pp. 407–8.

2. Arnold was there on Nov. 14 (Guthrie, 2:242).

To Arthur Hugh Clough

Fox How. Ambleside
My dear Clough	September 29, 1859
As soon as I heard from you I wrote to Froude urging *him* to do your Plutarch in Fraser,[1] having a fancy to reserve myself for the Edinburgh. I think I might be more useful in the Edinburgh, and I think Reeve would not refuse me an article there[2]—and then I could have my time, without having which I could not satisfy myself, as I write by no means easily, and should like to read through the best part of your translation, without speaking of other translations which I must skim, before reviewing it. But Froude says he is so busy he can do nothing—and adds a long rigmarole about your being so happy and so virtuous that it is not desirable to get literary work out of you—in that regular Carlylean strain which we all know by heart and which the clear-headed among us have so utter a contempt for—since we know very well that so long as *segnities* is, as Spinoza says,[3] with *superbia* the great bane of man, it will need the stimulant of literary work or something equally rousing, to overcome this, and to educe out of a man what virtue there is in him. I for my part find here that I could willingly fish all day and read the newspapers all the evening, and so live—but I am not pleased with the results in myself of even a day or two of such life.

To return to the review of your Plutarch—I incline to wait and see what I can do with Reeve—but if you prefer an article in Fraser, to come earlier, I will, as soon as ever I have done this French Report, see or write to Parker about it.—I think your notion of a selection very judicious—there is no sale for a book like a school sale.	With our united kindest regards to your wife, believe me,	ever your's

M. Arnold.—

I will give you a note to Wm Longman if you like, but it would be better I should speak to him when I come back to London at the end of this month, if that is not too late. I have some time ago talked to him about this Plutarch of your's. He is, as regards books, a thorough *tradesman*, though a capital fellow as regards everything else.

MS. Yale University.

1. Clough's Plutarch, published in Boston by Little, Brown in five volumes, in July. The "selection" of eight lives, " 'for the use of Schools,' " *Greek History from Themistocles to Alexander*, was published by Longman in July 1860 (Mulhauser, 2 : 570—78).

2. Henry Reeve (1813—95: *DNB*), on the staff of *The Times* from 1840, became editor of the *Edinburgh Review* in 1855 and remained there till his death. He appears to have known everybody in the Western world. He was Lansdowne's protégé, more or less, when Arnold was still a schoolboy, and he was in Paris—Arnold's brave new world was Reeve's *arrière-cour*—"at a time when Parisian society still retained much of its old brilliance and its old courtesies; when the world of intellect and art, of politics and of fashion still met on equal and familiar terms." The *Memoirs of the Life and Correspondence of Henry Reeve*, ed. John Knox Laughton (2 vols, 1898, from the preface of which the quotation is taken), is a fascinating and valuable record, starred with the names of most of the luminaries (whom he knew better, earlier, later than Arnold knew them) familiar here from Arnold's own diary and letters. Reeve's edition of the *Greville Memoirs* in eight volumes (1874—87, revised 1896) is an even more "fascinating and valuable record" than his own *Memoirs*.

3. "*Segnities*" (indolence, inertia), not in Spinoza, appears to be Arnold's elegant reduction of "Affectum Definitiones" no. 18, in *Ethics*, 3: "De Origine et Natura Affectuum" (also cited in Super, 2:160, 3:232): "To this emotion [i.e., *Superbia*, Pride, Self-conceit], a contrary does not exist, for no one, through hatred of himself, thinks too little of himself; indeed we may say that no one thinks too little of himself, in so far as he imagines himself unable to do this or that thing. For whatever he imagines that he cannot do, that thing he necessarily imagines, and by his imagination is so disposed that he is actually incapable of doing what he imagines he cannot do. So long, therefore, as he imagines himself unable to do this or that thing, so long is he not determined to do it, and, consequently, so long it is impossible for him to do it" (*Ethics*, tr. William Hale White, rev. Amelia Hutchinson Stirling, ed. James Gutman, 1949, Hafner, N. Y., p. 180)—with perhaps a recollection of *Paradise Lost* 1.320: "Awake, arise, or be for ever fallen."

William Wightman to Matthew Arnold

Pau
October 6, 1859

I thank you heartily, my dear Matt, for your letter & the kind wishes it contained. Considering that my clock of life has struck 75, I am doing pretty well as to health & activity, as you would have said, had you seen me, (as I most sincerely wish you had), climb up to the Plateau de Bious Artigues which commands so grand a view of the Pic du Midi d'Ossau that Lady Chatterton says that it is worth while to come all the way from England to see that alone. (Vide Murray's Hand Book France 287) In fact I have sadly wanted you to be with me in the wild romantic regions we have lately visited; not that I am without excellent company, but it is company that cannot do what you & I could do—for example we go to St Sebastian, an excursion which is followed immediately, by a very serious illness of 4 or 5 days of my lady, requiring the attendance at Bayonne of a very sensible French Physician, & greatly rejoiced we were that we were able to reach Bayonne, & that it had not come on at St Sebastian—Again, we go last Wednesday week to Eaux Bonnes in the Hautes Pyrenees, & while there we make an excursion to Gabas at the foot of the Pic du Midi d'Ossau, & thence Gina & I to the Plateau I have mentioned, Gina on a mule & I chiefly walking, but riding for a very little; the result has been the serious illness of Gina, who was fortunately able to return to Pau before she gave in & there she has had the advice of an English Physician who is still in attendance & is now with her at this very time—so that you see I have no great encouragement to do much even were I so disposed. The weather has been dreadfully hot for the last 3 weeks, the thermometer 83 in the shade & a cloudless sky, making it almost impossible to move about unless very early in the morning or very late in the Evening, neither of which times of the day suit us—The physician who attends Gina tells us that several deaths have occurred here from the effects of the heat. We have now been upwards of a fortnight at Pau & are in very agreeable apartments at the Hotel de France. [It] is in the Place Royale & from our windows we command a very beautiful landscape bounded by a most striking view of the Pic du Midi d'Ossau, by far the most picturesque of all the Pyrenean mountains that I have seen—If you look at Murray's France, titles Eaux Bonnes, Eaux Chaudes, Gabas, you will find a description of the places we have visited & the adjoining scenery—certainly of the most romantic grandeur, differing from Alpine scenery, mainly, in the absence of snow (except in small patches occasionally in crevices) & in the variety of the trees which clothe the sides of the mountains for the most part almost to their summits—

My lady's illness kept us longer at Bayonne than we intended, & as the town was very lively & chearful we were very well content with our stay there; but the inn was very noisy & crowded & not over clean—On our way from Bayonne to Pau we stopped at Orthez where Froissart was entertained to his great satisfaction by the Count de Foix & the Inn to which we went was La Belle Hotesse said by Murray (in whom we place implicit confidence) to be the [?]Lune of Froissart—

We were only one clear day at Bordeaux, which was long enough for us to see all that we wished to see there—indeed we could not well stay longer as our rooms (the best in the Hotel de France at 32 francs per day) were wanted for King Leopold who arrived the day we left—The vin ordinaire you recommended was 3 francs a bottle, & not 1½, & tho' good was not I thought so much superior to that which they gave us at the table d'hote, as the price would indicate.—The landlord remembered, & made honourable mention of you—And now, my dear Matt, my paper is near out, & I have hardly room for the kind remembrances with which I am charged from my lady Fanny & Gina together with my own to Mrs Arnold & your sisters, & all at Fox How, with best love to Flu & the little men & women believe me always   Yours sincerely & affectionately

Wm Wightman

We propose to remain here till the 17th—& to be in London on the 29th.

MS. Frederick Whitridge.

To the Editor of *The Times*

[c. October 25, 1859]

Is Gothic Architecture National?[1]

To the Editor of The Times

Sir,—I have been expecting that some of those who have a vested interest in the question would notice the letter of "E. A. F.," upon Gothic architecture, which appeared in your columns some days ago. Mr. Ruskin is at a loss for you[r] correspondent's name; but some of your readers will have recognized, or thought they recognized, a familiar and able expounder of Gothic architecture. The professors upon the other side are silent; will you allow one of the general public, with a sincere respect for Mr. Gilbert Scott's genius, but connected neither with the Goths nor the Greeks, to make a few remarks on "E. A. F.'s" ingenious letter.

The general public will, if it is wise, let alone his first assumption, that "Gothic and classic are, in a purely practical point of view, equally convenient, but that Gothic is the cheaper." To be sure, the one famous experiment which we all have before our eyes seems to contradict this assumption; the Houses of Parliament are eminently inconvenient and eminently dear. But then Sir Charles Barry is not a good Gothic architect, and Gothic architecture is only just beginning to be again understood. At any rate the Houses of Parliament are but a single experiment; it is certainly possible that future experiments may some day justify your correspondent's assumption, which is, he says, "really the common sense view."

Again, the general public may have its own opinion about his second assumption, that "Gothic and Grecian are just equal—they sit side by side as pure and perfect styles." One may think it strange that the art of the feudal age should be "just equal" with the art of the age of Pericles, the art of one of the poorest periods in the life of mankind with the art of one of the most brilliant. But then, as "E. A. F." tells us, "which style is the most beautiful must always be, to a great extent, a matter of taste;" and, as there is no disputing about tastes, we shall, if we are wise, leave this assumption likewise uncontested.

It is on a point where your correspondent probably imagines himself the most successful that he leaves us the most incredulous. It is on what he calls "the æsthetic question;" it is where he asserts that Gothic architecture is "emphatically," is "pre-eminently," the national architecture of England.

It might be so if there had been no solution of continuity between the feudal world and the modern world. It might be so if there had been no Revival of Letters, no Reformation, no Elizabethan Age, no Revolution of 1688, no French Revolution. As it is, it is not so.

Few will deny—certainly not your correspondent "E. A. F.,"—that there is an intimate correspondence between the condition of the society which invents an architecture and the character of that architecture. Change the condition of the society, and the character of the architecture will change also. Unless, therefore, your corespondent will maintain that the condition, the tendencies, of modern England are the same with the condition, the tendencies, of medieval and feudal England, it is evident that on the æsthetic ground his advocacy breaks down, and that Gothic architecture is in modern England no longer the national style, but an exotic and an anachronism.

But perhaps Gothic architecture was so characteristic a product of English genius that, however our social organization may alter, it must always remain our national style. How strange, in that case, that it should also have been a product of French and German genius, of the genius of two other nations both so unlike our own! Did it not strike "E. A. F.," when he wrote the words "Gothic architecture is the national architecture of England, France, and Germany," that a style produced in common by three such unlike nations can hardly have had its origins in the characteristic genius of each of the three, but must have had it in some circumstances common for a time to them all? This common property was the feudal organization which, from the 12th century to the 16th, held western Europe in the network of hierarchies,—hierarchies of priests, hierarchies of nobles, hierarchies of burghers. Under this common system France, England, and Germany had a common architecture; but that neither that system nor its architecture had root in the essential genius of all three nations two of them, at any rate, have ever since the 16th century been proving, by perpetually striving to free themselves from the first and by abandoning the second.

Gothic architecture is, correctly speaking, neither English architecture, nor French architecture, nor even German architecture; it is feudal architecture.

In the 16th century Gothic architecture "went," as your correspondent says, "out of fashion; it went out of fashion for everything." Yes, and why did it go out of fashion? It went out of fashion in consequence of a great event, or rather of a series of great events, which the term Renaissance brings to our minds, although that term properly denotes the revival of letters only. It went out of fashion because the heroes of the Renaissance—Columbus, Copernicus, Luther, Descartes, Shakespeare—launched the human spirit upon a career of freedom, progress, and sociability opposite to the bondage, stationariness, and isolation of the feudal world, whose symbol and handmaid Gothic architecture had been. It went out of fashion because modern society began, and with new aims and wants sought new styles of art in harmony with them. Gothic architecture was the pride of the feudal age, and well it might be, for it was its noblest fruit; still, it was the fruit of that age, and even its nobleness could not save it. Its magnificent expiring effort, the unfinished Cathedral of Strasburg, in the valley of the Rhine between revolutionized France and Germany, the cradle of feudalism, still attests at once the death of the feudal world and the destiny of Gothic architecture, to live or die with it.

I will not discuss the intrinsic beauty of the architecture of the Renaissance, as I will not dispute the intrinsic beauty of Gothic architecture. It may be that the architectural achievements of modern society are not, like the architectural achievements of feudal society, its proudest achievements. It may be that English architecture has not been sufficiently independent, sufficiently national; that it has too submisively allowed the influence of Italy, the foundress of modern art and civilization. But this is really not the question. The question is not whether the Tuileries or Whitehall are perfect buildings. The question is whether, for our secular buildings, at any rate (for our ecclesiastical buildings the question will come later), we shall work in the same direction as the architects of a modern and post-feudal state of society, or as those of a past and feudal one?

It was, no doubt, absurd to call the Jesuits patrons of Gothic architecture. But has "E. A. F." ever considered what the case of the Jesuits really does prove? Medieval and feudal Catholicism was falling to pieces, and the Jesuits undertook to save it. And how did they set about this? By mixing as much as possible of the form and spirit of modern society with the old doctrines of Catholicism. They made a bad mixture, I admit, but they owed to their modernism, to their partial conformity with the spirit of the age, a success which no other servants of the Roman Catholic Church have had since the Reformation. And this body, the only modern, the only able, the only successful body in the church, abandoned feudal architecture.

To have studied an age well makes us sensible to its merits, indulgent to

its faults; but to have studied an age exclusively makes us overrate it. This is
what has happened to some exclusive students of the Middle Age. They have
found much to admire in that age, taken by itself; and they have not comprehended it in its relation to other ages. They may clearly perceive, like your
able correspondent "E. A. F.," that there is an inseparable correspondence
between a style of architecture and the age which produces it, and that, if
they are to save Gothic architecture, they must save the feudal age; so they
think to save the feudal age by saying that it invented Parliaments! Then there
are the Gothic architects, who naturally believe that no style can equal that
to which they have devoted their powers. Heaven forbid that, like Brunelleschi, I should defy these gentlemen to defend Gothic architecture on its merits! To do that, one should be oneself an architect. But I defy them to prove
that Gothic architecture harmonious with the life of English society since the
16th century. To do this it needs only to have read history and to have one's
eyes open.   I remain, Sir,   your obedient servant,

A.

Text. The Times, Nov. 1, 1859, p. 10.

1. In this letter (published here for the first time since 1859) Arnold takes issue with
a letter in *The Times,* Oct. 19, p. 9, "Gothic or Classic—A Plain Statement of the Question," of which the opening sentence was: "There is a great controversy as to the proper
style of architecture for the new Foreign-office. Shall it be Gothic, or shall it be Classic?"
Two days later a letter by Ruskin, "The Turner Gallery" (*The Times,* p. 7; reprinted in
Works, 13:339–40), included this postscript: "I wish the writer of the admirable and
exhaustive letter which appeared in your columns of yesterday on the subject of Mr.
Scott's design for the Foreign-office would allow me to know his name."

His name was Edward Augustus Freeman (1823–92: *DNB*), who was at Trinity
College, Oxford, while Arnold was at Balliol, who won his spurs with his first book, *A
History of Architecture* (1849), and his prolific contributions to the *Saturday Review,* and
won fame as a distinguished and prolific historian. His inaugural lecture as Regius Professor of Modern History at Oxford, 1884, acknowledges his debt to and admiration of Dr
Arnold, but neither Dr Arnold's son nor this letter is mentioned in *The Life and Letters of
Edward A. Freeman,* ed. W. R. W. Stephens. Freeman's name crops up occasionally in these
volumes, and in a letter on Dec. 15, 1878, Arnold sums him up as "an ardent, learned, and
honest man, but . . . a ferocious pedant"—an estimate fully validated by *DNB.*

Gilbert Scott (1811–78; knt 1872: *DNB*), architect (St Pancras, Glasgow University) and architectural restorer, was at the heart of the controversy. "The competition for
the rebuilding of the war and foreign office in the autumn of 1856 was signalised by a
stormy conflict between the Gothic and classic schools of architecture, waged even in the
House of Commons. Scott's first design submitted in the competition was a sincere attempt to adapt the elements of French and Italian Gothic to the purposes of a modern
English institution. . . . In November 1858 he was appointed architect. . . . At this point
the classical opposition gathered strength, and its cause was taken up in ignorant warmth
by Lord Palmerston. . . . Parliament gave orders for an Italian design to be submitted in
comparison with the Gothic drawings. . . . Scott was thus forced either to abandoned his

appointment or to strike his colours as the Gothic champion. He chose the latter course"
(*DNB*).

Charles Barry (1795–1860; knt 1852: *DNB*), a first-rate *classicist* (Travellers' Club,
Reform Club, etc.), was the architect of the Houses of Parliament.

To Mary Penrose Arnold*

My dearest Mother   November 21, 1859

My drill spoiled my project of writing on Saturday—on Saturdays it is
from 4 to 6—just the letter writing time, as the post goes out from this club
at 6. Tonight the drill is from 7 to 9—a better time in some respects, but it
deprives one of one's dinner. For this however I am not wholly sorry, as in
the first place one eats and drinks so perpetually in London that I am rather
glad on two evenings in the week, Monday & Wednesday, to be relieved
from a regular dinner—in the second place it gives me an opportunity of
having supper at home on these two evenings and keeping one's own cook's
hand in. I like the drilling very much—it braces one's muscles, and does one
a world of good—you saw General Hay's speech[1] to us the other day—the
other corps which was joined with us, the London Scottish, is larger and
more advanced than we are, but we shall do very well, as we have a splendid
neighbourhood to choose from. Far from being a measure dangerous by its
arming the people,—a danger to which some persons are very senstive—it
seems to me that the establishment of these Rifle Corps will more than ever
throw the power into the hands of the upper and middle classes, as it is of
these that they are mainly composed—and these classes will thus have over
the lower classes the superiority, not only of wealth and intelligence, which
they have now, but of physical force. I hope and think that the higher classes
in this country have now so far developed their consciences that this will do
them no harm—still it is a consequence of the present arming movement
which deserves attention, and which is, no doubt, obscurely present to the
minds of the writers of the cheap Radical newspapers, who abuse the movement. The bad feature in the proceeding is the hideous English toadyism
with which lords and great people are invested with the commands in the
corps they join, quite without respect of any considerations of their efficiency. This proceeds from our national bane (Walter would laugh)—the
immense vulgar-mindedness and, so far, real inferiority of the English middle
classes.

It is announced, you see, that the Emperor is trying to moderate the
French newspapers, and I have not the least doubt either that he really wishes
peace with this country, or that he is resolved, even if war is inevitable, to

have to the last all the airs of moderation and studied avoidance of a conflict, on his side. The Times also is absurd and reasons as unscrupulously as an Old Bailey lawyer when it makes capital out of the Revue Britannique—what on earth should a set of refugees do, with nothing on earth to give them a chance in peace and their only hope in the scramble and thousand chances of a great war, but proclaim the imminence of that war with all their lungs? But there is a real danger in the intolerable arrogance and elation of mind which seems to beget itself in the French nation under a Napoleon.

I think I told Fan that my pamphlet is just sold out. It is improbable that I shall reprint it—still I wish you would ask Blanche Whately[2] when you next write what was the answer to it (I think in an appendix to some pamphlet or other) which she mentioned in a letter to me a few weeks ago. I should like to look at it in case I reprint my pamphlet. I heard yesterday that Cobden praised the pamphlet exceedingly.—I have got Papa's life, bound as you wished—what is to be done with it? I have not yet been able to speak to Walrond about Willy's monument—I have not seen him alone for one moment—but I will write to him in about a week. His wedding went off very well, and I enjoyed the day as much as I ever can enjoy having to see company—talk eat and drink champagne between the hours of 10 and 3 in the day time.[3] Flu went off to Devizes this morning, and returns this day week. I am busy this week so shall see little of the dear jolly little companions left me in Budge & Dick—they sleep with me by turns, however, and are to breakfast with me every morning. Tom goes to Eaton Place. Now I must stop and have a cup of coffee. I have had a thousand interruptions and a long expedition in the streets since I began. My love to dear Aunt Jane,[4] and to Fan. Rowland had better come to us next week, if possible. Ever my dearest Mother   your most affectionate son

M. A.—

MS. Balliol College.

1. Maj. Gen. Lord James Hay (1788–1862), second son of the 7th marquis of Tweeddale and retired on half-pay, was colonel commandant of the School of Musketry at Hythe. The Volunteer Rifle Corps had been sanctioned by the Government on May 12, 1859, in the (hysterical) fear of an invasion by Napoleon III (see *Annual Register*, pp. 262–64). Arnold, Clough remarked, is "learning the 'goose step' and other soldierly accomplishments as Member of the Queen's Volunteers or Pimlico Rifles, who drill thrice a week in Westminster Hall" (Mulhauser, 2:573). Hay's (gung ho) speech, at an inspection of the Scotch and Queen's Volunteers, was at Westminster Hall on Nov. 16 (*The Times*, Nov. 19, p. 10). A mildly sarcastic letter about it appeared in the *Examiner*, Nov. 19. Tennyson's poem "Riflemen Form!" (a warmed-over version of an earlier poem "Rifle-Clubs!!!," cooked up but not served in 1852 in response to an earlier, equally hysterical, fear of invasion), had been published in *The Times* on May 9.) See Tennyson, 2:20–21, 233n, and Swinburne, 1:29n.

2. Blanche Whately was one of the daughters of the archbishop, identified en masse in *OED* only as "female issue."

3. Walrond married Charlotte Grenfell at Bray Church on Nov. 17 (*Annual Register*). See above p. 168 n. 3. In India a commemorative medal for an annual award for Punjab scholars, "his grave on the Rock of Gibraltar, a tablet in Dharmsala Church," but "better than any of these, surely, he would like to be remembered by four words on the wall of Rugby Chapel: *Scilicet omnis noster erat* (Woodward, pp. 227–28).

4. Jane Penrose.

To Joseph Severn [1]

The Athenæum
2, Chester Square
My dear Severn   November 29, 1859

I was at Buckingham all yesterday, and did not come home till nearly 10 o'clock at night, too late to take advantage of your kind invitation.

I know the sonnet of Keats well—it contains two of the most magical lines which even he ever wrote. But I am glad you have given me an opportunity of seeing it in his own handwriting, and in a volume the *markings* of which are invaluable as proof where he got his *manner*. I have never doubted that the star continued to be spoken of all through the first eight lines of the sonnet; the only difficulty arises from Keats's somewhat incorrect use of the word "like" in line 4: one expects the star to be compared to some other person or thing, but it is not—Keats only means to say "as if thou wert Nature's solitary one."

I should have been glad to see Newton [2] again and should like to send him a copy of my Merope if you will tell me where he is to be found. If you will allow me I will send you a copy also as you will find there another Preface which may perhaps interest you. I hope this morning to go and look at the picture.   Ever very truly yours

M. Arnold.—

MS. Princeton University.

1. Joseph Severn (1793–1879: *DNB*), a painter, is remembered today as the best-known, and most selfless, of all Keats's friends. He accompanied Keats to Rome in 1820 and there "acted as nurse, cook, cleaner, secretary, entertainer, spiritual consoler, and confidant to the sick poet, who died in his arms" (*The Keats Circle*, ed. H. E. Rollins, 1:cxxxii). Arnold refers to the "Bright star" sonnet in the "holograph fair copy written opposite the beginning of *A Lover's Complaint* in the 1806 *Poetical Works of William Shakespeare* at Keats House, Hampstead" (*The Poems of John Keats*, ed. Jack Stillinger, p. 638).

2. Charles Thomas Newton (1816–94: *DNB*; knt 1887), the British consul at Rome, became Keeper of Greek and Roman Antiquities at the British Museum and married Severn's daughter in 1861 (whereupon Severn returned to Rome as consul). Ann

Mary (Severn) Newton (1832–66: *DNB*) had studied with Ary Scheffer in Paris in the mid-fifties and there had painted, among others, the countess of Elgin.

To Edward Walford[1]

The Judges Lodgings, York

My dear Walford   December 4, 1859

Your letter has been forwarded to me here. I am always very stupid at providing anything by a given time or for a special purpose, and just at this moment I have on my hands a Report on popular education on the continent which I was sent abroad this spring to collect materials for. So I must say to you, I am afraid, as I said to Thackeray the other day, that I am at the present moment doomed to entire literary sterility. Pray tell Lucas so, whom I, like everyone else, know from the Times, and not only from the Sandwich Islands.[2]

You must let me send you a copy (*not* for review) of a thing of mine which is and must be eminently unpopular, but which it gave me singular pleasure to compose—a tragedy on the Greek model. I send it to you as to one of the best scholars of my acquaintance, and in memory of those old Balliol days of which your letter reminds me—days the very remembrance of which begins to fade away, but which were some of the pleasantest of one's life. Believe me, my dear Walford,   ever very truly your's

M. Arnold.—

MS. Balliol College.

1. Edward Walford (1823–1897: *DNB*), "Bumsucker Walford," as Swinburne called him (blaming him for the loss of a manuscript and accusing him of sycophancy), antiquary, editor, and compiler, was at Balliol with Arnold (see above p. 37) and a decade before Swinburne. He was "ordained deacon in 1846, priest the next year. Statistics are imperfect, but Walford seems to hold the record for official religious vacillation, having deserted the Anglican Communion for the Roman in 1853 and 1871 and the Roman for the Anglican in 1869 and (about) 1896. From 1859 to 1865 he was first subeditor and then editor of *Once a Week*, and edited the *Gentleman's Magazine* from Jan. 1866 to May 1868" (Swinburne, 4:18; 2:177). He also compiled *County Families of Great Britain* (1860) and several annual peerages and similar volumes. In Feb. 1868 Arnold engaged him to tutor the boys for admission to Harrow.

2. Samuel Lucas (1818–68: *DNB*), journalist and author, was at Queen's College, Oxford, 1838–42, where he won the Newdigate Prize in 1841 for a poem called "The Sandwich Islands." He was a frequent contributor to *The Times* and collected several volumes of his pieces, of which the first was *Eminent Men and Popular Books from the "Times,"* 1859.

To Mary Penrose Arnold

York
My dearest Mother December 6, 1859

I write with the towers of the Minster in sight, and that is something—but it frets me to have come so far north and yet reached nothing in the way of country more reviving than this great York plain, and how I should like to make my way to you across the bracing hill country of the West Riding at this bracing time of the year. That cannot be—but tomorrow morning at 8 o'clock Budge and I start for Wharfeside—we shall go by a country which on the map looks promising and which at any rate is new to me—the country about Knaresborough: we shall be at Arthington before 10, and at Wharfeside,[1] I hope, before 11. We shall have from three to four hours there—but must leave at about ½ past 2 in the afternoon to get back here in time for a dinner with the Vernon Harcourts at the Residence House.[2] I cannot well leave the Judge for an evening—besides on a cross line of eastward, with several changes, and a child with one, one is glad to travel without luggage, which can be managed if one goes only for the day. We wanted K to come over to us here with Eddie[3] as Tom cannot move [in] this weather—indeed it was rather imprudent bringing him from London, and he has a toothache some cold and a bad colour, which makes us anxious about him—however I do not think he is going to be ill this time, but we must be careful of him, and, as he stays, Flu cannot leave him. K however declines coming which is natural enough as the journey is an abominable one and she not very enterprising—so Budge and I must go to her, and the journey with old Budge will be not bad fun. He is in great force—it was not him[4] but Tom that Major Johnson[5] saw and thought delicate. Budge was stopping in Eaton Place. We might have any amount of dining here, as York is one of the few provincial towns which still retain some resident magnates, besides the Cathedral dignitaries. Tomorrow we dine at the Residence, on Thursday with Mrs Fenton Scott,[6] on Friday we have people here and for Saturday and Sunday we are asked to Escrick[7] but I don't think we shall go as Lady Wightman is confined to her room by a bad cold and the Judge does not like to lose the enjoyment of his one free day Sunday, which he fancies he does lose if he has to do company all day—natural enough at his age. But Flu and I must at any rate go and see Stephen Lawley at the Rectory: and I think we shall go over for morning service and luncheon on Sunday and return in time for the Anthem at the Minster in the afternoon. On Monday we go back to London. The calendar is very heavy—about 100 prisoners—but I think the Judge will get done and follow us to London at the end of next week.

I was out all day nearly every day of Rowland's visit last week—but I used to go and see her when she was in bed at night. I think she was comfortable and the children behaved nicely to her—but I thought her not at all in a good state of health. I told her I would give her something she wanted for her leg, and that you should pay her and we would balance accounts. Yesterday she was to go the Crystal Palace with Mrs Tuffin and Dicky—that darling, we hear is quite happy and never asks for his brothers—but the morning of our departure his dear heart was quite full and every time he spoke of our going his sweet eyes filled with tears and we went away amidst a burst of grief from him. I think I told Fan that I may have to go back to Paris for a week after Xmas; I don't fancy the journey, but I shall be able to complete the seeing of some people & things that will be of use to me. I meant to send you a very good article on my pamphlet in the Atlas[8] but have mislaid the newspaper. After our return to London I will see that the Saturday Review is sent regularly. The first number of Macmillan's Magazine seems rather a failure: Thackeray's Magazine has a better start on that account. He will have an article by Captain Young of the Fox,[9] whom the Bensons know very well. I have had within the last ten days requests from him, from Fraser, and from Once a Week to do something for them—but cannot.[10] Write to me at the Judge's Lodgings here, if you can—and with love to my dear Fan and thanks for her letter believe me always my dearest Mother,   your most affectionate son

M. A.—

Flu's best love and thanks to Fan for her letter. I lose my drill here, which is a bore.[11] The present Dean of York is married to one of the Ladies Douglas whom you remember at Coton.[12]
I was very glad to represent our family at poor Uncle Buckland's funeral.[13] It was a dreary day and a dreary scene.

MS. Balliol College.

1. Home of the William Forsters.
2. William George Granville Venables Vernon Harcourt (1827–1904: *DNB*; knt 1873; *VF*, 5/11/99), grandson of Edward Harcourt (1757–1847), archbishop of York, and son of William Vernon Harcourt (1789–1871, of Nuneham Park, Oxford, canon of York), was born in the Old Residence, York, and educated at Trinity College, Cambridge, where he was one of the famed "Apostles." His precocity was conspicuous from his undergraduate days, and in 1855–59 he made a reputation by his frequent (unsigned) contributions to the brand-new *Saturday Review* and then, from Dec. 1861, over the name "Historicus," enhanced it with series of long letters to *The Times* on the subject of international law. At the time of this letter, he was a bridegroom of exactly a month (his wife, the former Maria Theresa Lister, died in 1863), and, though narrowly defeated in the General Election in May, he was clearly on the verge of a distinguished political career

(solicitor-general, home secretary, chancellor of the Exchequer three times, leader of the House), and he fulfilled expectations in every way—but one.

The British upper classes before, say, 1920, were not crippled by self-doubt, and Harcourt—rich, of "magnificent physique" and handsome (when young), his veins coursing with Plantagenet blood, was far from deficient in self-confidence: his superiority was outward, visible, and radiant. "Thus it was," wrote Horace G. Hutchinson (*Portraits of the Eighties*, p. 69), "that he was so useful a fighting man in the face of an avowed foe, but . . . somewhat worse than useless, for the at least equally valuable purpose of gaining friends." And thus it was that he was always a groomsman, never the groom. And thus it was that in 1894, on Gladstone's resignation, the queen summoned for the new ministry not Harcourt—Gladstone's hit man ("Babble and Bluster," according to *Vanity Fair* in 1892) the odds-on favorite—but the Earl of Rosebery, his *semblable et frère (cadet)*, younger by twenty years. (Harcourt was pictured six times in *Vanity Fair*, twice alone, four times in groups, from 1870 to 1899: mutability was not charitable.)

3. Edward Penrose Arnold, later, Arnold-Forster.

4. A rare usage in Arnold.

5. Edwin Beaumont Johnson (1825–93: *DNB*; knt 1875), later general; his father, Sir Henry Allen Johnson (1785–1860), 2d baronet, preceded Arnold's at Christ Church, Oxford, where he tutored the Prince of Orange (*DNB*; Foster)

6. Unidentified.

7. Escrick Park, seven miles SSE of York, was the seat of Beilby Richard Lawley (1818–80), 2d Baron Wenlock, older brother of Stephen and Frank Lawley and of Jane (d. 1900), who in 1846 married James Archibald Stuart-Wortley (1805–81: *DNB*), third son of 1st Baron Wharncliffe and recorder of the City of London and then, 1856–57, solicitor-general.

8. "Matthew Arnold on the Italian Question," *Atlas*, Sept. 3, 1859, p. 266 (anon.).

9. The first number of *Macmillan's Magazine* appeared in November, of Thackeray's *Cornhill Magazine* in January. Allen William Young (1827–1915: *DNB*; knt 1877) was the navigating officer for Capt. Francis Leopold McClintock (1819–1907: *DNB*) on the *Fox* in the successful search for Sir John Franklin and the *Erebus* and *Terror*. The *Fox* reached England on Sept. 21, and neither Young nor McClintock dawdled: Young's unsigned article, "The Search for Sir John Franklin (From the Private Journal of an Officer of the 'Fox')" appeared in the *Cornhill* in Jan. 1860, McClintock's book, *The Voyage of the "Fox" in the Arctic Seas: A Narrative of the Discovery of Sir John Franklin and His Companions*, published by Murray, appeared in Dec. 1859.

10. He gave in and sent "Men of Genius"—reprinted as "The Lord's Messengers"' (Allott, p. 490)—to Thackeray for the *Cornhill* in July. (See *Album*, pp. 12, 73–74.) For *Once a Week* see above p. 510 n. 1.

11. For the Volunteer Rifle Corps (see above p. 508 n. 1).

12. The Hon. and Very Rev. Augustus Duncombe (1814–80), son of the 1st Lord Feversham and a Worcester College man, was named dean of York in May 1858 (*Annual Register*); he married Harriet Christian Douglas (d. 1902), daughter of the 5th marquis of Queensberry, in 1841. Coton Hall, Warwickshire, four miles from Rugby, was a seat of her father (*Imperial Gazetteer*).

13. Rector of Trusham, South Devon (Boase), he died at Chertsey on Nov. 24, age 74 (*The Times*, Nov. 26, p. 1).

To Mary Penrose Arnold*

The Athenæum
London
My dearest Mother   December 19, 1859

Last week slipped away without my writing for my hours at the Training School, on which I counted, were so broken by people coming in to speak to me or ask me questions, that I had time for nothing. Tuesday Wednesday Thursday and Friday I had to be at the Westminster training school at ten o'clock—be there till ½ past 1—and begin again at 3, going on till half past 6—this with 80 candidates to look after and gas burning most of the day—either to give light or to help warm the room. In the middle of the day I had to dine with Scott, the Principal of the Training School. So I went out in the morning before I had seen little Lucy and did not get home at night till she had gone to bed. On Saturday I finished at the Training School at ½ past 2—but then I had my drill, which I find in my absence at York I have too much forgotten. Today I am free—but as I have to drill in the evening, I shall not be able to dine in Eaton Place, but shall come home to supper at ½ past 9, when the Du Quaires are coming in. Tomorrow I begin again at the Training School and continue till Friday, when I hope to be finally free, and to be able to work at my French Report till the end of January when I hope to send it in. I shall avoid going back to Paris if possible—though it is rather tempting in some ways when one hears of winter society having begun there and everybody being alive and gay. My great inducement in going back would be to see and talk to Cousin who has himself had a Report to make much like that on which I am engaged. I should also, now that I know and have read so much about popular education in France, much like to see Guizot again, and to ask him some questions. However I don't much think I shall go. The most difficult and important part of my Report is pretty well formed in my head now—and going back to Paris might give me a new start in some direction or other which would unsettle me and give me all to do again.

It is a very hard frost, but everyone who comes up to London from the country says how warm it is here to what they have left. And never, certainly, have I found our house more comfortable. Fanny Lucy insists in hard frosts on my having a fire in my dressing-room to get up by, as three sides of it are outside wall and we are afraid for the pipes in that part of the house—so my comfort is never better cared for than in very cold weather—for a fire to get up by is perhaps the greatest comfort in the world. We have a little iron bed now put up for Tom in the most sheltered corner of our bed-room, which is really the Isle of Madeira of the house—the thermometer there never hardly sinking below 60, though there is a fire in the room only in the evening—it suits Tom wonderfully and in this very cold weather his breathing seems perfectly free. Budge and Dick went with me and Flu to the Serpentine this morning about 11—it was a beautiful sight, with a bright sun shining and groups of people all over the ice—for an hour or so it all did very well, and I skated with Budge and Dick in my arms now & then, which delighted them exceedingly—but then the intense cold began to tell on Dick, who fell a roaring—and a little before 1 we all went home. Budge had a heavy fall on the back of his head—but his nose began to bleed and that relieved him— he did not cry at all, and in all matters of bearing pain or cold he is a very stout little boy. It has begun to snow this afternoon and they are all left at home: Budge made a good dinner and seems all right. I hear dear K has had a tooth out. I long to hear that this has relieved the discomfort in her face. Many thanks for your long letter—which told me a great deal—we were so very sorry to miss the Trevenen Penroses. Love to all and tell me how Row-land is—kiss Fan for me and believe me always   your most affectionate son—

M. A.—

Tell me what is done about Walter.

MS. Balliol College.

To Jane Martha Arnold Forster *

The Athenæum Club
My dearest K   December 24, 1859
    I must write a line home on my birthday—and I have long wanted to write to you who luckily find yourself at Fox How at this moment—so at the same time that I fulfil a long-entertained wish I can send my love to all at Fox How, and thanks to my dearest Mother, Fan Walter and Rowland for their affectionate good-wishes. Thank you, too, for your dear letter, my dar-ling K—if I do not often communicate with you it is not that I do not often think of you. There is no one about whom I so often think in connexion with my lectures, which have now entirely taken shape in my head and which I hope to publish at the end of 1860, giving five between this and then. I thought the other day that I would tell you of a Frenchman whom I saw in Paris, Ernest Rénan [*sic*], between whose line of endeavour and my own I imagine there is considerable resemblance, that you might have a look at some of his books if you liked. The difference is, perhaps, that he tends to

inculcate *morality*, in a high sense of the word, upon the French nation as what they most want, while I tend to inculcate *intelligence*, also in a high sense of the word, upon the English nation, as what they most want—but with respect both to morality and intelligence I think we are singularly at one in our ideas—and also with respect both to the progress and the established religion of the present day. The best book of his for you to read, in all ways, is his "Essais de Morale et de Critique" lately published—I have read few things for a long time with more pleasure than a long essay with which the book concludes—"Sur la poésie des races celtiques"—I have long felt that we owed far more, spiritually and artistically, to the celtic races than the somewhat coarse Germanic intelligence readily perceived, and been increasingly satisfied at our own semi-celtic origin, which, as I fancy, gives us the power, if we will use it, of comprehending the nature of both races. Rénan pushes the glorification of the Celts too far—but there is a great deal of truth in what he says and being on the same ground in my next lecture in which I have to examine the origin of what is called the "romantic" sentiment about women, which the Germans quite falsely are fond of giving themselves the credit of originating, I read him with the more interest.

How I envy you Rydal Lake! but the Serpentine is better than might be supposed, and very beautiful. The frost has been so hard that in spite of this thaw (thermometer at 45) the ice still bears—and Dicky and I on our pilgrimage to the city this morning were on it in St James's park. He and Budge were delighted with their party last night—there were 70 children present and the whole thing beautifully done: they were among the very youngest children there, but behaved very well, Flu says. They stayed till nearly 10 o'clock, but ate scarcely anything either at tea or supper, they were so excited—so they are none the worse today, for I am convinced it is through the stomach children generally suffer on these occasions. Dicky in a black velvet coat, white waistcoat, silk tartan skirt of red & black, and *white gloves*, was a sight to look at. Budge looked a duck, too, in a black velvet tunic and white trousers—and he also in white gloves. They had a magic lantern, dancing, and a magnificent Xmas tree: Flu says the way Budge dived in among the other boys and skirmished with them, was very amusing. Diddy clung generally to her.

I am much interested in Miss Hills's engagement[1]—I understand from the Walronds that she has a *history* and she looks as if she had. I mean no scandal, merely that she has had previous love-affairs, and that she is one of the few people whose looks induce one to wish to know all about them. I hear she is very well off. Curwen is rather a stupid match for her, I think, but her choice is not wide now Benson Harrison is married. Love to all—and tell my dear old Susy that I know I owe her a letter and that we sorrowed sincerely over the death of her horse, who probably died of carrying her on her incessant errands to do good. I must write to her. A happy Xmas to you all. Little Tom is very well for him, though he frightened us terribly the other night by throwing up a quantity of blood: but Dr Hutton says it was only from the throat, and that his lungs and heart are better than usual. Love to William: I don't understand about the Quaker Insurance offices—for volunteers only serve in case of invasion or insurrection, and in such cases the sovereign has power, by his admitted prerogative, to call on every man for armed service, on penalty of fine and imprisonment if he refuses, whether he be a volunteer or no.[2]   Your ever affectionate

M. A.—

Kiss the dear little children for me.

MS. Frederick Whitridge.

1. Clearly, the microworld of Windermere-Grasmere-Ambleside was abuzz, and Arnold has his little joke. Beatrice Cervinia Hills (d. 1876) married the Rev. Alfred Francis Curwen (1835–1920) on Jan. 2, 1861. She was the daughter of John Hills, Recorder of Rochester, he the son of Edward Stanley Curwen, Workington Hall, Cumberland, and The Island, Windermere. Benson Harrison (1786–1863), J.P., of Green Bank, Scale How, Ambleside, was twice married, the second time to a Wordsworth (his son, Matthew Benson Harrison [b.1824], at Belle Vue, had been married since 1845). (See Martineau; *County Families*; *Landed*; *Upper Ten Thousand*; Black's *Picturesque Guide to the English Lakes*, 1854, p. 74.) Florence Arnold-Forster, visiting Fox How from Ireland with her mother and father in Jan. 1882, had "afternoon tea at Mrs Benson Harrison's" and next day returned the invitation (Arnold-Forster, p. 365).

2. Forster "threw himself . . . with enthusiasm" into the Volunteer Movement: "It was difficult indeed to recognize in the captain of volunteers, who was eager above all things to perfect himself in his drill, who spent hours on the moors practising at the target, and who played the part of an indefatigable recruiting sergeant both at Bradford and at Burley, the son of the old Quaker preacher, whose whole life had been given to the promulgation of the doctrine of passive resistance" (Reid, 1 : 321).

To Thomas Arnold

⟨Education Department, Council Office, Downing Street, London:⟩
2, Chester Square
My dear Tom   December 29, 1859
    I have often looked at Newman's book on Universities[1] and read bits of it—and I am very glad to have it of my own—but still more glad to have it from you, and sent to me with such a pleasant note for my birthday.
    I cannot read it just yet for till I have done my French Report my reading is pretty much limited to what concerns that. I have had to read up and

down and right and left for it, for the French Education Department has published no Reports for the last ten years. You will be interested in reading it, I think, and I shall certainly send it you as soon as it is printed. I hope to have finished it by the end of January, and to have it printed in the course of February.

I am glad you saw my letter on Gothic architecture[2] which I said so little about that Fanny Lucy did not even know I had written it, till Edward, who had found it out by the style, teased me with it in her presence.

I am inclined to agree with you that no religious architecture affords so much satisfaction to the religious sense in its strongest degree as the Gothic. I doubt about its constructive excellence, if I rightly understand your use of the words: Ruskin is the most unsafe of guides; the école des Chartes have proved that the Gothic architects did not know Mathematics till they learnt them, quite late, from their opponents—and it was this ignorance, leading them to a system of perpetual buttressing and propping, that Brunelleschi reproached them with and built the Cathedral of Florence to shew what Mathematical architecture could do without supports. The Gothic cathedrals are perpetually out of repair from their vast system of external supports, exposed to the wind and rain, and for ever wanting to be tinkered. So it is said, at least, by those who should know. This only with regard to its constructive merits. But for social architecture I think it has deeper and inherent disqualifications. But this is a long story.

Come to London any time in the spring but when Mamma is with us, and we will take you in with delight. Love to the children, and our united love to you. Julia, I hear, is at Woodhouse.   Ever your affectionate
M. A.—

MS. Balliol College.

1. *The Scope and Nature of University Education,* 1859 (later, *The Idea of a University Defined and Illustrated,* 1873)—published in 1852 as *Discourses on the Scope and Nature of University Education, Addressed to the Catholics of Dublin.*
2. See above pp. 503–6.

To Mary Penrose Arnold*

⟨Education Department, Council Office, Downing Street, London:⟩
2, Chester Square
My dearest Mother   December 31, 1859
I have not much time, but must not fail to wish you many many happy new years. I keep planning and planning to pass Christmas and the New Year again at Fox How, where I have passed them so often and so happily, now,

alas! so long ago—but I do not see when it will be practicable. To make up, I think of you all more and oftener at this time of year than at any other.

I must tell you while I think of it that I had a little note from Tom on my birthday, sending me as a birthday present Newman's book on Universities—nothing I received that day pleased me more.

I think it is quite clear from what Uncle Trevenen says (I return his letters) that you must alter your will again, as it would not do to run the risk of the difficulty about the settlement money which he suggests. As to myself, if it were not for two considerations I should beg to be left as I stand in Papa's will: one is that the will actually presses harder upon me than he would probably have meant, just catching me and only just while it catches no one else—the other, that I shall want money if I am to have any chance of buying Fox How. But the "other funds at your disposal" of which Uncle Trevenen speaks, are not easy to be dealt with by will, I should think, at present, for after all their coming to you is not an absolute certainty. However you had better make Rowland's legacy safe at all events—for for that there will certainly be sufficient funds. As to the rest you had better take the advice of William Forster and Uncle Trevenen.

Lady Wightman is not, I think, in any immediate danger—but her attack, a sort of pleurisy, is a very serious one, because she nearly died of the same complaint some years ago, and is now in a very feeble and broken state, looking very much older than she did a month ago. She alarmed us all very much some days ago when she nearly sank in a succession of fainting fits which followed the application of leeches put on at her own earnest desire and rather against the doctor's wish. She cannot get rid of the pain in her side and till this is removed she cannot be considered out of danger. But she sleeps well at night, which is greatly in her favour.

Poor little Tom has been having, and has, one of his attacks—cough and fever—and yesterday was very ill indeed. But he struggles on in the wonderful way that you know, and in every hour that he gets a little ease, seems to recover his strength, which two or three hours of continuous cough try terribly. I hear his little voice now in the next room talking [to] his Mamma about Brown Jones and Robinson[1]—it is one of his good hours, but this afternoon he has been very unwell. The intensity of his feverishness is something curious—his little head and hands seem actually to give out heat as you sit near him. The others are very well indeed, and Lucy making a great start in liveliness—Budge and Dick went with us in the carriage this afternoon to make a call in the Regent's Park and as the people were out we took them on to the Zoological Gardens for an hour—it was Dick's [first] visit and he shouted and danced for pleasure at the animals—above all at the Lion who was in high excitement and growling magnificently. I am very fond of the Gardens myself, and there are many new things this year. I must stop and go on looking over papers. Did you see a long article in the Times on Clough's Plutarch?² it pleased me so much. Clough has just had the scarlatina and is at Hastings to get well. Were you not agitated to hear of Macaulay's death!³ It has made a great sensation. But the Times leading article on him is a splendid exhibition of what may be called the *intellectual vulgarity* of that newspaper. I had no notion Macaulay was so young a man. It is said he has left no more history ready, which is a national loss. I shall miss the post if I go on—so love and a happy new year to all.   Your ever most affectionate son

M. A.—

MS. Balliol College.

1. Richard Doyle's drawings, with captions, originally in *Punch* in 1850 (*The Plea-sure Trips of Brown, Jones, and Robinson*) or, as a volume in 1854, *The Foreign Tour of Brown, Jones, and Robinson.*

2. *The Times*, Dec. 12, 1859, p. 6: "not well done," said Clough, "though I fear only *too* well meant" (Mulhauser, 2 : 574).

3. Macaulay, age 60, died on Dec. 28. The long notice in the *Annual Register*, pp. 451 – 55, is "slightly abridged" from the account in *The Times* of this date, p. 7.

Appendixes
Index

Appendix A

(See Introduction, pp. xxxv–xxxvii)
To the left of certain dates on the unprinted right-hand pages of the
diaries for 1845, 1846, and 1847 are crosses, which demonstrably have nothing to do with chapel (attendance or avoidance), tardiness at prayers, or bad
weather, and are not explained in any way at any point. (Parentheses indicate
crosses on the *right* of the date.)

1845
January: 3, 5, 9, 11, 12, 24, 26, 30
February: 2, 8, 9, 10, 13, 15, 19, 24
March: 9, 23, 25, 30
April: 12, 16, 20, 22, 26
May: 2, 8, 10, 14, 18, 26, 27, 29, 31
June: 1, 5, 7, 13, 18, 22, 23, 24, 28
July: (1, 14, 16)
August: 9, 24
September: 4, 9, 13, 23, 25, 28
October: 5, 7, 18, 19, 29
November: (1, 6, 16, 23)
December: (5), 14, 15, 22, 26, 30

1846
January: (3, 10, 11, 13, 16, 23, 24, 25, 26, <27, 28, 29> 31)
February: 6, 10, 13, 16, 20, 24, 26, 28
March: 4, 6, 10, 11, 14, 18, 19, 23, 27, 28
April: 2, 4, 8, 16, 18, 21, 23, 27
May: 1, 2, 7, 9, 14, 16, 21, 23, 24, 27, 28, 30
June: 2, 4, 13, 22, 27
July: 5, 16, 19, 21, 24, 25, 27
August: 1, 3, 7, 9, 23, 25, 28, 29, 30, 31
September: 3, 6, 7, 12, 19, 21, 24
October: 4, 10, 16, 17, 18, 19, 24, 26, 30
November: (3, 9, 11, 23, 24)
December: (6, 9, 19, 21), 27

1847
January: (2, 4, 10), 27, 29
February: 8, 15, 19, 26, 28

March: 4, 13, 17, 21, 27, 31
April: 3, 12, 18, 19, 27, 28
May: [none]
June: 3, 13, <14,> 26
July: 8, 31
August: 7, 9, 11, 18, 19
September: 1, 5, 8, 11, 16, 30
October: (18, 28)
November: (8, 11, 18, 30)
December: (1, 14, 15, 22)

Appendix B

(Arnold's notes in Fauriel's Histoire de la poésie provençale; see above p. 415 n. 5)
M. Fauriel, *Histoire de la poésie provençal*, cours fait à la faculté de Paris. Paris, Jules Labitte, Librairie-Editeur, Passage des Panorama. 1846, 3 volumes. Williams & Norgate sticker. Jan. 1858, MA paid Williams & Norgate £20.3.6 (Guthrie, 2:222 see also p. 200).

Inserted, loose, in volume one a sheet folded to make four pages (watermarked: WHATMAN/1857).

The Burgundian kingdom of the Niebelungen is on both banks of the Middle Rhine, and has Worms for its capital.

The south Teutons (Germans) collected in the Middle Age the body of Niebelungen traditions in two Cycles: the Heldenbuch & the Niebelungen Lay.

The North Teutons (Scandinavians) collected them in two main Sagas: the Volsunga & the Wilkina Sagas.

Siegfried lived in the Niederland or Frankenland, (the right bank of the Lower Rhine) about the Middle of the 5th Century.

He begins by killing the Dwarf Fafnir, who, under the form of a Dragon, guarded an immense buried treasure on a lonely mountain, and by possessing himself of the treasure.

The Chriemhilde of the German tradition is the Gudruna of the Scandinavian.

[283–4] Both the German & Scandinavian works are only 'la fusion en un seul tout regulier et complet de chants populaires ou nationaux plus anciens composés isolement, en divers temps et par divers auteurs.'

Jornandes had read the songs of the Goths: the Emperor Julian had heard those of the German tribes on the right bank of the Rhine, & been struck with their barbarous melody. [p. 2] The other Edda was a collection of Scandinavian songs made by an Icelandic Ecclesiastic, named Saemund, at the *end of the 11th century*, probably to serve as documents for a history of his Country which he was engaged on. He was the first who *wrote them down*.

The younger Edda was a collection of old Scandinavian <religions> traditions & poems made by a learned Norwegian, Snorro Sturleson, *about the beginning of the 13th century*, just after the conversion of the Scandinavians to Christianity, and when their old legends were beginning to disappear.

The younger Edda contains no poem and cites no author contained or cited in the older Edda. Not one author of the pieces in the older Edda is known. The earliest poet cited in the younger Edda [p. 3] belongs to the Xth century.

[Lined off in a 'box' at the top of this page:]

The Niebelungen Lied contains about 10,000 lines.
The Horny Siegfried   ″   ″   750   ″
Walter of Aquitaine   ″   ″   1450   ″

The Volsunga Saga is a production probably of the beginning of the 13th century. It is "une espèce de resumé en *prose* des chants poétiques de l'Edda qui ont rapport aux Ni[e]belungen." As it was to serve as an orderly narrative of events, a great many poems which interfered with this object were left out.

The actual poem of the Ni[e]belungen had for its basis a latin narrative drawn up from local traditions & songs towards the end of the Xth century, by a Bishop of Passau om Hungary.

Louis the Debonnair[e] had the greatest aversion to all remains of the paganism of his Frankish ancestors: their songs probably fell into neglect in his reign.

Walter of Aquitaine is a Latin Poem having for its hero a Prince of Aquitaine.

The Wilkina Sage is a collection in prose of a number of romantic <traditions> stories, *made principally from German sources*, by a learned Norwegian Hiorn, about the middle of the XIIIth century.

[p. 4] J'ai entendu lire cette histoire à des clercs, à de savants latiniers, dans le livre ou [sic] se lisent les Gestes.

—Walter of Aquitaine, in its present form, was composed by a monk named Gerald, belonging to an abbey on the Loire, in the confines between Frankish Gaul & Aquitaine. It was probably founded on a story composed in the 7th century, in Aquitaine, in the semi-barbarous Latin which was then still spoken in that country.

—The only remain of the German national poetry of the Charlemagne era, is a fragment of about 60 lines, on an adventrue of Hildebrand, the follower of Dietrich of Bern.

—Walter (probably one of the Gallo-Roman dukes of Gascony or Aquitaine who reconquered the South of France from the Merovingians) is a *héros civilisé et chrétien*: his prayer over the bodies of his slain enemies shews this: but il n'y a pas, dans tout le poëme, un mot d'allusion aux usages chevaleresques. Nor is the love of Walter & Hildegunde a *romance love.*

I. 408 (in margin beside 'C'est indubitablement d'un Gaulois, d'un Gallo-Romain d'origine ou d'affection, qui s'est proposé de vanter les exploits.) 'd'origine, no; d'affection, possibly.'

I. 418 [in bottom margin]: Decbr 3rd, 1881.

I. [flyleaf at end]: Paulin Paris / Romancero Français / Techner, 1833 / article in vol. xxiii of Hist. Litt. de la France.

I. [facing flyleaf]: The two Eddas / 287–289'Wilkina Sage. / 386 /

penchant of Celts for things Greek—85
moral character of Marseilles schools—91–97.
Gaul civilised from Rome—113
rise of a new literature in South of France, 164
Greek in Provençal. 199
Walter the Monk—413
duties of chivalry—528

II. [flyleaf at end]:
good verse—34,-8,-9
the troubadour's end—39
syrventes—171.
Pierre Cardinal—174.
belle allégorie—180.
a beau passé imagined for chivalry—186
the Monk of Montandon—196.
Perdigon the troubadour—216.
the vers provencal [sic] the model of modern verse—221

[no penciling in volume iii, either in margins or on flyleaves]

Appendix C

No. III

The Etruscan Tombs at Perugia and Chiusi

(From Henry Robert Skeffington, *A Testimony: Poems*, W. D. Biden & Co., Kingston-upon-Thames, 1848, pp. 110–12. See above pp. 131–32.)

Let us enter; 'tis the palace where the disembodied sprite,
Kept his chill watch through the dreary dreary centuries of night.

Silent 'mid his silent brethren, each revolving on the past,
Listening to the distant echoes of the pulses of the blast—

As it snapped the slender cypress on the rugged mountain spread,
And the old oak-roots creaked to it, far above the sleeper's head.

Deep beneath the rock and torrent in the mountains's central gloom,
They are stretched on carvèd couches all around the painted room: [1]

By their side the wine-vase standing, but its draught may please not now,
And the lamp that cannot cheer them with its pale and sickly glow:

Waiting all, as in some danger, when the silent sages sit,
Watching through the wildered council, till GOD wake some wise man's wit;

Waiting all,—and o'er them hanging from the archèd roof of rocks,
Glows the death-sprite's solemn visage, and her twining serpent-locks. [2]

Who are these, and what attend they? Why hath death thus gathered hers?
Did men deem that silent ashes love associate-sepulchres?

Or perchance, not wholly hopeless when around the tomb they met,
Did they deem an inner life-pulse throbbed within their ashes yet?

And should gush forth when the spirit reached its summer-clime of truth,
With the form of their own Tages, all maturity, all youth?

Angel-voices may have whispered, borne,—aye, even on death's chill blast,—

While they groped out toward our future, as we grope back toward
  their past.

Is all silent? know we nothing? can philosophy not rear
Some dim theoretic ages from the social fossils here?

And amid the frightful clashing of her after-ages wild,
Hath the old world clean forgotten those, who tended her a child?

They are gone!—like seashore footsteps when the tide flows,—they are
  gone!
Swept by Heaven-won Regillus,[4] swept by fatal Vadimon.

Swept, that the strong eagle's pinion might fly forth in ample scope,
Fanned by which the Light might brighten that should shew us realms
  of Hope.[5]

Swept, poor prisoners of sorrow, to the doubtful dark of death,
That another generation might be told the name of FAITH.

Ah! for grief! what anguish took them when the fettered soul
  looked out,
Straining aching eye in vain to pierce the curtain of their doubt!

Ah! for grief! what longing seized it to have wings and wander hence,
As the torn soul in its phrenzy battered on the seas of sense!

Ah! for grief! what chill recoiling when the future that they sought,
Seemed an endless void before them—thoughtless, hopeless, dreamless,
  nought!

Ah! for grief! what curse was knowledge! what a burden was a mind,
Better be a beast—go, fat thee, feed, and propagate thy kind!

Have they perished then for ever?—Oh! Thou Beam of Light Divine,
That hast streamed on every nation from Thy Fount in Palestine!

That hast raised a victory-trophy, e'en in Hades[6] and the grave,
Who may tell what dawn Thou'lt flush around the prisoners of
  this cave!

1. The bassi relievi on the tombs are magnificent. Painted rooms are rare: however
there is one celebrated instance at Chiusi. The wine-vase and lamp are common append-
ages, as are also the lachrymatories, and various implements of workmanship, as used by
the deceased when alive.
2. The Medusa's head, the common ornament of the roof of the cavern.
3. Tages, the lawgiver of the Etrurians, was represented as a union of youth and age;
symbolizing that, to be good, laws should have the simplicity of the one, and the discretion
of the other; or, perhaps, the traditional claim of age added to the freshness of power of

youth;. Tages used to be described as having the form of a child and the head of an old man.

4. Regillus—the battle was won by the agency of Castor and Pollux, as the story ran. The Etruscan allies were quite crushed by this battle.

5. The Roman power seems to have been specially raised up for the spread of Christianity. It was an important means of its extension.

6. "By the which also He preached to the spirits in prison." The interpretation of the fathers of this passage always refers it to the salvation of just men who had died before the fulfilment of the promises of Messiah.

Index

Aggression Bill, 195
Alderson, Charles Henry, 105 n, 383, 416, 417, 418 n
Alderson, Edward Hall, 104, 105 n, 383 n
Alderson, Edward Pakenham, 105 n, 219 n
Alderson, Frederick Cecil, 342, 343 n
Alderson, Georgina Drewe, 105 n, 219
Alderson family, 133, 190, 191, 342
Alexander, William, 388 n
Alfred Club, 252 n
Alison, Archibald, 122, 125 n
Allott, Kenneth, xvii, xx, xxi, 74 n; "Matthew Arnold: Two Unpublished Letters," 70 n; *The Poems of Matthew Arnold*, xxi
Allou, M., 457, 459 n
Ambroise, Victor, 450 n
American Review, 337
Ampère, Jean Jacques, 259, 260 n
Andromeda and Other Poems, 270 n
Anstey, Charles Alleyne, 3, 5 n
Anstey, Thomas Chisholm, 106 n
Ape, 174 n, 193 n, 244 n, 410
Argyll, *see* Campbell, George Douglas
Armand, Jules, prince de Polignac, 84, 86 n
Arnal, Etienne, 436, 438 n
Arnold, Aldous, 66 n
Arnold, Charles Thomas ("Plug"), 64, 65–66 n, 117 n, 347, 405
Arnold, Edward Penrose ("Didu"), 2 n, 7, 16 n, 101, 124–25, 170 n, 175, 339, 487, 498, 518; letter to Mary Penrose Arnold, 72–74, 104–5; letter to parents, 13; letter to, 22–32; mentioned, 4, 20, 21, 69, 70, 81, 118, 126, 127 n, 133, 134, 141, 149, 158, 159, 181, 182,183, 184, 185, 191, 211 n, 267–68, 298, 308, 314
Arnold, Frances (sister of Thomas Sr.), *see* Buckland, Frances Arnold
Arnold, Frances Anne Hodgson, 333, 334 n

Arnold, Frances Bunsen Trevenen Whately ("Bonze"), 3 n, 10 n, 126, 170 n, 175, 346, 408, 512; letters to, 381–82, 406–7, 463–64; deletions to letters, xxvii; mentioned, 304, 446
Arnold, Jane Martha ("K"), 16 n, 511; autobiography, 18–19; engagement, 171; marriage, 175; letters to, 94–95, 97–98, 107–8, 116, 141, 143–44, 150–51, 151–52, 171, 177–78, 188–89, 206–7, 261–62, 276–77, 282–83, 286, 294–95, 301–2, 314, 319–20, 330–31, 335–36, 337–38, 340–41, 348–49, 355–56, 364–65, 374–75, 401–3, 410–11, 454–56, 469–71, 473–75, 478–79, 486–88, 515–16; letter to Mary Penrose Arnold, 12; letters to Tom Arnold, 81, 122–25, 158–64, 180–81, 316; letter to William Delafield Arnold, 80; letter from Tom Arnold, 137–38; mentioned, 1, 2 n, 6, 7, 10, 46, 63, 80, 133, 142, 153, 313, 389
Arnold, Lucy Charlotte, 470, 482, 489–90, 519; birth, 396 n, 410–11; christening, 414, 415 n
Arnold, Lydia, 19, 21 n
Arnold, Lydia (sister of Thomas elder), 80 n
Arnold, Martha Delafield, 2 n, 380 n
Arnold, Mary ("Small Wild Cat," "Baco"), 2, 6, 12, 13, 123; letter to C. Lydia Penrose, 35; letter to parents, 13; mentioned, 20, 32, 33, 58, 81, 122, 382
Arnold, Mary Penrose, 13, 35, 165 n, 175, 284; letters to, 58–60, 79–80, 91, 101, 133, 144–45, 146–47, 147–48, 149–50, 153, 240–41, 248, 265–66, 267–68, 277–78, 296, 297, 300–301, 304–5, 312–13, 315, 317–18, 320–21, 339, 346–47, 350–51, 357–58, 370–71, 378–79, 387–88, 389,

Arnold, Mary Penrose (*cont.*),
390–91, 391–92, 404–5, 408–9,
412–13, 414–15, 423–24, 432–33,
435, 446–47, 460–61, 466–68, 475–
77, 481–82, 489–90, 493–94, 497–
98, 507–8, 511–12, 514–15, 518–
20; letters to MA, 3–4, 6, 9; letters
to Tom Arnold, 22, 114, 142–43,
203, 209, 392–93; letter to Jane Penrose, 32–34; letter to Jane Penrose &
C. Lydia Penrose, 34, 35; letter from
Edward Penrose Arnold, 72–74,
104–5; letter from Tom Arnold, 138;
letter from Frances Wightman Arnold, 352–53; letter from Bunsen, 71;
mentioned, 1, 2n, 36, 45, 46, 64, 81,
122, 123, 124, 125, 126, 141, 158, 181
Arnold, Matthew ("Crab") 32–33, 122,
123, 124, 145–46; autobiography,
18–19; birth of son Thomas, 239n,
240; engagement, 196, 199, 203; on
Lake, 161; marriage, 209n, 210; tour
in France, 37–45; letter to parents,
12; letter recommending Clough,
228–29; letter recommending Price,
230; letter recommending Sandford,
229; mentioned, 1, 2, 7, 8, 14, 22, 34,
37, 45, 56, 70, 72, 73, 80, 81, 97, 114,
122, 123–24, 137, 142, 160, 162,
181, 163, 166, 170, 176n, 209, 215,
216, 217, 220, 223, 224, 225, 226,
316, 392–93, 407–8, 442
Arnold, Matthew (writings): "Balder
Dead," 301, 302n; "Cromwell,"
55n; "Dover Beach," xiii; *Empedocles
on Etna and Other Poems*, 143n, 245n,
250n, 254n, 272; *England and the Italian Question*, 419, 468, 481; *Essays in
Criticism, Second Series*, xiv, 52n;
"Forsaken Merman, The," 140n;
French Eton, A, xxxv; *God and the
Bible*, xiv; "Haworth Churchyard,"
311n, 315–16; letter to *The Times*,
503–6; "Memorial Verses," 173n;
Merope, 369, 370, 371, 372–73, 374,
375, 376–78, 379, 383, 385, 386;
Poems, Second Series, 300, 301n;
Popular Education of France, The, xxxv,

422; *Reports on Elementary Schools
1852–82*, 366n, 382n; "Schools in
the Reign of Queen Victoria," 58;
"Self-Dependence," 254n; "Sohrab
and Rustum," 263n, 277; *Strayed
Reveller, and Other Poems, The*, 134n,
144n, 272; "Westminster Abbey,"
53n; "Written in Kensington Gardens," 151–52
Arnold, Richard Penrose, 327n, 346, 352,
388, 393, 470, 482, 508, 512, 515,
516, 519; birth, 299n, 320n
Arnold, Sarah Anne Blissett, liv
Arnold, Susanna (aunt), 3n; death of, 11;
mentioned, 4, 7
Arnold, Susanna Elizabeth Lydia ("Babbat
Apbook"), 3n, 4, 13, 14, 175, 295n,
476; marriage, 259, 260n; letter to,
20–21, 68–69, 287–88, 351–52;
mentioned, 81, 122, 124, 125, 158,
159, 181, 212, 318, 379
Arnold, Theodore, 168n
Arnold, Thomas ("Prawn"), 12, 63n,
71, 72, 74n, 108n, 166n, 167, 176n,
211n, 221n, 300, 310n, 349n, 379,
514; marriage, 178n; tour in France,
37–45; letters to, 83–85, 211–12,
308–9, 359–60, 368–70, 385, 517–
18; letter to Mary Penrose Arnold,
138; letter to parents, 13; letters from
Mary Penrose Arnold, 142–43, 203,
209, 392–93; letters from Jane Martha Arnold, 81, 114, 122–25, 158–
64, 180–81, 316; letters from Mary
Arnold Twining, 166, 170, 175; letter from Palgrave, 106–7; letter from
Walrond, 96–97; *Passages in a Wandering Life*, 74n; mentioned, 1, 2, 4,
7, 10, 35, 36, 59, 64, 67, 69, 70, 77,
153, 155, 207, 277, 354n, 390, 482n
Arnold, Thomas (MA's father), xv, 23,
32n, 33, 34, 74n, 111n, 134n, 168n,
305n, 379; tour in France, 37–45;
letter to Jane Martha Arnold, 137–
38; letter to MA, 3–4, 5, 6, 10–11;
letter to Tom Arnold, 22; letter to
Frances Buckland, 45–6; letter to
Susan Delafield, 1–2; letter to Wil-

liam Empson, 45; mentioned, 9, 25, 28, 31, 32, 36, 67

Arnold, Thomas (MA's son), 244, 248, 262, 263 n, 265, 268, 301–2, 305, 316, 319, 321, 346, 348, 349, 356, 364, 387–88, 391, 392, 393, 470, 476, 482, 511, 517, 519; birth, 239 n, 240, 406, 409, 423–25, 432; letter to, 472

Arnold, Trevenen William ("Budge"), 168 n, 316, 319, 321, 346, 348, 349, 351, 356, 364, 388, 390, 392, 393, 403, 406, 423, 470, 482, 489, 508, 511, 515, 516, 519; birth, 278

Arnold, Walter Thomas ("Quid," "Corus"), liv, 3 n, 125; mentioned, 69, 81, 133, 181, 182, 183, 184, 267, 432, 433 n

Arnold, William (father), 2 n, 22

Arnold, William Delafield ("Widu"), 2 n, 13, 73, 74, 88 n, 125, 161, 162, 165 n, 175, 273, 274 n, 283, 313, 320, 321, 339, 409, 446; marriage, 267 n; death, 432, 433 n, 434, 435; letters to, 20–21, 331–32; letter from Jane Martha Arnold, 80; *Oakfield,* 74 n; mentioned, 81, 133, 151

Arnold, William Thomas (Tom's son), 166 n

Arnold-Forster, Edward Penrose, 267 n, 333 n, 446, 447 n

Arnold-Forster, Florence Mary, 267 n

Arnold-Forster, Frances Egerton, 267 n

Arnold-Forster, Hugh Oakeley, 173 n, 267 n

Arnold-Forster, Oakeley, 68 n

Arnold Newsletter, xvi

Arnould-Plessy, Jeanne Sylvanie Sophie, 449, 450 n

Ashburton, *see* Baring, William Bingham

Askew, Henry, 491 n

Askew, Mrs Henry, 489, 491 n, 498

Athenæum, 93 n

Auden, W. H.: "Matthew Arnold," xv

Bagehot, Walter, 102 n, 333 n

Bailey, Philip James, 82

Baillie, Evan P. Montagu, 440, 441 n, 442

Baillie, Frances, 440, 441 n, 442

Baines, Edward, 336

Baines, Matthew Talbot, 336 n

Baker, Mr, 488

Ball, William, 165 n

Balston, Henry, 34 n

Balston, William, 33, 34 n

Banks (gardener), 158, 164 n

Baring, Harriet Mary Montagu, 232, 233 n, 234

Baring, William Bingham, Lord Ashburton, 232, 233 n

Barraudot, M., 440

Barry, Charles, 503, 507 n

Barthélemy-Saint-Hilaire, Jules, 420, 425, 426 n

Batthyány, Lajos, 434 n

Batthyány, Mme, 434, 436

Bayley (unidentified), 191, 195

Bayley, F. W. N., 187, 193 n

Bayley, John Arden, 187, 193 n

Beale, A. J., letters to, 328, 345, 366, 368, 393, 406 n, 484

Beale, J. H., 322

Beattie, William, 353

Beauharnais, Hortense de, 438 n

Beaumarchais, Pierre Augustin Caron, 93 n

Beauwysse, comte de, 496

Beeloo, M., 458

Bell, Thomas (dentist), 69, 70 n

Belloc, Hilaire, 338 n

Belloc, Louis Swanton, 338 n

Bennett, William Cox, letter to, 287

Benoit, M., 451 n, 452

Benson, Florance John, 225 n

Benson, Henry Roxby, 225 n, 290, 291

Benson, Mary Henrietta Wightman, 200, 204, 308, 411, 412 n, 512; letter from Frances Lucy Wightman, 223–25

Benson, Miss (unidentified), 223, 224, 225 n

Bentinck, George, 110 n

Béranger, Pierre Jean, 77, 78 n, 120

Bertram, James, xli

Beugnot, Auguste Arthur, 426, 428 n, 434

Bhagavad Gita, 88 n, 89 n, 94 n

Bishop, Nadean, xvi

Blachford, T. J.: letters to, 430–31, 440

Blackett, Frances Mary (Fanny du Quaire), 75n, 266, 349, 424, 436, 437, 438, 440, 443, 449, 457, 465; letter to, 383–84
Blackett, John Fenwick Burgoyne, 75n, 105, 188n, 273, 282, 384n; letter to, 280–81; death, 337; mentioned, 115, 127, 145, 169, 186, 187, 190, 191, 192, 195, 196, 197, 198, 200, 204, 208, 211n, 266n
Blackett, Montagu, 384n
Blackie, John Stuart, 266n, 465
Blaen[?], Mme (unidentified), 427
Blakesley, J. W., 48n
Blanc, Louis, 92, 94n
Blaze de Bury, Henri, 293n
Blaze de Bury, Marie Pauline Rose, 293n
Bloxam (Bloxham), John Rouse, 59, 60n
Boag, Mrs, 85n
Bode, John Ernest, 353, 354
Boe, Jacques (Jasmin), 434
Bohn, Henry George, *A Catalogue of Books,* 109, 111n
Bolander (unidentified), 462
Bonafous, Abbé, 457, 458n
Bonfiguoli, Kyril, William Delafield Arnold Collection, xxxviii
Bonnerot, Louis, xvii
Bonney, Richard, 412, 413n
Boothby, Brooke, 187n
Boothby, George William, 187n
Boothby, Henry Brooke, 187n, 190, 191, 192, 195, 199
Bourbon, Francisco de Assisi de, 96n
Bowen, George Ferguson, 354–55n
Bowyer, George, 491
Boyle, George David, 266n
Bradley, George Granville, 97, 198, 201–2n; MA's recommendation of, 386–87
Bridges, Thomas Edward, 46, 47n
Bright, John, 198, 201n, 336, 385n, 405, 406n, 407, 411, 457
Brodie, Benjamin Collins (elder), 248
Brodie, Benjamin Collins, 49–50, 52n, 100n, 135, 140, 190, 193, 196, 197, 199, 200, 346, 425
Broglie, Achille Léonce Charles Victor, duc de, 425, 426n, 427, 440, 441

Brohan, Madeleine, 427, 428n
Brontë, Charlotte, 179, 180n, 258, 259n, 313
Brontë, Emily, 316
Brotherton Collection, xxxviii
Brougham, Henry Peter, 457, 459n
Broughton, Delves, 462, 463n
Broughton, Jane Bennett, 463n
Broughton, Rhoda, 463n
Brown, George, 292n
Browne, Edward Harold, 20, 21n, 22
Browning, Robert, 128, 129n, 383
Bruce, Augusta, 427, 428n, 437, 440
Bruce, Robert, 449, 450n
Buckingham, duke of, 20
Buckland, Caroline A. Ricketts, 332, 333n
Buckland, Charles Arnold, 339, 390n
Buckland, Charles Thomas, 333n
Buckland, Frances Arnold, 3n, 13, 16n, 79, 80n, 389, 390n; letter from TA, 45–46
Buckland, John, 2, 3n, 7, 46, 80, 204, 211n, 277, 300, 390n; travel with, 23, 28, 31
Buckland, Martha, 11; letter to, 19–20
Buckland, Matthew, 339, 389
Buckland, Thomas, 13, 16n
Buckland, William Arnold ("Willy," d. 1864), 19
Buller, Adelaide Louisa, 298, 299n
Buller, Edward, 299n
Buller, Mary, 459n
Buller, Reginald John, 298, 299n
Bunsen, Augusta Matilda, 72n, 187
Bunsen, Baron, 72n, 133, 190, 191, 192, 197, 199; letter to Mary Penrose Arnold, 71; mentioned, 98, 171, 404
Bunsen, Elizabeth Gurney, 72n
Bunsen, Emilia, 72n
Bunsen, Ernest, 72n
Bunsen, Frances, 72n
Bunsen, George, 72n
Bunsen, Henry, 71, 72n, 150, 190
Bunsen, Karl, 72n
Bunsen, Mary Charlotte Elizabeth, 72n
Bunsen, Theodor, 72n
Bunsen, Theodora, 72n

Burbidge, Thomas, 78, 135; *Ambarvalia,* 76–77n
Burg (Bury?), Mr, 105
Burgoyne, John Montagu, 150n, 187n, 195, 196, 443
Burgoyne, Mary Caroline, 150n, 449, 450n
Burgoyne, Mary Harriet Gore-Langton, 187, 190, 191, 193, 200, 208
Burgoyne, Montagu George, 187–88n
Butler, Charles, letters to, xxv
Buxton, Anna, 164n
Buxton, Charles, 303; *Memoirs of Sir Thomas Fowell Buxton, Baronet,* 164n
Buxton, Edward, 319
Buxton, Edward North, 320n
Buxton, Fowell, xxxii
Buxton, Thomas Fowell, 303n, 320n
Byron, George Gordon, Lord, xxvi, 120

Cadbury, James, 328, 345, 366, 406n
Caird, John, 405
Cameron, Lucy Lyttelton: *Memoirs of Emma and Her Nurse,* 341–42n
Campbell, Archibald Montgomery, 400, 401n
Campbell, George Douglas, duke of Argyll, 383, 384n
Carden, Lionel, 36, 37n
Cardolle, M., 469, 475, 477
Carly (unidentified), 33, 158
Carlyle, John Aitken, 135n
Carlyle, Thomas, 91, 92n, 93, 101, 109, 134, 135n, 145n, 156, 370; "The Repeal of the Union," 111n
Carpenter, Mary, 236n; letters to, 235, 334–35
Carré, M. de (unidentified), 443
Cartwright, William Ralph, 69, 242
"Caution to Poets, A," 250n
Cavan, Lady, 351
Cavour, Camillo Bensi conte di, 421n, 433, 434n, 496
Chapman, John, 261, 262n, 283
Charlotte (nursemaid), 406, 407n, 476, 482
Chasles, Philarète, 93n, 99, 431
Chastellux, Henri Louis, 428n

Chatelain, Jean Baptiste François Ernest Chevalier de, 305–6n
Christian Life, The: its hopes, its fears, and its close, 53
Chrzanowski, Albert, 450n
Circourt, Adolphe Marie Pierre, comte de, 420, 421n, 423, 426, 427, 492, 493, 494, 495, 496
Circourt, Anastasia de Klustine de, 420, 421n, 429, 438, 457
Clack, Thomas Edward, 221, 222n
Clack, William Courtenay, 221, 222n
Claremont, Lt. Col., 437, 439n
Clarendon, Lord, *see* Villiers, George William Frederick
Clark, Robin, 68
Clark, William George, 256
Clarke, Charles Cowden, 270n
Clarke, Loftus Longueville Tottenham, 459n
Clarke, Mrs Longueville, 457, 459n
Claude, Mary, 124, 126n
Claughton, Thomas Legh, 21n
Clayton, Augustus, 290n
Clayton, Fitz-Roy Augustus Talbot, 290–91
Clinton, Henry Pelham Fiennes Pelham, duke of Newcastle, 52, 414, 415n
Clothilde, Princess, 438, 439n
Clough, Arthur Hugh, 10, 94, 104n, 108n, 110n, 161, 165n, 168n, 176n, 209n, 211n, 229n, 241, 265n, 487, 501n, 508n, 520; letters to, xix, xx, 62–63, 64–65, 75, 76, 77, 78–79, 82, 86–87, 89–90, 92–93, 100, 102–3, 105–6, 108–9, 111–12, 113, 114–15, 116–17, 118–19, 119–21, 126–27, 128–29, 130–31, 131–32, 134–35, 135–36, 138, 139–40, 155–56, 167, 172, 176–77, 232–33, 233–34, 236, 237–38, 245–46, 249–50, 252–54, 258–59, 263–64, 268–69, 269–70, 270–71, 273–74, 275–76, 280, 281–82, 322, 484–86, 500; letter to Shairp, 70–71; MA's letter recommending, 228–29; *Ambarvalia,* 75, 76n; *Amours de Voyage,* 259n; *The Bothie of Toper-na-Fuosich,* 127n;

Clough, Arthur Hugh (*cont.*),
 "The Questioning Spirit," 75n;
 "Qui Laborat, Orat," 131n; men-
 tioned, 72, 73, 106, 107, 146, 186,
 187, 191, 192, 193, 195, 196, 197,
 198, 199, 200, 201, 204, 208, 280,
 359
Cobden, Richard, 102–3n, 105, 108,
 471–72n, 508
Cohn (Cohen), Albert, 436, 438n, 457,
 465
Coleridge, Alethea, 52n
Coleridge, Edith, 150
Coleridge, Haruey, 52n
Coleridge, Henry James, 53n
Coleridge, Henry Nelson, 150n
Coleridge, Jane Fortescue Seymour, 62n
Coleridge, John Duke, 52n, 135, 174n,
 259, 358, 413; letters to, 49–51, 53–
 55, 56–58, 60–61, 279; letter from
 John Manley Hawker, 56; *Memorials
 of Oxford,* 62; *Verses during Forty
 Years,* 62; mentioned, 59, 191, 315
Coleridge, John Taylor (nephew of poet),
 53n
Coleridge, John Taylor, 32n, 51n, 134,
 208, 312, 313, 393; mentioned, 37
Coleridge, Samuel Taylor, 62n
Coleridge, Sara, 150n
Colet, Louise, 496n
Collections of letters, xxxvii–xliii
Collins, William Wilkie, 134n
Coltman, George, 144n
Coltman, Miss (unidentified), 143
Coltman, Thomas (judge), 144n
Coltman, Thomas, 144n
Combe, Frances, 380n
Combe, George, 335, 336n
Combe, Harvey Christian, 380n
Committee of Council on Education,
 130n, 242; letters to, 231–32, 235,
 238, 243
Comte, Auguste, 92, 93n
Congreve, Richard, 65, 66n, 370, 371n
Conington, John, 52n, 127, 128n, 273
Conybeare, Charles Ranken, 359
Coote, Thomas, 255, 256n
Copleston, Edward, 363

Copley Fielding, Antony Vandyke, 147
Cornhill Magazine, 512, 513n
Correspondant, Le, 407
Cosway, William Halliday, 441
Cotton, Charles, 263, 265n
Cotton, George Edward Lynch, 97, 161,
 165n
Cotton, Richard Lynch: letter to, 361–
 62, 363n
Courier belge, Le, 110n
Cousin, Victor, 200, 420, 425, 426, 426n,
 488, 496n, 514
Cowley, *see* Wellesley, Henry Richard
 Charles
Cowper, Georgiana Tollemache, 401n
Cowper, William Francis, 399, 401n
Cox, William, 411, 412n
Crabb Robinson, Henry, 73, 74n, 173n
Crémieux, Isaac Moise (Adolphe), 92,
 94n
Crewdson, William Dillworth, 160, 165n
Croker, John Wilson, 211n
Crompton, Charles, 399, 401n
Crompton, Henry, 401n
Crompton, Mary, 401n
Cropper, James, 260n
Cropper, John Wakefield, 259, 260n, 287,
 318n, 352
Cropper, Lucy Ada, 352n
Culler, Dwight, xvii
Cumin, Patrick, 136, 140, 187, 193, 198,
 437, 490
Cunningham, Allan: Burns's *Works* with a
 Life, 153n
Curran, John Philpot, 263, 264n
Curwen, Alfred Francis, 517n
Curwen, Edward Stanley, 517n

Dalhousie, *see* Ramsay, James Andrew
 Broun
Daman, Charles, 60n
Dare, Joseph, 416
Dasent, George Webbe, 412n
Dauzet, M., 451n
Davies, Edward William Lewis, 498, 499n
Davies, John Llewellyn, 399, 401n
Davis, Arthur Kyle, Jr., xv–xvi, xvii, xxii
Davy, Mr & Mrs John, 142, 182, 184

Dawson, George, 368
De La Pryme, Charles: letter to, 251
De La Pryme, Sophia Cubitt, 251 n
de La Saussaye, 480
de La Villemarque, Theodore, 265 n
de Staël, Adelaide, 423, 425, 426 n, 427,
    440, 441; *Corinne*, 181 n
de Staël-Holstein, Albertine, 426 n
de Staël-Holstein, Auguste, 426 n
Deane (nurse), 278, 301, 302, 321
Deasy, Rickard, 399, 400, 401 n
Déjazet, Virginie, 431
Delafield, John, 380 n
Delafield, Joseph, 380 n
Delafield, Martha, *see* Arnold, Martha
    Delafield
Delafield, Susan, 1, 3 n, 18
Delafield, William, 379, 380 n
DeLaura, David, 78 n, 246 n, 265 n
Delcosso, M. O., 469 n
Deloche, M., 453, 454 n
Denbigh, Lady, 50, 52 n
Denison, George Anthony, 358
Denison, William, 169 n
Dent, John Dent, 462, 463 n
Derby, *see* Stanley, Edward George Geof-
    frey Smith
Devenham, Miss, 407
Diaries, xxxiv–xxxvii
Diary entries, 181–87, 190–93, 195–96,
    197–201, 203–5, 208, 210–11, 212–
    13, 214, 215–16, 218, 220, 223, 225,
    226–27, 230–31, 232, 426
Dickens, Charles, 478 n
Dieudonné, Emmanuel Augustin, comte
    de Las Cases, 148, 149 n
Dindorf, Wilhelm, 136
Disraeli, Benjamin, 413
Dodsworth, Mr, 104
Donnet, Ferdinand François Auguste, 451 n
Douglas, Harriet Christian, 513 n
Doyle, Richard, 520 n
Drouyn de Lhuys, Edouard, 429, 430 n
Ducie, Lady, 429, 430 n
Duckworth, John Thomas Buller, 457,
    458 n
Dumon (Dumont), Pierre Sylvain, 440,
    441, 441 n

Duncombe, Augustus, 513 n
Dunn, Henry, 205, 206 n, 207; lost letters,
    xxiv–xxv; letter to, 324–25
Dunsford, H., 35 n
du Quaire, Fanny, *see* Blackett, Frances
    Mary
du Quaire, Henri, 384 n, 420, 465, 514
Dutrey, M. C., 451 n

Economist, 102 n
Edinburgh Review, 501 n
Education Commission, 52
Edwards [?William Finch]: letter to, 381
Egmont: quoted, 183
Elgin, Lady, 427, 437, 440, 442
Eliot, George, 336 n, 338 n
Ellison, Noel, 358
Elwin, Whitwell, 260 n
Emerson, Ralph Waldo, 101 n, 106, 108 n,
    250, 254, 258
Empson, William: letter from Thomas
    Arnold, 45
English Review, 52 n
Entwisle, John, 7 n; mentioned, 6
Epictetus, 120
Etienne, Père, 440, 441 n
Eton Bureau, 61
Etty, William, 304, 305 n
Evans, Samuel H., 248
Everett, Edward, 198, 202 n
Ewald, Georg Heinrich August von, 115
Eyre, Charles Wasteneys, 24, 32 n, 43
Eyre, Lucy Dorothea Foulis, 24, 32 n,
    199

Faber, Frederick William, 51, 53 n, 381,
    382 n; *The Styrian Lake and Other
    Poems*, 53 n
Family letters, xxx–xxxiv; the Forsters,
    xxx–xxxii
Faraday, Michael, 133, 134 n
Farquhar, Lady, 15
Farquhar, Maria, 440, 441 n, 442
Farquhar, Thomas Harvie, 441 n
Farrar, F. W., 168 n
Farrer, Thomas Henry, 56
Faucit, Helena Savile, 388, 449, 450 n; let-
    ters to, 386, 387

Fauriel, Claude: *Histoire de la poésie proven-*
　çal, 415 n
Fell, William, 346, 347 n
Fellowes, Benjamin, 59, 141, 147, 266,
　272, 310 n, 312, 365
Fenwick, Isabella: letter from Words-
　worth, 63–64
Fenwick, Miss, 142
Ferrand, M., 451 n
Festus, 107, 108 n
Fielden, John, 477 n
Fielden, Samuel, 477 n
Fielden, Sarah Jane Yates, 476, 477 n
Fitzgerald, William Robert Seymour
　Vesey, 492
Fitzmaurice, Henry Petty, marquis of
　Lansdowne: letter to MA, 417, 418
Flahault de la Billarderie, Auguste comte
　de, 437, 438 n
Flaubert, Gustave, 496 n
Fleming, Fletcher, 163, 166 n, 182, 187
Fleming, John, 166 n
Fletcher, Archibald, 16 n, 142 n
Fletcher, Eliza, 16 n, 141, 142 n
Fletcher, Mary, 12, 16 n
Fletcher, Mrs, 277, 300, 358
Flocon, Ferdinand, 92, 94 n
Fontanès, Ernest: letters to, xix
Ford, Catherine Margaret Hodgson, 334 n
Ford, Charles, 334 n
Ford, Edith Mary, 334 n
Ford, Francis, 334 n
Ford, William, 334 n
Forster, John, 283 n
Forster, Robert, 207 n
Forster, William (father), death, 286
Forster, William Edward, xxxii, 74 n,
　110 n, 164 n, 171, 175 n, 196, 206,
　229 n, 260 n, 271, 313 n, 314, 330,
　336, 349, 356, 405, 411, 480, 487,
　488 n, 492, 519; letters to, 326, 376–
　78; letter to Ellis Yarnall, 284; men-
　tioned, 294, 389
Fould, Achille, 488, 490
Fox, Charles James, 32 n
Fox, Henry Richard Vassall (Lord Hol-
　land), 24, 32 n, 193 n
Franck, Adolphe, 426, 427 n, 434

Franklin, Benjamin, 189
Franklin, John, 165 n, 513 n
Fraser, James, 209 n
Fraser, John Farquhar, 208, 209 n
Fraser, William Augustus, 244
Fraser's Magazine, 308 n, 391
Freeman, Edward Augustus, 506 n
Freeman, Mr (unidentified), 33
Friedrich Wilhelm IV, 103 n
Fritry, M. (unidentified), 468, 469 n
Froude, James Anthony, 144, 145 n, 168 n,
　250, 261, 262 n, 264, 266, 269, 270,
　271, 272, 274, 277, 281, 282, 283,
　402, 404, 405, 500; letter to MA,
　375–76
Fry, Herbert: letter to, 350
Fulchers, the Miss, 328
Fuller, Margaret, 258, 259 n, 267
Furnivall (Furnevall), Frederick James, 73,
　74 n

Gambell, Isabella, 407
Garner, Mr & Mrs (unidentified), 221
Garnier-Pagès, Louis Antoine, 92, 94 n
Gascoyne-Cecil, James Brownlow William,
　marquis of Salisbury, 414, 415 n; letter
　to, 416
Gaskell, Elizabeth Cleghorn, 180 n; letters
　to, 278, 317; letter to MA, 315–16
Gell, Eleanor Franklin, 165 n
Gell, Frederick, 256
Gell, John Philip, 158, 161, 165 n, 256 n
Gell, William: *Itinerary of the Morea,* 372 n
Girardin, Marc, 86, 87 n, 93 n
Gladstone, William Ewart, 111 n, 127,
　195, 318 n, 388, 391, 485, 513 n; let-
　ter to, 483
Glynn (Glyn), George Grenfell, 198,
　202 n
Glynn, Georgiana Maria Tufnell, 202 n
Godlee, Mrs: letter to, 343
Goethe, 114, 166, 177 n, 285 n, 369; MA's
　thoughts on, 148; quoted, 186; *Con-*
　versations with Eckermann, 283; *Zahme*
　Xenien, 112 n
Gordon, Osborne, 127 n
Goulburn, Edward Meyrick, 161, 167,
　169 n, 198, 211, 212 n, 241

Goulburn, Julia Cartwright, 241, 242n
Gould, Mme, 421
Gould, Mrs, 434
Gramont, Antoine Alfred Agenor de, 87n
Granger (Grainger), Thomas, 58n
Grant, Alexander, 127n, 147n
Granville, Lord, *see* Leveson-Gower, Granville George
Gray, Thomas, 131n
Greenhill, Laura Ward, 45, 47n; letter to, 55
Greenhill, William Alexander, 47n
Greenwood, Robert Hodgson, 14
Greg, William Rathbone, 102n, 116, 117, 162, 498
Grenfell, Algernon, 9, 10n, 393, 393n
Grenfell, Edward Frederick, 393, 396n
Grenville, Lord & Lady, 15
Greswell, Richard, 57, 58n
Grey, Henry George, 71, 72n
Grote, George: *History of Greece,* 195, 196n
Grove, Emma Maria Powles, 134n
Grove, William Robert, 133, 134n
Guiccioli, Teresa (Mme Boissy), xxvi
Guizot, François, 83−84, 85−86n, 89, 95, 96n, 425, 426, 426n, 427, 436, 439n, 440, 441, 441n, 447, 454, 488, 494, 497, 514
Gully, James Manby, 189n
Gurney, Archer Thompson, 463
Guthrie, George James, 208, 209n, 221, 434, 434n
Guthrie, Kate, 209n, 438
Guthrie, William Bell, xxxiv
Gyulai, Ferencz, 450n

Haldimand, William, 396n, 477
Hallam, Arthur Henry, 129n
Hamilton, Captain, 8, 138
Hamilton, Christian Monteith, 496, 497n
Hamilton, J. G., 497n
Hamilton, Mr, 15
Hamilton, Walter Kerr, 390, 391n
Hamon, M., 427n
Hampden, Henrietta, 449, 450n
Hampden, Renn Dickson, 450n
Harcourt, Edward, 512n

Harcourt, William George Granville Venables Vernon, 511, 512n
Harcourt, William Vernon, 512n
Harden, Jane Sophia, 13, 15−16n, 33
Harden, John, 16
Harden, Robert Allan, 12, 16n
Hardenberg, Friedrich Leopold von (Novalis), 82n
Hare, Julius Charles, 47, 48n, 49
Harford, John B., 172n
Harford-Battersby, Mary Louisa, 72n
Harrington, Mr, 122
Harris (master of Deal Wesleyan School), 322
Harris, James Howard, earl of Malmesbury, 461n
Harrison, Benson, 191, 193n, 517n
Harrison, Matthew Benson, 193n
Harrison, Richard, 411, 412n
Harrison, Wordsworth, 412n
Hartwell, Francis Grant, 154n
Hartwell, Francis, 154, 193n
Hasler, Fanny Georgiana Jane (later, Lady Reay), 443
Hatton, Edward Hatton Finch, 187, 188n
Hauranne, Duvergier de, 449, 450n
Hawker, John Manley, 49, 52n, 56n; letter to John Duke Coleridge, 56; mentioned, 54, 55
Hawker, William Henry, 52n
Hawkes, John, 141
Hawkins, Edward, 45−46, 47, 50, 204, 205n, 312, 313n
Hawkins, Margaret, 313n
Hawkins, Mary Anne Buckle, 313n
Hawkins, Mary Frances, 313n
Hawtrey, Edward Craven, 59, 60n
Hay, James, 507, 508n
Haydon, Benjamin Robert, 270
Headland, E., 488n
Hearn, James, 125, 126n
Hearn, James Seckerson, 123, 124, 125n, 165n
Hebdomadal Council, 360, 361
Heber, Reginald, 107, 108n
Hedley, William, 360n
Heimann, Adolf, 245n
Heine, Heinrich, 148

Henley, Joseph Warner, 358
Hepworth, James: letters to, 326, 328–30, 347–48, 353, 382–83, 416
Hervé, Jean Florian, comte de Kergorlay, 427, 428 n, 442
Hiley, John Simeon, 388 n, 405, 497
Hill, Herbert, 17 n, 164 n, 183; letters to, 247, 371–72
Hill, Herbert, Jr., 17 n, 280
Hill, Mrs, 158
Hills, Beatrice Cervinia, 516, 517 n
Hills, John, 517 n
Hinchley, Annie, 322
Hinchliff (Hinchcliff), Thomas Woodbine, 399, 400 n
Hinds, Samuel, 160, 161, 165 n
Hodgkinson, G., 488 n
Hodgson, Frances Anne: marriage, 267 n
Hodgson, Hugh Norris, 334 n
Hodgson, John Anthony, 334 n
Hoijtema, M. van, 462
Holberton, Mrs. Vaughan, 204, 205 n
Holberton, Thomas Henry, 319, 320 n
Holberton, Vaughan, 350, 351 n
Holden, Eleanor Eliza White, 290 n
Holden, Henry, 290
Holland, Lord, *see* Fox, Henry Richard Vassall
Hook, Miss, 15
Hook, Mrs, 15
Horace: *Ars Poetica,* 121 n
How, Richard Thomas, 261 n
How, Richard, 261 n
How, William Briggins, 261 n
How, William Fitzwilliam, 260, 261 n
Howard, George William Frederick, earl of Carlisle, 482
Howard, Rachel, 261 n
Howley, William (archbishop of Canterbury), 57, 58 n
Hudson, C., 488 n
Hudson, George, 150 n
Hughes, Thomas, 154, 155 n, 195, 277 n; *Tom Brown's School Days,* 366 n
Huguenots, 208
Hull, Mrs, 147
Hull, William Winstanley, 23, 32 n, 43, 160
Hume, Joseph, 110 n

Hunt, George Ward, 190, 193 n
Hutton, Charles, 346, 347 n, 350, 409, 492, 498, 517
Hutton, Richard Holt, 333 n; letter to, 344
Hyett, Benjamin, 213 n
Hyett, William Henry Adams, 213–14 n; letter to, 213–14 n

Isabella II, 96 n

Jacqueret, Antoine Matthias Alexandre, 443 n
Jameson, Anna Brownell, 338
Jenkyns, Richard, 46, 47 n, 74 n
Jeune, Francis, 361 n
Joad, George, 488 n
John (servant), 14, 16 n, 33, 34
Johnson, Edwin Beaumont, 511, 513 n
Johnson, Henry Allen, 513 n
Josef, Heinrich Hermann, 450 n
Jourdain, Charles (unidentified), 440
Journal des débats, 93 n, 110 n
Jowett, Benjamin, 106, 128 n, 361 n

Keats, John, 134, 245, 270, 509
Keble, John, 133, 134 n, 358, 363
Kekewich, Trehawke, 190, 193 n
Keller, E., 120, 121 n
Kemble, Fanny, 89, 90 n
Kennedy, Benjamin Hall, 161, 165 n
Kergorlay, comte de, *see* Hervé, Jean Florian
King, Ada Byron, 112 n
King, Byron Noel, 112 n
King, Ralph Gordon Noel, 112 n
King (King-Noel), William, Lord Lovelace, 111, 112 n
Kingsley, Charles, 107, 168 n, 269, 277 n, 401 n, 402; *Hypatia,* 296; *The Saint's Tragedy,* 108 n
Knight, Charles, 141, 142 n
Kotzebue, August von, 377, 378 n
Kynaston, Herbert, 48 n

Laborde, Léon, marquis de, 426, 427 n
Laboulaye, Edouard René Lefebvre de, 426, 428 n, 437

Lacordaire, Jean Baptiste Henri, 447, 453–54n
Lake, Charles, 11n
Lake, Howard, 10, 11n
Lake, William Charles, 11n, 49, 50, 51, 52n, 53, 161, 167, 169n, 413
Lamartine, Alphonse, 84, 86n, 89, 90n, 91, 92–93, 98, 106n
Lambart, Anne Elizabeth Willes, 80n, 205
Lambart, Caroline Augusta Littleton, 351n
Lambart, Oliver William Matthew, 80n, 350
Lambart, Percy Francis, 351n
Lambart, Rodulph Augustus Arnold, 350, 351n
Landois, Narcisse, 427, 428n, 429
Landon, James Timothy Bainbridge, 126, 127n
Lanjuinais, Vicomte, 449, 450n
Lansdowne, Lord, 70n, 71, 72n, 73, 75–76n, 86, 88n, 97, 129, 146, 147, 179, 180n, 194, 195, 197, 201, 204, 205, 212, 283, 415n, 451, 456, 457, 501n
Lansdowne, Louisa Emma Fox-Strangways, 198; death, 200, 206n
Laprade, Victor Richard de, 420, 426n
Latham, Peter Mere, 346, 347n
Laurie, James Stuart, 335, 336n, 417
Lawley, Beilby Richard, 513n
Lawley, Francis Charles, 167n, 288, 291, 513n
Lawley, Stephen Willoughby, 167n, 511, 513n
Lawrence, Thomas, 360n
Leach, Henry, 6, 7n
Leake, Colonel, 370
Leake, William Martin: letter to, 367
Ledru-Rollin, Alexandre Auguste, 92, 94n
Lee, James Prince, 9, 10n
Leemans, M., 458
Leguinquis, M de, 443
Leith, George Hector, 290
Leveson-Gower, Granville George, 383, 384n; letter to, 418
Lewes, G. H., 370, 371n
Lewis, George Cornewall, 192, 194n
Liberty Bell, The, 335n
Lightfoot, John Prideaux, 405n

Lind, Jenny, 53, 97, 109, 111n
Lingen, Emma Hutton, 263, 265n, 399, 400
Lingen, Ralph Robert Wheeler, 117, 118n, 179, 187, 190, 192, 195, 199, 206, 229n, 234, 273, 281, 399, 400, 413, 416; letter to, 417
Lintott (dentist), 191, 194n
Lister, Maria Theresa, 512n
Literary Gazette and Journal of Belles Lettres, Arts, Sciences, 144, 145n
Lockhart, John Gibson, 153n, 188n, 259, 261, 262n; *Life of Robert Burns,* 153n
Longman, Thomas, letters to, 272, 274–75
Longman, William, 500
Lorain, Paul, 462, 463
Lost letters, xxiv
Louis Napoléon, 88n, 311, 478
Louis Philippe, 82n, 83, 84, 85n, 86, 96n
Lowe, Hudson, 149n
Lowe, Robert, 486n
Löwenstein, Prince, 72
Lowry, Howard Foster: *The Letters of Matthew Arnold to Arthur Hugh Clough,* xxi
Lucas, Samuel, 510
Lucas, William Henry: letters to, 70, 354
Ludlow, John Malcolm Forbes, 276, 277n, 401n
Luff, Mrs, 15
Lushington, Edmund, 127n
Lutteroth, Henri, 427, 428n
Lutteroth, Mme, 429, 436, 437
Lutwidge, H. P., 184, 187n

Macaulay, Thomas Babington, 136, 520
Macbean, [?]Frederick, 221, 222n
Mackarness, John Fielder, 49, 52n, 56
Mackenzie King, William Lyon, xxxix
Macmillan, Alexander: letter to, 365–66
Macmillan's Magazine, 512, 513n
Macpherson, Francis, 126, 127n
Macready, William Charles, 73, 89, 90n, 93n
Maedon, M. (unidentified), 468, 469n
Maffei, Scipio, 369, 370n
Magin, *see* Marrens-Magin, Alfred Joseph Auguste

Mair, Mary Charlotte, 439 n
Mallet, P. H., 301, 302 n
Marcet, Jane, 394, 396 n, 478 n
Marjoribanks, Mr, 325
Marlborough College, letter to Council of, 386–87
Marrens-Magin, Alfred Joseph Auguste, 437, 439 n, 448, 449, 450, 457, 465, 488, 491, 492, 493, 494, 495, 496
Marsden, Caroline Moore, 208
Marsden, John Howard, 208
Marsh, G. M., 290 n
Marshall, James Garth, 187, 188 n, 190, 192, 196, 198, 200, 202 n
Martin, Jacob L., 109, 110–11 n
Martin, Theodore, 386 n, 449, 450 n
Martineau, Harriet, 95 n, 101, 162, 179, 180 n, 254, 258, 313, 314, 315, 317, 335, 358, 370, 379, 411, 487, 490, 498; *British Rule in India,* 371 n; *Letters on the Laws of Man's Nature and Development,* 295; *A Retrospect of Western Travel,* 95 n; *Society in America,* 95 n; mentioned, 64, 107, 141, 142 n
Martineau, James, 295
Maskelyne, *see* Story-Maskelyne, Mervyn Herbert Nevil
Masson, David, 277 n
Masterman, Edward, 197, 201 n
Matthew Arnold's Letters: A Descriptive Checklist, xvi
Maude, John Hartwell, 193 n
Maude, Julia, 190, 193 n, 197
Maurice, F. D., 277 n, 401 n
Mayne, Lady, 409, 410 n, 494
Mayne, Richard, 410 n, 494, 497
Mayor, Charles, 66 n
Mayor, J., 66 n
Mazzini, Guiseppe: quoted, 184
McClintock, Francis Leopold, 513 n
Mérimée, Prosper, 384 n, 426, 427, 488, 490; letter to MA, 429
Merivale, Charles, 48 n
Michelet, Adèle Malairet, 438 n
Michelet, Jules, 89, 93 n, 377, 436, 438 n; letters to, 99, 431–32; letter to George Sand, 442; *Le Peuple,* 82–83 n

Mignet, Auguste, 420, 425, 426 n
Mill, John Stuart, 109, 111 n; *On Liberty,* 468, 471
Miller, John Cale, 358
Millot, M., 465
Milman, Henry Hart, 187, 188 n
Milner-Gibson, Thomas, 108, 110 n
Milnes, Richard Monckton, 101, 102 n 110 n, 326, 421 n, 457; letter to, 481; *Life, Letters and Literary Remains of John Keats,* 102 n, 129 n
Milton, John, 134, 136
Mioland, Jean Marie, 447, 448 n
Mitchell, Alexander, 442, 443 n, 488, 491, 494
Moberly, George, 21, 22 n, 60
Mohl, Jules or Julius, 420, 425 n, 427, 429
Mohl, Mary, 425 n, 440
Mole, Louis Matthieu, 84, 86 n
Molesworth, Andalusia Grant Carstairs, 188 n
Molesworth, William, 187, 188 n, 195, 196
Monnet, M. (Vevey landlord), 473
Montalembert, Charles Forbes René, comte de, 330, 331 n, 391, 407, 457
Montcalm, 429, 430 n
Monteagle, *see* Rice, Thomas Spring
Montez, Lola, 103 n
Montgomery, James, 304, 305 n
Montpensier, duc de, 96 n
Moorman, Mary, xxxvii, xxxviii
More, Hannah, 63 n
Morell, John Daniel, 207–8 n
Morier, James Justinian, 205 n
Morier, Robert Burnet David, 106, 127 n, 204, 205 n
Morley, John, 102 n; letters to, xix, xx
Morris, John Brande, 103 n
Morton, John Maddison: *Box and Cox,* 74 n
M'Queen, James, 290 n, 291
Mucklestone, Rowland, 127 n
Mueller, Friedrich Max, 168 n, 376, 404; letter to MA, 372–73
Mulhauser, Frederick L., xxv
Murray, John: letter to, 310
Murray's *Handbook for Travellers in Switzerland,* 120, 121 n

Musset, Alfred de, 491, 495
Musset, Paul, 496

Napier, Charles James, 141, 142 n, 365
Napier, William, 298, 299 n
Napier, William Francis Patrick: *The Conquest of Scinde*, 97, 98 n
Napoleon (Jerome), 439 n
Napoleon III, 438 n
Napoleon Bonaparte, 148, 438 n, 439 n
Nassau, Mme (unidentified), 431
National Review, 332, 333 n, 344 n
National, Le, 91 n, 101
National Society for Promoting the Education of the Poor in the Principles of the Established Church, 58 n
Neiman, Fraser, xvii
New, Herbert, 344
New Quarterly Review, 391
New Zealand Company, 74 n
Newcastle, duke of, *see* Clinton, Henry Pelham Fiennes Pelham
Newcastle Commission, xiv, 418–20; mentioned, 413, 414 n, 416
Newcastle Commission Journal entries, 420, 426–27, 429, 431, 434, 436–38, 440, 442–43, 448, 451, 453, 456–58, 462–63, 465, 468–69, 473, 475, 477, 480, 488, 491, 494, 496–97
Newman, Francis William, 100 n, 115 n, 135 n, 173 n
Newman, John Henry, 50, 51, 59, 115 n, 285 n, 297, 309; *The Scope and Nature of University Education*, 517–18
Newton, Ann May Severn, 509–10 n
Newton, Charles Thomas, 509
Nicholls, Fanny, 222–23 n, 308, 341, 391, 433, 470, 474, 476
Nokes, Mrs, 80
Norman (nurse), 379
Norton, Charles Eliot, 113
Novalis, *see* Hardenberg, Friedrich Leopold von

O'Connor, Feargus, 100 n, 108
O'Flaherty, Edmund, 291, 292 n
Oliphant, Laurence, 219, 220
Ollendorff, Heinrich Gottfried, 164 n

Ord, Ralph, 188 n
Ord, William, 187, 188 n
Original von Keller's Zweiter Reisekarte des Schweiz, 121 n
Orléans, Louis Philippe Albert, d', comte de Paris, 84–85, 86 n
Osborn, Mrs, 21, 22 n
Over, Mrs (unidentified), 382
Ovid: *Metamorphoses*, 121 n
Oxford Diaries of Arthur Hugh Clough, The, xxxv

Palgrave, Francis Turner: letters to, xix, 210; letters to Tom Arnold, 106–7, 127 n, 155; mentioned, 37
Pall Mall Gazette, The, 90 n
Palmer, Edwin, 128 n
Palmer, Roundell, 109, 111 n
Pape-Carpantier, Marie, 437, 439 n
Parker, John William, Jr, 308 n, 313; letters to, 307–8, 310, 311
Parkes, Bessie Rayner: letter to, 338
Pasley, Thomas, 60 n
Pattison, Mark, 127 n, 431
Payen, M., 469 n
Peachey, James: letter to, 197
Pearson, Hugh, 141
Peel, Laurence, 333, 334 n
Peel, Robert, 195 n, 334 n
Pélissier, Aimable Jean Jacques, 486 n
Penrose, C. Lydia: letter to, 36; letters from Mary Arnold, 34, 35
Penrose, Charles, 67, 68 n; *Eight Village Sermons*, 68 n; *Select Private Orations of Demosthenes with English Notes*, 68 n
Penrose, Elizabeth Cartwright, 5 n
Penrose, Emily, 37 n
Penrose, Francis Cranmer, 36, 37 n, 415 n
Penrose, Jane, 508, 509 n; letter to, 36; letters from Mary Penrose Arnold, 32–34, 35
Penrose, John (father), 5, 68 n, 415
Penrose, John (son), 36 n, 67, 68 n, 69, 489–90 n
Penrose, Mary, *see* Arnold, Mary Penrose
Penrose, Richard, xvii
Penrose, Susanna Brooke, 47 n; letter to, 36

Penrose, Thomas Trevenen, 5n, 17, 92n, 142n, 277, 300, 313, 519; letters to, 17, 66–67
Peterson, William S.: "G.W.E. Russell and the Editing of Matthew Arnold's Letters," xix
Peyrot, M., 453n
Phibey, Mrs, 408
Philippe, Frère (Matthieu Bransiet), 423n
Philips, Charlotte Delafield, 380n
Philips, John Williams, 299n
Philips, Nathaniel George, 380n
Phipps, Constantine Henry, 96n
Pickersgill, Henry William, 15, 17
Piguet, M., 477
Piou, M. O., 454n
Pitman, Isaac, 275n
Pitman, Rosella: letters to, 274, 303
Planche, Gustave, 491, 492n
Polk, James K., 88n
Pons, Louis, 3, 5n
Ponsonby, Mrs Spencer Cecil Brabazon, 205, 206n
Pope, Alexander, 369
Portal, Melville, 198, 202n, 204, 205
Portman, Edwin, 190, 193n
Poste, Beale, 202n
Poste, Edward, 200, 202n, 204, 275, 276n
Powell, Mrs, 80
Praslin, duchess of, 84, 86n
Pratt, Henry Sparrow, 257n
Price, Bonamy, 3, 4n, 48n, 49, 91, 92n, 97, 144, 145, 161, 163, 167, 272, 488; MA's letter recommending, 230
Prichard, Constantine Estlin, 61, 62n
Prior (unidentified), 23
Pritchard, Mrs, 159
Procter, Anne B., 436, 438n
Procter, Bryan Waller, 438n
Pryme, George, 251n
Pusey, Dr, 47n

Querini, Catherine, 412n
Querini, Mrs, 411, 412n
Quillinan, Edward, 16n, 163, 165n, 173n, 180n
Quillinan, Jemima, 166n
Quillinan, Rotha, 166n, 180n

Rachel, 109, 111n
Radetsky de Radetz, Joseph Venceslas, 217, 218n
Rahn, Charles (dentist), 412, 413n, 498
Ramsay, James Andrew Broun, earl of Dalhousie, 339, 340n
Randall, James, 358
Randon, Marshall Count, 452n
Rapet, Jean Jacques, 429, 430n, 434, 436, 437, 449, 457
Rauzan, Claire, duchesse de, 427, 428n, 429
Ravaisson-Mollien, Jean Gaspard Félix, 426, 428n
Rawnsley, Drummond, letter to, 170
Ray, Gordon N., xli
Reed, Henry Hope, 313n
Reeve, Henry, 191, 500, 501n
Reeves, Stanley, 368
Regnier de la Brière, François Joseph Pierre Tousez, 427, 428n, 449
Rémusat, Charles François Marie, comte de, 390n
Renan, Ernest, 426, 427n, 515
Rendu, Eugène, 423, 437, 438, 440, 491
Résigny, Marie Louis Jules d'Y de, 437, 439n
Revue des deux mondes, La, 93n, 94n, 259, 292
Rice, Thomas Spring, Baron Monteagle, 199, 202n
Richard, Charles, 443n
Richards, Joseph Loscombe, 405n
Richards, Westley, 68
Richards (Wightman servant), 222, 223n
Richardson, John, 16n
Ricketts, Elizabeth, 332, 333n
Ricketts, Henry, 333n
Ricketts, Marianne, 332, 333n
Riddell, James, 127, 128, 128n, 404, 405n
Rintoul, Robert Stephen, 283
Rizo-Rangabe, Rhalou, 410n
Robertson, Ellen, 9, 10n, 12, 13; letter to Mary Penrose Arnold, 13–14
Robertson, James, 450n
Robinson, Mr, 63
Rocher, M. C., 454n

Roess, André, 469 n

Rolleston (Rollestone), Robert, 163, 166 n

Romilly, Edward, 394, 396 n

Romilly, Lucy, 401 n

Romilly, Samuel, 396 n

Romilly, Sophia, 396 n

Roscoe, W. C., 388 n

Rossetti, Christina, 245 n

Rossetti, Dante, 245 n

Rossetti, William Michael, 244, 245 n

Rothschild, Alphonse de, 420, 424, 425 n, 433, 434 n

Rothschild, Annie de, 499 n

Rothschild, Anthony de, 499 n

Rothschild, Constance de, 499 n; journal entries, 407–8

Rothschild, James de, 425 n

Rothschild, Leonora de, 423, 425 n

Rothschild, Lionel Nathan de, 425 n, 499 n

Rothschild, Louisa de: letter to, 499

Rothschild, Nathan Mayer, 499 n

Roughsedge, Hornby, 158, 163, 164 n

Rouland, Gustave, 426, 427, 428 n

Rowan, Archibald Hamilton, 264 n

Rugby School: letter to trustees, 365

Rush, Richard, 88 n

Ruskin, John, 137 n, 222 n, 332, 336, 503, 518; *Modern Painters,* 333 n

Russell, Charles, xvii

Russell, George William Erskine, xiv; *Letters of Matthew Arnold,* xvii

Russell, John, xvii, 110 n, 194, 195, 266, 336, 384 n

Rutland, Miss, 2, 3 n, 9, 18

Ryder, Dudley, 134 n

Ryder, Dudley Francis Stuart, 134 n

Sacconi, Msgr., 429 n

Saint Augustine: quoted, 186

Saint-Georges, Pierre Thomas Marie de, 92, 94 n

Saint-Marc Girardin, *see* Girardin, Marc

Saint-Martin, Louis Claude de, 92 n

Sainte-Beuve, Charles Augustin, 91 n, 93 n, 294, 295 n, 307 n, 426, 491, 492, 494, 495; letters to, xix, 284–85, 292–93, 302, 306; letters to MA, 299–300, 303–4, 373; *Causeries du lundi,* 426 n

Sand, George, 103 n, 109, 155, 270 n, 330, 331 n, 473, 489, 491, 493, 495; *Château des désertes,* 202 n; *Consuelo,* 85 n; *François le champi,* 109, 110 n; *Indiana,* 63; *Jacques,* 63; *Teverino,* 109, 110 n; *La Daniella,* 452; *Elle et Lui,* 496 n

Sandars, Thomas Collett, 147 n

Sandford, Francis Richard John, 191, 273, 328, 433; MA's letter recommending, 229–30 n

Sansom, Thomas, 244 n, 248

Saunders, Charles Thomas, 325; letter to, 380

Scheffer, Ary, 457, 459 n, 462

Scheffer, Cornelie, 459 n

Scott, Gilbert, 503, 506 n

Scott, John, 208

Scott, Mrs Fenton, 511

Scott, Robert, 128 n

Scott, Robert: letters to, 360–61, 363

Sellar, William Young, 126, 127 n, 347

Senancour, Etienne Pivert de, 92 n

Senior, Nassau William, 36, 193, 194 n, 384 n, 421 n, 434 n, 438, 448, 449

Sergent, René Nicolas, 443 n, 447

Sermons and Essays on the Apostolical Age, 100 n

Severn, Joseph: letter to, 509

Sewell, William, 145 n

Seymour, George Turner, 62 n

Seymour, John Billingsley, 62 n

Shairp, John Campbell, 4 n, 135, 136–37 n, 161, 167, 277; letter from Clough, 70–71; "Balliol Scholars 1840–43," 168 n; mentioned, 96, 97, 198, 199, 241, 245

Shelley, Percy Bysshe, 245

Shephard, Thomas Henry, 126, 127 n

Sherwood, Mary Martha, 342 n

Shrimpton, Dr., 420

Shuttleworth, James Kay, 130, 336

Shuttleworth, Janet, 130 n

Simpkinson, John Nassau, 161, 165 n

Simpson, M. C. M., 439 n

Simpson, Mr, 14

Skeffington, Henry Robert, 131, 132 n; "The Etruscan Tombs at Perugia and Chiusi," xxiii

Skipwith, Gray, 34 n

Slade, Cicely Neave, 170 n, 436, 449

Slade, Frederick William, 239 n

Slade, George FitzClarence, 299 n

Slade, Gertrude Matilda, 343 n

Slade, Herbert Dawson ("Apollyon"), 239

Slade, Matilda Ellen Dawson, 242, 243 n

Slade, Sophia Louise, 343 n

Slade, Wyndham, 172 n, 190, 191, 211 n, 213, 348, 364, 411, 438, 440, 441, 448; letters to, xix, xx, 169, 173–74, 238–39, 242–43, 244–45, 288–89, 289–90, 291–92, 298, 327, 342–43; mentioned, 195, 196, 198, 199, 200, 210, 437

Smith, Albert Richard, 487, 488 n

Smith, Alexander, 259, 261, 262 n, 264, 266

Smith, Blanche, 241 n, 246 n, 250, 265 n, 323 n

Smith, Goldwin, 136, 137 n, 273, 279

Smith, Miss, 246

Sorell, Julia, 178 n

Sortain, Joseph, 340, 341 n

Southcombe, J. L. Hamilton, 58 n

Southey, Bertha, 17 n

Southey, Charles Cuthbert, 188 n

Southey, Cuthbert, 166 n

Southey, Kate, 163, 166 n

Southey, Robert, 17 n, 280 n

Souza, Mme de, 438 n

Spectator, 283

Spicer, John William Gooch, 204, 206 n

Spicer, Juliana Hannah Webb Probyn, 206 n

Spinoza, 177; quoted, 182, 183, 184

Spooner, Miss, 158

Spooner, William Archibald, 164 n

Spraggs, Mr & Mrs (unidentified), 20 n

Spy, 174 n, 390 n

Stanley, Arthur Penrhyn, 48 n, 50, 53 n, 99, 100 n, 142 n, 165 n, 188 n, 195, 202 n, 297, 301, 310, 312, 346, 358, 365, 367, 428 n, 488; mentioned, 45, 53, 54, 106, 115, 116, 117, 127, 163, 195, 199, 374

Stanley, Catherine Leycester, 187, 188 n

Stanley, Edward George Geoffrey Smith, earl of Derby, 195, 239, 384–85 n, 413, 433, 456, 461

Stanley, Bishop Edward, 165 n

Stanley, Edward John, 196 n

Stanley, Lord, of Alderley, Henry Edward John, 53 n, 186, 187 n, 192

Steinhauser, Pauline, 85 n

Stephen, Fitzjames, 380 n, 413, 487

Stephen, James Fitzjames, 390 n

Stephen, James, 333 n

Steward, Charles Holden, 223, 224, 225 n

Story-Maskelyne, Mary Lucy, 173 n

Story-Maskelyne, Mervyn Herbert Nevil, 172 n

Stowe, Harriet Beecher, 258, 259–60 n

Stuart-Wortley, James Archibald, 513 n

Stuart-Wortley, Jane Lawley, 513 n

Sugden, Edward Burtenshaw, 194 n

Sumner, George Henry: letters to, 353–54, 355, 359

Sumner, John Henry Robertson, 355 n

Sumner, Robert George Moncreiff, 355 n

Super, Robert H., xvii, xxi

Sutherland, duke of, 72 n

Swinburne, Algernon Charles, 102, 480 n

Tachard, M., 454 n

Taille, Mme, 75 n

Tait, Archibald Campbell, 161, 163, 164 n, 185, 392, 393; letters to, 47–48; mentioned, 52 n, 64, 97, 201 n

Tatham, Mr, 15

Tautphoeus, Jemima Montgomery: *The Initials A Novel,* 195, 197 n

Taylor, Henry: *Philip van Artevelde,* 74 n

Temple, Frederick, 37, 60 n, 117, 198, 210, 365, 381, 405; letter to, 129–30

Temple, Henry John, Lord Palmerston, 234 n

Temple, Jennetta Octavia, 406 n

Tennyson, Alfred, Lord, 102, 108 n, 137 n, 170 n, 210; *Maud and Other Poems,* 322, 323 n; mentioned, 306 n, 347

Tennyson, Emily, 170 n

Thackeray, William Makepeace, 258, 259 n, 510

Thierry, Amédée, 429
Thierry, Augustin, 429n
Thiers, Adolphe, 84, 86n, 426n, 429, 439n
Thirlwall, Connop, 48n, 49, 52n
Thomas à Kempis, 189
Thomas Arnold's Travelling Journals, 264, 265n
Thompson, Eleanor Wade, 202n
Thompson, John Vincent, 199, 202n
Thompson, Vincent Thomas, 202n
Thompson, William Hepworth: letter to, 367–68
Thomson, William, 410n
Thomson, Zoë Skene: letter to, 410
Thursby, Eleanor Mary Hargreaves, 9, 10n
Thursby, William, 9, 10n
Thursby, William Ford, 10n
Tinker, Chauncey Brewster, xxxviii
Tocqueville, Alexis de, 421n, 439n
Tomms, Captain, 449
Toovey, James: letter to, 237
Trench, Francis Chenevix, 129n
Trench, Richard (Chenevix), 128, 129n
Trench, William Steuart, 129n
Trevelyan, Charles Edward, 413, 414n
Trilling, Lionel, xvii
Trimmer, Sarah, 63n
Trousseau, Armand, 420, 423, 424, 425, 426, 432, 436; letter to MA, 430
Truman, Joseph, 321n
Tuffin, Mrs, 379, 380n, 413, 424, 429, 450, 476, 482, 489, 512
Turner, Edward Tindal, 70n
Twining, Louisa, 295, 351
Twining, Mary Arnold, 71, 72n, 108n, 160, 187, 199, 276, 351n, 497; marriage to Hiley, 388n; letter to, 146; letters to Tom Arnold, 145–46, 166, 170, 175; mentioned, 94, 95n, 181, 304, 313
Twining, Richard, 16n, 351n
Twining, William Aldred, 12, 16n, 72n, 295n
Two Sermons on the Interpretation of Prophecy, 53
Tyrwhitt-Drake, Thomas, 20, 22n

Vaillant, Marshal, 452n
van Citters, M., 458, 459n
Vane, Henry, 165n
Vaughan, C. J., 48n
Vaughan, Henry Halford, 190, 193n
Venard, Céleste, 496n
Vernon Smith, Emma Mary Fitzpatrick, 197, 201n
Vernon Smith, Robert, 201n
Veuillot, Louis, 479, 480n
Victor Emmanuel II, 439n
Viennet, Jean Pons Guillaume, 429
Villemain, 420, 425, 426, 427, 471, 494, 495, 496n
Villiers, Charles Pelham, 482
Villiers, George William Frederick, earl of Clarendon, 105, 106n, 194n
Virgil: *Georgics,* 118n
Visconti, Filippo Aurelio: *Musee Chiaramonti,* 127, 128n
Vittorio, Tommaso Alberto, 96n
Vivien, M., 480
Vollenhoven, Hendrik, 459n
Voltaire, 369
von Arnim, Mlle, 496
Voss, Johann Heinrich, 135n
Vuillemin, M., 477

Waddington, Thomas, 29, 32n
Waddington, William Henry, 32n, 423
Waite (unidentified), 56
Wale, Charles Brent, 163, 166n
Wale, Elizabeth Branch, 166n
Wale, Henrietta, 166n
Walford, Edward: letter to, 510; letter to *The Times,* 37
Walker, John: *Rhyming Dictionary,* 381, 382n
Walker, Mrs Thomas, 10, 11n
Wall, Charles Baring, 239n
Wall, Henry, 140n
Wall, Richard, 140n
Walrond, Charlotte Grenfell, 168n, 509n
Walrond, L. H., 192
Walrond, Theodore, 161, 168n, 176, 297, 327, 357, 394, 395, 396, 399, 400, 403, 509, 516; letter to Tom Arnold, 96–97; mentioned, 64, 72, 115, 167, 198, 211n, 238, 359, 404, 433, 508

Ward, John, 22n, 47n, 458, 459n
Ward, Martha Arnold, 21, 22n, 35, 47n, 158
Ward, Mrs Humphry, xix, xxxix, 85n
Ward, William, 437, 439n
Warden, Mr (unidentified), 33–34
Warrington (Warington), Elizabeth Billing, 221, 222n
Washington, George, 88n
Waterton, Fanny, 449
Waterton, Mr, 187
Waterton, Mrs (unidentified), 187, 190, 195, 443, 449
Watkin, Elvy (unidentified), 158
Watson, John, 290
Wayte, Miss, 240
Wayte, Samuel W.: letter to, 240
Webb, Miss (unidentified), 204, 206n
Webber (Wightman servant), 222, 223n
Wellesley, Henry Richard Charles, Earl Cowley, 417n, 418, 429, 431, 433, 437, 447, 465, 467, 478, 480, 485, 492
Westminster Assembly of Divines, 153, 154n
Whately, Blanche, 508, 509n
Whately, Edward William, 73, 74n
Whately, Elizabeth Jane, 166n
Whately, Elizabeth Pope, 36n
Whately, Henrietta, 60, 74n, 166n
Whately, Mrs, 141, 142, 144
Whately, Richard, 36, 327n
Whiteman, Bessy, 222n
Whiteman, John Clarmont, 221, 222n, 411
Whiteman, Sarah Horsley, 222n
Whitridge, Arnold, xvii, xxxvii
Whitridge, Eleanor, xxxix
Wightman, Charlotte Georgina Eleanor, 364, 365n
Wightman, Charlotte Mary Baird, 174n, 190, 200, 201, 205, 223, 308, 319, 349, 351, 497, 511, 519; letters from Frances Lucy Wightman, 214–15, 225–26
Wightman, Frances Lucy, 174n, 176n, 199, 200, 207, 357, 364, 389, 424,

458, 466, 467, 475, 476, 498, 511, 514, 516, 518; engagement, 196, 199, 203; marriage, 209n, 210; letters to, xix, 179, 194, 227, 228–29, 241–42, 251, 255, 256, 257, 257–58, 260–61, 286, 290, 295–96, 311–12, 323, 323–24, 393–94, 397–98, 398–400, 441–42, 443–44, 448–49, 451–52, 492, 494–96; letters to Mary Penrose Arnold, 352–53, 435–36; letter to Aunty, 220–22; letter to Mary Benson, 223–25; letters to Charlotte Wightman (mother), 214–15, 225–26; letter to William Wightman, 218–19; letter to Caroline Wood (sister), 216–17; mentioned, 190, 201, 204, 205, 208, 209, 214, 240, 242, 246, 248, 252, 263, 265, 266, 294, 308, 312, 316, 318, 321, 341, 346, 356, 379, 390, 391, 392, 403, 415, 420, 433, 468, 469, 482, 508
Wightman, Georgina ("Baby"), 192, 194n, 497, 502
Wightman, William, 174n, 189, 190n, 196, 199, 203, 316, 340, 357, 364, 385, 393, 497, 511; letter to MA, 501–3; letter from Frances Lucy Wightman, 218–19
Wilberforce, Samuel, 321n
Wilhelm I, prince of Prussia, 98n
Wilson, James, 102n
Wilson, John, 322n
Wilson, William James Erasmus, 125, 126n
Windham, William, 360
Winyard (Wynyard), Mrs, 63, 64
Winyards, 15, 17
Wiseman, Nicholas Patrick Stephen, 178, 191
Wodehouse, Roger, xxxviii
Wolff, Henry Drummond Charles, 174, 383; letter to, 421–22
Wolseley, Garnet, 167n
Wood, Caroline Elizabeth Wightman, 200, 201, 205, 218n, 268n; letter from Frances Lucy Wightman, 216–17
Wood, Charles Alexander, 222n

Wood, Edith Caroline, 217, 218n
Wood, Peter Almeric, 208, 218n, 222n, 268n, 327
Wood, Sophia Brownrigg, 221, 222n
Woodall, Mary Hebden, 463n
Wordsworth, Christopher, 175
Wordsworth, Dorothy (Dora), 13, 16n, 165n
Wordsworth, Mary Hutchinson, 13, 209n, 277, 300, 358; death, 411, 412n; letter to Thomas & Mary Penrose Arnold, 14–15
Wordsworth, William, 109, 110n, 123,

285n; death, 173n; letter to TA & MPA, 14–15; letter to Isabella Fenwick, 63–64; on Goethe, 166; "Resolution and Independence," 117n; mentioned, 6, 7n, 8, 9, 10
Wrightson, Mr (unidentified), 33
Wynter, Philip, 47n

Yarde-Buller, John Buller, 358
Yarnall, Ellis: letter from William E. Forster, 284
Young, Allen William, 513n
Young, Captain, 512

Victorian Literature and Culture Series

Daniel Albright
Tennyson: *The Muses' Tug-of-War*

David G. Riede
Matthew Arnold and the Betrayal of Language

Anthony Winner
Culture and Irony: *Studies in Joseph Conrad's Major Novels*

James Richardson
Vanishing Lives: *Style and Self in Tennyson, D. G. Rossetti, Swinburne, and Yeats*

Jerome J. McGann, Editor
Victorian Connections

Antony H. Harrison
Victorian Poets and Romantic Poems: *Intertextuality and Ideology*

E. Warwick Slinn
The Discourse of Self in Victorian Poetry

Linda K. Hughes and Michael Lund
The Victorian Serial

Anna Leonowens
The Romance of the Harem
Edited by Susan Morgan

Alan Fischler
Modified Rapture: *Comedy in W. S. Gilbert's Savoy Operas*

Emily Shore
Journal of Emily Shore
Edited by Barbara Timm Gates

Richard Maxwell
The Mysteries of Paris and London

Felicia Bonaparte
The Gypsy-Bachelor of Manchester: *The Life of Mrs. Gaskell's Demon*

Peter L. Shillingsburg
Pegasus in Harness: *Victorian Publishing and W. M. Thackeray*

Angela Leighton
Victorian Women Poets: *Writing against the Heart*

ALLAN C. DOOLEY
Author and Printer in Victorian England

SIMON GATRELL
Thomas Hardy and the Proper Study of Mankind

JEFFREY SKOBLOW
Paradise Dislocated: *Morris, Politics, Art*

MATTHEW ROWLINSON
Tennyson's Fixations: *Psychoanalysis and the Topics of the Early Poetry*

BEVERLY SEATON
The Language of Flowers: *A History*

BARRY MILLIGAN
Pleasures and Pains: *Opium and the Orient in Nineteenth-Century British Culture*

GINGER S. FROST
Promises Broken: *Courtship, Class, and Gender in Victorian England*

LINDA DOWLING
The Vulgarization of Art: *The Victorians and Aesthetic Democracy*

TRICIA LOOTENS
Lost Saints: *Silence, Gender, and Victorian Literary Canonization*

MATTHEW ARNOLD
The Letters of Matthew Arnold
Edited by Cecil Y. Lang